SAN FRANCISCO
RES
ACCESS

Orientation	4
Downtown/Union Square	10
Chinatown	32
North Beach	46
Fisherman's Wharf/The Embarcadero	62
Nob Hill/Russian Hill	72
Pacific Heights/Cow Hollow/The Marina	86
Japantown/Lower Haight	104
Civic Center/Hayes Valley/The Tenderloin	112
SoMa (South of Market/South Beach/Potrero Hill/Bayview–Hunters Point)	122
The Mission	142
Castro/Noe Valley	154
The Haight/Cole Valley/West Portal/Glen Park	166
The Sunset	174
The Richmond/Presidio Heights	184
Beyond the Bridges	202
Index	216

Second Edition ©1996 by **ACCESS**®PRESS. All rights reserved. No portion of this publication may be reproduced or transmitted in any form or manner by any means, including, but not limited to, graphic, electronic, and mechanical methods, photocopying, recording, taping, or any informational storage and retrieval systems without explicit permission from the publisher. **ACCESS**® is a registered trademark of HarperCollins Publishers Inc.

Orientation

From the aroma of roasting coffee that wafts through the air of **North Beach**, to the sights of fresh fish on ice in **Chinatown**, to the colorful pyramids of organic produce in the chic shops of **Pacific Heights**, to the host of great *taquerias* that dot the **Mission**, it's obvious that this city loves food. Residents here spend more money in restaurants than do their counterparts anywhere else in the country—easy to do in a city that boasts one restaurant for every 230 people, the highest proportion in the country.

Food has a long and colorful history in San Francisco. In 1849 the Gold Rush brought thousands of fortune seekers, mostly men, to the West Coast. There were enough saloons to intoxicate a city five times its size, and barkeepers soon figured out a way to attract customers and get them to rack up a bigger bar bill at the same time: the free lunch. It wasn't long before miners began to factor the quality of the food into their patronage, and the San Francisco restaurant trade was under way.

Restaurants also began to spring up in another male bastion: the bordello. In fact, Sally Stanford, one of the city's most renowned madams, became both a successful restaurateur and a mayor. Stanford, who ran her business out of an impressive Victorian house on **Pine Street**, retired from the world's oldest profession in 1950 and then opened **Valhalla**, a plush Victorian restaurant in **Sausalito**, a charming community just across the **Golden Gate Bridge**. In 1972 she won a seat on the Sausalito city council and was so popular that she became mayor in 1976. Later she was named honorary vice-mayor for life, which she jokingly turned around to "the mayor of vice."

Though the madam's restaurant is long gone, there are restaurants all over the city that are still thriving after more than a century: **Tadich Grill** opened its doors in 1849, followed by **Jack's** in 1864, and then **Sam's Grill**, which was founded in 1867 and has been owned by the same family since 1903. **Maye's Oyster House** also opened in 1867, and **Ristorante Fior d'Italia** dates to 1886. The restaurants of each succeeding decade provide a cultural blueprint of the city's growth: **Schroeder's**, a German restaurant near the **Embarcadero**, was established in 1893; **Bardelli's**, an old-style Italian restaurant near **Union Square**, dates to 1909; and in the Mission, **Roosevelt's Tamale Parlor** set up shop in 1922.

The city's rich culinary tapestry is enhanced by its location in the heart of one of the country's richest agricultural areas and its proximity to some of the best wine regions in the world: **Sonoma**, **Napa**, Santa Cruz, Mendocino, and Livermore. California wine, which many oenophiles now compare in quality to the best French labels, is making a strong showing on the international market.

And the fog, which San Francisco residents love to complain about, is another factor that fuels our passion: The cool temperatures stimulate the appetite. Where else in the country can you feel at home having a rich lamb stew, a hearty glass of wine, and a loaf of yeasty sourdough bread in the middle of August?

No longer mining for gold, today's visitors talk about the weather, the hills, and the European flavor of the city, but more than anything else they talk about the restaurants: from **Masa's**, **Rubicon**, and **Boulevard** to **Stars** and **Betelnut**. And no wonder. The city has come a long way from its Gold Rush roots.

When two dozen food writers around the country were asked for five words to describe San Francisco–style cooking, every one of them put "fresh" at the top of their list. In 1971 Alice Waters made that connection between land and plate and started a nationwide revolution when she opened **Chez Panisse** in **Berkeley**, which may be the only restaurant in the country with a full-time forager on staff to search for the best fresh products.

Today diners also can keep tabs on the way their meals are prepared. With a proliferation of open kitchens—among them **Stars**, **VIVANDE Porta Via**, **Boulevard**, **Hawthorne Lane**, **Postrio**, and **One Market**—many with a dining counter overlooking the cooks at work, the city has turned eating out into something of a spectator sport; in many cases you'll feel as though you have front-row seats at a master cooking class.

In keeping with this personal touch, chefs often identify the produce and the grower's name on the menu: Laura Chenel goat cheese, Liberty duck, or Star Route farms lettuce, to name a few. Good, fresh bread is another essential. Many restaurants bake their own, and the Bay Area nurtures at least a dozen small artisan bakeries. Look for breads by **Bakers of Paris**, **Boudin**, **Acme**, **Metropolis**, **Bread Workshop**, **Semifreddi's**, **Il Fornaio**, **Grace Baking**, and **Tassajara Bread Bakery.** And then there's the coffee: Specialty roasters abound—**Peet's Coffee & Tea**, **Spinelli Coffee Company**, **Capricorn Coffees**, **Caffè Trieste**, **Graffeo Coffee**, and **Peerless**—and everyone can tell you why his or her favorite is the best.

San Francisco is one of the most ethnically diverse cities in the country, and its culinary repertoire reflects that fact. Chinese restaurants have become so sophisticated that some specialize in one of the regional styles: Chiu Chow, Shanghai, Canton, Hakka, Hunan, Mandarin, Szechuan, and Peking. Diners can sample the native dishes of Burma, Cambodia, Laos, Malaysia, and Singapore. The rustic cuisine of Istria is explored at **Albona Restaurant**, and **YaYa Cuisine** features the exotic flavors of Mesopotamia. The newest trend is Mediterranean, a style that freely blends the flavors of France, Greece, Italy, Spain, Egypt, and Morocco. **Lhasa Moon**, in **Cow Hollow**, is the only Tibetan reataurant west of the Rockies. And **La Paz Restaurant and Pupuseria**, a new eatery in **SoMa**, is one of the many places in the city that serve Salvadoran cuisine.

So whether it's a dinner of grilled veal chop with parmesan-potato puree in the stylish surroundings at **Postrio**, or a midday cappuccino and biscotti break at **Caffè Trieste**, San Francisco is still going for the gold.

Orientation

How To Read This Guide

SAN FRANCISCO RESTAURANTS 96/97 ACCESS® is arranged so you can see at a glance where you are and what is around you. The numbers next to the entries in the following chapters correspond to the numbers on the maps.

The star ratings system takes into account the quality, service, atmosphere, and uniqueness of the restaurant. An expensive restaurant doesn't necessarily ensure an enjoyable evening; while a small, relatively unknown spot could have good food, professional service, and a lovely atmosphere. Therefore, on a purely subjective basis, stars are used to judge the overall dining value (see star ratings below). Keep in mind that chefs and owners often change, which sometimes drastically affects the quality of a restaurant. The ratings in this guidebook are based on information available at press time.

The restaurant price ratings, as categorized below, describe general price-range relationships among other restaurants and is based on the average costs of an entrée for one person, excluding tax and tip.

Restaurants

★	Good
★★	Very Good
★★★	Excellent
★★★★	An Extraordinary Experience
$	The Price Is Right (less than $10)
$$	Reasonable ($10–$15)
$$$	Expensive ($15–$25)
$$$$	Big Bucks ($25 and up)

Wheelchair Accessibility

Wheelchair accessibility is noted by a ♿ at the end of the entry. An establishment is considered wheelchair accessible when a person in a wheelchair can easily enter a building (i.e., no steps, a ramp, a wide-enough door) without assistance *and* if the rest rooms are on the same floor as the dining area and their entrances and stalls are wide enough to accommodate a wheelchair.

Symbols

Everything from soup to nuts, the following indicate where you can stop or shop:

baked goods

coffee/tea

cooking supplies/cookbooks

markets/food shops

tableware

wine/liquor

Map Key

1 Entry Number
City/Town
BART Station
Ferry
■ Point of Interest
80 Interstate Hwy
101 US Hwy.
1 State Hwy.
Freeway ═══ Tunnel
Highway
Tertiary Road

FYI

Area code 415 unless otherwise noted.

Drinking

The legal drinking age is 21. Bars stay open until 2AM. Wine and liquor are widely available and can be purchased in most grocery stores and supermarkets.

Hours

It's a good idea to call ahead to find out if a particular restaurant or shop will be open the day and time you plan to visit. Generally shops are open Monday through Saturday 9AM to 6PM, but keep in mind that this information may change with the seasons, the economy, or even the whim of the owner. Opening and closing times for shops, coffeehouses, and tearooms, etc. are listed by day(s) only if normal hours apply (opening between 8 and 11AM and closing between 4 and 7PM). In all other cases, specific hours are given (e.g., 6AM-2PM, daily 24 hours, noon-5PM).

Reservations

Most restaurants within the city accept reservations. Calling ahead is always a good idea, especially if the

Orientation

restaurant is popular. It's easier to get a table Monday through Wednesday nights than Thursday through Saturday, and earlier or later in the evening than the prime dinner hour of 7 to 8PM. Always call as far ahead as possible, but if you are shut out of the day and time you want, ask to leave your name on a waiting list. If you are staying in a large hotel, sometimes the concierge can secure a reservation for you at an always-busy restaurant. Many places have dining counters overlooking the kitchen to accommodate drop-in customers—they're also great for the single diner. But if you still can't get in to the hot spot of choice for dinner, go there for lunch—it will be less expensive and it should be uncrowded enough to allow you to actually see the room and hold a conversation.

Smoking
San Francisco has strict antismoking laws. It's illegal to smoke in any restaurant that has no bar; in all others, smoking is allowed only in the bar.

Tipping
A 15 percent gratuity to wait staff is standard in most dining spots, though 20 percent for good service is becoming more common. Generally, there is no need to tip the maître d' or the sommelier separately.

Food Tours
The best way to acquire an insider's view of two of the most food-intense neighborhoods—North Beach and Chinatown—is on a guided walking tour.

GraceAnn Walden (397.8530), a food columnist for the *San Francisco Chronicle* (and also the reviser of this book), leads a four-hour walking tour of North Beach each Saturday, including lunch at **Enrico's**.

Shirley Fong Torres (355.9657), known as the "Wok Wiz," offers a 3.5-hour tour of Chinatown daily, which includes a walk through an herb shop, an Asian supermarket, and a noodle factory, and concludes with a dim sum lunch. On Saturday, she expands the walk, calling it "I Can't Believe I Ate My Way Through Chinatown Tour." She also leads a two-hour walk through North Beach (lunch is arranged for an additional cost).

For coffee lovers, **Elaine Sosa** (673.WALK) conducts "Javawalk," a two-hour tour of coffeehouses Tuesday through Saturday, that starts at Union Square and winds through Chinatown, **Jackson Square**, and North Beach. Sosa covers the history and rituals of coffeehouse culture, stopping at a couple of North Beach cafes for a quick java fix, as well as at a coffee purveyor's where participants can watch the beans being roasted.

Fabulous Food Festivals and Street Fairs

San Francisco's fascinating ethnic diversity is joyously reflected in its many food festivals and street fairs held throughout the year. A few events that are located outside the city are unique—the celebration of wine in **Healdsburg**, of mustard in the **Napa Valley**—and give people a wonderful reason to get into their cars and go to a party. All of the celebrations tend to be crowded, noisy, fragrant, and colorful, brimming with local pride. The following are some of the most prominent, regularly scheduled festivities:

February
The **Chinese New Year Festival and Parade** is a weeklong celebration from the end of February into early March, climaxing in a colorful parade that snakes through **Chinatown**. It draws thousands of visitors and is aired live on local television stations. Traditional Chinese foods—sweet bean buns and dumplings, among others—are featured. ♦ Bounded by Kearny and Powell Sts, and Bush St and Broadway. 982.3000

Clam Chowder Cook-Off and Chowder Chase has, in addition to the cook-off, a number of booths along the boardwalk that sell clam chowder; fairgoers can do their own taste tests.
♦ Santa Cruz Beach Boardwalk, off Beach St (between Cliff and Third Sts). 408/423.5590

The **Russian Festival** celebrates Russian culture and showcases food, music, and crafts. Celebrants feast on kasha, pierogi, blini, and caviar, and wash it down with a variety of vodkas.
♦ 2450 Sutter St (between Divisadero and Broderick Sts). 921.7631

The **Tet Festival** commemorates the Vietnamese New Year and features such traditional foods as shrimp and pork spring rolls, hot rice noodles, and fish soups. ♦ Larkin St (at O'Farrell St). 885.2743

March
The **Napa Valley Mustard Festival** takes place in communities throughout the valley when the wild mustard blooms on the local hillsides. The festival features winery tours, wine tastings, and gourmet foods, most involving mustard in some guise. Vendors sell jars of mustard, and area restaurants offer intimate dinners of such dishes as quesadillas made with mustard and salmon with mustard sauce.
♦ Napa, Yountville, St. Helena, and Oakville, among other towns. 707/938.1133

April
Cherry Blossom Festival is held in **Japantown** and celebrates Japanese art,

7

Orientation

film, and Kabuki theater; it features teriyaki and tempura, among other favorite foods. There's also a traditional Japanese tea ceremony. ♦ Bounded by Octavia and Fillmore Sts, and Geary Blvd and California St. 563.2313

May

Carnaval Parade and Festival emphasizes multiculturalism and outrageousness in its parade, costumes, and cuisine. Food ranges from Brazilian to Thai to Creole to Filipino. ♦ Harrison St (from 21st to 16th Sts). 826.1401

Cinco de Mayo Parade and Festival commemorates Mexico's defeat of the French in 1862. Traditional Mexican and other Latin music is played, and food vendors offer barbecue, burritos, *flautas* (fried, stuffed tortillas), Mexican ices, margaritas, and beer. ♦ Civic Center Plaza, in front of City Hall (bounded by Polk St and Van Ness Ave, and Grove and McAllister Sts). 826.1401

Norway Day Festival is staged to promote cultural and economic cooperation between Norway and the United States. It showcases arts and crafts, music, and such Norwegian foods as open-face sandwiches featuring shrimp, salmon, or meatballs. Cooks prepare waffles, served with jam, and *lefse* (a crepe served with sugar and butter). ♦ Herbst Pavilion at Fort Mason (bounded by Bay St, Van Ness Ave, and Laguna St). 510/676.4708

Russian River Wine Festival stages wine tastings and intimate dinners at the wineries, featuring such entrées as salmon cakes and grilled Sonoma free-range chicken breast. Participants can also snack on more casual foods. ♦ Healdsburg Plaza (bounded by Matheson, Center, and Plaza Sts), Healdsburg. 707/433.6935

June

North Beach Street Fair reflects the area's Italian immigrant roots, as well as its past and present status as a mecca for artists and writers. The scene consists of music, paintings sold on the street, and much eating and drinking (sausage and pepper sandwiches, garlic chicken sandwiches, shish kabobs, cannoli, pizza, and cappuccino).

Union Street Spring Festival is essentially a garden party held in historic **Cow Hollow.** The street is closed to traffic from Gough to Steiner Streets, and a fashion show, waiters' race, and tea dancing take place. From the plethora of street vendors, you can buy tasty bagels with cream cheese, lace onions, gourmet sausages, focaccia stuffed with prosciutto or vegetables, fajitas, and hamburgers.

July

Jazz & All That Art on Fillmore is an enormous free jazz concert held on Fillmore Street. While you're moving to the groove, feast on buffalo wings, barbecued pork sandwiches, jambalaya, gumbo, and cheesesteaks. ♦ Fillmore St (between Jackson and Post Sts). 346.4446

Sonoma Salute to the Arts also features wine-country gourmet foods, especially goat cheese and foie gras; one of the two producers of foie gras in the United States is located in **Sonoma.** ♦ Sonoma Plaza (bounded by E First St and W First St, and Napa and Spain Sts), Sonoma. 707/938.1133

September

Folsom Street Fair is not for the timid—the booths here are devoted to leather, body piercing, and the like. This is where you can sample a variety of traditional Indian specialties, as well as knishes, barbecued oysters, steak and chicken tacos, and pizza.

October

German Festival features food provided by the restaurant **Suppenküche,** and includes sauerkraut, sausages, pretzels, strudel, and hearty German beer. ♦ Union Sq (bounded by Stockton and Powell Sts, and Geary and Post Sts). 775.1061

Orientation

All Aboard

In case breathtaking views and great food aren't enough, diners in Northern California can also enjoy a relaxing meal while sailing around **San Francisco Bay** or on a train cutting through the magnificent **Napa Valley** wine country. The following are a few options:

Hornblower Dining Yachts (788.8866) offers cruises around the bay at lunchtime on Friday, brunch break on Saturday and Sunday, and the dinner hour nightly. The service can't be beat, the vintage three-floor boat is wonderful—with a stately, cruise-line feel—and the views set the mood for romance. The food on the limited American menu, however, is pretty mundane. Reservations are required. Boats leave from **Pier 33**.

Pacific Marine Yachts Charters and Dining Cruises (788.9100) boasts a bountiful Sunday brunch cruise. The two-hour excursion includes not only a buffet and sparkling wine, but a close-up view of sea lions and pelicans in the bay. Food is cooked on board, so the brunch selections—ranging from eggs and Belgian waffles to salads, a meat carvery, and fish dishes—taste fresh. Book early, especially if you want a table by the window. There are also dinner-dance cruises on Saturday nights, and many customized private yacht charters are available. The boat leaves from **Pier 39**.

The **Napa Valley Wine Train** (707/253.2111, 800/427.4124) offers reservations-only brunch, lunch, or dinner excursions aboard a 1915 vintage train with Pullman lounge and dining cars. Over the course of a three-hour trip, a French/California–inspired three- or four-course meal is served to the passengers. Half the diners enjoy wine or cocktails in the lounge while the others sit down to eat at elegant damask-covered tables. Midway through the trip, the first group begins the meal (ending with dessert and coffee), and the second has dessert and coffee in the cocktail lounge. Board the train for lunch Monday through Friday, brunch on Saturday and Sunday, or dinner Tuesday through Sunday. Those passengers who want to be more spontaneous can order food à la carte or taste wines in the deli car, also by reservation. The train leaves from the **Napa** railroad station (1275 McKinstry St, near First St).

Downtown/Union Square

The epicurean epicenter of San Francisco is the Downtown area, encompassing Union Square and the **Financial District**. On any given weekday, about 225,000 people come here to work, play, shop, and eat. As one of the country's top financial centers, and encompassing its third-largest shopping district (after New York and Chicago), Downtown also claims the lion's share of the city's three- and four-star restaurants. They're splashy and special and they lure San Franciscans and tourists to the area specifically to dine. Downtown is home to **Aqua**, probably the most beautiful restaurant in the city, with its stunning architecture, lofty ceilings, and towering flower arrangements. The extraordinary **Redwood Room** in the **Clift Hotel** is a bar cloaked in aged redwood and featuring large reproductions of Gustav Klimt paintings on the bronzed walls. Other destinations are the romantic, exotic **Fleur de Lys**, which cossets guests under its tent of flowered fabric; the elegant, red-walled **Masa's**; and the exuberant **Postrio**, with its glitz and glamor.

Yet the fast pace of the area has also bred hundreds of places that cater to the quick-lunch crowd. Some aren't worth the price, while others are expert at preparing hearty deli sandwiches and bountiful salads.

The Financial District's heyday began on 12 May 1848, when Sam Brannan, editor of the town's first newspaper, announced that gold had been discovered in the foothills of the Sierras. The Gold Rush turned the local shopkeepers into bankers, since they had scales that could weigh the gold and safes for storing it. Other businesses proliferated, including eateries catering to lusty appetites. One San Francisco classic in particular, the nononsense "men's grill," harks back to this era, when lucky miners came to town for a thick steak, Champagne, and the company of a Barbary Coast damsel. These historic eateries exude a masculine ambience characterized by dark wood, tile floors, and bentwood chairs; most offer a simple French-Italian–inspired menu. Several of these old-timers are still popular (and today both women and men are welcome), including the **Tadich Grill**; **Sam's Grill**, with its warren of private booths for discreet encounters; and the classic, straightforward **Jack's**.

By the Civil War, genteel Union Square had become a hub of retail commerce, exemplified by the **City of**

Downtown/Union Square

Paris department store. It was known for its basement food hall, not unlike the one at Harrods in London and a precursor of **Macy's Cellar**. When the Dallas-based **Neiman Marcus** department store took over the space in the early 1980s, the **City of Paris** was demolished except for its impressive glass dome. Today people can sip a demitasse of bouillon and munch on hot popovers under the dome at **The Rotunda** and enjoy a civility that harks back to the top hat and white gloves era.

A host of fine merchants surrounds the square. But though branches of **Tiffany**, **Saks**, and **Macy's** can now be found in cities across the nation, the restaurants in Union Square retain their unique character. An innovative breed of dining establishment has arrived on the scene: **Rumpus**, tucked away in an alley off **Grant Avenue**, boasts a party atmosphere, and **Cafe Akimbo** on **Maiden Lane** offers unusual East/West combinations in bright, modern surroundings. In Union Square, you can pick up just the right cookie cutter or catch a cooking demonstration by a local chef in **Macy's Cellar**, buy exotic condiments from the **Epicurean Shop** at **Neiman Marcus**, or indulge in a luscious bonbon from **The Candy Jar**.

The **Embarcadero Center**, an eight-block complex of retail offices and residential space, contains some top-flight restaurants, including **Harbor Village**, one of the city's handsomest Chinese eateries, and **Splendido**, a Mediterranean oasis in the concrete jungle. An ever-increasing number of eateries near the complex draws diners from all over the Bay Area to the concrete caverns of the Financial District. There's **L'Olivier**, with its classic French country dishes; **Square One**, offering Mediterranean cuisine; and **MacArthur Park**, which boasts an all-American bill of fare. **Sol y Luna** has great tapas, and several evenings a week it becomes a sizzling nightclub. Another popular watering hole (if a more sedate one) is the **London Wine Bar** on **Sansome Street**; established 20 years ago, it was the first of its kind in California.

Admittedly, this is an expensive area of town to grab a bite in. But perhaps that's appropriate, given its gold-dusted history. Downtown, anyone can nourish the romantic illusion of living like landed gentry, even if only for a few hours.

YOUR SPACE

1 Your Space An eclectic mix of items to outfit the home is featured at this contemporary design studio, from unusual napkins and place mats to furniture (many pieces with metal accents) made by local artisans and a few antiques and recycled objects. ♦ By appointment only. 868 Post St (between Leavenworth and Hyde Sts). 928.8900; fax 928.0804 ♿

2 Burma House Cuisine ★$ The exotic flavors of Myanmar are showcased in a utilitarian environment distinguished only by the artificial vines twisting around the ceiling beams. Salads are highlights, particularly the ginger salad, tossed tableside with tender strips of young ginger, lentils, yellow peas, fried garlic, sesame seeds, and chilies, balanced by a squeeze of fresh lime. Or choose the equally refreshing tea salad, which has a peaty quality. Good options for the main course are the panfried string beans, with a wallop of chilies, and the Rangoon squid, which is scored and steamed, topped with peanuts, and served on a bed of spinach with a pungent sweet-and-sour sauce. The low prices and convenient location make this a good destination for theatergoers.
♦ Burmese ♦ M-F lunch and dinner; Sa-Su dinner. 720 Post St (between Jones and Leavenworth Sts). 775.1156 ♿

3 Cafe Titanic ★$ Entrepreneur Chip Conley has bought and refurbished small hotels all over San Francisco, adding restaurants to each. Now, he's replaced the ordinary coffee shop at the **Commodore International Hotel** with a delightful diner-cafe. The name, **Cafe Titanic**, fits in well with the nautical decor of the hotel in general, and the American fare is basic and tasty. For breakfast (served until the restaurant closes at 2:30PM), try eggs served

Downtown/Union Square

with applewood-smoked bacon, home fries, and fresh-baked muffins or scones; or ricotta-stuffed French toast served with warm fruit and real maple syrup. Good lunch choices include the "life preserver" burger, the exotic vegetarian Vietnamese sandwich with five-spice tofu, and the chicken prosciutto sandwich with melted fontina accented with sun-dried tomatoes and basil. The homemade soups are terrific, too. ♦ American ♦ Daily breakfast and lunch. 825 Sutter St (between Jones and Leavenworth Sts). 923.6800; fax 923.6804

4 Fleur de Lys ★★★★$$$$ Famed designer Michael Taylor, who defined the California look, decorated this elegant restaurant in 1969, yet it remains right up-to-date. Flowered fabric is fashioned into a room-size tent at the center of the room over an impressive arrangement of fresh flowers, making a perfect setting for the stunning French-Californian menu. Hubert Keller, who has worked with the great French chef Roger Verge, has removed much of the butter and fat from his cuisine. In addition to the impressive à la carte selections, he offers a four-course tasting menu beginning with a spectacular "Symphony of Fleur de Lys Appetizers" (which may include a crab cake, a sushi roll slice prepared with quinoa, and a slice of foie gras studded with pecans) and followed by an entrée such as venison tournedos on braised endive, herb-crusted rack of lamb, or sautéed veal medaillon. There's also an inventive, four-course vegetarian tasting menu that might feature wild mushroom ragout in a potato shell with caramelized vegetable *jus* or a mixture of quinoa, wild rice, and green peppercorns wrapped in cabbage leaves and served with a tomato and cumin seed sauce. For a modest fee, three different wines are matched to the savory courses of both menus. The setting is beautiful and the food is some of the best in the city, though occasionally one of Keller's experiments will fail (for instance, his idea of pairing mango puree with a fish terrine), and the wine list is pricey and lacks depth. ♦ French/Californian ♦ M-Sa dinner. Reservations recommended; jacket required. 777 Sutter St (between Taylor and Jones Sts). 673.7779; fax 673.4619

5 Lehr Brothers Bistro & Grill Formerly Lehr's Greenhouse, this dining room in the Canterbury Hotel has been a San Francisco institution since 1970, but it has recently received a complete face-lift. Now the space encompasses a bistro, grill room, oyster bar, and even a cigar room (one of the city's latest restaurant fads). One of the bistro's unique features is an entire wall stacked with premium spirits and liqueurs. The menu, by executive chef Phillip Michael Stevens, features classic continental dishes such as

dry-aged steaks, grilled sea scallops wrapped in pancetta, soups, and salads. ♦ Continental ♦ Grill: daily breakfast, lunch, and dinner. Bistro and oyster bar: daily lunch and dinner. 740 Sutter St (between Taylor and Jones Sts). 474.6478 &

WISHART

6 Wishart Celebrating 20 years in business, this delightful shop with an English feel is a find for the food lover who has everything. How about a silver-plated pizza cutter, ice-cream scoop, or Tabasco-sauce holder? There's also silver place-card holders, bottle stoppers, crystal brandy snifters and wine-glasses, salt and pepper shakers, and other accessories. One of the top draws: a special silver-plated coffeepot, a favorite of connoisseurs. ♦ Tu-Sa. 664 Post St (between Taylor and Jones Sts). 474.7442 &

7 Ar Roi ★★$ With a Deco-inspired interior and extremely friendly service, this Thai eatery is a cut above most of the neighborhood competition. While many Thai chefs in this country tone down their spices, the one here embraces fiery flavors. The chicken salad is pungent and sinus-clearing, with the citrus overtones and the spiciness a refreshing contrast to the crisp, cold iceberg lettuce and the profusion of ground chicken. Shrimp with red curry in coconut milk hits the palate sweet but leaves in a blaze of fire that can only be doused by rice. Other worthy dishes are the chicken with coconut milk soup (a classic starter), and chicken wings with chili sauce topped with crisp, fried basil leaves. ♦ Thai ♦ M-Sa lunch and dinner; Su dinner. 643 Post St (between Taylor and Jones Sts). 771.5146

7 China Moon Cafe ★★$$$ Barbara Tropp has turned a Deco-style diner into a bright, popular Chinese cafe that has received volumes of national publicity. In truth, the dishes haven't changed in years and the food isn't much better than what you'll find at similar places for less than half the cost. However, the Western-style service and sensibilities combine nicely with the Asian food. Top dishes include the "strange-flavor" eggplant, and the stir-fry chicken and vegetables on a crisp noodle pillow. Desserts, particularly the ginger ice cream drizzled with chocolate sauce, are first-rate. ♦ Chinese/California ♦ Daily dinner. Reservations recommended. 639 Post St (between Taylor and Jones Sts). 775.4789; fax 775.1409

8 City of Paris ★★$$ Named after the legendary department store (now a **Neiman Marcus**), this Art Nouveau bistro turns out some excellent straightforward food. The open kitchen is dominated by a rotisserie. To start, the cabbage salad combines salty lardons of bacon and chunks of blue cheese,

13

Downtown/Union Square

with a lemony dressing bringing everything together. One of the top main-course choices, and by far the best value, is the roast chicken, served with crunchy double-cooked fries. Wine prices are excellent, but the service can be a little disjointed. ♦ Californian/Bistro ♦ M breakfast and dinner; Tu-Su breakfast, lunch, and dinner. 550 Geary St (between Taylor and Jones Sts). 441.4442; fax 928.6813

8 Brasserie Savoy ★★★$$ With its marble floors, zinc-topped bar, and high ceilings with ornate moldings, this place looks and feels like a Parisian brasserie. A flurry of chefs has come and gone over the past several years, but now Dean James Max has settled in and is creating some of the best casual French food in the city. The three-course pretheater dinner is a good value, generally beginning with a simple salad and ending with rich crème brûlée. On the à la carte menu, the duck confit is perfectly highlighted by French lentils, *frisée* (curly endive), and a red wine vinaigrette. The roast chicken set on a bed of mushrooms and garlic mashed potatoes is comfort food at its best. ♦ French ♦ Daily dinner. Reservations recommended. 580 Geary St (at Jones St). 474.8686; fax 441.2700

9 Dottie's True Blue Cafe ★$ Pancakes and house-baked breads are the lure of this breakfast and lunch spot. A recent change in ownership has brought an increase in vegetarian offerings, especially at lunch, like the roasted eggplant sandwich with goat cheese and tomatoes, a black bean chili, and vegetable-filled tarts. ♦ American ♦ M-F breakfast and lunch; Sa-Su breakfast. 522 Jones St (at O'Farrell St). 885.2767

10 Original Joe's Italian Restaurant ★$ This Italian-American spot has a strong following despite its location in the Tenderloin, a slowly improving neighborhood that still carries a rather rough reputation. The excellent hamburger—a huge, loosely formed log of ground meat served on a chewy, hollowed-out French roll—may be one of the reasons for its appeal. (Ask for your burger to be flame-grilled rather than fried.) The red vinyl booths and moody lighting likewise speak of another era. The waiters in vintage tuxedos are as classic as the retro food, and the cooks working behind the counter in the open kitchen are as crusty as the bread. ♦ Italian ♦ Daily lunch, dinner, and late-night meals. 144 Taylor St (between Turk and Eddy Sts). 775.4877; fax 775.6563

11 Cityscape Restaurant ★★$$$ Located on the 46th floor of the **San Francisco Hilton and Towers**, this is one of the best sky-top restaurants in town. Created by chef David Lawrence, the food may not be perfect, but it's good enough, especially with the spectacular vistas from just about any table. Enjoy the 360° view while you dine on California crab cakes, pepper-crusted, cherrywood-smoked pork chops, or seared sea bass. ♦ Californian ♦ M-Sa dinner; Su brunch and dinner. Reservations recommended. 333 O'Farrell St (between Mason and Taylor Sts). 771.1400; fax 673.5163

12 Napa Valley Winery Exchange In keeping with its name, this shop stocks mostly Napa Valley wines among its 500 selections. The staff also helps customers plan trips to the Napa Valley and arranges personal appointments for winery tours and tastings and will ship purchases, too. A quarterly newsletter includes the staff's pick of those wines introduced in the last three months. ♦ M-Sa. 415 Taylor St (between O'Farrell and Geary Sts). 771.2887; fax 441.9463

13 Grand Cafe ★★$$$ This former ballroom turned-brasserie in the **Hotel Monaco** in the theater district has soaring 30-foot ceilings and an eclectic, somewhat cluttered decor that makes it seem like the place has been here forever. The open kitchen produces such appetizers as puffy shrimp and scallop beignets with remoulade sauce and eggplant stacked on goat's milk ricotta and balsamic vinaigrette. Chef Nelson Cognac's entrées are equally impressive: duck confit, cassoulet, paella, and pasta dishes. There's also a bar where sandwiches, soups, and pizzas baked in a wood-burning oven are served; it's open until midnight Fridays and Saturdays and until 11PM the rest of the week. ♦ Californian/ Continental ♦ Daily breakfast, lunch, and dinner. 501 Geary St (at Taylor St). 292.0101; fax 292.0150

14 French Room ★★$$$$ With a massive crystal chandelier and Louis XV decor, this beautiful restaurant in the **Clift Hotel** inspires many people to take a chance on the Californian-French food, which can be inconsistent. The menu choices span the globe, which probably reflects the hotel's many international guests. For breakfast (as well as Sunday brunch), there's Belgian waffles, *huevos rancheros* (fried eggs served over a corn tortilla with spicy tomato sauce), smoked-salmon eggs Benedict,

14

Downtown/Union Square

egg-white frittatas for the low-cholesterol set, and even a full Japanese menu, while the lunch and dinner menus might feature anything from Cajun-blackened prime rib to lobster cioppino. ♦ International ♦ M breakfast; Tu-Sa breakfast and dinner; Su brunch. 495 Geary St (at Taylor St). 775.4700; fax 441.4621 ♿

14 Redwood Room ★★$$$ One of the best examples of Art Deco design in America, this dining room in the **Clift Hotel** is entirely paneled in redwood from a 2,000-year-old tree. Soaring 22-foot fluted columns and an elegant 75-foot bar decorated with fine Italian marble highlights and Klimt reproductions complete the magnificent look. The "bistro" menu lists a nice selection of snacks and light lunch choices. Start with a traditional French onion soup or a hearts of romaine salad with creamy Caesar dressing. The terrific entrées include the Clift burger with crisp Canadian bacon and melted Swiss cheese, smoked turkey club sandwich with avocado, and chicken or shrimp stir-fry with Shanghai noodles. ♦ Californian/French ♦ Bistro menu 11AM-11PM. 495 Geary St (at Taylor St). 775.4700; fax 441.4621 ♿

15 California Pizza Kitchen ★$ Put on dark glasses to enter this chrome yellow, black, and white world of strange pizzas. In the worst of California tradition, this chain's parlor offers thin, slightly sweet crusts topped with such idiocies as barbecued chicken, Thai chicken with peanuts, duck with hoisin sauce, and Canadian bacon with pineapple. Stick with the traditional and you'll have no regrets, especially since the prices for pizza and pasta are reasonable for the area. ♦ Gourmet Pizza ♦ Daily lunch and dinner. 438 Geary St (between Mason and Taylor Sts). 563.8911; fax 563.2143 ♿

15 David's Delicatessen ★$ The true deli connoisseur may be disappointed by this place, the city's most famous Jewish deli. However, the sandwiches are generous, piled high with lots of pastrami or corned beef, and the Reuben and the blintzes are standouts. Full dinners include Hungarian goulash, stuffed cabbage, and beef brisket. For dessert, you can choose among any of more than a hundred homemade pastries, including dense cheesecake and "decadence," a gooey concoction made with five kinds of chocolate. Service is efficient and friendly. ♦ Deli ♦ Daily breakfast, lunch, and dinner. 474 Geary St (between Mason and Taylor Sts). 771.1600; fax 931.5442 ♿

15 La Scene Cafe and Bar ★$$$ A pleasant spot before or after the theater, this richly appointed room is graced with sketches of performers who have appeared at the **Curran Theatre.** The food here has been unreliable in the past, but chef Rebecca Gray, a recent arrival, is trying to turn the kitchen around. The ever-changing à la carte menu features such dishes as apple and fennel salad with gorgonzola and walnuts dressed with a pear vinaigrette; spicy calamari dipped in lemon-caper aioli; polenta napoleon with goat cheese, basil pesto, and mushroom ragout; and grilled salmon in butternut squash sauce with roasted Peruvian potatoes. The pretheater three-course fixed-price menu is a great deal. ♦ Provençal/Mediterranean ♦ Daily breakfast; Tu-Sa dinner; daily bar (with a limited menu M, Su). Reservations recommended. 490 Geary St (at Taylor St). 292.6430; fax 441.8788 ♿

16 Floréal This charming flower shop fashions unique, sophisticated centerpieces, with the unusual touch of fruits and vegetables; an arrangement might include pomegranates, kiwi, and a profusion of fragrant lavender. It's worth a visit for inspiration alone; check out the whimsical art pieces featuring fruit and food motifs, freeze-dried produce that looks great in arrangements, and elegant garlands for all seasons. ♦ M-Sa. 533 Taylor St (at Geary St). 885.4261; fax 885.0342 ♿

17 Gold Leaf The theme at this store is food and flowers, with thousands of miniature ceramic fruits, vegetables, and flowers that are so detailed they look like shrunken versions of the real thing. The collection also includes wonderful button covers, mini-teapots, earrings, bells, and magnets that follow the same food-obsessed theme. ♦ M-Sa. 611 Post St (between Taylor and Jones Sts). 885.4004; fax 673.6177 ♿

18 Postrio ★★★$$$ Wolfgang Puck's Northern California outpost looks like a slice of LA. With customers who appear to be from central casting descending a dramatic

Downtown/Union Square

staircase into the impressive dining room, it's a great place to people watch. However, although the ambience is influenced by Hollywood, the inventive food is rooted in San Francisco's strong Italian and Asian heritage. Chefs (and brothers) Steven and Mitchell Rosenthal have put their own spin on Puck's signature cuisine with such creations as garlic lamb stir-fried with mint and fresh chilies, smoked salmon served on a giant blini, and grilled quail accompanied by a soft egg ravioli (pierce the pasta, and the yolk of a quail egg oozes forth). Other standouts include Puck's version of roasted Chinese duck, served with a changing array of sauces such as pineapple-ginger vinaigrette. The service is smooth and professional. While everyone seems to come here for lunch or dinner, most people don't realize it's also a great downtown breakfast spot. Don't miss the oyster and pancetta omelette. ♦ Californian ♦ M-F breakfast, lunch, and dinner; Sa-Su brunch and dinner. 545 Post St (between Mason and Taylor Sts). 776.7825; fax 776.6702

19 Pacific ★★★$$$ Try as it may, the management of the **Pan Pacific** hotel, where this establishment is located, has never been able to turn it into a local destination. There's no street access, so diners must take an elevator up to the restaurant, which is elegantly appointed but has an impersonal feel. Yet the food has never been better than it is under Takayoshi Kawai, the former executive sous-chef at **Masa's** (see page 19). Sautéed lobster is accented with the earthy perfume of truffles and the crunch of barely cooked cabbage; squab is also touched with truffles, this time in a creamy, rich risotto. In another inspired combination, breast of pheasant is paired with braised cabbage and mashed potatoes mixed with truffles. ♦ Californian ♦ M-F breakfast, lunch, and dinner, Sa-Su brunch and dinner. 500 Post St (between Mason and Taylor Sts). 929.2087; fax 921.4756

The Tadich Grill has been a downtown institution since it opened in 1849. But a glance at the 1962 menu shows how times have changed. Back then, a diner could order an abalone steak for $2.60 or a whole crab sauté for $4.25. An "alligator pear"—known as an avocado these days—with Louis dressing was $1.25.

20 Yakety Yak Coffee House ★$ Brightly painted in primary colors, this rambling, rustic cafe attracts an artistic crowd, especially the students at the **Academy of Art Institute** across the street. The counter is lined with all kinds of delicious pastries and munchies, and the coffee has a marvelously strong and bitter edge. ♦ Coffeehouse ♦ Daily. 679 Sutter St (between Mason and Taylor Sts). 885.6908

21 White Horse Tavern ★$ This tavern, in the **Hotel Beresford,** replicates an Edinburgh pub, and as might be expected, the cooks do a splendid job with grilled meats. Portions are large, preparations are straightforward, and prices are excellent. The large hamburger is a challenge to finish, and the corned beef and cabbage consists of a half-dozen thick slices of meat and half a head of cabbage cut into wedges and arranged on the plate with a boiled potato. ♦ British ♦ M, Su breakfast and lunch; Tu-Sa breakfast, lunch, and dinner. 635 Sutter St (between Mason and Taylor Sts). 673.9900; fax 474.0449

22 Zingari ★★$$$ Formerly the **Ristorante Donatello** (which was one of the top Italian eateries in the city several years ago), this dining room in the **Donatello Hotel** continues to serve excellent Italian fare. Owner/chef Giovanni Scorzo has chosen to feature dishes from all over Italy, presented in an elegant, refined style with such menu offerings as broiled calamari topped with fresh tomatoes and basil, grilled and smoked mozzarella cheese served with portobello mushrooms and radicchio (which the menu calls "wild chicory"), and veal loin stuffed with truffles and fontina cheese, as well as risotti, pasta dishes, and salads. Named after the Italian word for "gypsies," the intimate dining room boasts Venetian marble accents. ♦ Italian ♦ Daily breakfast, lunch, and dinner. 501 Post St (at Mason St). 441.7100; fax 885.8842

23 Christophe ★$$$ Classic French food in a pink-washed Art Deco setting makes this restaurant a festive spot for dining before or after the theater. The best deal is the pretheater fixed-price menu, which might consist of ravioli with sun-dried tomatoes, mixed salad, thin medaillons of pork piccata,

Downtown/Union Square

and a fresh-fruit pudding. ◆ French ◆ M, Su dinner; Tu-Sa lunch and dinner. Reservations recommended. 405 Mason St (at Geary St), Second floor. 771.6393; fax 771.6496

23 Biscuits and Blues ★$$ Well-known restaurateur Regina Charboneau specializes in "hot biscuits and cool blues." The biscuits, shrimp and corn fritters, and vinegar-laced greens *are* exceptional, but otherwise the kitchen can be uneven. Among the main courses on the abbreviated menu are grilled or fried catfish and chicken, a daily special such as jambalaya, Caesar salad topped with crisply fried shrimp, and a vegetarian plate of pickled black-eyed peas, mashed potatoes, pureed sweet potatoes, and those wonderful greens. The walls of this basement-level speakeasy are covered with shrines to blues singers, and masses of candles flank the slightly raised stage. There is live music every night. ◆ Southern ◆ Cover from 9PM to 1AM. Tu-Sa dinner. 401 Mason St (at Geary St). 292.2583; fax 834.2754

24 Sushi Bune ★★$ Popular and fun for a quick lunch, this spot's chefs place sushi and sashimi on little boats that float around the sushi bar's moat; diners at the counter grab what they want as it sails by. At the end of the meal the server counts up what the diner consumed, calculating prices by the size or shape of the raft. Full dinners are also offered, and the tempura is better than average. ◆ Japanese ◆ Daily lunch and dinner. 389 Geary St (at Mason St). 781.5111

25 New Delhi Restaurant ★$$ Set in a onetime hotel ballroom, this eatery is graced by elaborate columns that lend it a vestige of grandeur. Among the offerings the tandoori chicken and the vegetable turnovers stand out. For a quick bite, sit at the ornate mahogany bar and order appetizers. ◆ Indian ◆ M-Sa lunch and dinner; bar daily until 2AM. 160 Ellis St (between Cyril Magnin and Mason Sts). 397.8470; fax 397.1024

26 Nanbantei ★★$$ One of the few *yakitori* bars in the city, this is an ideal stop for grazers. The 27 skewered and grilled tidbits include tiny lamb chops, meaty ginkgo nuts, fiery Japanese peppers wrapped in thin baconlike strips of pork, juicy cuttlefish wrapped in *sic* (a pungent Japanese herb), sweet scallops with just a hint of smoke, and tender marinated chunks of filet mignon. Diners can sit at the tables, but the best show is at the bar, where the chefs work with the precision of ballet dancers. ◆ Japanese ◆ Daily dinner. 115 Cyril Magnin St (at Ellis St). 421.2101; fax 834.2754

27 Puccini & Pinetti ★$ Operated by the Kimpton hotel group, which manages more than a dozen restaurants around town, this casual dining spot presents a menu that emphasizes straightforward pasta dishes, a few salads, and well-prepared panini, all at reasonable prices. Particularly good menu choices are angel hair pasta with summer vegetables and basil oil, spicy *penne arrabiatta,* in a tomato sauce with chili flecks and bits of sausage, and grilled half-chicken with rosemary potatoes. ◆ Californian/Italian ◆ Daily lunch and dinner. 129 Ellis St (at Cyril Magnin St). 392.5500; fax 392.2650

28 Kantaro ★$ Light wood columns and white walls hung with lanterns give this Japanese restaurant style that belies its low prices. The best dish is teriyaki; the chicken version is moistened with a sauce that adds only a touch of sweetness. The tempura are crisp and excellent in flavor, although the coating is on the heavy side. Sushi or sashimi are fine for a quick lunch, and also popular is the Chirashi-sushi or scattered sushi, a bowl of vinegary rice topped with sliced raw fish, daikon, pickled ginger, cucumbers, and other fresh-tasting ingredients. ◆ Japanese ◆ Daily lunch and dinner. 124 Ellis St (at Powell St). 986.2339; fax 986.4312

29 John's Grill ★$$ A classic San Francisco grill established in 1908, this eatery caters to the two-martini-lunch businessman. With a moody, dark wood and brass interior, it's no surprise that this was a favorite hangout of author Dashiell Hammett (as well as his fictional character Sam Spade). Like all grills of the period, its food has an Italian flavor. Specialties include steaks and pork chops with baked potatoes (one of Sam's favorites). The chicken Jerusalem (with artichokes and mushrooms) is a good rendition of a classic. To wash down your food, try the "Bloody Brigid," a sweet and sour vodka drink named for the dame that "done in" Sam Spade's partner, Miles Archer, in *The Maltese Falcon.* ◆ American ◆ M-Sa lunch and dinner; Su dinner. 63 Ellis St (between Stockton and Powell Sts). 986.0069; fax 982.2583

30 Tad's Steaks ★$ Cheap, fast, and filling characterize the fare at this cafeteria-style steak house established in the mid-1940s. The nine-ounce strip steak or a roasted half-chicken, served with salad, potatoes, and rolls, is only adequate, but it's a bargain. ◆ American ◆ Daily breakfast, lunch, and dinner. No credit cards accepted. 120 Powell St (between Ellis and O'Farrell Sts). 982.1718

17

Downtown/Union Square

31 Dojima An ★★$$ Noodles are the specialty at this sleek, minimally decorated Japanese spot. The menu lists 23 different combinations made with either *udon* (thick, chewy white noodles) or *soba* (spaghetti-like buckwheat noodles), along with 11 *donburi* (rice topped with meat and vegetables). Best bets include the Japanese mountain vegetables and the cold noodles with grated daikon. The tempura, teriyaki, and other choices aren't nearly as special. ♦ Japanese ♦ Daily breakfast, lunch, and dinner. 219 O'Farrell St (at Powell St). 956.0838

KULETO'S

32 Kuleto's Italian Restaurant ★$$ The large open kitchen gives this trattoria a boisterous feel. Sitting at the counter can be fun: Watch the always-harried chefs pull wonderful pizzas from the oven and exceptional roasted meats from the rotisserie. Pastas are good, too—especially the penne with lamb sausage and red chard in a marinara sauce—though on particularly busy nights the food can be lackluster. The adjoining **Caffè Kuleto** serves espresso drinks, focaccia, panini, and gelato at outdoor tables during the day. ♦ Italian ♦ Daily breakfast, lunch, and dinner. 221 Powell St (at O'Farrell St). 397.7720; fax 986.7050

33 New Joe's $ Like **Original Joe's** (see page 14), this place serves classic Cal-Ital fare—a throwback to the 1950s, when tomato sauces were cooked for hours and beef was king. The wheelchair-accessible entrance is through the adjacent **Handlery Hotel.** ♦ Italian ♦ Daily breakfast, lunch, and dinner. 347 Geary St (between Powell and Mason Sts). 397.9999; fax 989.1544

34 Compass Rose ★$$$ Formerly just an afternoon tea spot, this place in the lobby of the **Westin St. Francis Hotel** has been converted to a full-service restaurant. Both the dining area and the adjacent bar feature dark wood paneling, high ceilings, and a quiet, subdued atmosphere the bar also has hand-crafted, cut glass accents. The menu offers typical California cuisine presented with somewhat inconsistent quality. Start your meal with crispy shrimp tempura or a plate of assorted vegetables with basil-yogurt dip, then move on to pan-seared salmon with fried capers, *ahi* tuna, or broiled Black Angus tenderloin. At the bar, you can munch on some of the appetizers from the regular menu, as well as pizza topped with smoked chicken. A full tea is still served in the afternoon. ♦ Californian ♦ Daily lunch, afternoon tea, and dinner. 335 Powell St (on Union Sq, between Geary and Post Sts). 774.0167; fax 403.6850

34 Dewey's ★$ Also in the lobby of the **Westin St. Francis,** this sports bar is a fun place to grab a bite and catch your favorite team on one of the many TV sets. Decent cappuccino and excellent house-baked pastries hit the spot at breakfast, while pizzas and sandwiches step up to the plate for lunch and dinner. Decorated in traditional pub style, with wood paneling, scattered tables, and bar stools, the bar features over 50 different beers. ♦ Sports Bar ♦ Daily breakfast, lunch, snacks, and dinner. 335 Powell St (on Union Sq, between Geary and Post Sts). 774.0169; fax 403.6850

34 Dutch Kitchen $$$ Although this hotel cafeteria is rather drab and dreary (especially compared to the opulent surroundings of the **Westin St. Francis**), it is one of the only restaurants in the city that offers a traditional Japanese breakfast (salads, breads, etc.) in addition to the standard morning fare. The food is okay, but very overpriced. ♦ American/Japanese ♦ Daily breakfast. 335 Powell St (on Union Sq, between Geary and Post Sts). 774.0264; fax 403.6850

34 My Sister's Garden Ceramic plates from Portugal and Italy, including the Nino Brucca collection, bring the southern European countryside to this shop in the lobby of the **Westin St. Francis** hotel. ♦ Daily. Main entrance 427 Post St (at Powell St). 397.0550

35 Morton's of Chicago ★$$$$ Although this upscale steak chain offers a great piece of beef, diners pay an exceedingly high price. And even at that price, the meat comes ungarnished; every side dish carries a separate price tag. Waiters are trained like seals to "tell" the menu, punctuating their recitation by displaying the raw ingredients—a potato, a bunch of broccoli, and a live lobster, for instance. For dessert, avoid the soufflés and stick with the Key lime pie. The basement setting, with dark woods and low lighting, has a retro mood. ♦ Steak house ♦ Daily dinner. 400 Post St (at Powell St). 986.5830; fax 986.5829

World Famous
Sears FINE Food
BREAKFAST LUNCH

35 Sears Fine Foods ★★$$ Hordes line up at this no-nonsense breakfast and lunch spot. With its classic breakfasts, bare-bones environment, and motherly waitresses, the place is an institution. The most popular dish is the Swedish pancakes. ♦ American ♦ W–Su breakfast and lunch. 439 Powell St (near Post St). 986.1160

Downtown/Union Square

36 Cafe SFA ★★$$ On the fifth floor of **Saks Fifth Avenue,** this department-store dining room is among the best of its kind. Booths curve around the room, affording a bird's-eye view of **Union Square,** and the convivial mix of well-dressed buyers, executives, and the ladies-who-lunch bunch provides ample people-watching opportunities. The imaginative menu includes a delicious crab sandwich, grilled Asian pork chops with a wild rice and spinach pancake, and smoked chicken and arugula salad with tarragon vinaigrette. ♦ Californian ♦ M-Sa lunch. 384 Post St (at Powell St). 986.4758; fax 986.0643 &

37 Scala's Bistro ★★★$$ In the **Sir Francis Drake** hotel, this dining room has quickly become one of Union Square's top restaurants and a magnet for the fashion crowd. The tin ceiling, Craftsman-looking lights, and striking open kitchen combine to spectacular effect. The bilevel dining area is broken up with booths and partitions that make just about every table seem intimate. The menu features both French country and Italian influences, including one of the best versions of fried calamari in town. Carpaccio is enhanced by shaved raw artichokes and nutty parmesan cheese. Among the pastas, the bow ties with wild mushrooms and asparagus never fail to satisfy. Meat courses include marinated pork tenderloin with rich au gratin potatoes and wilted greens, and a roast chicken that emerges bronzed and succulent from the brick oven in back. The Bostini cream pie is truly memorable—actually a bowl of rich custard topped with a tender cupcake of orange chiffon, all doused in chocolate sauce. ♦ Italian ♦ Daily breakfast, lunch, and dinner. 432 Powell St (between Post and Sutter Sts). 395.8555; fax 395.8549 &

37 Harry Denton's Starlight Room ★★$$ Harry Denton has a long history in San Francisco as a great host, bar and restaurant owner, and party animal, and now he has brought his boisterous personality to the newly refurbished rooftop nightclub at the **Sir Francis Drake** hotel. The room is decorated in sumptuous glamor reminiscent of classic 1930s movies, with voluminous silk drapery in ruby red and gold, crystal chandeliers, and high-backed velvet booths. But undoubtedly the major asset is the spectacular 360° view, which can be had from almost every table in the place. The menu features elegant appetizers and light entrées, including caviar, jumbo shrimp cocktail, oysters on the half shell, and chilled smoked beef tenderloin. Desserts here range from the light (angel food cake) to the deliciously decadent ("Death by Chocolate," a sinfully rich chocolate mousse cake), and a dizzying array of cocktails, specialty drinks, and wines is available. A full orchestra and vocalists perform dance music Monday through Saturday nights, and taped music is played on Sundays. ♦ American ♦ Cover. Daily dinner. 432 Powell St (between Post and Sutter Sts). 395.8595; fax 391.8719 &

37 Cafe Espresso ★★$ Few coffee bars are as pretty as this corner cafe in the **Sir Francis Drake.** At breakfast, grab a newspaper from the racks at the front window, order a bowl of granola or a pastry, and settle back for a gentle morning wake-up. The rich yellow walls, bistro-style chairs with marble tables, and the Old World marble-topped bar give the interior a sophisticated look. The straightforward fare includes sandwiches on fresh rolls or focaccia and such salads as Caesar, Chinese chicken, and Thai shrimp. End the meal with Snicker Doodle cookies and a cup of cappuccino or espresso. ♦ Cafe ♦ Daily breakfast, lunch, and dinner. 432 Powell St (between Post and Sutter Sts). 395.8585 &

MASA'S

38 Masa's ★★★★$$$$ Julian Serrano uses his Spanish heritage and French training to create some of the most innovative food in town. Instead of an à la carte menu, a four-course and a six-course tasting menu are offered. Serrano sautés chunks of rich foie gras to a crisp veneer and serves them with perfect vegetable morsels bathed in a truffle sauce with a hint of sweetness from Madeira. Lamb noisettes with green peppercorns in a velvety Zinfandel sauce is perfectly complemented by a rich Bordeaux. More than 20 vintages on the award winning wine list (including the exquisite Château d'Yquem) can be enjoyed by the glass, which facilitates matching the right wine to each course. The recently refurbished dining room now has a sleek elegance, with modern art on the red walls and Hutschenreuther china and Christofle silver table settings. Though the service is smooth and efficient, it can also be a bit cold and impersonal. ♦ French ♦ Tu-Sa dinner. Reservations recommended; jacket required. 648 Bush St (at Powell St). 989.7154; fax 989.3141 &

39 Campton Place Restaurant ★★★$$$$ Probably the best-known and most elegant hotel restaurant in the city, this establishment in the **Campton Place** hotel elevated its former chefs Bradley Ogden and Jan Birnbaum to national stature. The present chef is Todd Humphries, who worked in Gray Kunz's kitchen at Lespinasse in New York, and Humphries's creations reflect some of the same innovative flavor combinations that Kunz pioneered. Consider such dishes as duck breast with baby turnips, kumquats, and kafir lime leaves; scallops with salsify (an oyster-flavored root), vanilla, and ginger; and

19

Downtown/Union Square

pork chops with cardamom, cabbage, apples, bacon, and chestnuts. Another specialty is power breakfasts: The corn sticks are famous and the prices steep. ♦ American ♦ Daily breakfast, lunch, and dinner. Reservations recommended; jacket recommended. 340 Stockton St (at Campton Pl). 955.5555; fax 955.5596 &

Anjou Restaurant

40 Anjou ★★$$ A charming French ambience pervades this two-level dining room. The menu created by chef-owner Pierre Morin strikes a balance between tradition and innovation: There's moist duck confit on portobello mushrooms and herb polenta; asparagus with puff pastry in a morel-studded cream sauce; a casserole of prawns and artichokes; and lamb chops with fresh flageolets. On the classic side, consider such dishes as the thin-cut New York steak with extra-crisp fries, the calves' brains sautéed with sage, or the *tarte tatin* (upside-down apple tart) for dessert. ♦ French bistro ♦ Tu-Sa lunch and dinner. 44 Campton Pl (off Stockton St, between Post and Sutter Sts). 392.5373

41 Napper's ★★$ Located on the ground floor of the **Grand Hyatt Hotel** on **Union Square**, this cafeteria has such whimsical touches as tables set on mannequin legs. On nice days, dine around a fountain on a brick terrace overlooking **Union Square**. Sandwiches are fairly priced and include shrimp salad, crab salad, and roast turkey; there are also hot dogs and chili dogs. Salads are another good luncheon value: The cobb has grilled chicken, bacon, blue cheese, and vegetables, and the creamy Caesar is available plain or with chicken. There's also a daily changing soup special and hearty chili con carne. ♦ American ♦ Daily breakfast, lunch, and early dinner. 345 Stockton St (between Post and Sutter Sts). 398.7687; fax 403.4888 &

41 Plaza ★$$ Like **Napper's** (see above), this grand, full-service restaurant is in the **Grand Hyatt Hotel**, but the same cobb salad costs more than twice as much here. However, the mezzanine-level room is impressive: A stained-glass dome, latticework walls, a fountain, and a slate floor create a garden pavilion, complete with coconut palm-trees, and the wall of windows overlooking **Union Square** provides picture-postcard views. Aside from sandwiches, there are such well-prepared hot dishes as roast chicken in a golden brown gravy or shrimp-chicken-vegetable stir-fry over rice. Evenings bring a fixed-price menu and free valet parking at the hotel entrance. And the Sunday Champagne brunch is popular. ♦ American ♦ Daily breakfast, lunch, and dinner; Su brunch. 345 Stockton St (between Post and Sutter Sts). 398.1234; fax 392.2536 &

42 Cafe Akimbo ★★$$ East and West meet comfortably at this 38-seat, third-floor cafe tucked away on Maiden Lane. Although the walls and support beams across the ceiling are painted in a rainbow of colors, the atmosphere is serene. Few chefs do as good a job with cross-cultural cooking as Daniel Yang, a former flight attendant who is the (self-taught) chef and co-owner. Starters include chilled soft tofu with a confetti of dried flowers and shrimp, all accented with a lemon-soy dressing, and grilled flank steak, drizzled with a honey-sesame vinaigrette. Among the entrées, pan-cooked chicken is paired with a sweet-potato and curry sauce, and a confit of duck leg is imaginatively served with an apricot sauce and ginger-glazed carrots. The ginger crème caramel makes a refreshing and comforting finish. ♦ Californian ♦ M-Sa lunch and dinner. 116 Maiden La (between Grant Ave and Stockton St), Third floor. 433.2288; fax 433.2298 &

43 The Epicurean Shop The top floor of **Neiman Marcus** is the place to go for high-quality (and expensive) provisions, including smoked salmon, caviar, wine and spirits, cheeses, cookies, pies, cakes, and specialty products. Designer table accessories are also available. Made-to-order gift baskets are a specialty. ♦ Daily. 150 Stockton St (at Geary St). 362.3900 ext 2177; fax 291.9816 &

THE ROTUNDA

43 The Rotunda ★★$$ The centerpiece of this elegant restaurant on the fourth floor of **Neiman Marcus** is the impressive stained-glass dome from the **City of Paris** department store, the site's former occupant. The dome lends a warm, romantic glow to the tiered dining room that wraps around the atrium. Other nice touches are the tiny cups of bouillon and delicious popovers with flavored butters that automatically appear on each table. Popular dishes include the lobster club sandwich, the oven-roasted chicken with mustard sauce, and the smoked-salmon salad. Desserts range from a tall root-beer float to an impressive lemon layer cake sprinkled with coconut. ♦ Californian ♦ Daily lunch and tea. Reservations recommended. 150 Stockton St (at Geary St). 362.4777 &

Downtown/Union Square

level, there's also furniture, candles, and toys. Prices are generally lower than at department stores, too. ♦ Daily. 125 Grant Ave (between Geary and Post Sts). 986.4000; fax 986.8280

52 Christofle Known for its beautiful sterling silver flatware, tea sets, trays, and wine buckets, this branch of the French chain also presents a fine collection of china, all displayed in elegant surroundings. ♦ M-Sa. 140 Grant Ave (between Geary and Post Sts). 399.1931; fax 399.1779

NOSHERIA

52 Nosheria ★$ The fragrant aroma of freshly baked bread entices diners to this cafeteria-style eatery, whose focaccia sandwiches make a tasty, quick lunch. In addition to the indoor seating, there are tables outdoors, in the street, but the setting is pretty bare: marble tables and ice-cream-parlor chairs, without plants or other embellishments. It's very pleasant on a sunny day, though (except for the pesky pigeons). ♦ Italian ♦ Daily breakfast, lunch, and dinner. 69 Maiden La (between Kearny St and Grant Ave). 398.3557

53 Candelier A veritable inspiration for setting a beautiful table, this shop features more than a thousand candles (and various holders), displayed cunningly in seasonal exhibits. For one, an entire table was covered with what appeared to be a bountiful array of fruits and vegetables, interspersed with cookbooks; closer inspection revealed that the grapes, raspberries, asparagus, ears of corn, pears, and fruit tarts were actually candles. There's also a well-chosen assortment of dinnerware, place mats, napkins, soaps, and bath products (the scent of the vanilla soap is addictive). ♦ M-Sa. 60 Maiden La (between Kearny St and Grant Ave). 989.8600; fax 989.9263

54 Gump's With its opening here in March 1995, this retailer, which has been selling luxury goods since 1861, has reestablished itself as one of the premier stores on **Union Square**. Within its beautifully remodeled 1910 Beaux Arts building, a spectacular 32-foot-high atrium vaults over a museum-quality 18th-century Ching dynasty Buddha; the selling area lies around the perimeter. No other store in San Francisco has as impressive a selection of fine crystal, silverware, and china; the "Great Wall of China" on the second floor offers more than 200 patterns. The extensive tabletop collection includes such treasures as antique Georg Jensen gravy boats ($13,000), an artistic Sabbatini silver tea service ($2,100), and Steuben glass from the 1920s and 1930s (priced from $525 to $25,000). The Baccarat collection features such unique pieces as a crystal and cobalt-blue chandelier ($38,000). In addition to its exquisite displays of jade jewelry and pearls, the store is known for fine Chinese porcelains and modern European and American art glass; its new location boasts an even larger selection. A new bed, bath, and linen department offers a wealth of elegant place mats and napkins. Even if you can only afford to browse, it's a not-to-be-missed San Francisco classic. ♦ M-Sa. 135 Post St (between Kearny St and Grant Ave). 982.1616; fax 984.9379

55 Williams-Sonoma The well-known cookware chain got its start almost 40 years ago, when it was launched by Chuck Williams. (Williams originally owned a hardware store in Sonoma, hence the name.) The merchandise at this flagship store, beautifully displayed on two floors, offers the serious cook the best in equipment. Lately, however, the china and glass made in Europe specifically for the chain store is less unique in design than it used to be, and in many cases it can't go into the dishwasher or microwave. ♦ Daily. 150 Post St (between Kearny St and Grant Ave). 362.6904; fax 362.2852. Also at: San Francisco Centre, 865 Market St (at Fifth St). 546.0171; 2000 Chestnut St (at Fillmore St). 929.2520

56 Teuscher Chocolates of Switzerland In business more than 60 years, this tiny, expensive chocolate shop has a glittery, party atmosphere. Of the hundred varieties of chocolates flown in from Zurich weekly, the most popular is the Champagne chocolate, containing a splash of Dom Pérignon in the center. All the chocolates can be elaborately boxed for impressive gifts. ♦ M-Sa. 255 Grant Ave (between Campton Pl and Sutter St). 990.2700; fax 398.2031

57 Rumpus ★★★$$ Noisy and bright, as its name implies, this stylish spot never-theless has a civilized edge. And great food streams from chef Charles Price's glass-enclosed kitchen: penne with tomato and sausage, risotto with shrimp and okra, juicy roast chicken enlivened with garlic, and New York steak with mashed sweet potatoes. The Caesar salad is one of the best in town, and the wine list, which

Downtown/Union Square

THE FRESHMARKET℠

43 Fresh Market Cafe ★$ Relatively inexpensive, this third-floor cafe at **Neiman Marcus** is popular with the retail crowd, which comes for sandwiches (chicken curry in pita, tuna-pecan salad), salads (cobb, Caesar, or that 1950s classic, sweet lemon soufflé), and the daily-changing soups. Carrot cake and pound cake are both good ways to cap a meal or enjoy a midday respite from shopping. ♦ Cafe ♦ M, Th-F breakfast, lunch, and early dinner; Tu-W, Sa-Su breakfast and lunch. 150 Stockton St (at Geary St), Third floor. 362.3900 ext 2169 &

43 Espresso Bar $ A quick and easy stop for basic sandwiches, sweets, and coffee, this cafe on the lower level of **Neiman Marcus** offers a convenient pick-me-up to shoppers, especially those perusing the adjoining men's clothing department. ♦ Cafe ♦ Daily breakfast, lunch, and snacks. 150 Stockton St (at Geary St). 362.3900 ext 2334 &

44 Macy's Cellar Just about everything any at-home cook needs can be found in this huge basement-level department of **Macy's**. It boasts walls of pottery dishes, appliances, cutlery, bar stools, gadgets, and a whole section of specialty food products, including oils, mustards, pastas, and condiments. Non-cooks will be happy, too, with the take-out deli featuring Wolfgang Puck's pizza, **Boudin** breads and cakes, and Tom's cookies (they're fabulous). There's even a wine shop. ♦ Daily. 170 O'Farrell St (at Stockton St). 397.3333 &

45 Fresh Choice $ For a healthful break from shopping, this chain eatery is quick, easy, and emphasizes low-fat food. It features an extensive salad bar, breads, pastas (often mushy), and desserts, including fresh fruit. ♦ American ♦ Daily lunch and early dinner. 120 Stockton St (at O'Farrell St), Basement. 989.6861; fax 989.6863 &. Also at: 150 Fourth St (between Howard and Mission Sts). 777.2075; fax 777.2076 &

46 Ghirardelli Chocolates Chocoholics who don't want to fight the crowds at **Ghirardelli Square** can buy a wide range of chocolates in more peaceful surroundings here. Many of the choices are great for giving: A 10-ounce milk chocolate cable car may be the ultimate edible gift, and the 10-ounce can of unsweetened cocoa makes unbeatable hot chocolate. ♦ Daily. 44 Stockton St (at Market St). 397.3615; fax 397.7626 &

46 Planet Hollywood $$$ Number 25 in this worldwide chain of eateries owned by Sylvester Stallone, Arnold Schwarzenegger, and Bruce Willis, this spot is strictly for the fanatical movie buff. Cluttered with movie photos, costumes, and artifacts (including the ark from *Raiders of the Lost Ark*, one of the half-human robots from the *Terminator* series, and a representation of Stallone's *Demolition Man* character frozen in a block of ice), it's more of a theme park than a restaurant; gastronomically, your best bet is the simple hamburger. But kids (and kids at heart) will probably have a good time. (You might want to bring earplugs, though—the sound system continually blasts high-decibel rock music.) And don't forget to buy a T-shirt. ♦ American ♦ Daily lunch and dinner. 2 Stockton St (at Market St). 421.7827 &

47 Eppler's Bakery ★$ This 110-year-old enterprise, now with five locations, feels like a cozy hometown bakery. Its ovens turn out more than 300 products, including cakes, cookies, Danish, and doughnuts. Nothing is a standout, but the pastries are sweet and gooey. Coffee drinks, pastries, sandwiches, and other light lunch fare can be eaten in-house. ♦ Cafe ♦ M-Sa 6AM-7PM; Su 7AM-6PM. 750 Market St (at Grant Ave). 392.0101. Also at: Numerous locations throughout the city

48 Armani Cafe ★★$$ For light eaters, a horseshoe-shape espresso bar right in the middle of **Emporio Armani** offers great coffee drinks, wine, aperitifs, focaccia sandwiches, designer pizzas, freshly made salads, and fresh-grilled seafood and meats. The tables are set up in a circle around the preparation/serving area. ♦ Cafe ♦ Daily lunch. 1 Grant Ave (at O'Farrell St). 677.9010; fax 677.9212 &

49 Cafe Dolci Cramming a lot into a closet-size space, this black-and-white, high-tech espresso bar/candy shop offers three kinds of chewy caramels, truffles, bags of sweets, biscotti, and great cups of Spinelli coffee—all to go. Easy to miss, it's next door to the **Wells Fargo Bank**. ♦ M-F. No credit cards accepted. 740 Market St (at Grant Ave). 392.9222 &

50 Morrow's Nut House Innumerable nuts fill this tiny specialty shop, and all kinds of fancy tins line the walls behind the glass-covered bins of fresh-roasted nuts. There's also trail mix and fleshy dried apricots and papayas, among other fruits. ♦ M-Sa. 111 Geary St (at Grant Ave). 362.7969 &

51 Crate & Barrel This Chicago-based retail chain has an excellent selection of stylish merchandise for the kitchen, bath, and beyond, including dishes and wineglasses in just about every shape and size. On the lower

21

Downtown/Union Square

concentrates on Rhône and Italian varietals from California wineries, is tops. For dessert, order the chocolate brioche bread pudding or the apple tart composed of lightly browned slices of fruit draped over a mound of custard resting on a crisp circle of puff pastry; the latter takes 20 minutes, but is worth the wait. ♦ American ♦ M-Sa lunch and dinner; Su dinner. 1 Tillman Pl (off Grant Ave, between Post and Sutter Sts). 421.2300; fax 421.2316

58 The Candy Jar This tiny shop has been an institution on Union Square for 17 years. The display cases hold truffles, bonbons, marzipan fruits, and other sweets, some made without sugar. Individually wrapped candies and toffees line the shelves and bins, and everything can be gift-boxed. ♦ M-Sa. 210 Grant Ave (between Post and Sutter Sts). 391.5508. Also at: 2065 Oakdale Ave (at Industrial Ave). 550.8846; fax 550.8359

59 Sonoma Valley Bagel Co. ★★$ The latest addition to San Francisco's growing number of bagelries, this pleasant eatery boils its bagels in a kettle instead of oven-baking them, which makes them nice and chewy. There are 13 varieties, including jalapeño, cranberry, and sun-dried tomato with basil, and low- and no-fat spreads to go with them. The menu is rounded out with bagel sandwiches, hot dogs served on bagel buns, soups, and salads. There's both indoor and outdoor seating, or you can get your bagel to go. ♦ American ♦ Daily breakfast and lunch. 266 Sutter St (between Kearny St and Grant Ave) 951.0133; fax 951.8540

60 Café Claude ★$$ The zinc bar, where patrons can linger as long as they like, and the lively ambience make this a French haven, especially for lunch. Nighttime often brings live jazz. The menu revolves around typical bistro fare, with a few specials chalked on a blackboard. The onion soup is hearty and delicious, and the *croque monsieur*, a puffy delight of warm cheese and ham, is served with a small salad. Grazers will love the charcuterie platter, which includes pâté. If cassoulet is on the menu, don't pass it up, and wash it down with a Côtes du Rhône. And for dessert, what else but chocolate mousse? ♦ French ♦ M-F breakfast, lunch, and dinner; Sa dinner. 7 Claude La (off Bush St, between Kearny and Grant Ave). 392.3505

61 Le Central ★★$$ On a chilly night, come to this brasserie for the soul-warming cassoulet with beans, confit, and juicy pieces of sausage. The grilled steak topped with Roquefort sauce also is great, though the pile of crisp french fries it's served with is even better. Crab cakes are as good here as in Maryland, but for a lighter, earthier appetizer try the beet salad topped with sieved egg. The best dessert is the crème caramel, which has a brûléelike consistency. The narrow room

lined with tables and rough brick walls has a European feel, reinforced by the efficient maitre d' and the waiters. ♦ French ♦ M-Sa lunch and dinner. Reservations recommended. 453 Bush St (between Claude La and Grant Ave). 391.2233; fax 391.3615

Rendezvous du Monde

61 Rendezvous du Monde ★★$$ Tiny and cute, this family-owned, 50-seat spot has a hideaway appeal. The changing menu lists some interesting salads and such simple noshes as roasted potatoes with aioli, caponata with grilled focaccia, or *brandade* (a puree of salt cod and potatoes) with toast points. The fish selection might include halibut with an olive-and-lemon paste on a bed of corn and sugar snap peas. Don't miss the *pots de crème* (custard) for dessert. ♦ French/ Italian ♦ M breakfast and lunch; Tu-Sa breakfast, lunch, and dinner. 431 Bush St (between Claude La and Grant Ave). 392.3332

62 Cafe de la Presse ★★$ The atmosphere is oh-so-European at this newsstand/cafe, and it has become the cornerstone of an emerging "French Quarter." Linger over cereal, pastries, pancakes, or simple egg dishes in the morning and straightforward salads, sandwiches, and cold plates at lunch. Just so you'll know you're still in America, there are hamburgers, as well as quiches and pasta. ♦ American/French ♦ Daily breakfast, lunch, and dinner. 352 Grant Ave (at Bush St). 398.2680; fax 249.0916

63 The Hot Shop With four locations in the Bay Area, this take-out shop does for burritos what California chefs have done for pizza, stuffing them with all kinds of nontraditional ingredients. Here are such fillings as lamb Mediterranean, Chinese chicken, sweet and hot duck, and Bombay curry, to name a few. ♦ M-Sa. 359 Kearny St (at Pine St). 989.8077; fax 989.8078

64 Occidental Grill ★★$$ Here's a new twist on the traditional San Francisco grill. Even though a restaurant has operated on this site since 1909 and its latest incarnation evokes those old days with a dark wood bar, green-glass lights, and semiprivate booths, the food has a 1990s pedigree

23

Downtown/Union Square

dubbed "contemporary grill fare." Stick with the simpler offerings: grilled double chicken breast with wild boar bacon, smoked pork chop with horseradish mashed potatoes and cranberry ketchup, and "Thai'd up" skirt steak with red curried peanut slaw and shoestring taro potatoes. ♦ American ♦ M-F lunch and dinner. 453 Pine St (between Montgomery and Kearny Sts). 834.0484

65 Specialty's Cafe and Bakery At lunchtime, Financial District workers line up here to take out sandwiches, soups, and salads. This carryout shop (which has three locations around the city) has made a name for itself by baking all its breads and pastries in-house, although sometimes the bread can be leaden and the sweets disappointing. ♦ M-F 6AM-6PM. No credit cards accepted. 312 Kearny St (between Bush and Pine Sts). Daily specials 896. BAKE; catering, delivery, and customer service, all locations 512.9550 ⌕. Also at: 22 Battery St (at Market St); 150 Spear St (between Howard and Mission Sts)

66 Cafe Bastille ★★$$ Perfectly capturing the atmosphere of a French bistro, this charming cafe on a pedestrian street attracts both a business clientele and a good share of young bohemians, who come in for the nightly live jazz as well as the food. Try the onion soup, steamed mussels, roast chicken breast, or pâté. Even though the cafe is in the shadow of the 52-story **Bank of America** monolith, you can sit at one of its outdoor tables and pretend you're in Paris. ♦ Bistro ♦ M-Sa lunch and dinner. 22 Belden Pl (between Bush and Pine Sts). 986.5673; fax 986.1013

66 Cafe Tiramisù ★★★$$ The captivating smells of sautéed garlic and onions alone would lure passersby into this chic cafe, whose walls look as if they're painted with ancient frescoes. Everyone receives a friendly welcome, and the Italian food is just as warming: risotto with earthy mushrooms, osso buco with soft polenta, and roasted whole fish with nuances of smoke. In all, this eatery is one of the best places in the area for a hearty Italian meal. Outdoor seating is available, too. ♦ Italian ♦ M-F lunch and dinner; Sa dinner. Reservations recommended. 28 Belden Pl (between Bush and Pine Sts). 421.7044; fax 421.3009

66 Plouf ★★★$$ Local restaurateurs Eric Klein and Olivier Azancot, along with French-born Jocelyn Bulow, have opened this tiny new dining spot dedicated to seafood in general and mussels and oysters in particular. (The name, appropriately, is the French word for "splash.") Featured here are mussels prepared in several different sauces and accompanied by crisp french fries, an oyster bar, and a number of seafood dishes, all at bargain prices. There are some tables outside in the pedestrian alleyway. ♦ Bistro ♦ M-F lunch and dinner; Sa dinner. 40 Belden Pl (between Bush and Pine Sts). 986.6491 ⌕

67 Sam's Grill ★★$$ In business for more than 50 years, this is the best of the old-time grills; it's so retro, it's back in style. The masculine, clubby decor has dark wainscoting and enough coat hooks to accommodate an army. The back is lined with curtained booths, just right for a clandestine meeting. It's the perfect stage for the veteran waiters, who work hard to maintain a gruff demeanor (underneath they're really quite charming). Top choices include sweetbreads served on toast points with crisp slices of bacon and roasted potatoes, minute steak, celery Victor, French pancakes (thin crepes drizzled with lemon juice and powdered sugar), and comforting rice pudding (the fish dishes, however, are sometimes overcooked). Wines are fairly priced. ♦ American ♦ M-F lunch and dinner. 374 Bush St (between Montgomery and Kearny Sts). 421.0594; fax 421.2632

68 Cafe Pacifica/Sankt Gallen Brewery $ A curious hybrid, it's both a brew pub and a dim sum restaurant. The beige-colored angled ceiling, white walls, dark wood, and tall windows make it a clean, peaceful retreat. Unfortunately, the dim sum is slightly gummy and only mediocre, and the fried rice is underseasoned. But the beers brewed in the three copper tanks up front are good. ♦ Dim sum/Brewery ♦ Daily lunch and dinner. 333 Bush St (at Montgomery St). 296.8203; fax 296.9348 ⌕

68 Kelly's on Trinity ★★$ Kelly Mills, who won acclaim as chef at the **Four Seasons Clift** hotel, gave up the fast track to open this cafeteria-style lunch spot several years ago. The pastel green and yellow color scheme, printed upholstery, and windows overlooking Trinity Place make it more pleasant than most quick-hit restaurants. Chili and three types of soup are offered each day, and the salads range from steak with mushrooms, green beans, and croutons to Asian chicken with celery, eggplant, and a Thai dressing. Sandwiches are prepared on freshly made rolls, and the cookies and desserts—particularly the apple bread pudding—are excellent. ♦ Cafeteria ♦ M-F breakfast and lunch. 333 Bush St (at Montgomery St). 362.4454; fax 362.2813 ⌕

Downtown/Union Square

69 FAZ ★★$$ The business-lunch crowd flocks to this sleek spot in the **Crocker Galleria.** Light wood partitions divide the long, narrow room, adding intimacy; the color scheme of ocher accented with plum and olive provides an earthy, rustic ambience. The menu blends the flavors of the Middle East and California: Housemade potato chips share top billing with a salad topped with pomegranate seeds, toasted walnuts, and a pomegranate vinaigrette. At lunch, portobellos on rosemary focaccia make a popular sandwich, and any of the pastas—perhaps *riso* (rice-shaped pasta) with baby artichokes in a light tomato sauce—are good choices. For dessert there's honey-soaked baklava with three kinds of nuts, and black-and-white chocolate torte on a buttery crust, resting in a pool of caramel sauce. ♦ Middle Eastern/Californian ♦ M F lunch and dinner; Sa dinner. Reservations recommended. 161 Sutter St (between Montgomery and Kearny Sts). 362.0404; fax 362.5865 ♿

69 John Walker and Co. Liquors Thick burgundy carpets and richly paneled cases that display wine as elegantly and meticulously as art set this wine and spirits store apart. There's a special emphasis on Bordeaux and other French wines, although the Italian and California offerings are nothing to dismiss, either. More than 150 customers store wine with the shop; some have overbought, and their older vintage wines are listed on a sheet at the counter for resale. The selection of half bottles, large bottles, and miniatures is impressive. The staffers are particularly adept at locating hard-to-find wines; they also gift wrap and ship purchases.
♦ M-Sa. 175 Sutter St (between Montgomery and Kearny Sts). 986.2707; fax 421.5820 ♿

69 Perry's Downtown ★★$$ **Perry's,** one of the city's most popular watering holes, has been a fixture on trendy Union Street for two decades. Not content to rest on his laurels, Perry Butler, the legendary restaurateur/barman behind that operation, has opened a downtown version that's every bit as good as the original. It's got the same look (hardwood and tile floors, wood panels, and brass accents reminiscent of East Side New York) and the same menu of all-American classics (burgers, chili, Caesar salad, lobster club sandwich, soups, and salads). For dessert, be sure to try the apple brown Betty. ♦ American ♦ Daily lunch and dinner. 185 Sutter St (between Montgomery and Kearny Sts). 989.6895; fax 433.4409 ♿. Also at: 1944 Union St (between Laguna and Buchanan Sts). 922.9022

70 Metropol ★★★$ Albert Rainer, who built a loyal clientele at **Hyde Street Bistro** in Nob Hill, has expanded his empire with this stylish eatery. It offers more bang for the buck than just about any other. The dark wood molding, marbleized walls, black marble floors, polished cherry tables, and whimsical Italian lights make a dashing setting for the delicious fare. Highlights include roasted eggplant salad with goat cheese and greens, and seafood salad with fennel, carrots, and celery in a tarragon vinaigrette. House-baked bread is the foundation for such sandwiches as roast beef with pickled onions and horseradish. Another good choice is the calzone bursting with artichokes. For grazers, almost every savory course can be ordered in a half portion. The desserts are made in-house: Try the dark-and-white chocolate mousse torte.
♦ Californian ♦ M-Sa lunch and dinner. 168 Sutter St (between Montgomery and Kearny Sts). 732.7777; fax 732.7778 ♿

71 Brasserie Chambord ★$$ The food here has never reached the heights of the other French restaurants in the area, but the classics are a sure bet, especially filet mignon with peppercorns. Particularly appealing to those who work and shop in the area are the lighter choices and main-course salads. Next door is the **Crêpe Escape,** under the same ownership, which serves crepes, coffee, pastries, and light meals from 9:30AM to 3PM. ♦ French ♦ M-Sa breakfast, lunch, and dinner; Su breakfast. Reservations required. 152 Kearny St (at Sutter St). 434.3688; fax 434.9039 ♿

72 City Eats $ The **Crocker Galleria's** food court, run by Marriott, offers hundreds of indoor seats and a dozen or so cafeteria-style options for the busy office workers who grab lunch here, including **Phoebe's Bar, The Monterey Pasta Company, Niji Japanese Grille, Standing Room Only,** and **Tortola.**
♦ Food court ♦ M-Sa lunch. 50 Post St (between Montgomery and Kearny Sts). 433.0306 ♿

72 Gloria Jean's The heady coffee aroma in this bean-and-brew store in the **Crocker Galleria** is infused with a chocolaty raspberry scent—a tip-off to the shop's focus on flavored coffees, including hazelnut cinnamon, butter pecan, and banana cream. Flavored coffee is anathema to the local

Downtown/Union Square

connoisseur, so few retailers in the area carry as wide a selection (50 varieties) as this fast-growing chain. ♦ M-Sa. 50 Post St (between Montgomery and Kearny Sts). 393.7755; fax 391.8965 ♿. Also at: Numerous locations throughout the city

73 Carnelian Room ★★$$$ Panoramic views of the Golden Gate and Bay Bridges dazzle diners at this eatery on top of the **Bank of America World Headquarters** building. At night the room is dark and romantic, the brass chandeliers and dark wood paneling giving it a solid, traditional feel. The food has taken some pretty hard knocks over the years, but a meal here can be a pleasant experience if you order simply. The best way to go is the three-course, prix-fixe menu; it's not only a good value but also offers the most straightforward dishes, with three choices in each category. The starting course may be sautéed Dungeness crab cakes or potato gnocchi with truffled gorgonzola cream. Entrées may include veal medaillons in lemon sauce with prosciutto and sage, and grilled mustard-glazed salmon served with Provençal vegetables and thyme *jus*. For dessert, the chocolate hazelnut roulade and the custardy bread pudding are good choices. The award winning wine list is one of the most extensive in California. ♦ French ♦ M-Sa, cocktails and dinner; Su brunch and dinner. 555 California St (at Kearny St), 52nd floor. 433.7500; fax 291.0815 ♿

74 Jack's ★★★$ Not one to give in to culinary trends, this restaurant (opened in 1864 and operated by the same family since 1903) has held its ground; now its simple, straightforward style has returned to fashion. The menu is a hit parade of classics. The sand dabs meunière are a must, and the house version of rex sole has no competition: The delicate fillets are arranged to cover the plate and simply drizzled with butter, herbs, and a splash of lemon. To start, nothing beats the plate of tiny, barely crunchy *haricots verts* (green beans) doused with vinaigrette. Daily specials may include coq au vin, spring lamb stew, or leg of lamb with lentils. And where else can diners still find jellied consommé (which is kind of like a beefy Jell-O) and cherries jubilee? The long, narrow dining room is lined with elaborate coat hooks, and the ceiling is brightened with gilded ornamentation; starched white tablecloths and dark bentwood chairs add attractive, tailored touches. The waiters, many of long service, seem a bit grumpy but betray themselves by the twinkle in their eyes; if you order the wrong thing they will offer their own recommendations. ♦ American ♦ M-F lunch and dinner; Sa dinner. Reservations recommended. 615 Sacramento St (between Montgomery and Kearny Sts). 986.9854

75 Palio d'Asti ★★★$$ One of the best spots for pasta, it's a handsome place, with cement beams making a dramatic contrast to the polished wood trim and the gleaming white, glass-enclosed kitchen. Many of the pastas are housemade; they're all dressed creatively with such flourishes as artichoke hearts, parmesan cheese, mint, and Italian parsley. Unfortunately, the restaurant is now open only for lunch (it can be rented in the evening for special functions). ♦ Italian ♦ M-F lunch only. Reservations recommended. 640 Sacramento St (between Montgomery and Kearny Sts). 395.9800; fax 362.6002 ♿

76 Paninoteca Palio d'Asti ★★$ A lower-priced offshoot of **Palio d'Asti** (see above), this spot features stylish fare to carry out or eat in. The panini made on house-baked breads are excellent. Choices run from the *san rocco* (roast of the day) to the *tanaro*, a rich combination of mascarpone cheese, chives, and smoked salmon. Be sure to try the dense biscotti. ♦ Italian ♦ M-F breakfast and lunch. 505 Montgomery St (between Sacramento and Commercial Sts). 362.6900; fax 362.0700 ♿

77 Vertigo Restaurant & Bar ★★★$$$ Named for the famous movie Alfred Hitchcock filmed in the city, this restaurant was an instant hit when it opened in 1995. Located on the ground floor of the **Transamerica Pyramid**, it is as spectacular as the much-photographed building. Copper mesh covers the peaked ceiling, and a dramatic light fixture snakes overhead. The rich woods, huge flower arrangements, circular banquettes, and open kitchen give the three-tiered dining room an expansive feel. The seasonal menu features local organic ingredients and highlights French, Italian, and Asian cuisines. Earlier this year, the restaurant hired a new chef, Jeff Inahara, who's cooked at Patina in Los

Downtown/Union Square

SCOTT'S SEAFOOD GRILL & BAR

98 Scott's Seafood ★$$$ The terrace here is a popular spot for lunch; the inside dining room is country French. Unfortunately, the food never soars. The selection of fresh fish changes daily; grilled sand dabs and local petrale sole, served with lemon-caper butter, are among the specialties. ♦ Seafood ♦ M-Sa lunch and dinner; Su dinner. 3 Embarcadero Center (Sacramento St, between Drumm and Davis Sts). 981.0622; fax 296.9501 &; Also at: 2400 Lombard St (at Scott St). 563.8988; fax 563.1897 &

99 Confetti le Chocolatier Cases of truffles and shelves of imported chocolate bars, jelly beans, and marzipan (the pig faces are particularly fun) fill this candy shop; pastry and coffee are also served. A center display features seasonal and holiday-themed treats. ♦ Daily. 4 Embarcadero Center, Drumm St (between Sacramento and Clay Sts). 362.1706 &

99 Splendido ★★$$$ Tucked away in a high-rise shopping center is this Mediterranean oasis, with a domed brick ceiling at the entry, a rough rock fireplace, whimsical lights, and an open kitchen. The food has slipped a bit but still can be excellent, particularly the pasta, brick-oven pizza, and grilled lamb served with such interesting side dishes as fried shallots and white bean–garlic flan. ♦ Mediterranean ♦ M-F lunch and dinner; Sa-Su dinner. 4 Embarcadero Center (Drumm St, between Sacramento and Clay Sts). 986.3222; fax 434.3530 &

99 Harbor Village ★★$$ Elegantly appointed with rosewood and teak, and somewhat pricier than other Hong Kong–style restaurants, this place features excellent dim sum at lunch. At night the waiters resolutely try to steer non-Asian patrons to the most mundane dishes, so stand firm. Some popular choices include the minced squab and Peking duck, but ask about any seasonal or chef's specialties. The special prearranged banquets also can be exceptional, and the half-dozen opulent private dining rooms are perfect for celebrations. The best way to get the full impact of this dining experience is in a group, where you can order lots of dim sum dishes or several entrées and share. ♦ Cantonese ♦ Daily lunch and dinner. 4 Embarcadero Center (Drumm St, between Sacramento and Clay Sts). 781.8833; fax 781.8810 &

99 SRO! ★$ Designed for the eat-quick and take-out crowd (hence the name), this spot offers varied and interesting lunches, including lasagna, chicken, salads, and cheeses. The wine section features Californian and European selections and hosts regularly scheduled tastings. There are tables inside, but the choice dining spots are outside overlooking the impressive **Villancourt Fountain** in **Justin Herman Plaza**. ♦ Cafe ♦ Daily lunch. 4 Embarcadero Center (Drumm St, between Sacramento and Clay Sts). 986.5020; fax 399.1267 &

100 Levy's Bagels & Co. This recent arrival brings a New York twist to the deli business with its traditional boiled and baked bagels (plus such unconventional, unnecessary varieties as blueberry). The turkey is house-roasted, and the chopped liver, tongue, and knishes round out the hit parade. Owners Marie and Robert Levy urge busy customers to fax in their orders. ♦ M-W 6AM-6:30PM; Th, F 6AM-5PM; Sa 7:30AM-2PM; Su 7:30AM-1PM. 21 Drumm St (at California St). 362.5580; fax 362.5581 &

ECLIPSE CAFE

101 Eclipse Cafe $$ Located in the **Hyatt Regency Hotel**, this cafe offers standard hotel fare at inflated hotel prices. ♦ American ♦ Daily breakfast and lunch (until 2PM). 5 Embarcadero Center (Drumm St, between Market and California Sts). 788.1234; fax 398.2567 &

13 views

101 Thirteen Views $$ Salads, sandwiches, and pizzas are available all day long at this **Hyatt Regency Hotel** eatery. ♦ American ♦ Daily breakfast, lunch, and dinner. 5 Embarcadero Center (Drumm St, between Market and California Sts). 788.1234 &

101 Equinox $$$ The **Hyatt Regency Hotel** is home to Northern California's only revolving restaurant. The views are the main draw, but it's a safe enough bet for Sunday brunch or cocktails. ♦ American ♦ M-Sa, cocktails, and dinner; Su brunch, cocktails, and dinner. 5 Embarcadero Center (Drumm St, between Market and California Sts). 788.1234; fax 398.2567 &

Chinatown

Stand on the corner of **Stockton Street** and **Broadway** on a Saturday or Sunday morning to see the real Chinatown. The sidewalks overflow with shoppers going about their everyday chores. Spending one afternoon here will teach you more about Asian food than a year of studying all the latest Chinese cookbooks. Stand beside a woman as she carefully chooses snow peas—one by one—for her family's dinner. Or strike up a conversation about where to get the best barbecued pork in town and watch the sparks fly (people can get pretty passionate about their favorite barbecue spot).

The second most densely populated area in the United States (behind New York City's Harlem), Chinatown is home to the largest concentration of Asian residents outside of Asia. Popular with both tourists and locals, it attracts about 10 million visitors annually. And it's the weekend destination for

Chinatown

waiter browbeats the customers, ordering them to set tables, wash their hands, etc. This is that place, but the waiter has died, taking his act with him. Nevertheless, this 81-year-old place remains one of Chinatown's most venerable restaurants, and the reasonable prices and okay food keep it well patronized. Try the *congee* (rice porridge), noodle dishes, and wonton soup with duck. ♦ Chinese ♦ M-Sa lunch and dinner. No credit cards accepted. 813 Washington St (at Grant Ave). 982.0596

9 Kowloon Vegetarian Restaurant ★$
The window displays of figurines and pastries are deceptive; this is a vegetarian spot, one of the few that serve meatless dim sum. An array of vegetables, soy products, and wheat gluten stand in for the meat in traditional dishes. The egg rolls are delicious, with a mushroom-vegetable filling that's packed with flavor. Dumplings are equally good, filled with mushrooms, faux chicken, and vegetables; the *siu mai* (pork dumplings), made with taro root, mushrooms, and carrots, are terrific. You won't even miss the poultry in the *kung pao* "chicken," with tofu, green peppers, peas, corn, celery, carrots, mushrooms, and a handful of crunchy toasted peanuts in a slightly spicy sauce. Other preparations include curried "pork," assorted "gluten-over-rice" concoctions, and fried, crispy walnuts. ♦ Chinese/Vegetarian ♦ Daily lunch and dinner. No credit cards accepted. 909 Grant Ave (at Washington St). 362.9888

9 Mee On Company
Barely big enough to notice, this candy shop, which has been in business more than 70 years, is a storehouse of preserved and sugared treats: coconut, lotus nuts, water chestnuts, winter melon, kumquats, ginger (the best), and lotus roots, to name a few. They're stashed in bins and sold by the quarter pound. Also available are chewy dried papaya and preserved plums. ♦ Daily. No credit cards accepted. 812 Washington St (at Grant Ave). 982.4456 &

10 Silver Restaurant ★$
The glittering silver marquee raises expectations of glamour, so the utilitarian interior here is something of a letdown. The main draw is the inexpensive food, especially during crab season (November through April), when a whole crab is usually priced at about $8; also attractive are the round-the-clock service and friendly, attentive staff. Overall, the food is okay, and the *congees* and the thin noodles with wontons and a choice of toppings (including excellent barbecued pork or duck) make a fine end to a long night of partying. The place is usually packed at 2AM, when the bar crowd stops by for "breakfast." ♦ Chinese ♦ Daily 24 hours. 737 Washington St (between Kearny St and Grant Ave). 433.8888 &

11 World Ginseng Center
This supermarket-size ginseng emporium is a good place to buy the aromatic, gnarled roots of that medicinal herb. There's ginseng from America, China, and Korea in just about every form: extract for tea, tea bags, medicinals, and candies. Prices go as high as $1,000 a pound for the prized Wisconsin wild ginseng. ♦ Daily. 801 Kearny St (at Washington St). 362.0928 &

12 Star Lunch ★$
With only 12 seats at the kitchen counter, this eatery is one of the smallest in Chinatown. Diners can feel a blast of heat as the cook turns out popular Shanghai chow mein dishes with either pork or chicken. It's a good place to sample pig's feet in noodle soup or salted cabbage and shredded pork. ♦ Chinese/Shanghai ♦ Tu-Su lunch until 5PM. No credit cards accepted. 605 Jackson St (at Kearny St). 788.6709

12 J & J Restaurant ★★★$
Crowds line up outside this top dim sum parlor. Inside, the decor is much like other Hong Kong–style restaurants, with paneled walls and crystal chandeliers. But the dumplings here have some of the best fillings around, boldly flavored by their main ingredients: The *ha gow* (shrimp dumplings) taste only of shrimp and ginger, for example. The pork balls are encased in a flour dumpling and served with a red vinegar sauce; the dumplings shaped like cocks' combs contain chopped shrimp, cilantro, and fresh water chestnuts, which add a sweet, crunchy burst of flavor; and the silken bean-curd skins have a tender interior. When the dim sum carts are stored for the evening and the full menu is offered, look to the seafood specialties, which are fresh as can be; their key ingredients are scooped up live from the fish tank. ♦ Chinese ♦ M dinner; Tu-Su lunch and dinner. 615 Jackson St (at Kearny St). 981.7308 &

Chop suey was invented in 1856 when a group of miners showed up after closing at a Chinese restaurant in San Francisco. To accommodate them the chef combined various leftovers and created this now ubiquitous stir-fry dish.

Chinatown

Mastering the Dim Sum Experience

No San Francisco culinary experience is complete without a sampling of dim sum. These delicious tidbits are a local institution; only Hong Kong has more dim sum parlors, and that's where the tradition originated.

Generally, dim sum are served for brunch; most dim-sum houses open around 10AM and close in the middle or late afternoon. Typically, waiters circle the dining room pushing carts stacked with covered bamboo or stainless- steel containers filled with steamed or fried dumplings, shrimp balls, spring rolls, steamed buns, and Chinese pastries. Just point to the items that look appealing as they roll by; the dim sum won't be listed on a menu, and the waiters often speak no English, so ordering is done by gesture.

Although dim sum may appear to be exotic, most fillings are pretty straightforward—pork, shrimp, cabbage, mushrooms, and ginger appear in many guises. Such unfamiliar delicacies as duck or chicken

Cha Siu So
Flaky buns

Floweret Siu Mai
Meat-filled dumplings

Jow Nn Hueng Gai
Chicken lollipops

Jow Ha Gok
Shrimp turnovers

Ng Heung Ngau
Braised beef shank

Dan Tar
Custard tart

Pot Sticker (Kou Teh)
Meat-filled dumplings

Gee Yoke Go
Savory pork triangles

Siu Mai
Steamed pork dumplings

Pot Sticker Triangles
Meat-filled wonton skins

Cha Siu Bow
Steamed barbecued pork buns

Chinatown

17 Royal Jade ★★$
The modern Hong Kong–style room looks like many others, but the dim sum here are more creative and better balanced. In a variation on *siu mai,* for example, the chef drapes dough over whole shrimp coated with ground mixed spices with a whisper of tangerine and tops it with a meaty mushroom cap. The wrappings on the tapioca-flour dumplings are chewy, but so thin that they reveal the contents within. The *ha gow* (shrimp) filling is one of the best in town. ♦ Chinese ♦ Daily breakfast, lunch, and dinner. 675 Jackson St (between Kearny St and Grant Ave). 392.2929

18 New Woey Loy Goey Restaurant ★$
This modest place has built a reputation for its rice and noodle dishes at rock-bottom prices. More than 60 rice plates and 35 noodle dishes are offered; try the cashew chicken rice plate and the garlic chicken with crispy noodles. ♦ Chinese ♦ Daily lunch and dinner. No credit cards accepted. 699 Jackson St (at Grant Ave). 399.0733

19 Ten Ren Tea Company of San Francisco, Ltd. Ellen and Mark Lill's pretty shop specializes in green tea, which in recent years has become the darling of the health-conscious. More than a dozen varieties are sold from large gold-metal cans lining the rich wood shelves. Two glass cases along one side hold an impressive display of teapots for sale. The other half of the store is devoted to ginseng, also reputed to have healing qualities. The shop is orderly and very clean, and a carved table sits in the center for free tea tastings; a raised area in back is reserved for the Chinese tea ceremony, which is performed every morning for city-tour groups (or for private groups—call to make arrangements). The staff are helpful and willingly answer questions. ♦ Daily 9AM-9PM. 949 Grant Ave (between Washington and Jackson Sts). 362.0656; fax 750.8242 ♦

20 Yong Kee For more than 30 years this bakery has produced superior steamed pork buns, with moist, light dough and finely ground fillings. The noodle rolls, however, are thick and almost mushy, lacking that bit of rubber band resistance that marks the best. ♦ Tu-Su. No credit cards accepted. 732 Jackson St (at Grant Ave). 986.3759

21 Ginn Wall Company An all-purpose Chinese cookware store, it stocks a little bit of everything: bowls, some cookbooks, tart molds, moon-cake presses, steamers, woks, rice cookers, cast-iron grill pans, and a surprisingly wide variety of knives, cleavers, pastry tips, and cookie cutters. There's even a selection of seeds for Chinese vegetables. The owners are cheerful and friendly. ♦ M-W; F-Su. 1016 Grant Ave (between Jackson St and Pacific Ave). 982.6307 ♦

22 Golden Gate Bakery Yellow custard tarts are displayed at just about every bakery and on every dim sum cart in the city, but the best are at this tiny, crowded shop. The tart shells are made with butter for a crust as flaky as puff pastry, and the seductively good custard has just a hint of salt (typical of Chinese pastries). They're kept warm so they always taste freshly baked—and they're good enough to delight even the finest French pastry chef. ♦ Daily. No credit cards accepted. 1029 Grant Ave (between Jackson St and Pacific Ave). 781.2627

23 Mayerson Food Company Always crowded, this produce-and-meat market is known for its high-quality Chinese ingredients. Fat taro root, massive radishes, and sweet *dau meu* (pea sprouts) vie for space. Most of the hard-working employees do not speak English, so you're on your own if you have questions. ♦ Daily. No credit cards accepted. 1101 Grant Ave (at Pacific Ave). 398.4618 ♦

24 Four Sea Supermarket One of the most impressive fish markets in Chinatown (or in the city, for that matter), it displays 25 kinds of fish on ice and in tanks; meat is sold along one side. Here you can find eel curled like snakes ready to strike, live turtles up to 18 inches long, live frogs, blue crab, tiny catfish, geoduck (pronounced *gooey*-duck), and silver-skinned pike three feet long. Everything is butchered to order, which is no sight for the sensitive, but certainly ensures freshness. ♦ Daily. No credit cards accepted. 1100 Grant Ave (at Pacific Ave). 788.2532 ♦

24 New On Sang Poultry Company The front window is stacked with wire cases holding guinea fowl and blue chickens (they have blue skin and white feathers); the latter, reputed to have curative powers, are a popular ingredient for soup. Inside, the poultry that has made this place famous is quickly cut up behind glass windows. Chicken and parts are displayed on one side, fish on the other. The same company owns **San Francisco Chicken/New On Sang Market,** a stylish rotisserie and deli on Clement Street in the Richmond district. ♦ Daily. No credit cards accepted. 1114 Grant Ave (at Pacific Ave). 982.9228 ♦. Also at: 617 Clement St (at Seventh Ave). 752.4100; fax 750.8242 ♦

39

Chinatown

25 Yuen's Garden ★★$ As at so many Chinatown shops, the windows at this restaurant/store are decked with hanging roasted birds, but these have a particularly good color, and the selection is above average. The tea-roasted quail has an exquisite five-spice taste, and even the chicken wings retain their succulence. The shop also offers walnut-hued squab cooked with the head on, soy-sauce chicken, poached chicken, roasted Rock Cornish game hens, tea-smoked duck, and pressed duck. Rice-flour crepes, chewy and delicious, are made to order in the window by a friendly old woman, then filled with sugar, chopped peanuts, and coconut, or savory pork, peanuts, and dried shrimp. The food can be taken out or eaten at one of the tables (the place seats 50). ♦ Chinese ♦ Daily lunch. No credit cards accepted. 1131 Grant Ave (between Pacific Ave and Broadway). 391.1131 ら

26 New Hop Yick Meat Market Fresh meats line one side of this popular market, while the other side is reserved for sausage, pressed ducks, and Smithfield ham, which is very popular in Chinese cooking. Mountains of crisp pork skins fill the window. ♦ Daily. No credit cards accepted. 1155 Grant Ave (between Pacific Ave and Broadway). 989.0247 ら

26 Kwong Jow Sausage Manufacturing Company Connoisseurs recommend this place for its Chinese-style sausage called *lop cheong*. Made from beef, pork, or duck liver, the chewy, slightly sweet sausages cover an entire wall of the shop; smoked bacon and other cured products are also sold. The rest of the space is occupied by the butcher shop, where the sausage meat is prepared. ♦ Daily. No credit cards accepted. 1157 Grant Ave (between Pacific Ave and Broadway). 397.2562 ら

27 Taiwan Restaurant ★★★$ The Northern-style food is so good at this dining spot that people should line up at the door for it. Unfortunately, many pedestrians walk on by because the restaurant looks as though it's part of a bank. But the steamed dumplings are superb: With just the right amount of meat and cabbage, they gush slightly as you bite into the tender, slightly chewy shell. Crispy chicken and Shanghai noodles are also excellent, as are the turnip cakes, which are crunchy outside and creamy just below the surface. If you've never been a fan of tripe soup, try the version here: It's tender and mild, with long strips of greens and pickled vegetables in a delicate broth with just a hint of spice. The decor is straightforward: A brass hood separates the kitchen from the entrance, and the small dining room in back is decorated in gray and plum with faux-granite Formica tables. This place also has an extremely popular and equally good sister restaurant in the Richmond district. ♦ Chinese ♦ M-F lunch and dinner; Sa-Su brunch and dinner. 289 Columbus Ave (at Broadway). 989.6789. Also at: 445 Clement St (at Sixth Ave). 387.1789 ら

28 New Sun Hong Kong ★★$ Even if the food weren't good, it would almost be worth visiting this two-level corner restaurant for its views of Columbus and Broadway, where the worlds of Chinatown and the predominantly Italian North Beach collide. *Congee* is the most popular dish at every meal. Hot pots are another specialty, and they're always earthy and comforting. One of the best features smoky chicken with mushrooms and onions in a rich sauce that's spicy with flecks of coarsely ground black pepper. If the street view becomes dull, focus attention on the glass-enclosed kitchen, which gets a bit steamy during peak hours. All in all, it's a satisfying show. This place is great for night owls, too—it stays open until 3AM. ♦ Chinese ♦ Daily breakfast, lunch, and dinner. 606 Broadway (at Grant Ave). 956.3338; fax 956.3345 ら

29 Gold Mountain Restaurant ★★$ The blush-colored dining room with red accents is so long and so crowded that the captains carry walkie-talkies. Crowded rooms, however, mean crowded carts, brimming with all kinds of fresh dumplings. The *ha gow* here is simple but delicious: the plump shrimp is lightly accented with ginger. The *siu mai*, traditional steamed dumplings, are dressed up with whole shrimp on top. One of the most unusual preparations is a ground shrimp mixture, dotted with carrots and a whole cilantro leaf, dipped in a tempuralike batter and deep-fried. Soup carts dish up *congee*; others have griddles so that the pot stickers can be warmed and crisped before serving. Noodle dishes, served at dinner, are also excellent. Try the *chow fun*, wide white noodles that are nearly paper-thin. ♦ Chinese ♦ Daily breakfast, lunch, and dinner. 644 Broadway (between Columbus Ave and Stockton St). 296.7733; fax 296.7782 ら

29 Kim Do Company A hodgepodge of garish ceramic figurines, shaving cream, garden tools, kitchenware, and trinkets can be found here, much of it stacked in the middle of the floor. The discerning shopper can unearth some bargains, such as huge coffee mugs with lids, individual soy bowls, china spoons,

Chinatown

Shopping in Chinatown—
A Flavorful Adventure

Whether you're a seasoned master of Chinese cookery or don't know soy sprouts from bean sprouts, a visit to San Francisco's Chinatown can be educational. It gives you a terrific opportunity to explore another community's history, culture, and cuisine. The need for food is common to all people; the only difference between societies is in the ways they satisfy that need.

In China, many foods are seen as curative, almost medicinal, as well as simply nutritious—in fact, the old adage "You are what you eat" could be translated in Chinese culture as "Eat to stay healthy." A nursing mother, for example, is encouraged to eat silver carp in order to stay healthy and strong and to ensure a constant supply of milk for her baby. The use of herbal therapy to relieve pain and other symptoms of illness—so prevalent for centuries in China—has begun to take root in the US.

The best way to shop in Chinatown is to start with a plan. Pick out a recipe for a dish that you would like to cook, draw up your shopping list of ingredients, and set out. Need a canned or bottled sauce? **May Wah Trading Company** is sure to have it. Does your recipe call for a bit of salty Smithfield ham? Pick up a slice or two at **Metro Foods Company**. Or seek out that elusive blue-skinned chicken at **New On Sang Poultry Company**.

With its bustling streets and foreign atmosphere, Chinatown can be somewhat intimidating to venture into, and many of the people you are dealing with are recent immigrants, so they haven't had a chance to learn much English. But patience, friendliness, and persistence pay off in the end. You can communicate volumes by smiling, gesturing, and pointing. But if you really need some good advice, seek out young staffers, who usually are English-speaking. Relax and let yourself get swept up in all the activity, and you'll undoubtedly find shopping in Chinatown a unique, fascinating experience.

---

40 Sun Duck Market A case in back of this top-rated fish and poultry market holds a selection of chickens and ducks, including Petaluma-raised Peking duck. Dried and fresh fish fill the rest of the cramped quarters. The doorway is usually tended by an employee overseeing a plastic tub filled with flopping black bass; they're sold almost as fast as they can be caught. ♦ Daily. No credit cards accepted. 1107 Stockton St (at Jackson St). 956.8030 &

NEW PING YUEN

40 New Ping Yuen This bakery specializes in moon cakes, which look like dense, round pies with a design embossed on the crust. These pastries are traditionally exchanged at the Autumn Buddhist Moon Festival in September and at family celebrations. Here they come in all sizes and with various fillings, including red bean paste, sweet sesame seeds, lotus seeds, salty pork, egg yolk, and chicken. The bakery also is known for its baked buns, which have either a juicy pork filling, or drier chicken or beef filling. ♦ Daily. 1125 Stockton St (between Jackson St and Pacific Ave). 433.5571 &

41 J R New Orange Land One of the top shops for Chinese produce, its bins line both sides of the sidewalk, creating traffic jams that make bumper cars seem civilized. If it's a Chinese vegetable and it's in season, it'll probably be here, and at an excellent price. For years, it's been known for its bargain-priced oranges and other citrus fruits. ♦ Daily. No credit cards accepted. 1055 Stockton St (at Jackson St). 982.8188 &

42 Dick Lee Pastry The drab warehouse kitchen here turns out sweet gelatins, steamed pork buns, and Chinese cupcakes, which are sold at an equally dreary retail counter. (A smaller, marginally more pleasant cafe is next door, but most of the business that this place gets seems to be takeout.) Its popularity is puzzling, since everything has a flat taste. ♦ M-Tu, Th-Su. No credit cards accepted. 777 Jackson St (at Stockton St). 397.0788 &

42 Feng Huang Pastry While most pastry shops in Chinatown are Cantonese, this 27-year-old bakery prefers the Mandarin style. Here are *the* best rice-noodle rolls, which come stuffed with various meat combinations (this shop even supplies many Bay Area Chinese restaurants with the rice-noodle dough for *chow fun*). And don't overlook the turnovers filled with coconut and fried to a crisp crunch. The buns are wonderful, too, with a dry, firm texture and a slightly sweet pork filling. The place is nothing to look at, but the quality of the ingredients and the final products are beyond compare. ♦ Daily (but the shop closes some Thursdays; call to check). No credit cards accepted. 761 Jackson St (between Grant Ave and Stockton St). 421.7885 &

43 Golden Gate Fortune Cookie Company The aromas of almond and sugar waft down Ross Alley, where this cramped factory has been making fortune cookies for more than 30 years. The process is relatively straightforward. Batter is poured into a mold and baked on a circular conveyor belt. Grandmotherly workers pluck up each hot, flat disk,

43

Chinatown

place a paper fortune in the center, and quickly fold it into the distinctively shaped cookie. In addition to the usual predictions of health and wealth, X-rated fortunes are available. Visitors can watch the cookies being made and, for a glimpse into the future, buy them here, too. ♦ Daily. No credit cards accepted. 56 Ross Alley (off Jackson St, between Grant Ave and Stockton St). 781.3956 ♿

44 Gourmet Kitchen With so many shop windows hung with ducks, ribs, and other roast meats, it's hard to know which is best, but this place has won legions of fans for its roast pig and duck. A close look reveals that the skin is evenly colored and crisp. ♦ Daily. No credit cards accepted. 1051 Stockton St (between Washington and Jackson Sts). 781.7988 ♿

44 New Golden Daisy Company Roast suckling pig is the specialty of this take-out deli. The butcher slices pieces to order from an upside-down hanging pig. The skin is darker and crispier than most, making the meat seem all the more rich and succulent. Pans stacked in the front window proffer chicken feet in a rich brown sauce, as well as fried chicken wings, pork ribs, and delicious smoked bacon. The pressed duck, which looks like a cartoon character flattened by a steamroller, has an intense, salty flavor and is used to make soup. The deli also makes superb "Chinese tamales"—rice and other ingredients wrapped in lotus leaves and steamed. ♦ Daily. No credit cards accepted. 1041 Stockton St (between Washington and Jackson Sts). 392.0111 ♿

Chinese restaurants may have one name according to their English sign and quite another if you can read the Chinese characters on their signage. The four characters on the sign adorning the Empress of China Restaurant translate to multistory house, empress, wine, and liquor. Also in translation, the sign on Sam Lok Restaurant reads: shop, joyful, heart, cooked rice—with nary a mention of Sam Lok.

In *How to Cook a Wolf*, the writer M.F.K. Fisher tells a true story of a San Francisco college student who lived for two years during the Depression on about seven cents a day by eating ground wheat at every meal and drinking a gallon of milk each week. He supplemented his diet almost every day with a piece of fruit stolen from a nearby Chinese-owned pushcart. After he graduated from college, he sent the pushcart owner ten dollars; he received four dollars in change, and an invitation to a New Year's party in Chinatown. He went.

45 Kam Lok ★$ The dishes served at this basement eatery can best be described as Chinese soul food—about as close to peasant fare as you're likely to find. This is the place for pork with salted egg yolk, and Chinese water spinach with shrimp paste. Among connoisseurs this place is known for its extremely hot wok, which makes for superior stir-fries. The menu includes nearly 25 rice plates topped with stir-fried ingredients, 25 soups, and 11 clay-pot dishes, including pork with eggplant. Virtually everyone hunkered over bowls of noodles here is a Chinatown resident, and may pause in mid-slurp to stare at newcomers. ♦ Chinese ♦ Daily lunch and dinner. No credit cards accepted. 834 Washington St (between Grant Ave and Stockton St). 421.8102

45 Lucky Creation ★★$ Shared tables are the norm in this blue-tiled hole-in-the-wall, but the food is something to savor: This is, by far, the best vegetarian restaurant in town. One of the tastiest dishes is mixed vegetables in a golden nest—a crisp potato basket lined with perfectly cooked broccoli florets and filled with oyster, button, and straw mushrooms, wood ears, and white fungus, all bathed in an intense brown sauce. Another standout is an array of mushrooms, celery, green bell pepper, and carrots, all cut like stars and daisies. Taro is shaped like a goldfish, deep-fried until crisp, and served with a sweet-and-sour sauce. Another good choice is fresh-tasting pan-fried noodles topped with mushrooms, bean sprouts, and celery. ♦ Chinese/Vegetarian ♦ M-Tu, Th-Su lunch and dinner. 854 Washington St (between Grant Ave and Stockton St). 989.0818

SUPERIOR

46 Superior Trading Company This 40-year-old business is one of the city's most respected purveyors of Chinese medicinal herbs and teas. The wood drawers that line the wall make the place look like a cross between an old-time bank and an apothecary. ♦ Daily. No credit cards accepted. 837 Washington St (between Grant Ave and Stockton St). 982.8722 ♿

47 Wycen Foods Inc. Off the beaten path, but going strong since 1948, this meat-processing plant sells cured duck gizzards, chicken liver sausage, cured dried duck, Chinese-style bacon, and pork rinds. Smoked fish and beef jerky also are available. ♦ Daily. No credit cards accepted. 903 Washington St (at Stockton St). 788.3910 ♿

Chinatown

48 Little Paris Coffee Shop ★★$
This tiny, modest shop is a good place to try one of the most distinctive cross-cultural foods to be embraced by the Asian population here, *bahn mi*. Part Vietnamese and part French, these sandwiches are much cheaper than their American counterparts, and usually a lot more interesting. They're constructed on a French roll (crisp outside, chewy inside) that's slathered with mayonnaise and stuffed with such fillings as pâté, smoked chicken, barbecued pork, and pork sausage, then piled with shredded pickled daikon, carrots, cilantro, onions, and cucumbers and splashed with chili vinegar. There are also big bowls of *pho* with all kinds of fresh garnishes, including cilantro, bean sprouts, and lemon slices, and a dozen puddinglike desserts. Altogether, it makes a quick, filling, and inexpensive meal.
◆ Vietnamese/Cafe ◆ Daily lunch and dinner. No credit cards accepted. 939 Stockton St (between Clay and Washington Sts). 982.6111 &

49 H-P Seafood Market A drab-looking seafood market, it sells only fish freshly netted from its dozen tanks. The tanks are stocked with a comprehensive selection, including shark and five kinds of turtles. One small counter is devoted to cutting up customers' selections. ◆ Daily. No credit cards accepted. 848 Jackson St (between Stockton and Powell Sts). No phone &

49 L & H Seafood Similar to **H-P Seafood Market** (see above), this shop has fewer kinds of fish, but a particularly large selection of live crabs. ◆ Daily. No credit cards accepted. 838 Jackson St (between Stockton and Powell Sts). No phone &

50 New Hong Kong Noodle Company The raw wood shelves and boxes in back make this look more like a warehouse than a noodle factory, but it turns out fresh, thick, and chewy Shanghai noodles to cook at home. Also on hand are all kinds of frozen dim sum, including sesame rice balls and pot stickers, and packages of dried noodles. ◆ Daily. No credit cards accepted. 874 Pacific Ave (at Powell St). 433.1886 &

51 Mee Heong Bakery With one case filled with soft drinks, another with pastries, and a single row of tables, what's the draw at this bakery-cafe? Steamed buns. They're made with airy, moist dough and have such fillings as pork and lotus paste. ◆ Daily. No credit cards accepted. 1343 Powell St (between Pacific Ave and Broadway). 781.3266

52 Kam (H.K.) Po Kitchen ★$ People from all walks of life can be seen enjoying the wholesome, tasty fare at this exceptionally clean corner cafe. Most of the *congee* dishes are very cheap; even more elaborate preparations are a bargain. Try soup, lo mein, or rice dish that features barbecue. The take-out section in front offers roast pig, poultry, and ribs. If you're planning a large buffet party, this is the place to get enormous pans of chow mein or roast meat at a pittance. ◆ Chinese/Takeout ◆ Daily lunch and dinner. No credit cards accepted. 801 Broadway (at Powell St). 982.3516

53 Imperial Tea Court A calming oasis in between Chinatown and North Beach, this modern tea shop with dark wood accents offers high-quality teas and tables where people can sip. For a fee, tea masters guide tastings that demonstrate how the brew changes character as it goes from the first steeping to the fourth and final one; connoisseurs consider the second and third prime. Many teas here cost more than $100 a pound: The Junshan Yinzhen is $545; Sword of the Emperor is $365, and the popular Imperial Dragon Well is $280 (small samples are also available at a reasonable price). The staff is so helpful that a visit here seems like a college course in the myriad qualities of tea.
◆ Daily 11AM-6:30PM. 1411 Powell St (at Broadway). 788.6080; fax 788.6079

54 Des Alpes Restaurant ★★$ The dining room behind the cozy bar looks just as a Basque dining hall should: packed with tables, crowded with families having a good time, and imbued with a warm, comfortable ambience. The seven-course prix-fixe menu is keyed to the days of the week and features staggering quantities of such fare as sweetbreads, oxtail stew, lamb stew, and trout—all at an incredible price. This is one of the best deals in the city, and the waiters have a spirit as bountiful as the food. ◆ Basque ◆ Tu-Su dinner. Reservations recommended Friday through Sunday. 732 Broadway (between Stockton and Powell Sts). 391.4249

Want to learn more about Chinese vegetables, calligraphy, or the Chinese zodiac? You can buy books and posters on these subjects at the Chinese Culture Center located on the third floor of the Holiday Inn at 750 Kearny Street. In addition to cards, books, and jewelry, there are rotating exhibits of art and crafts. A recent exhibit featured antiques used on the set of the movie *The Joy Luck Club*. The center is open Sunday from 12PM-4PM and Tuesday through Saturday from 10AM-4PM. Admission is free.

North Beach

North Beach is fueled by coffee. The dense concentration of quaint coffeehouses and the heady aroma of roasting beans scenting the air practically mesmerize strollers into passing first one hour, then two, over a leisurely cup.

According to local lore, the first cappuccino in the United States was served in North Beach in 1956 by John Giotta at **Caffè Trieste**. The cafe, now run by his son, still attracts a diverse group with its dark Italian espresso, made at the roasting facility next door. North Beach also boasts two other roasters: **Caffè Roma Coffee Roasting Company** and **Graffeo Coffee**, which has been selling coffee since 1935. Comparing coffees and absorbing the different atmosphere at each cafe is an excellent way to experience the area's essence.

Certainly coffee, as well as North Beach's European, laid-back atmosphere, helped seduce the Beat Generation into taking root here in the 1950s, particularly at **Enrico's** on **Broadway**. The bohemian spirit lingers today, with many writers and painters clinging to rent-controlled apartments around **Telegraph Hill**.

There's more than just java here, though, as the scent of bread baking and the perfume of sautéed garlic attest. North Beach is virtually synonymous with "Little Italy," and its Italian culinary history reaches back to the first immigrants from Genoa, who arrived in the 1840s, followed by the Ligurians, the Luccans, and finally, in the late 1880s, the Sicilians.

Despite their strong presence in North Beach today, Italians were not the first to settle the area. The original Gold Rush–era settlers were Chinese fishermen, who later gave way to Irish and German immigrants who clustered on Telegraph Hill. The first Italians called this section of San Francisco "Little City" and recreated Italy here, with legitimate theaters and concerts and three newspapers all in Italian. The Genovese established truck farms and got into the produce business, the Luccans were storekeepers, and the Sicilians established many of the eateries along **Fisherman's Wharf**. The Sicilian influence on the neighborhood is apparent every October, when a procession honoring the Madonna del Lume (Madonna of Light), a religious observance from that part of Italy, departs from **Saints Peter and Paul Catholic Church** and heads toward Fisherman's Wharf for the blessing of the fishing fleet.

Look no farther for evidence of North Beach's Italian soul (or, at least, stomach) than the focaccia at **Liguria Bakery**; biscotti from the **Italian/French Bakery**; air-dried sausage from **Molinari Delicatessen**; fat *cotechino* sausages and delicious mascarpone *tortas* from **Prudente Meat Market and Deli**; the irresistible *sacripantina* at **Stella Pastry**; and a rum-soaked *zuccotto* at **Victoria Bakery Co**. And after you've taken in the culinary sights, don't miss **Biordi**, where owner Gianfranco Savio has gathered a magnificent assortment of traditional and modern Italian pottery.

Capp's Corner and **LaFelce** provide the classic Italian family-dining experience, complete with red-and-white-checkered oilcloths, walls covered with photographs and mementos, and bargain-priced five-course meals. But even in North Beach, that kind of old-style eatery is beginning to give way to trendier, more tourist-oriented spots, including the **Stinking Rose**, which offers an all-garlic menu.

Other shifts are evident, such as the latest twist in North Beach's demographic profile. The neighborhood abuts **Chinatown**, and ever since Chinese immigration to San Francisco peaked in the 1980s, the Asian influence in the area has grown. The 1990 census revealed that only about 12 percent of North Beach residents were of Italian heritage; 65 percent were of Asian descent. Chinatown, traditionally demarcated from North Beach by Broadway, has begun creeping across the divide. The two worlds collide at Broadway and **Grant Avenue**, in a dizzying kaleidoscope of language, sights, and smells. The growing Asian influence has resulted in a bit of cross-pollination at some North Beach restaurants. **The House** on Grant Avenue serves *soba* noodles and tempura, all seasoned with Italian flair, while **Enrico's** serves steamed clams in a broth perfumed with lemongrass.

Nevertheless, although new influences such as that of the Asian community, and the addition of strip clubs and flashing neon which has made this area nearly as colorful as Las Vegas, plenty of classic European flavor remains. In fact, during the 1990s a new wave of Italian immigrants

North Beach

has been opening restaurants in the neighborhood, including **Steps of Rome**, **L'Osteria del Forno**, and **Ristorante Ideale**.

No tour of North Beach would be complete without a cappuccino finale. For the best cup, head for **Mario's Bohemian Cigar Store**. This 19th-century hangout makes a fitting spot for the inevitable realization that even the most leisurely day spent exploring the neighborhood has somehow rushed by. Well, relax and linger a little longer; you've just discovered the magic of North Beach.

湖南小喫 *Hunan Restaurant*

1 **Hunan Restaurant** ★$$ Owner Henry Chung introduced spicy Hunan food to San Francisco in a 20-seat hole-in-the wall back in 1974. No matter how large his restaurant has expanded since then, there's always a full house. Devotees keep coming back for Diana's special, a deep-fried pie filled with pork, cheese, and onions; the house-smoked duck; and ham with peppers and onions, which is hot enough to clear the sinuses. ♦ Chinese ♦ Daily lunch and dinner. Reservations recommended. 924 Sansome St (between Broadway and Vallejo St). 956.7727; fax 956.5772 &

2 **Centerfolds** ★★$$$ The main event here is the topless dancing, but a full menu is also served at this dark, retro club with brick walls, black booths, and red-filtered lighting. If you don't mind bare-breasted women gyrating near your table while you eat, the food is actually pretty good, especially the grilled New York steak with mashed potatoes and wilted spinach and the oysters on the half shell (which you should not dip into the bland sauce that comes on the side). The fried buttermilk-battered calamari is also deftly prepared. A large selection of single malt scotches and Champagnes is available at the bar. ♦ American ♦ Cover. M-F, Su 11:30AM-1AM; Sa-Su 5:30PM-1AM. Reservations recommended. 932 Montgomery St (at Broadway). 834.0661; fax 834.9126

3 **The Helmand Restaurant** ★★★$$ Afghani food, little known in this part of the world, is worth exploring in this pretty, romantic place with flowers on each table and low-key service. A specialty is lamb, served three ways: sautéed with yellow split peas, onions, and vinegar; speared into kabobs, marinated with onion and sun-dried baby grapes, and charbroiled; or marinated, sliced, and served on Afghan bread with sautéed eggplant. *Aushak* is a kind of Afghan ravioli, tender pillows of pasta stuffed with leeks and served with a yogurt sauce, carrots, yellow split peas, and a beef sauce. The combinations seem exotic, but the flavors are sublime, and a good wine list matches the refined food. ♦ Afghani ♦ M-F lunch and dinner; Sa-Su dinner. 430 Broadway (between Montgomery and Kearny Sts). 362.0641 &

BRANDY HO'S

4 **Brandy Ho's** ★$ This glitzy Chinese eatery, located in a building featuring award-winning modern architecture by John Goldman, is wrapped with enough neon to rival the flashing lights that snake down Broadway. The facade has 23-foot red columns topped with a porcelain garland of red peppers (which figure prominently in the restaurant's cuisine). The Hunan menu features pungent house-smoked meats, including chicken, duck, and ham served with whole cloves of garlic. Most of the dishes have a fiery undercurrent, but some are listed as "Not Hot With Pepper." One of the most popular preparations is the *kung pao* chicken, which is sautéed with peanuts, bamboo shoots, water chestnuts, and onions. The staff is happy to help customers make selections. ♦ Hunan ♦ Daily lunch and dinner. Reservations recommended Friday and Saturday. 450 Broadway (at Kearny St). 362.6268. fax 362.3098 &. Also at: 217 Columbus Ave (at Pacific Ave). 788.7527; fax 788.7528

4 **The Old Place** ★★$$ This dining spot used to be **Vanessi's**, a legendary Italian restaurant operated in the 1950s by savvy entrepreneur Modesto Lanzone and his partner, Bart Shea. But Shea took **Vanessi's** to Nob Hill in the 1980s, and now Lanzone and his son Eugene have taken over the old space. The look is still the same—an open kitchen, red leather upholstery, and seating at counters as well as tables—but chef Keith Williamson's menu features some fresh, interesting takes on Italian cuisine. Top choices include

North Beach

handmade tortellini filled with zucchini and ricotta; fire-grilled fillet of beef with foie gras enveloped in a Madeira glaze; and pan-seared saddle of rabbit served with garlic-thyme au jus and a spinach and carrot flan. And the frothy zabaglione, which was a smashing hit in **Vanessi's** heyday, is as good as ever. ◆ Italian ◆ Daily lunch and dinner. 498 Broadway (at Kearny St). 772.9115;. fax 567.0764 ♿.

5 Enrico's ★★★$$ From a safe perch on the heated outdoor patio, diners can observe the bawdy goings-on of the neon jungle around them while enjoying chef/owner Rick Hackett's Italian-inspired fare. (There's also indoor seating, with live entertainment nightly.) The pizzas, cooked to a turn in the wood-burning oven, have a yeasty, thin crust. They are available in classic versions, like the margherita (with roasted garlic and tomato sauce), or topped with such creative combinations as shrimp, corn, and ricotta. The mussels with olive oil, garlic, and Italian parsley are among the best in the city. Also excellent is the Tuscan-style T-bone steak served with white beans. Hackett has recently added a tapas menu, making this place popular for a late-night bite. The desserts are great, too, especially "Mickey Mousse," which presents several small chocolate cakes sitting in a pool of crème anglaise. ◆ Italian/Mediterranean ◆ Daily lunch and dinner. Reservations recommended. 504 Broadway (at Kearny St). 982.6223; fax 397.7244 ♿.

6 Tommaso's ★★$ *People* magazine proclaimed it one of the country's top three pizza places, but success hasn't spoiled this little spot, which is credited with producing San Francisco's first brick-oven pizza some 60 years ago. All the crisp, thin-crust pizzas, spread with just the right amount of topping, are superb. So is the pasta, served with freshly made, sensible, traditional sauces. When you do plain and simple as well as this, there's no need to do anything else. ◆ Italian ◆ Tu-Su dinner. 1042 Kearny St (between Pacific Ave and Broadway). 398.9696; fax 909.9415.

6 Cho-Cho Restaurant ★$$ One of the oldest Japanese restaurants in the city, this place has developed a following among the Hollywood set. It was featured in the movie *Rising Sun,* and regular customers include Francis Coppola and George Lucas. It has the atmosphere of a well-worn Japanese country inn, with rough wood beams, baskets, and massive tables. The open kitchen is framed by shelves holding hand-thrown pottery. Top food choices include sukiyaki, tempura, and a spinach salad with roasted red peppers, bacon, sesame seeds, and a special, ginger-laden sauce. ◆ Japanese ◆ M-F lunch and dinner; Sa dinner. 1020 Kearny St (between Pacific Ave and Broadway). 397.3066 ♿.

7 Caffè Macaroni ★$$ The quality of the food at this cute but modest trattoria has deteriorated a bit lately, but it has remained a popular neighborhood spot. Reliable entrées include a dish of crab, mussels, and octopus served over black pasta flavored with squid ink, puffy gnocchi with gorgonzola sauce, pork with fennel-seed sauce, and chicken breast sautéed with porcini mushrooms. ◆ Italian ◆ M-F lunch and dinner; Sa dinner. Reservations recommended. No credit cards accepted. 59 Columbus Ave (at Jackson St). 956.9737.

8 San Francisco Brewing Company This brewpub offers 20 types of specialty beers, plus house brews, and caters to the Financial District crowd. The interior is virtually the same as it was at the turn of the century. Suspended above the impressive mahogany bar, with its gilded top and beveled-glass mirrors, is a long fan that looks like a Willy Wonka contraption and gently turns a series of palm fans. The tile moat around the bar is actually the original spittoon. There's history here, too: Boxer Jack Dempsey worked as a bouncer, and Babyface Nelson was captured in what is now the women's room. On most nights you can hear blues, jazz, and other live music. The experience is great, but the food is an afterthought, though you can't go wrong with a hamburger. ◆ Daily. 155 Columbus Ave (at Pacific Ave). 434.3344 ♿.

9 Campo Santo ★$ Looking like a folk-art celebration of the Day of the Dead, with kitschy Madonnas and candles everywhere, this quirky spot is a find for those who have overdosed on Italian food and want to enjoy Mexican-inspired fare. Unfortunately, a change in ownership has caused a downturn at this once very popular alternative in the

49

North Beach

trattoria-dense North Beach. The food is less exciting now, and the flavors are somewhat muddied. There are several vegetarian entrées, as well as burritos, chicken mole, and a few creative variations of traditional Mexican dishes, such as salmon tacos with grilled onions and prawn quesadillas with tomatoes and cactus. ◆ Mexican ◆ M lunch; Tu-F lunch and dinner; Sa dinner. Reservations recommended for parties larger than four. 240 Columbus Ave (between Pacific Ave and Broadway). 433.9623

9 Tosca Cafe $ The special cappuccino in this popular hangout is actually made without coffee: It's a frothy cup of steamed milk with brandy and chocolate. The bar is also known for its "white nun," made with steamed milk, Kahlúa, and brandy. No food is served, but things are always hopping here. The gleaming copper espresso machine at the end of the bar, the dark, spacious interior, and the Italian opera on the jukebox give the place a unique character. (Best nights to hear the arias are Monday, Tuesday, and Wednesday; disco music blasting from a nearby nightclub the rest of the week greatly diminishes the experience.) You might see Nicolas Cage lounging by the bar when he is in town. ◆ Coffeehouse ◆ Daily 5PM-2AM. No credit cards accepted. 242 Columbus Ave (between Pacific Ave and Broadway). 986.9651

10 Vesuvio ★$ One of the most popular gathering places for the 1950s Beat generation, this bar still has a bohemian, beatnik feel. ◆ Bar ◆ Daily. No credit cards accepted. 255 Columbus Ave (at Jack Kerouac Alley, near Broadway). 362.3370

11 Little Joe's ★$$ The menu proclaims "Rain or shine, there's always a line," which is a bit of hyperbole these days, as other Italian restaurants open almost every week. The food here is hearty and 1950s plain. Specialties include sautéed calamari steaks with white wine, garlic, and tomato sauce; fish stew in a garlicky tomato sauce (served with a bib, if you wish); and pasta with prawns, tomato, and cheese. ◆ Italian ◆ Daily lunch and dinner. 523 Broadway (at Columbus Ave). 982.7639; fax 433.7066

12 Basque Hotel and Restaurant ★$$ This family-style place, where the Basque cooking is hearty, homey, and spicy, serves an inexpensive fixed-price five-course meal with two entrées. Main courses include barbecued lamb steaks and nightly specials: trout, lamb stew, roast chicken, or beef tongue on Wednesday, Friday, and Sunday; red snapper, oxtail stew, lamb shank, sweetbreads, and duck confit on Tuesday, Thursday, and Saturday. ◆ Basque ◆ Tu-Su dinner. 15 Romolo Pl (off Broadway, between Kearny St and Columbus Ave). 788.9404

13 Yee Cheong General Contractors Although this crammed shop doesn't look like much, it's excellent for bargain-priced Asian cookware. You'll find a good selection of woks, tongs, and other kitchen tools and gadgets. ◆ Daily. No credit cards accepted. 1319 Stockton St (at Broadway). 398.7395

14 The House ★★★$$ Modern in both look and food, this cross-cultural restaurant is the brainchild of Larry Tse, an accountant who put away his calculator to tie on an apron. Choose among such appetizers as shrimp in a heady Chinese barbecue sauce with hot sesame oil; Caesar salad strewn with golden bay scallops; wonderful taro spring rolls, no bigger than a pinkie; garlicky fried chicken wings; and tempura with a substantial batter. Outstanding main courses include sea bass with ginger soy sauce, served with gingery bok choy and roasted or mashed potatoes; veal chop with oyster sauce and shiitake mushrooms; warm noodles with strips of barbecued pork; and stir-fried calamari with bean-paste noodles. Desserts might be a dense chocolate-truffle torte or a thick apple crumb pie. The decor—granite floors, honey-colored tables, and modern Italian lights hanging from the ceiling—makes an appropriate setting for the cutting-edge food. ◆ Asian/Californian ◆ Tu-Sa lunch and dinner. 1230 Grant Ave (at Columbus Ave). 986.8612

The Italian/French Bakery in North Beach bakes approximately 6,000 loaves of bread a day. Its most popular product is a half-sour, crusty bread called the "bastone." In Italian *bastone* means "the club," which is precisely what the long, thick loaf resembles.

North Beach

15 The Stinking Rose ★$$ The name refers to garlic, and the tag line on the menu—"We season our garlic with food"—isn't stretching the truth. The most popular dish is the *bagna calda* (a hot skillet of oven-roasted garlic in olive oil and butter with a hint of anchovy), which spreads on bread like butter. The nongarlic dishes on the menu are marked with a vampire, but lasagna is the only savory course safe for Dracula. For dessert, skip the garlic ice cream with caramel mole sauce and chill out on the lemon sorbet. The restaurant has an enormous following, primarily tourists. Those who haven't had their fill of garlic can buy products made from the pungent cloves. ♦ Italian/American ♦ Daily lunch and dinner. Reservations recommended. 325 Columbus Ave (between Grant Ave and Vallejo St). 781.ROSE; fax 781.2833

16 Steps of Rome ★$ A young, attractive Italian crowd gathers here to meet over cups of espresso. Good antipasto salads and pasta dishes are also available. ♦ Cafe ♦ Daily breakfast, lunch, and dinner. No credit cards accepted. 348 Columbus Ave (between Grant Ave and Vallejo St). 397.0435

17 Columbus Cutlery One of the oldest and most respected cutlery stores in the city, this is where many professional chefs buy their knives and have them sharpened. The shop packs a complete selection of knives, scissors, and utensils into a space that feels no bigger than a phone booth. There's always a crowd waiting for service, and the couple who own the shop can be a bit cranky—though they will answer your questions. ♦ M-Tu, Th-Sa. 358 Columbus Ave (between Grant Ave and Vallejo St). 362.1342

18 Mona Lisa #3: The Island of Garlic ★$$ Sicilian food is the specialty at this old-line restaurant, where one whiff reveals the kitchen's favorite seasoning: garlic. The menu features more than 20 pasta dishes, including a tamed-down version of fettuccine carbonara that's made with ham instead of bacon. But veal piccata gets a kick from lots of capers, and all the pastas and meat courses come with a bowl of good minestrone. The place has a cozy, lived-in look, thanks to the ceiling that's sponge-painted with rainbow colors, fish nets hanging near the bar, and the tables set with black-and-white checkered cloths. ♦ Italian ♦ Daily lunch and dinner. Reservations recommended. 353 Columbus (at Vallejo St). 989.4917; fax 986.6662

18 Molinari Delicatessen This Italian deli, which dates from 1896, is so crammed with fresh and packaged food that it can be claustrophobic. But squeeze yourself in to pick up some of the fresh tortellini and ravioli and the air-dried salami. The display case contains a mouthwatering assortment of meats and such cheeses as gorgonzola, *cambozola,* and Italian fontina. Fresh sausage selections include hot or mild Sicilian; French, which is made with white wine; and excellent *bresaola* (air-dried beef). You'll also find a wonderful selection of olive oils, vinegars, and pastas, and the imported wines are a real bargain. ♦ Daily. No credit cards accepted. 373 Columbus Ave (at Vallejo St). 421.2337

19 Caffè Puccini ★$ The strains of Italian opera emanating from this popular cafe (nicknamed "The Pooch" by its loyal patrons) attract a diverse, music-loving, and artistic crowd. The bar that stretches along the back wall is surrounded by displays of pastries and sweets; the tortes and tarts are particularly good. ♦ Coffeehouse ♦ Daily. 411 Columbus Ave (at Vallejo St). 989.7033

20 Biordi Hand-painted Italian pottery fills this large, 50-year-old ceramics shop. The display is an education in classic and modern majolica designs; trying to decide among the lovely items that pack the floor-to-ceiling shelves can lead to sensory overload. Shoppers will find dishes, bowls, platters, vinegar and oil cruets, pitchers, vases, and even tables. Look for the Renaissance-style plates from Deruta and the beautiful pastel fruit and flower pottery patterns of Castelli. ♦ Daily. 412 Columbus Ave (at Vallejo St). 392.8096; fax 392.2608

21 U.S. Restaurant ★★$ The topsy-turvy arrangement of the rooms, the well-worn interior, and the long-cooked Italian/American food offer up a classic slice of North Beach. This is a popular spot for strapped college students, tourists looking for a bargain, and officers from the nearby police station. Hotcakes are a specialty at breakfast, and ham and two eggs make a filling, low-cost start to the morning. Each day brings four or five specials, all at rock-bottom prices. Regulars

North Beach

come on Wednesday for the stewed tripe or baked ham with ravioli, and on Friday for the stewed rabbit or calamari. ♦ Italian/American ♦ Tu-Sa breakfast, lunch, and dinner. No credit cards accepted. 431 Columbus Ave (between Vallejo and Green Sts). 362.6251

22 Calzone's $$ Black tile and bright neon accents give the facade a space-age look that seems jarring alongside the more traditional storefronts here. But past the doorway, this place is strictly Old World: green walls lined with foodstuffs, a bare tree wrapped in tiny white lights, and a bar positioned under a canopy of miniature liquor bottles. The food isn't a standout, although the pizza is better than average. One plus: Complimentary limo service is offered to and from the Financial District for parties of up to 15. ♦ Italian ♦ Daily lunch and dinner. 430 Columbus Ave (between Vallejo and Green Sts). 397.3600; fax 397.3446

22 Stella Pastry Everything has been made on the premises since this traditional Italian bakery opened in 1942. Be sure to try the specialty, *sacripantina,* layers of sponge cake brushed with maraschino liqueur and zabaglione. Other noteworthy selections include tiramisù, a creamy dessert with layers of ladyfingers, liqueur, mascarpone, and cocoa; biscotti; amaretti, macaroonlike cookies topped with pine nuts; cannoli; and panettone. ♦ M-F 7:30AM-7PM; Sa 7:30AM-midnight; Su 9AM-6PM. No credit cards accepted. 446 Columbus Ave (between Vallejo and Green Sts). 986.2914

Eighty percent of all avocados in the US are grown in California.

General Mariano Guadalupe Vallejo may have been a California pioneer, but his daughter was renowned in her own right as a cook. Here's her recipe for Spanish eggs: Add two cups of peeled, seeded, and chopped tomatoes to a large skillet. Thicken with bits of crustless bread. Add two or three jalapeño peppers (for hotter flavor, mince the peppers beforehand) and a finely sliced onion. Add a little butter, salt, and pepper. Simmer gently 20 minutes to meld the flavors, then break three whole eggs on top. Baste with the sauce until the eggs are set.

---

23 Caffè Trieste ★$ An eclectic clientele—bohemians, musicians, white-collar types, and tourists—flocks here to relax, converse, and enjoy some of the best coffee in North Beach. They can also find pastries and, at lunch, a limited number of sandwiches, like turkey or ham and cheese on focaccia. The company imports, roasts, and distributes its own beans. The retail shop next door often is covered in a haze from the beans roasting out in the open for all to see. The favorite brew here is the Italian roast espresso, a rich, smooth blend that's just on the edge of bitterness. Every Saturday afternoon, the restaurant holds a singalong, with patrons and staff performing arias together. ♦ Cafe ♦ Daily. 601 Vallejo St (at Grant Ave). 392.6739

23 Basta Pasta $$ Popular with tourists because of the splashy decor and sophisticated-looking menu, this eatery offers little that you can't find elsewhere. The pasta often is overcooked and soggy and the pizza quickly goes limp. ♦ Italian ♦ Daily lunch and dinner until 1:30AM. 1268 Grant Ave (at Vallejo St). 434.2248; fax 421.4489 ♿

24 North Beach Pizza ★$ A full menu is available (heavy on pasta), but most diners concentrate on the pizza, which many claim is the best in the city (though we find it to be inconsistent). Ten combinations are offered, including one with pepperoni, mushrooms, and cheese, and another with clams, garlic, and cheese—all smoothed over the slightly doughy crust. You can call for pizza delivery 24 hours a day. ♦ Pizzeria ♦ Daily lunch and dinner. 1310 Grant Ave (at Vallejo St). 433.2444; fax 433.7217 Also at: 1499 Grant Ave (at Union St). 433.2444; fax 433.7217

25 Ristorante Ideale ★★★$$ Maurizio Bruschi, who was a part-owner of **Bonta** in the Marina District and **Pazzia** on Third Street, spotlights the foods of Rome at his restaurant, which is decorated in warm pumpkin tones. The one-page menu is filled with not-to-be-missed selections. Start with a simple salad or fried Arborio rice dumplings stuffed with mozzarella. For pasta, try the *pappardelle* (broad noodles) with a tomato-based lamb sauce, or penne with a combination of fresh and smoked salmon in a creamy tomato sauce. Delicious entrées include the baby lamb chops, grilled pork loin

North Beach

with wild fennel, and Cornish hen roasted with herbs. ♦ Italian ♦ Tu-Su dinner. Reservations recommended. 1309 Grant Ave (at Vallejo St). 391.4129

26 Mo's Gourmet Hamburgers ★★$ The top hamburger in the area, prepared over a revolving coal-fired grill, it has a slightly smoky flavor with a crusty exterior and juicy interior. The old-fashioned shakes, served in the metal containers, are winners, too. And nostalgia buffs go wild for the frothy root-beer float. ♦ Hamburgers ♦ Daily breakfast, lunch, and dinner. 1322 Grant Ave (between Vallejo and Green Sts). 788.3779 ♿

27 The Nature Stop This natural-foods grocery is a godsend for local residents. There's a deli featuring mostly vegetarian selections and sandwiches, a juice bar with wheat-grass shooters, and a small produce section with five kinds of mushrooms and other choice seasonal items. Bread comes from **Tassajara**, **Semifreddi's**, and **Metropolis**. A whole wall of bins has foods in bulk, including a dozen granolas, and shelves hold nonfat snacks, a half-dozen flavors of honey, and an herbal tea section that includes "Daily Detox . . . For today's toxic environment." ♦ M-F 9AM-10PM; Sa-Su 10AM-9PM. 1336 Grant Ave (between Vallejo and Green Sts). 398.3810; fax 398.1537 ♿

28 La Bodega ★$ Decorated in bright, bold colors, this Spanish restaurant features a lovely abstract brush painting of flamenco dancers. A complimentary bowl of olives sets the stage for the rest of the meal. Try the thinly sliced chorizo, and follow it with the paella or the chicken served over vegetable-studded rice. Every night after 8PM, there's live entertainment. ♦ Spanish ♦ Daily dinner. 1337 Grant Ave (between Vallejo and Green Sts). 433.0439 ♿

29 Figoni Hardware Co. Here is a classic: a vintage 1907 hardware store, complete with scarred wood floors, bare lightbulbs hanging from the 15-foot ceiling, and helpful salespeople who are almost courtly in their long, blue coats. The surprise is the wide array of great kitchenware, including cast-iron grill pans, gadgets, and basic Italian pottery. Among the Italian food-making equipment look for ravioli rolling pins, pasta machines, and parmesan cheese graters. ♦ M-Tu, Th-Sa. 1352 Grant Ave (between Vallejo and Green Sts). 392.4765

30 Maykedeh ★★$$ By most accounts this is the best Persian restaurant in the city, a rating based somewhat on the pleasant decor: White tablecloths and fresh flowers lend an airy atmosphere. To start, try the tender lamb tongue with lime, sour cream, and saffron, or the dolmas (stuffed grape leaves). Among the best dishes are such house specials as the marinated *poussin* (broiler chicken), slightly charred by flames, or the hefty skewers of perfumed ground lamb and beef, which have been marinated in lime and onions. ♦ Persian ♦ Daily lunch and dinner. Reservations recommended Friday and Saturday. 470 Green St (at Grant Ave). 362.8286 ♿

30 Bocce Caffè ★$$ This stylish restaurant has open-beam ceilings, swirling fans, terra-cotta floors, and an attractive patio surrounding a fig tree. The menu includes a good selection of inexpensive dishes, including lasagna, cannelloni, gnocchi, and pizza. But watch out for the house specials, perhaps grilled fish of the day or risotto: They can cost twice as much, but don't taste twice as good. Stick with the basics and you'll be happy, especially in such nice surroundings. ♦ Northern Italian ♦ Daily lunch and dinner. 478 Green St (at Grant Ave). 981.2044 ♿

30 North End Caffè A haze of smoke envelops this hangout with high ceilings, a mezzanine, and an atmosphere that makes it feel as if its history goes back further than the 1980s. The place has worked its way into the fabric of local poets' lives, and readings are held regularly. The young crowd seems content to play chess or backgammon and ponder existence over a strong cup of coffee. ♦ Daily. No credit cards accepted. 1402 Grant Ave (at Green St). 956.3350

31 Danilo Italian Bakery An all-purpose bakery specializing in Tuscan recipes, this shop makes a lot of things very well, among them breads, bread sticks, biscotti, focaccia, and panettone (including the very special anise-flavored *buccelatto*). One of the unique treats is a *torta di verdura*, a dense pie made with Swiss chard, liqueur, raisins, and pine nuts. ♦ Daily. No credit cards accepted. 516 Green St (at Grant Ave). 989.1806 ♿

32 New Pisa Restaurant ★$ A classic North Beach restaurant that serves family-style food, this place is a sister to the better-known **Capp's Corner** (see page 60). The fixed-price menus (including salad, soup, pasta, main course, and spumoni) are the same at both,

53

North Beach

but the atmosphere here is more refined, with booths that afford some privacy. Go on Friday for the fisherman's stew with all kinds of shellfish. Throughout the week, the leg of lamb, herb chicken with mushrooms and rosemary, and housemade sausage score points. ♦ Italian ♦ Daily lunch and dinner. 550 Green St (between Grant and Columbus Aves). 989.2289; fax 989.2025

33 Savoy Tivoli In business since 1907, this watering hole for the postcollegiate singles crowd has a "rec room" with three pool tables, a well-worn bar, and a very European feel. Bar food is available, but young people really come to drink, mingle, and hang out. ♦ Tu-Th 5PM-2AM; F-Su 3PM-2AM. No credit cards accepted. 1434 Grant Ave (between Green and Union Sts). 362.7023

34 Cafe Jacqueline ★★★$$ Soufflé's the thing at this cozy, romantic restaurant with candles and flowers on the tables—in fact, it's the only thing. Owner Jacqueline Margulis stations herself behind a big bowl of eggs, ready to whisk them by hand into airy, flavorful delights. Each soufflé is designed to serve two; they aren't cheap, but they're absolutely wonderful. Savory selections might include salmon and asparagus, shiitake mushrooms, or white corn with ginger and garlic. The dessert soufflés—raspberry, Grand Marnier, and chocolate—are too good to choose among. The only other dishes offered are salad and soup to enjoy before the soufflé extravaganza. ♦ French ♦ W-Su dinner. 1454 Grant Ave (between Green and Union Sts). 981.5565

35 Prudente Meat Market and Deli An institution, this great market has been in the Rossi family since it opened in 1910 as **R. Iacopi and Co.** In June 1995 it was sold to a goddaughter of former owner Leo Rossi and the name was changed. Among the delicacies prepared on the premises are pancetta, Parma-style prosciutto, and house-cured dry jack cheese. The family also has a longstanding tradition of sausage making; the excellent varieties sold here include hot Calabrese, aromatic, garlicky Toscana, and slightly sweet Sicilian. Rossi's ex-wife, Darlene, originated the famous *tortas*: homemade mascarpone cheese layered with such fillings as basil and sun-dried tomatoes, smoked salmon, porcini mushrooms, black olives and pine nuts, and figs and almonds. Don't miss the nightly entrées (chicken cutlets, roasted vegetables and garlic, and rich gourmet sandwiches), which are available only for takeout. ♦ Daily. 1462 Grant Ave (at Union St). 421.0757; fax 421.0759

36 Italian/French Bakery The *bastone* (club loaf) here repeatedly earns top marks in tasting contests. This bakery also has a deserved reputation for its Dutch crunch sourdough, bread sticks, and crisp biscotti in such flavors as walnut, hazelnut, chocolate chip, anise, and almond. ♦ Daily 7AM-6PM. 1501 Grant Ave (at Union St). 421.3796

37 Lo Coco's Restaurant ★★$$ Few restaurants prepare lusty Sicilian food as well as this intimate spot. Many of the sauces are intensely flavored. The *pasta con sarde,* from a recipe that dates back more than a thousand years, is made of saffron pasta tossed with anchovies, fennel, pine nuts, currants, and bread crumbs. The flavor is haunting. Also satisfying are any of the pastas with a hearty Neapolitan tomato sauce. The pizzas here are wonderfully light and crisp; the crust is so good, in fact, that the simplest toppings are best. The pepperoni, for instance, comes out crisp around the edges and with a fresh-tasting tomato sauce and green onions. The housemade cannoli, stuffed with ricotta cheese and preserved cherries, also is excellent. All these delights are served up amid a comfortable, cafelike atmosphere, with brick walls, terra-cotta floors, and windows that open onto the street. ♦ Italian ♦ Tu-Sa dinner. Reservations recommended Friday and Saturday. 510 Union St (between Grant Ave and Stockton St). 296.9151

38 Caffè Malvina ★★$ Compared to others in the area, this cafe has an expansive feel: A sea of well-spaced tables and bentwood chairs is surrounded by a curving bar and windows that open to the bustle of passersby. The coffee, roasted and ground at the restaurant's facility south of Market Street, is rich and bracing. Another reason to come here is the terrific salads: Sweet rock shrimp are combined with sliced button mushrooms, bacon, and baby spinach with a warm lemon dressing. Another winner is the *quattro stagione,* featuring marinated garbanzo and kidney beans, artichoke hearts, roasted peppers, mushrooms, and avocado on a bed of mixed greens. Sandwiches and *pizzetta* are better than average. ♦ Cafe ♦ Daily. 1600 Stockton St (at Union St). 391.1290

North Beach

any of the pastas, which may be paired with lobster, pesto, calamari, shrimp, scallops, or four kinds of cheese. It's worth a visit just to see the wealth of colorful, Sicilian-inspired artwork covering the walls and ceiling and competing for attention with the Christmas lights that crisscross overhead. ♦ Italian ♦ Tu-Sa lunch and dinner. Reservations recommended. No credit cards accepted. 574 Green St (at Columbus Ave). 981.1251

53 European Delights The shelves of this no-frills shop groan with glass jars filled with more than 300 kinds of candies and confections. Among the sweets are hard candies, chocolates, and more flavors of jelly beans than you could ever imagine. Coffee beans are available, too, and they can grind them on the premises. ♦ Daily. No credit cards accepted. 521 Columbus Ave (between Green and Union Sts). 398.7782 &

Everything You Ever Wanted to Know about Pairing Wine and Food, But Were Afraid to Ask

Maybe it's all those wine-loving Italians who settled in San Francisco in the 19th century, or perhaps it's the fertile wine-growing regions a short drive away. Whatever the reason, this is one of the top wine buying and wine drinking cities in the nation.

But with the multitude of wines now available, as well as new culinary trends, selecting a wine to accompany a meal or snack has become more complicated. The rules are no longer so simple as red with meat, white with fish. And the seasoning or sauce served with the main ingredient can affect your choice. For example, oysters on the half shell are great with a Sauvignon Blanc—but choose a Chardonnay if they're served in a cream sauce.

Wine can even stand in for other beverages now. Beer's always been a classic with pizza, but when the pizza is topped with smoked salmon and caviar, as at **Postrio**, or sprinkled with wild mushrooms or fresh corn, as at **Enrico's**, a crisp Sauvignon Blanc or an easy-drinking Pinot Blanc might make a better match.

Today many restaurants offer extensive selections of wines by the glass, so it's easy to experiment. If the wine tastes good with your food, you've made the right decision. Here are some suggestions for adventurous wine pairing.

Appetizers
Asparagus: Sauvignon Blanc/Fumé Blanc
Carpaccio: Barbera, Rhône blends
Caviar: Brut sparkling wine or brut Champagne
Crudités: Chardonnay, Pinot Blanc, Zinfandel
Foie gras: Sauternes, late-harvest Riesling
Oysters (raw): Brut sparkling wine, Champagne, Sauvignon Blanc, Chenin Blanc
Pasta with cream sauce: Chardonnay
Pasta with tomato sauce: Sangiovese, Zinfandel, Rhône blends
Scallops: Sauvignon Blanc, Chardonnay, Pinot Noir, Semillon

Main Courses
Fish and Shellfish: Sauvignon Blanc/Fumé Blanc, Chardonnay, brut sparkling wine, Champagne, Pinot Blanc, Pinot Gris, Viognier
Lamb: Syrah, Rhône blends, Cabernet
Poultry: Chardonnay, Merlot, Gamay Beaujolais, Pinot Noir, Zinfandel
Pork: Pinot Noir, Zinfandel, Gamay Beaujolais, Merlot
Beef: Cabernet Sauvignon, Syrah, Barbera, Zinfandel, Rhône blends

Rabbit: Riesling, Pinot Noir, Zinfandel
Sausage: Riesling, Gamay Beaujolais, Syrah, Zinfandel
Veal: Chardonnay, Barbera, Merlot
Venison: Rhône blends, Zinfandel, Pinot Noir, Cabernet Sauvignon

Ethnic Foods
Chinese: Chardonnay, Pinot Blanc, Merlot
Spicy Chinese: Dry (and off-dry) Riesling, Gewürztraminer
Mexican: Chenin Blanc, Gamay Beaujolais
Thai: Gewürztraminer, Riesling, Pinot Blanc, Chenin Blanc

Cheeses
Soft: Brut or rosé sparkling wine, Sauvignon Blanc, Pinot Noir
Hard: Cabernet Sauvignon, Zinfandel, Muscat, late-harvest Riesling

Desserts
Most desserts pair well with demi-sec sparkling wines, late-harvest Rieslings, ice wines, Muscat, or Zinfandel. Chocolate and Cabernet Sauvignon were made for each other.

North Beach

L'Osteria del forno

53 L'Osteria del Forno ★★★$ If we had to pick one "find" in North Beach, this would be it. Few places have such a wonderful feel: This hole in the wall is what you'd expect in North Beach, with tables wedged into the front windows, and the service friendly and casual. The kitchen turns out *the* best focaccia sandwiches, excellent pasta, and a roast of the day, usually beef or a delectable pork that has been marinated and braised in milk. All this for what amounts to small change. ♦ Italian ♦ M, W-Su lunch and dinner. Reservations recommended. No credit cards accepted. 519 Columbus Ave (between Green and Union Sts). 982.1124

54 Caffè Roma Coffee Roasting Company ★$ Java gets no fresher than at this popular coffeehouse, which is dominated by its roasting machine. The aromatic, bitter-tinged coffees go well with the pastry selection here. The cafe portion has been remodeled to create an idealized 1990s version of a 1920s cafe: a black-and-white tile floor, swirling fans, and dark wood shelves holding all kinds of coffee-related merchandise. In the retail area you can also purchase coffee by the pound. Note, however, that there are no public restrooms here. ♦ Coffeehouse ♦ Daily. 526 Columbus Ave (between Green and Union Sts). 296.7662; fax 800/296.ROMA

55 Gold Spike $ The family-style meals on our last visit here were mediocre, but this dingy restaurant does boast a real conversation starter: Thousands (maybe millions) of yellowing business cards stud the ceiling and walls. Entrées include standards like osso buco and pot roast. ♦ Italian ♦ M-Tu, Th-Su dinner. 527 Columbus Ave (between Green and Union Sts). 421.4591

56 Ben & Jerry's It caused quite a controversy when this East Coast–based chain opened a branch here several years ago. Residents worried that the neighborhood would soon turn into Anytown USA. Well, North Beach has managed to hold on to all its individuality even as this shop dishes up its famous ice cream as well as baked goods and espresso drinks. The top seller here is the ice cream studded with chocolate-chip cookie dough. ♦ Daily. 543 Columbus Ave (between Green and Union Sts). 249.4684; fax 249.2655 ♿. Also at: 79 Jefferson St (at Mason St). 249.2662 ♿; 1480 Haight St (at Ashbury St). 249.4685; fax 249.4682 ♿

56 Il Pollaio ★$ Grilled chicken doesn't come any better than at this pie-shaped wedge of a cafe, whose picture windows overlook Columbus Avenue—though the quality is inconsistent (sometimes the meat comes out dry and burned). Other entrées—such as lamb chops, pork chops, and rabbit—are spiced and grilled in the Argentine manner. Don't miss either of the side orders: crisp french fries or marinated eggplant. Soup, a couple of salads, and two desserts round out the short menu. ♦ Argentine/Italian ♦ M-Sa lunch and dinner. 555 Columbus Ave (between Green and Union Sts). 362.7727

56 Ristorante Volare ★$$ For the last eight years, Giovanni Zocca has operated **El Menudo,** one of the best *taquerias* in the Outer Mission. Now, in keeping with his Italian heritage, he has opened this new Sicilian eatery in North Beach. The waiter may try to "help" you by steering you to the more traditional, mundane dishes, but insist on ordering the Sicilian specialties, such as penne served with a sauce made from tomatoes and fresh ricotta, or Sicilian antipasti featuring *bottarga* (preserved tuna roe), crabmeat, and vegetables. And leave room for the tiramisù, which is so heavenly it's almost sinful. (And if you see a guy standing outside the restaurant singing *Volare* at the top of his lungs, don't worry—that's Giovanni. Singing on the street outside is his way of attracting customers.) ♦ Italian ♦ Daily lunch and dinner. 561 Columbus Ave (between Green and Union Sts). 362.2774; fax 362.1353

57 Rose Pistola ★★$$ Restaurateur/chef Reed Hearon has had no trouble keeping busy in San Francisco the past few years. First he opened the hot, hip **Lulu** in the SoMa district, then he and partner Louis Clement created **Cafe Marimba,** a new-wave presentation of Mexican food. Now Hearon has opened this Italian eatery in North Beach. The food is in the tradition of the early Ligurian and Genoese immigrants to North Beach—highlights include cioppino, porcini risotto fritters with fontina cheese, braised calamari and artichokes with polenta and pizzas baked in a wood-burning oven. The dining room is accented with Italian glass tile, chrome, and mahogany. Live jazz is offered after 9PM. ♦ Italian ♦ Daily lunch and dinner (to 1AM Friday and Saturday). 532 Columbus Ave (between Stockton and Union Sts). 399.0499 ♿

58 Mario's Bohemian Cigar Store ★★$ For many locals this 100-year-old cafe encapsulates everything that's right about North Beach: The surroundings are comfortable but unpretentious, the staff is friendly, and the cappuccino is the best in the area. When the Crimani family took over

North Beach

the bar in 1971, they added windows that overlook **Washington Square Park** and transformed it from a hangout for elderly Italian men into an upbeat, bustling spot. The focaccia sandwiches are excellent, the ricotta cheesecake perfect for a midafternoon snack. The place stays open until midnight most evenings (except Sunday, when it closes at 11PM). ♦ Cafe/Italian ♦ Daily breakfast, lunch, and dinner. 566 Columbus Ave (at Union St). 362.0536. Also at: 2209 Polk St (between Vallejo and Green Sts). 776.8226; fax 776.3388 &

59 Michaelangelo Cafe ★$$ With all the people inside and lines often snaking outside, this cafe can be as busy as Grand Central Station at rush hour. While waiting for a seat, peek in through the large windows to see an impressive tableau: The tables are covered with prints of some of Michelangelo's ceiling work, the walls with elaborately framed oil paintings. Top menu choices include the calamari salad, served on lettuce with a lemony dressing, and the pastas, which are sometimes oversauced (fans nonetheless favor the thick bolognese sauce with meat and mushrooms). One of the best dishes is the potato gnocchi in a creamy tomato sauce. ♦ Italian ♦ Daily dinner. No credit cards accepted. 579 Columbus Ave (at Union St). 986.4058

59 Coit Liquors A knowledgeable staff and a great selection of Italian wines set this wine- and-liquor store apart from the rest. The staff prides itself on tasting wines at least four nights a week, and the experience shows: When customers ask questions, they get the right answers. ♦ Daily until midnight. 585 Columbus Ave (at Union St). 986.4036; fax 296.7825 &

pasta pomodoro

60 Pasta Pomodoro ★★$ This pasta house offers incredible deals and generous portions. Plus, the gnocchi, coated in gorgonzola sauce and spiked with diced tomato, are better than preparations that cost twice as much. The dozen or so pastas include *penne putanesca* (with black and green olives and a slightly spicy tomato sauce); rigatoni with roast chicken, cream, mushrooms, and sun-dried tomatoes; and spaghetti with calamari, mussels, and scallops in a light tomato sauce. The Caesar salad is light on the garlic and anchovy, but big shavings of parmesan compensate. A few sandwiches round out the menu, and for dessert there's tiramisù, biscotti, or gelato. Clean and spare, with seating at a U-shaped counter or tables along the walls, the place is designed to ensure quick turnover. ♦ Italian ♦ Daily lunch and dinner. No credit cards accepted. 655 Union St (between Columbus Ave and Powell St). 399.0300; fax 399.0377 &. Also at: 2027 Chestnut St (at Fillmore St). 474.3400; fax 474.4511 &

Gira Polli

60 Gira Polli ★★$ The stippled walls and high-tech lighting make an interesting juxtaposition to the wood-fired rotisserie, where diners can watch the flames lick at the dozens of chickens lazily bronzing. Few places do chicken better; here it's served with Palermo-style potatoes, cooked in broth and baked with white wine and herbs until they're tender. There are a few salads, soups, and pastas—all fine, but not nearly as special as the chicken. For dessert, the light, lemon-flavored cheesecake will satisfy any sweet tooth. A popular take-out menu offers complete family-style dinners for four (with garden salad, pasta with pesto, two chickens, potato and vegetable, and biscotti) at an amazing price. ♦ Italian/Takeout ♦ Daily dinner. 659 Union St (between Columbus Ave and Powell St). 434.4472; fax 434.3762

61 Little City Antipasti Bar ★$$ One of the first restaurants in the city to cash in on the grazing trend, this place offers dozens of small Italian appetizers, in the tapas mode. They may include grilled tuna on white beans with a dollop of aioli; ground lamb patties accentuated with an Arabic salad of cucumbers, peppers, and croutonlike pita chips; or grilled baby artichokes with a tomato-tarragon aioli. But the best-seller is straight out of the 1980s: roasted garlic with baked brie. The decor is warmed by brick walls, a bar that takes up a good portion of the room, and fine paintings by local artists. An overflow dining room, often set up for private parties, opens at peak times; it's less interesting, but has a great collection of photos from North Beach and Italy. The restaurant is a good late-night destination, as it stays open until midnight every night. ♦ Italian ♦ Daily lunch and dinner. 673 Union St (at Powell St). 434.2900; fax 434.1501

62 Washington Square Bar and Grill ★★$$ This place has been a political and celebrity hangout since it opened in 1973,

59

North Beach

thanks to its jovial former owner, Ed Moose, who sold it in 1990 and opened up **Moose's** (see page 55) just across the square. After a few tough years, the "Washbag," as locals fondly call this establishment, was given a new lease on life in 1995 when Peter Osborne—who also owns the **Buchanan Bar and Grill** in the Marina—bought the restaurant and spruced up the interior. But he left all the memorabilia that gives it the feel of a casual men's club, and has kept up the tradition of live piano music at night. The crowds have returned, and the place captures the spirit of North Beach, particularly with its classic Italian/Californian menu. Standout dishes include smoked salmon with warm potato pancakes, fried calamari, petrale sole with capers and lemon, veal chop with mushrooms, and a warm apple tart with caramel sauce. ♦ Italian/Californian ♦ M-F lunch and dinner; Sa-Su brunch and dinner. 1707 Powell St (between Union St and Columbus Ave). 982.8123; fax 982.5718

63 Anthony's ★$$ Lobster at rock-bottom prices has put this Italian seafood restaurant on the map. The kitchen also turns out a fine pizza, which is lightly grilled over mesquite, then baked in a wood-fired oven with a choice of innovative and traditional toppings. One of the most popular pies is made with lobster and shrimp. Many shellfish favorites—prawns, clams, and scallops—are also served over pasta. ♦ Italian/Seafood ♦ Daily dinner. Reservations recommended. 1701 Powell St (at Union St). 391.4488; fax 391.0528

64 Capp's Corner ★★$$ At this quintessential neighborhood Italian joint, the rows of red-and-white–checkered tables are so close that you nearly eat with your neighbor. Completing the picture, a group of buddies at the long wooden bar seems perpetually engaged in animated conversation, half watching the TV suspended overhead. The waitresses may seem a bit brusque at first, but actually they're very friendly. The food has that old-style appeal, with a multicourse bargain that includes soup and salad, pasta, a main course, and spumoni. The leg of lamb is excellent, as are the braised veal shanks served with baked polenta. The braised pork loin with mushroom sauce can be a tad dry, but the flavor is outstanding. ♦ Italian ♦ M-F lunch and dinner; Sa-Su dinner. Reservations recommended. 1600 Powell St (at Green St). 989.2589

65 O'Reilly's Bar & Restaurant ★★$$ Owned by Irish-born restaurateur Miles O'Reilly, this eatery gives the mostly Italian neighborhood of North Beach a taste of the "aulde sod." O'Reilly has introduced some genuine Irish objects into the decor, including an 18th-century globe-shaped street lamp from Dublin and a handsome mahogany bar topped by stained-glass canopy from Cork.

On the walls are pen-and-ink drawings of prominent Irish men and women; most striking is the whimsical mural depicting some of Ireland's greatest writers, including Yeats, Joyce, Wilde, and Brendan Behan. Chef Larry Doyle (who formerly worked at **Stars** and **Stars Cafe** under Jeremiah Tower) wants to put Irish food on the map—and he doesn't mean corned beef and cabbage (which is actually an American creation). His menu features traditional dishes, such as lamb stew, "boxty" (smoked salmon draped over a light potato cake), and a "fry-up" of fish, chips, cockles, and mussels. At the bar, you can get Guinness and other varieties of ale, served warm at 45° the way they do in real Irish pubs. ♦ Irish ♦ M-Sa lunch and dinner; Su brunch and dinner. 622 Green St (between Stockton and Powell Sts). 989.6222

TRATTORIA
Contadina

66 Trattoria Contadina ★★$$ Somewhat off the beaten path, this restaurant draws mostly locals with its well-prepared Italian food and warm and welcoming service. (Celebrities dine here too, or so the framed glossies of Kirstie Alley, Melanie Griffith, and Jack Scalia attest.) Few dishes in North Beach are as appealing as the veal medaillons covered with a cream sauce infused with the earthy, nutty flavors of porcini mushrooms. While the other entrées, including osso buco, don't reach that pinnacle, they still are satisfying. But the specialty here is stuffed pastas, each cooked to perfection with just the right amount of sauce. All meals come with a salad. If you want something more substantial, begin with the paper-thin carpaccio or the marinated calamari. ♦ Italian ♦ Daily dinner. Reservations recommended. 1800 Mason St (at Union St). 982.5728

67 Graffeo Coffee Mention great coffee and the name Graffeo always comes up; this retail store, which dates from 1935 and roasts its own beans, has a cultlike following. The rich house blend combines beans from Colombia, Costa Rica, and New Guinea, and connoisseurs consider the Swiss water–process decaffeinated Colombian to be the best of its kind. ♦ M-F 9AM-5PM; Sa 9AM-6PM. 735 Columbus Ave (between Filbert and Greenwich Sts). 986.2420, mail order 800.222.6250; fax 986.1577

60

North Beach

68 Buca Giovanni ★★$$$ A romantic, cavelike setting showcases terrific Italian dishes and grilled meats. All pastas are made on the premises, and the chef is a master at preparing rabbit. (His two specialties come together marvelously in the fettuccine with house-smoked rabbit.) Fans have a hard time choosing among rabbit entrées, whether it's roasted with grappa and oyster mushrooms; or grilled, seasoned with rosemary, and accompanied by roasted potatoes with balsamic vinegar; or sautéed with porcini mushrooms, sage, garlic, and wine. Those who prefer not to think of rabbits as a meal will be very happy with the scampi with oyster mushrooms or the lamb medallions with black olives and capers. Also be sure to order white beans seasoned with olive oil, garlic, and fresh herbs. The tiramisù makes a perfect ending. ♦ Italian ♦ Tu-Sa dinner. Reservations required. 800 Greenwich St (near Columbus Ave). 776.7766

69 Caffè Freddy's Eatery ★$ Just a few blocks from the North Beach hubbub, this brightly painted corner restaurant caters to a young clientele with what the staff refers to as "affordable gourmet" Italian fare. The menu comprises mostly salads, sandwiches, and pizzas, all served in large portions. Some of the more unusual offerings include an open-face sandwich of hot goat cheese and smoked salmon with a spinach vinaigrette, and a *pizzetta* with slices of new potatoes, mozzarella, parmesan, provolone, and a sprinkling of fresh rosemary. There's also a selection of low-calorie dishes made without oil or dairy products. One drawback: Service can sometimes be brusque. ♦ Italian/American ♦ Daily breakfast, lunch, and dinner. 901 Columbus Ave (at Lombard St). 922.0151

70 Zax ★★★$$ Husband-and-wife team Mark Drazek and Barbara Mulas share culinary duties at one of the best chef-owned restaurants in the city. This out-of-the-way place has a soothing, modern decor: A wide celadon stripe painted around the room subtly contrasts with the gray walls, while the apricot ceiling adds a pleasant glow; the large flower arrangement and polished wood chairs complete the look. Starters on the changing menu might include a puffy goat cheese soufflé to complement a mixed green salad dressed with a mixture of vinegar and aged sherry. The entrée might be well-peppered salmon cooked to a bronze finish and propped on mashed potatoes infused with garlic, served with a warm salad of white corn and baby spinach. For dessert, don't miss the wonderful *gallette,* an old-fashioned apple tart in which a delicious buttery crust curls over the top. ♦ French/Mediterranean ♦ Tu-Sa dinner. 2230 Taylor St (between Columbus Ave and Francisco St). 563.6266

71 Albona Restaurant ★★★$$ Owner Bruno Viscovi re-creates the intriguing food of his homeland at the only Istrian restaurant in northern California. (Istria, a peninsula below Trieste, belonged to Italy for 2,000 years before becoming part of Yugoslavia after World War II.) Thanks to Istria's position on the spice-trade route, almonds, honey, dates, raisins, cumin, and paprika were integrated into its cuisine. Central European influences added goulash, sauerkraut, and strudel. Viscovi prepares uncommon fare, and he describes his dishes with such a poetic cadence that diners hang on his every word. The ravioli filled with cheese, pine nuts, and golden raisins are served in a browned sirloin-tip sauce with a hint of sweet spices and cumin. The panfried gnocchi, served in the same sirloin sauce, are puffy, slightly crispy mouthfuls that are so specific to Viscovi's hometown that they are unknown even 10 miles away. One of his top recommendations is the roasted free-range chicken cooked with a wine glaze; also worth trying is the *brodetto,* a ragout of fish, squid, and shellfish in a rich balsamic sauce. The moody lighting and comfortable chairs make a pleasant backdrop to the dramatic food. ♦ Istrian ♦ Tu-Sa dinner. Reservations recommended Friday and Saturday. 545 Francisco St (at Taylor St). 441.1040; fax 441.5107

72 Julius' Castle ★$$$$ Even after the owners of this romantic, elegant restaurant perched on the hills near **Coit Tower** refurbished the interior, installed an exhibition kitchen, and hired a new chef, the food here still doesn't match the surroundings. Pasta with broccoli rape and garlic isn't nearly as special as it should be, and the kitchen insists on using mealy potatoes to showcase sautéed scallops in a refreshing cucumber sauce. Sea bass, served with garlic mashed potatoes and a mountain of fried leeks is dry and overcooked, while the pheasant comes to the table blood-red in the middle. Many patrons don't seem to mind, though. With its rich paneled interior, soft lighting, and panoramic vista of the bay, this place has probably kindled more flames than any other dining spot in the city. ♦ Continental ♦ Daily dinner. Reservations required; jacket required. 1541 Montgomery St (at Greenwich St). 392.2222; fax 986.8197

Fisherman's Wharf/ The Embarcadero

Ever-popular with tourists, Fisherman's Wharf is mostly avoided by locals, probably because of the amusement-park atmosphere it has acquired over the years. But they don't know what they're missing; this area has a long history of seafaring and fishing, and it also has a number of fine restaurants, many of which boast patios or wharfside windows that make the most of their spectacular views of the **Golden Gate Bridge**, the **Bay Bridge**, **Alcatraz**, and the shimmering water of **San Francisco Bay**.

The waters of the bay were once so rich with fish and shellfish that archaeologists have been able to identify Native American settlements (such as that of the Ohlone people, who lived here for centuries until they died out in the 19th century) by the mounds of oyster shells contained in the substrata of the banks. From around the time of the Gold Rush in the mid–19th century until the early 20th century, fisherfolk streamed here from Italy and used their own time-honored traditions to net, hook, or scoop a living from the sea. The main catches were salmon and crab. As recently as 1970, more than 300 vessels regularly fished the waters. Today, only about 120 boats are moored in the harbor, and most of those travel beyond the bay to nab their daily catch of rock cod, salmon, and Dungeness crab. And there hasn't been much shipping or receiving on the docks here since the 1960s, when the advent of container ships caused most of this activity to shift across the bay to Oakland, a more convenient location. What remains is almost a honky-tonk caricature of a bustling port, with lots of touristy T-shirt and souvenir shops, a wax museum, and dance clubs.

Nevertheless, the area still evokes some of the romance of the time when San Francisco's economy was linked to the sea—particularly if you visit in the early morning. Just stroll down **Fish Alley** (which is also known as **Richard Henry Dana Street** in honor of the famous local author), where each day's catch is cut and filleted for sale to the city's markets and restaurants. Or go to **Pier 47** and watch as the fishing boats—each fitted with enormous net-retrieving equipment and topped by towering outriggers—chug out of the harbor. Farther down the Embarcadero, pilot ships are sent out to guide cruise ships and large container freighters through the bay's tricky waters.

And the wharf can still sate any appetite for fresh seafood in every incarnation—from the simplest, purest oysters on the half shell at **A. Sabella's Restaurant** to juicy *ahi* tuna steak at **Scoma's** to "walkaway" crab cocktail or tasty fish-and-chips to go at **N. Alioto's** streetside stand. All three spots have been family-owned and -operated for generations.

In the past, the food proffered by the wharf's seafood houses was traditional almost to the point of stuffiness. Nowadays, though, a wide variety of cooking styles can be found here. Even stalwarts such as **A. Sabella's** and **The Waterfront Restaurant** have updated their menus and added more contemporary creations. (So no one will look at you strangely if you ask for your fish to be cooked medium rare.) A bit apart from the wharf's hubbub, you can sample the inventive fare at the popular and stylish **Fog City Diner** and **Chez Michel**.

The wharf area is also home to three distinct retail-entertainment-dining hubs: **Ghirardelli Square**, the **Cannery**, and **Pier 39**. The buildings that make up **Ghirardelli Square** were once manufacturing plants owned by Domingo Ghirardelli, the Italian-born confectioner who arrived in San Francisco in 1849 and is best known for the chocolate that still bears his name. In the 1960s, the Ghirardelli family sold the business, the new owner moved the chocolate production to San Leandro (in the

63

Fisherman's Wharf/The Embarcadero

East Bay), and the square underwent an impressive redevelopment. Today it bustles with free entertainment and an interesting assortment of shops and eateries. The only remnant of its chocolaty past is the **Ghirardelli Chocolate Manufactory**, a wondrous combination of seductive soda fountain, elegant chocolate shop, and miniature chocolate factory.

The brick building that houses the **Cannery** was built at the turn of the century as a fruit- and vegetable-packing plant; under the Del Monte company's ownership, it became the world's largest peach-canning facility. It was sold in 1964 and reopened in 1967 as a collection of shops, galleries, and restaurants.

Pier 39, which was developed in 1978, attracts more than 10 million visitors a year to its shops and food vendors and restaurants. It's the place to pick up such snacks and souvenirs as flavored coffees at **San Francisco Tea and Coffee Co.** and delicious peanut-butter fudge at **The Fudge House**.

Despite its excessive commercialization, Fisherman's Wharf remains an area worthy of notice by anyone who loves the sea and seafood. And plans are underway to make it more attractive and easier to visit for both visitors and residents. Future improvements (scheduled to be completed at press time) include the redesign of the Embarcadero, the addition of a trolley line to the wharf, and the opening of **Underwater World**, a new aquarium at **Pier 39**.

1 The Waterfront Restaurant ★★$$
Popular for lunch and brunch, this favorite (which was being remodeled at press time) capitalizes on its grand view of the Bay Bridge and **Treasure Island**. The menu is dominated by fresh fish, naturally, and recently the preparations have been updated and Asian flavors incorporated into the formula.
◆ Seafood ◆ M-Sa lunch and dinner; Su brunch and dinner. Pier 7 at The Embarcadero and Broadway. 391.2696; fax 391.7125

2 deStijl Cafe ★★$ Call it hip or cutting edge, this busy cafe is a magnet for television talent and local architects who work in the area. The room has a cool feel, with a color scheme of black, faded red, and orange, dramatic wood-back chairs, and light wood tables. Breakfast choices include granola, excellent waffles, and fresh fruit dishes. The lunch menu tends to be inspired by the Middle East: It might include red lentil *kibbeh,* a lentil patty stuffed with chickpeas and spinach and topped with a creamy yogurt sauce; a sandwich of grilled chicken with tahini-and-cumin sauce; and a clear vegetable broth with cracked wheat, spinach, and a touch of cumin and cinnamon. For dessert, try the oatmeal cookies, and don't miss the incredible strawberry-rhubarb pie if it's available.
◆ Californian ◆ M-Sa breakfast and lunch; Su breakfast. Reservations required on Thursday 1 Union St (at Front St). 291.0808

3 Il Fornaio ★★$$ One of the prettiest Italian restaurants in the city, the dining room looks out on the well-manicured Levi's Plaza. There's outdoor seating for dining on sunny days, but there is also a heated patio that's pleasant in chilly weather. The pizzas are appealing, as is any meat or pasta dish that emerges from the wood-burning oven. Try the eggplant pizza with black olives and smoked mozzarella, or the focaccia pizza with gorgonzola, pine nuts, and sweet onions. Other specialties include ravioli stuffed with lobster and ricotta and topped with a lemon-cream sauce, and spinach linguini with rock shrimp and tomatoes. It's also a great place for a weekend brunch. The house-baked breads are wonderful; pick up a loaf to go at the adjoining bakery. ◆ Italian ◆ M-F breakfast, lunch, and dinner; Sa-Su brunch and dinner. Reservations recommended. 1265 Battery St (at Greenwich St). 986.0100; fax 986.2210

4 Happy Valley Chinese Seafood Restaurant ★★$$ This stylish restaurant located in Levi's Plaza specializes in Mongolian hot pot, but unlike the less-expensive wannabes in the Richmond district, it uses

Fisherman's Wharf/The Embarcadero

nothing but high-quality ingredients. The hot-pot process is similar to preparing fondue: A pot of bubbling broth is brought to your table, as well as some just-caught seafood, a selection of ground dumpling pastes, noodles, and fresh vegetables. You pick up your food with chopsticks or small baskets and put it into the pot (they're done when they float to the top). Drink the flavorful broth at the end. For those who want their meals already cooked, the menu also features typical Cantonese stir-fry and braised dishes. ♦ Chinese ♦ M-F lunch and dinner; Sa-Su dinner. 1255 Battery St (at Filbert St). 399.9393; fax 399.9399 ౘ. Also at: 2346 Lombard St (between Pierce and Scott Sts) 922.9179 ౘ.

5 Fog City Diner ★★$$ One of the most visited restaurant in the city, it fueled the diner trend when it opened about a decade ago. At night the chrome exterior and neon glow like a space station in orbit; the interior, swathed in rich wood and brass, looks more like a stylish 1930s men's club. Yes, there's such diner fare as burgers, fries, and "black cows," but with a decidedly upmarket flair; the ketchup is homemade and the menu is rounded out with numerous Californian specialties, including crab cakes, stuffed *pasilla* (fresh chili peppers), and all kinds of California-style fish and meat dishes. ♦ American ♦ Daily lunch and dinner. 1300 Battery St (between Greenwich and Lombard Sts). 982.2000; fax 982.3711 ౘ.

6 The Fudge House This locally owned shop makes fudge and candy-dipped fruits before your eyes. There are dozens of fudge flavors (the peanut butter is excellent), as well as caramel apples, chocolate-covered strawberries, white chocolate–covered red licorice, chocolate-dipped bananas, English toffee, peanut clusters, and pecan logs. ♦ Daily. Pier 39 (Building K, Level 1). 986.4240; fax 743.1485 ౘ.

7 Alcatraz Bar and Grill ★$ The prison cell at the entrance (go ahead, step inside and take a picture) and the sign "Have you done time in our retail shop?" let you know right away that this is a tourist haunt. Still, the menu is one of the most reasonably priced on **Pier 39,** if you can get by the pun-filled menu: The "Preliminary Hearings" include good onion rings and deep-fried calamari with a popcornlike crunch. The "Warden's Dinner Menu" includes clam chowder or tossed salad with such main courses as "killer shrimp" (spicy prawns served with rice). There are

also burgers and pizzas, and other cutely named categories, but if we follow the theme any further we might have to cop a plea. ♦ American ♦ Daily lunch and dinner. Pier 39 (Building M, Level 1). 434.1818; fax 434.2266 ౘ.

8 We Be Knives Pocketknives and hunting and kitchen knives fill the display cases and cover the walls of this specialty shop. All the best brands for cutting up in the kitchen are here, including Wüsthof and Gerber. ♦ Daily. Pier 39 (Building O, Level 1). 982.WEBE; fax 331.1479 ౘ.

9 Casa de Fruta An "orchard outlet," this shop stocks all kinds of dried fruits and nuts, packaged and in bulk. Gourmets will find three kinds of apricots, red flame raisins, dried blueberries and cranberries, and more. Popular snack items include a dried vegetable mix containing green beans, taro, and sweet-potato chips; taco-seasoned corn nuts; and Cajun-seasoned fava beans. Packaged gift products, including salsas, sauces, and vinegars, are also available. ♦ Daily. Pier 39 (Building P, Level 1). 989.3012; fax 647.0258 ౘ.

10 Chocolate Heaven The sign over the door proclaiming this "The Greatest Chocolate Store in the World" is only a bit exaggerated; the shop does boast an incredible selection of imported and domestic chocolates. Rarely will you find boxes of Hawaiian Host, Perugina, Lindt, Ghirardelli, Joseph Schmidt, Blum's, Cremaretto from Italy, Ferrero Rocher, and Nob Hill under one roof. The walls are lined with bins of chocolates sold by the piece. Novelties include jalapeño jam chocolates and cream-filled seashells from Belgium. ♦ Daily. Pier 39 (Building D, Level 1). 421.6551 ౘ.

11 Blue Chip Cookies Be warned: These big, gooey cookies can be addictive. The chocolate chip is a winner. ♦ Daily. Pier 39 (Building B, Level 1). 989.9411 ౘ. Also at: Rincon Center, 101 Spear St (at Mission St). 896.5267; fax 989.1746 ౘ.

12 Eagle Cafe ★$ Once a ticket office and baggage room for the **McCormick Steamship Line,** this rustic, turn-of-the-century building looks like a longshoreman's hangout. It became a cafe in 1928 and was lifted and moved to the present location in 1978. A century of scars shows on the walls, which are covered with white railroad car siding.

Fisherman's Wharf/The Embarcadero

The tiny kitchen, set behind a green Formica counter, turns out bountiful breakfasts and lunches. French toast, housemade corned-beef hash, and fluffy buttermilk pancakes are top morning choices. At lunch there's a list of sandwiches and hearty, reasonably priced blue plate specials, including meat loaf or roast beef with mashed potatoes, vegetables, and sourdough bread. ♦ American ♦ Daily breakfast and lunch; bar until 10PM. Pier 39 (Building A, Level 2). 433.3689

Old Swiss House

13 Old Swiss House ★★$$$ This place looks like a little slice of the Alps: Swiss-style stencils decorate the perimeter of the pitched room, which is dominated by a hexagonal fireplace, and lace curtains soften the ocean-front view. Although most menus on the wharf are almost carbon copies of one another, this one is distinguished by such hearty European specialties as medaillons of pork sautéed in butter and topped with cognac-infused morels; lamb, served with a cranberry glacé; and pan-fried veal stuffed with ham. ♦ Swiss/Continental ♦ Daily lunch and dinner. Pier 39 (Building C, Level 2). 434.0432

14 San Francisco Tea and Coffee Co. Geared to the tourist, this shop stocks more flavors of coffee and tea than just about any other in the city. Coffee flavors include peaches 'n' cream, macadamia nut, and Irish cream. Coffeepots, teapots, and other related equipment are for sale, including mugs with handles in the shape of toucans, dinosaurs, fish, and alligators. ♦ Daily. Pier 39 (Building D, Level 2). 421.5119

Dante's

15 Dante's Fresh Italian Seafood ★$$$ The dark wood appointments, dark green carpets, and white tablecloths lend a traditional ambience to this handsome, glass-fronted dining room with a picturesque view of the East Bay. Maine lobster is prepared three ways: in cioppino; stuffed with prawns and wrapped in prosciutto; or sautéed in garlic butter. The mesquite-grilled selections, including swordfish, salmon, and halibut, are generally good. Upstairs there's a warm and cozy bar for sitting and sipping. ♦ Seafood ♦ Daily lunch and dinner. Pier 39 (Building N, Level 2). 421.5778; fax 434.2266

16 Yet Wah $ The only Chinese restaurant on **Pier 39**, its menu has a middle-of-the-road appeal, but the lunch buffet can get sorry-looking by 3PM. It is part of a chain known for generic, yet well-prepared, food; however, each branch is individually owned, so the quality varies from one to the other. ♦ Chinese ♦ Daily lunch and dinner. Pier 39 (Building M, Level 2). 434.4430

17 Neptune's Palace ★$$$ Located at the end of **Pier 39** (and under the same ownership as **Dante's**), this spot offers the best view of the hundreds of sea lions and seals that sun and frolic in the calm, protected waters here. The sprawling dining rooms, one resembling a garden, another a Victorian parlor, also have a dramatic and melancholy view of Alcatraz Island. The menu reads like a book, but skip to the section that offers the daily catches. Generally, eight fish are available, and diners can choose the preparation: grilled with wasabi (Japanese horseradish) butter; baked with hot-and-sour mushrooms; pan-fried with a spicy black bean sauce; blackened and cooled with cucumber yogurt; or poached with a citrus hollandaise. Thirty wines are offered by the glass. ♦ Seafood ♦ Daily lunch and dinner. Pier 39 (Building K, Level 2). 434.2260; fax 434.2266

18 Cost Plus World Market A one-stop bargain-shopping paradise, this warehouse-size store stocks everything from country- or Shaker-style tables and chairs, to all kinds of glassware and pottery, to an enormous selection of specialty foods, including coffees, teas, and wines. With a large collection of baskets, napkins, and the like, it's easy to gather all the makings of a beautiful gift basket. ♦ Daily 9AM-9PM. 2552 Taylor St (at Bay St). 928.6200; fax 921.2657

19 Foggy's ★$ A good cup of coffee isn't easy to come by in this neighborhood, which makes this spot (which used to be called **Foggy Bay Coffee Company**) a real find for those who need to refuel. Tea is also available and there is a nice selection of pastries to enjoy with a "cuppa" at one of the small tables. ♦ Coffeehouse ♦ Daily. 570 North Point St (at Taylor St). 474.2070

20 Cafe Pescatore ★$$ One of the most attractive dining options in the wharf area, the place has a welcoming trattoria atmosphere, with an impressive exhibition kitchen. The wood-burning oven turns out crisp-crusted pizzas. Some dishes can be uneven; stick with the stews and roasts, including the roast chicken. The location, a block away from the crowds, adds a civilizing note. On warm days

Fisherman's Wharf/The Embarcadero

diners can sit on the patio and watch the passersby. ♦ Italian/Seafood ♦ Daily breakfast, lunch, and dinner. 2455 Mason St (at North Point St). 561.1111; fax 561.1199 ♿

BEN & JERRY'S®

21 Ben & Jerry's Largely a walk-and-lick operation, this popular ice-cream shop does offer inside tables to those who want to relax with a sundae; the shop also shares the patio in back of the **TraveLodge at the Wharf** hotel with **Johnny Rockets** (see below). Wheelchair access is through the hotel. ♦ Daily. 79 Jefferson St (at Mason St). 249.2662 ♿. Also at: 543 Columbus Ave (between Green and Union Sts). 249.4684; fax 249.2655 ♿; 1480 Haight St (at Ashbury St). 249.4685; fax 249.4682 ♿

21 Johnny Rockets ★★$ At this 1950s-style diner/hamburger joint, you can enjoy a root-beer float and fries while seated around the poolside patio. On a sunny day, looking at the pool ringed by palm trees will make you think you're in Florida. ♦ American/ Hamburgers ♦ Daily breakfast, lunch, and dinner. 81 Jefferson St (at Mason St). 693.9120; fax 693.9404 ♿. Also at: 1946 Fillmore St (at Pine St). 776.9878; fax 776.1189 ♿

22 The Candy Barrel Wine barrels brimming with all kinds of treats give this sweetshop a nostalgic feel. There are more than 25 flavors of locally produced saltwater taffy, including watermelon, coconut, passion fruit, caramel pecan, and licorice swirl, as well as individually wrapped hard candies. Another local specialty not to be missed is Judy's coconut almond brittle—simply marvelous. Just down the street, and under the same ownership, **Doc's International Candy Shoppe** (131 Jefferson St, between Mason and Taylor Sts, 771.8908) offers an equally vast selection. ♦ Daily. 333 Jefferson St (between Jones and Leavenworth Sts). 771.5526 ♿.

22 N. Alioto ★★$ Here's a streetside stand with a difference: The fish-and-chips and other seafood offerings look fresh and taste it, too. If you can't visit the wharf without indulging in a crab cocktail, this is the place for it. ♦ Seafood ♦ Daily. 155 Jefferson St (between Mason and Taylor Sts). 776.7300 ♿

22 Boudin Sourdough Bakery & Café ★$ Since opening on North Beach's Grant Avenue back in 1849, this bakery chain has expanded to 18 locations in San Francisco. This branch offers a glimpse, behind glass, of the sourdough bread–making process. It also houses two eateries, the original in front, with a few tables, and a cafe/bakery in the parking area behind (at Taylor Street between Jefferson Street and The Embarcadero). The menu is the same at both, and offers sandwiches on sourdough bread. A specialty at all **Boudin** cafes is clam chowder served in a hollowed-out sourdough loaf, allowing diners to eat the bowl, if that's their pleasure. ♦ Cafe ♦ Daily breakfast, lunch, and light dinner until 8PM. 157 Jefferson St (between Mason and Taylor Sts). 928.1849; fax 776.1778. Also at: 619 Market St (between New Montgomery and Third Sts). 281.8200 ♿; 399 10th Ave (at Geary Blvd). 221.1210; fax 221.3854 ♿

23 A. Sabella's Restaurant ★★★$$$ When the Sabella family emigrated here from Sicily in 1871, they made their living by fishing the bay. They opened this seafood restaurant in 1920, and they've been in business here ever since. Today, the third generation of Sabellas runs the place. The huge banquet-style room has floor-to-ceiling windows overlooking the wharf, and a bar in the back is warmed by a fireplace that would look right at home in an Aspen ski lodge. Special dishes include crab legs à la Mama (mixed with scallions, mushrooms, garlic, and white wine and baked in puff pastry). Chef Michael Sabella has updated the menu, adding dishes with an Asian influence, such as whole cracked crab with a light, fermented black-bean sauce. The fresh seafood offerings change daily and include such combinations as broiled salmon on sautéed spinach and tarragon *riso,* a rice-shaped pasta. The lounge next door features live entertainment on weekends and mystery-theater packages that include the whodunit, as well as a three-course meal, tax, and parking. ♦ Seafood ♦ Daily lunch and dinner. 2766 Taylor St (at Jefferson St), Third floor. 771.6775; fax 771.6777 ♿

24 Tarantino's $$$ A view of the boat basin is assured, thanks to the tiered seating at this restaurant, which has been here since 1946. But although he food can be fine, the preparations often seem slipshod. Pasta is made in-house and is used as a bed for some of the specialties, including scallops and prawns in a smoky tomato sauce, redolent of garlic. Best bets include steamed clams with butter and

67

Fisherman's Wharf/The Embarcadero

garlic; grilled sand dabs; rex sole, served boned; and abalone, dipped in an egg batter and served with a butter sauce. ◆ Seafood ◆ Daily lunch and dinner. 206 Jefferson St (at Taylor St). 775.5600; fax 749.2097 ♿

25 Fishermen's Grotto ★$$$ Like many of its neighbors, this place has a cracked crab stand in front, a casual sit-down seafood eatery on the ground floor, and a more formal restaurant upstairs. In the winter, the fireplace in the cocktail lounge is inviting. Although some seafood preparations are in a 1950s time warp—crab on shredded iceberg lettuce with Louis dressing, crab au gratin bubbling in enough cream to stop a healthy heart—the simply steamed mussels and the sautéed fish are about as fresh as you'll find. Skip the commercial-tasting desserts from a tray. ◆ Seafood ◆ Daily lunch and dinner. 9 Fisherman's Wharf (at Taylor St). 673.8100; fax 673.7984

25 Alioto's ★★$$$ Not to be confused with **N. Alioto**, this is the oldest restaurant on the wharf and one of the most popular as well. It is *the* place for cioppino, the seafood stew that it claims to have invented. The streetside stand offers cracked crab, while **The Oysteria**, an oyster bar on the first floor, is fine for a light repast. The upstairs dining room is washed in a quiet brown color scheme that lets the colorful view of gently rocking boats stand out. Sicilian specialties are mixed in with such standard Cal/Ital dishes as ziti with pine nuts, raisins, tomatoes, and flakes of fresh-tasting fish. The seafood risotto here is one of the best in town; another great entrée is abalone wrapped in a light egg coating. Nunzio Alioto is one of the top sommeliers in San Francisco, and his list of excellent wines includes many bargains, particularly among the Italian vintages. ◆ Seafood ◆ Daily lunch and dinner. 8 Fisherman's Wharf (at Taylor St). 673.0183; fax 673.3894 ♿

A San Francisco original, steam beer is named for the way it used to be brewed. The process used lager yeast at ale temperatures; the resulting brew was so effervescent that, when a keg was tapped, the beer erupted like steam escaping a pipe. These days, steam beer is still produced (Anchor Steam Beer is one of the leading brands), but more modern methods are used.

26 Tokyo Sukiyaki Restaurant and Sushi Bar ★★$$ After a day at the garish wharf, you'll welcome the serenity of this sleek spot decorated with celadon walls and movable bamboo screens. Sit Western-style, kneel on tatami mats at low tables, or perch at the elevated sushi bar. Two menus are offered, regardless of where the diners are seated: One lists such typical dishes as tempura and teriyaki, and a smaller menu, written in Japanese and English, presents traditional rice and noodle dishes and a variety of sake and spirits. Sushi is better elsewhere, but do try the beef sukiyaki with scallions, mushrooms, tofu, and noodles; *shabu shabu* (slices of beef cooked in broth and served with sesame and vinegar sauces); and some of the cooked fish dishes, including the salt-broiled flounder. ◆ Japanese ◆ M-F dinner; Sa-Su lunch and dinner. 225 Jefferson St (between Taylor and Jones Sts). 775.9030; fax 775.3872

27 Everyday Cafe ★$ An instant hit with both locals and visitors, this recently opened coffee shop offers three kinds of java, as well as tea and Lappert's ice cream, an exotic bran that is imported from Hawaii (try the Kona coffee-fudge flavor). Owner Holly Smith offers bagel sandwiches, fresh pastries, and croissants at breakfast, and the rest of the day she serves a wide variety of sandwiches, homemade soups, and salads. ◆ American ◆ Daily breakfast, lunch, and dinner until 7PM Jan-Apr, Sept-Dec; until 11PM May-Oct. 448 Beach St (between Taylor and Jones Sts). 346.6047 ♿

28 The Sweet Factory Big Plexiglas tubes, mounted on the walls, display an extravaganza of hard candies in such eye-catching colors as lime green, Pepto Bismol pink, and passionate purple. Snacking on these Day-Glo–hued morsels is a high-tech way to get low-tech cavities. Other sweets include chocolates, jelly beans, and gummies. ◆ Daily. 333 Jefferson St (at Jones St, in the Anchorage Mall). 474.4731 ♿

29 Pompei's Grotto ★$$ Compared to the banquet-size dining rooms that predominate in the area, this quaint room, decked out in checkered tablecloths, paneled walls, and gently whirling fans, has an intimate, almost romantic ambience (but it's popular with

Fisherman's Wharf/The Embarcadero

families, too). The restaurant dates from 1946, and the food has a similar pedigree, with all kinds of seafood mixed in with Italian specialties. ♦ Italian ♦ Daily lunch and dinner. 340 Jefferson St (between Jones and Leavenworth Sts). 776.9265; fax 776.9646 ♿

30 Scoma's ★★$$ Believe it or not, this venerable but rundown seafood house is the highest-grossing restaurant in San Francisco, packing people in just about every day of the year. It's the kind of joint where disinterested waiters sling your food at you on the run and present the check before dessert even arrives. But it attracts locals (who frequently are seated without waiting) and tourists alike. Much of the charm of this place is its dockside location. As for the food, the fish is generally very fresh, and portions are generous, but the presentation is fatally flawed. Oysters on the half shell, for instance, are mishandled, buried in ice, and sloppily served. Best bets are the grilled fish steaks served with simple sauces. ♦ Seafood ♦ Daily lunch and dinner. Pier 47 (at Jones and Jefferson Sts). 771.4383; fax 775.2601 ♿

30 Lou's Pier 47 Club This noisy, boisterous nightclub offers live blues music performances and dancing, along with a full bar and a pub-style menu of burgers and snacks. With its funky, hip atmosphere, it has become very popular and trendy very quickly. ♦ Daily 6:30PM-midnight. 300 Jefferson St (near Pier 47). 771.0377

⊛ THE CANNERY

31 The Cannery Constructed in 1909 as the Del Monte Fruit Company's peach-canning plant, this building was remodeled in 1968 by **Joseph Esherick & Associates** following the successful redevelopment of **Ghirardelli Square** (see page 70). The three-story complex contains shops, restaurants, a comedy club, galleries, and a movie theater. Its sunken courtyard, which is filled with flowers and century-old olive trees, hosts musicians, mimes, and other talented street performers. ♦ 2801 Leavenworth St (at Jefferson St). 771.3112; fax 771.2424 ♿

Within The Cannery:

Cannery Wine Cellar and Gourmet Market This sprawling market, with an exposed network of pipes and wires overhead, seems an unlikely place for a serious wine-and-liquor store. But amid the clutter of tourist merchandise are stocked more than 300 kinds of beers, 160 single-malt scotches, and a good collection of California wines. Shelves of gourmet products, including mustards, jams, olive oils, and vinegars, round out the food selections. ♦ Daily. 673.0400; fax 673.0461 ♿

Confetti's Dazzling cases of chocolates and candies from some of the top purveyors in the Bay Area and the country are the attraction here. For lower-cal treats, walk out the door to the corner, where sister shop **Confetti California Fruits and Nuts** carries a terrific selection of California-grown nuts and dried fruits. ♦ Daily. 928.1256 ♿

Jack's Bar $ A resplendent English interior—with paneling that dates back to the 17th century, a carved fireplace, and patterned plaster ceiling—makes this pub stand out from the other restaurants on the wharf. One of several similarly named taverns under the same ownership, it offers a menu of fresh seafood appetizers and other bar food, including sandwiches, salads, and daily specials. The real draw, though, is the selection of beers—nearly 70—on tap. ♦ Seafood ♦ Daily lunch and dinner. 931.6400; fax 931.6404 ♿. Also at: 3200 16th St (at Guerrero St). 552.1633

Cafe Rigatoni $$ Neapolitan-inspired dishes are the specialty at this pizza and pasta place and include—surprise—rigatoni, coated with a plain tomato sauce or one with sausage, and sautéed Tuscan chicken breast, which comes crusted with fennel, cumin, and coriander. The restaurant makes its own sausage—the flavor changes daily—and serves it with polenta. Choose between indoor dining and alfresco seating amid lush greenery and beautiful concrete fountains. ♦ Italian ♦ Daily lunch and dinner. Courtyard. 771.5225 ♿

32 Buena Vista Cafe ★$ You haven't had Irish coffee until you've had it here, because of the drink's quality as well as its history. That soul-satisfying brew, blended with Irish whiskey and topped with whipped cream, was first served in the United States at this place in 1952, after Stan Delaplane, a longtime *San Francisco Chronicle* columnist, tasted it in Shannon Airport and brought the idea back. The cafe's not much to look at: Round wooden tables sit on an old tile floor, the scarred walls look as if they've seen a hundred coats of glossy paint. The bar menu offers casual, tasty fare, such as hamburgers with cheddar or outstanding Reuben sandwiches, and blackboard specials

69

Fisherman's Wharf/The Embarcadero

include corned beef and cabbage, and macaroni and cheese. ♦ American ♦ Daily breakfast, lunch, and dinner; bar until 2AM. No credit cards accepted. 2765 Hyde St (at Beach St). 474.5044; fax 474.2207 ♿

32 Little Rio Cafe and Pizzeria ★$ This is one of many similar restaurants around the Bay Area that offer a menu of pizza and Brazilian fare. Colorful Latin flair wins out in the decor department with splashy tablecloths, but pizza is clearly the most popular item. There's even a Carmen Miranda dessert pizza, slathered with butter, cinnamon, sugar, bananas, and cheese (order at your own risk). Pasta and Brazilian dishes round out the menu, which includes marinated beef sautéed with onions and served with rice and beans, and, every weekend, *feijoada*, a black-bean and pork stew that is considered the national dish of Brazil. A good selection of bottled beers from Brazil, El Salvador, Peru, and other exotic places also is showcased. ♦ Brazilian/Pizzeria ♦ Daily lunch and dinner. 2721 Hyde St (between North Point and Beach Sts). 441.3344 ♿

32 Chez Michel ★$$$ A complete departure from the usual wharf-area restaurant, this upscale establishment has pale gray walls, matching plantation shutters at the windows, mirrors, and wood beams. Indirect lighting illuminates an eye-catching domed ceiling. However, the overall mood is cold and the color scheme unflattering, casting a gray wash onto diners' faces. The kitchen's creations, a throwback to the 1980s, range from very good to just passable. Appetizers include duck confit on *frisée* (curly endive) and salad with tough pieces of octopus in an overwhelming citrus marinade. Representative main courses are tender slices of rosy duck breast glistening in an overly sweet raspberry sauce and chicken stuffed with wild mushrooms. But the attentive, unpretentious service and the reasonably priced wine list remain major assets. ♦ French/Californian ♦ Tu-Su dinner. 804 North Point St (at Hyde St). 775.7036; fax 775.1805 ♿

33 Ghirardelli Square During the Civil War this was the site of a woolen mill, but it was the famous chocolate factory built here in 1896 by Domenico Ghirardelli that gave the square its name. The factory was converted into the city's most attractive commercial complex by **Wurster, Bernardi & Emmons Inc.** and **Lawrence Halprin & Associates** from 1962 to 1967. The location is blessed with a view of the bay, and at night the buildings are festively outlined with strings of lights. The **Mermaid Fountain** in the central plaza, designed by local artist Ruth Asawa, is a good resting and meeting spot. Free entertainment usually is taking place somewhere within the square, and the information booth (located smack in the middle of the square) has a detailed guide to the shops and restaurants. ♦ 900 North Point St (across from Aquatic Park). 775.5500; fax 775.0912 ♿

Within Ghirardelli Square:

Ghirardelli Chocolate Manufactory ★★$ You're unlikely to find better ice-cream concoctions than those at this magical combination soda fountain, chocolate shop, and chocolate factory. The soda fountain dishes up huge, scrumptious sundaes and steaming mugs of delicious hot chocolate topped with mounds of whipped cream; on warm days try the strawberry or vanilla soda. Next door, the elegant chocolate shop's dark wood cases are filled with sweet temptations. The mini-factory is in back; there, three exposed belts gently rotate a paddle that stirs the vat of molten chocolate. ♦ Ice-cream parlor ♦ Daily. Clocktower Building, First floor. 771.4903; fax 775.0912 ♿

The Mandarin ★$$$ With its brick walls, windows overlooking the bay, country-style setting, and formal service, this is one of the city's most upscale Chinese restaurants. For more than 30 years it was owned by Cecilia Chiang, who introduced many now-standard dishes to the United States. She sold her place to one of her employees several years ago; since then, the interior has frayed a bit around the edges and the food's innovative edge has dulled. Still, the sesame-coated fried-prawn appetizer, the prawns served in a mayonnaise sauce with honey-coated walnuts, and the minced squab in lettuce cups are never-fail dishes. ♦ Chinese ♦ Daily lunch and dinner. Woolen Mill, Fourth floor. 673.8812; fax 673.5480 ♿

McCormick & Kuleto's ★$$$ Far and away the most impressive-looking restaurant on the wharf, this seafood house has a view of the lighted **Aquatic Park** and a striking design by **Pat Kuleto**, who has worked his magic on many of the city's best restaurants. The tiered interior features rich wood-and-brass appointments and tortoiseshell-glass lights shaped like boats. The food can be excellent, but with 400 seats plus private receptions and banquets, consistency is a problem. Dozens of fresh fish are featured each day. Order what looks simplest and you may well have a very good meal. ♦ Seafood ♦ Daily lunch and dinner. Webster Building, Courtyard level. 929.1730; fax 567.2919 ♿

Fisherman's Wharf/The Embarcadero

Adjoining McCormick & Kuleto's:

Crab Cake Lounge ★★$ It looks like a typical wharfside bar, its brick walls covered with pictures, but this place serves up plenty of good, affordable eats. More than a half-dozen varieties of oysters are offered on the half shell, as well as salads, crab, mussels, grilled trout, hamburger, and a dozen or so pizzas cooked in the brick oven. The bar features at least 10 single-malt scotches and as many Cognacs, Armagnacs, and bottled beers, including a special seasonal draft. ♦ Seafood ♦ Daily lunch and dinner. 929.1730; fax 567.2919 ♿

Big Sky Ranch ★★$$ A world of cowboys and country is tucked away in the **Cocoa Building.** An etched cowboy motif at the windows, rustic hickory chairs, and a western-print fabric evoke *Bonanza's* Ponderosa—a welcome change from the Mediterranean and Asian places that dominate the city. The hearty, homestyle preparations include corn chowder, crispy corn cakes, and quesadillas to start, followed by pot roast, baby back ribs, chicken potpie, apple pie, and berry cobbler.

(Note that the Hungarian owners, who used to operate **Paprikas Fono** at this location, have retained a separate menu featuring stuffed cabbage and other favorites from the old country.) ♦ American/Hungarian ♦ Daily lunch and dinner. Cocoa Building, Third floor. 441.1223 ♿

Gaylord India Restaurant ★$$$ No Indian restaurant in the city matches the elegance of this one, awash in pink and red and mahogany, with a wall of glass overlooking Jefferson Street. On recent visits, however, the food was a bit sloppy and tired, though the tandoori selections still are outstanding. ♦ Indian ♦ Daily lunch and dinner. Chocolate Building, Third floor. 771.8822; fax 771.4980 ♿

Operetta Italian dining and kitchen accessories are the backbone of this store, along with a few well-chosen food items and antiques. Be sure to look for the tapestry table runners and tablecloths that incorporate a vegetable-and-fruit motif into the design. ♦ Daily. Woolen Mill, Third floor. 928.1676 ♿

Scan Trends This shop carries tabletop accessories by such important Scandinavian names as Royal Copenhagen and George Jensen. You'll find more than 30 dinnerware patterns, flatware, candlesticks, serving trays, and other items to set a beautiful table. ♦ Daily. Woolen Mill, Third floor. 775.2217; fax 707.996.7790 ♿

Bests

Jeanette Etheredge
Owner, Tosca Cafe

Bix: They treat me like a movie star. Plus they have the best club sandwich in town.

Fog City Diner: The food makes me feel like I'm in high school again, and I had a great time in high school!

Enrico's: Great pizza—a close second to **Tommaso's.**

I love the food shop at **Neiman Marcus:** great cheeses, Petrossian caviar. The closest we have to Harrod's food hall in London. I wish they would turn the whole floor into a food hall.

Cammy Blackstone
On-air Personality, KFRC Radio

Polly Ann Ice Cream: This shop has the most unusual ice cream flavors, made in-house, including *lilikoi,* guava, green tea, red bean, lychee, and taro. For pet owners, they give you a special "doggie cone," no charge.

Original Joe's Italian Restaurant: Joe grinds his own chuck daily. The burgers are damn good!

Speckmann's: The storefront is a German deli where you can buy sausages, cheese, and breads—all imported or made here in German style. The restaurant entrance is on the side street. The bratwursts, knockwursts, and schnitzel are divine, and with mashed potatoes, a side of red cabbage, and a *weiss bier,* I'm in heaven.

Valentine's Cafe: My favorite place to go with a vegetarian or a vegan. The stuffed butternut squash with veggie gravy and mashed potatoes, or Thai noodles with grilled vegetables, or mushroom samosas with chutney. You almost don't miss meat.

Tom Luddy
Film Producer, American Zoetrope

My favorite restaurants, all Chinese, in no particular order: **Fountain Court, Dragon House, Yuet Lee, Harbor Village, R & G Lounge, Oriental Pearl Restaurant,** and **Hunan Homes.**

Also, **The House,** which is semi-Chinese.

Non-Chinese: **Caffè Macaroni** and **Zuni Cafe.**

Best of all: **Chez Panisse,** but it's in Berkeley.

Nob Hill/Russian Hill

Nob Hill and Russian Hill, two of San Francisco's most famous areas, have completely different personalities. Russian Hill, which is closer to the water, has always enjoyed a bohemian spirit that attracts artists. It nurtured such famous writers as George Sterling, Ambrose Bierce, and Robert Louis Stevenson. It's also home to the **San Francisco Art Institute**, which was founded in 1871, and squiggly **Lombard Street**, known as the "crookedest street in the world." But Russian Hill's artsy unconventionality is not reflected in the food found here. The restaurants tend to be small and cater to a neighborhood clientele that ranges from well-heeled executives to blue-collar families.

Polk Street, the main shopping strip that serves both neighborhoods, has undergone something of a revival, especially the western end stretching toward the bay. It houses a four-star French restaurant, **La Folie**, and a popular singles' bar and restaurant, **Johnny Love's**. Several ethnic restaurants and elegant carryouts have added a gourmet patina to the street: **Leonard's** offers up great cheeses; **Pure T** churns up tea-flavored ice cream (which may sound weird but is delicious); **Auntie Pasta** provides great fixings for an Italian dinner; **The Real Food Company** features just-picked organic produce; and **The Jug Shop** stocks a wide selection of wines at competitive prices.

Higher up, near Nob Hill, the scene is somewhat tattered. Known as "Polk Gulch," it was the center of gay culture before the Castro emerged in the 1970s. It still has a smattering of bars, but the merchants are struggling to find an equilibrium.

Farther up still, the best doughnuts in the city can be found at **Bob's Donut and Pastry Shop.** And don't miss the wonderful take-out seafood at the venerable **Swan Oyster Depot,** which has a marble counter where you can enjoy a bowl of clam chowder.

A more exclusive ambience pervades Nob Hill. Rising steeply from Polk Street, Nob Hill is distinguished on the skyline by its landmark **Grace Cathedral.** Built on the spoils of commerce, the area began to attract visitors after the advent of the cable car, which made scaling the hills easier. This is where the "Big Four" staked their claims: Here Charles Crocker, Leland Stanford, Mark Hopkins, and Collis Huntington all raised hilltop mansions, which were destroyed in the 1906 earthquake and fire. Today the area is home to some of the city's most distinctive hotel restaurants: **Fournou's Ovens** at the **Stanford Court; The Big Four** at the **Huntington;** the campy **Tonga Restaurant and Hurricane Bar** (whose South Seas theme extends to hourly rainstorms) at the **Fairmont;** the tony **Nob Hill Restaurant** and the panoramic **Top of the Mark** at the **Mark Hopkins Inter-Continental San Francisco;** and **The Dining Room** at the **Ritz-Carlton San Francisco.** A fresh addition to the Nob Hill restaurant scene is the stunning **Charles Nob Hill,** whose fabulous food and attentive service have made it an immediate hit.

Tucked away in the residential sections of both Russian and Nob Hills are some of the cutest restaurants in town, such as the popular **Allegro Ristorante Italiano.** Other interesting eateries are situated along the **Hyde Street** cable car line and are frequented mostly by locals: They head to the **Hyde Street Bistro** for its creative mix of Austrian-Californian cuisine; **Zarzuela** for its excellent tapas; **Café Chaise** for a good light meal; and **Sinclair's Petit Cafe** for all-American fare.

---

1 Maye's Oyster House $$ Dating back to 1867 and at this location since 1904, this Italian-style seafood restaurant blazes no new culinary trail, but if you stick to the simplest dishes you'll do just fine. ♦ Italian ♦ Daily lunch and dinner. 1233 Polk St (between Sutter and Bush Sts). 474.7674

2 Freed Teller & Freed's One of the oldest specialty coffee merchants, this establishment is still the Rolls-Royce of purveyors. The knowledgeable staff can explain all the different beans and roasts in great detail. Another bonus: rows of jars holding bulk spices, including a terrific selection of whole peppercorns from exotic-sounding places. Ask and they will help you create your own blend of tea or coffee. ♦ M-Sa. 1326 Polk St (between Bush and Pine Sts). 673.0922; fax 673.3436. Also at: Embarcadero Center, West Tower (Sacramento St, between Battery and Sansome Sts). 986.8851; fax 986.8853

3 Coconut Grove ★★★ $$$ Entering this elegant supper club is like walking into a 1930s movie. A massive dome painted with screen legends of the 1930s and 1940s, stylized metal palms scattered about the two-story dining room, a center stage, white leatherlike booths, exquisite crystal and silver on every cloth-draped table, and waiters in white coats and black ties, give the place a pleasant dash of decadence. The classic continental menu, however, has been revamped for the 1990s. A mesquite-grilled salmon fillet is paired with lentils, angel hair pasta is accented with succulent smoked chicken, and barbecued back ribs come with onion rings and spicy-ginger glaze. The crowning touch to any meal here would be the macadamia tart—the crunchy nut crust and dense center of browned coconut are made all the richer by the warm chocolate sauce and slices of caramelized bananas that cover everything. Nightly shows feature such notables as Nancy Wilson, Debbie Reynolds, Tom Jones, and the house vocalist, Cami Thompson. The entree prices have been

Nob Hill/Russian Hill

reduced somewhat, but the wine list is pricey. ♦ American ♦ Cover (even if you don't see the show). M, Th-Su dinner. 1415 Van Ness Ave (between Bush and Pine Sts). 776.1616 ♿

4 Crustacean ★$$$ Roast crab is the dish to order at this upscale Vietnamese restaurant. On the third floor of a glass-fronted building, diners enjoy a neon-lit, vaguely Deco-looking space and have a bird's-eye view of Polk Street, which can diplomatically be described as urban. Try the "multivitamin rolls" (a New Age name for spring rolls) and the pungent garlic noodles, to contrast with the sweetness of the crab. Other dishes tend to be less successful. ♦ Seafood ♦ Daily dinner. 1475 Polk St (between Pine and California Sts), Third floor. 776.2722; fax 776.1069 ♿

5 Cordon Bleu ★$ Bare bones all the way, this Vietnamese restaurant compensates with extremely low prices and excellent five-spice chicken. While not a place to linger (smoke from the kitchen sometimes infiltrates the dining room), it's a popular stop for people heading to the many movie houses in the area. ♦ Vietnamese ♦ Tu-Sa lunch and dinner; Su dinner. No credit cards accepted. 1574 California St (between Larkin and Polk Sts). 673.5637

5 Emerald Garden ★★$$ This restaurant was created in an alleyway, so the brick buildings on either side serve as its walls. The pink accents and leafy potted plants make everything seem intimate and comfortable. Some of the best items are the crepes, fried appetizers, and Saigon-style pork chops, which are marinated in soy sauce with sugar and black pepper, grilled over charcoal, and basted with rum. ♦ French/Vietnamese ♦ M-F lunch and dinner; Sa-Su dinner. Reservations recommended. 1550 California St (between Larkin and Polk Sts). 673.1155; fax 673.1253 ♿

6 Aromi ★★$$ Owner-chef Hoss Zare's stock-in-trade is lusty Italian food: veal shanks in a gutsy tomato sauce with white beans and wilted winter greens; risotto cakes stuffed with gorgonzola, shiitake mushrooms, and roasted garlic; sweetbreads laced with Marsala; and a bed of soft polenta soaked with an intense mushroom sauce. Other dishes worth ordering include penne with tomato and vodka, *pappardelle* (wide noodles) with veal, and linguine with grilled salmon, olives,

capers, and fennel. For dessert, chocolate cake with a medley of fruit sauces drizzled over the plate and *budino* (a warm chocolate soufflé cake) can't be beat. French doors separate an ornate, marble-floored bar from the attractive dining room, with its dark wood floor, bentwood chairs, and single flower on each table. More French doors lead to a heated patio overlooking the seedy urban bustle of Polk Street. ♦ Italian ♦ M, Su dinner Tu-Sa lunch and dinner. 1507 Polk St (at California St). 775.5977

6 Main Squeeze ★$ This juice bar/coffee shop has won many awards for its knockout design, which includes glazed cement floors and curving tabletops inset with constellations. Scattered throughout are bright green flats of wheat grass, which not only lend decoration but are squeezed into juice "shots" for health-conscious patrons. In case you haven't guessed, the emphasis here is on low and nonfat preparations, fruit smoothies, and loads of salads. Near the counter, patrons can check out a chart of essential vitamins and minerals and the best foods for getting them. ♦ Cafe ♦ Daily breakfast, lunch, and dinner. 1515 Polk St (between California and Sacramento Sts). 567.1515; fax 567.1515 ♿

6 Swan Oyster Depot ★★★$$ For more than 75 years this tiny storefront fish market has showcased some of the finest local products—salmon, sole, rockfish, sand dabs lingcod, and oysters—as well as fish from other areas and a fine selection of smoked seafood. It's equally popular as a lunch destination for the steamy bowls of chowder and oysters on the half shell served at the old fashioned marble counter. And if you like fish for breakfast, you can find it here. ♦ Seafood ♦ M-Sa breakfast, lunch, and early dinner. No credit cards accepted. 1517 Polk St (between California and Sacramento Sts). 673.1101

6 See's Candy These quaint candy stores, done in black and white, look as if they were plucked from a different era, and the sweet, elderly salesclerks from central casting. As you wait for your hand-packed order, the clerk will slip you a chocolate. For an unusual treat try the chocolate-covered candied ginger. ♦ M-Sa. 1519 Polk St (between California and Sacramento Sts). 775.7049; fax 775.7049 ♿

7 Ruth's Chris Steak House ★$$$ Popular with tourists, this New Orleans–based steak house chain has 45 locations around the

74

Nob Hill/Russian Hill

21 Johnny Love's ★$$ John Meheny, with his good looks and 150-watt smile, became so popular as a bartender around town that he developed the nickname Johnny Love. Now he has his own place, and it's a singles' paradise. On weekends, when the live music cranks up at 10PM (it goes on until 2AM), lines wrap around the block. It's such a scene that bar hoppers may forget there's also some pretty good food to be had (until 10PM only). Fried calamari with two dipping sauces is at the top of the list, but regulars also go for mini-pizzas, juicy burgers, quesadillas, and pasta. ♦ Eclectic/American ♦ Daily dinner. 1500 Broadway (at Polk St). 931.6053; fax 931.1712 ♿

21 Golden Turtle ★★★$ The city's prettiest Vietnamese restaurant is set in a converted house, where husband and wife Kham Dinh Tran and Kim-Quy Tran have created an intimate, upscale dining room with intricately carved wood murals. Kim-Quy is the chef, and she has a knack for balancing the sweet and spicy, crunchy and soft, and hot and cold elements that make this cuisine so intriguing. Try the cigar-shaped imperial rolls stuffed with ground pork, prawns, and crab; the platter of mint leaves, rice noodles, cilantro, marinated carrots, cucumbers, and spicy fish sauce that get rolled up together in lettuce leaves; or the rosy beef salad accompanied by black sesame seed–studded toasts. The kitchen is particularly adept with beef, whether minced and wrapped in edible leaves or skewered and grilled. The quail, flamed tableside in rum sauce, is also a must. And five-spice chicken and such fish as whole steamed sea bass with ginger and cilantro taste vibrant and fresh. In fact, nearly every dish is a winner. The only downside: The service is gracious, but not always efficient. ♦ Vietnamese ♦ Tu-Su lunch and dinner. 2211 Van Ness Ave (between Broadway and Vallejo St). 441.4419; fax 441.4419 ♿

22 The Bagelry One of the oldest and most popular bagel emporiums in the city, it draws customers with its 14 varieties (more on weekends) and a big selection of flavored cream cheeses. ♦ Daily; W until noon. 2134 Polk St (between Broadway and Vallejo St). 441.3003; fax 441.8708 ♿

22 The Real Food Company The premier health food store in San Francisco has a deserved reputation for the best in organic produce at premium prices. There's always a great selection of whatever is in season, along with many hard-to-find and unusual items, excellent fresh fish and meat, the city's best selection of dried beans, and all kinds of grains, flours, and specialty products, such as olive oils, natural body moisturizers, and vitamins. ♦ Daily. 2140 Polk St (between Broadway and Vallejo St). 673.7420; fax 673.1787 ♿. Also at: 3939 24th St (between Sanchez and Noe Sts). 282.9500; fax 282.9190 ♿; 1023 Stanyan St (at Carl St). 564.2800; fax 564.4882 ♿

22 The Real Food Company Deli ★$ Patrons have come to expect a wide selection here of bread from the best bakeries, well-prepared meat and vegetarian dishes, salads, and cheeses. The desserts, however, tend to be uneven. There's seating inside and outside for about 25 altogether. ♦ Deli/Takeout ♦ Daily. 2164 Polk St (between Broadway and Vallejo St). 775.2805; fax 673.1787 ♿. Also at: 1001 Stanyan St (at Carl St). 564.1117; fax 564.4882 ♿

23 Auntie Pasta Headquarters for six take-out shops, this one specializes in complete Italian meals. There's always a good selection of fresh pastas and sauces, made daily without preservatives. Some of the better soups include carrot ginger and mushroom barley. You'll also find breads, olives, wine, dips, and frozen filled pastas. ♦ Daily. 2139A Polk St (between Broadway and Vallejo St). 776.9420; fax 776.8512 ♿. Also at: 741 Diamond St (between 24th and Elizabeth Sts). 282.0738; fax 282.4205; 1501 Waller St (at Clayton St). 681.4242; fax 681.0227 ♿; 3101 Fillmore St (at Filbert St). 921.7576; fax 921.1547 ♿

¡WA-HA-KA!
OAXACA MEXICAN GRILL

23 WA-HA-KA! (Oaxaca Mexican Grill) ★$ This chic *taqueria* has a Russian Hill pedigree but Mission District prices. Specializing in burritos with black beans and brown rice, the restaurant uses no lard and offers several lower-fat options, such as fish tacos and shrimp fajitas. The fresh salsa bar is a plus, and the sangria makes a cool refresher. ♦ Mexican ♦ Daily lunch and dinner. 2141 Polk St (between Broadway and Vallejo St). 775.1055 ♿. Also at: 1489 Folsom St (at 11th St). 861.1410; fax 861.1410 ♿; 1980 Union St (at Buchanan St). 775.4145 ♿

The first foreign-language cookbook to be printed in the US, *El Cocinero Español, obra que contiene mil recetas* (The Spanish Cookbook, a work that contains a thousand recipes), by Encarnación Piñeda, was published in San Francisco in 1898.

77

Nob Hill/Russian Hill

24 Starbucks Coffee The Seattle-based chain, with more than 500 coffee bars across the country, entered the San Francisco market with a vengeance only a few years ago, but they've quickly taken hold in just about every neighborhood. The **Starbucks** blend, somewhat milder than most, is made from Central American beans. ♦ Daily. 2163 Polk St (at Vallejo St). 921.1351 ♿. Also at: Numerous locations throughout the city

25 Royal Ground Coffee A branch of the chain started by Ramzi Faraj, this neighborhood stop is most popular on weekend mornings, when the locals gather for pastries and a brew. Like the other locations, this place is simple, comfortable, and funky. And it's hard to beat the selection of 40 to 50 kinds of beans available whole or ground to order. ♦ M-F 6:30AM-11PM; Sa-Su 8AM-11PM. 2216 Polk St (between Vallejo and Green Sts). 474.5957. Also at: Numerous locations throughout the city

25 Pure T ★★★$ This one-of-a-kind teahouse/ice-cream parlor observes the philosophy that's printed in bold letters on the wall: "Be Well and Enjoy Life to the Fullest." The stylish, Japanese-inspired interior, in earthy greens and browns, is a great place to do just that. Kick back with a pot of tea and rice wafers, or indulge in a dish of tea-flavored ice cream, which is the only variety served here. Although tea may seem like an unlikely flavor base for ice cream, it creates haunting, sophisticated blends. More than a dozen flavors are on hand, with new ones invented every day. The black currant is a good place to start; then sample the Earl Grey, German fruit, jasmine, and litchi. You can buy teas and pints of ice cream to take home, and unique brewing pots and cups, too. ♦ Teahouse/Ice-cream parlor ♦ M, W-Su from noon. 2238 Polk St (between Vallejo and Green Sts). 441.7878; fax 441.6878 ♿.

26 Mario's Bohemian Cigar Store Cafe ★★$ A 60-seat branch of the original North Beach cafe, this one's decor boasts green wainscoting, yellow walls, and a mahogany bar. The menu is the same as at the North Beach location: grilled chicken, turkey, or meatballs, all served on warm focaccia bread; such main courses as cannelloni and polenta with sausages; and exceptional espresso drinks and fresh pastries. Like its sister, this branch stays open until midnight most evenings except Sunday (when it closes at 11PM). ♦ Italian ♦ Daily lunch and dinner. 2209 Polk St (between Vallejo and Green Sts). 776.8226; fax 776.3388 ♿. Also at: 566 Columbus Ave (at Union St). 362.0536

26 Salonika ★$$ Named for a small seaport city in northern Greece, this place has a brick-and-mirror interior, softened by white tablecloths and fresh flowers. For starters, try the garlicky chilled eggplant topped with crumbled feta cheese. The lemon roast chicken with roasted potatoes is also popular, as is the sour, housemade yogurt, drizzled with honey and topped with walnuts. ♦ Greek ♦ Tu-Su dinner. 2237 Polk St (between Vallejo and Green Sts). 771.2077; fax 771.5097 ♿

26 Wren & Culpeper's Vintages There may be better wine stores in the city, but few are as chic. The walls are covered with art, and the tasting bar is elegantly set with place mats and glasses. Customers can sample three selections, which change regularly, and wine classes and special tasting sessions are given on occasion. Most of the bottles are from small American wineries. ♦ Tu-Su. 2253 Polk St (at Green St). 346.2713; fax 346.2718 ♿

27 Matterhorn Swiss Restaurant ★★$$$ Ignore the garishly lit entry; inside, most of the furnishings were crafted in Switzerland, from the chairs and tables up to the beamed ceiling. Hand-painted glass panes depicting Alpine scenes divide the room into dining alcoves. Chef-owner Andrew Thorpe creates rich fare rooted in classic techniques. Start with corn soup, full of sweet kernels and two light chicken quenelles. Among the main dishes are crisp sautéed halibut, which gets a flavor boost from a thin layer of smoked salmon. Pork tenderloin is wrapped in bacon and topped with an oniony breading. And the julienned veal, presented in a cream sauce with mushrooms, is worth the cholesterol surge. The crème brûlée looks like a mound of whipped cream, but tastes every bit as good as the more familiar version with the caramelized crust. ♦ Swiss ♦ Tu-Su dinner. 2323 Van Ness Ave (between Vallejo and Green Sts). 885.6116; fax 459.1967 ♿

28 Rex Cafe ★$$ The overhead fans are still here, but little else remains from the former **Casablanca** restaurant. Featuring an updated fern-bar look, this place attracts a good crowd

Nob Hill/Russian Hill

after 10PM. Most patrons come for the lively bar scene, but the American-style fare can also be satisfying. ♦ American ♦ Daily dinner; Sa-Su brunch. 2323 Polk St (between Green and Union Sts). 441.2244; fax 441.2292 ♿

28 Aux Délices ★★$ The room is spare, with booths separated by open-slat partitions, and the Vietnamese food is fresh and light. Fans come for marinated panfried catfish; chicken with lemongrass; and crisp, gossamer spring rolls served with pungent fish sauce. ♦ Vietnamese ♦ M-Sa lunch and dinner; Su dinner. 2327 Polk St (between Green and Union Sts). 928.4977 ♿

La folie

29 La Folie ★★★★$$$$ Without question, this is one of the top Californian/French restaurants in the city. French-born Roland Passot, his brother George (the sommelier), and his American wife, Jamie, have created a dreamy, casually elegant environment in which puffy white clouds dance across the sky-blue ceiling and rich, yellow print fabric hangs from the French windows and frames the doors. A copper hood creates a focal point above the open window to the kitchen. Passot's presentations are breathtaking, and the recently updated menu (which changes seasonally) is better than ever. There might be roast quail leg stuffed with foie gras, backed by a lyonnaise salad topped with a poached quail egg; *rôti* (roast) of squab and quail; rack of lamb; or fricasseed lobster. Passot also offers an à la carte menu, a five-course Discovery Menu, and a four course vegetarian menu. ♦ Californian/French ♦ M-Sa dinner. 2316 Polk St (between Green and Union Sts). 776.5577; fax 776.3431

29 Green World Mercantile Browsers will find a large selection of tea, pottery, cookware, and recycled glassware at this sunny, yellow-washed shop, which specializes in organic and ecologically correct products. A newsletter announces upcoming events and product demonstrations and offers inspiring reading. This place keeps late hours every night—a rarity among stores of this type. ♦ Daily 10AM-10PM. 2340 Polk St (between Green and Union Sts). 771.5717; fax 771.2809 ♿

29 Little Thai Restaurant ★$ A fish tank greets diners as they enter this tiny eatery, where the support column in the middle has been transformed into a palm tree trunk, with fronds shooting overhead. The coconut-milk chicken soup with chilies, lemongrass, and loads of mushrooms and vegetables is the highlight of the menu; the satays and curries are better than average. ♦ Thai ♦ Daily dinner. 2348 Polk St (between Green and Union Sts). 771.5544

30 City Discount In the garage of an old Victorian building, this rambling store offers home and restaurant supplies, including restaurant-quality bowls, whisks, ladles, and some food items. Oddly, a collection of furniture fills the back of the store. There's nothing exotic here, but it's fun and funky. ♦ Daily. 2436 Polk St (between Union and Filbert Sts). 771.4649

31 Art Institute Cafe ★$ The eatery at the **San Francisco Art Institute** offers a taste of the art student's life. Make your choices at the cafeteria line, then enjoy your meal—fresh salads, interesting sandwiches—inside or out with great views of the bay. You can even catch some art displays at the **Institute** while you're there. ♦ American ♦ Call ahead; hours vary. 800 Chestnut St (between Jones and Leavenworth Sts). 749.4567 ♿

"GOOD AS FATHER USED TO MAKE"

32 Swensen's Ice Cream This is the original parlor, dating to the 1940s, that launched a huge ice-cream corporation. There may be better ice cream these days, but here you can watch the ice-cream maker at work in the front window. (The classic ice creams are made in-house, but the yogurt and fat-free creations are produced in Arizona.) Many people double park in front of the shop just to grab a cone. ♦ Daily till 10PM. 1999 Hyde St (at Union St). 775.6818 ♿

32 Zarzuela ★★★$ With its rough wood, stucco, and brick walls, this charming tapas place has a warm, welcoming look. Service is as friendly as you'll find anywhere; mention that you like a dish and the waiter may bring out the chef so you can tell him personally. Among the top hot tapas, lamb tenders are seared to a caramelized crustiness, all the

Nob Hill/Russian Hill

better for the garlic-laced gravy that pools in the bottom of the plate. Scallops are golden outside and still silken inside and surround tender, wilted greens. The shrimp are spiced, cooked, cooled, and drizzled with a tomato-laced mayonnaise. Grilled vegetables, including eggplant and squash, get a boost from the smattering of olive oil and lemon. Big plates are also offered, including several rice dishes, but the tapas are so good we've never ventured beyond. ♦ Spanish ♦ Daily lunch and dinner. 2000 Hyde St (at Union St). 441.6913

33 ZA Pizza ★$$ Top-quality ingredients go into these New York–style pizzas, while artsy inclinations are reflected in the picture-lined space and the inventively named pies: Vincent Van Dough (tomato and garlic), Pesto Picasso, and MOMA (mushrooms, onions, marinated artichokes). There's also a selection of fresh, crisp salads. Because the place has only 25 seats, more than half the pizzas made are for carryout; you can also buy slices. In addition, there's **LITTLE ZA**, for take-out pizza by the slice only (at 2162 Polk St, between Broadway and Vallejo St, 922.8005; fax 771.4675 &). ♦ Pizza ♦ M-Th dinner; F-Su lunch and dinner. 1919 Hyde St (between Green and Union Sts). 771.3100; fax 771.4675

34 Frascati Ristorante ★$$ A popular neighborhood gathering place, this charming but cramped restaurant serves respectable Italian food. Diners gather for the meat dishes particularly osso buco (veal shank) with risotto, and daily variations on veal scallopini. ♦ Italian ♦ M, W-Su dinner. 1901 Hyde St (at Green St). 928.1406; fax 928.1983

35 Sinclair's Petite Cafe ★★$ Mark Sinclair, who enjoyed such success at **Paragon**, left to take over this tiny corner eatery (which used to be **Le Petit Cafe**). The space is cozy and comfortable, with simple wooden tables, high ceilings, and bookshelves lining the walls. His menu stresses hearty comfort food; good bets include *focaccia crostini* with aged blue brie and marinated tomatoes, panfried oysters with tomato-horseradish tartar sauce, chicken à la king over buttered fettuccine, grilled salmon with new potatoes and smoked salmon salad, and meat loaf with homemade ketchup and chive mashed potatoes. There's also a nice selection of Pacific Coast microbrews. ♦ American ♦ Tu-F breakfast, lunch, and dinner; Sa-Su brunch and dinner. 2164 Larkin St (at Green St). 776.5356; fax 776.3495 &

Child's Play

It's a rite of passage experienced by many an adult restaurant goer: one day the bottles of wine, flowers, and candlelight disappear, replaced by plastic-topped tables and food wrapped in waxed paper. Suddenly a family includes a younger member and dining out becomes a different experience. But there's no need to worry—San Francisco has many child-friendly places that an adult can also enjoy:

1 Alcatraz Bar and Grill Children of all ages will be thrilled by the mock prison cell at the entrance, the faux-prison decor, and such offerings as "killer shrimp." Pizza, burgers, and onion rings are featured; there's also a children's menu.

2 Cafe Marimba The vivid colors and folk art are fun to look at in this bustling Mexican restaurant, which serves family-style platters loaded with grilled chicken, pork ribs, and rock shrimp as well as enchiladas and quesadillas. Childish exuberance will go unnoticed amid the din created by the twentysomething crowd.

3 Ghirardelli Chocolate Manufactory Nobody can resist indulging in a luscious sundae, float, or a steaming cup of chocolate with whipped cream at this wonderful ice-cream parlor–cum–chocolate factory, where you can watch the chocolate being made.

4 Hard Rock Cafe Teens are happy to line up and wait (sometimes for hours) to grab a hamburger and gawk at the rock memorabilia at this link in the worldwide chain.

5 J & J Restaurant Great for dim sum, this eatery is always crowded with families and carts of Chinese appetizers that command everyone's interest.

6 Mel's Drive In Preteens and nostalgia buffs love the 1950s-style vinyl booths and tabletop jukeboxes; such diner eats as burgers and fries, meat loaf, fried-egg sandwiches—and, of course, cherry Cokes.

7 Miss Pearl's Jam House The *Gilligan's Island* decor, tropical-inspired food, and general mayhem appeal to preteens as well as to an older rock 'n' roll crowd.

8 Pizza Inferno Square pizza is the specialty of this aptly named parlor, where devilishly colored, swirling-patterned murals cover the floor, walls, and ceiling. The pizzas are good, too.

9 St. Francis Fountain Not much has changed at this honest-to-goodness soda fountain since 1918: There are still grilled cheese sandwiches, blue-plate specials, scrumptious homemade ice cream in 20 flavors, and wonderful peanut brittle.

10 Toy Boat Dessert Cafe Children delight in riding the mechanical bucking horse in the center of the dining room and they can't resist the vast collection of toys lining the wall. Coffee drinks and old-fashioned berry pie will appeal to adults; the kids will go for the peanut-butter–and–chocolate-cookie sandwich.

Nob Hill/Russian Hill

i Fratelli

36 i Fratelli ★★$$ A longtime favorite, this Italian eatery moved into larger, more comfortable quarters several years ago. The chefs, working in the open kitchen of an L-shaped dining room, turn out generous portions of pasta. The menu is heavy on salads, and there's sautéed spinach with big chunks of garlic. Seafood and a few vegetarian selections are available, and roast chicken and mushrooms should keep fowl fans happy. ♦ Italian ♦ Daily dinner. Reservations recommended. 1896 Hyde St (between Vallejo and Green Sts). 474.8240; fax 474.5553 &

37 Café Chaise ★★$$ Owners Rae Dunn—a graphic designer—and Michael Berke transformed this space into a chic "attic" motif, with concrete floors, gold walls, and mismatched chairs. Eva Allard shows what a talented chef can do with a six-burner stove: She roasts a free-range *poussin* (broiler chicken) to perfection and perches it on a nest of garlic mashed potatoes and white-corn kernels tossed with nasturtium butter. Grilled tuna is served with a white bean and celery salad and moistened with a lemony anchovy vinaigrette, and grilled trout is surrounded by a corn and squash hash. The vegetarian onion soup and beet salad with the surprising addition of juicy watermelon are two great ways to begin the meal, and either the espresso or watermelon granita ensures a perfect ending. ♦ French ♦ Tu-F dinner; Sa brunch and dinner; Su brunch. 1556 Hyde St (at Pacific Ave). 775.5556 &

38 Nob Hill Noshery Cafe ★$ Located near the **Powell Street** cable-car line, this deli-style cafe gets lots of tourist traffic. Bagels and coffee are the choice for breakfast, and the substantial sandwiches make a filling lunch. In between, there's a "nosh" menu of lighter tide-me-overs. ♦ Deli ♦ Daily breakfast, lunch, and dinner. 1400 Pacific Ave (at Hyde St). 928.6674

38 Ristorante Milano ★★$$ From the day it first opened in 1985, this Northern Italian restaurant has been building a loyal following. The contemporary decor is a mix of Asian and Italian accents, but the food and service are endearingly European. Top choices are the risottos, skewered chicken livers with grilled endive, and pasta *puttanesca* (a spicy, tomato-based Sicilian specialty). The tiramisù, a creamy dessert made with espresso, ladyfingers, and mascarpone cheese, is outstanding. ♦ Northern Italian

♦ Tu-Su dinner. 1448 Pacific Ave (between Hyde and Larkin Sts). 673.2961; fax 826.0448

39 Hyde Street Bistro ★★$$ Albert Rainer, the dashing chef-owner, greets and charms customers at the door of his pleasant, modest restaurant. He also produces some outstanding food. His Californian/Austrian approach translates into a captivating vegetable strudel with layers of flaky pastry, excellent roast chicken with the barest whisper of cumin, and rustic veal fricassee with wild mushrooms and spaetzle. His tuna and salmon preparations are also without equal. In the grand European tradition, the chef's brother, Klaus, turns out desserts that would be at home in far more formal—and expensive—settings. Of special note, on this busy street, is the availability of valet parking. ♦ Austrian/Californian ♦ Daily dinner. Reservations recommended. 1521 Hyde St (between Jackson St and Pacific Ave). 441.7778; fax 441.3407

39 Hyde Street Seafood House and Raw Bar ★$$ This charming, nautically inspired restaurant has a cozy feel and welcoming service. The best dish is the seafood in papillote. ♦ Seafood ♦ Daily dinner. 1509 Hyde St (between Jackson St and Pacific Ave). 928.9148; fax 921.9148

40 Allegro Ristorante Italiano ★★$$$ Tucked into an affluent residential area, this pretty place is ruled by Angelo Quaranta, who specializes in the foods of central and southern Italy. It's a favorite haunt of San Francisco politicos and top executives. Regulars stick to the gnocchi or cannelloni, but you can't go wrong with any of the pastas. *Bruschetta* (thick slices of toasted bread spread with a chopped-tomato mixture) and Cornish hen are our top choices. ♦ Italian ♦ Daily dinner. Reservations recommended. 1701 Jones St (at Broadway). 928.4002; fax 885.4396 &

41 Alfred's ★★★$$$ The dark room says "classic steak house," and indeed this is a classic; it's been in business since 1928. The specialty here is the delicious New York cut, grilled over mesquite and accompanied by ravioli, baked potato, or french fries. Or choose from such pastas as cannelloni and fettuccine Alfredo. Appetizers have an Italian bent and include antipasto; the Caesar salad is made table-side. ♦ Steak house ♦ Daily dinner. 886 Broadway (at Mason St). 781.7058; fax 397.1928

42 Charles Nob Hill ★★★★$$$ To staff his new, wonderful restaurant (formerly **Le Cafe**), owner Charles Condy has called on the same talented people who also run **Aqua**, his other outstanding San Francisco establishment. Here, executive chef Michael Mina and chef de cuisine Jason Weiner work together in perfect sync to create a

Nob Hill/Russian Hill

memorable dining experience. The tiny room, with bright white walls, gauzy window fabrics, recessed lighting, and slipcovered chairs, seats only 50 people, ensuring an intimate ambience. And almost all the dishes are a delight to behold (and taste), including paillard of salmon kissed by horseradish beurre blanc and set off by marinated red beets; scallop and truffle potpie; and bouillabaisse generously spiked with lobster pieces. As at **Aqua**, the wine list here is long and carefully crafted to complement the food. ♦ Contemporary ♦ Tu-Sa dinner. Reservations recommended. 1250 Jones St (at Clay St). 771.5400; fax 771.3542

43 Nob Hill Cafe ★★$$ This charming cafe spreads over two storefronts: One room, with the stove wedged in at the front window, accommodates just a few tables; the other has forest green walls, fresh flowers on each table, and a terra-cotta floor. The printed menu emphasizes pasta—generous portions served in large bowls—with a few starters and pizzas to round out the offerings. Try the penne with tomato, cream, and vodka, or a stellar carbonara (cream with bacon). The pizza has a crisp, almost blackened crust and a cheese-and-tomato topping; additional ingredients are available at an extra charge. All main courses, such as fillet of sole or veal piccata, appear as blackboard specials. If it's available, don't miss the wonderful veal stew, which is flavored with fresh bell peppers and contains puffy gnocchi. Chocolate fans will swoon over the dense chocolate ganache, lightened with a generous dollop of whipped cream and served in a parfait glass. Many of the wines are reasonably priced, making this a great place for everyday meals as well as special occasions. ♦ Italian ♦ Daily lunch and dinner. 1152 Taylor St (between Sacramento and Clay Sts). 776.6500; fax 474.2000

San Francisco claims about 3,200 eating and drinking establishments, or one restaurant for every 230 residents.

44 The Big Four ★★$$$$ Few rooms capture that turn-of-the-century men's club ambience as well as this one, located in the **Huntington** hotel. An oasis of dark paneling, forest green leather, and sparkling beveled-glass windows, it offers a glimpse of what the privileged life must once have been like. It's a great place to have a drink to begin or cap off an evening. Game dishes are a specialty, and so is buffalo—an unusual offering these days and usually one of the main courses. ♦ French/Californian ♦ M-F breakfast, lunch, and dinner; Sa-Su breakfast and dinner. Reservations recommended. 1075 California St (between Mason and Taylor Sts). 474.5400; fax 474.6227

45 The Fairmont Lobby ★★$$ The opulent lobby of the **Fairmont** hotel, with soaring columns, black walls, red-and-black-patterned carpet, and enough gilt to paint the Golden Gate Bridge, is a grand place to enjoy a cup of tea. Offered every afternoon, the fixed-price tea includes delicate sandwiches, pastries, cookies, and scones, which are served with a little pot of Devonshire cream. ♦ Teahouse ♦ M-Sa 3-6PM; Su 1-6PM. 950 Mason St (at California St). 772.5000; fax 837.0587

45 Tonga Restaurant and Hurricane Bar $$$ Disneyland meets the South Pacific at this one-of-a-kind restaurant on the terrace level of the **Fairmont**; hourly lightning and thunderstorms are staged here, with water pouring down over a central pool. A waterfall behind the low-lit bar and artificial orchids and other plants evoke the tropics, as do the funky drinks (such as the Bora-Bora Horror, a mixture of rum, banana liqueur, Grand Marnier, and pineapple juice). The nightly hors d'oeuvres (including egg rolls, pot stickers, curried mussels, and barbecued pork loin) are a bargain, but the dinner menu is not well executed. The whole place is campy and can be fun with the right group of friends. ♦ Asian ♦ Daily dinner. 950 Mason St (at California St). 772.5278; fax 837.0587

45 Masons Restaurant ★★$$$ One of the most striking rooms in the city, this restaurant on the arcade level of the **Fairmont** has an

Nob Hill/Russian Hill

understated elegance, a beautiful wood ceiling, and deep chairs upholstered in pastel stripes and patterns. Flames from the copper-lined grill in the middle of the room romantically reflect in the leaded glass windows. A three-course fixed-price dinner, with choices from the regular menu, is offered before 7PM and is the best bargain. Starters include grilled prawns arranged on a mound of couscous flecked with corn, red pepper, and beets. Entrées lean to straightforward grilled preparations, like lamb chops served on soft polenta. For dessert there's chocolate soufflé or warm apple tart with caramel sauce. ♦ American ♦ Daily dinner. 950 Mason St (at California St). 772.5233; fax 837.0587 &

46 Fournou's Ovens ★★$$$ Although the chefs come and go, this restaurant, in the **Stouffer Stanford Court Hotel,** remains a popular destination. Its classic European ambience complements a good wine list and some intriguing food combinations created by chef Ercolino Crugnale. The terrific appetizers might include gnocchi with vegetables in a truffle broth, or pasta with rock shrimp and sun-dried tomatoes. The filet mignon, served on a bed of corn kernel–studded mashed potatoes, is topped with a parmesan cheese wafer and a square of foie gras with fried leeks and smoky tomato vinaigrette. One of the best bargains around is the Twilight Supper, served from 5:30PM to 6:30PM, featuring two or three courses. ♦ American ♦ Daily breakfast, lunch, and dinner. Reservations recommended. 905 California St (at Powell St). 989.3500; fax 391.0513 &

47 The Dining Room ★★★★$$$$ Chef Gary Danko, a protégé of Madeleine Kamman, presides over the kitchen of this establishment in the **Ritz-Carlton San Francisco** hotel and turns out some of the most creative Californian/French food in the city. The setting is formal and luxurious, ideal for romance and celebration. The five-course tasting menu, paired with wines, is always available and changes six times a year. It might include such seasonal specialties as glazed oysters with leek fondue or roast lobster with chanterelles, tomato, corn, and tarragon. ♦ Californian/French ♦ Tu-Sa dinner. Reservations recommended. 600 Stockton St (between Pine and California Sts). 296.7465; fax 291.0147 &

47 The Terrace ★★★$$$ This place, also at the **Ritz-Carlton San Francisco,** has an elegant French interior and also the prettiest outdoor dining facility in the city. Protected from the elements on three sides by the 85-year-old Neo-Classical hotel, the formal garden is lined with boxwood, roses, and azaleas and boasts a circular, tiered fountain. Under the guidance of the hotel's executive chef, Jean-Pierre Dubray, the Italian-inspired menu offers such interesting selections as a

plate of delicate greens with squares of puff pastry filled with caramelized onions and artichoke hearts, and Tuscan-style chicken, served flattened and ringed with zucchini and roasted potatoes. This spot is perfect for a leisurely lunch, accompanied by any of the 15 wines served by the glass. ♦ Italian ♦ Daily breakfast, lunch, and dinner. 600 Stockton St (between Pine and California Sts). 296.7465; fax 291.0147 &

47 The Lobby Lounge This bar, on the fourth floor of the **Ritz-Carlton San Francisco,** offers live music, a formal English-style tea, and a unique sushi service. ♦ Tea daily 2:30-4:30PM; sushi M-Sa until 8PM; bar M-Th, Su until midnight; F-Sa until 2AM. 600 Stockton St (between Pine and California Sts). 296.7465; fax 291.0147 &

48 Top of the Mark Dating from 1939, this renowned sky-high lounge, which boasts glorious views from its 19th-floor perch in the **Mark Hopkins Inter-Continental San Francisco,** set the standard for those that came after it. It's an elegant, charming place to watch the sun set or to take in the twinkling lights of the city. Food is served only on Sunday, when an elaborate, expensive buffet brunch is offered. ♦ M-Th 4PM-1AM; F-Sa 4PM-2AM; Su brunch 10AM-2PM. 1 Nob Hill (between Powell and Mason Sts). 392.3434; fax 421.3302 &

In the 1870s the most popular drink in San Francisco was the Pisco Punch, first served at the famous Bank Exchange Saloon. Although the precise recipe died with its creator, bar owner Duncan Nichol, here's an updated version.

Pisco Punch (serves one)
1 tablespoon Pernod
1½ ounces brandy or Pisco Peruvian brandy, if available
1 ounce grape juice
shaved ice
6 ounces chilled pineapple juice
Coat the inside of a tall glass with the Pernod, pouring out the excess. Add the brandy, grape juice, and ice. Top with pineapple juice to the brim.

Nob Hill/Russian Hill

The Daily Grind

Going out for a cup of coffee in San Francisco is not motivated merely by caffeine addiction: Here it's a relaxing social ritual. A lot of schmoozing, flirting, and just plain hanging out has shifted from bars to coffeehouses. But in San Francisco's coffee culture, the brew is still more important than the meeting-and-greeting scene. Local connoisseurs fiercely debate rival coffeehouses' blends and grinds, not to mention their muffins, scones, and brownies.

It seems that every neighborhood in the city has at least one specialty coffeehouse; most have more. In fact, the San Francisco telephone directory has 22 listings beginning with the word "java," from **Java Joint** to **Javaholic**. Local chains include **Spinelli, Peet's, Pasqua,** and **Royal Ground** (which also operates under other names, including **Jammin' Java, Muddy Water,** and **Coffee Zone**).

National coffee chains have not overlooked the San Francisco market, either. **Starbucks** created quite a stir when in came to town in 1992. The business community in **North Beach,** a neighborhood with Italian roots and its own venerable coffeehouse tradition, actually rose up and denied the Seattle-based coffee chain a use permit. But obviously **Starbucks** has its supporters, because in four short years it has spawned 10 branches throughout the city.

In addition to the big boys, many independent operators are perking around town. Here are some of the more interesting ones.

Everyday Cafe (44 Beach St, at Taylor St, 346.6047 &) is a new addition to **Fisherman's Wharf.** This full-service spot offers several varieties of coffee, including latte, cappuccino, and espresso, as well as exotic ice cream, pastries, sandwiches, and soups. A seat at one of the outdoor tables is a great vantage point for people watching at the Wharf. ♦ Open daily 7AM-11PM May-Sept; daily 7AM-7PM the rest of the year.

The Gathering Cafe (1326 Grant Ave, between Vallejo and Green Sts, 433.4247) is ground zero for listening to cool jazz nightly and sipping hot coffee drinks, beer, or wine in the heart of bohemian North Beach. The pastries are good too. ♦ Open M-F 7PM-2AM; Sa-Su 11AM-2AM.

The Grove (2250 Chestnut St, between Pierce and Scott Sts, 474.4843; fax 474.9734 &), in the midst of bustling **Chestnut Street,** is a quiet place to grab a cappuccino, mocha coffee, or espresso. Pastries and other sweets share the menu with savory international entrées such as lasagne and burritos. There are some vegetarian dishes as well. ♦ Open M-W 7AM-11PM; Th-Sa 7AM-midnight; Su 8AM-11PM.

Java Beach Cafe (1396 La Playa, at Judah St, 665.5282 &) is the best place to grab a latte, drag a plastic chair outside, and catch the last rays of sunlight a stone's throw from **Ocean Beach** in the **Sunset.** It attracts an eclectic following of surfers, Russian émigrés, mothers with kids, and a sprinkling of clean-cut motorcyclists. Besides coffee, there are a few vegetarian concoctions on the menu, like veggie lasagna. ♦ Open M-F 6AM-11PM; Sa-Su 7AM-11PM.

Muddy Waters Coffee (521 Valencia St, at 16th St, 863.8006 &) is popular with students at the nearby **New College.** Besides a wide selection of brews, the menu also offers bagels, pastries, scones, and other light bites. ♦ Open M-Th 6:30AM-11PM; F-Sa 6:30AM-midnight; Su 7:30AM-11PM.

Spike's Coffee & Tea (4117 19th St, between Castro and Collingwood Sts, 626.5573), smack in the middle of the **Castro,** the city's gay epicenter, is a nice friendly place where people meet, flirt, and sip coffee—often with their pups in tow. All the typical coffee drinks are on hand, as are beans, tea, and a good variety of sweets, from pastries to candies. ♦ Open daily 6:30AM-7PM.

Tart to Tart (641 Irving St, between Seventh and Eighth Aves, 753.0643; fax 753.3274 &) serves the whole gamut of hot beverages—espresso drinks, traditional and flavored coffees, teas—to go along with some of the best pastries in town. This place in the Sunset offers salads and sandwiches for heartier appetites. ♦ Open daily until 2AM.

Yakety Yak Coffee House (679 Sutter St, between Mason and Tyler Sts, 885.6908), a brightly painted cafe in a cluster of towering apartment buildings, provides warmth and charm to this downtown neighborhood. Staggeringly popular with coffee sippers, flirty Generation X-ers, and older folks, the place is always jumping. There are some outdoor tables, too. ♦ Open M-Sa 7AM-10PM; Su 8AM-10PM

Downtown/Union Square

dubbed "contemporary grill fare." Stick with the simpler offerings: grilled double chicken breast with wild boar bacon, smoked pork chop with horseradish mashed potatoes and cranberry ketchup, and "Thai'd up" skirt steak with red curried peanut slaw and shoestring taro potatoes. ♦ American ♦ M-F lunch and dinner. 453 Pine St (between Montgomery and Kearny Sts). 834.0484

65 Specialty's Cafe and Bakery At lunchtime, Financial District workers line up here to take out sandwiches, soups, and salads. This carryout shop (which has three locations around the city) has made a name for itself by baking all its breads and pastries in-house, although sometimes the bread can be leaden and the sweets disappointing. ♦ M-F 6AM-6PM. No credit cards accepted. 312 Kearny St (between Bush and Pine Sts). Daily specials 896.BAKE; catering, delivery, and customer service, all locations 512.9550 &. Also at: 22 Battery St (at Market St); 150 Spear St (between Howard and Mission Sts)

66 Cafe Bastille ★★$$ Perfectly capturing the atmosphere of a French bistro, this charming cafe on a pedestrian street attracts both a business clientele and a good share of young bohemians, who come in for the nightly live jazz as well as the food. Try the onion soup, steamed mussels, roast chicken breast, or pâté. Even though the cafe is in the shadow of the 52-story **Bank of America** monolith, you can sit at one of its outdoor tables and pretend you're in Paris. ♦ Bistro ♦ M-Sa lunch and dinner. 22 Belden Pl (between Bush and Pine Sts). 986.5673; fax 986.1013

66 Cafe Tiramisù ★★★$$ The captivating smells of sautéed garlic and onions alone would lure passersby into this chic cafe, whose walls look as if they're painted with ancient frescoes. Everyone receives a friendly welcome, and the Italian food is just as warming: risotto with earthy mushrooms, osso buco with soft polenta, and roasted whole fish with nuances of smoke. In all, this eatery is one of the best places in the area for a hearty Italian meal. Outdoor seating is available, too. ♦ Italian ♦ M-F lunch and dinner; Sa dinner. Reservations recommended. 28 Belden Pl (between Bush and Pine Sts). 421.7044; fax 421.3009

66 Plouf ★★★$$ Local restaurateurs Eric Klein and Olivier Azancot, along with French-born Jocelyn Bulow, have opened this tiny new dining spot dedicated to seafood in general and mussels and oysters in particular. (The name, appropriately, is the French word for "splash.") Featured here are mussels prepared in several different sauces and accompanied by crisp french fries, an oyster bar, and a number of seafood dishes, all at bargain prices. There are some tables outside in the pedestrian alleyway. ♦ Bistro ♦ M-F lunch and dinner; Sa dinner. 40 Belden Pl (between Bush and Pine Sts). 986.6491 &

67 Sam's Grill ★★$$ In business for more than 50 years, this is the best of the old-time grills; it's so retro, it's back in style. The masculine, clubby decor has dark wainscoting and enough coat hooks to accommodate an army. The back is lined with curtained booths, just right for a clandestine meeting. It's the perfect stage for the veteran waiters, who work hard to maintain a gruff demeanor (underneath they're really quite charming). Top choices include sweetbreads served on toast points with crisp slices of bacon and roasted potatoes, minute steak, celery Victor, French pancakes (thin crepes drizzled with lemon juice and powdered sugar), and comforting rice pudding (the fish dishes, however, are sometimes overcooked). Wines are fairly priced. ♦ American ♦ M-F lunch and dinner. 374 Bush St (between Montgomery and Kearny Sts). 421.0594; fax 421.2632

68 Cafe Pacifica/Sankt Gallen Brewery $ A curious hybrid, it's both a brew pub and a dim sum restaurant. The beige-colored angled ceiling, white walls, dark wood, and tall windows make it a clean, peaceful retreat. Unfortunately, the dim sum is slightly gummy and only mediocre, and the fried rice is underseasoned. But the beers brewed in the three copper tanks up front are good. ♦ Dim sum/Brewery ♦ Daily lunch and dinner. 333 Bush St (at Montgomery St). 296.8203; fax 296.9348 &

68 Kelly's on Trinity ★★$ Kelly Mills, who won acclaim as chef at the **Four Seasons Clift** hotel, gave up the fast track to open this cafeteria-style lunch spot several years ago. The pastel green and yellow color scheme, printed upholstery, and windows overlooking Trinity Place make it more pleasant than most quick hit restaurants. Chili and three types of soup are offered each day, and the salads range from steak with mushrooms, green beans, and croutons to Asian chicken with celery, eggplant, and a Thai dressing. Sandwiches are prepared on freshly made rolls, and the cookies and desserts—particularly the apple bread pudding—are excellent. ♦ Cafeteria ♦ M-F breakfast and lunch. 333 Bush St (at Montgomery St). 362.4454; fax 362.2013 &

Downtown/Union Square

concentrates on Rhône and Italian varietals from California wineries, is tops. For dessert, order the chocolate brioche bread pudding or the apple tart composed of lightly browned slices of fruit draped over a mound of custard resting on a crisp circle of puff pastry; the latter takes 20 minutes, but is worth the wait. ♦ American ♦ M-Sa lunch and dinner; Su dinner. 1 Tillman Pl (off Grant Ave, between Post and Sutter Sts). 421.2300; fax 421.2316

58 The Candy Jar This tiny shop has been an institution on Union Square for 17 years. The display cases hold truffles, bonbons, marzipan fruits, and other sweets, some made without sugar. Individually wrapped candies and toffees line the shelves and bins, and everything can be gift-boxed. ♦ M-Sa. 210 Grant Ave (between Post and Sutter Sts). 391.5508. Also at: 2065 Oakdale Ave (at Industrial Ave). 550.8846; fax 550.8359

59 Sonoma Valley Bagel Co. ★★$ The latest addition to San Francisco's growing number of bagelries, this pleasant eatery boils its bagels in a kettle instead of oven-baking them, which makes them nice and chewy. There are 13 varieties, including jalapeño, cranberry, and sun-dried tomato with basil, and low- and no-fat spreads to go with them. The menu is rounded out with bagel sandwiches, hot dogs served on bagel buns, soups, and salads. There's both indoor and outdoor seating, or you can get your bagel to go. ♦ American ♦ Daily breakfast and lunch. 266 Sutter St (between Kearny St and Grant Ave) 951.0133; fax 951.8540

60 Café Claude ★$$ The zinc bar, where patrons can linger as long as they like, and the lively ambience make this a French haven, especially for lunch. Nighttime often brings live jazz. The menu revolves around typical bistro fare, with a few specials chalked on a blackboard. The onion soup is hearty and delicious, and the *croque monsieur,* a puffy delight of warm cheese and ham, is served with a small salad. Grazers will love the charcuterie platter, which includes pâté. If cassoulet is on the menu, don't pass it up, and wash it down with a Côtes du Rhône. And for dessert, what else but chocolate mousse? ♦ French ♦ M-F breakfast, lunch, and dinner; Sa dinner. 7 Claude La (off Bush St, between Kearny St and Grant Ave). 392.3505

61 Le Central ★★$$ On a chilly night, come to this brasserie for the soul-warming cassoulet with beans, confit, and juicy pieces of sausage. The grilled steak topped with Roquefort sauce also is great, though the pile of crisp french fries it's served with is even better. Crab cakes are as good here as in Maryland, but for a lighter, earthier appetizer try the beet salad topped with sieved egg. The best dessert is the crème caramel, which has a brûléelike consistency. The narrow room

lined with tables and rough brick walls has a European feel, reinforced by the efficient maitre d' and the waiters. ♦ French ♦ M-Sa lunch and dinner. Reservations recommended. 453 Bush St (between Claude La and Grant Ave). 391.2233; fax 391.3615

Rendezvous DU MONDE

61 Rendezvous du Monde ★★$$ Tiny and cute, this family-owned, 50-seat spot has a hideaway appeal. The changing menu lists some interesting salads and such simple noshes as roasted potatoes with aioli, caponata with grilled focaccia, or *brandade* (a puree of salt cod and potatoes) with toast points. The fish selection might include halibut with an olive-and-lemon paste on a bed of corn and sugar snap peas. Don't miss the *pots de crème* (custard) for dessert. ♦ French/ Italian ♦ M breakfast and lunch; Tu-Sa breakfast, lunch, and dinner. 431 Bush St (between Claude La and Grant Ave). 392.3332

62 Cafe de la Presse ★★$ The atmosphere is oh-so-European at this newsstand/cafe, and it has become the cornerstone of an emerging "French Quarter." Linger over cereal, pastries, pancakes, or simple egg dishes in the morning and straightforward salads, sandwiches, and cold plates at lunch. Just so you'll know you're still in America, there are hamburgers, as well as quiches and pasta. ♦ American/French ♦ Daily breakfast, lunch, and dinner. 352 Grant Ave (at Bush St). 398.2680; fax 249.0916

63 The Hot Shop With four locations in the Bay Area, this take-out shop does for burritos what California chefs have done for pizza, stuffing them with all kinds of nontraditional ingredients. Here are such fillings as lamb Mediterranean, Chinese chicken, sweet-and-hot duck, and Bombay curry, to name a few. ♦ M-Sa. 359 Kearny St (at Pine St). 989.8077; fax 989.8078

64 Occidental Grill ★★$$ Here's a new twist on the traditional San Francisco grill. Even though a restaurant has operated on this site since 1909 and its latest incarnation evokes those old days with a dark wood bar, green-glass lights, and semiprivate booths, the food has a 1990s pedigree

23

Chinatown

HOUSE OF NANKING

13 House of Nanking $ This tiny, grungy place has inexplicably developed a cult following, mostly of Caucasian college students. Customers line up outside for as long as an hour for the privilege of squeezing in at a small table and being rushed through a meal that will probably last half as long as the wait. The dishes, a mishmash of culinary styles, are prepared with the same hot, salty sauce and presented sloppily, with no finesse. ♦ Chinese ♦ M-Sa lunch and dinner; Su dinner. No credit cards accepted. 911 Kearny St (between Jackson St and Columbus Ave). 421.1429

13 Palermo Ristorante ★$ At the border of Chinatown and North Beach, the former **Carretto Ristorante Italiano** has been replaced by yet another Sicilian restaurant. The interior is very pretty, featuring a diorama displaying antique puppets imported from Palermo and bric-a-brac from the Old Country. Owner David Mufty is half Sicilian and half Pakistani, but he proudly asserts the fact that chef Bruno Carrenza is 100 percent Sicilian. Get the Pollo Palermo (tender breast of chicken with ham and mushrooms in a butter-marsala sauce) or swordfish grilled and perfumed with garlic, olive oil, and lemon juice. Tiramisù and cannoli are great choices for dessert. ♦ Italian ♦ M-Sa lunch and dinner. 939 Kearny St (between Jackson St and Columbus Ave). 296.9796; fax 296.9797

14 DPD Restaurant ★★$$ Some of the best Shanghai noodles in the city are served at six well-worn Formica tables in a battered yellow-and-green building. The spicy, thick noodles, which turn mahogany-colored in the wok, are like manna when served with Chinese cabbage and strips of pork. The noodle soups are just as enticing, whether topped with pork chops, beef tendon, or smoked fish. On the seafood menu try the hot braised prawns and the scallops in garlic-and-ginger sauce. Daily specials often include vegetable wontons with pork and such non-noodle dishes as steamed fish. The blackboard specials can be excellent, but the noodle dishes are not to be missed. ♦ Chinese/Shanghai ♦ Daily lunch and dinner. No credit cards accepted. 901 Kearny St (at Columbus Ave). 982.0471

The fortune cookie was invented in San Francisco around the turn of the century by Makota Hagiwara, the chief gardener of the Japanese Tea Garden in Golden Gate Park.

15 Hunan Homes ★★$ Decorated in shades of pink, this dining spot boasts a fun, comfortable atmosphere and first-rate cuisine. Among the dishes are Hunan-style smoked ham, stir-fried with cabbage, leeks, and green pepper; and eggplant doused with garlic and mixed with bits of ground pork. Platters of prawns or beef with green pepper and onions are tossed with chili sauce and ground pork and served sizzling. It's a popular hangout for celebrated director Francis Coppola and his entourage. ♦ Chinese ♦ Daily lunch and dinner. 622 Jackson St (between Kearny St and Grant Ave). 982.2844

16 Jackson Pavilion ★$ One of only a handful of Chinese-owned restaurants specializing in American food (known as *sai choy*), this is where local Chinese-Americans go for omelettes and prime ribs. Try the omelette with strips of ham, turkey, onions, bell peppers, and mushrooms, served with commercial preshaped hash browns (crisp and greasy) and lavishly buttered toast. The menu runs to pork chops and the like, but there are a few *ramen* noodle combinations. ♦ American ♦ Daily breakfast, lunch, and dinner. 640 Jackson St (between Kearny St and Grant Ave). 982.2409

17 Great Eastern Restaurant ★★★$$ Fish is the thing to order at this typically noisy bilevel eatery with ornate crystal chandeliers: It couldn't be fresher. The tanks are filled with crabs, abalone, prawns, oysters, scallops, frogs, and various fin fish, which are priced by the pound. Order a whole steamed fish and the waiter will bring the flopping creature to the table for your inspection. The kitchen literally makes the most of its ingredients, transforming the bones of a cod, for instance, into a rich soup with a spicy bite, then cutting the rest of the fish into chunks to stir-fry with sugar snap peas and other vegetables. The prawns, fresh from the aquarium, are incredible steamed in the shell (you peel them yourself) and prepared with a generous dose of minced garlic. Among the nonseafood dishes, both quail and squab are popular. ♦ Chinese ♦ Daily lunch and dinner until 1AM. 849 Jackson St (between Kearny St and Grant Ave). 986.2500 ♿

17 Golden Flower Restaurant ★$ One of the few Vietnamese spots in Chinatown, it's popular for *pho* (Vietnamese noodle soup made from pork bones and oxtails). Choose among 12 beef preparations, each presented in a big bowl with side garnishes of bean sprouts, mint, cilantro, chilies, lemon wedges, and chili sauce. The classic finish is filtered coffee, which slowly drips into a cup containing spoonfuls of sweet condensed milk. ♦ Vietnamese ♦ Daily lunch and dinner. No credit cards accepted. 667 Jackson St (between Kearny St and Grant Ave). 433.6469 ♿

Chinatown

feet are sometimes offered, but they are easy to detect and reject, if you so desire. Noodle dishes may also be available, but they will be listed on a menu with English translations, rather than offered from the cart.

Each table is set with a container of brick-red chili oil, bottles of soy sauce, and white vinegar. Chili sauce and vinegar are mixed to make a sauce for pot stickers, and soy sauce and chili oil are blended to accent just about everything else.

The carts circulate continuously, so you can order in stages, taking a few items each time they pass. In the old days, the bill was figured by the number of little plates left on the table, but today, a printed bill is updated by the servers as the meal progresses. It never adds up to much, though—you'll have to eat a lot of food to spend more than $10 a person.

Every dim sum restaurant does things a little differently, but here's a thumbnail guide to some of the most popular items.

Fans
filled wonton skins

Jap Gaw Ja Lee
Mixed-fruit gelatin

Gee Cheung Fun
Steamed rice-noodle rolls

Jing Joon
Glutinous rice flavored with dried shrimp, sausage, or other meats, and steamed in a lotus leaf. Commonly called Chinese tamale

Ngau Yuk Siu Mai
Steamed beef meatballs, often on a bed of greens

Chun Guen
Spring Rolls

Ha Gow
Shrimp dumplings

ow
paste-filled buns

37

Nob Hill/Russian Hill

14 The House of Prime Rib ★$$ This eatery has been a San Francisco institution for nearly 50 years, and the staff is as cordial as you'll find anywhere (though the service can be a bit rushed when it's busy). This is the best place to get a slab of prime rib, carved tableside. The warren of richly appointed, clubby rooms, most with fireplaces, belies the reasonable prices. Included with each entrée are side dishes and salad (watch it being tossed in a spinning bowl filled with ice), but if that doesn't fill you up, seconds are even offered. ♦ American ♦ Daily dinner. 1906 Van Ness Ave (between Washington and Jackson Sts). 885.4605; fax 921.0854

15 Bell Tower ★★$ This comfortable bar/restaurant won the hearts of the Russian Hill crowd in short order. The older set comes in early; the younger crowd follows, either before, during, or after a night on the town. Chef Gary Ferry, who used to work in the kitchen at Stars, has refined the menu here, adding a grilled bluenose bass served with basil mashed potatoes and an olive-caper relish, and succulent roast chicken. The half-pound burger and french fries combo is good and very reasonably priced. ♦ Californian/American ♦ Daily lunch and dinner until midnight. 1900 Polk St (at Jackson St). 567.9596

16 Jug Shop People drive for miles to shop at this sprawling wine store, drawn by the enormous selection, as well as the discounted prices. Here you'll find more than 2,000 wines, 400 beers, and just about every spirit imaginable. The clerks know their stuff and are fun, friendly, and helpful. They'll assist you in selecting and also shipping wines. A wine-tasting bar is open every Friday and Saturday. And wonder of wonders, there's even parking at the corner. ♦ Daily. 1567 Pacific Ave (between Larkin and Polk Sts). 885.2922; fax 885.6612

17 Kiki's Paris 1920 ★★$$ The spirit of Paris pervades this brasserie, which has such authentic details as front windows painted in burgundy and gold leaf, a large bar, and high-quality people watching. The classic brasserie fare—roast chicken, prime rib, duck confit, steak and fries—has improved considerably of late, thanks to new chef Jason Markowich. There's also a reasonably priced oyster bar. Finish with luscious profiteroles, filled with ice cream and topped with warm chocolate sauce at the table. ♦ French ♦ Daily dinner. 2080 Van Ness Ave (at Pacific Ave). 567.7600; fax 567.7687

18 Harris' Restaurant ★★★$$$ The best steak house in San Francisco also sports the most sophisticated decor, with dark wood paneling, a bucolic mural, and deep, tufted booths. Start with a martini and steak tartar or a Caesar salad and then try the New York cut, which has a caramelized exterior kissed with mesquite and a pink, juicy interior. The 100-plus wine list is appropriately weighted to full-bodied reds. For dessert the pecan pie is excellent. ♦ Steak house ♦ Daily dinner. Reservations recommended. 2100 Van Ness Ave (at Pacific Ave). 673.1888; fax 673.8817

19 Leonard's More than 200 types of cheese make this sunny, corner specialty store a prime draw. You'll also find many different grains and dried fruits as well as freshly ground peanut butter. The owner, Leonard Born, usually imparts great tidbits of information to his patrons about their purchases. ♦ Daily. 2001 Polk St (at Pacific Ave). 921.2001

19 Tai Chi Restaurant $ It's not much to look at and the food's never been critically acclaimed, but this tiny restaurant does a land-office business. The most popular dish on the menu is Hunan General Tso's chicken, in hot sweet-and-sour sauce. ♦ Hunan/Mandarin ♦ M-Sa lunch and dinner; Su dinner. 2031 Polk St (between Pacific Ave and Broadway). 441.6758

20 Pasha ★$$$ This exotically decked-out oasis transforms an urban setting into a little piece of Morocco, with tented fabric draping from the ceiling, colorful rugs, low wood tables, and deep sofas. To cap it off, a belly dancer undulates by in a swirl of sequins and gauzy material. It seems a bit touristy when the dancer plucks people from their tables to join her, but the food is anything but hokey. The easiest, and most fulfilling, way to go is with the combination dinners (made for sharing), which consist of seven appetizers and four smaller-portioned main courses. Otherwise you might try quail with lime and sage, grilled chicken brochette, or smoky prawns served with basmati rice. ♦ Moroccan/Middle Eastern ♦ Tu-Su dinner. Reservations recommended. 1516 Broadway (between Polk St and Van Ness Ave). 885.4477; fax 885.4477

Nob Hill/Russian Hill

United States. The steaks, drowned in butter (unless you specify otherwise), are prime but pricey; vegetables, potatoes, and salads are ordered separately, pushing the tab even higher. Also, the service isn't what it should be at these prices. ♦ Steak house ♦ Daily dinner. 1700 California St (at Van Ness Ave). 673.0557; fax 673.5309

8 Hard Rock Cafe ★$ Even if you didn't notice the life-size black-and-white cow outside you couldn't miss this link in the popular chain because of the continuous line of people waiting to get in. This is where the younger set wants to hang out, snarf down burgers, and then take home a T-shirt bearing the famous logo. ♦ American ♦ Daily lunch and dinner. 1699 Van Ness Ave (at Sacramento St). 885.1699; fax 885.0701

9 Acquerello ★★★$$$ The service is consistently flawless at this chic, romantic Italian restaurant, and the *nuova cucina* (nouvelle cuisine) is imaginatively conceived and artfully presented. Chef/owner Suzette Gresham creates an ever-changing array of dishes that may include thin slices of raw beef stuffed with pickled vegetables in a lemon and truffle-oil sauce; quail stuffed with apple and thyme and presented on zucchini-and-potato pancakes; or tuna in a fennel-and-dill crust with saffron sauce and a refreshing confit of lemons. ♦ Italian ♦ Tu-Su dinner. Reservations recommended. 1722 Sacramento St (between Polk St and Van Ness Ave). 567.5432; fax 567.6432

10 Bob's Donut and Pastry Shop Early morning traffic jams are common in front of this small, bare-bones bakery, as Mercedes, trucks, and taxis vie for a space so that drivers can rush in to get the city's best doughnuts. In a world filled with generic shops offering cookie-cutter products, these goods are made from scratch. The fried versions come out extra puffy and light with a thin, crackling glaze of sugar; the cake varieties crumble seductively with each bite; and the buttermilk bars have just a hint of tartness. The coffee is also freshly made and strong. ♦ Daily 24 hours. 1621 Polk St (between Sacramento and Clay Sts). 776.3141

10 Double Rainbow Ice Cream The almost magical rainbow reflected on the sidewalk in front of this parlor draws a wide cross section of people right in—some even sport the colors of the rainbow in their hair. "Double bow," as many refer to it, has been a favorite of ice-cream aficionados since the original shop opened on Castro Street in 1976. Ice cream is the star, but the frozen yogurts and baked goods are increasingly popular. ♦ M-Th, Su 11AM-11PM; F-Sa 11AM-midnight. 1653 Polk St (between Sacramento and Clay Sts). 775.3220. Also at: 407 Castro St (at Market St). 621.2350; 1724 Haight St (between Cole and Shrader Sts). 668.6690

Julie Ring's Heart and Soul

11 Julie Ring's Heart and Soul ★★$$ Julie Ring has launched such funky theme spots as the 1950s-style **Julie's Supper Club** and the lively Caribbean **Miss Pearl's Jam House.** Now she's exploring the sophisticated 1940s with a supper club that features piano music and jazz combos nightly. Dark green walls, red carpet, black accents, and a wrought-iron railing around the mezzanine give the room a moody, intimate atmosphere, and just about every table has a great view of the raised stage. The food is well executed and reasonably priced. Start with mussels served with aioli and pungent barbecue sauce, a classic whole-leaf Caesar salad, or a seafood sampler of shrimp and oysters with a variety of sauces. Main courses include a juicy steak with quartered portobello mushrooms and mashed potatoes; fettuccine with lemon, arugula, and a waft of chilies; and an earthy *posole,* pork stew with hominy, onions, and garlic. The homey desserts include fruit crisp and strawberry-rhubarb pie. ♦ Californian ♦ Cover. M, Su snacks; Tu-Sa dinner. 1695 Polk St (at Clay St). 673.7100; fax 673.6799

12 Polk St. Beans and Cafe $ Although it began as a retail store, this place has slowly evolved into an eclectic coffeehouse serving inexpensive soups and hot and cold sandwiches. You can still buy beans, teas, and coffee paraphernalia (pots, mugs, filters) here, but most people prefer to while away a few hours enjoying their coffee—especially on Thursday, when poetry readings, singing, or even tap dancing takes center stage, and on Friday and Saturday, when it stays open until midnight. Live bands play from time to time. The only thing missing from this recreation of a Beat hangout is the smoke. ♦ Coffeehouse ♦ Daily. 1733 Polk St (between Clay and Washington Sts). 776.9292

WING LEE RESTAURANT

13 Wing Lee Restaurant ★★$ What you lose in elegant decor you gain in good food at this recently remodeled, family-owned Chinese cafe. Specialties include sizzling-rice soup; panfried noodles with chicken; and pork with fresh, nutty lotus root. For an impromptu dinner party, take home one of the bronzed roast ducks that hang upside down from hooks in the front window. ♦ Chinese ♦ M, W-Su lunch and dinner. 1810 Polk St (between Washington and Jackson Sts). 775.3210

Nob Hill/Russian Hill

48 Nob Hill Restaurant ★★$$$$ Located in the **Mark Hopkins Inter-Continental San Francisco** and largely patronized by hotel guests, this restaurant serves food with a French accent. The menu changes often and might include consommé of pheasant with poached quail egg and chives, sea bass steamed with fennel and served with a parsnip-caviar mousse and grilled portobello mushrooms, or roast loin of veal with sun-dried–cherry sauce. One of the best deals is a prix-fixe, three-course dinner offered nightly. The interior has a clubby, Old World atmosphere in the tradition of grand-hotel dining. ♦ Californian/French ♦ Daily breakfast, lunch, and dinner. Reservations recommended. 1 Nob Hill (between Powell and Mason Sts). 616.6944; fax 421.3302

49 Rue Lepic ★★$$$ This cheerful corner storefront, with an open kitchen carved out of one side of the room, has a lot of charm. Each table in the intimate, 35-seat dining room is set with a silver vase and a pink rose, and the French food can be wonderful. The best deal is the five-course fixed-price menu. Few restaurants can pull off red wine sauces with fish, but the grilled salmon in red wine here will surprise you. Such classic desserts as crème brûlée and chocolate mousse are also excellent. ♦ French ♦ M-F lunch and dinner; Sa-Su dinner. 900 Pine St (at Mason St). 474.6070; fax 474.6187

50 Vanessi's ★$$$ During its glory days in North Beach, this Italian restaurant inspired the open kitchens seen at **Stars** and other places around the city. Unfortunately, after its migration to Nob Hill in 1986, both its food and its atmosphere have suffered. But the dining room, decked out in red upholstered chairs, is still pleasant, with a retro feel, and they still serve great hot zabaglione, a Marsala-laced egg dessert that's made to order and froths over the serving glass. Other specialties are veal chops and pasta. ♦ Italian ♦ M-F lunch and dinner; Sa-Su dinner. Reservations recommended. 1177 California St (at Jones St). 771.2422; fax 771.7122

51 Buffalo Whole Food & Grain Company Started in 1975 by Rob Mitchell, this full-service store packs a lot into its little space. With an emphasis on organically grown foods, the shop has an adequate selection of produce and more than 200 items sold in bulk. The extensive variety of vitamins and supplements seems overwhelming, but the knowledgeable staff is happy to help. ♦ Daily. 1058 Hyde St (between Pine and California Sts). 474.3053. Also at: 598 Castro St (at 19th St). 626.7038; fax 626.7511

Bests

Fred Gebhart and Maxine Cass
Travel Writers; Co-authors, *On the Road Around California*

The Dining Room at the **Ritz-Carlton Hotel**: Some of the best food in town and easily the best service.

Wor Won Ton soup at the **Eight Immortals**: A Chinese seafood combo in a real San Francisco neighborhood restaurant.

Gold Spike Restaurant: Family-style Italian dinners from the 1950s, served on red-checked tablecloths with candles dripping down the Chianti bottles.

Michele Anna Jordan
Author, *The Good Cook's Book*;
Freelance Restaurant Critic

Zuni Cafe: I love Judy Rogers's cooking. The service is excellent and the clientele lively and diverse.

North India Restaurant: When I crave Indian fare, nothing satisfies me like the fish *masala* here.

Julie Ring's Heart & Soul: I adore the Gothic bordello decor, plus Julie's spicy fries.

Ron Palmtag
Chief Concierge, Park Hyatt Hotel

For the best sushi in San Francisco, I like **Hamano Sushi** in **Noe Valley**. Be sure to order the *bincho maguro*, a great taste of white tuna. Also try the *gomo ao* spinach if you've reached your limit on fish. If you still have room after dinner, walk to **24th** and **Castro Streets**, for some ice cream at **Rory's**. I also like to stroll **Fillmore Street** and stop at **VIVANDE Porta Via** for a great Italian lunch—especially the pizza rustica, made only on Fridays. Then walk over to **Alta Plaza Park**, where from **Jackson** and **Pierce Streets** you can see the Victorians of **Pacific Heights** and **San Francisco Bay**, as well.

85

Pacific Heights/ Cow Hollow/ The Marina

Pacific Heights, Cow Hollow, and the Marina are three of the city's most affluent areas. The main business districts run north and south along **Fillmore Street** (in Pacific Heights) and east and west along **Union Street** (in Cow Hollow) and **Chestnut Street** (in the Marina). Pacific Heights, which sits on a hill above the other two neighborhoods, enjoys expansive views of the bay and is studded with mansions that cling to the hillsides and house some of the city's most prominent citizens. Union Street has evolved in recent years from a shopping mecca into a restaurant and bar destination for thirty-somethings. Chestnut Street also has exploded with new restaurants and bars in the aftermath of the 1989 earthquake, which hit the Marina area hard; these places tend to appeal to the postcollegiate singles who moved into the apartments vacated by the many longtime residents who left after the quake.

Pacific Heights/Cow Hollow/The Marina

to two other locations. All three sport the usual bare-bones backdrop that goes with this down-home fare. The thick red barbecue sauce veers toward the sweet end of the spectrum, but it goes particularly well with the hot links. Aficionados might be disappointed; at times the ribs can taste warmed over.
♦ Barbecue ♦ Daily lunch and dinner. 1911 Fillmore St (between Bush and Pine Sts). 922.2436 ♿. Also at: 2800 Sloat Blvd (at 47th Ave). 681.3071; 2800 Leavenworth St (Anchorage Center, between Jefferson and Beach Sts). No phone

1 Oritalia ★★★$$ Bruce Hill combines Italian and Asian cuisines in one of the few successful fusion restaurants in the city. Try the wonderful portobello mushrooms, sliced and stacked like Lincoln Logs and doused in a fresh plum sauce, or the mixed shrimp, salmon, and calamari served *moo shu* style with whole wheat Mandarin pancakes. On the Western side of the menu, salmon may be wrapped in pancetta and served with white beans and broccoli rabe, or a chicken breast will be accompanied by mashed celery root with artichokes and tarragon. The decor is also a marvelous cross-cultural blend, with Japanese accents, rich wood, and contemporary design combining to stunning effect.
♦ Asian/Italian ♦ Daily dinner. 1915 Fillmore St (between Bush and Pine Sts). 346.1333; fax 346.0610 ♿

2 Osome ★★$$ Many enthusiasts consider this one of the city's top neighborhood Japanese restaurants. The neutral colors and light wood give it a peaceful, casual feel, and the menu offers more than 40 kinds of sushi and sashimi. One of the most interesting is the *sakekawamaki*, which is grilled salmon skin with green onions. The *shabu shabu*, thin slices of beef, vegetables, and yam noodles cooked table-side in a broth, is a treat here.
♦ Japanese ♦ Daily dinner. 1923 Fillmore St (between Bush and Pine Sts). 346.2411

2 Cedanna This shop specializes in modern home furnishings, mostly by local artists, that almost qualify as folk art. With inventory ranging from rough granite tables to rusted-metal objects, like candleholders and lamps, it is a good place to look for unusual

accessories and gifts. ♦ Daily. 1925 Fillmore St (at Pine St). 474.7152; fax 726.3834 ♿

3 Mainline Gifts Among the wares at this trendy gift shop are fashionable place mats, candleholders, and other items for setting an interesting table. ♦ Daily. 1928 Fillmore St (at Wilmot Alley). 563.4438; fax 563.7528

3 Johnny Rockets ★$ The burgers are actually quite good at this 1950s-theme chain. This branch boasts large windows overlooking the street, plus a sunny patio in back; the shiny tile, polished chrome, and long counter give it all a well-scrubbed appeal. The burgers are served in old-fashioned paper wrappers, and the helpful waiters, decked out in traditional pointed caps, are so accommodating they even pour the ketchup for you.
♦ American/Hamburgers ♦ Daily lunch and dinner; F-Sa until 2AM. 1946 Fillmore St (at Pine St). 776.9878; fax 776.1189 ♿. Also at: 81 Jefferson St (at Mason St). 693.9120; fax 693.9404 ♿

4 Rory's Twisted Scoop As if the ice cream alone were not indulgence enough, the specialty here is add-ins, which include chunks of Reese's Peanut Butter Cups, M&Ms, and nuts. This is the shop's original location (there is also a Noe Valley store) and is where the ice cream for both units is produced. The shop also makes its own waffle cones and features several nonfat yogurts, including banana peanut butter and Ghirardelli chocolate. ♦ Daily 11:30AM-10PM; F-Sa until midnight. No credit cards accepted. 2015 Fillmore St (between Pine and California Sts). 346.3692. Also at: 4101 24th St (at Castro St). 648.2837 ♿

5 The Straw, The Jar and The Bean "An environmental natural-food store" is how the owners bill this small, trendy shop, which features an excellent selection of high-quality products from specialty growers and manufacturers. An array of grains, seeds, and beans is sold in bulk; there's also a line of medicinal herbs, vitamins, and skin-care products. A flyer explains the effort that went into making the store environmentally friendly. For example, the galvanized sheet metal used in the construction was not hot-dipped (which would release toxic fumes), the stones for the counters were salvaged, and

Only a decade ago, Fillmore Street was known mostly for its secondhand stores; these endure, but have been joined by chic flower shops, design galleries, and pretty cafes. Food lovers will find decadent pyramid cakes at **Le Chantilly**, Southern Italian takeout at **VIVANDE Porta Via**, and more than 200 bargain-priced Champagnes and sparkling wines at **D&M Liquors**. The dining-out options abound too. For example, **Oritalia** offers a creative blend of Asian and Italian fare, and the locals pack into **Via Veneto** and **Jackson Fillmore Trattoria** for Italian specialties, **Alta Plaza Bar and Restaurant** for contemporary California cuisine, **La Méditerranée** for Middle Eastern fare, **Leon's** for barbecue, the **Elite Cafe** for creole food, and **Osome** for Japanese dishes.

Union Street is one of the city's most popular shopping strips, where Victorian homes now serve as the setting for more than 300 boutiques, restaurants, and antiques stores. Here, pick up crusty bread studded with olives at **Il Fornaio Panetteria** and specialty foods at **Full Moon Foods and Mercantile**. The area is also home to fine eateries, with strong leanings to Italian, including **Pane e Vino**, **Bonta Ristorante**, **Radicchio**, and **Prego Ristorante**. And **Perry's**, a pioneer of the singles' scene when it opened more than 20 years ago, still draws crowds (including some of the original habitués). **Betelnut** is probably the most inventive restaurant to open on Union Street in some time; the concept—a stylish Asian beer house—was a hit from day one. And **Lhasa Moon**, a new Asian restaurant on **Lombard Street**, is the West Coast's first Tibetan eatery.

Farther down Fillmore Street at **Greenwich Street** in Cow Hollow is the infamous "Bermuda Triangle," a cluster of restaurants and bars that is a weekend hub of singles' action. Here are the **Balboa Cafe**, **Baja Cantina**, the new **City Tavern**, and the popular **Plumpjack Cafe**.

A few blocks farther down the hill, in the Marina, Chestnut Street is a popular hub, especially on Sunday mornings, when people congregate, sitting on the sidewalks and milling about the numerous coffeehouses (including **Peet's Coffee & Tea** and **Starbucks**) that have opened in the last decade. Many of the restaurants, too, appeal to the young, or at least the young at heart. **Cafe Marimba** serves up regional Mexican fare in a colorful, noisy setting; **Sweet Heat** and **Andalé Taqueria** are stylish, healthful *taquerias;* and **Paragon** mixes great cocktails and good food. Newcomers include **Flying Kamikazes** on Steiner Street and **Babaloo Restaurant** and **Allegria**, two spots on Lombard Street that make the most of the tapas trend.

The Marina's changes have created an interesting dichotomy of old and new. Such longtime establishments as **Lucca**, an extraordinary Italian deli, have been joined by cutting-edge stores catering to the young and upwardly mobile, including **s. f. Gourmet**, with an incredible selection of precooked food ready to be taken home and reheated. As eclectic as its collection of residents, the area offers culinary delights to satisfy a variety of appetites.

details

1 Zinc Details Collections from more than 40 artists and craftspeople, among them 10 glassblowers, make this a great place to find a cutting-edge gift. Browse through the brightly colored frosted vases, delicate porcelain bowls, and wood furniture painted in a rainbow of colors. Fans of art glass probably won't be able to resist treating themselves to something, too. ♦ Daily. 1905 Fillmore St (at Bush St). 776.2100; fax 510/841.9700 &

1 Leon's Bar-B-Q ★$$ San Francisco may not be a barbecue kind of town, but it has supported Leon McHenry's rib joint for more than 30 years and prompted Leon's expansion

Pacific Heights/Cow Hollow/The Marina

the woods used were from such fast-growing trees as birch. ♦ Daily. 2047 Fillmore St (between Pine and California Sts). 922.3811; fax 922.0407 &

5 Elite Cafe ★★$$ One of the few New Orleans–style restaurants in the city, it dishes up authentic cajun and creole fare. You'll find great-tasting raw oysters, seafood chowder, soft-shell crabs, baby back ribs, and pecan pie. The dark wood appointments, oyster bar in the window, and tall booths along the wall give the place a clubby ambience. Most of the time the service is professional and friendly, although occasionally, when they're jammed, it can be a bit curt. ♦ Creole/Cajun ♦ M-Sa dinner; Su brunch and dinner. 2049 Fillmore St (between Pine and California Sts). 346.8668; fax 346.9324 &

6 Grand Central Market Several independent purveyors sell under one roof at this grocery store, a combination that ensures personal service as well as the convenience of a one-stop supermarket. The produce isn't the best in town (that honor goes to **The Real Food Company** stores), but it's better than at many chain markets. The bakery is fairly standard, although it carries a good selection of breads from the best Bay Area producers. Excellent sandwiches and take-out food can be found at the deli area, and the meat market, one of the few remaining independents in the city, is a top draw with its wonderful beef, organic chicken, lamb, sausage, and fish. And the staff will capably roll a crown roast or butterfly a leg of lamb on request. ♦ Daily. 2435 California St (between Fillmore and Steiner Sts). 567.4902; fax 567.3215 &

7 Rasselas ★★$$ The city's best Ethiopian restaurant has the added attraction of nightly jazz performances. The comfortable dining room's high ceilings have been draped with swags of canvas to create an intimate, tentlike atmosphere, and the music spilling over from the bar area makes for a pleasant evening. The food mainly consists of stews, scooped up with a spongy bread called *injera*, which looks like a folded napkin. Main courses include fiery morsels of chicken topped with eggs, and tender cubes of beef in a thick, spicy sauce. Vegetarian entrées abound, one of the best being red and yellow lentils with greens, flavored with ginger and garlic. ♦ Ethiopian ♦ Two-drink minimum (if you come only for the music). Daily dinner. 2801 California St (at Divisadero St). 567.5010 &

Sugar built one of the city's most impressive homes, the Spreckels Mansion at 2080 Washington Street in Pacific Heights. Constructed in 1912 by sugar czar Claus Spreckels, the Beaux Arts structure is now owned by novelist Danielle Steel.

---

8 Food Inc. ★★$ Terrific carryout food and specialty products can be found at this charming storefront cafe with large windows. Homemade scones, pastries, and plum cakes are offered for breakfast, along with egg dishes and waffles. Lunchtime sandwiches include pear and brie, smoked salmon with cucumber, and Mediterranean chicken with olives and asparagus. There are always a few housemade soups and salads, including Caesar, pasta, or warm goat cheese with mixed greens. Hot specials, available for eating in or out, might be stuffed peppers or eggplant parmigiana. ♦ Cafe/Takeout ♦ M-Sa 9AM-9PM; Su 9AM-3PM. 2800 California St (at Divisadero St). 928.3728; fax 928.0494 &

9 Mi Burrito $ A loyal following has kept this Mexican eatery in business for more than 20 years. It has a spiffy, colorful decor, but the burritos, tacos, and enchiladas—while filling—are mediocre. ♦ Mexican ♦ Daily lunch and dinner. 2408 California St (between Fillmore and Steiner Sts). 563.3509; fax 928.3378 &

10 Le Chantilly Yellow walls and white-and-gold French provincial appointments lend elegance to this exclusive chocolate and pastry shop. Noteworthy delectables include impressive pyramid cakes made with Valhrona chocolate, and Ipanema cake layered with Cointreau and bitter chocolate mousse. More than a dozen kinds of truffles are sold, flavored with the likes of caramel and Cognac or white chocolate and mint. ♦ Daily. 2119 Fillmore St (between California and Sacramento Sts). 441.1500; fax 441.1380

10 VIVANDE Porta Via ★★★$$ Owner/chef Carlo Middione has gained national attention through his popular cookbooks and cooking show, and with good reason: He makes the best pasta in the city, as well as some marvelous desserts. His bustling trattoria specializes in Southern Italian fare; it also houses a deli that showcases prepared foods and high-quality specialty products to take out. (Customers can also sit at the counter and be served lunch.) Dining is a casual affair at tables that are arranged along a rough brick

Pacific Heights/Cow Hollow/The Marina

wall decorated with scores of ceramic pig heads. All the dishes are simply prepared and rich in flavor: Lamb chops are pounded flat and lightly sautéed; risotto is enhanced with lemon. For takeout, there's an impressive selection of Italian cheeses, such salads as white beans with caviar, and entrées that have saved many last-minute dinner parties. ♦ Italian/Takeout ♦ Daily lunch and dinner; deli, daily lunch; takeout 11:30AM-10PM. 2125 Fillmore St (between California and Sacramento Sts). 346.4430; fax 346.2877

11 Fillamento If it's new and different, you will find it first at this oh-so-chic furniture/accessory shop. Its three floors are filled with designer furniture, cutting-edge ceramics, and trend-setting glassware from some 2,000 vendors, of which more than 200 are local artisans. Owner Iris Fuller changes the merchandise so often that shoppers who want to keep up to date should drop by at least once a month. ♦ Daily. 2185 Fillmore St (between California and Sacramento Sts). 931.2224; fax 931.6304

12 R.H. This stylish shop's beautifully selected array of pottery and accessories for the home and garden includes herb topiary trees (English myrtle, lavender) and interesting table settings. ♦ Daily. 2506 Sacramento St (between Fillmore and Steiner Sts). 346.1460

13 Tea & Company This market/cafe offers an updated take on tea. There's brewed tea to sip (and seating for 25 sippers), bulk teas to buy, chocolates and jams to accompany your tea service, and—talk about being immersed in a subject!—even tea soaps. ♦ Daily 7AM-11PM. 2207 Fillmore St (at Sacramento St). 929.TEAS; fax 929.8385 ♿

14 La Méditerranée ★★$ Rock-bottom prices have helped this Middle Eastern eatery maintain a loyal following since it opened in 1979; the entrées even come with salad or a cup of soup. Start with the wonderful, lemony hummus, then try the ground lamb kebabs or the chicken drumsticks marinated and baked in pomegranate juice. The long, narrow restaurant can feel a little cramped, but the food is good, the service convivial. ♦ Mediterranean ♦ M-Sa lunch and dinner. 2210 Fillmore St (at Sacramento St). 921.2956 ♿. Also at: 288 Noe St (at Market St). 431.7210 ♿

14 D&M Liquors The owners of this extraordinary wine shop claim to have the widest selection of Champagne outside France, and experience tells us they're probably right. They stock about 200 Champagnes, including 10 to 15 vintages of Dom Pérignon. What's more, the prices are better than at most other shops. And long before the single-malt scotch craze, this store carried about 150 selections. Other finds include vintage Calvados from as far back as 1955 and Armagnac dating to 1932. ♦ Daily. 2200 Fillmore St (at Sacramento St). 346.1325; fax 346.1812 ♿

15 Ten Ichi ★★$$ This venerable Japanese restaurant provides a simple, modern setting for its creative food, with blush-colored sponge-painted walls, polished wood accents, and an L-shaped sushi bar. The staff has fun naming the *maki* (rice and seafood wrapped in seaweed) rolls: There's Jurassic Park, with crab and vegetables; ELT (barbecued eel, lettuce, tomatoes, and avocado); and rainbow rolls, with five kinds of fish. Purists may sneer at some of the combinations, but if you're not overly serious about sushi, this place is fun. Try the golden, crisp tempura, the subtly sweet and never cloying teriyaki, or the sukiyaki, whose tasty broth contains chewy *udon* (white) noodles as well as the traditional glass noodles, chunks of button mushrooms, and still-crunchy scallions. Particularly friendly service enhances the meal. ♦ Japanese/Sushi ♦ M-F lunch and dinner; Sa-Su dinner. 2235 Fillmore St (between Sacramento and Clay Sts). 346.3477; fax 346.1816 ♿

16 Via Veneto ★★$$ With butter-colored walls painted with a harlequin pattern, plus a lively open kitchen, this Italian restaurant is chic and appealing. The 10 pastas on the menu—all good—are sauced sparingly, the way it's done in Italy. The fiery *penne alla puttanesca*, pungent with olives and anchovy, is our top choice. Also try the grilled chicken breast brushed with olive oil and served on a bed of spinach, or the classic veal with white wine, lemon butter, and capers. The tiramisù is an excellent way to end the meal. ♦ Italian ♦ M-Sa lunch and dinner; Su dinner. 2244 Fillmore St (between Sacramento and Clay Sts). 346.9211; fax 346.6948 ♿

16 La Posada ★$$ After a few margaritas and an order of nachos, most diners forget that Mexican food in San Francisco tends to be mediocre. But by comparison to what's out

Pacific Heights

there, the fare here is actually pretty good. The *taquitos,* small rolls of fried tortillas stuffed with ham and cheese, are tasty, while the guacamole served alongside is spicy and refreshing. The enchiladas, with a choice of fillings, are some of the best dishes on the menu. Strangely, the decor isn't Mexican; the place looks more like a Victorian-style fern bar. ♦ Mexican ♦ M-Sa lunch and dinner; Su brunch and dinner. 2298 Fillmore St (at Clay St). 922.1722

17 Alta Plaza Bar and Restaurant ★★$$ Few restaurants rise from the ashes, but this one came back better than ever. After three years as the **Fillmore Grill** singles' scene, it was reborn under its original name; it now attracts a neighborhood crowd for early dining, followed by gay night owls. The bar is a popular gathering place until the wee hours. The decor has been spruced up with white-painted walls, and an open mezzanine overlooks the bar action. Chef Amey Shaw has created a solid, Italian-inspired menu. Best bets include an excellent Caesar salad; sautéed mushrooms; roast chicken with garlic mashed potatoes and broccoli rabe; and barbecued flank steak with a sweet-and-spicy sauce and fiery black beans. ♦ Californian ♦ M-Sa dinner; Su brunch and dinner; bar until 2AM. 2301 Fillmore St (at Clay St). 922.1444; fax 922.1767

18 Pauli's Cafe ★$$ With large windows overlooking Fillmore Street, this corner cafe is at its best for breakfast. The menu features omelettes with myriad fillings and buttermilk pancakes with real maple syrup. At dinner it's a come-as-you-are kind of place; for the same price you can find more stylish surroundings and better food elsewhere on Fillmore Street. ♦ Californian ♦ Daily breakfast, lunch, and dinner. 2500 Washington St (at Fillmore St). 921.5159

juicy NEWS

19 Juicy News A newsstand/juice bar, it carries many hard-to-find foreign food magazines, frozen yogurt, and freshly blended fruit concoctions. ♦ Daily. 2453 Fillmore St (at Jackson St). 441.3051

20 Jackson Fillmore Trattoria ★★★$$ Although this place is homey and unassuming, it serves top-notch Italian food and caters to the affluent Pacific Heights crowd. There's almost always a wait, especially for tables; many customers choose to sit at the diner-style counter overlooking the antipasto selections. Few appetizers can be better than the grilled portobello mushrooms, the size of a saucer, tender and juicy with olive oil, sprinkled with cheese and garlic, arranged on a bed of peppery arugula. The gnocchi, occasionally on the menu, are as light as a feather and worth an hour's wait. Sure bets among the entrées are such braised dishes as the woodsman-style chicken with sausage, mushrooms, and beans. End the meal with hot zabaglione, a frothy mixture of Marsala and eggs that practically spills over the wineglass in which it's served. ♦ Italian ♦ Daily dinner. Reservations accepted for three or more people. 2506 Fillmore St (at Jackson St). 346.5288

21 The Meetinghouse ★★$$ Joanna Karlinsky and John Bryant Snell have taken over the space once occupied by **La Fiammetta** and transformed the serene Italian into an American original with Shaker-style decor, sunny yellow walls, and an American-centered menu. Appetizers include a crisp flatbread with caramelized onions, fingerling potatoes, sage, and sheep's milk ricotta; oyster stew with celery root and fennel; and potted rabbit with cranberry conserve. There are such delightful entrées as braised pork with juniper, and pan-roasted chicken with wild mushroom *jus,* savory bread pudding, and winter greens. But save room for the terrific desserts; it's hard to choose a favorite among the luscious Meyer lemon meringue pie, caramelized banana cream tart with dark rum sauce, and the chilled coconut-and-guava soup with pineapple sorbet. ♦ American ♦ W-Su dinner. 1701 Octavia St (at Bush St). 922.6733; fax 661.8565

22 Gourmet Carousel ★★$ In a neighborhood bereft of Chinese restaurants, this one is a nice surprise—and a bargain. A dinner for six featuring eight dishes even includes the 7 UP on the table. Be sure to try the pot stickers, crystal prawns (large shrimp stir-fried with vegetables), and pork with eggplant. Fearless eaters can opt for pork bellies in a clay pot, deep-fried intestines, crabmeat and fish-stomach soup, or pigskin with rice noodles. The pleasant room has a clean, simple look, with black metal chairs and white-clothed tables. ♦ Chinese ♦ Tu-Su dinner. 1559 Franklin St (at Pine St). 771.2044

23 Sushi Chardonnay ★$$ It doesn't look like much—the well-worn interior is crowned by an industrial-style ceiling crisscrossed by pipes—but this Japanese restaurant has earned a reputation for its sushi buffet. It's an all-you-can-eat extravaganza, with 28 sushi and several tempura choices for a flat, per-person price. Just don't let your eyes get bigger than your stomach, because you'll be charged $1 for each piece left uneaten on your plate. ♦ Japanese ♦ M-F lunch and dinner; Sa-Su dinner. 1785 Union St (at Octavia St). 346.5070; fax 346.0581

Who Says There's No Free Lunch?

The restaurant tradition of offering a free lunch originated during San Francisco's Gold Rush to encourage bar patrons to stick around and consume more alcohol. It lives on today in Happy Hour, when a number of bars with restaurants offer free or almost-free nibbles on weekdays during the late afternoon or early evening.

City of Paris (550 Geary St, between Taylor and Jones Sts, 441.4442) offers hot buffalo wings, mini crab cakes, olives, cold cuts, and onion rings at no charge Monday through Friday 5 to 7PM.

In the **Fairmont Hotel, Tonga Restaurant and Hurricane Bar** (950 Mason St, at California St, Terrace level, 772.5278) puts out an all-you-can-eat spread with eight different dishes, including chow mein, roast duck, and crudités. For the $5 tab, plus a one-drink minimum (about $2.50), it's one of the best deals in town, Monday through Friday 5 to 7PM.

New Joe's (347 Geary St, between Powell and Mason Sts, 392.9999) features a different dish daily (M-F 4:30-6:30PM) at no charge. Typical offerings are pizza slices or pasta.

Liverpool Lil's (2942 Lyon St, between Greenwich and Lombard Sts, 921.6664) serves one dish free Monday through Friday 4 to 6PM. Meatballs, tortellini, and chicken wings are representative of the fare.

Buchanan Grill (3653 Buchanan St, between Bay and North Point Sts, 346.8727) sets out finger sandwiches Monday through Friday between 5 and 7PM; Monday night during the football season brings on hot dogs with the works. Depending on the day, there may also be barbecued chicken or pasta.

---

24 Radicchio ★★$$ A generous spirit permeates this 50-seat Italian eatery that uses—you guessed it—radicchio in many dishes. The bitter purple lettuce makes a great wrapper for scallops and brings Caesar salad up to date. The kitchen is particularly proud of its black-and-white *tagliolini*, thin noodles made with squid ink and served with a saffron-infused sauce and a generous scattering of rock shrimp. Our favorite, however, is the penne with tomatoes, fresh artichokes, garlic, and herbs. For the meat course, try the flank steak served over mushrooms, or the New Zealand lamb chops. The tile floor in back and the mirrors that reflect the wine racks against one wall give the room an intimate feel. Owners Verniero Monti and Giacomo Ciabattini do wonders in the front of the house and with the food. ♦ Italian ♦ Tu-Su dinner. 1809 Union St (at Octavia St). 346.7373; fax 346.7374

25 Pasand Madras Cuisine ★$ One of the few places serving southern Indian food, which includes tandoori preparations and the milder *masala* dishes, this dark and moody spot also features live jazz. Specialties include *masala dosa*, a thick pancake made with lentil flour and stuffed with potatoes. The meat curries are also popular. ♦ Indian ♦ Tu-Su dinner; jazz W-Su until 1AM. 1875 Union St (between Octavia and Laguna Sts). 922.4498

25 Starbucks Coffee The Seattle-based chain, with more than 600 coffee bars across the country, entered the San Francisco market with a vengeance at this location back in 1992. Since then, its shops have been moving into just about every neighborhood and competing with the other major players. **Starbucks** blend, somewhat milder than most, is made from Central American beans. ♦ Daily. 1899 Union St (at Laguna St). 921.4049 &. Also at: Numerous locations throughout the city

26 Bepples Pies Thick-crusted pies beckon passersby from an open window overlooking the kitchen, which turns out all kinds of deep-dish pies—fruit, cream, and savory. The savory pies, dense with chicken, herbs, carrots, peas, and other vegetables and crowned with a golden crust, make a great, quick meal at home; just heat them up and dig in. But be sure to ask for whatever is the freshest; at times, the pies can taste a tad old. Eat-in meals, including salad and soup, are available at the Chestnut Street branch. ♦ Daily until midnight. No credit cards accepted. 1934 Union St (between Laguna and Buchanan Sts). 931.6225 &. Also at: 2142 Chestnut St (between Steiner and Pierce Sts). 391.6226

26 Perry's ★★$$ Perry Butler escaped from Manhattan back in 1969, bringing with him the

Pacific Heights/Cow Hollow/The Marina

idea for this typical Upper East Side New York saloon. Originally popular as a singles' place, it has retained a fiercely loyal clientele over the years, but now the old regulars bring their kids. A smattering of singles can still be found at the traditional bar, which is reminiscent of the 1970s. Offerings include veal chops, steaks, calves' liver, *ahi* tuna, and such bar favorites as chicken fajitas, quesadillas, and excellent burgers and fries. ♦ American ♦ M-F breakfast, lunch, and dinner; Sa-Su brunch and dinner. 1944 Union St (between Laguna and Buchanan Sts). 922.9022. Also at: 185 Sutter St (between Montgomery and Kearny Sts). 989.6895; fax 433.4409 ♿

27 Baton Rouge Cajun Roadhouse $
Huntley Castner and Greg McNally have married the newest branch of their **WA-HA-KA! (Oaxaca Mexican Grill)** to this spicy Cajun-themed joint. The two lively and brightly painted restaurants share a bar/party space that appeals to young locals out for a good time. Here, look for the likes of peel-and-eat crawfish and shrimp served with grilled corn and red potatoes, all served on newspaper; jambalaya; and po-boy sandwiches. ♦ American ♦ Daily lunch and dinner. 1980 Union St (at Buchanan St). 929.7890 ♿

27 WA-HA-KA! (Oaxaca Mexican Grill) $
This is the third branch of a *taqueria* chain specializing in healthful Mexican fare, made without lard. Start with the fresh chips served with a delicious roasted tomato salsa. In the Northern Californian style, the burritos are stuffed to bursting with meat, beans, cheese, shredded lettuce, and rice. Also offered are quesadillas and tasty grilled meats. ♦ Mexican ♦ Daily lunch and dinner. 1980 Union St (at Buchanan St). 775.4145 ♿. Also at: 2141 Polk St (between Broadway and Vallejo Sts). 775.1055 ♿; 1489 Folsom St (at 11th St). 861.1410; fax 861.1410 ♿

28 The Brazen Head Restaurant ★★$$
There's no sign to mark the entrance of this quaint place nestled in a residential area, and that is part of its mystique and charm. Inside, low, low lighting sets the stage for romance, with candles and flowers on each wooden table to enhance the mood. The classic food is all well prepared, including the onion soup and the garlicky Caesar salad. The meltingly tender filet mignon is accented with sautéed mushrooms and scalloped potatoes. Chicken breast is crusted with pepper and sautéed in a pungent brandy sauce. Other classics include lamb chops with mint jelly, veal piccata, and petrale sole amandine. Because they serve late, this place is popular with chefs and waiters. ♦ Continental ♦ Daily dinner until 1AM. No credit cards accepted. 3166 Buchanan St (at Greenwich St). 921.7600; fax 921.0164

29 Prego Ristorante $$ When it opened more than a decade ago, this was one of the first restaurants to serve New Wave Italian food in American-brasserie surroundings. It's still a stylish place, with an open kitchen and long, narrow windows overlooking the street. There are pizzas and meats from the rotisserie, but the fare can vary wildly in quality from one day to the next. Let's hope the kitchen gets back on track soon. ♦ Italian ♦ Daily lunch and dinner until midnight. 2000 Union St (at Buchanan St). 563.3305; fax 563.1561 ♿

27 Betelnut ★★★$$ George Chen has collaborated with Cecilia Chiang, the former owner of the **Mandarin,** and the Real Restaurant folks (they own **Fog City Diner**) to make this the restaurant of the moment. Thanks to the raves of local diners and reviewers, it's almost impossible to get in. Chef Barney Brown's (he's half Korean) pan-Asian menu includes delicious Singapore chili crab, spicy coconut chicken from Thailand, and a wonderful appetizer of sun-dried anchovies, peanuts, and chili from Taipei. All the food goes well with the Asian and American brews on tap and in bottles. The bar at the front has a somewhat mysterious air, with large, unusual looking ceiling fans, paintings of sensuous Asian beauties, and the sense that Peter Lorre or Sidney Greenstreet is about to be seated. ♦ Pan-Asian ♦ Daily lunch and dinner. 2030 Union St (at Buchanan St). 929.8855; fax 929.8894 ♿

27 Cafe de Paris L'Entrecôte ★$$ The best features of this brasserie are the glassed-in patio built around a tree that overlooks Union Street, and the delicious hangar steak with crispy french fries and a wonderful sauce. The balance of the menu is just so-so, however. Still, the setting is bright and sunny during the day, glittering and romantic at night. ♦ French/Californian ♦ Daily lunch and dinner. 2032 Union St (at Buchanan St). 931.5006; fax 931.5383 ♿

Pacific Heights/Cow Hollow/The Marina

30 Amici's East Coast Pizza ★★$ The aroma of fresh-baked pizza filling this roomy place should be enough to convince you to stick with pizza and salad here. The pies have a medium-thick crust that's crisp enough to stand up to whatever toppings you concoct. Free delivery makes this one of the best take-out choices in town. ♦ Pizzeria ♦ Daily lunch and dinner; F-Sa until 1AM. 2033 Union St (between Buchanan and Webster Sts). 885.4500; fax 885.0152

30 Z-Gallerie Wonderful glasses and plates made by area artisans can be found at this poster-and-frame shop, which also carries trendy furniture and all kinds of decorative accessories. ♦ Daily. 2071 Union St (between Buchanan and Webster Sts). 346.9000

31 Writer's Bookstore Here's where cookbook collectors from all over the Bay Area come to find great deals on current releases. Its selection and prices outclass the much-hyped chains. ♦ Daily. 2848 Webster St (between Green and Union Sts). 921.2620

32 Yoshida-Ya ★★$$ One of only a handful of *yakitori* bars in the city, it is set in an expansive room with tasteful appointments. The extensive menu also offers tempura, sushi, and more, but the *yakitori* dishes—skewered and grilled combinations—are the best. Highlights include mushrooms stuffed with ground chicken; beef with pungent Japanese mustard; marinated shiitake mushrooms; and Japanese eggplant with ginger. ♦ Japanese ♦ Daily dinner. 2909 Webster St (at Union St). 346.3431; fax 346.0907

Without the influence of Italian immigrant growers, who brought the necessary seeds with them, there wouldn't be acres and acres of artichokes growing around Half Moon Bay, 20 miles south of San Francisco. Other commercial crops linked to the influx of Italians are bell peppers, eggplant, broccoli, and fava beans. Some of the first farms were established in the Outer Mission in the late 19th century by Italian immigrants.

32 Gordon Bennett A potpourri of accessories for the home and garden is featured at this delightful shop, including casual tabletop and kitchen wares, a small selection of first-rate packaged food, rusty garden sculptures, and seeds and bulbs. ♦ Daily. 2102 Union St (at Webster St). 929.1172; fax 929.7525

33 La Nouvelle Patisserie There was a time when this French patisserie drew raves for its delicate and delicious pastries. But as the volume of business increased and a second location opened, the quality diminished; many of the products now have a mass-produced taste. Mousse cakes may have ice crystals in the center, and the puff pastry tastes more like phyllo. ♦ Daily. 2184 Union St (at Fillmore St). 931.7655; fax 931.0544

34 Union Street Coffee Roastery ★$ It may strike some as pretentious, but the bespectacled college-student types sitting on bags of coffee beans for hours while they pore over their Proust give this cafe a distinct personality. We think it makes a perfect retreat on a rainy or wintry day. The coffee is well balanced and strong; the pastries and light snacks are standard issue, but filling. The coffee served here is roasted at the **Chestnut Street Roastery**, which is also a cafe (2331 Chestnut St, between Scott and Divisadero Sts, 931.5282). ♦ Coffeehouse ♦ Daily. 2191 Union St (at Fillmore St). 922.9559

35 Doidge's ★★$ Although it's a little frayed around the edges, this home-style cafe is a veritable breakfast institution; it draws throngs, especially on weekends. Choose from more than a dozen omelettes, including one filled with an unusual peach-walnut chutney, and 10 kinds of toast. The eggs benedict are beautifully done, and the French toast and housemade scones also win raves. ♦ American ♦ Daily breakfast. Reservations recommended. 2217 Union St (between Fillmore and Steiner Sts). 921.2149

35 Full Moon Foods and Mercantile Low-fat organic foods are highlighted at this deli and specialty-foods store, which has a small produce section, packaged goods, and such bulk products as granola and dried beans. The deli case features roasted vegetables, curried potatoes, and roasted chicken, among other dishes. The shop also makes entertaining a snap with its special holiday menus. At Thanksgiving, for example, it prepares quarts of gravy, rolls, roasted-garlic–and-thyme stuffing, grilled yams, and even a vegan pumpkin pie; all the host has to do is roast the turkey. ♦ Daily. 2263 Union St (between Fillmore and Steiner Sts). 567.5755

Pacific Heights/Cow Hollow/The Marina

35 Bonta Ristorante ★★★$$ The flower boxes under the windows add a cheerful, European-style welcome to this always-crowded Italian restaurant. The tables are a bit close together, but that just contributes to the friendly, party atmosphere. An excellent starter is the smoked buffalo mozzarella, baked and crowned with sautéed mushrooms. Also try the ravioli stuffed with sea bass, ricotta, and spinach and covered with a creamy tomato sauce; the angel-hair pasta tossed with scallops and fresh tomatoes; or the marvelous beef fillet topped with bitter radicchio and soothed with a balsamic vinegar sauce. For dessert, don't miss the warm pear crisp with hazelnut gelato. ♦ Italian ♦ Tu-Su dinner. Reservations recommended. 2223 Union St (between Fillmore and Steiner Sts). 929.0407

36 Il Fornaio Panetteria One of the top bakeries, known for its breads and *grissini* (bread sticks), it also boasts rich wood surroundings that make it one of the prettiest. Choose from more than a dozen kinds of breads spanning the regions of Italy. The specialty breads are a treat, too: The *pane alla olive* (with green olives and olive oil) and *pane alle noci con uva* (with walnuts and raisins) are both wonderful with cheese. The bakery also features a variety of delicious cookies, cakes, fruit tarts, and nut tarts, all made from traditional Italian recipes. ♦ Daily. 2298 Union St (at Steiner St). 563.3400; fax 563.0642

37 Pane e Vino ★★$$ The intimate dining room of this top-notch trattoria is dominated by a long, narrow table displaying a prosciutto ham, decorative vegetables, and parmesan cheese. The homey environment, the fresh aromas that greet you as you enter, the simply prepared but robust food, and the convivial spirit all evoke the best of Italy. This spot is so popular that even those with reservations may have to wait to be seated, but the food is worth it. All the pastas are superb, and if they're on the menu, try the braised rabbit (or any other long-simmered meat) or the whole roasted fish. ♦ Italian ♦ M-Sa lunch and dinner; Su dinner. Reservations recommended. 3011 Steiner St (at Union St). 346.2111; fax 346.0741

38 La Canasta ★$ This is a good place to grab a quick bite, Mexican style, in a neighborhood that seems to host nothing but Italian eateries. The only seating is on a bench outside, but the food is so tasty that fans don't mind sitting there and trying to balance their *chalupas* (tortillas layered with beans, meat, cheese, and guacamole), burritos, and tamales—and inevitably splattering their clothes. (If you'd prefer eating at a set table, delivery is available for dinner.) The *chiles verdes* burrito with pork and the *tortas* (Mexican sandwiches made with crisp-crusted, nutty-tasting rolls) are outstanding. ♦ Mexican ♦ Daily lunch and dinner. No credit cards accepted. 2219 Filbert St (at Fillmore St). 921.3003; fax 202.8582. Also at: 3006 Buchanan St (at Union St). 474.2627; fax 202.8582

Turin-born Joseph Coppa opened his eponymous restaurant on the corner of Montgomery and Merchant Streets around the turn of the century. The place was quickly adopted by the local bohemians—writers (including Jack London) and artists living in nearby North Beach. These artists left behind a lasting gift—a number of brightly colored murals on the wall. Among the images are painted quotations from several great philosophers (by Porter Garnett) and a frieze of stenciled black cats (artist unknown).

San Franciscans were the first to taste the products of S & W Foods (a local enterprise named for its founders, Sussman and Wormser). Today, it's one of the largest canning companies in the world.

Pacific Heights/Cow Hollow/The Marina

39 Auntie Pasta Like the handful of its sister outlets, this corner shop carries lots of fresh, frozen, and packaged pasta and sauces, along with wine and just about everything else needed to put together a dinner at home. The ever-changing take-out menu might include Thai chicken rolls or baby crab cakes with jalapeño remoulade; entrées run the gamut from shepherd's pie to honey-glazed chicken breast. ◆ Daily. 3101 Fillmore St (at Filbert St). 921.7576; fax 921.1547. Also at: 741 Diamond St (between 24th and Elizabeth Sts). 282.0738; fax 282.4205; 2139A Polk St (between Broadway and Vallejo St). 776.9420; fax 776.8512; 1501 Waller St (at Clayton St). 681.4242; fax 681.0227

40 Brew City Personal Brewery The city's first do-it-yourself brewery opened in 1994. Customers choose a beer from about 40 recipes, then the trained staff guides them through the two-hour brewing process, resulting in 13.5 gallons of beer. It must be cold fermented on-site for several weeks, when customers return to bottle it (bottles and personalized labels are included). The whole tab comes to a little more than a hundred dollars, or less than $5 for the equivalent of a six pack. The smell of hops permeates the warehouse-size room, which is dominated by six copper tanks and a self-bottling line. No beer is served on premises, but customers can taste their own brew during the process. It makes a terrific personalized gift for your favorite "hop head." ◆ Tu-Sa 11AM-6PM. Appointments recommended one week in advance. 2198 Filbert St (at Fillmore St). 929.2255; fax 929.2256

41 Bugatti's Espresso Cafe ★$ This venerable neighborhood coffeehouse caters to sleepy-eyed residents who don't want to put up with the mob scene on Union or Chestnut Streets. Pastries and coffee are good, but the simply prepared egg dishes are the real draw. ◆ Coffeehouse ◆ Daily breakfast, lunch, and dinner. 3001 Webster St (at Filbert St). 922.4888

42 PlumpJack Cafe ★★$$ One of the city's most popular restaurants, this place has a celebrity pedigree: It was launched by Andrew and Billy Getty (sons of billionaire Gordon Getty) and Gavin Newsom (whose father, Bill, is a retired judge). The taupe-and-green-gray color scheme is appealing, as are all the subtle design details: A metal screen in front of the window enmeshes the traffic outside in a soft-focus artistic haze; a gold yin-yang–like fixture hovers over the center of the room, its oval shape repeated on the waiters' vests and on the buttons of the tufted banquettes. But the room can get noisy when it's packed, thanks to the many hard, uncushioned surfaces. Chef Maria Helm makes some terrific appetizers, including *bruschetta* topped with roasted beets, baby lettuces, goat cheese, and roasted garlic; gravlax with blini on the side; and a salad made from lettuce, gorgonzola, beets, and walnuts. The wine list offers some of the best bargains in the city: its wines are priced at retail cost, without the premium usually paid in restaurants. But the entrées are sometimes salty and overseasoned with rosemary. ◆ Californian/Mediterranean ◆ M-F lunch and dinner; Sa dinner. Reservations recommended. 3127 Fillmore St (between Filbert and Greenwich Sts). 346.9870; fax 346.9879

43 City Tavern $$ This eatery replaced the **Golden Gate Grill**, a singles' place known as much for its donnybrooks as its fare. The tone is more sedate now, but—between the poorly trained waitstaff and the middle-of-the-road menu—it's destined to be no more than a second choice for those singles who can't get into the other watering holes nearby. ◆ American ◆ Daily dinner. 3200 Fillmore St (at Greenwich St). 567.0918

43 Balboa Cafe ★$$ Billy Getty and Gavin Newsom of **PlumpJack Cafe** (see above) recently bought this venerable bar and American eatery and gave it a beautiful face-lift. The society crowd and their kids are returning to rub shoulders, grab a bite, and down a few. The burger is still terrific, but make sure you get it on a hamburger bun—trying to eat one served on a baguette will run up your cleaning bill. ◆ American ◆ Daily lunch and dinner. 3199 Fillmore St (at Greenwich St). 921.3944; fax 346.9879

44 PlumpJack Wines A companion to **PlumpJack Cafe**, this handsome wine store has become one of the city's best. The selection of boutique Californian wines is phenomenal, and all are elegantly displayed in surroundings worthy of the carriage trade—but at terrific prices. This is where you'll find wines you've never heard of, or small-vineyard wines that go only to the select few; because of the Getty-Newsom connection, all the wine makers want to showcase their wares here. ◆ Daily. 3201 Fillmore St (at Greenwich St). 346.9870; fax 346.9879

Pacific Heights/Cow Hollow/The Marina

45 Holey Bagel Here's a bagel to delight the most discriminating aficionado. The bagels are simmered in water, then baked to create a dense, chewy texture. The number of varieties now totals 18, with more than a dozen schmears. The shop also features such specialties as *rugalach* (filled crescent-shaped cookies), muffins, and croissants. And there's an espresso bar, a New York–style deli, and full-service catering. This bagelry has been in business since 1979 and has expanded to eight branches around the Bay Area; at press time, the chain was considering changing its name to **Manhattan Bagel**. ♦ Daily. 3218 Fillmore St (at Greenwich St). 922.1955; fax 626.2453 ♿. Also at: 3872 24th St (between Vicksburg and Sanchez Sts). 647.3334; fax 647.0824 ♿; 1206 Masonic St (at Haight St). 626.9111; fax 626.2730; 1789 Fourth St (at Harvest Ave), Berkeley. 510/525.9445; fax 510/525.8105 ♿

46 Cassis Bistro ★★★$$ The neighborhood has embraced this sunny little bistro. It has cheerful blue-and-white striped banquettes, a copper-fronted bar that makes a pleasant place to wait for a table, and chef Erik Leroux's comforting bistro fare. There's an addictive individual onion tart, as well as warm sausage embedded in a slice of rosemary toast and paired with a veal sauce. Entrées include a toothsome spinach ravioli in a garlicky tomato sauce, several fish dishes, and a tender chicken breast. If it's offered, don't pass up the *tarte tatin;* it's one of the best in the city. The staff is very friendly and the whole experience is restorative. ♦ French ♦ Tu-Sa dinner. 2120 Greenwich St (between Webster and Fillmore Sts). 292.0770

47 North India Restaurant ★★★$$ At the best Indian restaurant in the city, chef-owner Parvesh Sahi perfectly captures the complexity of Indian spices, giving each dish a distinct, bright flavor. All the curry dishes showcase his talent, as do the full-flavored and succulent tandoori preparations—don't miss the sweet tandoori prawns. If you're intimidated by the extensive menu, order one of the fixed-price meals, which include many of the best dishes. Everything, including the breads, is made to order; glass windows offer glimpses of the chefs toiling in the pristine kitchen. The room, done in burgundy and pink, with rich, rose-colored wood, makes a comfortable backdrop for the food. One caveat: Service can be slow at some times and pushy at others. ♦ Indian ♦ M-F lunch and dinner; Sa-Su dinner. 3131 Webster St (at Lombard St). 931.1556; fax 931.1527 ♿

48 Byblos ★★$$ An array of *mezes,* the Middle Eastern version of tapas, makes the best meal at this pleasant Lebanese eatery. Labibi Maamari, mother of owner Anis Maamari, holds forth from the partly open kitchen. Choose from her more than 20 small appetizers, including *sambusik,* flaky braided pastries seasoned with ground chicken and pine nuts; *baba ganooj,* a spread of smoky grilled eggplant infused with garlic; dill cakes, crisp fritters with loads of herbs; *crisor,* an outstanding version of hummus; and fantastic stuffed grape leaves plump with rice. The larger plates can be uneven, but lamb chops with pomegranate sauce and beef kabobs are winners. The house version of baklava is particularly good because it's not excessively sweet. ♦ Lebanese ♦ M-Sa lunch and dinner; Su dinner. 1910 Lombard St (at Buchanan St). 292.5672

49 Allegria ★★$$ The tapas trend in San Francisco continues at this excellent dining spot. Cold dishes include authentic Spanish cured ham and imported pimientos, quail cooked in wine and sherry vinegar, and toast with anchovies, tomato, and manchego cheese; hot ones include meatballs, tripe Madrid style, and steamed mussels. But this restaurant also offers a dynamite paella, available in three versions (seafood, chicken and seafood, and vegetarian). And don't miss the thick crepes enveloped in a silky caramelized milk sauce for dessert. ♦ Spanish ♦ M-Tu dinner; W-Su lunch and dinner. 2018 Lombard St (at Webster St). 929.8888; fax 929.9215

50 Babaloo Restaurant $ The dishes at this tapas parlor have a decidedly Cuban influence. There's prawns with roasted paprika, salt, and garlic; turkey chorizo; and banana and pepper–stuffed shrimp in a *poblano* pepper sauce. The menu also offers several soups and salads, a burger served on Cuban bread, and grilled, marinated pork loin with chips and chayote slaw. You can wash it all down with any of the 16 microbrewed beers on tap or the tropical fruit–spiked sangria. ♦ Cuban/Tapas ♦ Daily dinner. 2030 Lombard St (between Webster and Fillmore Sts). 346.5474 ♿

51 Mel's Drive-In ★$ A favorite with the preteen set, this idealized 1950s-style diner has a welcoming neon glow outside and an authentic look inside, with vinyl booths and tabletop jukeboxes. What to order? Hamburgers, cherry Cokes, banana splits, and, for a throwback to the days before cholesterol became a household word, fried-egg sandwiches spread with mayo. ♦ American ♦ Daily breakfast, lunch, and dinner. No credit cards accepted. 2165 Lombard St (between Fillmore and Steiner Sts). 921.3039; fax 921.3521. Also at: 3355 Geary Blvd (at Stanyan St). 387.2244; fax 387.1259 ♿

Chicken Tetrazzini—that rich, delicious mélange of chicken, macaroni, cheese, and a mushroom velouté sauce—was created in honor of a famous San Francisco–based coloratura soprano, Luisa Tetrazzini.

97

Pacific Heights/Cow Hollow/The Marina

52 Cafe Adriano ★★$$ This storefront jewel is wrapped in a rich green-and-yellow interior, with nicely contrasting copper-pipe chandeliers and other copper accents. Start with arugula salad with celery and pears glistening in a walnut-oil dressing, or the timbale of gorgonzola and mascarpone cheese. To follow, try either the tiny gnocchi with broccoli, anchovies, and olive oil, or the linguine with shrimp, clams, scallops, and snap peas in a light garlic-and-tomato sauce. Winning entrées include grilled *ahi*, brushed with pesto and served on Tuscan white beans seasoned with olive oil and bites of raw tomato. And the veal sprinkled with parmesan cheese and drizzled with truffle oil makes a savory foil for the mashed potatoes and spinach served alongside. ♦ Italian ♦ Tu-Su dinner. 3347 Fillmore St (at Chestnut St). 474.4180; fax 474.4511

52 Pasta Pomodoro ★★$ Run by the same people who own **Cafe Adriano** (see above), this quick-fix pasta house offers excellent pastas, salads, and sandwiches, all at rock-bottom prices. Tagliatelle is prepared with tomato, chicken, or alfredo sauce; a bowl of polenta is sprinkled with tomato-basil sauce or gorgonzola cheese. There's only counter seating, but called-in orders are ready in five minutes, which makes this neighborhood joint popular for takeout. ♦ Italian/Takeout ♦ Daily lunch and dinner. No credit cards accepted. 2027 Chestnut St (at Fillmore St). 474.3400; fax 474.4511 &. Also at: 655 Union St (between Columbus Ave and Powell St). 399.0300; fax 399.0377 &

53 Williams-Sonoma Another branch in the popular nationwide chain of housewares shops, it stocks all kinds of must-have kitchen gadgets and specialty foods. ♦ Daily. 2000 Chestnut St (at Fillmore St). 929.2520 &. Also at: 150 Post St (between Kearny St and Grant Ave). 362.6904; fax 362-2852 &; San Francisco Centre, 865 Market St (at Fifth St). 546.0171 &

54 Noah's Bagels The green-and-white hexagonal floor tiles, dark green vinyl-covered stools, and tile work behind the bins of bagels and New York memorabilia give this place a snazzy look. The bagels here are more breadlike than bagel-like, since they are steamed before baking rather than boiled, but they are tasty, particularly when spread with the wide selection of schmears. Espresso and good coffee are also available.

♦ Daily. No credit cards accepted. 2075 Chestnut St (at Steiner St). 775.2910; fax 775.1243 &. Also at: 742 Irving St (at Ninth Ave). 566.2761; fax 566.9258 &

55 Tây Việt ★★$ It's a tiny sliver of a restaurant, barely big enough for two rows of tables, but with its high ceiling hung with leaf-shaped white chandeliers, the white walls, and the changing artwork, this place has all the panache of an art gallery. The Vietnamese food offered here is as light and delicate as you could wish. Top choices include the imperial rolls, which are stuffed with mint and crabmeat, among other ingredients, and served with a refreshing dipping sauce; the quail, flamed table-side and served with salt and pepper and a wedge of lime; and beef fondue, featuring paper-thin slices of beef that quickly cook in a vinegar broth. Roast chicken, flavored with five-spice powder, and aromatic barbecued pork are other fine options. ♦ Vietnamese ♦ Daily lunch and dinner. 2034 Chestnut St (between Fillmore and Steiner Sts). 567.8124 &

56 Parma Ristorante ★★$$ The waiters at this fun, relaxed destination seem to have come from central casting; they banter with guests, peppering their speech with "Mamma Mia." The red banquette running the length of the brick wall makes diners feel they're sitting at a communal table, and the food is classic trattoria fare. There's minestrone thick with vegetables and several preparations of veal, including saltimbocca. One of the best pastas features sausage and tomato sauce spiked with vodka, which adds a complex, lingering spiciness. ♦ Italian ♦ M-Sa dinner. 3314 Steiner St (between Lombard and Chestnut Sts). 567.0500

56 Sweet Heat ★★$ The slowly swinging palm fans over the service counter and the mismatched tables and chairs look as if they came straight from Old Mexico, but the food here has a modern, healthful bent. Spicy chicken wings are cooled with a nonfat cilantro-yogurt dipping sauce, and fire-roasted corn is slathered with either cilantro pesto or hot chipotle salsa. Tacos are stuffed

Pacific Heights/Cow Hollow/The Marina

with calamari or scallops, and burritos are plumped with fish or one of several other combinations, all at very reasonable prices. Even the Caesar salad gets a zippy twist with chili-flecked croutons, salsa, and Mexican cheese. ♦ Mexican ♦ Daily lunch and dinner until midnight. No credit cards accepted. 3324 Steiner St (between Lombard and Chestnut Sts). 474.9191; fax 292.6874 &

56 Caffe Centro ★★$ Airy and modern, this cafe has seating on a patio as well as inside; the dining room is enlivened by a light wood bar and a floor painted in muted yellow, green, and orange. Among the tasty choices on the menu is a warm spinach salad matched with French butter pears and gorgonzola-topped croutons. Several pastas and sandwiches are offered; heartier entrées include grilled pork chops with crispy potato pancakes and fresh plum sauce, and a rib-eye steak with red-wine butter. This spot is especially popular for brunch, which includes oatmeal with brown sugar, eggs with chicken-apple sausage, or scrambled eggs with smoked salmon and cream cheese, served with brioche. ♦ Cafe ♦ Tu-F dinner; Sa-Su brunch and dinner. 3340 Steiner St (between Lombard and Chestnut Sts). 202.0100; fax 202.0153 &

56 Barney's Gourmet Hamburgers ★$ This branch of the well-known local chain has been spruced up with painted wood paneling and sailboat cutouts functioning as artwork. The menu is the same here as at the other locations: dozens of burgers, including some made with turkey or vegetables. Another draw is the outdoor patio in back. ♦ Hamburgers ♦ Daily lunch and dinner. No credit cards accepted. 3344 Steiner St (between Lombard and Chestnut Sts). 563.0307 &. Also at: 4138 24th St (between Castro and Diamond Sts). 282.7770; fax 282.1920 &

57 Izzy's Steak & Chops ★★★$$ One of the city's top steak houses, it boasts a lively, saloonlike ambience. The memorabilia-covered walls and the dark wainscoting—topped with a shelf that's lined with every steak sauce and condiment ever made—add considerable charm. The one thing to order here is steak. The assortment of accompaniments—potatoes, roasted carrots and onions, steamed broccoli, and especially the creamed spinach—are excellent, too. ♦ Steak/Seafood ♦ Daily dinner. Reservations recommended. 3349 Steiner St (between Lombard and Chestnut Sts). 563.0487; fax 563.4956 &

57 Flying Kamikazes ★★$$ The name of this funky, New-Wave Japanese restaurant in the Marina says it all—if you're looking for the traditional sushi experience, this place isn't for you. Rather than serene music in the background, teakwood furnishings, and low lighting, you get bright yellow and red decor, uncushioned brick seating, piped-in reggae music, and Godzilla movies playing on a screen behind the bar. But the preparations of sushi are inventive and tasty. There's a menu of small appetizer plates (the Japanese version of tapas) that includes *hamachi* (yellow tail), *ahi* tuna potstickers served with a chili-soy vinegar dipping sauce, and a smoky-tasting grilled giant squid with a velvety roasted-pepper mayonnaise. Executive chef Kioshi Hayakawa turns out fine *nigiri* sushi, such as *ikura* (salmon roe), *maguro* (tuna) or *unagi* (grilled water eel). He has also designed 22 varieties of sushi rolls, including the Flying Kamikaze (spicy tuna and crunchy asparagus wrapped in sushi rice and then enclosed with albacore tuna). ♦ Sushi ♦ Daily dinner. 3339 Steiner St (between Lombard and Chestnut Sts). 567.4903 &

58 Peet's Coffee & Tea Started in Berkeley in 1966, this coffee bar and retail chain has grown to 20 shops (this was the first in San Francisco) and has amassed a following, thanks in part to the rich, earthy taste of the house blend produced by coffee roaster Alfred Peet. The high-ceilinged shop retains its old architectural moldings, and 30 kinds of beans from around the world are prominently displayed. If you buy a pound of coffee you get a free cup of the featured brew; or a free cup of tea for the purchase of a half pound of tea. Coffee and tea paraphernalia are also for sale. ♦ Daily. 2156 Chestnut St (between Steiner and Pierce Sts). 931.8302 &. Also at: Numerous locations throughout the area

58 Andalé Taqueria ★★$ Only in the Marina district would a taco place be as nattily put together as this architectural gem. A profusion of tables clutters an outdoor patio in front, all warmed by a corner fireplace. Inside, a copper pot filled with lacy palms, stippled walls, and wrought-iron fixtures gussy up what is really a fast-food restaurant. Diners order at a counter in front of the kitchen; the food is brought to the table. No lard, canned food, or preservatives are used. Traditional dinners feature *chiles rellenos*, tacos, and tamales, although the best menu choices here are the tacos and burritos filled

99

Pacific Heights/Cow Hollow/The Marina

with rotisserie-roasted chicken or mesquite-grilled beef. The *agua fresca* (freshly made fruit juices) and sangria are also excellent. ♦ Mexican ♦ M-F lunch and dinner; Sa-Su breakfast, lunch, and dinner. No credit cards accepted. 2150 Chestnut St (between Steiner and Pierce Sts). 749.0506 ♿

s. f. gourmet

58 s. f. gourmet A chic shop, it greets customers with an eight-foot replica of a pear hanging from the high entryway ceiling. Inside are such housemade take-out delights as Caesar salad, roasted vegetables, and Chinese chicken salad. Soups include Mexican vegetable, spicy tomato, roasted onion, and corn-and-chili chowder. Among the numerous main courses ready to heat and eat are stuffed pasta shells, vegetable potpie, stuffed peppers, hearty beef stew, and rosemary garlic chicken. The store also stocks bread from the popular **Grace** and **Semifreddi's** bakeries, along with cheeses, bottled waters, beers, wines, packaged products, and specialty items like piquant pickled asparagus and green beans. ♦ Daily. 2128 Chestnut St (between Steiner and Pierce Sts). 441.4800; fax 441.2864 ♿

58 Lucca Delicatessen The whole roast chicken with its bronzed skin flecked with black pepper, the marinated artichoke hearts, the pasta in meat sauce, and the roast turkey parts, all on view in the front window, speak volumes about the quality of this Italian deli. Inside, the tantalizing aromas of garlic and roasting meats make you want to buy one of everything—if you can ever reach the counter, which is always three-deep on weekends. In addition to the smoked tongue, sausage, and all manner of prepared take-away foods, the deli stocks pastas, wine, and other packaged goods. Very good selections of cheese and cold cuts are other draws. ♦ Daily. No credit cards accepted. 2120 Chestnut St (between Steiner and Pierce Sts). 921.7873; fax 921.2402 ♿

58 Pottery Barn This California-based chain just opened its largest store here to carry most of the items previously available only through its catalog. Customers can now see for themselves those rustic pine tables and colorful stained-wood chairs, country cabinets to hold spices and mixing bowls, stainless steel flatware (including some with faux-bone handles), hand-painted pottery, bright kitchen towels, everyday bistro ware in white porcelain, and yellow pottery bowls that replicate Church Gresley's 1864 design. It all adds up to lots of style for not too much money. ♦ Daily. 2100 Chestnut St (at Steiner St). 441.1787; fax 441.5311 ♿. Also at: 1 Embarcadero Center (Battery St, between Sacramento and Clay Sts). 788.6810; fax 788.4819 ♿

59 Home Plate ★★$ Although this place changed hands a few years ago, the crowds that converge for breakfast every weekend don't seem to mind; it has become a neighborhood fixture. The interior has a pleasant minimalist look, with white walls and tables squeezed in a little too tightly. The house-baked scones and coffee that arrive as you sit down make a nice start to the day. Then most people opt for one of the egg dishes—standard combinations, but done very well here. ♦ American ♦ Daily breakfast and lunch. 2274 Lombard St (at Pierce St). 922.4663

60 The California Wine Merchant With its wooden shelves holding the bottles upright for easy browsing, this narrow shop is like a wine library. As the name implies, nearly all the wines are from California, and prices are better than at many of the high-volume shops. Personal service is the key here; the staff is happy to suggest appropriate wines for dinner, and the shop offers free local delivery; it also will ship anywhere in the US for a fee. A monthly newsletter highlights current releases and new arrivals. ♦ M-Sa. 3237 Pierce St (between Lombard and Chestnut Sts). 567.0646 ♿

61 The Chestnut Street Grill ★$ More than a hundred sandwiches named after well-known locals, and a penchant for making up whimsical quotations, have put this cafe on the culinary map. For example, the Andy Leitner sandwich "ruins roofs and razors," and consists of organic peanut butter, tomatoes, and bacon. The lengthy menu also lists more than a dozen burgers. The checkered tablecloths, bentwood chairs, brown ceiling, and white walls contribute to the place's cozy feel, but many people prefer the garden tables in back on sunny days. ♦ American ♦ Daily lunch and dinner. 2231 Chestnut St (between Pierce and Scott Sts). 922.5558; fax 922.5274 ♿

World Wrapps

61 World Wrapps ★$ The name refers to this place's flavored tortillas, which are stuffed

Pacific Heights/Cow Hollow/The Marina

with globally inspired designer combinations of meats and vegetables. There's mango salsa and grilled snapper in a spinach tortilla; Peking duck with *hoisin* sauce in a plain tortilla; barbecued chicken in a tomato tortilla; and teriyaki tofu in a whole wheat tortilla. Fruit smoothies are the featured drinks and the varieties include raspberry; banana date; pineapple ginger; and peanut butter banana. The food can be carried away or eaten in the bright blue-and-white room furnished with multicolored tables and chairs. ♦ International ♦ Daily. No credit cards accepted. 2257 Chestnut St (between Pierce and Scott Sts). 563.9727 ♿

62 Judy's Cafe ★$ The quaint, sunny interior and down-home breakfasts offer a little taste of country life in the big city. The menu features a dozen omelettes prepared with a twist: taco style, with ground chuck and salsa; Italian, with sausage, mushrooms, and marinara sauce; Russian, with black caviar and cream cheese; and Nordic, with smoked salmon. The Texas version is filled with chili, and the farm-style omelette comes with ham, onions, and home fries. Or opt for one of the more traditional egg dishes, all of which are served with pumpkin loaf, blueberry muffins, English muffins, or honey-wheat toast. Sandwiches and soups are lunchtime mainstays. ♦ American ♦ Daily breakfast and lunch. No credit cards accepted. 2268 Chestnut St (between Pierce and Scott Sts). 922.4588

The Grove
SAN FRANCISCO

62 The Grove ★$ One of the best places to hang out in and get a feel for the neighborhood, this eatery is as comfortable as a well-worn leather chair. The rough plank flooring, dark wood wainscoting, heavy wood tables, and craftsmanlike lights and chairs add warm touches to the dining room's rustic interior. Display cases in back hold an array of sweets and pastries and such savory preparations as lasagna and burritos that can be heated up in the microwave. ♦ Coffeehouse ♦ Daily breakfast, lunch, and dinner until 11PM; W-Sa until midnight. 2250 Chestnut St (between Pierce and Scott Sts). 474.4843; fax 474.9734 ♿

62 E'Angelo Restaurant ★★$ One of the city's most popular pasta houses, it has squeezed an open kitchen and a dining room into a narrow storefront. It's so crowded that parties fewer than six might as well be sharing tables. The fake wood paneling, linoleum, and blue-checkered tablecloths aren't much to look at, but no one seems to mind the downscale decor. Animated veteran waiters practically dance around the tables, and the simple pastas and salads are homey and satisfying. The carbonara combines thick noodles, mushrooms, and nubbins of crisp bacon enveloped in a delicious cream sauce. Eggplant parmigiana is liberally doused with housemade tomato sauce, mozzarella, and parmesan. Meat courses, such as leg of lamb, tend to taste warmed over, but such side dishes as garlicky sautéed spinach and crisply roasted potatoes are truly outstanding. Another winner is the thin-crusted pizza topped with anchovies, mushrooms, or salami. ♦ Italian ♦ Tu-Sa dinner. No credit cards accepted. 2234 Chestnut St (between Pierce and Scott Sts). 567.6164; fax 928.3727 ♿

Some Like It Hot
A FIERY FOOD EMPORIUM

63 Some Like It Hot! A Fiery Food Emporium The pungent aroma of chili pervades this bright shop, which is lined with more than a hundred kinds of tantalizingly hot sauces imported from around the world. Check out Habañero Hot Hot Hot! Pepper Sauce, and Ol' Gringo Gourmet Green Chile Sauce from Hatch Valley, New Mexico. They even publish a 12-page catalog, so you can keep up with what's hot without having to leave your home. ♦ Tu-Su. 3208 Scott St (between Lombard and Chestnut Sts). 441.7468, 800/806.4468; fax 510/482.1192 ♿

63 Saji Japanese Cuisine ★★★ $$ This modest little place may not look like much from the outside, but a wealth of expertly prepared sushi awaits within its walls. Sit at the bar and watch owner Hideki Makiyama do his magic with the sparkling fresh fish, or sit on cushions at one of the low-slung tables in the tatami room. Any of the *nigiri* sushi is wonderful, but once you've tried a few pieces ask a chef to make you one of his specialties. In addition to sushi there's a full Japanese menu that features dishes such as chicken teriyaki, tempura, and crispy soft-shell crab. ♦ Japanese ♦ Tu-Su dinner (until midnight Friday and Saturday). 3232 Scott St (between Lombard and Chestnut Sts). 931.0563

Pacific Heights/Cow Hollow/The Marina

64 Paragon ★★$$ The crowd of young diners at this handsome, bar-dominated restaurant gives it the feel of an ongoing college party—except that the food is every bit as good as the cocktails. The short, changing menu might include scallops topped with a mound of fried leeks, flank steak with garlic mashed potatoes and onion rings, and seared *ahi* tuna with a citrus aioli, ringed with potato chips and a salad of baby greens. ♦ American ♦ Daily dinner. 3251 Scott St (between Lombard and Chestnut Sts). 922.2456; fax 922.1740

64 Olive's Gourmet Pizza ★★$$ A slice of North Beach in the Marina, this eatery produces terrific pizzas with a delectable cornmeal-and-olive-oil crust. Toppings range from the traditional to the creative, but they never stray too far from the mainstream. A shrimp pizza is accented with red onions, diced lemons, and capers. Another features several types of cheese, andouille sausage, corn, red peppers, onions, and Italian herbs. The mushroom-and-roasted-eggplant pizza tastes so meaty that you'd hardly believe it's vegetarian; and the pizza with fennel-spiced sausage, roasted green peppers, tomato sauce, and mozzarella merits its status as a classic. A few well-prepared pastas and salads round out the menu. Try the dense almond cake for dessert. ♦ Italian ♦ Daily lunch and dinner. No credit cards accepted. 3249 Scott St (between Lombard and Chestnut Sts). 567.4488

65 Scott's Seafood ★$$ Popular with out-of-towners and local traditionalists, this seafood spot sails on safe waters with predictable preparations that disappoint only because they don't excite. The grilled fish is the best bet. This is also a good place to sample the classic San Francisco fish stew, cioppino. Other pluses are the comfortable, slightly nautical setting with dark wood and brass, and the crisp service. ♦ Seafood ♦ Daily lunch and dinner. 2400 Lombard St (at Scott St). 563.8988; fax 563.1897 ♿. Also at: 3 Embarcadero Center (Sacramento St, between Drumm and Davis Sts). 981.0622; fax 296.9501 ♿

65 Samui Thai Cuisine ★★$ Named for an island off the coast of Thailand, this place evokes a tropical atmosphere with a long fish tank and a couple of artificial palm trees. It is one of the few restaurants offering southern Thai fare. To best explore the flavors of that region, try the seafood specials and the hot-and-sour shrimp soup. Other good dishes include the green-papaya salad, which makes a refreshing, crunchy contrast to the soup. The coconut-flecked Thai crepe wraps around a filling of chicken and peanuts. Broiled eggplant gets a lift from both mint and basil. ♦ Thai ♦ Tu-Sa lunch and dinner; Su dinner. 2414 Lombard St (at Scott St). 563.4405; fax 563.3793

65 Lhasa Moon ★★$ Owner Losang Gyatso and his girlfriend, Tsering Wangmo, have opened the first Tibetan restaurant west of the Rockies. Featured on the menu are a number of homestyle Tibetan dishes, some of which have Indian influences (such as a sauce made with onions, tomatoes, and ginger). Stews, soups, and hand-rolled pasta are also offered. Standouts include *momos,* a juicy dumpling similar to Chinese pot stickers that can be filled with a mixture of beef and herb-flavored vegetables, chicken, or a combination of vegetables; *churul,* blue cheese soup with minced beef; lamb curry; herbed fried chicken; and shredded beef with sliced potatoes and spinach. A few of the dishes are flavored with *emma,* a Tibetan wild peppercorn. The interior is painted white with hunter green wainscoting, and in keeping with their heritage, the owners display framed photographs of Tibet before it was occupied by China on the walls, and Tibetan music plays in the background. ♦ Tibetan ♦ Tu-F lunch and dinner; Sa-Su dinner. 2420 Lombard St (at Scott St). 674.9898

66 Bechelli's Coffee Shop ★★$ This is the real thing: an honest-to-goodness Deco-style diner with a horseshoe-shaped counter. The walls are lined with stills from films that opened in the theater next door back in the 1940s. It all conjures a nostalgia for the golden age of film, and for the food of that time. The hamburger and thick french fries are a delight, and the all-American, housemade apple pie, cherry pie, and chocolate cake are classic. ♦ American ♦ Daily breakfast and lunch. No credit cards accepted. 2346 Chestnut St (between Scott and Divisadero Sts). 346.1801

67 Cafe Marimba ★$$ Louise Clement and Reed Hearon, who put together the wildly popular **LuLu**, here turn their talents to Mexican food. Highlights include the mole dishes from Oaxaca and the large family-style

Pacific Heights/Cow Hollow/The Marina

platters, each heaped with grilled chicken, pork ribs, rock shrimp, or mushrooms with tomato salsa. Among the unusual seafood dishes are tacos filled with octopus or red snapper. More traditional enchiladas and quesadillas also are offered, all served with housemade sauces. The decor is stunning: Two palm trees are stationed at the front entrance, and the boldly colored interior boasts a collection of Mexican folk art. The downside is the noise level and some sloppiness in the presentation—sometimes the entrées are not hot enough, temperature-wise. ♦ Mexican ♦ M dinner; Tu-F lunch and dinner; Sa-Su brunch and dinner. 2317 Chestnut St (between Scott and Divisadero Sts). 776.1506; fax 776.5104 &

67 Cucina Paradiso ★$$ An airy two-story setting, a bustling open kitchen, and exceptionally welcoming service earn this simple Italian place extra points. The patio in back is surrounded by white trellises and flowering plants. The arugula salad, simply dressed and topped with a few grapes and shavings of parmesan, is a completely satisfying starter. Heartier appetites will be sated by the crisp ball of fried risotto with a melted-cheese center. And don't miss the saltimbocca—slices of veal sautéed with white wine, sage, and a thin slice of prosciutto, served with parmesan-dusted spinach and a risotto that changes nightly. ♦ Italian ♦ Daily dinner. 2373 Chestnut St (at Divisadero St). 563.0217 &

THE BUCHANAN GRILL

68 Buchanan Grill ★★$$ "Classic" describes this busy bar/restaurant, where every inch of wall is covered with pictures of sports personalities. Many people eat in the green-wainscoted area opposite the bar, but the back room, with six skylights, is quieter. Those who like their Buffalo chicken wings explosively hot will go for the ones here; they're doused in red-hot pepper sauce and accompanied by cooling celery sticks and blue cheese dipping sauce. Also try the crisp onion-potato pancake, topped with smoked salmon and capers and drizzled with sour cream. Main courses include such comfort food as pot roast and mashed potatoes in a rich mushroom gravy; there's also grilled salmon with avocado salsa, a stellar steak sandwich with sautéed onions and mushrooms, and a juicy, thick hamburger. And don't miss the thin-crusted hot apple tart, topped with a melting scoop of vanilla ice cream. ♦ American ♦ Daily lunch and dinner. 3653 Buchanan St (between Bay and N Point Sts). 346.8727; fax 346.8781 &

greens RESTAURANT

69 Greens Restaurant ★★$$ The Zen Buddhists who opened this place in 1979 brought vegetarian food into the mainstream; the bright flavors and creative combinations captivated even dedicated meat eaters. Now, however, other restaurants offer light, meatless fare, and it has fallen behind; some dishes are rich in cheese and oil. Still, there are always treats on the nightly changing menu: *enchiladas verdes* with mushrooms, peppers, corn, red onions, two cheeses, and green sauce; curried vegetables; and light-as-air eggplant fritters, which come with a teriyaki-style dipping sauce and English cucumbers in an orange marinade. Another winner is the pizza with two kinds of mushrooms, onions, and two kinds of cheese. Among the best desserts are apricot-boysenberry cobbler, rich mocha *pots de crème* (custard), and chocolate-raspberry tart with whipped cream. Note: The five-course prix-fixe menu on Saturdays is a very good buy. The wine list, which covers nine pages, is exceptional. An added bonus is the spectacular location on a pier overlooking the bay and the Golden Gate Bridge. The expansive dining room boasts a lofty, exposed-beam ceiling and striking flower arrangements. The bakery, just inside the door, features great breads and also sells take-out items. ♦ Vegetarian ♦ M dinner; Tu-Sa lunch and dinner; Su brunch. Reservations recommended. Fort Mason, Building A (at the foot of Buchanan St). 771.6222 &

Bests

Francis Ford Coppola
Film Director/Producer

Yank Sing: The best dim sum.

Brandy Ho's: A stylish restaurant with terrific food.

Tommaso's: In their 60th year in **North Beach.** The first pizzeria in North Beach.

Hunan Homes: Spicy specialties are great.

Japantown/Lower Haight

Japantown—"Nihonmachi" to its residents—is a surprising oasis, a pristine village located within the approximate boundaries of **Octavia** and **Fillmore Streets**, and **Geary Boulevard** and **California Street**. After World War II, when Japantown's residents returned from internment camps to find their former homes occupied, they scattered about the city and into the suburbs. Although the city's Japanese-Americans have fully integrated into the Bay Area, the heart of their community remains here.

The area's commercial and cultural focus is **Japan Center**, which covers a three-block stretch around Fillmore and **Laguna** Streets. It houses the North American headquarters of the **Ikenobo Ikebana Society**, the flower-arranging school, with its artful displays in the windows, as well as the **Kintetsu** and **Kinokuniya** shopping malls; they are connected by the arched **Webster Street Bridge of Shops**, fashioned after the Ponte Vecchio in Florence. Other attractions include the cobblestoned **Buchanan Mall**, with flowering plum and cherry trees, and **Peace Plaza**, with its towering pagoda, a gift from Japan. Relax with a shiatsu massage or enjoy a refreshing communal bath at the **Kabuki Hot Springs** (1750 Geary Blvd at Fillmore St, 922.6002).

An 800-car parking lot makes the center easily accessible. And a block away is **Nichi Bei Kai** (1759 Sutter St at Buchanan St, 921.1782; fax 931.1826), housing a cultural center and a small, peaceful room especially designed for the traditional Japanese tea ceremony (call for an appointment). The tearoom was actually brought from Japan and reassembled here.

To people unfamiliar with Japanese culture, Japantown may seem intimidating, but the staffs at restaurants and shops are generally friendly and welcoming. There are three major grocery stores, several bakeries and confection shops, and a great-for-browsing hardware store that stocks both Japanese and American wares. The Japanese aesthetic can be explored at the **Maruwa Foods** supermarket, with its displays of perfect, sushi-quality fish fillets; at sister shops **Asakichi** and **Asakichi II**, where bamboo shelves hold an impressive collection of metal and china teapots; and at **Ma-Shi-Ko Folkcraft**, with its antique oval sushi carriers.

Of the more than 40 traditional Japanese restaurants, **Mifune**, done in cheerful red with dark wood appointments, is a wonderful place to enjoy a generous bowl of *soba* (buckwheat) or *udon* (white) noodles. Sample tempura and a broad range of dishes in a rustic setting at **Sanppo**. One of the most popular eating attractions, though not necessarily the best, is **Isobune Sushi**, where sushi dishes travel around the counter on waterborne rafts. **YOYO Tsumami Bistro**, a new eatery at the Miyako Hotel, is a very good choice for a full dinner or drinks and *tsumami* (small plates of appetizers).

That this clean, orderly, almost serene area should butt up against the Lower Haight, which typifies urban grittiness, perfectly illustrates the diversity of San Francisco neighborhoods. In recent years, **Haight Street** has reinvented itself—evolving from the druggy peace-and-love era of the sixties through the outrageous punk rebellion to a new era of individuality in search of freedom. Here, body-pierced young people with brightly colored hair and leather clothing live in harmony with young marrieds with kids, gay couples, and seniors.

Ethnic restaurants, done on the cheap, cluster here. Catering to the young folk in the area, prices are low, service is casual (but can be absentminded), and many of the offerings are vegetarian. **India Oven** produces great tandoori and gutsy Indian food in soothing surroundings; **Thep Phanom** is one of the best Thai restaurants in the city and has the look of a well-heeled grandmother's parlor; and the **Squat & Gobble Cafe** serves hearty, fresh breakfasts and lunch to a mob of post-punk patrons. The Lower Haight may look rough, but it can be fun.

---

1 Neecha Thai ★★$ A neighborhood favorite, this place offers well-balanced Thai combinations that straddle the sweet-sour axis. No new ground is broken, but the coconut-chicken soup, chicken with basil, and Thai crepe are all winners. What with the brick and dark wood, the place is reminiscent of an English pub. ♦ Thai ♦ M-F lunch and dinner; Sa-Su dinner. 2100 Sutter St (at Steiner St). 922.9419 &

2 Tre Fratelli ★$ The food and the plain decor don't dazzle, but that doesn't dissuade the local fans who come for pasta and a simple salad. The service can be slow, but people feel as comfortable here as they do in their own home. ♦ Italian ♦ Daily dinner. 2101 Sutter St (at Steiner St). 931.0701; fax 447.5553 &

3 Patisserie Delanghe This is one of the top stops for classic French pastries. Owner Dominique Delanghe has a great feel for balance, which makes all her creations sparkle without being overly sweet. Napoleons are our favorites; order ahead and pick them up right before you want to serve them. The filling is cool and creamy, and the puff pastry crumbles at the touch of a fork. In fact, Delanghe's puff pastry is so excellent that many professional caterers buy sheets of the raw dough here. ♦ Tu-Su. 1890 Fillmore St (at Bush St). 923.0711 &

4 Trio Cafe ★$ Several years ago, under different owners, this was the gathering place for a cross section of affluent business mavens, designers, and artists. All the hubbub has died down, but the cafe is still popular for

Japantown/Lower Haight

a light breakfast and all-day fare, including poached eggs, scones, *pizzettas,* and simple open-face sandwiches. The sunny blue-and-white environment lends a cheery note to an early morning café au lait. ♦ Cafe ♦ Daily breakfast and lunch. 1830 Fillmore St (between Sutter and Bush Sts). 563.2248

4 Pizza Inferno ★$ True to this place's hellish name, the ceiling, walls, and floor are painted in a swirling pattern that seems to give off a red, vertiginous glow. Amid such surreal surroundings, the square pizzas, with a thin, crisp crust, fit right in. In addition to the classic toppings are some interesting variations, including one version with goat cheese, mozzarella, and walnuts, and another with spicy Thai chicken and cilantro or peanuts. The house salad with balsamic vinaigrette is a good way to start. ♦ Pizzeria ♦ Daily lunch and dinner. 1800 Fillmore St (at Sutter St). 775.1800

5 Cafe Kati ★★★$$ Kirk Webber is an artist, and this whimsical neighborhood restaurant is his studio. Few places in the city offer such interestingly designed presentations. In his version of Caesar salad, the romaine leaves are bunched together and stand straight up in the center of the plate. His desserts look like replicas of a Japanese garden. This all could come off as silly, except that it's fun, and the flavors are always wonderful. The monthly-changing menu offers a host of intriguing combinations: steamed mussels and Thai salmon sausage with red curry; chicken breast stuffed with roquefort and walnuts and moistened with sage brown butter; crispy salmon fillet with Chinese five spices and a light oxtail broth; and filet mignon with house-dried tomatoes and a frothy herbed zabaglione. With all that fussing, dishes can emerge from the kitchen slowly. This is not the place to grab a bite; it's designed for an evening's entertainment, in cozy surroundings. ♦ Eclectic/Californian ♦ Tu-Su dinner. 1963 Sutter St (between Webster and Fillmore Sts). 775.7313; fax 379.9952

Sushi is delicious with a dipping sauce of soy sauce and wasabi (green Japanese horseradish). The proper way to dip sushi is to pick it up gently, then rotate it so that just the fish touches the soy-wasabi mixture. Dipping the rice causes it to fall apart. Place the whole piece of sushi in the mouth, with the fish side touching the tongue first.

5 Yamada Seika Confectionery For the past 15 years, the husband-and-wife team here has been turning out delicate rice crackers and sweet confections, many stuffed with bean paste. The sweets at this petite shop are displayed in the case in front and dried peas and other snacks and crackers occupy the side shelves. The husband is always toiling among the large sacks of flour and bakery equipment; the wife is so shy that she'll bolt to the back if asked too many questions. ♦ Tu-Su. 1955 Sutter St (between Webster and Fillmore Sts). 922.3848

6 Benkyodo Confectioners ★$ A popular gathering place for Japanese-Americans, this modest cafe features traditional bean-paste confections and light lunches. ♦ Japanese ♦ M-Sa breakfast and lunch. 1747 Buchanan St (at Sutter St). 922.1244

6 Sushi-A ★★★$$ The "A" of the name just might refer to the quality of the food here, because most of the numerous offerings are winners. The sushi and sashimi are exceptional, the tempura is light and feathery, and the clay-pot seafood dishes are not to be missed. The prawn, for example, combines at least a dozen shrimp, noodles, several types of mushrooms, scallions, cabbage, and tofu in a very light broth; the dipping sauce magically brings the food to life. If you can't make up your mind, try a combination dinner or the *kaiseki* dinner, which consists of many small portions geared to the season. The gray ceilings and recessed lighting create a restful backdrop for the exemplary fare. ♦ Sushi/Japanese ♦ M, Th-Su lunch and dinner. 1737 Buchanan St (at Sutter St). 931.4685; fax 931.4120

7 Yakitori West $$ Although it's popular with tourists, there's better food elsewhere in Japantown. The sukiyaki has a barnyard flavor, the tempura is heavy, and the sushi doesn't taste fresh. The once-pleasant room with shoji screens and lanterns now looks a little tired. ♦ Japanese ♦ Daily lunch and dinner. 1707 Buchanan St (at Post St). 567.6552

7 Sanppo ★★$$ Celadon walls, dark wood screens, and the inset wood ceiling give this tiny spot a Japanese country feel. Although the food covers a broad range, it's all done surprisingly well. Offerings include yakitori (grilled skewered meat and vegetables), *nabemono* (clay-pot dishes), *udon* and *soba* noodles, *donburi* (rice), a particularly delicate and delicious tempura, and many other specialties, mostly seafood. Popular dishes include grilled seafood and *katsu*-marinated salmon, in which the fish is flavored with the lees of sake. Eggplant sandwiched between slices of marinated beef is a great choice for meat eaters. The meal comes with a pleasant miso soup and a salad with a light mustard

Japantown/Lower Haight

dressing. ♦ Japanese ♦ Tu-Sa lunch and dinner; Su dinner. 1702 Post St (at Buchanan St). 346.3486

8 Super Koyama This neat and clean full-service Japanese grocery store has a good selection of produce, packaged goods, and sweets. The fish is a standout. No other store in the city has such a wide selection of sushi-quality seafood. ♦ Daily. 1790 Sutter St (at Buchanan St). 921.6529

9 Sanko Cooking Supply For fun souvenirs, come here to buy those plastic sushi replicas seen in all the Japantown restaurant windows. The shop also carries teapots, sake sets, chopstick rests, rice cookers, rice bowls, serving plates, kitchen equipment, and just about everything else related to Japanese cooking and eating. ♦ Daily. 1758 Buchanan St (at Sutter St). 922.8331; fax 922.8365

10 Iroha ★★$$ Dark wood screens between the tables and rich red walls give this second-floor restaurant an upmarket look. Skip the heavy tempura and try the house specialty, *ramen* noodles, which come with toppings of chicken, beef, pork, seafood, or vegetables. Other winning dishes include *yakitori* and *gyoza* (Japanese pot stickers). ♦ Japanese ♦ Daily lunch and dinner. 1728 Buchanan St (at Post St). 922.0321

10 Soko Hardware Lovers of hardware stores and gadgets will be happy browsing this shop, where most of the wares are Japanese. This is the place for inexpensive tea and sake sets, rice bowls, vases, rice cookers, hibachis, cleavers, and utensils. Varieties of chopsticks and chopstick rests number more than a hundred and are very reasonably priced. There's also a great selection of American products, including the indispensable Swing Away can opener. ♦ M-Sa. 1698 Post St (at Buchanan St). 931.5510; fax 931.4927

10 Soko Interiors The window of this shop, next door to **Soko Hardware** (see above), displays primarily cement garden sculptures; inside, more upscale housewares are for sale, including tea sets. Either ask for admittance at **Soko Hardware** or call the store for an appointment. ♦ M-Sa by appointment. 1672 Post St (between Laguna and Buchanan Sts). 931.5510; fax 931.4927

11 Uoki K. Sakai Company The spitting image of an American neighborhood grocery store, except its eight-foot shelves are lined with soy sauces and row after row of dried fish no bigger than minnows. Although packaged products predominate, there's a small selection of produce, meat, free-range chickens, and fish. ♦ Daily. 1656 Post St (between Laguna and Buchanan Sts). 921.0515

11 Korea House ★★$$$ Join the crowds at this dark, woody restaurant for a late-night, do-it-yourself barbecue. In addition to such typical fare as thinly sliced beef and marinated chicken, there are a few exotic meats to toss on the table's grill, including beef tongue and tripe. ♦ Korean ♦ Daily lunch and dinner; F-Sa until 3AM. 1640 Post St (at Laguna St). 563.1388; fax 563.3480

12 Cafe Majestic ★★$$$ Many people consider this restaurant in the **Hotel Majestic** one of the most romantic in the city. The Victorian ornamentation, flickering candles, gilded mirrors, and piano music put diners in the mood to woo. The seasonal menu has both Mediterranean and Asian accents: Roast breast of duck may be matched with shiitake mushrooms and Beijing pancakes; rack of lamb may be presented on a bed of lentils with spaghetti squash and mushrooms; scallops may be served in a broth perfumed with basil and ginger. Occasionally the kitchen misses slightly, but the excellent service and ambience are ample compensation. ♦ Californian ♦ Daily breakfast and dinner; Su brunch. 1500 Sutter St (at Gough St). 776.6400; fax 673.7331

13 Asakichi More than 60 individual teapots and many styles of rice bowls are crowded into this tiny, pretty shop in **Japan Center**. Also on display are unique tea sets, pottery, and rectangular sushi plates. ♦ Daily. Kinokuniya Building, 1581 Webster St (at Post St). 921.2147; fax 921.2147. Also at: Webster St Bridge. 921.3821; fax 921.3821

Japantown/Lower Haight

14 Isuzu Restaurant ★★$ The grandmotherly waitresses' friendly smiles light up this place. With round rice-paper lanterns, bamboo partitions, and red accents, it looks a bit like an upscale cafeteria, but the interesting menu boasts a wide selection, and the food is quite good. Spicy *udon* noodles are brought to the table in a lidded iron pot; nestling inside with the noodles are prawns, tofu, chunks of fish, carrots, cabbage, and scallions, all studded with chili flakes. The tempura has a light, feathery texture, and the standard array of sushi is better than average. Numerous clay-pot dishes also are offered. ♦ Sushi/Japanese ♦ M, W-Su lunch and dinner. Kinokuniya Building, 1581 Webster St (at Post St). 922.2290 ♿

15 Maruwa Foods Each shelf at this spotless modern grocery store is perfectly stacked, as if waiting to be filmed for a commercial. Most products are Japanese, and there's a full case of take-out fare, including breaded fish and noodle salads. The produce department stocks such ingredients for stir-fries as vacuum-packed slices of lotus root and cabbage, and the fish selections include sushi-quality octopus, tuna, and cuttlefish. Pork, beef, and chicken are thinly sliced for sukiyaki, and several kinds of marinated fish are ready to be taken home and placed on the grill. ♦ Daily. 1737 Post St (at Webster St). 563.1901; fax 563.0716 ♿

16 YOYO Tsumami Bistro ★★★$$ A few years ago, Elka Gilmore blew into town and opened **Elka**, a Franco-Japanese bistro in the **Miyako Hotel** that was a great success for a while. After Gilmore moved on to other things, the quality took a nosedive, and the place closed soon after. But now it's reopened with a new name and a new twist on the same idea. For starters, don't miss the ginger-pickled salmon with wasabi crème fraîche; the *ahi* tuna tartar with miso and eggplant; or the roasted fennel with star anise and olives. Entrées include tempura salad; roasted cod with succotash; and braised lamb shank with *azuki*-bean ragout. The dining room is striking (yet more comfortable and casual than in its previous incarnation), with saturated colors, mobilelike light fixtures that seem to be in flight, and very good black-and-white photographs. The upstairs bar and cocktail area is perfect for a *tsumami* (a small plate of appetizers) or two. ♦ Franco-Japanese ♦ Daily lunch and dinner. 1611 Post St (at Laguna St). 922.7788; fax 921.0417 ♿

17 Seoul Garden ★★$$ Deep in the heart of Japantown is one of the city's most beautiful Korean restaurants, which comprises two booth-lined rooms. On the grills set on the tables, diners get to cook their own marinated squid, beef, chicken, and seafood. Chef-prepared specialties include steamed fish and braised ribs. The *kimchi* (pickled cabbage) here is particularly good and packs a spicy punch. ♦ Korean ♦ Daily lunch and dinner. Tasamak Plaza (at Geary Blvd and Buchanan St). 563.7664 ♿

18 Isobune Sushi $ At what is probably the most popular sushi bar in Japantown, diners pluck their selections from little boats that float around the counter while two sushi chefs continuously replenish the stock. At the end of the meal the waitress tabulates the bill according to the empty trays in front of each diner. Unfortunately, the sushi leaves a little to be desired, and the rice often is mushy. Best bets are the bright orange flying-fish roe that burst in the mouth and the bright-green fish roe flavored with wasabi. One tip: Keep an eye on what the chef places on the boat and nab quickly to avoid any raw fish that's circled the counter too many times. ♦ Sushi ♦ Daily lunch and dinner. Kintetsu Mall, 1737 Post St (at Webster St). 563.1030; fax 921.3857 ♿

19 Koji Osakaya ★★$$ *Yakitori*, noodles, teriyaki, sushi—you name it, it's on the menu here. But it's best to bypass the sushi for the excellent *ramen* noodles in either miso or light soy broth, topped with deep-fried pork, vegetables, or barbecued meats. The crunchy tempura is served with an enticing, earthy dipping sauce with grated daikon. White walls and dark wood screens between the tables give this restaurant a clean, casual look, and the service is particularly pleasant. ♦ Japanese ♦ Daily lunch and dinner. Kintetsu Mall, 1737 Post St (at Webster St). 922.2728; fax 567.4211 ♿

20 Benihana of Tokyo ★$$$ Billed as the "Japanese Steakhouse," this chain is known for its chefs' fancy knife work as they cook to order on the hot iron grills inset on each table. All dinners include onion soup, salad, shrimp appetizer, vegetables, rice, and ice cream. ♦ Japanese/Steak house ♦ Daily lunch and dinner. Kintetsu Mall, 1737 Post St (at Webster St). 563.4844; fax 563.8022 ♿

Japantown/Lower Haight

21 Murata's Café Hana ★$ Perfect for a shopping break, this spot offers nothing but rich treats, including cream cakes and cookies, to have with coffee or tea. The free-form black tables spill out into the mall. ♦ Coffeehouse ♦ Daily. Kintetsu Mall, 1737 Post St (at Webster St). 567.9133; fax 567.1710 ♿

22 May's Coffee Shop $ In a corner of the rectangular kitchen here, workers pour a thin batter into fish molds, squeeze in bean paste, press the halves together, and bake them. The result is a slightly sweet golden-brown goldfish (not the standard fishbowl variety); they're sold piping hot, a dollar apiece. Along with cheap but filling teriyaki, the cafe serves such Western diner food as hamburgers, hot dogs, and breakfasts. ♦ Cafe ♦ Daily breakfast and lunch. Kintetsu Mall, 1737 Post St (at Webster St). 346.4020 ♿

23 Mifune ★★$ People line up for quick bites at this inexpensive noodle emporium featuring 20 hot dishes, a dozen cold, and about as many *donburi* dishes. Each combination can be ordered with either *udon* or *soba*. The minimal interior with dark wood and red walls gives the bustling place a sleek look. ♦ Japanese ♦ Daily lunch and dinner. Kintetsu Mall, 1737 Post St (at Webster St). 922.0337 ♿

24 Kushi Tsuru ★★$$ This is a top stop for broiled salmon, mackerel, or eel, all crisply coated and slightly smoky. Other offerings include battered, skewered, then deep-fried meats and vegetables that are crisper and more substantial than tempura. The pork is a standout (the beef less so), and the whole asparagus spears are delicious. Tempura and sushi are respectable, but not outstanding. The *bento* box (a compartmentalized tray) contains tempura, tuna sashimi, cooked squash and daikon, broiled salmon, sushi rolls, and rice. Noodle cravers who can't get into **Mifune**, next door, can sample the fine *udon* here. ♦ Japanese ♦ M, W-Su lunch and dinner. Kintetsu Mall, 1737 Post St (at Webster St). 922.9202 ♿

25 Asakichi II Dozens of cast-iron teapots fill the bamboo shelves that zigzag across the center of this narrow shop, a sister to **Asakichi** (see page 107). The teapots look more like museum pieces than functional kitchen equipment, but functional they are;

they include detailed instructions on how to use and care for them. Also on display are wind chimes, sculptures, and other cast-iron and bronze pieces. ♦ Daily. Webster St Bridge (near Post St). 921.3821; fax 921.3821 ♿. Also at: Kinokuniya Building, 1581 Webster St (at Post St). 921.2147; fax 921.2147 ♿

26 Kame Sushi ★★$ One glance at the fish in the display case will tell what connoisseurs already know: This is where to find some of the freshest sushi in town. It's a tiny, inconspicuous spot, with only a few tables, vinyl chairs, a television set, and an eight-seat sushi counter presided over by a single sushi master. Try the octopus, halibut, and the wonderful tuna. ♦ Sushi ♦ Tu-Su lunch and dinner. Kinokuniya Building, 1581 Webster St (at Post St). 921.5215 ♿

27 Sapporo-ya ★$ With a noodle machine in the window and stacked boxes of noodles near the door, it's no surprise this country-style restaurant is most popular for its giant bowls of *ramen* noodles. An unusual offering is *okonomiyaki*, a rice-flour and egg pancake that is filled with either a shrimp or beef mixture, then sprinkled with dried bonito flakes and drizzled with Worcestershire sauce. ♦ Japanese ♦ Daily lunch and dinner. Kinokuniya Building, 1581 Webster St (at Post St). 563.7400 ♿

28 Ma-Shi-Ko Folkcraft Of particular interest here is the brushed Mashiko pottery, whose images are delicately painted on, often with enamel, a decorative technique that goes back seven centuries. The shop also sells interesting antique oval sushi carriers, cherry-wood teapots, cedar or kiri-wood vases, and classic Japanese pottery and serving pieces. ♦ M, W-Su. Kinokuniya Building, 1581 Webster St (at Post St). 346.0748 ♿

29 Kinokuniya Bookstore This sprawling bookstore has the best inventory of Japanese books and magazines in the city. In addition to Japanese-language cookbooks, there are several shelves of all kinds of Asian cookbooks in English. The collection explores many traditional culinary arts, including sushi making, and also carries such newer-fangled titles as *New Salads: Quick Recipes from Japan*. Browsers will find vegetarian and macrobiotic guides, a selection of Japanese food magazines, as well as gardening books

109

Japantown/Lower Haight

that show how to grow Japanese vegetables at home. ♦ Daily. Kinokuniya Building, 1581 Webster St (at Post St). 567.7625; fax 567.4109 &

SPAGHETTI WESTERN

30 Spaghetti Western ★$ Plentiful portions and a grunge atmosphere are what this Haight hangout is all about. A dizzying black-and-white floor, bright colored walls, cow skulls, and yokes add up to a quirky decor. Eggs come in many guises: in an Irish breakfast with brown bread, bacon, and home fries; in a Cajun version with andouille sausage; and with chilies and cheese for a Mexican preparation. Other draws include fluffy homemade biscuits and moist pancakes served with maple syrup. The lunch menu includes hamburgers, vegetable burgers, and grilled chicken with chilies. Service is a little scattered but good-natured, which seems to suit the mood of the crowd. ♦ Californian ♦ Daily breakfast and lunch. 576 Haight St (between Fillmore and Steiner Sts). 864.8461

30 The Mad Dog in the Fog ★$ At this brew pub, locals like to kick back with a pint of bitters, throw a few darts, and scarf up some pub grub—there's a good version of shepherd's pie, a ploughman's lunch, and sausages and potatoes. The vinyl chairs may be a bit torn and shabby, but the barnlike space is comfortable and welcoming. ♦ English/Irish ♦ Daily lunch and dinner. 530 Haight St (between Fillmore and Steiner Sts). 626.7279 &

Some Japanese restaurants offer a special multicourse dinner that's arranged in advance with the chef, usually on a day's notice. Called a *kaiseki* dinner, it may include up to a dozen small dishes. Traditionally the meal begins with an hors d'oeuvre, followed by a clear soup, raw fish, special side dish, a broiled dish, a boiled dish, salad, a fried dish, rice-miso soup, and a pickled vegetable. Green tea, fruit, and a sweet dish conclude the repast. The cost is usually about $50 per person.

Many Japanese restaurants display plastic models of the dishes they offer on their menus. Don't be put off by these "fakes," especially if you don't know your *soba* from your *udon*. (Hint: They're both noodles served in soup with other savory ingredients.)

---

31 Ali Baba's Cave ★$ Although the name has changed (it was **Narghile Cafe & Restaurant**), the Middle Eastern food and ambience here have remained pretty much the same. From the kitchen come platters of falafel, hummus, cabbage rolls, and dolmas. Sandwiches and couscous are also available, as are many types of coffee, including strong Turkish cappuccino. The place has a peaceful yet slightly exotic feel, thanks to the green fabric swags covering the ceiling and stucco walls, and the pounded copper surface behind the bar. ♦ Middle Eastern ♦ Daily lunch and dinner until midnight; F-Sa until 2AM. 531 Haight St (between Fillmore and Steiner Sts). 255.7820; fax 255.7820

31 Todos Santos ★$ A cheerful little joint, it features cheap but tasty Mexican food. The walls are a veritable shrine to the Virgin Mary, the tables covered in clear plastic over bright fabrics, and the rafters hung with angels. The waitress, with nose and lip pierced, is herself an angel of Haight Street. Specialties include burritos with *chorizo* (spicy sausage) and black beans, a mildly spiced enchilada, *huevos rancheros,* fajitas, nachos, and other typical fare. ♦ Mexican ♦ M-F lunch and dinner; Sa-Su breakfast, lunch, and dinner. No credit cards accepted. 521 Haight St (between Fillmore and Steiner Sts). 864.3721; fax 864.3721 &

32 Rose Garden ★$ White lace curtains separate the pretty pink interior from the grunge just outside the door at this pleasant Vietnamese place. Specialties include barbecued prawns, pork, or lemongrass beef, served with vegetables and rice noodles; diners roll everything up in rice paper. ♦ Vietnamese ♦ M-Sa lunch and dinner. 509 Haight St (at Fillmore St). 621.1500 &

32 Haight & Fillmore Whole Foods Although this full-service natural-foods store opened well after the Age of Aquarius, it's steeped in that era. With a peeling linoleum floor and faded walls, the crowded quarters can be overwhelming, but there's a good selection of produce, bulk items, and other staples. ♦ Daily. 503 Haight St (at Fillmore St). 552.6077

33 Kate's Kitchen ★★$ Breakfast buffs put this place at the top of their list, for good reason. Thick wedges of French toast are perfumed with orange zest and sprinkled with fresh berries and maple syrup. The hash, made with chunks of corned beef, potatoes, fried onions, carrots, and celery, is a great platform for two over-easy eggs. Sausage gravy is a perfect match for two biscuits laced with cheese and scallions, and buttermilk pancakes get a twist with cornmeal and a light lemon syrup. For lunch, there's a rich chicken soup to combat the sniffles, freshly made lemonade, and a meat loaf sandwich that, served either hot or cold, is worth a special

Japantown/Lower Haight

trip. To end such a homey meal, try the freshly baked fruit pies, often still warm from the oven. The boxy dining room has a quasi-country look with blue-and-white–checkered tablecloths and cordial waitresses outfitted in 1950s-style housedresses. ♦ American ♦ Daily breakfast and lunch. No credit cards accepted. 471 Haight St (at Fillmore St). 626.3984

34 Squat & Gobble Cafe ★★$ You haven't experienced sensory overload until you've walk into this crowded, aptly named cafe. Those who don't sport a pierced nose, purple hair, grungy pants, and a ripped, baggy T-shirt may feel out of place. Take a number, order, jockey for a table (which is probably heaped with dirty dishes), then wait for your number to be called. Why come here? Because these people know something about good food, and the portions are large. Crepes have either sweet fillings or such savory combinations as feta, artichokes, olives, and tomatoes; sandwiches are made with toasted multigrain bread and served with sautéed potatoes; and puffy omelettes practically push the sautéed potatoes off the oversize plates. ♦ American/Creperie ♦ Daily breakfast, lunch, and dinner. No credit cards accepted. 237 Fillmore St (between Waller and Haight Sts). 487.0551 &

34 India Oven ★★$$ The aroma of curry and roasting meats is the first hint that the food here is fresh and exciting. The dining room, an airy Victorian storefront, has a contemporary feel, with white tablecloths, flowers, modern art on the walls, and an open kitchen with a tandoori oven. Although the service can be a little erratic and slow, patience is rewarded by the creative twists given even standard dishes. The lamb squonge is stuffed with pistachios, and the chicken *masala* in a tomato sauce has a cumin kick. ♦ Indian ♦ Daily lunch and dinner. 233 Fillmore St (between Waller and Haight Sts). 626.1628; fax 626.3945

35 Studio Cafe ★$ The chalkboard specials hold the most promise at this all-natural cafe and include vegetarian lasagna, polenta with turkey sausage, and *torta rustica* (marinated artichoke hearts, ricotta, and spinach in a corn bread crust). The housemade dishes are supplemented by first-rate pastries from **La Seine.** The decor has a homespun quality: The tables look like flea-market finds, and what appear to be recycled pieces of wood and tin are nailed to the wall and painted white. ♦ American ♦ Daily breakfast, lunch, and dinner until 6PM. No credit cards accepted. 248 Fillmore St (between Waller and Haight Sts). 863.8982

36 Thep Phanom ★★★$ Hands down, this Lower Haight spot serves the best Thai food in the city. The homey surroundings—lots of wood and folk art—and the friendly service are serendipitous. Don't miss the fried quail or the chicken wings stuffed with glass noodles. The meat salads, particularly the chicken or beef, have an extraordinary sweet-sour balance. The Thai crepes also are good, as is the chicken with basil and the chicken and coconut-milk soup. ♦ Thai ♦ Daily dinner. 400 Waller St (at Fillmore St). 431.2526 &

37 Bean There ★$ Bamboo chairs, a painted concrete floor, and artistically brushed walls give this coffeehouse an up-to-date look. Sixteen coffees are for sale in bulk, as are 26 teas, including lemon hibiscus, apricot decaf, honey ginseng, and a mixture of mango, banana, and pineapple. Customers can choose a coffee blend, and the staff will grind and brew it to order. There also are soups, sandwiches, focaccia, and pastries. In one corner are free newspapers for perusing and a collection of mugs, teapots, and other coffee- and tea-related items for sale. It's a fun place to sit and sip outdoors. ♦ Coffeehouse ♦ Daily. 201 Steiner St (at Waller St). 255.8855 &

What's the difference between sushi and sashimi? Sushi refers to combinations made from vinegared rice and raw fish (or other ingredients), and sashimi is the raw fish served by itself.

111

Civic Center/ Hayes Valley/ The Tenderloin

The Civic Center has long been the political and cultural heart of the city; it houses the impressively domed **City Hall**, as well as the **San Francisco Public Library, War Memorial Opera House**, and **Louise M. Davies Symphony Hall**, venues for performances of operas, symphonies, and ballets. With curtain times to consider, and the daily schedules of city, state, and federal workers, many of the area eateries are geared to fast lunches and quick bites for preperformance noshers. But the district also boasts some fine destination restaurants—places like **Stars**, Jeremiah Tower's frenetic brasserie, and the **Zuni Cafe**, where a loyal crowd enjoys roast chicken and probably the best Caesar salad in the city. Vegetarians adore **Millennium**, the first restaurant in town to forgo not only meat but all dairy products and most added oil. After the show, head to the plush, romantic **Act IV** for a nightcap. Also located here, the **California Culinary Academy** trains professional chefs and runs two restaurants open to the public (of course, the food varies with the talents of the student chefs).

The two neighborhoods surrounding the area, Hayes Valley and the Tenderloin, are separated by **Van Ness Avenue**, the major north-south thoroughfare connecting San Francisco to Marin. Once a glorious avenue lined with some of the city's most impressive homes, it's now drab and commercial, cluttered with car dealerships and San Francisco's only collection of fast-food restaurants. **Hayes Street** received a much-needed boost when the interstate, which cut through the heart of the neighborhood, was damaged and torn down after the 1989 earthquake. The street has been revitalized with new apartment buildings and a growing mix of restaurants, antiques shops, art galleries, and avant-garde clothing stores. Visitors as well as locals are drawn to the **Hayes Street Grill** for seafood, **Ivy's Restaurant and Bar** for American dishes, **Geva's** for Jamaican specialties, and the monastic-looking **Suppenküche** for modern German fare.

Perhaps the most interesting feature of the neighborhood's renaissance is the profusion of coffeehouses, cafes, and wine bars. **Place Pigalle** cafe provides sofas for cozy chats over wine, beer, coffee, and snacks, as well as live weekend entertainment and monthly art shows, and **Mad Magda's Russian Tea Room & Mystic Cafe** offers psychic readings in addition to tea, coffee, and light fare. **Momi Toby's Revolution Cafe** attracts 1960s-style political zealots and stages poetry readings on Monday nights. The 1994 opening of **Hayes and Vine**, a stylish wine bar, was a sure sign that the neighborhood had indeed been discovered by the mainstream. Still, the district's diversity is evident in such spots as **Moishe's Pippic**, a Chicago-style deli known for Vienna beef frankfurters and corned-beef sandwiches, and **Powell's Place**, which dishes up soul food along with first-rate fried chicken.

It's a big cultural leap across Van Ness Avenue to the Tenderloin, which suffers the highest crime rate in the city, although an influx of Vietnamese immigrants has helped soften the rough edges. Fortunately, some of the best cafes are located right on the Tenderloin's edge, along the relatively safe **Larkin Street**. Try the great fried quail at the Cambodian **Phnom Penh**; excellent clay-pot dishes at **Lee Kee**; and wonderful *bahn mi* (Vietnamese-French sandwiches) at **Saigon Sandwich**.

Whatever gentrification the area boasts has come by way of **Miss Pearl's Jam House**. Located in the **Phoenix Hotel**, a favorite of visiting rock 'n' roll bands, it lures a young, affluent crowd with Caribbean fare in a "Gilligan's Island" setting. The Sunday brunch and the oyster bar around the pool are particularly popular. Daylight is the best time to explore the area east of Larkin, but even then it's a go-at-your-own-risk proposition.

---

1 Carta ★★$$
Under chef-owner Rob Zaborny (who spent 13 years at the **Hayes Street Grill**), the Mediterranean-accented menu offers about a dozen small plates and five large ones. For appetizers, Zaborny makes his own dolmas (stuffed grape leaves), batter-fried okra and eggplant with a dipping sauce, Greek meatballs in a tomato sauce, and leeks grilled with goat cheese and pistachios. Main courses include moussaka, grilled tuna with artichoke gratin, or marinated roast chicken with spinach pie. Desserts could be honey-walnut cake, Greek rice pudding, or Meyer lemon ice with almond cookies. The setting is a storefront with an open kitchen in back; blue glassware on the tables adds a stylish note. ♦ Mediterranean ♦ Tu-Su dinner. Reservations recommended. 1772 Market St (between Gough and Octavia Sts). Phone and fax 863.3516

Civic Center/Hayes Valley/The Tenderloin

2 Floogie's Swamp Cafe ★★$$ Jasper (Jazz) Boudreaux, who hails from Montegut, Louisiana, 75 miles south of New Orleans, has brought down-home Cajun food to San Francisco. The 1920s-style eatery has a classic Cajun look: ceiling fans, a corrugated tin roof covering a section of the bar, a saffron, green, and orange color scheme, and New Orleans memorabilia from Boudreaux's private collection. The space is tiny—just 48 seats, including the ones at the counter. The menu consists of such quintessential New Orleans fare as jambalaya, gumbo, barbecued shrimp, chicken-fried steak, and soft-shell crab, all prepared according to Boudreaux's family recipes. The "Swamp Cafe Sampler" combines small tastes of many of these dishes, with red beans and rice on the side. ♦ Cajun/Seafood ♦ Daily lunch and dinner. 1686 Market St (at Gough St). 864.3700

3 Zuni Cafe ★★★$$$ Most people who know and love food will put this restaurant at the top of their list of favorites. Since opening 15 years ago with a menu of Southwestern fare (hence the name), the cafe has developed a Mediterranean flavor under the direction of chef-owner Judy Rodgers. Signature dishes include a grand selection of oysters, roast chicken with bread salad (bread and greens in a Champagne vinaigrette), juicy ground-to-order hamburgers on house-baked focaccia, and frosty espresso granita (coffee-flavored shaved ice). The Caesar salad is the best in the city. The unusual pie-shaped, two-story structure housing the restaurant has a bohemian feel, dovetailing with the eclectic crowd: artistic types, gays out on the town, and the city's most prominent citizens, all appearing to mix comfortably. ♦ American ♦ Tu-Su breakfast, lunch, and dinner. Reservations recommended for dinner. 1658 Market St (at Franklin St). 552.2522; fax 552.9149

4 Bistro Clovis ★★$$ The style here comes straight from a Parisian wine bar, captured in the straight-back cane chairs, the impressive bar that commands one side of the room, the crocheted cafe curtains at the windows—and the menu. Classic country flavors come alive in the onion soup, shepherd's pie, smoked salmon, mushroom crepes, and light-as-air salmon mousse with marinated cucumbers.

Be sure to do some wine sampling, too: Three two-ounce tastes of different wines are available at a modest fee. ♦ French bistro ♦ M-Sa lunch and dinner. Reservations recommended. 1596 Market St (at Franklin St). 864.0231

5 Incontro ★$ This Italian spot is the newest venture of Ted Zuur and Joe Arias, two seasoned industry professionals (they met while waiting tables at **Ristorante Milano**). Under chef Andreas Maniscalco (formerly of Sausalito's **Spinnaker**) the kitchen turns out budget-priced pastas, risotti, polenta, and antipasti. An excellent choice is the *pasta primavera*. The 50-seat space is painted in a happy light blue and peach, with a dark blue ceiling; it's got a very casual, carefree atmosphere. ♦ Italian ♦ M-F lunch and dinner; Sa-Su dinner. 41 Gough St (at Page St). 436.9355; fax 334.1141

6 Eliza's ★★★$$ Here's a stunning setting for fine Chinese fare. The restaurant preserved a Matisse-like mural and the art glass inherited from its French predecessor, and serves tea in Wedgwood demitasse cups and food on sophisticated Italian plates in a rainbow of colors. Start with the pot stickers and a refreshing celery salad, followed by a delicious sizzling-rice soup. Sunflower beef features thin slices of meat in a vibrant sauce surrounded by enoki mushrooms. Sesame chicken has a nutty flavor and is enhanced with julienned vegetables. Desserts are an afterthought, but what comes before is so good that only a sugarholic would object. ♦ Californian/Chinese ♦ M-F lunch and dinner; Sa dinner. Reservations recommended. 205 Oak St (at Gough St). 621.4819

7 Thepin Thai Cuisine ★$ This pretty restaurant is popular with those who want a quick bite before the symphony (**Louise M. Davies Symphony Hall** is just four blocks away). The best bets are the chef's specialties and any of the salads that feature squid, duck, or chicken. But the food can be disappointing, missing the balance between sweet and acid and resulting in dishes that taste a bit sour. ♦ Thai ♦ M-F lunch and dinner; Sa-Su dinner. 298 Gough St (at Fell St). 863.9335

8 Nuts About You The child in us all will be captivated by this small shop's counter lined with jars of nuts and candies, including seven types of chocolate bark. Grown-up tastes will enjoy savory snacks, coffees, and such dried fruits as cranberries, apples, and blueberries. Three small tables in the front allow the few patrons lucky enough to snare a seat to huddle over a cup of housemade brew. Mugs, wicker baskets, gift wrap, dozens of ribbons, and greeting cards are also for sale in this charming, one-stop gift emporium. ♦ Daily. 327 Hayes St (between Franklin and Gough Sts). 864.6887

Civic Center/Hayes Valley/The Tenderloin

8 Hayes and Vine ★★$ This classy wine bar is a perfect stop before or after attending one of the nearby cultural events. It's a stylish, comfortable place to unwind. Thick cushions on the light wood chairs are upholstered in purple-and-gold-striped fabric, an attractive contrast to the earthy mustard-and-brick color scheme. The free-form white onyx bar glows (it's lit from below) and a black sculptural frame suspended above it holds gleaming stemware. Here, 350 bottles of wine are ready to be uncorked, and up to 35 wines can be ordered by the glass. Taste three similar wines—perhaps Pinot Blancs from California, Germany, and France—or compare the Rhônes of California and France. Food options are minimal, but enhance the wine: There's caviar, pâté, cheese plates, and biscotti.
♦ Wine bar ♦ M-Th 5PM-midnight; F-Sa until 1AM. 377 Hayes St (between Franklin and Gough Sts). 626.5301; fax 626.5278 ♿

9 Caffè Delle Stelle ★★$$ A recent move to a bigger space (formerly occupied by the **Vince** restaurant) just a few doors from the original location gives this trattoria more refinement and charm. Rustic pastas shine, whether with potatoes, sage, and truffle oil or blended with coarsely chopped tomatoes, garlic, arugula, and olive oil. Salads, especially the mixed greens with walnuts and blue cheese, are a good way to begin. The mildly flavored, creamy tiramisù is a good way to end. ♦ Italian ♦ M-Sa lunch and dinner. Reservations recommended. 395 Hayes St (at Gough St). 252.1110; fax 863.5224 ♿

10 Hayes Street Grill ★★$$$ One of the city's most renowned seafood houses, it has built a reputation on serving the freshest fish with a choice of a half-dozen sauces. Salads all have unusual twists, such as grilled calamari with fennel, red onion, and arugula, or shrimp with grapefruit and lime. The 1930s-style light fixtures, bentwood chairs, white walls, and white tablecloths give the place a comfortable look. The service is erratic—anywhere from grill-room–surly (Heaven help you if you want to send anything back!) to diner-friendly. ♦ Seafood ♦ M-F lunch and dinner; Sa-Su dinner. Reservations recommended. 320 Hayes St (between Franklin and Gough Sts). 863.5545; fax 863.1873 ♿

10 Cafe Corbas ★$ Even those not into working out will enjoy the treats at this health-food bar attached to the **Muscle System** gym (which caters to well-toned gays). Hop onto a stool at the small counter for a smoothie (made with low-fat yogurt, bananas, and apple juice), a Dagwood sandwich, or a "pocket pie" (vegetable-filled dumpling). Cookies, sodas, muffins, and all kinds of coffee drinks are also on hand to satisfy the occasional indulgence.
♦ Cafe ♦ M-F. No credit cards accepted. 364 Hayes St (between Franklin and Gough Sts). 863.8590 ♿

11 City Picnic ★$ Passersby would never guess that this self-service restaurant has one of the most charming outdoor patios in the city. Tables cluster on cobblestone walkways, surrounded by flowers and grass under a canopy of Japanese maples. Stair-step benches on one side make a great spot for eating a sandwich (try the barbecued pork) and catching a few rays. There's also a good salad bar, Asian noodle salad, and Japanese *udon* soup. For the healthy set there are yogurt drinks mixed with fruit, bran, or whatever is trendy at the moment.
♦ American ♦ M-Sa 8AM-4PM. 384-A Hayes St (at Gough St). 431.8814

IVY'S

11 Ivy's Restaurant and Bar ★★$$$ Surprisingly, this place has never received its due, because its American-inspired food is really on the cutting edge. Showstoppers include an appetizer of tender chicken, stuffed with herbs, wrapped in paper-thin sheets of phyllo, and lightly moistened with a Champagne sauce. The ever-changing menu might include rabbit, sautéed and served with grilled potatoes and a creamy mushroom sauce, or halibut, given a zip with a cream-based jalapeño sauce. Dessert might be lime pound cake with fresh peaches, or peanut-butter pie with pralines and whipped cream. The service can be amateurish, but not enough so to detract from the food. ♦ Californian ♦ M-F lunch and dinner; Sa dinner; Su brunch and dinner. Reservations recommended. 398 Hayes St (at Gough St). 626.3930 ♿

12 Pendragon Bakery and Cafe ★$ On a busy corner, this popular spot turns out good muffins, scones, and salads. The shortbreads

115

Civic Center/Hayes Valley/The Tenderloin

and cookies are particularly tasty, especially the Louisiana jumble, a huge cookie with chocolate chips, oatmeal, coconut, raisins, and an underlying flavor of brown sugar and butter. Savory hot dishes include vegetable roulade with a bronzed pastry and tamale pie. The few tables in front make it a good place for a quick bite. ♦ Cafe ♦ M-F 5AM-5PM; Sa-Su 6AM-5PM. 400 Hayes St (at Gough St). 552.7017

12 Stelline ★$ This cheerful eatery, with the kitchen half hidden behind stacks of beautifully arranged Italian products, is much more stylish than the low prices would indicate. Generous portions of pasta come with tossed salad and garlic bread. But if you want to "splurge" try one of the large salads, the best being mixed greens surrounded by warm roasted potatoes, or one of the desserts, including a respectable tiramisù. This place is under the same ownership as **Caffè Delle Stelle** (see page 115). ♦ Southern Italian ♦ M-F lunch and dinner; Sa dinner. No credit cards accepted. 429 Gough St (at Ivy St). 626.4292; fax 626.4282

13 Moishe's Pippic ★$ Midwesterners flock to this Chicago-style deli for the Vienna all-beef hot dogs, served heaped with Day-Glo green pickle relish and loads of mustard slathered on squishy poppyseed buns. Many Easterners swoon over the hot pastrami on chewy rye bread, but it's really pretty standard. And who else but a deli devotee could drool over the chopped liver sandwich with schmaltz? ♦ Deli ♦ M-F 8AM-4PM; Sa 9AM-4PM. No credit cards accepted. 425-A Hayes St (at Gough St). 431.2440

What today appears on menus as an "oyster loaf"—half a loaf of bread, hollowed out, toasted, then filled with fried oysters and condiments—was invented at Gobey's Restaurant in the late 1880s. Considered a sure-fire cure for hangovers, in those days the dish was called "The Squarer."

---

14 Geva's ★★$$$ The best and brightest Caribbean restaurant in San Francisco evokes the alluring islands with its coral walls lighting fixtures shaped like banana leaves, grassy patio used on warm evenings, and tantalizing menu. Begin with a refreshing beet salad, then try the spicy jerk pork chops, tamed with cucumber-yogurt sauce served on the side. Clams, mussels, and shrimp in a seafood stew help to cool the spiciness of the broth and are topped with a lacy network of fresh herbs. Bread pudding makes a soothing finish for the fiery meal. ♦ Caribbean ♦ Tu-Sa dinner. 482-A Hayes St (between Gough and Octavia Sts). 863.1220

15 Place Pigalle ★$ Art mixes with alcohol a this cafe. In front, inviting sofas are arranged in cozy, conversational groupings; the back room is dedicated to monthly art exhibits and artsy metal tables. From the copper-topped bar come about 10 wines, 10 beers, and an array of coffee drinks. The limited menu of light nibbles features smoked salmon, vegetable sandwiches, quiche, and cheese plates. Tuesday nights bring poetry readings, and there's live music several times a week. ♦ Cafe ♦ Daily dinner. No credit cards accepted. 520 Hayes St (between Octavia and Laguna Sts). Phone and fax 552.2671

16 Powell's Place ★$ Soulful food draws locals to this bare-bones restaurant, owned by Emmit Powell, the well-known gospel singer. Great fried chicken, greens, and homemade pies top the list. You'll also find chicken-fried steak, pork chops, and braised short ribs. Just don't expect California-fresh vegetables; corn and some others taste as if they were picked by the Green Giant. ♦ Soul food ♦ Daily breakfast, lunch, and dinner. 511 Hayes St (at Octavia St). 863.1404; fax 863.2368

17 Mad Magda's Russian Tea Room & Mystic Cafe ★$ "Great Food, Mystic Arts, reads the sign over this intimate cafe, summing up the focus here on baked goods, excellent coffee, and psychic readings (ask at the counter for a reading from early afternoon on). Tea is served in china pots and flowered cups from the 1940s. The cafe also offers soups, including borscht, a standard array of sandwiches and salads, and blintzes on weekends. A patio in back offers a hodge-podge of tables and chairs, set amid large splashes of greenery and vibrant clusters of

Civic Center/Hayes Valley/The Tenderloin

pink and orange impatiens. ♦ Tearoom/Deli ♦ Daily lunch, afternoon tea, and dinner. 579 Hayes St (between Octavia and Laguna Sts). 864.7654

18 Suppenküche ★★$$ Popular with a hip crowd, the city's best German restaurant (whose name means "soup kitchen") serves the new, lighter kind of food gaining increasing favor in Germany. Top dishes include venison with red cabbage and cranberry sauce, bratwurst, chicken stew, and pork schnitzel with spaetzle. The cross in the corner of the dining room and the long, communal benches give the place a monastic look. ♦ German ♦ Daily dinner. Reservations recommended for parties over five. 601 Hayes St (at Laguna St). 252.9289

19 Momi Toby's Revolution Cafe $ The closest thing to the Age of Aquarius these days, this quirky coffeehouse offers poetry readings on Monday nights. Any day of the week, it's the place local hippies, beatniks, and other bohemians linger over strong cups of coffee. All the savory food is brought in and microwaved on the premises, including enchilada pie, lasagna, soup, and one sandwich: tuna salad on a bagel. ♦ Coffeehouse ♦ Daily breakfast, lunch, and dinner. 528 Laguna St (between Fell and Hayes Sts). 626.1508

20 Vicolo Pizzeria ★★$ If you like cornmeal-crusted pizza, you'll like this place; if you don't, seek the pie of your dreams elsewhere. The pies have thick, crisp, cornmeal crusts and a choice of more than 30 combination toppings. Try the roast eggplant with blue cheese and garlic, or the fennel with mozzarella, fontina, red onions, and red bell peppers. A plus is that you can order by the slice to see if you like the combination. Green salads or marinated vegetable mixtures, such as black beans with jicama, are also available. Order at the counter, and the server will bring the food to the table. ♦ Pizzeria ♦ Daily lunch and dinner. 201 Ivy St (at Franklin St). 863.2382; fax 863.7202 ♿

21 Act IV $$$ One of the most beautiful rooms in the city is located at the **Inn at the Opera** hotel. Filled with wonderful oil paintings and flower arrangements, an ornate bar, dark wood appointments, an oversize fireplace, and deep, plush banquettes, it's the perfect spot for a drink and a simple nibble after a concert or to cap an evening. At press time, the owner had overhauled the concept with an all-American menu featuring steaks, chops, and housemade condiments and relishes. ♦ European/Californian ♦ M-F breakfast, lunch, and dinner; Sa breakfast and dinner; Su brunch and dinner. 333 Fulton St (at Franklin St). 863.8400; fax 861.0821 ♿

22 Backstage ★★$$$ In keeping with its name, this restaurant has a theatrical feel, with wide moldings, columns, massive wrought-iron chandeliers, and a whimsical papier-mâché relief of angels stretching along the entire wall. The eclectic American food may include smoked trout sandwiched between two crisp potato pancakes; grilled green tomatoes drizzled with aioli and served with a corn and roasted-pepper salad; or roast chicken breast with bacon-scented mashed potatoes and a hearty mushroom sauce. ♦ American ♦ M lunch; Tu-F lunch and dinner; Sa dinner. 687 McAllister St (at Gough St). 673.9353; fax 558.8253 ♿

23 Stars Cafe ★$$ Jeremiah Tower's less expensive version of **Stars** has an impersonal, corporate feel. The bar, which extends along one wall of the multilevel brasserie, has become a holding tank for expectant diners, since reservations are accepted only for large parties. Those waiting are poorly rewarded for their patience by a gougingly expensive by-the-glass wine list. Best food bets include hummus with fried *pappadams* (thin, crisp, lentil wafers), grilled rib-eye steak with mashed potatoes, and wood-oven–fired pizza. Among the outstanding, diverse desserts are a root-beer float, a mixed-berry napoleon, and a banana-cream pie with mounds of whipped cream. ♦ Californian ♦ Daily lunch and dinner. 500 Van Ness Ave (at McAllister St). 861.4344; fax 861.4322 ♿

24 Caffe Trinity ★★$ At the end of **City Hall Plaza,** amid tacky T-shirt stores and pawnshops, this jewel has the rich appointments found in espresso cafes in the best part of town—painted murals trimmed in gold leaf, Venetian glass chandeliers, a marble-and-mahogany bar, and matching bistro tables.

117

Civic Center/Hayes Valley/The Tenderloin

The simple food is as lovely as the setting. Rich, strong coffee is served in oversized bowls. Breakfast features muffins, bagels, scones, and freshly squeezed juices. Sandwiches, some of the best anywhere, include roast beef and turkey and are made with focaccia or a fresh-baked roll. Several pasta salads and freshly made soups are fine choices for a quick, light lunch. ♦ Cafe ♦ M-F breakfast and lunch. 1145 Market St (between Seventh and Eighth Sts). 864.3333 ♿

25 Millennium ★★$$ "Optimal health cuisine," which eschews meat, most oil, and dairy products, can present chefs with a stiff challenge. They've met it here. Start with the grilled portobello mushroom glazed with a sweet-and-spicy Moroccan sauce, or grilled rosemary polenta brightened with chopped red and yellow tomatoes. Main courses include a saffron and corn risotto, topped with a smoky stew featuring three beans and chunks of butternut squash; and chanterelle purse—phyllo dough filled with chanterelle and shiitake mushrooms, braised leek tofu "ricotta," and a barley-millet pilaf—served over a roasted shallot sauce and asparagus. Desserts are low-fat takeoffs on all-American favorites, including a nondairy butterscotch custard with an apple and cranberry compote.

The cheerful setting, in the basement of a former carriage house for the 1920s-era **Abigail Hotel,** has a black-and-white tile floor, wall sconces, and sponge-painted walls. The wine list has a good selection of organic labels; organic beers are also offered. ♦ Vegetarian ♦ Tu-F lunch and dinner; Sa-Su dinner. 246 McAllister St (between Hyde and Larkin Sts). 487.9800; fax 487.9921

26 Spuntino ★$$ This high-tech Italian eatery has adopted the chaotic ordering process that's common all over Italy: semi–self-service. Diners order at the counter, pay, and head for a table to wait for the food. They have to fetch their own water and bus their own tables if they want the dishes cleared before they tackle dessert. The best way to go here is a salad (enough for two) and a simple pasta. Pizzas can be good but are sometimes underbaked and soggy, and the desserts look better than they taste. Given the food, ambience, and service, the place is a bit overpriced. ♦ Italian ♦ Daily breakfast, lunch, and dinner; Sa-Su brunch. 524 Van Ness Ave (between McAllister St and Golden Gate Ave). 861.7772; fax 861.7160 ♿

26 Stars ★★★$$$$ Jeremiah Tower's 12-year-old restaurant is still the archetypal American brasserie, and there's always a buzz at the tables, the bar, and the open kitchen overlooking the pizza oven. The daily-changing menu gives mouthwatering twists to combinations that sometimes overstretch. Appetizers might include grilled apples with blue-cheese mousseline, *frisée* (curly endive) marinated onions, and toasted pecans; or poached sea scallops and lobster risotto made with saffron tomatoes and tarragon. Among the main courses might be grilled tuna with sun-dried tomato sauce, zucchini cut in noodlelike strips, and accents of artichokes and pesto; or grilled duck breast with truffle-scented parsnip puree, shiitake mushrooms, and a tart/sweet pomegranate *demi-glace* (rich brown sauce). Desserts range from a lemon soufflé with lemon-ginger sauce, to a pear-and-cranberry dumpling, to a refreshing tangerine ice. Just about everything on the menu is a winner, but the kitchen sometimes can't keep up with the crush of pretheater diners. Best to go at off-peak hours, or on a nonperformance weeknight. ♦ Californian ♦ Daily lunch and dinner; limited bar menu daily 2PM-5:30PM and after 11:30PM. Reservations recommended for dinner. 150 Redwood St (at Van Ness Ave). 861.7827; fax 554.0351 ♿

27 J.T.'s Bistro ★★★$$$ Jeremiah Tower has closed **Starbake,** his bakery adventure adjacent to **Stars,** and in its place opened this bistro, where he offers a five-course prix-fixe meal. Dishes include a black truffle custard with chestnuts pheasant with white corn soufflé and watercress sauce; and such desserts as white peaches with pineapple–passion fruit sorbet, napped with raspberry sauce and garnished with rose petals. Puffers may retire after dinner to the **Stellar Cigar Society Room** upstairs, where they can light up and enjoy full liquor service, leather sofas, television, and stogie-filled humidors. ♦ New American ♦ Daily dinner. 555 Golden Gate Ave (between Polk St and Van Ness Ave). 861.7827; fax 554.0351 ♿

28 Max's Opera Cafe ★$ What it lacks in finesse, it makes up for in quantity, like pastrami sandwiches as big as Arnold Schwarzenegger's biceps; one sandwich easily serves four. The blue-plate specials run from a chicken-wing dinner to barbecued brisket of beef, all served in such ample portions that leftovers are a given. Everything is large, but calorie counters can choose from

Civic Center/Hayes Valley/The Tenderloin

such low-fat selections as salads with an oil-free mustard dressing, broiled chicken breast with tomato vinaigrette, and a turkey salisbury steak. The waitstaff also provides entertainment, breaking into song throughout the evening. Located at the **Opera Plaza** apartment complex. ♦ Deli ♦ Daily lunch and dinner. 601 Van Ness Ave (at Golden Gate Ave). 771.7301; fax 771.2456

29 VIVANDE Ristorante ★★★$$$ Carlo Middione, who draws raves for his wonderful **VIVANDE Porta Via** in Pacific Heights, branched out by opening this impressive trattoria in the **Opera Plaza** complex. Known for his Southern Italian cooking, Middione has crafted a rustic menu where every pasta dish is a housemade winner—tagliatelle is tossed with oyster and shiitake mushrooms in a light olive-oil sauce. If rice is your fancy, try the risotto with sweet shrimp and fresh lemon. The buttery sea bass is served on a lightly charred wedge of cabbage that's drizzled with lemon oil and surrounded by roast potatoes. Finish the meal with the famous earthquake cake—a flourless chocolate cake with a cracked top. The Italian wine list is a bold move in a city where most restaurants offer California labels. The frescoes, the bold orange-and-cream– striped lampshades on the ceiling fixtures and floor lamps, the orange-fronted brick oven, and the oversize wood chairs—which are branded with the distinctive "V" logo—are all examples of Middione's painstaking attention to detail. Be sure to peek in the rest room to see the intricately painted, vaguely bawdy scenes— they're the talk of the town. ♦ Italian ♦ Daily lunch, tea, and dinner until midnight. 670 Golden Gate Ave (between Van Ness Ave and Franklin St). 673.9245; fax 673.2160 ♿

San Francisco THAI BAR-B-Q

30 Thai BBQ ★★$ Good noodle dishes with a variety of meat and vegetable toppings— including squid, beef meatballs, and duck— are the staples here. Also available are such barbecued dishes as grilled prawns, trout, oysters, and veal, all served with carrot salad and sticky rice. To start, try the flaky spring rolls or the chicken satay with peanut sauce. The cloth napkins and stylishly cool interior are unexpectedly elegant touches, considering the rock-bottom prices and in-a-hurry service. ♦ Thai ♦ M-F lunch and dinner; Sa dinner. No credit cards accepted. 730 Van Ness Ave (between Turk and Eddy Sts). 441.1640 ♿

31 SF Scone Works Mary Ann Woomer turns out some of the best scones in town in this small storefront. Baked throughout the day, they are dense but still crumbly, and come in such imaginative flavors as sun-dried cranberries and crystallized ginger with pecans. Those who want to eat scones fresh from the oven at home can buy them unbaked and frozen. ♦ M-F 6:30AM-4PM. 814 Eddy St (at Van Ness Ave). 922.0635

32 California Culinary Academy The West Coast's premier cooking school offers several training programs, including a 16-month professional chef's course. For the less committed culinarian, the continuing education department offers a series of one-shot or concentrated classes in catering and baking, as well as a kid's culinary college. In addition to preparing all the foods offered in the attractive ground-level retail shop, the students in the professional course run two dining rooms, but quality varies so widely that getting a good meal is as iffy as flipping a coin. ♦ 625 Polk St (between Turk and Eddy Sts). 771.3536; fax 775.5129 ♿

Within the California Culinary Academy:

Academy Grill $ Popular for lunch, this cafe is located in the culinary academy's basement. Among the offerings are burgers, deli items, and blue-plate specials: turkey florentine on Mondays, fried chicken on Wednesdays, and seafood gumbo on Fridays. ♦ American ♦ Call ahead; hours vary with school sessions. 771.3536; fax 775.5129 ♿

Careme Room ★$$$ Set in a two-story atrium, this impressive room boasts soaring columns and walls of glass that let diners peek in on the culinary classrooms and kitchens. Early in the week, table service is provided (including tableside preparations of Caesar salad and flaming desserts); Thursday and Friday offer buffets. Most dishes are continental classics; the menu continually changes. The high-priced wine list provides as much grief as pleasure: It's common to order a vintage listed on the menu but be served something else because the selection wasn't available. ♦ French/Californian ♦ Call ahead; the hours vary with school sessions. Reservations recommended. 771.3536; fax 775.5129 ♿

When word of the Gold Rush reached the East Coast and subsequently Europe in the 1850s, restaurateurs and French chefs swarmed to California to cash in on the boom. Although the 49ers had a reputation for being crude, many were educated, sophisticated men who supported such elegant restaurants as Winn's Fountain Head, where diners enjoyed venison steaks, oysters, and partridge in a setting of rich Oriental rugs, rosewood chairs, and tables topped with Italian marble.

Civic Center/Hayes Valley/The Tenderloin

33 Miss Pearl's Jam House ★★$$ Fans flock to this funky shipwreck, where weather-beaten doors serve as wainscoting and an inverted canoe is the canopy over the bar. Like the 1950s-style **Phoenix** hotel next door, it attracts the rock 'n' roll set and can get quite noisy. The half pound of peel-'em-yourself shrimp is a good value; jerk chicken and leg of lamb drizzled with an herb-and-garlic sauce round out the menu. Friday nights bring a Happy Hour at the oyster bar near the hotel's pool, also perfect for weekend brunch. ♦ Caribbean/Soul ♦ Tu-Su dinner; Sa-Su gospel brunch. Reservations recommended for large parties. 601 Eddy St (between Larkin and Polk Sts). 775.5267; fax 775.4992

34 Saigon Sandwich ★★$ The French influence found all over Vietnam adds a delightful twist to the fare at this typical Vietnamese cafe. The "Saigon sandwiches" here are made with French rolls slathered with mayonnaise and a pâté-like spread and heaped a meat filling that might be pork or barbecued chicken. Then, for a wonderful crunch, cilantro and a few lightly pickled vegetables are added, including jalapeño, daikon, carrots, and onions. Most sandwiches are very cheap and absolutely delicious. ♦ Vietnamese ♦ Daily breakfast and lunch until 5PM. 560 Larkin St (at Eddy St). 474.5698

35 Bien Dong ★$ Incredibly cheap and surprisingly good Vietnamese food distinguishes this corner place from the look-alike storefronts up and down the block. Specialties include shrimp spring rolls, chicken with lemongrass over rice, and tofu with sautéed vegetables. ♦ Vietnamese ♦ Daily breakfast and lunch. 601 Larkin St (at Eddy St). 673.7604

35 Pacific Restaurant ★$ Open from morning to night, this Vietnamese eatery is known for its *pho* (beef and rice-noodle soup). The "soup" contains more noodles than broth, but those with big appetites can also opt for one of the inexpensive rice dishes. ♦ Vietnamese ♦ Daily breakfast, lunch, and dinner. 607 Larkin St (at Eddy St). 441.6722

36 Phnom Penh ★★$ Sure, the atmosphere at this dining spot is drab, but the wonderful Cambodian food makes this a most inviting oasis. The fried quail, served with a salt-and-pepper dipping sauce, is so good it could be offered at **Stars** for triple the price. Other recommended dishes include eggplant with pork and shrimp in a sauce perfumed with coriander and green onions, and grilled chicken marinated with ginger. ♦ Cambodian ♦ M-Sa lunch and dinner. 631 Larkin St (at Willow St). 775.5979

36 Pagolac ★★$ Although this 50-seat place may look at first glance like a dreary Vietnamese coffee shop, it is spotless, which bodes well for the food. The best items to order here are the *com dai* (about 30 combinations of meat and vegetables served over rice), all very reasonably priced. Appetizers feature fragrant grilled pork balls served with rice noodles and pickled vegetables: Put a bit of each ingredient on rice paper and wrap it all up. For dessert try the sweet red-bean paste layered with coconut milk and flavored gelatin and served in a parfait glass. ♦ Vietnamese ♦ M-Tu, Th-Su lunch and dinner. 655 Larkin St (between Willow and Ellis Sts). 776.3234

36 Hai Ky Mi Gia ★$ Students on a tight budget crowd into this Chinese restaurant day and night for the single dish on the menu: noodles in broth. ♦ Chinese ♦ Daily lunch and dinner until 6PM. 707 Ellis St (at Larkin St). 771.2577

37 New Chieu Fong Company Despite the somewhat run-down neighborhood, connoisseurs trek out to this market featuring Southeast Asian and Chinese products; it is one of the best in the city. Shoppers will find good produce, including young ginger, lemongrass, bitter melons, and lots of fresh noodles. There's also a fresh-fish display case, a wide variety of meats, which are butchered on-site, and dry goods. ♦ Daily. 724 Ellis St (between Larkin and Polk Sts). 776.7151

38 Racha Cafe ★$ This Thai restaurant has won fans among chefs. Although much of the food has been a bit disappointing in the last few years (mainly because of the overuse of oil), you can always count on the meat salad, coconut-and-chicken soup, and fried rice. ♦ Thai ♦ Daily lunch and dinner. 771 Ellis St (at Polk St). 885.0725

39 Thang Xuong Market With aisles barely wide enough to walk down with a hand-held basket, this tiny full-service market packs in lots of merchandise. Prices are lower here than at the **New Chieu Fong** market around the corner. ♦ Daily. No credit cards accepted. 724 Larkin St (between Ellis and O'Farrell Sts). 474.4004

Civic Center/Hayes Valley/The Tenderloin

40 Kam Wah ★★★$ This Chinese-Vietnamese restaurant located on the edge of the Tenderloin is really two eateries in one. In the front, there's a counter where you can buy roast duck and barbecued pork to go. Behind it is a bare-bones dining room—little decor and no ambience, but well-prepared food at dirt cheap prices. During crab season (November through April) the restaurant offers a terrific Vietnamese-style crab (coated with salt and pepper, stir-fried, and served with sliced jalapeño and green onions). Other favorites include succulent mussels flavored with Thai basil and onions; and all of the vegetable dishes, especially *dau meu* (snow pea shoots stir-fried with garlic). ♦ Chinese/Vietnamese ♦ Daily breakfast, lunch, and dinner until 9:30PM. 730 Larkin St (between Ellis and O'Farrell Sts). 928.2938

41 Soups ★$ The menu proclaims "Good Food Dirt Cheap," which is true, but this restaurant also has a mission. Owner Richard Gaule opened it in the economically depressed Tenderloin district with the idea of hiring and training neighborhood residents to take over the cafe. The setting is plain but cheerful, with pink soup bowls stenciled around the molding below the ceiling. The short menu offers both vegetable and meat soups, and the very reasonable prices include a half-bowl refill, coffee, tea, or milk, and even tax. ♦ American ♦ M-Sa 10AM-6:30PM. 784 O'Farrell St (at Larkin St). 775.6406 &

42 German Cook ★★$ A warm ambience prevails at this tiny German restaurant. Diners can perch at the four seats at the counter in front of the open kitchen or sit in a wooden booth painted with delicate flowers. Everything has a lived-in look, but the waitress sparkles and has more than enough energy to cover the room by herself. Great, filling combinations include stuffed cabbage, sauerbraten with potato pancakes, and bratwurst with a fine consistency and a crisp, browned exterior. ♦ German ♦ M-Su dinner; W-F lunch. No credit cards accepted. 612 O'Farrell St (between Leavenworth and Hyde Sts). 776.9022

Bests

James McNair
Cookbook Author/Food Photographer

Here's a short list of places I shop for recipe testing, food photography needs, and to stock up my **Napa Valley** kitchen, when I'm in San Francisco:

Happy Supermarket for Asian groceries.

Super Koyama for Japanese groceries.

Haig's Delicacies for Indonesian, Indian, and Middle Eastern staples.

Antonelli's Fish and Poultry (in **Cal-Mart**) for fresh fish and smoked chickens.

Bryan's for immaculate fish, poultry, and meats.

Peet's Coffee and Tea for the finest caffeine.

The Real Food Company for dried beans, grains, and fresh produce.

Joseph Schmidt for chocolate gifts and indulgences.

Fillamento for tableware.

Nancy L. Snyderman, M.D.
Surgeon; Medical Correspondent, ABC News

Neecha Thai: Green curry chicken is the best, kind waiters. Good for a date or with children.

Jackson Fillmore: Great food. I won't wait for a table; instead I sit at the counter.

Doidge's: Best breakfast in the world—I'm not kidding! Freshly squeezed OJ, hot chocolate, and a breakfast casserole are my favorites.

Square One: Consistently exceptional cuisine and great wine list. The only place I'll eat raw oysters.

Wavy Gravy
Activist/Clown

As a transplanted New Yorker, I "gravy-tated" to **Moose's** in **North Beach.** Not only for its excellent eats and awesome ambience, but also for its blue neon moose sign and moose fountain. They serve primo pasta and "boss" burgers.

Sally Bernstein
Editor, "Sally's Place," an Internet Web Site Dedicated to Food, Wine, and Travel

For an intimate night on the town, where I can sip Champagne and devour an artistic lobster salad, I would dine at Roland Passot's **La Folie.** But when I feel like standing in line to sit elbow to elbow and eat some of **Chinatown**'s best Chinese food, then I would head to the **House of Nanking.**

My favorite San Francisco shop is **Thomas E. Cara, Ltd.** on Pacific Avenue. He's been in business since 1946 selling and repairing beautiful espresso machines.

SoMa (South of Market)/ South Beach/ Potrero Hill/ Bayview– Hunters Point

The South of Market area, popularly known as SoMa, has evolved into one of San Francisco's most eclectic and artsy frontiers—and one of the city's most fun and casual districts for food. Bounded by **San Francisco Bay, Van Ness Avenue**, and **Market Street**, SoMa began as an industrial area. Several foundries established headquarters here in the 1850s, as did light industrial companies, wholesalers, and the **Southern Pacific Railroad**. When these industries moved out in the 1970s, blue-collar families and members of San Francisco's artistic community moved in, converting the cavernous warehouses into residential spaces. Still home to a community of families and artists today, SoMa has become a trendy neighborhood, ever-changing with the arrival of new restaurants, discos, and comedy clubs.

One cause of SoMa's rebirth was undoubtedly the 1981 arrival of the **Moscone Convention Center**, which was followed in 1989 by the **San Francisco Centre**, a vertical mall that is anchored by **Nordstrom**. The addition of such hotels as the **Marriott** and the **Sheraton Palace** also changed the face of the area. More recent spurs to SoMa's development include the 1994 debut of the dazzling **Yerba Buena Gardens** arts complex and cultural center, and the 1995 unveiling of the **San Francisco Museum of Modern Art**.

SoMa (South of Market)/South Beach/Potrero Hill/Bayview–Hunters Point

The 1989 Loma Prieta earthquake actually provided another boon. Thanks to the temblor's devastation, the **Embarcadero Freeway** that had long blocked SoMa from the waterside had to be dismantled. As a result, gorgeous views of the bay have been opened up, giving rise to a new section of town known as South Beach, which is west of **The Embarcadero** and south of the **Bay Bridge**. The biggest residential building project in San Francisco in more than 30 years is currently being planned for South Beach; construction has not yet begun, however, due to lack of funds. One of South Beach's best views of the Bay Bridge can be had from the patio of **Palomino Euro Bistro**, a glitzy branch of the Seattle-based chain at the **Hills Brothers Plaza** (once a coffee factory). The housemade beers and lively crowd at **Gordon Biersch Brewery Restaurant**, one of the area's finest brew pubs, also make it worth a stop.

Potrero Hill, an up-and-coming residential area, is also enjoying a renaissance. Set on a hill above SoMa, it boasts some of the city's sunniest weather and awe-inspiring panoramas. The neighborhood's main shopping strip, a three-block stretch along **18th Street**, is so small-town picture-perfect that it could be a movie set. Yet the shops and restaurants here are charmingly diverse: There's **Aperto**, a fine Italian trattoria; **Eliza's**, for delicious Chinese food with a California twist; **San Francisco Bar-B-Que**, a Thai noodle house; **Asimakopoulos Cafe**, a top Greek spot; **The Daily Scoop**, an old-fashioned ice-cream parlor; and **Farley's**, an inviting coffeehouse.

Another bustling area is at SoMa's northern corner, around **Rincon Center**—a massive complex of offices, shops, restaurants, and apartments just south of **Market Street** and off The Embarcadero. Clustered within a few blocks of each other, such impressive places as **Boulevard** and **Harry Denton's** have made this the city's new Restaurant Row.

Changes may also be in store for one of the poorest neighborhoods in the city: Bayview–Hunters Point. This area runs along **Third Street** from **Army Street** to **Bayshore Boulevard** through what remains of San Francisco's light industrial, warehouse, and manufacturing districts. Most of the restaurants in this chiefly African-American neighborhood specialize in soul food, fried fish, and barbecue, with a few Chinese places here and there.

As with any burgeoning area, the attrition rate for restaurants has been high; but the quality of the eateries opening here has consistently improved. Among the wonderful spots with staying power are **LuLu**, known for great seafood and rotisserie meats and its impressively vast warehouse setting; **Fringale Restaurant**, a top French bistro; the pretty and lively **Bistro Rôti**; **Wu Kong**, with its impressive menu of Shanghai specialties; the Parisian **South Park Cafe**; and the **The Fly Trap**, which offers new twists on San Francisco classics in a tailored beige-and-brass environment. Other noteworthy spots are **Basil**, a sophisticated restaurant that melds California and Thai cuisines, **Kyo-ya**, one of the top Japanese eateries in the city; and **Hawthorne Lane**, a dining spot owned by Anne and David Gingrass, who—with Wolfgang Puck—put **Postrio** on the map.

Though the SoMa area still has rough edges, its fresh and appealing mix is drawing everyone from white-collar conventioneers to grungy twentysomethings and stylish types of all ages, all eager to explore the culinary diversity here.

SoMa (South of Market)/South Beach/Potrero Hill/Bayview–Hunters Point

1 Ferry Plaza Farmers' Market Located on the beautiful waterfront in front of the **Ferry Building**, this certified market features fresh seasonal produce and such special events as a "Shop with the Chef" tour, during which a well-known cook chooses produce and offers shoppers advice on preparing it; some chefs include a cooking demonstration. There are also monthly tastings of one type of produce, such as greens, and activities for children, including cooking classes. The market has grown so popular that a second branch has now opened near the **Hyatt Regency;** it's held on Tuesdays. ♦ Tu 11:30AM-3PM; Sa 8AM-1:30PM. Tuesday market: Market St (near the Hyatt Regency). No phone; Saturday market: Ferry Plaza (at The Embarcadero end of Market St, near the Ferry Building and World Trade Center). 981.3004.

2 One Market Restaurant ★★$$$ Celebrity chef Bradley Ogden made a name for himself at the illustrious **Campton Place;** then he moved to Marin County and opened the much-praised **Lark Creek Inn.** Now Ogden's returned to San Francisco to serve up his signature American-Californian cuisine. Ogden is in the process of making his menu more casual, with such dishes as meat loaf, pork chops, roasted vegetables, and grilled beef tenderloin. This venture is every bit as successful as the others, but the food quality is more variable—sometimes marvelous, sometimes just okay. And although the stylish interior design cost millions, the sea of tables, hard-surfaced floor, and high-tech open kitchen in back drive the noise level to deafening heights. ♦ Californian ♦ M-F lunch and dinner; Sa dinner; Su brunch and dinner. Reservations recommended. 1 Market St (at Steuart St). 777.5577; fax 777.3366 ♿

3 Boulevard ★★★$$$ Two of the city's top talents joined together for this venture—Nancy Oakes, formerly of **L'Avenue,** whom *Food & Wine* has heralded as one of the country's top new chefs, and **Pat Kuleto,** who has designed some of the city's best restaurants (most notably **Postrio**). Here **Kuleto** has created a room with three distinct areas: the bar, defined by a domed brick ceiling and an intricate peacock-patterned tile floor; the informal central section, with an open kitchen and a counter; and the dramatically lit, more formal dining area. Oakes is known for her lusty combinations and innovative presentations. The menu changes often, but try anything that includes quail, or the napoleon made with mashed potatoes and mushrooms. Vanilla-cured pork loin gets varying treatments and never misses the mark. The wine list is a little pricey, but features some excellent, hard-to-find California wines. ♦ French/Californian ♦ M-F lunch and dinner; Sa-Su dinner. Reservations recommended. 1 Mission St (at Steuart St). 543.6084; fax 543.8631 ♿

3 Palindrome ★$ It may be a hole-in-the-wall, but the surroundings are classy and the coffee is smooth and strong. The sandwiches are built on terrific bread, and the extremely friendly service is another bonus. ♦ Coffeehouse/Takeout ♦ M-F 6AM-6PM. No credit cards accepted. 131 Steuart St (between Howard and Mission Sts). 357.0753; fax 357.1753 ♿

3 Bistro Rôti ★★★$$ Any seat in the house offers a good view of the action here: There's a lively bar scene up front; in the middle, a chef tends a rotisserie at an open brick fireplace; and, in the back of the room, counter seats overlook an open kitchen and tables have views of the Bay Bridge. The food has a French twist, as evidenced by such offerings as french fries with lemon aïoli, or the grilled duck breast salad with peaches and a Port vinaigrette. The fireplace turns out grilled lamb sirloin, served with a silky polenta, and spit-roasted chicken, with garlic mashed potatoes. The griddled salmon with a thin mustard glaze and shiitake mushrooms, and the duck confit with lentils and roast garlic are also standouts. Dessert offerings include cherry-and-apricot brioche pudding, and an excellent crème brûlée topped with either light or dark chocolate. Although the food can be inconsistent, the service is efficient and the pretty surroundings make up for the occasional lapses. ♦ Californian/French ♦ M-F lunch and dinner; Sa-Su brunch and dinner. Reservations recommended. 155 Steuart St (between Howard and Mission Sts). 495.6500; fax 495.3522 ♿

3 Harry Denton's ★$$ Operated by one of the city's most celebrated party guys, this posh, late-night watering hole is a favorite after-hours haunt. The action at the bar (there's a cover charge for the live music after 9PM Thursday through Saturday) is better than the homey fare, although that can be pretty good, too. Pot roast with mashed potatoes and gravy is the signature dish. Other options include the blackened meat loaf (no, it wasn't burned, it's supposed to be that way); oak-fired pizzas; spaghetti marinara with rock shrimp and pesto; and country-style chicken with artichokes, escarole, and white

125

SoMa (South of Market)/South Beach/Potrero Hill/Bayview–Hunters Point

beans. Parties of six or more can take advantage of an inexpensive five-course family-style dinner. ♦ American ♦ Daily breakfast, lunch, and dinner. Reservations recommended. 165 Steuart St (between Howard and Mission Sts). 882.1333; fax 979.0471

4 Rincon Center This multiuse complex contains several ethnic restaurants and many lunch places catering to office workers. What distinguishes the food court is that many of its eateries are branches of local restaurants, rather than generic chains. ♦101 Spear St (at Mission St)

Within Rincon Center:

CHALKERS Billiard Club

Chalkers Billiard Club ★$ Shoot a game of pool and have a bite to eat at this elegant billiard parlor boasting more than 30 antique and custom pool tables. Appetizers veer toward the chip-and-dip genre: salsa with chips, tuna pâté, roasted-garlic almond spread, or country pâté with sourdough bread. Main courses include hearty salads, a pasta or two, and a large variety of sandwiches, including Mexican chicken, a salmon burger with jack cheese, and Italian sausage with marinara sauce. The most popular (and best) comestibles, however, are the 10 draft beers or the dozen wines available by the glass. ♦ American ♦ Daily lunch and dinner. 512.0450

Blue Chip Cookies Top choices at this sweet-treat stop include chocolate chip, peanut butter, and white chocolate macadamia nut. ♦ M-F. 896.5267; fax 989.1746. Also at: Pier 39 (Building B, Level 1). 989.9411

Sorabol Noodles ★$ The area's top Korean restaurant is a scaled-down version of the older original in Oakland. The menu features barbecue, noodles (try the seaweed noodles with beef, chicken, or pork), and a few side orders such as pot stickers and stir-fried vegetables. ♦ Korean ♦ M-F lunch until 4PM. 896.5959. Also at: 3251 20th Ave (at Winston St), Oakland. 510/753.5959

San Francisco has a long coffee tradition. During the Gold Rush, such entrepreneurs as James Folger sold specially roasted beans to miners and other fortune seekers. At the turn of the century, the Hills Brothers invented vacuum packing, which brought good coffee to a broader audience. Today, hundreds of coffee bars dot the city's culinary landscape.

Burger Gourmet ★$ All kinds of juicy hamburgers and fixings are available at one of the most popular lunch places around. ♦ American ♦ M-F breakfast and lunch. 777.9200

Speedsters ★$ Rush in here and pick up a salad—cobb, spinach, tuna, or pasta. Good homemade soups round out the menu. It's all fast, fresh, and tasty. ♦ American ♦ M-F lunch until 4PM. No credit cards accepted. 974.5170

Tampico $ A safe bet for a quick Mexican fix. Burritos are filled with steak, pork, sausage, chicken, or cheese. Wash it all down with a fresh strawberry, pineapple, mango, banana, watermelon, or tangerine *agua fresca* soda. ♦ Mexican ♦ M-F lunch until 4PM. No credit cards accepted. 543.8616

Village Pizza ★$ Here's an outlet of the popular local pizza chain. Choose either a thick- or thin-crust pie, with all kinds of toppings, including clams and garlic. ♦ Pizzeria ♦ M-F lunch and dinner; Sa lunch until 4PM. 243.0666; fax 243.0917

A·ROMA
espresso · panini

Aroma $ Primarily an espresso bar and coffeehouse, this stylish cafe also serves up light eats. ♦ Coffeehouse ♦ M-Sa. 896.5282

Wazam $ The menu features a few tandoori specials, curries, and Indian breads, all at incredibly low prices. ♦ Indian ♦ M-F lunch and dinner until 6:30PM; Sa lunch until 3PM. 974.1111

Thai-to-go $ One of the best items is the green papaya salad with string beans, chilies and a refreshing lemon dressing. Otherwise, expect the typical array of curries, plus noodle soups topped with beef, chicken, or barbecued pork. ♦ Thai ♦ M-F lunch. No credit cards accepted. 777.6989

Rubin's $ Standard deli sandwiches and hot specials like burgers, chicken breast, focaccia with turkey and melted cheese, and a rotisseried half chicken are all available here. ♦ Deli ♦ M-F breakfast and lunch. No credit cards accepted. 974.1545

Arabi $ This is a good place to pick up egg dishes in the morning. Lunchtime fare includes kebabs and Middle Eastern salads. ♦ Middle Eastern ♦ M-F breakfast and lunch. No credit cards accepted. 243.8575

Thatcher's Dozens of flavors of sweet and savory popcorn, all available for sampling, are made here. Among the unique concoctions are low-fat caramel, honey vanilla and nuts,

SoMa (South of Market)/South Beach/Potrero Hill/Bayview–Hunters Point

cookies and cream, pistachio crunch, sour cream and onion, jalapeño, barbecue, and white cheddar. ♦ M-F. 957.9601, mail-order sales 800/926.2676; fax 957.1217 ♿. Also at: 180 Howard St (at Main St). 957.9601; fax 957.1217 ♿.

Wu Kong Restaurant ★★★$$ One of the city's prettiest Chinese restaurants, complete with glittering chandeliers and fine art, it's also the place to sample the cuisine of Shanghai province. For an appetizer, try the drunken squab or drunken chicken (chilled and served in a wine sauce). Another must-have, whether as part of dinner or dim sum, is the Shanghai dumpling (a savory pork filling wrapped in gossamer-light noodle dough), which is best eaten in one bite. The near-perfect panfried noodles are thick and doughy, and the crystal shrimp taste as if the prawns had jumped out of the tank and landed in the hot, silken sauce. ♦ Chinese ♦ Daily lunch and dinner. 957.9300; fax 957.0696 ♿.

Jimmy Bean's ★★$ The menu at one of the most popular lunch spots in **Rincon Center** focuses on quesadillas, with fillings that range from duck with shiitake mushrooms and braised fennel, to grilled eggplant with potato and roasted tomato, scallops with parsley pesto, and grilled vegetables with chipotle-and-cilantro pesto. The superb sandwiches include roast leg of lamb with red onions and eggplant, and pork loin with pears, arugula, red onions, and a red-pepper sauce. If none of these hits the spot, try one of the *soba* (buckwheat) noodle salads, chicken or seafood skewers, or *pizzettas*. ♦ Californian ♦ M-F breakfast and lunch. 495.2590; fax 495.2711 ♿.

5 Palomino Euro Bistro ★$$ An offshoot of a Seattle-based chain, this eatery in **Hills Brothers Plaza** affords diners the best view of the Bay Bridge. The menu revolves around the wood-burning oven: Pizzas have cracker-thin crusts, and two of the best main courses are spit-roasted chicken and cedar-planked salmon with a hint of flavor picked up from the cedar. Even the apple tart gets a turn in the wood oven and comes out with a bronze glaze that is topped off with a drizzle of caramel sauce. ♦ Mediterranean ♦ M-F lunch and dinner; Sa dinner; Su brunch and dinner. 345 Spear St (between Harrison and Folsom Sts). 512.7400; fax 512.7358 ♿.

6 Gordon Biersch Brewery Restaurant ★$$ The three types of beer (all brewed in-house), lovely view of the Bay Bridge, and lively after-work crowd are reasons enough to check out this pub, but the food served in the upstairs dining loft is also pretty good. Try the garlic lamb, grilled and served with cucumber salad and flat bread, or the fried rock shrimp with a lemon-chili dipping sauce. Lunch selections are primarily salads and sandwiches, but dinnertime brings a full menu: baby back ribs with garlic fries, wild mushroom ravioli, and seared scallops with roasted *pasilla* chilies and fettuccine. Check out the rich chocolate *pots de crème* (custard) for dessert. Service can be erratic at busy times, however, and bar noise sometimes intrudes on the dining area. ♦ Californian/ Brew pub ♦ Daily lunch and dinner. 2 Harrison St (at Steuart St and The Embarcadero). 243.8246; fax 243.9214 ♿.

7 Delancey Street Restaurant ★$$ This self-described "ethnic American bistro" makes a social statement as well as a culinary one. It's run by residents of the Delancey Street Project, a residential community and training program for former down-and-outers. The handsome copper bar, hand-crafted by the residents, and the wood and brass appointments create a modern bistro look. The outdoor patio provides a lovely view of the Bay Bridge and the waterfront area. On any given day, the menu might include matzo-ball soup, Szechuan noodles with peanut sauce, Moroccan vegetable stew, or salmon mousse in phyllo. The American fare includes such staples as meat loaf, pot roast, barbecued baby back ribs, and chicken. ♦ American ♦ Tu-F lunch and dinner; Sa-Su brunch and dinner. 600 The Embarcadero (at Brannan St). 512.5179 ♿.

8 Red's Java House ★$ In contrast to all the new development going on around The Embarcadero since the freeway tumbled in the

127

SoMa (South of Market)/South Beach/Potrero Hill/Bayview–Hunters Point

1989 earthquake, this diner looks like an old crab shack. But for 35 years it has been a working-class gathering spot; now it's being invaded by the white-collar crowd. The double cheeseburgers served here are legendary, and there's no need to delve much deeper. ♦ American ♦ M-Sa breakfast and lunch. Pier 40 (off The Embarcadero, at Townsend St). 495.7260 ♿

9 Town's End Restaurant and Bakery ★★$$ The bakery here turns out chewy sourdough rye, poppy-seed wheat baguettes, parmesan bread sticks, and all kinds of delectable treats; in the restaurant, the basket of bread that graces the table is one of the best parts of the meal. The dining room is set off by curved partitions that combine with the bay views for a nautical ambience. The menu changes daily, but typical creations include a crisp triangle of polenta topped with shiitake, chanterelle, and portobello mushrooms; housemade ravioli stuffed with caramelized onions; and fettuccine with rock shrimp in a light, but intensely flavored, tomato broth. If you're lucky, chocolate angel-food cake or lemon meringue pie will be among the day's desserts. ♦ American ♦ Tu-F breakfast, lunch, and dinner; Sa brunch and dinner; Su brunch. 2 Townsend St (at The Embarcadero). 512.0749; fax 512.0927 ♿

10 Caffe Centro ★★$ The perfect out-of-the-way retreat, an hour spent here is almost as relaxing as a weekend in the country. With bright paintings on the wall, a floor painted in warm tones of gold, green, and red, and an attractive wood bar, this mellow space is the ideal spot for savoring a light breakfast and a leisurely perusal of the morning paper. The menu changes slightly for lunch, but the mood is just as free-spirited. Try one of the generous salads or a focaccia sandwich with grilled vegetables or chicken. Good choices for dessert are the brownies and cookies, which taste like they're freshly baked. ♦ Cafe ♦ M-F breakfast, lunch, and early dinner; Sa breakfast and lunch until 4:30PM. 102 South Park Ave (between Brannan and Bryant Sts). 882.1500; fax 882.1502 ♿

10 South Park Cafe ★★★$$ Here's a little bit of Paris overlooking the urban oasis of **South Park**. With the long, narrow room painted in ocher, the cozy bar, and the brief menu, the atmosphere is French cafe all the way. There's blood sausage, steamed mussels, roast pork tenderloin with potato puree, and duck breast with honey, ginger, and cinnamon. Desserts include a classic crème brûlée, profiteroles, and a bittersweet chocolate cake. ♦ French ♦ M-F breakfast, lunch, and dinner; Sa dinner. 108 South Park Ave (between Brannan and Bryant Sts). 495.7275; fax 495.7255 ♿

10 Ristorante Ecco ★★$$ The simple but stylish dining room, which looks out onto **South Park**, basks in warm earth tones. More dramatic is the impressive bar, which is set beneath a soaring ceiling along with some tables that accommodate dining room overflow. As at so many places, changes in the kitchen have caused the food to falter a bit. Still, an always reliable choice, *linguine al Ecco*, is one of the best dishes on the menu—an unlikely mix of linguine, pears, pecans, gorgonzola, and parmesan (ask to have it split into two portions for an appetizer). Another option for starters is the deep-fried squid with fennel and red onion. Main courses include *poussin* (broiler chicken) stuffed with olives, salmon served on white beans, or rabbit braised in red wine with mushrooms. ♦ Italian ♦ M-F lunch and dinner; Sa dinner. Reservations recommended. 101 South Park Ave (between Brannan and Bryant Sts). 495.3291; fax 495.7225 ♿

11 Collections Gift Store It's quite a surprise to find this refined shop amid the urban sprawl here, and it's worth seeking out for the good selection of coffees and chocolates and stellar inventory of specialty foods. In addition, the shop sells great candles and candlesticks, water pitchers shaped like pelicans, handmade plates and platters emblazoned with fish, and even seed packets to grow a fragrant herb garden. ♦ M-Sa. 380 Brannan St (between Second and Third Sts). 546.9298; fax 546.9397

12 Lumbini Garden statuary fills the windows of this shop, but the interior is stocked with all kinds of artsy ceramic bowls and plates, some handmade by local artisans. Most items have a produce motif: earrings shaped like carrots, candles that replicate avocados, teapots that look like a head of cabbage, and the like. ♦ M-F noon-8PM. 156 South Park Ave (between Second and Third Sts and Brannan and Bryant Sts). 896.2666; fax 896.2995 ♿

SoMa (South of Market)/South Beach/Potrero Hill/Bayview–Hunters Point

13 Ruby's Pizza ★★$ The place for delicious pizza with a thick cornmeal crust; just add a salad of fresh red-leaf lettuce, blue cheese, and creamy herb vinaigrette for one terrific meal. Or try one of the pastas, or such traditional entrées as braised duck leg with baked polenta. Butter-colored walls, arched partitions, and fresh flowers on the tables give the room a warm, romantic glow. One caveat: Service has never been particularly efficient, and the place always seems understaffed.
♦ Pizzeria/Italian ♦ Tu-F lunch and dinner; Sa-Su dinner. 489 Third St (between Bryant and Harrison Sts). 541.0795; fax 541.0503

14 The Wine House A warehouse-style shop with brick walls and wine stacked up in crates, it has one of the city's best inventories of French wines. Bordeaux, Burgundy, and Rhône selections are particularly strong; the store stocks multiple vintages of many of the best houses, including Château d'Yquem. Domestic and other non-French wines are also available. The knowledgeable staff can answer just about any question you can pose.
♦ M-Sa. 535 Bryant St (between Third and Fourth Sts). 495.8486; fax 495.4720

15 Bizou ★★$$ Loretta Keller made her reputation at **Stars** before moving to SoMa to open her own place, an old-time bistro with hanging light fixtures and glazed mustard-colored walls. The bar dominates the room, and the bar-side tables (by the windows overlooking Fourth Street) are perfect for those with romance in mind. Lately the quality of the food has dipped a bit, mainly because many of the dishes are too salty; however, the tempura-fried green beans, in a delicate batter with a bit of crunch and served with a fig dip, is still one of the best dishes of all time. The slow-simmered and gently baked dishes are just the thing on a foggy day. Sizzling Catalan shrimp and fresh grilled sardines are popular. Desserts are memorable, especially the summer berry pudding, with its dense, moist, cakey texture and plenty of fruit. ♦ French ♦ M-F lunch and dinner; Sa dinner. Reservations recommended. 598 Fourth St (at Brannan St). 543.2222; fax 543.2999

16 Fringale Restaurant ★★★★$$ Chef Gerald Hirigoyen has created just about the best casual French restaurant you'll find outside of France. What's more, he's maintained his reasonable prices, despite his soaring popularity (*Food & Wine* has named him one of the country's 10 best new chefs). Some of the standout dishes on his Basque-influenced menu include macaroni gratin with mushrooms; not-to-be-missed mussels flecked with parsley and crisp pieces of fried garlic; and a meltingly tender pork tenderloin confit. Hirigoyen used to be a pastry chef, so look forward to finishing up with a rich crème brulée, custardy fruit *clafouti* (sort of a cross between a flan and a fruit-filled pancake), or a Basque chocolate cake. The restaurant's bright yellow facade and interior, curved bar, and large fresh flower arrangements are all the more charming in the semi-industrial location. Most of the staffers are French and are just as appealing as their surroundings. The place has become so popular that there's often a wait, even with a reservation.
♦ French ♦ M-F lunch and dinner; Sa dinner. Reservations recommended. 570 Fourth St (between Brannan and Bryant Sts). 543.0573; fax 905.0317

17 Pazzia ★$ The utilitarian interior and the kitchen exposed in back attract the young crowd that gathers at this popular spot at lunchtime and late in the evening. Pizzas have a cracker-thin crust, pastas are perfectly dressed with classic sauces, and the roast chicken with crisp roast potatoes is truly satisfying. ♦ Italian ♦ M-F lunch and dinner; Sa dinner. 337 Third St (between Harrison and Folsom Sts). 512.1693; fax 542.8455

18 Max's Diner and Bakery ★$ A sign on one side of the door reads "This is a good place for a diet." A sign on the other side says "This is a bad place for a diet." Both are true. Sandwiches are huge, big enough to feed two people. There are also traditional blue-plate diner specials, low-fat dishes, and lots of salads. Check out the "Salary Savers" section of the menu, where a turkey dinner with mashed potatoes and vegetables is a bargain. Cakes, pies, and crisps—in huge portions—are fine desserts. ♦ American ♦ Daily lunch and dinner, F-Sa until midnight. 311 Third St (between Harrison and Folsom Sts). 546.6297; fax 546.9231

129

SoMa (South of Market)/South Beach/Potrero Hill/Bayview–Hunters Point

19 Canton Restaurant ★★$ The dim sum at this pleasant, if plain, spot can rival the best in the city. And because the location is far from the bustle of Chinatown, there's less competition for the carts of wonderful dumplings that come rolling by. The parchment-wrapped chicken (actually wrapped in foil) is bronzed and gooey, and it practically melts in your mouth. The *ha gow* (shrimp with ginger and onions in a tapioca-flour dumpling) is simple and delicious. Even if it's not on the menu, order the bok choy in oyster sauce; the sautéed, but crunchy, bright green cabbage is perfectly topped by a light, salty sauce. ♦ Chinese/Dim sum ♦ Daily lunch and dinner. 655 Folsom St (between Second and Third Sts). 495.3064 &

THE FLY TRAP Restaurant

20 The Fly Trap ★★★$$ With walls washed in beige and punctuated by brass-framed architectural prints, this attractive room provides a modern stage for revitalized versions of San Francisco classics. For appetizers try the celery Victor (poached and served with hard-boiled egg, vinaigrette, and anchovies), sautéed chicken livers with polenta, or crab cakes. Main courses include sautéed sweetbreads with mushrooms, calves' liver with bacon and onions, and chicken Jerusalem (with artichoke hearts). The chef, Robert Morgenstein, has done a superb job maintaining the character of traditional dishes while cutting much of the fat, a feat few have accomplished with such style and success. ♦ Californian ♦ M-F lunch and dinner; Sa dinner. 606 Folsom St (at Second St). 243.0580; fax 243.9539 &

21 Hawthorne Lane ★★★$$$ One of the newest (and hottest) restaurants in town, this place was opened by David and Ann Gingrass, who made a name for themselves at Wolfgang Puck's **Postrio**. The Gingrasses have created a warehouse-size dining room that's as grand as their former digs. Metal sculptures of cherry blossoms serve as banisters and as polished insets in a light wood screen at the entrance. Crisscrossing earthquake-bracing beams rise up to a huge skylight in the middle of the room. Another ceiling window above the open kitchen is filled with metal pipes from the exhaust fans that are as decorative as they are functional. The menu has equally unique offerings. Boldly flavored, the American food has a few Asian accents mixed in. Try grilled tenderloin of beef with spicy greens in fresh spring rolls; seared Maine scallops with mâche, Cabernet sauce, and horseradish crème fraîche; or slices of Sonoma lamb with artichoke risotto and tomato tarragon sauce. Another specialty is seared foie gras served with a rich chopped onion sauce and a vegetable-and-bread stuffed onion. Desserts also have an artistic bent: A light cheesecake, topped by a rich lemon curd, is on a poppy-seed cake and accompanied by swirls of blueberry sauce and whole blueberries; and a flaky almond tart with fresh peaches is served with delicate fresh peach ice cream topped with puff pastry and a chocolate butterfly. ♦ Californian ♦ M-F lunch and dinner; Sa-Su dinner. 22 Hawthorne St (at Howard St). 777.9779; fax 777.9782 &

22 Caribbean Zone ★$$ The airplane cabin suspended above the dining room is not just for decoration—it's a cocktail lounge that serves drinks with names like Sex in the Jungle, Goomba Boomba, and Belize Breeze. The dining room below offers a lush Kon Tiki setting, complete with an indoor waterfall. Not surprisingly, food isn't the major draw here, but it's pretty good. The tropics-inspired menu lists lots of munching options: conch fritters with a lime-mustard mayonnaise, grilled prawns with chipotle and orange juice, and panfried green plantains with salsa. Those who stick around for a main course can order paella, jerk chicken, salmon with sesame seeds, or smoked pork loin with grilled pineapple and rum. ♦ Caribbean ♦ M-F lunch and dinner; Sa dinner. 55 Natoma St (between First and Second Sts). 541.9465; fax 974.641

23 Eddie Rickenbacker's ★★$$ For a while this was a hot spot; now it's settled down into a popular after-work meeting place. The decor is an incongruous mix of Victoriana and sports bar, typified by the two enormous crystal chandeliers and three motorcycles hanging from the ceiling. The Caesar salad is good, as are the hamburgers and the crisp french fries. More substantial choices include grilled salmon, roast chicken, and other straightforward dishes. ♦ American ♦ M-Sa lunch and dinner. 133 Second St (at Mission St). 543.3498; fax 543.7526 &

MONDO CAFFE

24 Mondo Caffe ★★$ In marked contrast to the drab stretch of Mission Street on which it's located, this stylish cafe is visually arresting, with a patterned concrete floor, a polished wooden counter with a molded black cement top, sponge-painted walls, and copper-mesh–covered lights. The simple

SoMa (South of Market)/South Beach/Potrero Hill/Bayview–Hunters Point

menu features focaccia sandwiches, frittatas, and a few appetizers (try the whole stuffed artichoke). Don't pass up the vegetable sandwich; it's layered with wilted greens, mushrooms, and paper-thin slices of zucchini, topped with cheese, flattened and grilled into a melting, yet crisp, masterpiece, and served with a pile of ultrafresh greens. Another good sandwich is made with thin slices of pork loin and topped with a generous dollop of tuna mayonnaise. ♦ Italian/Cafe ♦ M-F breakfast, lunch, and dinner until 7PM. 602 Mission St (at Second St). 882.1682; fax 882.1683 ♿

25 Garden Court ★★$$$$ There's no prettier room in San Francisco than this one in the lobby of the **Sheraton Palace** hotel. Beneath a spectacular glass roof, a sea of elegant tables, chairs, and willowy palms is arranged over a richly patterned carpet. The optimum time to visit is for afternoon tea; the aristocratic aura and attentive service bring a Victorian fantasy to life. But try it for other meals, too, as it's been much improved by more attentive service and chef Kerry Heffernan's updated menu. The chicken and beef salads are good choices. ♦ Contemporary ♦ Tu-Sa breakfast, lunch, afternoon tea, and dinner; Su brunch. Reservations recommended. 2 New Montgomery St (at Market St). 392.8600; fax 243.8062 ♿

25 Kyo-ya ★★★$$ One of the city's best Japanese restaurants lies within the **Sheraton Palace** hotel; the melt-in-the-mouth tuna sashimi here is unsurpassed. Full dinners begin with a vibrant miso and a small plate of pickled vegetables. Main courses include shrimp tempura—five prawns encased in a lacy batter—served with a rock-shrimp cake and fresh vegetables. The grilled sea bass is perfection, marinated and cooked to a mahogany hue, with a moist, snow-white interior. The ambience is serene, the decor, almost austere. Silk partitions separate the sushi bar from the dramatically lit dining room with black lacquered chairs and fresh flowers on each highly glossed wood table. ♦ Japanese ♦ M-F lunch and dinner; Sa dinner. 2 New Montgomery St (at Market St). 392.8600; fax 243.8062 ♿

25 Maxfield's $$ A cozy grill rounds out the dining options at the **Sheraton Palace** hotel. The specialty is spit-roasted meats, like leg of lamb and Cornish game hen. ♦ American ♦ Daily lunch and dinner. 2 New Montgomery St (at Market St). 392.8600; fax 243.8062 ♿

26 Doudin Sourdough Bakery & Cafe ★$ With its rich wood-and-brass interior, this could be a movie set for a turn-of-the-century grill. There are fresh baguettes and some of the best sourdough in the city. The cafe offers continental breakfasts as well as a bountiful selection of sandwiches, soups, and salads. ♦ Cafe ♦ M-F 6AM-6:30PM; Sa 9AM-4PM. 619 Market St (between New Montgomery and Third Sts). 281.8200 ♿. Also at: 157 Jefferson St (between Mason and Taylor Sts). 928.1849; fax 776.1778. 399 10th Ave (at Geary Blvd). 221.1210; fax 221.3854 ♿

CAFFÈ MUSEO

27 Caffè Museo ★★$ The **San Francisco Museum of Modern Art (SFMOMA)** has a cafe as chic as its environs. The eye-catching decor consists of wooden pegboards, a slatted ceiling, a striped granite floor, and leather directors' chairs. The cafeteria is run by Real Restaurants, which brought the Bay Area such eateries as **Bistro Rôti, Mustards Grill, Ristorante Tra Vigne,** and **Bix.** Sandwiches, including an excellent grilled vegetable version, are made with focaccia, and the salad choices range from barley with mushrooms and artichokes to saffron rice studded with bits of zucchini and whole rock shrimp. Skip the *pizzetta,* which tastes like an airy focaccia crust pulled from a grocery store freezer. ♦ Mediterranean ♦ Tu-Su breakfast, lunch, and dinner until 6PM, Th until 9PM. 151 Third St (between Howard and Mission Sts). 357.4500; fax 357.4506

29 California Creole Cafe $$ The glass walls, granite floor, and bare tables provide an airy setting for down-to-earth New Orleans–style food. Trouble is, Creole spice blends are used too liberally, making just about everything taste much the same. Best bets include barbecued chicken wings, gumbo, and peach cobbler. ♦ Californian/Creole ♦ M-W, Su lunch until 6PM; Th-Sa lunch and dinner until 9PM. 720 Howard St (at Third St), Terrace level. 974.1762; fax 974.6907 ♿

29 Pasqua ★$ This chain's branch within the impressive **Yerba Buena Gardens** arts complex has a breezy open-air atmosphere. Surprisingly comfortable stainless-steel chairs and matching tables fill the glass-walled room and cluster under umbrellas on the outside terrace. At the cafeteria-style counter choose from fresh-baked muffins, scones, cookies, and desserts to go with coffee. Breakfast includes a choice of egg dishes, while lunchtime offerings consist of pizza, salads, and sandwiches made with seeded baguettes and such fillings as smoked turkey with lemon, thyme, and caper sauce; roasted eggplant with ricotta; or roast beef with parmesan, sun-dried tomatoes, and a roasted red pepper sauce. ♦ Cafe ♦ Daily breakfast and lunch until 5PM. 730 Howard St (between Third and Fourth Sts). 541.9962; fax 541.9964 ♿

SoMa (South of Market)/South Beach/Potrero Hill/Bayview–Hunters Point

29 OPTS Cafe ★★$$ A visual and culinary treat awaits diners on the second floor of the **Visual Arts Center** at the **Yerba Buena Gardens** complex. A wall of glass overlooks the gardens, and a curving purple wall contrasts vividly with the lime green–and-white walls elsewhere in the building. The food has an equally creative bent and is often tailored to match the special shows at **SFMOMA**. Part of the menu is devoted to a "featured artist," where local chefs supply their favorite recipes. Then there's the "permanent collection," which includes a terrific Caesar salad with loads of crispy croutons; Moroccan chicken pie wrapped in phyllo, sprinkled with powdered sugar, and served with an eggplant and pomegranate salad; and a sandwich of smoked chicken and sausage with fennel confit and mustard on sourdough bread. Don't pass up the lemon tart or the multilayered chocolate cake, better than Mom ever dreamed of making. ♦ Cafe ♦ Tu-Su 11AM-5PM. Third and Mission Sts. 896.1770 ♿

29 Kinoko ★$$$ This Japanese place within the **Marriott** offers sushi and sashimi; combination entrées—chicken and shrimp or steak and lobster—are cooked table-side. ♦ Japanese ♦ Daily dinner. 55 Fourth St (between Mission and Market Sts). 896.1600; fax 777.2799 ♿

29 View Lounge The 39th floor of the **Marriott** hotel is an ideal place to enjoy an appetizer, a dessert, or a nightcap with the glittery skyline of San Francisco laid out before you. ♦ Daily. 55 Fourth St (between Mission and Market Sts). 896.1600; fax 777.2799 ♿

30 Fresh Choice $ This cafeteria chain should be the *last* choice, at least for pasta, which is mushy and dull. But it's an option for those looking to save time or money—just stick to the all-you-can-eat salad bar. There are at least a half-dozen dressings, all kinds of greens and toppings, such pretossed salads as Caesar and Chinese chicken, as well as stuffed baked potatoes, muffins, and bread. The large interior is pleasant, as fast-food places go. ♦ Cafeteria/Salad bar ♦ Daily lunch and dinner. 150 Fourth St (between Howard and Mission Sts). 777.2075; fax 777.2076 ♿. Also at: 120 Stockton St (at O'Farrell St), Basement. 989.6861; fax 989.6863 ♿

31 Chevys ★★$$ This enormous branch of the chain is supposed to look like a Mexican dive—bright colors, stacked boxes of beer—but the cardboard boxes that serve as partitions are empty; so it all comes across as less than authentic, thanks in part to its location in a glassy modern office building. The food can be very good, however. Tortillas are made in-house, and the chips and salsa are some of the best around. True to the "fresh Mex" trend, many of the dishes are low in fat and cholesterol. The fajitas are excellent but avoid the *chiles rellenos* (stuffed chili peppers), which have a thick, greasy batter. ♦ Mexican ♦ Daily lunch and dinner. 150 Fourth St (at Howard St). 543.8060; fax 543.0410 ♿. Also at: 2 Embarcadero Center (Front St, between Sacramento and Clay Sts), Promenade level. 391.2323; fax 391.4404 ♿

32 LuLu ★★★$$ One of the best meals in San Francisco can be had at this recently expanded spot. Formerly three separate eateries, they are now connected throughout and serve the same menu (but each space has different hours). Fish and tender cuts of meat come slow-cooked from a rotisserie or a wood-burning oven. The food, presented on Italian pottery platters, is served family style. Best appetizer choices are the fried artichokes topped with thin shavings of parmesan cheese, and the roasted mussels with drawn butter. For entrées consider the roast chicken or the grilled rib eye for two, served over a bed of thinly sliced potatoes and artichokes. Don't miss the fire-roasted chestnuts with white truffle honey. Warm chocolate cake, with a gush of molten chocolate in the center, is the most popular dessert. The dramatic **Main Room** has a soaring ceiling with a skylight, seating on two levels, and an open kitchen; the **Bis** is a much smaller, more intimate space; and the **Cafe** has the most casual ambience. ♦ French/Italian ♦ Main Room: M-F lunch and dinner; Sa-Su brunch and dinner. Bis: Daily dinner. Cafe: M-F breakfast, lunch, and dinner; Sa-Su dinner. Reservations recommended for the Main Room and the Bis. 816 Folsom St (at Fourth St). 495.5775; fax 495.7810 ♿

Le Charm
French Bistro

33 Le Charm ★★$ Who would think that anyone would open a stylish French bistro in one of the ugliest strips south of Market Street? Well, husband-and-wife team Alain Delangle, former sous-chef at **Sherman House**, and Lina Yew, previously a pastry chef at **Fleur de Lys**, have done just that. They've created a charming place, with pretty lights, soft yellow walls, an outdoor patio, and a

SoMa (South of Market)/South Beach/Potrero Hill/Bayview–Hunters Point

copper-topped bar that separates the kitchen from the 45-seat dining room. Try the rich onion soup; sizzling-hot sautéed chicken livers; garlic roasted chicken with mashed potatoes and greens; or salmon topped with bread crumbs on a bed of spinach and mashed potatoes. Save room for the thinly glazed orange crème brûlée or the French apple tart. The lunch crowd is as diverse as the neighborhood: The reasonable prices attract filling-station attendants, artists, and postal workers, as well as the chi-chi crowd. ♦ French ♦ M lunch, Tu-F lunch and dinner; Sa dinner. 315 Fifth St (at Folsom St). 546.6128 ♿

34 Cadillac Bar and Grill ★$ Pop in here around Happy Hour, when an array of free munchies can be had with the purchase of a margarita or a beer. Nibbling away on chimichangas or nachos, you'll be full before you know it. The warehouse-sized restaurant, behind the **Fifth and Mission Garage,** offers a few standouts, including multigrain chips and salsa; nachos smothered in guacamole, cheese, jalapeños, and sour cream; tamales; and enchiladas. ♦ Mexican ♦ Daily lunch and dinner. 325 Minna St (off Fifth St, between Mission and Howard Sts). 543.8226; fax 543.8682 ♿

35 San Francisco Centre Across the street from the **Powell Street** cable-car turnaround, this vertical shopping mall of 90 stores is anchored by **Nordstrom,** and boasts multiple places to eat as well as to shop. The concourse level of the center is ringed with cafeteria-style restaurants. None of them will bring you back for more, but they're convenient for shoppers and people working nearby. ♦865 Market St (at Fifth St). 495.5656; fax 512.6770 ♿

Within the San Francisco Centre:

The Pub $ You gotta love the look of this authentic re-creation of an English watering hole. Located just off **Nordstrom**'s men's store, the pub attracts a mostly male lunchtime crowd and satisfies hearty appetites. Selections include the ploughman's plate of cheese, all kinds of appetizers, crab cakes, pizza, and a steak sandwich. ♦ English/American ♦ Daily breakfast (all day), lunch, and dinner. N1 level. 978.5152 ♿

Champagne Exchange $$ The wall-length display of Champagnes and sparkling wines underscores the focus of this burgundy-and-gray **Nordstrom** restaurant, whose food was designed to match the drink. The bill of fare highlights lighter meals, with lots of seafood, such as prawns, salmon, and caviar, and several entrée salads. The concept here of pairing food with wine started out wonderfully, but has become tired because of the slipshod preparation. ♦ Californian ♦ Daily lunch. N3 level. 978.5153; fax 978.5089 ♿

City Centre Grill $$ A panoramic view of the cable-car turnaround is the draw of this **Nordstrom** eatery, where tables are set with white tablecloths, brass lanterns, and fresh flowers. The regular menu of sandwiches and salads is augmented by daily specials and more substantial fare, such as a filet mignon with mushrooms and a bourbon sauce. Solo diners can sit at the granite counter in front of the open kitchen. You can see that the cooks are trying, but the results are still disappointing. ♦ Californian ♦ Daily lunch and dinner. N4 level. 978.5155 ♿

Cafe Express $ Adjacent to the **City Centre Grill,** this spot features sandwiches, soups, and salads. Diners order at the counter and take a seat, and the food is brought to the table. The blue-plate special—soup, salad, and half a sandwich—is a great deal. Quality varies, however; some days the salads are crisp and cold, other times, warm and limp. ♦ American ♦ Daily lunch and dinner. N4 level. 621.4778; fax 978.5080

Williams-Sonoma A link in the chain of housewares shops, it stocks all kinds of must-have kitchen gadgets and specialty foods. ♦ Daily. Second floor. 546.0171 ♿. Also at: 150 Post St (between Kearny St and Grant Ave). 362.6904; fax 362.2852 ♿; 2000 Chestnut St (at Fillmore St). 929.2520 ♿

Autumn Harvest This shop has one of the best selections of edibles in the city, many from California. Along with the standard olive oils, flavored vinegars, and pastas are such unusual foodstuffs as court bouillons with thyme or dill and all kinds of flavored nuts, including honey-orange or anise almonds and chili-lemon pistachios. ♦ Daily. Concourse level. 543.0705; fax 543.1512 ♿

La Nouvelle Patisserie $ Old-fashioned marble-and-iron tables set the tone at this cafe, conveniently located by the center's Fifth Street entrance. The sandwiches, quiche, salads, and wide assortment of sweets are of varying quality. ♦ Cafe ♦ Daily. Street level. 979.0553 ♿. Also at: 2184 Union St (at Fillmore St). 931.7655; fax 931.0544 ♿

In the late 18th and early 19th centuries, the area that is now San Francisco (then known as Yerba Buena) was covered with seven large ranchos, which raised beef cattle to produce meat, hide, and tallow.

SoMa (South of Market)/South Beach/Potrero Hill/Bayview–Hunters Point

Farmers' Markets

Whether they are professional chefs or just like to cook as a hobby, San Franciscans are obsessed with getting the freshest available produce. To meet this demand, a number of outdoor markets selling food right from the farm are cropping up everywhere—at last count there were 65 in the nine counties that comprise the Bay Area. At three different locations in San Francisco, on four different days, just-picked fruits and vegetables are trucked in by local farmers. A trip to a farmers' market is a fun way for visitors to learn more about the Bay Area food scene. And although a tourist staying in a hotel may not need fresh produce, other nonperishable goods are also sold at these markets, including honey, flavored oils and vinegars, dried flowers, and local crafts. Each market has its own unique character and special features, making it a refreshing change from cookie-cutter chain supermarkets. For instance, the wildly popular **Ferry Plaza Farmers' Market** has stands offering small samples from some of the city's top restaurants and organizes a tour called "Shop with the Chef," during which a well-known cook picks out produce at the market and gives shoppers ideas on how to prepare dishes using the selections; tours also include organized tastings and activities for children. Listed below are some of the best markets in San Francisco:

Alemany Farmers' Market Located in a gritty, industrial part of the city, this 50-year-old market is a great place to learn about and buy Asian produce. You can also get California-grown fruits and vegetables, dried fruits and nuts, honeys, and jams. ♦ Sa 6AM-5PM. ♦100 Alemany Blvd (between Hwy 101 and Prentiss St, near the intersection of Hwys 101 and 280).

Ferry Plaza Farmers' Market One of the newest markets in the city, it has fast become the most popular—so much so that a second branch has opened near the **Hyatt Regency**, at the foot of **Market Street**; it's held on Tuesdays. The vendors here sell all kinds of food and produce—and even beautiful dried-flower bouquets. Be sure to check out the stand where chef David Gingrass of **Hawthorne Lane** restaurant sells his specialty sausages. ♦ Tu 11:30AM-3PM; Sa 8AM-1:30PM. ♦ Tuesday market: Market St (near the Hyatt Regency). No phone; Saturday market: W Ferry Plaza (at the Embarcadero end of Market St, near the Ferry Building and World Trade Center). 981.3004.

Heart of the City Market This market held near the **Civic Center** draws people from all over San Francisco. City Hall clerks, senior citizens, and Asian families from the **Tenderloin** can be seen jostling each other at the farm stands, trying to get that perfect red apple, fresh lettuce, or sweet corn on the cob. ♦ W, Su 7AM-5PM. ♦ United Nations Plaza (intersection of Hyde and Market Sts, in the Civic Center).

36 Bistro M ★★$$$ Michel Richard, best known for Citrus in Los Angeles, came north in 1994 with this handsome 160-seat bistro in the **Milano** hotel. The light wood appointments, modernistic ceiling mural, and arched windows overlooking the street all add to the fresh-scrubbed ambience. Richard, a former pastry chef, isn't afraid of butter and cream and uses both with abandon; the results range from extraordinary to mundane. The menu features 23 starters and about 18 main courses. Best bets are onion soup; oxtail encircled by vegetables and penne pasta; and steamed vegetables with garlic aioli. For dessert, try the crème brûlée sandwiched between sheets of puff pastry, or the delicious, cakelike apple brioche bread pudding. ♦ Californian/French ♦ Daily breakfast, lunch, and dinner. 55 Fifth St (between Mission and Market Sts). 543.5554; fax 543.5843 ⅍

37 Raza's $ This dinerlike eatery in the **Aston Pickwick Hotel** is known for its footlong hamburger, served on a baguette. ♦ American ♦ Daily breakfast, lunch, and dinner. 85 Fifth St (at Mission St). 495.4849 ⅍

38 M & M Tavern ★$ A block from the *Chronicle* and *Examiner,* this beloved greasy spoon is a real journalists' hangout. And the food's actually not greasy; every item is freshly prepared. Burgers are fat and juicy, and the hand-cut fries are the best (ask for them crispy). Any of the daily specials—like liver with onions, mashed potatoes, and mixed vegetables, or corned beef and cabbage—will fill you up for a pittance. The staff treats everyone like regulars, making this a cozy home away from home for locals and visitors alike. ♦ American ♦ M-Sa breakfast, lunch, and dinner. 798 Fifth St (at Howard St). 362.6386 ⅍

39 Wine Club With its stacked rows of crates and bottles, this shop is far from posh, but the extraordinary wine selection makes it a connoisseur's delight, and the prices are hard to beat—it's unusual to be able to locate a hard-to-find wine *and* get a deal at the same time. In the back, there's a tasting bar and a small cache of serious wine paraphernalia for sale. Make a special trip. ♦ Daily. 953 Harrison St (between Fifth and Sixth Sts). 512.9086

SoMa (South of Market)/South Beach/Potrero Hill/Bayview–Hunters Point

40 The Line-Up ★$$ As popular for its drinks as its food, this is a good place to settle in at the bar with a margarita and crunch on a few chips. The Mexican fare here includes all the standards—we're talking tacos, *chiles rellenos,* and enchiladas. It's owned by the same people who run **La Posada** in Pacific Heights and **Leticia's** in the Castro.
♦ Mexican ♦ Daily lunch and dinner. 398 Seventh St (at Harrison St). 861.2887

41 The Up & Down Club $$ Part owner and supermodel Christy Turlington lends this place cachet. Upstairs is a bar and a disc jockey; downstairs is a restaurant with live jazz performances most nights. The short menu runs to such nibbles as polenta sticks with gorgonzola, deep-fried calamari, and duck quesadillas with red-pepper salsa. A few pastas and such main courses as seafood ragout and grilled rib eye round out the offerings. ♦ Californian ♦ Restaurant M-Th, Sa dinner 8-10PM; F 7:30-10PM; bar M, W-Sa from 10PM to 2AM. 1151 Folsom St (between Seventh and Eighth Sts). 626.2388; fax 626.4750

41 Julie's Supper Club ★★$$ Every night is like a fraternity party at this 1950s-style joint. Push through the twentysomething crowd to the bar and sip a martini (the drink of choice here) while waiting for a table. After a few years of seesawing quality, the kitchen is on the upswing again. The menu showcases finger food like fried wontons, fried calamari, and chicken brochettes. For the main event, the grilled New York steak, leg of lamb, or pork chops will provide the fuel for partying the night away. ♦ American ♦ M-Sa dinner. Reservations recommended. 1123 Folsom St (at Langton St). 861.0707

41 San Francisco Patisserie Cafe ★★$ The trompe l'oeil window and the crack painted on the cement wall in back give this industrial-chic cafe whimsical appeal. The stylish decor is a bit cold, but the friendly service and well-crafted food warm up the place. A long bar holds the makings for a great cup of coffee and a sweet snack. From the kitchen come interesting breakfast and lunch dishes. Try the *koba* (a torpedo of ground lamb and herbs that's rolled in cracked wheat, fried to a crisp crust, and drizzled with a roasted-pepper-and-tomato sauce) or *croque madame,* a toasted ham sandwich dipped in melted cheese and topped with two eggs sunny side up. The delicious breads and sweets are baked in-house. ♦ Coffeehouse/Takeout ♦ M-F breakfast and lunch until 5PM; Sa until 3PM. 1155 Folsom St (between Seventh and Eighth Sts). 703.0557

42 Half Shell Restaurant and Oyster Bar ★★$$ Many locals rate this among their favorite seafood houses. Hidden by a weathered fence, the former lumberyard features a lovely brick walkway that leads to an airy dining room of natural wood and exposed beams. The seafood selection ranges from striped bass with butter sauce and fried capers, to a mixed seafood grill drizzled with jalapeño puree. The service can be chaotic—just be warned, and have a good time anyway. ♦ Seafood ♦ M-F lunch and dinner; Sa dinner. 64 Rausch St (between Folsom and Howard Sts). 552.7677; fax 552.5032

43 Ideal Deli ★$ This "Mexicatessen" is the place to try *tortas* (Mexican sandwiches) or to pick up a plump burrito stuffed with a choice of meat and beans—and don't forget the excellent salsa. Specials include chicken in red chili sauce, pork with green chilies, and beef Colorado with chilies. Sure, it looks like a dive, but a crowd of satisfied regulars keeps the kitchen busy, so they're clearly doing something right. ♦ Mexican/Takeout ♦ M-F breakfast, lunch, and dinner. 1198 Folsom St (at Eighth St). 626.6043

44 Appam Indian Cuisine ★$ One of the prettier Indian restaurants, it's outfitted with a mahogany bar, murals of temple dancers and Indian landscapes, and a blue-tiled open kitchen; the small dining area overlooks a garden patio. Start with *samosas* (flaky pastries filled with curried potatoes and peas) and the stuffed breads. The kitchen specializes in *dum pukht* (clay-pot dishes) of meat and vegetable curries that are topped with dough and baked until golden and bubbling. Tandoori preparations, including squid and lamb, earn raves. ♦ Indian ♦ Daily dinner. 1259 Folsom St (between Eighth and Ninth Sts). 626.2798

45 Basil ★★$$ This is one of the prettiest Thai restaurants in the city, with a sleek decor that includes a wall of glass bricks, a polished cement bar against a wall of midnight blue, yellow accents, wood floors, white tablecloths topped with butcher paper, and bistro-style chairs. The kitchen updates traditional fare: Huge prawns are splayed on a platter and seasoned with white pepper and garlic; spring

SoMa (South of Market)/South Beach/Potrero Hill/Bayview–Hunters Point

rolls are cut on the diagonal to reveal a bright tangle of purple cabbage; beef short ribs get a lift from a mild, basil-laced curry with a confetti of lime leaves; and New Zealand mussels are steamed with Chardonnay. Save room for dessert: sweet coconut rice served with half a sliced mango. ♦ Thai ♦ M-F lunch and dinner; Sa dinner. 1175 Folsom St (between Eighth and Ninth Sts). 552.8999; fax 552.8889

46 Icon Byte Bar & Grill $ Connect to the Internet while grabbing a "byte" at this fun and trendy spot, where customers stand in line to go on-line. In addition to Information Highway access, there's frequent live entertainment, Happy Hours, and alcohol-free "smart" martinis that are designed to perk up the brain. The restaurant recently changed hands, however, and the new owners do not seem as enthusiastic about the concept as the previous ones; the place has become more of a novelty attraction than a restaurant (the food is decidedly uneven in quality). For spicy palates there's Cajun-spiced fries, jambalaya with shrimp and sausage, and Cuban steak with chili-laden roasted-tomato salsa. Tamer eaters can try soft polenta with roasted garlic and fried sage, or roast chicken with new potatoes. ♦ American/Continental ♦ M lunch; Tu-F lunch and dinner; Sa dinner. 299 Ninth St (at Folsom St). 861.BYTE; fax 861.2989; e-mail iconbytebar.com

47 WA-HA-KA! (Oaxaca Mexican Grill) ★★$ A converted warehouse has become a popular refueling stop on the nightclub circuit in this part of town. The kitchen turns out excellent burritos and good, gooey quesadillas; the bar features scores of tequilas to sample straight up or in margaritas. ♦ Mexican ♦ M-F lunch and dinner; Sa brunch and dinner; Su dinner. 1489 Folsom St (at 11th St). 861.1410; fax 861.1410. Also at: 2141 Polk St (between Broadway and Vallejo St). 775.1055; 1980 Union St (at Buchanan St). 775.4145

48 Twenty Tank Brewery One of only four brew pubs in San Francisco, this gigantic watering hole features six house-brewed ales. Nachos and a few other beer-friendly noshes are on hand, and there's a shuffle-board table for entertainment. ♦ Daily 11:30AM-1:30AM. No credit cards accepted. 316 11th St (between Harrison and Folsom Sts). 255.9455; fax 255.MEAL

49 11 Ristorante + Bar ★★$$ Before its makeover, it was called **Undici** ("11" in Italian). Now the tone is slightly more casual and bar-oriented, and the dramatic two-story interior makes a comfortable venue for watching the party-happy crowd. The menu lists portobello mushrooms with polenta, steamed mussels or clams in a white-wine garlic sauce, pizza, and pasta. The half-dozen main courses include roast chicken with garlic mashed potatoes; a classic petrale sole with lemon, capers, and white wine; and peppered New York steak with brandy sauce. Live music, mostly jazz, is featured regularly. The place stays open until midnight on Friday and Saturday. ♦ Italian ♦ M-Sa dinner. 374 11th St (between Harrison and Folsom Sts). 431.3337

50 Hamburger Mary's ★$ Pierce your nose, dye your hair (purple or cherry red would be appropriate), add a tattoo, and you'll fit right in at this alternative universe. The decor looks like a collection of stuff from somebody's attic. The hamburgers are the main draw, although other sandwiches and soups can be very good. Still, the grazing is not nearly as satisfying as the gazing. ♦ American ♦ Tu-Su lunch and dinner. 1582 Folsom St (at 12th St). 626.5767; fax 626.1985

51 Manora's Thai Cuisine ★★$$ There are two kinds of Thai restaurants: those that lean toward the sour side and those that veer to the sweet. This simple and unassuming spot is one of the best examples of the sweet type. Devoted customers swear by the curries, the pork infused with garlic and pepper, and the minced fish steamed in banana leaves. ♦ Thai ♦ M-F lunch and dinner; Sa-Su dinner. 1600 Folsom St (at 12th St). 861.6224. Also at: 3226 Mission St (at Valencia St). 826.4639

52 Big Nate's Bar-B-Que ★$ Owned by basketball superstar Nate Thurman, this is your standard linoleum-and-Formica barbecue joint. The business consists mostly of takeout and catering, with a few seats for eating in-house. The ovens groan with bronzed chickens, crinkled sausage, charred hunks of brisket, and glazed slabs of ribs. Each of the sauces—mild, medium, and hot—carries an undercurrent of sweetness that combines perfectly with the smoky meats. ♦ Barbecue/Takeout ♦ Daily lunch and dinner. 1665 Folsom St (between 12th and 13th Sts). 861.4242; fax 861.1633

SoMa (South of Market)/South Beach/Potrero Hill/Bayview–Hunters Point

53 Homestead Ravioli Since 1917, this factory has been turning out stuffed pastas. At least a half-dozen kinds are offered in one- or two-pound boxes at near-wholesale prices. In addition to the traditional beef- or cheese-stuffed versions, there's ravioli filled with mushrooms, or sun-dried tomatoes and almonds, or a lean mix of seasoned veal, pork, and turkey. All are free of MSG and preservatives and can be frozen for several months. ♦ M-F 7AM-noon and 1PM-3:30PM. 120 14th St (at Folsom St). 864.2992 &

54 Woodward's Garden ★★★$$ Practically abutting the multilevel freeway, this place in a brick building on a dingy corner is a true find. Inside, the kitchen dominates an L-shaped room big enough for just nine tables. The menu, which changes weekly, showcases everything good about California cuisine. Whether it's a massive pork chop accompanied by a hillock of mashed potatoes and a vibrant tomato-and-mushroom ragout, or roasted salmon topped with aioli and arranged over a bed of white beans and spinach, it's fresh and delicious. Lemon *pots de crème* and moist ginger cake with fruit compote and rum-scented whipped cream show up from time to time, along with other satisfying sweets. ♦ American ♦ W-Su dinner. No credit cards accepted. 1700 Mission St (at Duboce Ave). 621.7122 &

55 Costco Some of the best beef in the city is for sale at this members-only warehouse store (but the rather high membership fee makes it impractical for visitors to join). The meats are sold in bulk, which means you'd better have a big freezer (or a lot of friends) to stock up here. The steaks are of excellent quality, though, and the pork, lamb, and chicken are as good as or better than in most supermarkets. Check out the frozen-food aisles for designer items like Wolfgang Puck's pizza, Amy's lasagna and enchiladas, Nancy's bite-sized quiches, and more. There's also a wide assortment of olive oils, **Starbucks** coffee, and occasional bargains on wine. ♦ Daily. 450 10th St (at Harrison St). 626.4288; fax 626.4599 &

GEORGE'S

56 George's Global Kitchen ★$ "Think globally, eat locally," says George, and you could hardly get more global than his cross-cultural cuisine, or more local than his quaint little diner tucked beneath the freeway. With a partly exposed kitchen and a dining counter, the atmosphere is homey and the eclectic fare ranges from lamb quesadillas with a Yucatecan salsa to Thai salad with rock shrimp in a spicy dressing, grilled salmon served with white beans, and meat loaf with garlic mashed potatoes. ♦ Californian ♦ M lunch; Tu-F lunch and dinner; Sa dinner. 340 Division St (between 10th and Bryant Sts). 864.4224; fax 864.2332 &

57 Trader Joe's This branch of the popular Southern California discount specialty-foods chain offers nearly a thousand items under its own label, and many brand-name close-outs. Here's the place to pick up chili-lime tortilla chips and salsas, fruit juices, refrigerated sandwiches, salads, enchiladas, lasagnas, quiches, and frozen dinners. Also stocked are jams, vinegars, pickled vegetables, breads, and cookies. The wines offered are fine for everyday drinking; most are low-priced. ♦ Daily. 555 Ninth St (at Bryant St). 863.1292 &

58 Stamp Francisco A mesmerizing array of rubber stamps, many with food themes, is sold here. With an ink pad and stamps of pears, berries, clusters of cherries, or ornate crossed forks and knives, anyone can create cool business cards, invitations, or stationery. It's easy to drop $50 quickly, so keep tabs on what you're tossing into the shopping basket. ♦ Tu-Sa. 466 Eighth St (between Bryant and Harrison Sts). 252.5975; fax 252.5978 &

59 Kiss ★★$$$ Hidden within a commercial-looking building is this romantic oasis: Fabric drapes from the ceiling, fresco-inspired murals cover the walls, and more gauzy drapery is loosely tied around each table. The creative food is a blend of East and West, and might include fillet of chicken with orange sauce, pork tenderloin with poached pears and red wine–and-cinnamon sauce, or venison in port sauce. The only downside is that too many of the entrées are sweetly sauced. ♦ Californian/French ♦ M-Sa lunch and dinner. 680 Eighth St (between Townsend and Brannan Sts). 552.8757; fax 552.8758 &

60 Sally's ★★$ The bright blue corrugated-tin building looks more like an auto-body shop than a restaurant, but this cafeteria-style eatery draws people from all over town, especially for the omelettes and baked goods. The hunks who work out at the nearby **World Gym** stop by for such low-fat items as Chuck's stir-fry (egg whites scrambled with carrots, celery, and mushrooms) and oatmeal

137

SoMa (South of Market)/South Beach/Potrero Hill/Bayview–Hunters Point

pancakes with walnuts, raisins, and brown sugar. **Sally's Upstairs Cafe** (also cafeteria style) highlights veggie burgers, burritos, and salads; **Sally's Bakery** packages luscious scones, cookies, coffee cakes, muffins, breads, and savories to go. ♦ American/Cafe ♦ Daily breakfast and lunch. 300 DeHaro St (at 16th St). 626.3354, bakery 626.0838; fax 626.6155 ♿

60 Rustico ★$$ Famous for its excellent crisp-crusted pizza, this eat-in/take-out spot is small, but attractive. If none of the dozen or so fresh-tasting topping combinations appeals, create your own from a list of 25 ingredients. A few sandwiches, salads, soups, and pasta dishes round out the menu. ♦ Pizzeria/Takeout ♦ M-F 8AM-8PM; Sa 10AM-5PM; Su 11AM-4PM. 300 DeHaro St (at 16th St). 252.0180; fax 255.1533 ♿

61 Garibaldi's Cafe $$ Don't mistake this once-popular spot for the similarly named restaurant in the Presidio. This place has lost much of its charm, thanks to the uneven quality of the food. Pastas are often underseasoned and oversauced, and the food is crowded onto plates like diner specials—but at white-tablecloth prices. Still, the old-fashioned barroom, with a wood bar and porthole windows, has style; the adjacent dining room is decked out in corrugated-tin siding, painted cement, and mirror strips around the windows. There's a take-out window around the corner. ♦ Cafe ♦ M lunch; Tu-F lunch and dinner; Sa dinner. 1600 17th St (at Wisconsin St). 552.3325 ♿

62 Restaurant 2001 ★★$$ This cute little restaurant/bar, owned by Barbara and Paul Jellison, sits smack dab in the middle of a sea of warehouses and industrial buildings. The menu consists of straightforward, contemporary renditions of classic American fare; particularly good choices are the pork chops and all of the chicken dishes. With its subdued lighting and intimate atmosphere, this is a great spot for a romantic lunch or dinner. ♦ American ♦ Tu-Sa lunch and dinner; Su dinner. 2001 17th St (at Kansas St). 621.2001 ♿

63 Asimakopoulos Cafe ★★$$ One of the city's only Greek restaurants, it has garnered raves from residents and the local press for over ten years. One bite of the spinach in phyllo appetizer will make you a believer, too. The entrées are equally good, including skewered pork, chicken and lamb dishes, and moussaka. Save room for the flaky and delicious baklava; it's not overly sweet, so the flavors of the nuts and pastry shine through. On Tuesday or Sunday nights, bring a burning question along with an appetite; a fortune teller is on hand to read the coffee grounds in the bottom of your cup. ♦ Greek ♦ M-F lunch and dinner; Sa-Su dinner. 288 Connecticut St (at 18th St). 552.8789; fax 552.8798

64 Goat Hill Pizza ★$ The sourdough crust sets these pizzas above those of the competition. This popular Italian place also serves pasta, salads, and soups. Many regulars time their pizza feasts to coincide with the live music featured Thursday through Saturday nights. ♦ Pizzeria ♦ Daily lunch and dinner. 300 Connecticut St (at 18th St). 641.1440; fax 641.7262 ♿

65 Aperto ★★★$$ There are few decorative frills here, but count on the lusty smells emanating from the open kitchen to provide enough atmosphere. The food is excellent, but it doesn't break any new creative ground. Crisp triangles of polenta topped with fresh chopped tomatoes and a dollop of melting gorgonzola make a good first course. To follow, the roast chicken—topped with wedges of salty, pungent, preserved lemons and surrounded by roast potatoes and calamata olives—is a tasty choice. Best desserts are fresh fruit granita and warm chocolate soufflé cake. The high ceiling and windows on two sides add an airiness that helps disguise the fact that the tables are squeezed together. Since reservations are not accepted, hordes tend to line up, eyeing the occupied seats hungrily. ♦ Italian ♦ M-F lunch and dinner; Sa-Su brunch and dinner. 1434 18th St (at Connecticut St). 252.1625 ♿

66 Thanya and Salee ★★$ This top Thai eatery offers meticulous preparations of such standard dishes as duck salad, coconut-

SoMa (South of Market)/South Beach/Potrero Hill/Bayview–Hunters Point

chicken soup, and pad thai, as well as more unusual fare. Sweet corn salad is infused with chilies, lime, thinly sliced red onion, roasted peppers, zucchini, and large cilantro leaves. Hot-and-sour prawn soup is scented with lemongrass and smoothed with coconut milk. Don't pass up the southern Thai barbecue chicken with a mildly spicy red-curry dipping sauce or the garlic-marinated pork, which is crisply fried and served with a green chili sauce redolent of fresh lime. The mirror-backed bar under a replica Thai temple roof, the thick carpeting, and the tables freshly laid with white butcher paper and flowers contribute to the comfortable mood. ♦ Thai ♦ Daily lunch and dinner. 1469 18th St (at Connecticut St). 647.6469; fax 647.2910 ♿

66 Eliza's ★★★$ Ping and Jan Sung have crafted a Chinese restaurant that subtly reworks familiar preparations, giving them a modern California twist. Sunflower beef (thin slices of meat in a rich satay sauce spiked with scallions) is encircled by a burst of white enoki mushrooms. The sweet China prawns are matched with snow peas and toasted pine nuts in a velvety ginger sauce. Salmon is paired with asparagus tips in an equally refined black-bean sauce. The stylish decor features grand Matisse-like paintings, hand-crafted lights, and potted orchids on each table. Tea is served in white Wedgwood demitasse cups, and the food is presented on pastel Italian pottery. And all this creativity doesn't cost any more than a meal at the corner cafe. The only downside is dessert—nothing but fortune cookies and ice cream. ♦ Chinese ♦ Daily lunch and dinner. 1457 18th St (at Connecticut St). 648.9999 ♿

66 Just For You Cafe ★$ This narrow little place is no more than a row of stools at a scarred wooden counter, with one table tucked into the front window. But on weekends customers line up for breakfast and for lunch specials that include shrimp creole, gumbo, and other New Orleans specialties. At dinner the menu takes on a Cajun edge with such dishes as red beans and rice and jambalaya. ♦ Creole/Cajun ♦ Daily breakfast, lunch, and dinner. 1453 18th St (between Missouri and Connecticut Sts). 647.3033

66 The Daily Scoop ★$ With its tile floor, parlor chairs, and authentic soda fountain, this old-fashioned ice-cream parlor offers a glimpse of the past. People think it's been around forever, but the place is less than 20 years old. The owner adds to the nostalgia with his growing collection of memorabilia that includes classic blenders and mixers. Double Rainbow ice cream is served in such flavors as banana-fudge-walnut. ♦ Ice-cream parlor ♦ Daily 7:30AM-10PM. 1401 18th St (at Missouri St). 824.3975 ♿

67 Hazel's Kitchen Somehow, this closet-sized take-out place produces fabulous food. The aqua-and-white color scheme and the display of Bauer pottery add a bright note and reflect the homey character of the limited menu. A day's offerings usually include several sandwiches dressed with an herb-and-mustard mayonnaise, a refreshing soup (perhaps carrot-ginger), and salads. The Greek salad of pungent feta, cool mint, cucumbers, black olives, and tomatoes is outstanding. ♦ Daily. 1331 18th St (between Texas and Missouri Sts). 647.7941 ♿

67 Mager's Wine Shop Just about the perfect neighborhood wine shop offers a small but well-selected array of California, French, and Italian wines. It also carries a small assortment of gourmet condiments and Joseph Schmidt chocolates. ♦ Daily. 1319 18th St (between Texas and Missouri Sts). 282.6650 ♿

67 Farley's ★$ A local institution, this coffeehouse has captured the spirit of the emerging Potrero Hill neighborhood, which has some of the most spectacular city and bay views in San Francisco. The wood floors and slatboard siding and ceiling lend a lived-in look that sets the tone of the place. People sit for hours, playing board games, nursing cups of the robust house blend of coffee, and perusing the large selection of magazines for sale. The pastries and light snack items are generally very good, and whole and ground beans are sold for home use. ♦ Coffeehouse ♦ Daily. No credit cards accepted. 1315 18th St (at Texas St). 648.1545

68 San Francisco Bar-B-Que ★$ With that name, this sounds like a traditional barbecue joint, but there are no slabs of ribs and brisket here. Actually, the menu lists all kinds of Thai-style noodles topped with chunks of barbecued meats. The portions are big and filling, and prices are rock-bottom ♦ Thai ♦ Tu-F lunch and dinner; Sa-Su dinner. No credit cards accepted. 1328 18th St (between Texas and Missouri Sts). 431.8956

In 1868 the fabled Poodle Dog restaurant opened at Bush Street and Grant Avenue. Although the food served in its first-floor dining room and second-floor banquet rooms was highly prized, the restaurant was better-known for the private dining rooms on the third, fourth, and fifth floors. These could be reached by a private entrance, and each was furnished with a large sofa and locks on the doors. Many a diner and his lady friend stayed the night.

139

SoMa (South of Market)/South Beach/Potrero Hill/Bayview–Hunters Point

The Good Life Grocery

69 The Good Life Grocery Produce, cheese, packaged goods, bread from several of the city's best bakeries, and a limited meat selection (free-range chickens, sausages, and fresh fish) have made this a one-stop grocery store for the neighborhood. Although the quarters are small, it's one of the best natural-food stores in the city. ♦ Daily. 1524 20th St (between Missouri and Connecticut Sts). 282.9204 &

KLEIN'S

70 Klein's Deli ★$ Few delis are as personal as this one, where the female owners have named every sandwich after famous women: The Abzug celebrates Bella with tongue, muenster cheese, and dark rye bread; the Audrey Hepburn features salmon pâté on a sourdough roll; and the Minnie Mouse puts three kinds of cheese on a kaiser roll. It's become a popular hangout and working-lunch spot for an artsy set of graphic designers, architects, and photographers. A small, reasonably priced selection of wine and a few choice packaged specialty foods fill a nook in the back of the store. ♦ Deli ♦ Daily breakfast, lunch, and dinner until 7PM; Su till 5:30PM. 501 Connecticut St (at 20th St). 821.9149; fax 821.0518

71 La Paz Restaurant and Pupuseria ★★$ This clean, well-lit hole-in-the-wall across the street from **San Francisco General Hospital** is quite a find. Not only does it serve well-prepared authentic Salvadoran fare, the prices are incredibly low—an entire meal can cost as little as $6. The delicious *pupusas* (tortillas stuffed with cheese alone or meat and cheese) are served with a sharply flavored cole slaw, and the pork or chicken tamales are so light they practically float over your plate. Other dishes include tongue in salsa, chicken in red sauce, and beef cooked with tomatoes, peppers, and eggs. It's a bit out of the way, but the journey is well worth it. ♦ Salvadoran ♦ Daily breakfast, lunch, and dinner. 1028 Potrero Ave (near 22nd St). 550.8213

72 The Candy Jar Outlet Those with a serious sweet tooth and a penchant for bargains bypass the posh retail branch on **Union Square** and head for its outlet here, where truffles in more than a dozen flavors cost 30 to 50 percent less. Some goods are slightly flawed, some are overruns, but most are simply sold at wholesale prices. The sales counter, located in front of the candy factory, proffers such sweet treats as oversized turtles, chocolate-covered Oreos, imported hard candies and jellies, and cooking chocolate, plus gift boxes, wrapping paper, and ribbon. ♦ M-Sa. 2065 Oakdale Ave (at Industrial Ave). 550.8846; fax 550.8359 &. Also at: 210 Grant Ave (between Post and Sutter Sts). 391.5508 &

73 Heritage House Located in an industrial building on a sparsely traveled street in the warehouse district, this china, crystal, and flatware showroom glitters with up to 1,500 china patterns from the likes of Minton, Christian Dior, Fitz & Floyd, Lenox, Noritake, Rosenthal, Royal Doulton, Royal Worcester, Villeroy & Boch, and Wedgwood. In silverware, all the big names are covered, including such specialty producers as Georg Jensen, WMF Fraser, and Yamazaki. Crystal suppliers include Baccarat, Riedel, Waterford, and St. Louis. Many items are discounted by 20 to 40 percent. The store maintains a bridal registry; it will also replace broken pieces for half the retail price. ♦ M-F; Sa and evenings by appointment. 2190 Palou Ave (at Industrial Ave). 285.1331; fax 285.9840

74 James & James Ribs 'n' Thangs ★★★$$ This rib joint, located on a stretch of small shops and bars in Bayview–Hunters Point, is a magnet for barbecue mavens from all over the city. The restaurant is classy (as barbecue joints go) and comfortable, with antique tables and chairs, a large open kitchen, and a barbecue pit. Paintings and posters of prominent African-American heroes from Malcolm X to Martin Luther King grace the walls. Upon entering, you'll be greeted by the luscious smell of barbecued meats and the blare of loud rock music. The most popular choice here (particularly with barbecue novices) is the "two-way," which offers a choice of two barbecued meats (such as beef, sausage links, chicken, or pork ribs), and a choice of two side dishes (creamy potato salad, cole slaw, collard greens, barbecued beans, cornbread muffins, or corn on the cob). White or wheat bread is also available so you can sop up the sauce (mild or hot) that's slathered over the meat. Other menu options include fried catfish, snapper, sole, and prawns. For dessert, try a slice of the moist and tasty sweet potato pie. ♦ Barbecue/ soulfood ♦ Tu-Su lunch and dinner (until 2AM Friday and Saturday). 5130 Third St (at Shafter Ave). 671.0269

75 Moshi Moshi ★★$ In a landscape dominated by warehouses, this bright corner restaurant serves skillfully prepared Japanese food. Start with the fine *gyoza* (Japanese dumplings), then move on to one of the classics—steak teriyaki, shrimp tempura, or chicken yakitori. The sushi is much better than at many places in Japantown, the service

SoMa (South of Market)/South Beach/Potrero Hill/Bayview–Hunters Point

attentive, and the simple look of light wood tables and chairs and celadon walls attractive. Throw in the low prices, and this place warrants a special trip. ♦ Japanese ♦ M-F lunch and dinner; Sa-Su dinner. 2092 Third St (at 18th St). 861.8285; fax 861.8291 &

76 Economy Restaurant Fixtures The best place in the city to shop for restaurant-grade pots, pans, and tableware is now even better. In early 1995 the store moved from its location on Howard Street to a new warehouse that's more than twice as big as the old shop. Professional stoves, industrial-strength cleaners, and cotton towels are among the thousands of other items on sale here. It's the spot to find an oversized stock pot or to pick up enough glassware to host a party (glasses come in boxes of 36). Prices are very low, and for an even better deal, check out the used equipment and tableware where the prices can be dirt cheap. ♦ M-Sa. 1200 7th St (at Irwin St). 626.5611; fax 252.9627 &

77 42 Degrees ★★★$$ It's unusual to find an exceptional late-night dining establishment in San Francisco (the joint doesn't start jumping until 9PM), another reason that this chic restaurant is so welcome. Located in a warehouse-size space that once housed **Caffe ESPRIT** (it's next to the **ESPRIT** factory store), this place sports a high-tech look—there's a curving black metal staircase—with a dash of nightclub style. Dine on purple banquettes upstairs while enjoying a view of the bay; eat downstairs in front of the exposed kitchen or near the 22-foot high windows that are opened in pleasant weather; or enjoy a lunchtime focaccia on the patio. Owner/chef Jim Moffat, who's also partner in **The Slow Club** in the Mission, offers a menu that changes daily and might include grilled quail and rich duck confit on a heap of truffled risotto with morels; and a whole *poussin* with hard cider sauce, baked apples, and rice studded with sour cherries. Also featured is a wide variety of small dishes that's perfect for the drinking crowd. Try the stuffed artichoke or grilled asparagus with cherries and a light vinaigrette. Sweets lovers will be quite content with the rich chocolate *pots de crème* or strawberries and blackberries over a warm pecan shortcake. ♦ Californian ♦ M-Tu lunch; W-Sa lunch, dinner, and late-night meals. 235 16th St (off Third St). 777.5559; fax 777.0278 &

78 The Ramp ★$$ Sunny weekends guarantee long waits at this bare-bones eatery, thanks to its large deck overlooking the bay. The menu includes average egg dishes, sandwiches, and burgers. In the summer there's live jazz, salsa, or rock Thursday through Sunday evenings, as well as outdoor barbecues on weekend afternoons through early evening. As cool weather sets in, the kitchen turns out hearty stews to ease the chill. It's a fun crowd—an eclectic mix of laborers, society matrons, singles, and gays. ♦ American ♦ M-F breakfast and lunch; Sa-Su brunch. 855 China Basin St (at Mariposa St). 621.2378

79 Mission Rock Resort ★$ With its terrace overlooking the slips and boats in dry dock on China Bay, this bar-restaurant attracts a fun-loving group of regulars. Sunday brunch, with the standard array of egg dishes, is a big draw, as are the barbecue and live music sessions on sunny weekend afternoons. The fare runs to burgers and deep-fried seafood—scallops, oysters, prawns, and fish-and-chips, served until 3PM. And the bar keeps hopping long after the kitchen closes. ♦ American ♦ M-Sa breakfast and lunch; Su brunch. 817 China Basin St (north of Mariposa St). 621.5538 &

80 Jelly's: A Dance Cafe ★$$ The outdoor terrace that opens onto the bay is a popular spot for lunch, when selections include a BLT with french fries, fish-and-chips, Caesar salad, and grilled chicken breast on a French roll. Daily lunch specials draw inspiration from far-flung destinations like the American Southwest, Italy, and France. Formerly a dinner spot as well, now the place hosts private parties at night. ♦ International ♦ M-F lunch; Sa-Su brunch. 295 Terry A. Francois Blvd (near Mission Rock and Third Sts). 495.3099; fax 495.2884

The Mission

North Beach was a magnet for the Beat generation of the 1950s; the Haight captured the hearts of the flower children of the 1960s; the Castro was the mecca for the gay movement of the 1970s; and the Mission is becoming home to what writer Herb Gold and others have dubbed the "New Bohemia"—the favorite hangout of young, white, underemployed coffeehouse philosophers, former punk rockers, and political activists.

Sandwiched between Potrero Hill to the east, the Castro to the west, and Downtown to the north, the Mission is more diverse culturally and culinarily than any other neighborhood in San Francisco. This flat, expansive area, one of the warmest and sunniest in the city, has a long history as an ethnic enclave, beginning with the Irish and Germans in the 19th century and continuing with Italians, Mexicans, and most recently Central Americans and Asians.

This diversity has given birth to a veritable United Nations of restaurants, including Brazilian, Peruvian, Salvadoran, Spanish, Italian, French, Chinese, Cambodian, Laotian, Korean, Thai, and Indian places. Most are true mom-and-pop operations, but the low rents are beginning to attract such destination establishments as **Mangiafuoco**, as well as many of the city's most innovative kitchens: The **Flying Saucer**'s eccentric chef creates wild, cross-cultural plates, and the **Rooster** serves peasant fare from southern Europe and Asia.

One indicator of the area's growing sophistication was the transformation of **Picaro**. For more than a decade, it was a popular gathering place for the New Bohemians, who would linger for hours discussing art, films, and life. But in 1994, **Picaro** was turned into one of the city's hottest tapas bars, and now it's been joined by the nearby **Paella Movida**. Sylvie Le Mer's creperie, **Ti Couz**, continues to attract the urban set as well as the bridge-and-tunnel crowd.

The Mission is a laid-back kind of neighborhood, designed for hanging out, which is what draws the current generation of dreamers. There's a cafe for just about every persuasion: **Radio Valencia** has quickly become the place to showcase new jazz acts, and **Cafe Tisane** is the spot to linger over a cup of herbal tea, while conversation at **Cafe Macondo** centers on soccer. And 1960s idealism lives on at **Rainbow Grocery**, one of the few true communal efforts still prospering. In utilitarian surroundings, it has accumulated the city's best collection of natural foods, fresh herbs, and food items in bulk.

Despite the diversity, the real heart of the Mission is Central American. Much of the neighborhood's Central American character can be found on **Mission Street** and along **24th Street**, the bustling area that contains the bulk of the city's Latino restaurants, markets, and bakeries. The Mission, like many other parts of the city, suffers from some street crime, gang activity, and drug problems. It's safe to visit during the day, when the streets are filled with ordinary folks going about their lives. At night, however, visitors should exercise common-sense precautions: Always try to know where you're going, and pay attention to where you are and what is happening around you. Don't flash cash or expensive jewelry and keep an eye on your wallet or purse. And if in doubt, take a taxi to and from your destination. Just remember that the road to culinary nirvana isn't always smooth, but it is always worth the trip.

The Mission

1 Dominguez Mexican Bakery People have been known to drive for miles for the *churros* here. The long twists of doughnutlike dough, fried crisp and rolled in sugar, can be addictive, so fans buy them in dozens to freeze (with little loss in quality). The display windows contain electric pink, blue, and green cookies and gingerbread that look garish but taste wonderful. The bakery is also known for its breads; they're all winners. ♦ Daily. No credit cards accepted. 2951 24th St (at Alabama St). 821.1717

"La Victoria"

1 La Victoria Mexican Bakery For 30 years this bakery has been turning out delicious, plump, and moist macaroons called *cocadas* and Mexican wedding cookies dusted with powdered sugar. Unlike those at some other bakeries, the sweet breads here have the traditional dry, sandy texture. ♦ Daily. No credit cards accepted. 2937 24th St (between Florida and Alabama Sts). 550.9292

2 Casa Lucas This Latino market carries many products from the Caribbean and Central America that can't be found elsewhere: canned breadfruit for Jamaican dishes; the burnished palm oil important to Brazilian cuisine; cans of small Colombian potatoes; and a whole shelf of fruit products, including a good deal of guava. The produce section boasts such hard-to-find seasonal fruits as green coconuts, bitter oranges, and huge Mexican mangoes. ♦ Daily. No credit cards accepted. 2934 24th St (between Florida and Alabama Sts). 826.4334 ♿

3 La Palma A rapid-fire slapping sound means tortillas are being made by hand at this "Mexicatessen." A line of women pats the dough into tortillas and then places them on the griddle, where they release a seductive aroma of corn. The steam table along the back wall offers all kinds of take-out specialties, including wonderful tamales swathed in corn husks, *papusas* (stuffed tortillas), and *chiles verdes* (pork, chilies, and onions in a green sauce). The shelves hold several kinds of red and green salsas, which make perfect accompaniments to the best tortilla chips in the Bay Area. There's also an exceptionally large selection of canned, ground, dried, and bottled chilies. ♦ Daily. No credit cards accepted. 2884 24th St (at Florida St). 647.1500; fax 647.1710 ♿

4 St. Francis Fountain ★★$ Still looking much as it did when it opened in 1918, this is a childhood fantasy come true. It is flanked by a soda fountain on one side and a display case of candy on the other; the peanut brittle alone is worth a special trip. Sit at the counter or at one of the tables in back and indulge in a soda or a cone of luscious homemade ice cream in one of 20 flavors. More substantial fare includes the wonderful comfort food of days gone by, like grilled cheese sandwiches and daily blue-plate specials. ♦ American/Ice-cream parlor ♦ Daily lunch and dinner. No credit cards accepted. 2801 24th St (at York St). 826.4200

5 Roosevelt's Tamale Parlor ★★$ Very good Tex-Mex food has been packing fans into this eatery since 1922. With its bright blue ceiling, glowing Pepsi clock, and baseball pennants, it's a deceptively simple joint. Tamales are a specialty, and so are the combination platters, which include great enchiladas, *chiles rellenos* (stuffed chili peppers), and tacos. The green-chili burrito, with chunks of stewed pork and pungent strips of chilies, is marvelous. ♦ Mexican ♦ Tu-Su lunch and dinner. No credit cards accepted. 2817 24th St (between York and Bryant Sts). 550.9213

6 Casa Sanchez Mornings are the time to visit this family shop: That's when the staff is busy working amid steaming vats of corn and cranking up dough machines that turn out fresh tortillas in all sizes. Connoisseurs head for the regular corn tortillas, recognized as the city's best. The shop also sells staples and such take-out fare as sausages, stuffed *poblano* chilies, and excellent salsas, particularly *salsa verde* (green sauce) made with tomatillos. ♦ Daily. No credit cards accepted. 2778 24th St (between Hampshire and York Sts). 282.2400; fax 550.4463 ♿

The Mission

7 Universal Cafe
★★★$$ Despite the hard-to-find location in an unlikely industrial-residential neighborhood, this place attracts a wide range of young (or young-at-heart) diners with its excellent food. (Its conversion from a coffee-roasting company into a sunny, high-style, urban hangout has also attracted the attention of design magazines.) At lunch the sandwiches on focaccia are unsurpassed: Try the grilled beef tenderloin with gorgonzola, roast chicken with aioli, or Italian meat loaf with provolone. At dinner the candlelit room takes on a magical glow. Great appetizers include the grilled flatbread topped with sautéed arugula, prosciutto, and asiago cheese; warm greens with pancetta and leeks; or baked gnocchi with oyster mushrooms and scallions. Only about three main courses are offered on any given evening; they might include roast chicken with tomato *coulis,* semolina, and braised greens, or roast salmon with avocado-leek salad and crispy potatoes. For dessert, try the seasonal fruit crisps. ♦ Cafe ♦ Tu-F breakfast, lunch, and dinner; Sa-Su brunch, lunch, and dinner. 2814 19th St (at Bryant St). 821.4608; fax 285.6760 ♿

8 The Slow Club ★★$$ Never mind the name—a fast-paced crowd fills this trendy cafe with its quasi-industrial feel and slick, California-inspired menu. From the closet-size kitchen behind a colorful plywood bar comes a United Nations of flavors. The menu changes daily, but appetizers might be an array of tapas, a designer salad, or soft polenta enriched with parmesan and brightened with fava beans. Entrées might include monkfish presented on risotto or braised short ribs with roasted apples. Seductive endings: a rich *pots de crème* (custard) or polenta pound cake topped with fruit compote. ♦ Californian ♦ M lunch; Tu-F lunch and dinner; Sa dinner. 2501 Mariposa St (at Hampshire St). 241.9390 ♿

According to the National Restaurant Association, San Franciscans spend spend $978 per person annually for food consumed outside of the home.

The fortune cookie was invented in San Francisco during the turn of the century by Makota Hagiwara, chief gardener of the Japanese Tea Garden in Golden Gate Park.

9 Eichelberger's $$ Named for legendary drag actress Ethel Eichelberger, the draw of this exotic-looking spot is its live entertainment, which ranges from banjo music to cabaret to singers on trapezes. The Egyptian-inspired interior has a New Age air that attracts an eclectic, oh-so-trendy crowd. Go for the experience, not for the American food, which is uneven. ♦ American ♦ Tu-Sa dinner, F-Sa until 1AM. 2742 17th St (at Florida St). 863.4177

10 Chava's Mexican Restaurant ★★$ Brightly painted in primary colors, this eatery is particularly popular on weekends, when it serves goat and *menudo,* the hearty tripe stew that Mexicans consider the only cure for a hangover; many other places cook up this rich, hominy-studded stew, but few do it better. The kitchen is also known for its egg dishes, especially the *huevos rancheros.* Other top draws are the housemade corn tortillas and the *chiles verdes.* ♦ Mexican ♦ Daily lunch and dinner. No credit cards accepted. 3248 18th St (at Shotwell St) 552.9387

11 Rainbow Grocery This natural-foods co-op, owned by a very ecologically aware collective, stocks a staggering array of vitamins, herb extracts, and amino supplements, plus a truly amazing range of foodstuffs, including produce, cheese, and top-quality organic fruits and vegetables. The crowded aisles are filled with bins of flours, grains, and fruits, including dried persimmons, mangoes, and papayas. More than 30 teas, 80 spices, and 200 roots and herbs (including Irish moss and Jamaican dogwood) are also sold in bulk. One thing is certain—you won't find environmentally harmful products on the shelves. Under the same roof (and ownership) is a general store that carries everything from housewares to natural-fiber clothing to gemstones. ♦ Daily. 1899 Mission St (at 15th St). 863.0620, general store 863.9200; fax 863.8955 ♿

12 San Francisco Herb Company Spices in *serious* bulk—that is, one-, five-, or 20-pound portions—are all that this wholesale-retail shop sells. The savings are huge, too, so many people divide their purchases with friends. All the standard seasonings are available, as are spices used for ethnic cooking, such as annatto, lemongrass, and chicory root. The store also carries seeds for sprouting, including mung bean, radish, alfalfa, and clover. ♦ M-F 10AM-4PM. 250 14th St (between S Van Ness Ave and Mission St). 861.3018; fax 864.4440 ♿

13 Greek American Food Imports This small shop is packed with all the products needed to put an authentic Greek meal on the table, including wine. Several kinds of phyllo are available, both fresh and frozen; the selection

The Mission

of cheeses includes *kasseri* (similar to cheddar) and feta from the United States, Greece, and France. A display case in front holds baklava and other pastries. ♦ Tu-Su 10AM-1PM. No credit cards accepted. 223 Valencia St (at Duboce Ave). 864.0978 ♿

14 Pauline's Pizza ★★$ A prime stop for pizza with crisp, cornmeal-dusted crusts, this spot has even been spiffed up recently. The cloth-covered tables and enthusiastic service make clear that this is no ordinary pizza parlor, but the bars across the windows hint that it's not in the best neighborhood. Pizza toppings run from the traditional to combinations that would make even Wolfgang Puck shake his head in wonder: Consider smoked ham, braised leeks, fontina cheese, and bell-pepper puree, for instance. The best-known dish is pesto pizza, in which the vibrant topping is spooned over a prebaked crust. The salad is generous enough for sharing. ♦ Pizzeria ♦ Tu-Sa dinner. 260 Valencia St (between 14th St and Duboce Ave). 552.2050 ♿

15 Pancho Villa Taqueria ★$ Similar fresh fare is offered here as at its sister *taqueria* **El Toro** (see below), but in spacious, bare-bones surroundings. There's a larger selection of fruit drinks, as well as such dishes as tequila-marinated prawns, served with rice and beans. ♦ Mexican ♦ Daily lunch and dinner. No credit cards accepted. 3071 16th St (between Mission and Valencia Sts). 864.8840; fax 864.3484 ♿

16 Taquería La Cumbre ★$ In its heyday, 20 years ago, this was the best *taqueria* in town. But over the years, it grew into a large chain, and the style and food have become more impersonal. But the food is still pretty good: The made-to-order burritos weigh in at well over a pound each, the *carne asada* (beef) is a winner, and the burritos made with tongue or pork stomach have legions of fans. However, many of the authentic Mexican specialties have been eliminated. ♦ Mexican ♦ Daily lunch and dinner. No credit cards accepted. 515 Valencia St (at 16th St). 863.8205; fax 863.2322 ♿

16 Cafe Istanbul $ A peaceful oasis, this blue-tented room with cushions on the floor is the place to relax with tea made with anise, sage, apple, or licorice, or to linger over a Turkish coffee. Light snacks include falafel, hummus, and other standard Middle Eastern fare. The service is relaxed, too—almost to the point of nonexistence. ♦ Middle Eastern ♦ Daily lunch and dinner. No credit cards accepted. 525 Valencia St (between 17th and 16th Sts). 863.8854

17 Bombay Bazar Pungent incense pervades this well-stocked Indian grocery store, which sells most items in bulk. The selection of beans and grains is far wider than at any health-food store. Gunnysacks of basmati rice are stacked high, and *dal* (lentils) seem to come in every color of the rainbow. On one shelf alone are more than 20 kinds of flour. Drums of raw peanuts and garbanzo beans and huge bins of *masala*, cumin, and other spices are offered at rock-bottom prices. ♦ Tu-Su. 548 Valencia St (between 17th and 16th Sts). 621.1717 ♿

18 The Slanted Door ★★$ Decorated in soothing shades of blue and featuring paintings by local artist Judy North, this restaurant is a great addition to the Mission's Restaurant Row. The menu changes weekly, but it always features such well-prepared Asian dishes as stir-fried beans, five-spice chicken, and curried tofu. The desserts, however, are undistinguished; finish your meal with a pot of jasmine pearl tea instead. ♦ Asian ♦ Tu-Su lunch and dinner. 584 Valencia St (at 17th St). 861.8032; fax 861.8329 ♿

18 Amira ★$$ Ceilings draped with purple fabric, low tables topped with brass trays, and artfully painted walls lend an exotic air to this "pan-Arabic" restaurant. It's like a visit to a foreign land, even without the belly dancers, who entertain on weekends. The walnut dip, a specialty of the chef, is the best way to begin. Follow with one of the couscous dishes, succulent kabobs, or another of the Middle Eastern standards. (Be prepared to linger over your meal, though: To say that the service is slow is an understatement.) ♦ Middle Eastern ♦ Tu-Su dinner. 590 Valencia St (at 17th St). 621.6213

18 El Toro Taqueria ★★$$ The owners are so meticulous that they regularly scrape off the flyers that are plastered on the lampposts in front of their corner restaurant. The fresh-tasting food, even better than at **Pancho Villa Taqueria** (see above), reflects that same

The Mission

persnicketiness. Offerings include the standard soft tacos, a burrito generously filled with plump shrimp, and a tamale made with a *masa* (corn) dough that's so light it's almost a soufflé. ♦ Mexican ♦ Daily. No credit cards accepted. 598 Valencia St (at 17th St). 431.3351

19 La Hacienda Rows of colorful piñatas hang above a marble floor and below an ornate gilded ceiling—clues that this popular grocery once was a bank. It has one of the best selections of chilies in the Mission, a small produce aisle, meats, cheeses, and canned goods. There are also at least a hundred different kinds of religious candles—even one to light to win the lottery. ♦ Daily. 3100 16th St (at Valencia St). 431.8445; fax 431.8455 &

19 Ti Couz ★★★$ Sylvie Le Mer's Breton creperie is a winner—so popular, in fact, that it expanded next door a couple of years ago. The interior design comes straight from a French village, but the real focus is at the counter, where the cooks make crepes in assembly-line fashion. There are dozens of fillings: Savory ones include sausage, mushrooms, and ratatouille, while the sweet options might be apples, caramel, or chocolate. The beverage of choice is hard cider—a novelty in San Francisco—which is perfect with the light fare. At the adjacent bar, the cozy seating is conducive to conversation. Young, old, rich, poor, conservative, liberal—everyone comes here. ♦ Creperie ♦ Daily lunch and dinner. 3108 16th St (at Valencia St). 252.7373; fax 252.7712 &

19 Picaro ★★$ Bright, bold colors and flavors dominate this warehouse-size tapas bar. The bar is painted in tribute to Miró, and the art on the walls evokes Picasso and Dalí. The tables are arranged helter-skelter, and the service can be painfully slow, but the kitchen successfully turns out a laundry list of tapas, which are as big as the entrées at most restaurants. Grilled mussels are redolent of garlic, the grilled quail needs nothing more

than a gentle squeeze of lemon, and chicken croquettes ooze béchamel sauce. The beet-and-mushroom salad is an excellent antidote for all the garlic. For dessert, try the chocolate mousse, rice pudding, or creamy custard. ♦ Spanish/Tapas ♦ Daily lunch and dinner. No credit cards accepted. 3120 16th St (between Valencia and Guerrero Sts). 431.4089; fax 431.4089 &

20 Maya Taqueria ★$ Although it looks as big as a dance hall, this busy *taqueria*'s dimensions can't dwarf the enormous portions of its food. It's all hearty (and priced at rock-bottom), but the specialty is the Azteca taco, a flour tortilla stuffed with beans, rice, a choice of meat, cheese, and salsa. It's heated quickly, ladled with spicy enchilada sauce, and crowned with creamy guacamole sauce and tangy sour cream sauce that help quell the chili-induced fire. ♦ Mexican ♦ Daily lunch and dinner. No credit cards accepted. 3198 16th St (at Guerrero St). 621.8025

21 Katz Bagels ★$ The chewy, slightly doughy bagels here come in 18 varieties, from traditional versions to dill cheddar and jalapeño. Smear them with a choice of spreads that includes honey date and dill cucumber, and eat in or carry them out. Loyal Mission residents keep this place hopping; they, and their diverse lifestyles, are celebrated by color portraits of them covering the walls. ♦ Cafe ♦ Daily. No credit cards accepted. 3147 16th St (between Valencia and Guerrero Sts). 552.9122; fax 642.1255

21 Cafe Macondo $ Another of the scores of coffeehouses in the area, this one is a must-visit for anyone who wants to read up on what's happening in South American soccer. The place serves tamales, quesadillas, quiche, and some pastries. ♦ Coffeehouse ♦ Daily. 3159 16th St (at Guerrero St). 863.6517

21 Malai Lao Restaurant ★$ One of the few Laotian restaurants in the city, this small storefront eatery has tasty food. The *larh gai* (chicken with rice flour) here is similar to the Thai version, but better. Grilled quail is served with a dipping sauce of salt, pepper, and lemon—an accompaniment familiar to those who frequent Vietnamese and Thai restaurants. Another interesting dish is the fish steamed in banana leaves. ♦ Laotian/Thai ♦ M-F lunch and dinner; Sa-Su dinner. 3189 16th St (at Guerrero St). 626.8528

22 Jack's Elixir Bar A tavern has stood on this spot since 1932. In 1988, the place was purchased by Bill Carlson, who has turned six other locations throughout the city into multi-tap venues, all incorporating **Jack's** in the name (i.e., **Jack's Bar** in Fisherman's Wharf). There are no fewer than 50 beers on tap here (try the Pyramid apricot—it's fabulous). The wood bar, with a silver footrest and chrome stools, is the focal point of this dark room;

147

The Mission

there also are tables below the windows. No food is served. ♦ Daily 2PM-2AM. 3200 16th St (at Guerrero St). 552.1633. Also at: The Cannery, 2801 Leavenworth St (at Jefferson St). 931.6400; fax 931.6404 ♿

23 Paella la Movida ★★$$ Named for the movement that came into being in Spain after the death of Franco in 1975, this new addition to the Mission's restaurant scene does indeed serve a very good paella, as well as some of the best tapas around (but at a rather high price). The dining room is decorated in a rainbow of colors, including bright yellow walls, a green wood floor, and red tables; paintings depicting Spanish landscapes and street scenes hang on the walls. ♦ Spanish ♦ Tu-F dinner; Sa-Su brunch and dinner. 3228 16th St (between Guerrero and Dolores Sts). 552.3889 ♿

24 Anna's Danish Cookies With Danish butter cookies this crisp and rich, it's no wonder this family business has been going strong for more than 60 years; it ships up to 300 boxes of cookies across the country every day. (The cookies also are available in diatetic and chocolate-dipped versions.) The storefront windows and the shelves behind the service counter are filled with marvelous ceramic cookie jars in the shapes of pineapples, strawberries, whimsical animals, and Victorian houses. ♦ Tu-Sa. 3560 18th St (between Valencia and Guerrero Sts). 863.3882 ♿

25 Canto do Brazil ★$ Bright green walls, yellow cafe curtains, and colored oilcloth tablecloths transform this small storefront into a fun setting for Brazilian food. The deep-fried croquettes made with chicken or beef are outstanding; the *feijoada* (the bean-based national dish of Brazil), which is made on weekends, is one of the best in the city. ♦ Brazilian ♦ Tu-Su dinner. 3621 18th St (at Guerrero St). 626.8727

26 Carl's Pastry In business for 45 years, this bakery produces superb American-style pastries in 1950s surroundings. The bear claws, with a crispy exterior and a flaky interior, are a sharp contrast to the doughy versions found at most places. Carl's special, an almond, cinnamon, and buttercream ring, generally sells out first thing in the morning. If you want a treat for your pooch, pick up a bag of Bone Appetit, a bakery-made version of dog biscuits. ♦ Tu-Su. 600 Guerrero St (at 18th St). 552.1141

The City of Paris, an elegant, but long-closed, San Francisco department store (Neiman Marcus is now on its site), ran an advertisement in the 1950s inviting the public to "come in and see our $10,000 display of Alsace-Lorraine pâté de foie gras with truffles."

27 Jivano's Cutlery Service Make an appointment to explore the fine selection of new and used knives here. Even when the place is closed and the curtains are drawn, you can drop your dull knives through the door slot with your name and phone number; they'll be sharpened to about the best edge in town. ♦ By appointment only. 3674 18th St (at Dolores St). 552.7997

28 Burger Joint ★$ The neon decor of this diner, with vivid aqua tabletops and vinyl booths in lime green and red, draws crowds—and so do the hamburgers made with chic Niman-Schell beef and the chicken-breast sandwiches made from free-range chicken. The limited menu also includes hot dogs, a vegetarian burger, and milk shakes. ♦ American/Hamburgers ♦ Daily lunch and dinner. No credit cards accepted. 807 Valencia St (at 19th St). 824.3494 ♿

29 Timo's Tapas Bar ★★$ Tapas lovers flock to this popular bar; it's aglow in bright colors, from the aqua-and-blue–trimmed exterior to the tables of electric yellow and black Formica. Among the outstanding tapas are grilled mushrooms punched up with garlic and parsley; new potatoes drizzled with aioli; and a masterful, chunky salt-cod and potato cake, crisp outside and creamy within. Other showstoppers include a ramekin of shrimp, glistening with butter and olive oil and studded with crisp slices of garlic, and duck confit ringed by baby turnips. Dish after dish is fresh and vibrant. Unfortunately, the service is amateurish. ♦ Spanish ♦ Daily dinner. 842 Valencia St (between 20th and 19th Sts). 647.0558

30 La Rondalla ★$$ It's always Christmas at this Mexican restaurant, which is bedecked with blazing tree lights 365 days a year and has developed something of a cult following (it's also a late night hangout for bar-hoppers). Stuffed birds and other kitsch fill the dining rooms and compete with the strolling mariachis for attention. The open kitchen turns out delicious guacamole and *carne asada*, and several creations made with goat meat. ♦ Mexican ♦ Tu-Su lunch and dinner until 3AM. No credit cards accepted. 901 Valencia St (at 20th St). 647.7474

31 VAL 21 ★★$$ The corrugated-tin walls are softened by a curved, emerald green bar, red-cushioned chairs, and cobalt blue vases of fresh tulips, all contributing to a finished,

The Mission

dramatic look. It's a fitting setting for the California-inspired menu, which changes every six weeks but always includes several impressive vegetarian dishes (for example, the twice-baked miniature pumpkins, one stuffed with mushrooms and the other with ratatouille). A roasted baby chicken may be glazed with cranberries and served with cornbread dressing and wilted chard; *ahi* tuna may be paired with coconut-scented couscous, baked baby bananas, and pineapple salsa. Desserts include a hearty, spiced bread pudding with cranberries and a dense, steamed chocolate pudding. ♦ Californian ♦ M-F dinner; Sa-Su brunch and dinner. 995 Valencia St (at 21st St). 821.6622 &

31 Valencia Whole Foods As far as selection goes, this natural-foods store doesn't compare to **The Real Food Company** or **Rainbow Grocery,** but it's leagues ahead in terms of its presentation. The bulk merchandise is stored in wood- and glass-fronted bins, the vitamins are perfectly aligned behind the counter, and the shelves display all kinds of high-quality convenience products, like organic dry soup mixes. ♦ Daily. 999 Valencia St (at 21st St). 285.0231; fax 285.5267 &

32 Fina Estanpa ★★$ It's nothing fancy, but the food keeps this place packed with regulars. Among the tapas from Spain and Peru are marinated beef hearts, and potato slices drizzled with a feta-based sauce and topped with hard-cooked egg and black olives. There's also excellent paella, and fried chicken nuggets tossed with marinated onions and tomatoes. The shrimp in garlic, served both as a tapas and a main course, is a stunner. The decor features faux-wood paneling, a matted red carpet, and tables topped with glass. ♦ Spanish ♦ Tu-Su lunch and dinner. 2374 Mission St (between 20th and 19th Sts). 824.4437

33 Bruno's ★★★$$ From the moment it opened in the 1940s, **Bruno's** was a popular favorite among labor leaders, city politicians, and just plain folks. It seemed that everybody loved to come here and feast on classic Italian dishes like veal parmigiana and *spaghetti bolognese*. In the 1990s, it wore out its welcome a bit, closing for four years. But now **Bruno's** is back, reopened by restaurant veterans (and Mission residents) John Varnedoe and Wayne Neithold. Together, they've created a retro setting that celebrates and yet refines the old, friendly ambience of the place. The partners rescued the restaurant's 14 handsome red leather booths from a salvage yard, shined up its original stained-glass light fixtures, and moved the kitchen to the back of the main dining room. Chef James Ormsby's best appetizers include seared *ahi* tuna served on herb-perfumed lentils, and velvety braised oxtails with mashed potatoes blended with parsnips. Featured entrées are seared scallops paired with herb gnocchi, and salmon with a mushroom "roof" served on quinoa. Desserts are also special, particularly the chocolate mousse and any warm fruit crisp. And there's a lounge that serves snacks. ♦ Mediterranean ♦ Restaurant Tu-Su dinner; lounge daily until 1AM. 2389 Mission St (at 20th St). 550.7455; fax 642.9059 &

34 Mi Rancho Market An all-purpose source of imported and local Latino food supplies, the market is equipped with a butcher shop, a bakery, and a wine section that stocks bottles from Chile and Argentina. Unlike many of the smaller stores in the Mission, this one—bigger, and with a more complete selection of merchandise—has a supermarket atmosphere. ♦ Daily. No credit cards accepted. 3365 20th St (between Shotwell St and S Van Ness Ave). 647.0580; fax 647.0582 &

35 Casa Felix Produce and packaged goods are stacked high at this popular store specializing in Latino products. It offers great deals on produce, baked goods, dried chilies, spices, and canned foods. ♦ Daily. No credit cards accepted. 2567 Mission St (between 22nd and 21st Sts). 824.4491. Also at: 2840 Mission St (between 25th and 24th Sts). 824.4474 &

36 Lucky Pork Store This shop stocks a wide variety of hard-to-find organ meats—pig's head for headcheese, pig's feet for pickling, pork intestines for sausage casings, for example. Suckling pigs can be ordered, and goat meat is available most days. The constant traffic ensures freshness. ♦ Daily. 2659 Mission St (between 23rd and 22nd Sts). 285.3611 &

MISSION MARKET
FISH & POULTRY

37 Mission Market Fish & Poultry To find this vendor, walk through the marketplace clutter of the enclosed Mission mall. At the rear, under a red awning, you'll find free-range chickens, fresh turkey parts, fat stewing hens, and the like. Everything is freshly cut on-site. The seafood includes an array of clams, oysters, shrimp, and other shellfish, and many kinds of fish, including tilapia from Taiwan, "Gasper Goo" from Louisiana, and carp. ♦ M-Sa. 2590 Mission St (at 22nd St). 282.3331 &

The Mission

37 Mission Meat Market Just across the aisle from the seafood and poultry market, this meat market is the place to find Harris Ranch beef and all kinds of lamb and pork, including pork hearts. The honeycomb tripe is especially good. ♦ M-Sa. No credit cards accepted. 2590 Mission St (at 22nd St). 282.1030 ♿

38 Esperpento ★★$ The Spanish name loosely translates as "weird," but the restaurant and the customers just look artsy. With bright pink walls stippled with yellow splotches, hand-painted tabletops, and Daliesque paintings, the compact room feels like an artists' retreat. Nearly 40 tapas are offered for big-time noshing. Chicken croquettes come out crisp, golden, and moist inside with béchamel sauce. Squid is infused with its own ink; most people will probably prefer the more familiar fried calamari. Try the shrimp, which come from the kitchen sizzling in olive oil studded with garlic and red chili flakes. The paella is an excellent rendition of this classic dish of rice, seafood, chicken, and pork, served in the traditional cast-iron skillet. ♦ Spanish/Tapas ♦ M-Sa lunch and dinner. 3295 22nd St (at Valencia St). 282.8867; fax 282.8867 ♿

38 The Rooster ★★$$ Peasant cooking from southern Europe and Asia draws diners to this stylishly rustic new spot. The floor has the texture of sandpaper, the walls look scraped of a century of paint, and the chandeliers are made of rusted iron and shards of glass. Starters might be polenta with mushrooms, mussels in a spicy Asian-inspired broth, or roasted beets with crumbled creamy goat cheese. Entrées include such clay-pot dishes as lamb *tajine* (a Moroccan stew with olives and couscous) and beef stew in a red wine sauce perfumed with orange, as well as paella. Roast chicken and mashed potatoes get a twist with a compote of prunes and apricots. Dessert is not a strong point, except for the poached pear: One half is poached in red wine, the other in white wine, then the fruit is reassembled and presented upright on the plate with the red-wine poaching liquid. ♦ Mediterranean/Asian ♦ Daily dinner. 1101 Valencia St (at 22nd St). 824.1222; fax 824.1222

39 Radio Valencia Cafe ★$ Young people love this energetic bar/coffeehouse, where they huddle around the tables—actually painted cable spools. All the standard coffee drinks are offered, as well as five beers on tap and Wyder's Pear Cider. The food is prepared to order, and the main attractions are sandwiches, focaccia, and pizzas. There's live blues and rock on Friday nights, bluegrass on Saturday, and jazz on Sunday; the jazz has a modest music charge, but there's no cover. ♦ Cafe ♦ M-F dinner until midnight; Sa-Su lunch and dinner. 1199 Valencia St (at 23rd St). 826.1199 ♿

40 Lucca Ravioli Co., Inc. Loyal customers take a number and stand in line, and their patience is rewarded by great homemade ravioli, fresh pasta, Italian cheese, sausage, superb cold cuts, sauces, frozen pesto, and excellent Italian wines—all at reasonable prices. No wonder this place has been in business for more than 70 years. ♦ M-Sa. 1100 Valencia St (at 22nd St). 647.5581; fax 647.1948 ♿

40 Saigon Saigon ★★$ A bright urban oasis in a drab section of the Mission, this place sets a cheerful tone with the flower arrangements at the door. Begin with softshell crabs with a spicy dipping sauce, papaya-beef salad with nuances of fresh mint, or a gingery duck salad. Move on to black-peppered catfish or lamb kebabs with peanut sauce. If you insist on dessert, the crème caramel is simple, soothing, and satisfying. ♦ Vietnamese ♦ M-F lunch; Sa-Su dinner. 1132 Valencia St (between 23rd and 22nd Sts). 206.9635

41 Le Trou ★★$$ Robert Reynolds, the chef and owner, now divides his time between San Francisco and France, where he runs a cooking school, but he leaves his romantic restaurant in capable hands. Although it's just a storefront, the flickering candles on the ledges above the banquettes and the embroidered napkins at each place setting lend an upscale feel. The fixed-price menu, which changes seasonally, features some very good rustic combinations grounded in the French classics. Starters might be a refreshing pasta with lemon, prosciutto, and olives, smoothed with gruyère, or a mussel flan with a hint of cider and leeks. Main courses include duck prepared three ways: confit, sautéed breast, and duck-liver flan, served with spiced prunes and lentils. Another option might be sea bass

The Mission

marinated in Arabic spices, then sautéed and served with spinach and raisins. Dessert might be a classic warm *tarte tatin* (upside-down apple tart) or mocha-raspberry cake.
♦ French ♦ Tu-Sa dinner. Reservations required. 1007 Guerrero St (at 22nd St). 550.8169; fax 550.0643

41 Mangiafuoco ★★$$ This 50-seat dining spot serves incredible risotto, featherweight gnocchi, and great pasta, including the eponymous *mangiafuoco*: fettuccine coated with tomato sauce, topped with seafood, and then baked in parchment paper. Other excellent choices are the salads and the carpaccio drizzled with mustard. Since the restaurant's name means "fire eater," it's ironic that grilled dishes are its weak point; they aren't bad, they just pale in comparison to the other preparations. The cozy interior has hand-painted tabletops, ocher walls, halogen lighting, an open kitchen, and picture windows overlooking a row of Victorian houses. ♦ Italian ♦ Daily dinner. No credit cards accepted. 1001 Guerrero St (at 22nd St). 206.9881

FLYING SAUCER

42 The Flying Saucer ★★★$$$ The far-out food and decor have made this quirky restaurant a winner from the day it opened. There are black wooden booths, pressed-tin panels, and folk art on the walls, and a store mannequin lying across the ledge above the window. The menu, crafted by chef-owner Albert Trodjman, changes every six weeks and reflects what he calls "world-beat cuisine," meaning unusual cross-cultural combinations and dramatic presentations. Duck confit may share a plate with cabbage-peanut salad and ginger-infused Asian noodles. Rack of lamb might be coated with pecans and served with wild rice and a tart mint-fig compote; salmon might be blackened and served with spicy shrimp bread pudding. ♦ Californian ♦ T-Su dinner. Reservations recommended. 1000 Guerrero St (at 22nd St). 641.9955

43 Taqueria Goyaz ★$ The Mission hardly needs another *taqueria*, but this spot has a twist: In addition to the standard Mexican selections (the pork burritos are excellent), it offers a range of Brazilian fare. Skewers of marinated beef are served on a bed of greens, and the Brazilian-style grilled chicken is tender and succulent. The plain environment doesn't encourage lingering, but prices are low even by Mission standards. ♦ Mexican/Brazilian ♦ Daily lunch and dinner. 3392 24th St (at Valencia St). 821.4600; fax 695.9295

44 Muddy's Coffee House $ With all its clutter and its faux-grungy crowd, this coffeehouse fits right into the neighborhood. Most people come here for a dose of caffeine and to hang out. There's also the standard array of pastries and other cafe fare. ♦ Coffee-

house ♦ Daily breakfast, lunch, and dinner. 1304 Valencia St (at 24th St). 647.7994. Also at: 521 Valencia St (at 16th St). 863.8006; 260 Church St (at 15th St). 621.2233

45 Suriya Thai Restaurant ★★$$ Chef-owner Suriya Srithongt adds pizzazz to her dishes with such fanciful garnishes as radishes carved into elephants, elevating this spot a step above most of the competition. The decor features Asian antiques, bamboo-backed chairs, and large urns of bamboo. The food veers toward the sweet side, making it popular with Western palates. Best dishes include chicken salad, garlic-pepper pork with red peppers and scallions, and chicken wrapped in banana leaves with cashews and raisins. The shrimp with ginger makes a dazzlingly hot contrast to the sweeter items. ♦ Thai ♦ Tu-F lunch and dinner; Sa-Su dinner. No credit cards accepted. 1432 Valencia St (between 26th and 25th Sts). 824.6655

46 Latin Freeze *Paletas* (fruit purees frozen on a stick) are produced at this tiny shop in dozens of seasonal flavors, including papaya, mango, melon, pineapple, coconut, and strawberry; all taste as if they were made from fresh-picked fruit. For a refreshing change, try the intriguingly sour tamarind. ♦ Daily. No credit cards accepted. 3338 24th St (between Mission and Bartlett Sts). 282.5033

47 23rd and Mission Produce The produce overflows onto the street at this clean shop, which has some of the best-priced fruits and vegetables in the city. Don't be discouraged by the long lines at the checkouts; the system is so efficient, you'll be through in a flash. ♦ Daily. No credit cards accepted. 2700 Mission St (at 23rd St). 285.7955

48 Dianda's Italian and American Pastries Just before the holidays, aficionados of Italian baked goods line up around the block to pick up their special orders. After one taste, you'll understand why. The amaretto cookies are soft and delicious; the fillings for zuppa inglese and zabaglione tortes are whipped by hand in copper bowls. *Paneforte*, a dense Italian fruitcake popular at Christmas, is moist and somewhat lighter here; it's available year-round. ♦ Daily. No credit cards accepted. 2883 Mission St (at 25th St). 647.5469

48 La Taqueria ★★$ The terra-cotta-colored floor and Mexican-tile walls here are always scrupulously clean, as is the open kitchen that turns out juicy grilled steak, tender *carnitas*

The Mission

(pork), and moist chicken, all wrapped in delicate flour tortillas. The salsa, even in winter, is fresh and vibrant, and the quesadillas are also good. *Agua fresca* sodas, which come in at least a half-dozen flavors, taste like the fruit's very essence (the cantaloupe and tangerine are incredible). The friendly service and rock-bottom prices are icing on the cake. ♦ Mexican ♦ Daily lunch and dinner. No credit cards accepted. 2889 Mission St (at 25th St). 285.7117 ♦

49 La Traviata ★★$$ An elegant outpost in a drab part of the Mission, the narrow room boasts an arched wooden ceiling, window frames holding mirrors instead of glass, and bronze carpeting that matches the upholstery on the booths and chairs; the tables are adorned by fresh pink roses and candles under frosted pink shades. Pictures of opera stars and scenes from famous operas bedeck the walls, and opera music plays continuously—a fitting backdrop for the dramatic fare. The gnocchi are wonderful—light, slightly chewy puffs of potato dough in a creamy tomato sauce with a hint of sweet spices. The tortellini is served in a white cream sauce perfumed with nutmeg. And don't miss the stews: The lamb stew is rich with the flavor that comes from slow simmering, yet the meat remains juicy. Other selections on the classic menu include veal with artichokes and chicken rolled around prosciutto and served with a mushroom sauce. Desserts mostly come from **Dianda's Italian and American Pastries** (see page 151), but the creamy tiramisù is made in-house. Avoid the cannoli: It's prepared in advance and tastes like it. ♦ Italian ♦ Tu-Su dinner. 2854 Mission St (near 25th St). 282.0500 ♦

50 Taqueria San Jose ★★★$ This is one of the best taco and burrito joints in the city. The grilled beef burrito is always worth sampling, and aficionados of more unusual Mexican fare can also find tripe, brains, chicken, pork stomach, and other delicacies on the menu. Prices are good and portions are big. ♦ Mexican ♦ Daily lunch and dinner. No credit cards accepted. 2830 Mission St (at 24th St). 282.0203

51 El Pollo Supremo ★★$ The bright yellow-and-orange exterior has dulled over time and the colorful interior looks the worse for wear, but this modest place produces some of the best chicken in the city, either to eat in or to take out. The limited menu also offers such side dishes as yucca (a starchy root) in garlic sauce, but chicken is the main event. ♦ Rotisserie/ Mexican ♦ Daily lunch and dinner. No credit cards accepted. 3150 24th St (at Shotwell St). 550.1193; fax 550.2433

52 El Nuevo Frutilandia ★$ The dishes of Cuba and Puerto Rico are showcased in this small storefront restaurant with vivid coral walls and a cozy dining counter. Plantains, rice, and yucca show up in many of the mildly seasoned dishes—for example, in a Brazilian tamale, which is steamed in a plantain leaf. Lunch includes Cuban sandwiches, while dinner features substantial plates like chicken breasts in a bright green salsa. The nightly specials generally include a homey braised dish, always a good choice. ♦ Cuban/Puerto Rican ♦ Daily lunch and dinner. 3077 24th St (at Folsom St). 648.2958 ♦

53 Manora's Thai Cuisine ★★$ This is one of the most popular Thai restaurants in the city, in spite of all its ordinary trappings—a tattered green awning, white walls inside, and white tablecloths covered with glass. Dishes tend to be on the sweet side, similar to those at its sister restaurant in SoMa. Top choices include fish steamed in a banana leaf, pork with garlic and pepper, and chicken with lemongrass and coconut milk. ♦ Thai ♦ Tu-Su dinner. 3226 Mission St (at Valencia St). 550.0856. Also at: 1600 Folsom St (at 12th St). 861.6224

54 Mitchell's Ice Cream Even though it's a bit off the beaten track, this parlor is a local legend. The ice creams are as rich as gelato, and many come in exotic tropical flavors, including avocado, litchi, *ube* (a root similar to a yam), *langka* (a tart melon), and *buko* (baby coconut). The Mexican chocolate ice cream has an enticing whisper of cinnamon, and the rich caramel is studded with toasted pecans. Three display cases hold half gallons for takeout, and an attendant sequestered behind glass, much like a bank teller, sells coffee and cones to those who want to lick and run. ♦ Daily. No credit cards accepted. 688 San Jose Ave (at 29th St). 648.2300 ♦

55 Angkor Borei ★★$ San Francisco was the first city in the United States to have a Cambodian restaurant. Although that one has closed, it paved the way for the others, of which this modest place is among the best.

The Mission

Juicy grilled beef balls, encasing water chestnuts and presented with pickled vegetables, are a wonderful introduction to this aromatic cuisine. Delicate Cambodian spring rolls, which crack like a thin layer of ice, are stuffed with vegetables, noodles, and pork. Green curries are laced with the fresh tastes of basil and lemongrass. The simple room in the outer Mission isn't up to the caliber of the food, but it's pleasant enough. ♦ Cambodian ♦ Daily lunch and dinner. 3471 Mission St (between Cortland Ave and 30th St). 550.8417

56 Inca ★★$ This small blue-and-white Peruvian cafe specializes in seafood; the deep-fried seafood platter—prawns, red snapper, mussels, clams, and calamari—is a standout. Also excellent is the appetizer of marinated and grilled beef heart with fried potatoes. Just be warned that service in this mom-and-pop operation can be slow. ♦ Peruvian ♦ M, W-Su lunch and dinner. No credit cards accepted. 3515 Mission St (at Cortland Ave). 821.5852; fax 206.0783 &

57 The Liberty Cafe ★★★$$ Finally, the Bernal Heights neighborhood has its first three-star hangout, thanks to this charming cafe. The menu features about four appetizers and as many main courses, but each is perfectly executed. Spears of asparagus are drizzled with a jalapeño-shallot vinaigrette, sprinkled with crisp bread crumbs, and topped with two halved quail eggs, and the Caesar salad is among the best in the city. Chicken potpie has a burnished puff-pastry crust and a lightly thickened filling of roasted pearl onions, carrots, and big chunks of potatoes and chicken. A whole trout is coated in a cornmeal crust, pan-seared, and served with lemony spinach, sautéed baby artichokes, and browned potatoes. For dessert the banana cream pie is unbeatable: a buttery, crisp crust; rich, creamy custard studded with slices of fruit; and billowy whipped cream. The decor of this 38-seat cafe is simple but attractive, with sky blue wainscoting and golden walls stenciled with ivy. White-clothed tables are topped with butcher paper and set with ceramic candleholders from Guatemala. All in all, it's an excellent destination. ♦ American ♦ Tu-F lunch and dinner; Sa brunch and dinner; Su brunch. 410 Cortland Ave (at Bennington St). 695.8777 &

58 The Good Life Grocery One of the city's most complete natural-food stores, it offers an impressive display of organic produce, plus a full-service deli featuring prepared salads and sandwiches. In addition, it carries beer and wine. ♦ Daily. 448 Cortland Ave (between Andover and Bennington Sts). 648.3221 &

59 Alemany Farmers' Market This market has been around for nearly 50 years and features all kinds of California-grown fruits and vegetables, as well as hard-to-find Asian products, dried fruits, nuts, eggs, herbs, honeys and jams, and crabs and oysters from Half Moon Bay. Street musicians often set up around the market. ♦ Sa 6AM-5PM. 100 Alemany Blvd (between Hwy 101 and Prentiss St, near the intersection of Hwy 280). 647.9423 &

Lights, Camera, Dinner!

Thanks to San Francisco's spectacular scenery and proximity to Hollywood, scores of movies have been filmed here, among them the Alfred Hitchcock classic *Vertigo,* Clint Eastwood's five "Dirty Harry" films, and the James Bond flick *A View to a Kill.* Whoopi Goldberg spent two weeks filming *Sister Act* in **Noe Valley,** and Steve McQueen careened through **Potrero Hill** in *Bullitt.* San Francisco's distinctive restaurants and food emporiums have played supporting roles in the following movies:

Ristorante Fior d'Italia was the setting for a meeting between David Caruso and co-star Linda Fiorentino in *Jade* (1995).

The cavernous old **American Can Company** factory stood in for Cape Canaveral when *The Right Stuff* (1983) was shot here. The **Cow Palace,** a venue for exhibitions and conventions, was the setting the film makers used for a barbecue President Lyndon Johnson hosted for the astronauts.

In one scene of *The Graduate* (1967), Dustin Hoffman is seen sitting in **Berkeley**'s **Mediterranee Caffè**—still a popular student hangout.

Kim Novak and Jimmy Stewart supped at the elegant but now-closed **Ernie's** in *Vertigo* (1958).

The hilarious dining scene in *Mrs. Doubtfire* (1993), when Robin Williams, in drag as a nanny, loses his false teeth, was filmed in the Bridges restaurant in San Ramon, about 30 miles east of San Francisco.

All the scenes set in the butcher shop featured in *So I Married an Axe Murderer*—the 1993 farce starring Mike (*Wayne's World*) Myers—were shot at the former **R. Iacoppi & Company** in **North Beach.** Last year, the owner sold the store to his goddaughter, Josette Prudente. With her husband, Daniel, she has turned it into the **Prudente Meat Market & Deli.**

Castro/Noe Valley

A stroll past **Chloe's Cafe** on a Sunday morning can tell even casual observers everything they need to know about the Castro and Noe Valley, two neighborhoods settled on the eastern slopes of **Twin Peaks**. While waiting outside for a table, two men lean against the building, holding hands; a young father bounces his baby on his knee while the mother looks on; and two women pushing a stroller down the sidewalk zigzag around the crowd. If there's anything unusual about the scene, no one seems to notice, because the neighborhood is inhabited by gay men, lesbians, and young heterosexual couples with children. In the Castro and Noe Valley, Boys Town meets Baby Town. That's a big change from a decade ago. When young heterosexuals moved into the area, and the **Walgreen's** at **18th and Castro Streets** began to carry Pampers, it was front-page news in the mainstream press.

The center of San Francisco's gay culture for the past 25 years or so, the Castro has never been known for great food, but it does have a keen sense of culinary humor. **RoCocoa's Faerie Queene Chocolates,** for example, with fairies flying from the ceiling and faux-pearl–encrusted candy cases, is a campy (and pricey) place to buy Belgian chocolates. And although the phrase "hot 'n' hunky" may have certain connotations to some people, it also happens to be the name of a popular diner in this neighborhood specializing in hamburgers. Still, there's a lot to recommend here: delicious cross-cultural meals at **Ma Tante Sumi,** sparkling fresh oysters at **Anchor Oyster Bar,** and creative American fare at **Ryan's Restaurant,** whose downstairs deli features some of the best takeout in the city.

Good wine shops and cheese shops can be found along Castro and **Market** Streets, and a few blocks up, the excellent specialty grocer **Harvest Ranch Market** displays nature's bounty in baskets. Just about everywhere you look there's a coffeehouse, and none is as popular as **Cafe Flore.** Known by the gay locals as "Cafe Hairdo," it's a prime place to relax and get a snapshot view of the neighborhood.

Coffeehouses fuel Noe Valley, too, a quaint neighborhood of Victorian storefronts and homes. The main shopping strip, **24th Street,** is the home of the original **Spinelli Coffee Company,** a well-known specialty roaster. Also on the street, **The Real Food Company** offers wonderful organic produce, **Caruso Wine and Liquor Store** can set you up with a great wine from a small California producer, and the **Noe Valley Bakery & Bread Co.** is one of the top spots for baked goods. The restaurants didn't used to appeal to anyone from beyond the neighborhood, but that's beginning to change. In the last few years **Bacco Ristorante Italiano** and **Firefly** have brought three-star dining status to this three-star neighborhood. And then there are the latest additions: **Miss Millie's,** a fantastic place to enjoy Sunday brunch; and **John Cunin's No-Name Restaurant,** whose eclectic cuisine and bargain prices have made its no-name a household word.

---

1 It's Tops Coffee Shop ★★$ Amid all the glitzy faux diners popping up, it's a treat to find an authentic one like this place, which dates to 1935. Even the table-side jukeboxes play nothing more recent than early Beatles tunes. The knotty pine covering the walls and peaked ceiling are original; the eight bright orange booths and the counter with 12 stools were installed in the 1950s. The classic breakfasts include waffles, pancakes, and omelettes. The hamburgers are terrific— loosely formed, crisp on the outside, and sandwiched between grilled, cornmeal-dusted buns. Dinners include excellent grilled chicken breast, lamb chops, or liver and onions. The pies are average-tasting, but the homemade brownies and the milk shakes are exceptional. It's a great stop for night owls, as it's open late several nights a week. ♦ American ♦ M-Tu, Su breakfast and lunch; W-Sa breakfast, lunch, and dinner until 3AM. 1801 Market St (at Guerrero St). 431.6395; fax 431.6395

2 The Orbit Room ★$ This trendy hangout cranks up early in the morning and continues into the wee hours. Daytime bites include sandwiches of roast beef or turkey, and salads topped with tuna, lemon chicken, or stilton cheese. There are strong espresso drinks, pastries, and desserts. At night the focus is on the bar, which stocks a full line of spirits and nine beers on tap (plus 12 bottled brews). The decor is impressive: the Deco building, the intricate period ceiling, cement vases on the tables, and large ornate windows overlooking the street. ♦ Coffeehouse/Bar ♦ M-Th 7AM-midnight; F-Su until 2AM. 1900 Market St (at Laguna St). 252.9525 ♿

3 Dame—a restaurant ★★$ Though it's just a hole-in-the-wall kind of place—no atmosphere to speak of—this eatery is a hot hangout for locals in the know. The menu offers a modest selection of well-prepared American dishes. Starters include Caesar salad, gorgonzola french fries, and Prince Edward Island mussels steamed in a roasted red pepper broth. Entrées, which change often, include fettuccine with grilled chicken, spinach, roasted onions, and pesto; and moist

Castro/Noe Valley

and tasty smoked pork loin served with rosemary polenta and oven-roasted vegetables. Friendly and fun, this is a great place to mingle with neighborhood residents. ♦ American ♦ Tu-F lunch and dinner; Sa dinner; Su brunch. 1815 Market St (between Guerrero and Dolores Sts). 255.8818

4 Mecca ★★$$ This new supper club is a stylish addition to the Castro district. The centerpiece of the place is a circular bar that seats 28; surrounding it are five distinct dining rooms, each with a different ambience. The atmospheres range from French bistro to 1930s supper club, but the menu throughout (by acclaimed chef Lynn Sheehan) is Mediterranean. ♦ Mediterranean ♦ M-Sa dinner. 2029 Market St (between Dolores and Church Sts). 621.7000 &

5 Amazing Grace Vegetarian Restaurant ★$ The amazing thing about this clean but earthy-looking restaurant, with its slatted-wood ceiling and chairs, is that it's been in the same location since 1969, serving cafeteria-style vegetarian food at rock-bottom prices. The pungent smell of curry pervades the place. You'll find a southern Indian version with carrots and cashews and another with mushrooms. The salad bar offers more than 30 items. ♦ Vegetarian ♦ M-Sa lunch and dinner. No credit cards accepted. 216 Church St (at Market St). 626.6411 &

6 Just Desserts This is the original retail location (there are now a dozen) that the Hoffmans, a husband-and-wife team, founded over 20 years ago as an outlet to sell their immensely popular cheesecakes. Their made-it-big story may be unique: The company, which has also acquired the popular **Tassajara Bread Bakery,** maintains strict quality control and still uses butter and hand-cracked eggs. Such care really shows in its popular cheesecakes and super-moist chocolate cake. Just about any of the baked goods—pastries, cookies, and pies—are winners. ♦ Daily. 248 Church St (between 15th and Market Sts). 626.5774; fax 626.7212 &. Also at: 836 Irving St (at 10th Ave). 681.1277; fax 681.0308

6 Muddy Waters Coffee $ Rough brick walls, worn plank floors, dark wood tables, and window seats filled with alternative newspapers and announcements give this new place an authentic coffeehouse feel. The *lattes* are served in glasses, so be prepared to nurse burned fingers. Any bitter edge the coffee may have is smoothed by plenty of milk. You'll find lots of sweets and snacks, as well as coffee beans for sale. The best part is watching the people: Some leave their dogs outside and bring their bikes inside. ♦ Cafe ♦ Daily. No credit cards accepted. 260 Church St (at 15th St). 621.2233 &. Also at: 521 Valencia St (at 16th St). 863.8006 &; 1304 Valencia St (at 24th St). 647.7994

7 Nippon Sushi ★★$ Since there's no signage at this 1980s-era eatery, locals have taken to calling it "No-Name Sushi." Although it's just a sliver of a place—with a well-worn sushi bar, bare tables, and only 26 seats, including at the counter—its good, inexpensive sushi attracts a cultlike following; fans begin to line up before 6PM. Upon being seated, customers are served a pot of toasted-barley tea, which goes well with the tasty *maki* (rice and seaweed with fish or vegetables rolled in the center). There's no telephone—only a pay phone that is never answered—and no liquor license, but that hasn't dampened its popularity one whit. ♦ Japanese ♦ M-Sa lunch and dinner. No credit cards accepted. 314 Church St (at 15th St). No phone

8 Thai House Bar and Café ★$ Opened only a few years ago, this outpost of **Thai House Restaurant** (see page 157) features an outdoor patio and a full bar. The warm meat salads and the soups are good, although main courses can be oily. Try the chicken satay, panfried shrimp, or chicken and coconut-milk soup. ♦ Thai ♦ Daily lunch and dinner. 2200 Market St (at 15th St). 864.5006 &. Also at: 151 Noe St (at Henry St). 863.0374

9 John Cunin's No-Name Restaurant ★★★$$ John Cunin is nothing if not a smart entrepreneur who keeps ahead of (and sometimes starts) the latest trends. The opening of his **Cypress Club** five years ago helped spark the renaissance of the supper club in San Francisco, and Gate Five, a Cunin-owned seafood spot in Marin, has been a smash hit with both locals and visitors. Now, he's opened a stylish and moderately priced dining establishment here in the Castro, a neighborhood that has always been short on contemporary cuisine. The sunny walls and fanciful light fixtures (with sculptured metal, opaque shades, and bulbs in various interesting shapes) set a friendly and almost magical tone, preparing you for the wonderful food to come. Star appetizers include warm duck confit salad with seasonal fruits, spiced pecans and pomegranate vinaigrette; wild mushroom soup with puff pastry; and grilled sea scallops with shaved fennel and citrus

Castro/Noe Valley

salad. Leading entrées are herb brioche–crusted pork loin served with yams and sage-buttered escarole; fillet of salmon poached in Champagne accompanied by potato puree; and a whole roasted guinea hen. The chocolate cake with Champagne-citrus granita is a heavenly way to round out the meal. The full bar serves a wide variety of cocktails, and the vintages on the wine list have been carefully chosen to complement the foods. ♦ Contemporary American ♦ M-Sa lunch and dinner; Su brunch and dinner. 2223 Market St (between Sanchez and Noe Sts). 431.0692 &

10 Thai House Restaurant ★$ Smaller than the branch on Market Street (see page 156), this place has a more intimate feel and a more loyal neighborhood clientele. The menu is virtually the same, although the food tends to be a little better balanced. Best bets include the shrimp rolls, the yellow (with turmeric) chicken curry, and the sirloin with spinach in peanut sauce. ♦ Thai ♦ Daily dinner. 151 Noe St (at Henry St). 863.0374. Also at: 2200 Market St (at 15th St). 864.5006 &

11 Metro Bar and Restaurant ★$ Customers flock to this restaurant, up a flight of stairs, for the pot stickers, General Tso's chicken in hot sweet-and-sour sauce, and the squid *kung pao* (in a spicy sauce with peanuts). The bar, opposite, serves as a way station and is also a popular gay watering hole featuring drink specials on most nights. Its narrow outdoor patio wrapping around two sides is a prime place to hang out and watch the street action on Market. ♦ Chinese ♦ Daily dinner; bar M-F 2:30PM-2AM; Sa-Su 1PM-2AM. 3600 16th St (at Market St). 703.9750; fax 241.9493

11 La Méditerranée ★★$ This Middle Eastern–inspired restaurant offers good food in intimate surroundings at excellent prices. The lemony hummus with fresh herbs is a good starter. Among the popular main courses are the "Levant" sandwiches, pinwheels of cream cheese and other ingredients, which change daily; ground lamb kebab served with rice; and chicken drumsticks marinated in pomegranate sauce and baked. Main courses come with salad or a cup of soup. ♦ Middle Eastern ♦ Tu-Su lunch and dinner. 288 Noe St (at Market St). 431.7210 &. Also at: 2210 Fillmore St (at Sacramento St). 921.2956 &

1 Cafe Flore $ Probably the most popular coffeehouse with the gay community, this place looks like an overgrown lean-to and is easy to miss because of the planters obscuring the windows. The patio is the place to be on fine days, and the cozy, crowded interior is warming in the chilly winter. Quarters are so close, in fact, that at Christmas the tree is suspended upside down from the ceiling. Nobody is ever hassled;

frustrated poets spend hours writing in their diaries, while other customers nurse their brew, trying to catch the eye of potential dates. People don't come for the food, but on good days the eggs are fine and the organic greens taste as fresh as you'll find. Either way it doesn't seem to matter; this is the best place to explore the heart of the Castro. ♦ Californian ♦ M-Th, Su 7:30AM-11PM; F-Sa 7:30AM-midnight. 2298 Market St (at Noe St). 621.8579

12 Harvest Ranch Market One of the top specialty groceries, this place is always lively. People fill up the benches outside, eating takeout from the elaborate salad bar. Produce, most of it organic and looking hand-selected, is displayed in baskets, and breads from all the best bakeries fill the front window. The bins of bulk items, good olive oils, condiments, and hard-to-find products make this a popular destination. ♦ Daily 9AM-11PM. 2285 Market St (at Noe St). 626.0805; fax 626.0809

13 Ginseng Mania While ginseng shops are popular in Chinatown, this is one of the few in a non-Asian neighborhood. Richard Kim has created a stark black-and-white emporium with everything ginseng: teas, tablets, gum, candy, and extracts. Ginseng, the wonder herb of Chinese medicine, is said to relieve stress, detoxify the body of alcohol, and help in diabetes, cancer, hypertension, and arteriosclerosis. Medicinal or not, his smoothies made with fruits (apple, banana, and mango, among others) and rice milk are delightfully refreshing. ♦ Daily. No credit cards accepted. 2312 Market St (between Noe and Castro Sts). 552.2111 &

14 Pozole ★★$ It looks like a Mexican folk art museum, but it's a burrito parlor specializing in low-fat, low-salt Mexican food, and the quesadillas and burritos have interesting fillings. The *burrito Californiano* combines cactus, *pasilla* (dried chili pepper), tomatoes, and roasted garlic; the *Mexicano* has chicken and roasted peppers with tomatillo and lime. Order at the counter and the food is brought to you. ♦ Mexican ♦ M-Th dinner; F-Sa lunch and dinner until midnight; Su lunch and dinner until 11PM. 2337 Market St (between 16th and Castro Sts). 626.2666; fax 252.8083 &

15 Double Rainbow Ice Cream This is the original parlor (opened in 1976) that spawned the immense growth of this popular ice cream. Barely big enough for more than a handful of patrons, the busy shop turns out lots of quality ice cream and frozen yogurt. ♦ Daily. 407 Castro St (at Market St). 621.2350 &. Also at: 1653 Polk St (between Sacramento and Clay Sts). 775.3220 &; 1724 Haight St (between Cole and Shrader Sts). 668.6690 &

Castro/Noe Valley

Pasta Primer

San Francisco is pasta-obsessed. Even people who pride themselves on knowing their way around the culinary landscape will be faced, sooner or later, with a shape they didn't know existed. Here's a look at some of the pastas in area restaurants and supermarkets:

Bucatini		**Orecchiette**	
Capellini		**Orzo**	
Capelli d'angeli		**Pappardelle**	
Conchigliette		**Penne**	
Farfalle		**Ravioli**	
Fettuccine		**Rigatoni**	
Fusilli		**Rotelle**	
Gnocchi		**Spaghetti**	
Lasagna		**Tagliatelle**	
Linguine		**Tortellini**	
		Vermicelli	
Macaroni		**Ziti**	
Mostaccioli			

Castro/Noe Valley

15 RoCocoa's Faerie Queene Chocolates
Owner Jeoffrey Douglas says he's serious about chocolate, but not to the extent that he found in the exclusive shops in Europe, where chocolates are treated like precious jewels. He's put a drag-queen twist on his shop by draping the ceiling and walls with pink and white satin, gilding just about everything that could be painted, and adding dried nosegays and dozens of flying fairies (they're for sale, too). He's even glued pearls around the edges of the two cases that hold the pricey Belgian, French, and American chocolates. Douglas makes his own fudge—peanut butter and chocolate leading the pack. Among the specialty items: a chocolate phallus for the bawdy; delicate, pink-chocolate long-stem roses for the romantic. You can fax your orders. ♦ Daily noon-10PM. 415 Castro St (at Market St). 252.5814; fax 255.2016

15 Castro Cheesery This may be called a cheese shop, but when you walk in and smell the wake-up aroma of fresh ground beans you know that coffee is the real attraction. Stacked in the corner, ceiling high, are plastic sacks of beans, and the area behind the counter displays more than 40 varieties, plus 20 flavored blends. Most of the coffees are surprisingly cheap; among the premium types are Kona, Yemen Mocha, and Jamaican Blue Mountain—considered by many to be the finest in the world. There is cheese, of course, a dozen cheddars and nine blues, but when it comes to aroma, coffee wins by a nose. ♦ Daily. 427 Castro St (at 17th St). 552.6676; fax 552.0663 &

16 Rossi's Delicatessen Although small, this Italian-style deli makes great use of its space. Besides sandwiches and salads, you'll find a good sampling of wines, a growing collection of coffee beans, and a surprising selection of coffee filters. ♦ Tu-Sa 8AM-10PM; Su 10AM-8PM. No credit cards accepted. 426 Castro St (at Market St). 863.4533 &

17 Slider's Diner ★$ Hamburgers are the tour de force of this newish restaurant featuring a 25-item self-service condiment bar. The burgers are thick and juicy, with thick fries to match—you order and pick up from the counter. It's a quick in and out, although some people linger to enjoy the music videos, concerts, and games that play on the television suspended from the ceiling in the clean, tiled dining room. ♦ Hamburgers ♦ Daily lunch and dinner until midnight. 449 Castro St (between 18th and Market Sts). 431.3288; fax 431.3288 &

17 Cliff's Variety Established in 1936, this one-stop hardware store carries a large assortment of kitchenware, small appliances, and dishes. It's one of the most complete variety stores in the city. ♦ M-Sa 9:30AM-8PM. 479 Castro St (between 18th and Market Sts). 431.5365; fax 431.0803 &

18 Cafe Lupann's ★$$ Although the atmosphere suggests fine dining, the food and service can be uneven. Retro appetizers go from fried brie wedge (1970s) to pâté and escargot (1960s French). Main courses are more interesting: American pot roast, pork tenderloin grilled and served with Bourbon sauce and dried cherries, and boneless chicken breast topped with a spicy cucumber-and-mint yogurt sauce. ♦ Californian ♦ Daily dinner. 4072 18th St (between Hartford and Castro Sts). 552.6655

19 Bad Man Jose's ★★$ A terrific place for a quick snack, this self-serve parlor features interesting burritos made of whole-wheat tortillas, black beans, brown rice, and grilled chicken or steak. Ingredients taste fresh and prices are low. The pleasant, modern surroundings are a plus, too, with a granite bar (ideal for the single diner) and, along the opposite wall, tables with straight-back wooden chairs. ♦ Mexican ♦ Daily lunch and dinner. No credit cards accepted. 4077 18th St (between Hartford and Castro Sts). 861.1706; fax 861.2426

19 Hot 'N' Hunky ★$ Yet another chrome-and-tile burger joint, this one capitalizes on the gay clientele in both its name and its interior appointments, such as pictures of Marilyn Monroe. Fans contend that this eatery has the best burger in the city; we'd argue otherwise, but they are thick and the fries are crisp. ♦ Hamburgers ♦ M-Th, Su lunch and dinner until midnight; F-Sa lunch and dinner until 1AM. No credit cards accepted. 4039 18th St (between Hartford and Castro Sts). 621.6365

20 Rosie's Cantina ★$ This pleasant and open corner restaurant features a straightforward menu of burritos, tacos, enchiladas, and other simple Mexican fare. After ordering at the counter, you can sit at one of the scattered tables or have your food wrapped to go. ♦ Mexican ♦ Daily lunch and dinner. No credit cards accepted. 4001 18th St (at Noe St). 864.5643 &

21 Taqueria Zapata ★$ This spare, cafeteria-style taco joint offers a large choice of fillings. Be patient, though; the many choices tend to slow and confuse both customers and employees. ♦ Mexican ♦ Daily lunch and dinner until midnight. No credit cards accepted. 4150 18th St (at Collingwood St). 861.4470 &

Castro/Noe Valley

MA TANTE SUMI

22 Ma Tante Sumi ★★$$ Featuring a creative menu that blends Japanese and French dishes, this small, intimate space, with tables on several levels, has a cozy aura and cross-cultural accents. The wasabi-cured salmon with pickled ginger is always a popular starter and so is the warm goat cheese served with *shiso* (a peppery Japanese herb), Asian pears, and walnut vinaigrette. Some of the more unusual dishes include grilled tuna with *wasabi-tobiko* (Japanese horseradish with flying-fish roe); pan-roasted duck with *hoisin* vinaigrette; and roast chicken with lemon and garlic sauce and a sesame *udon* (white noodle) salad. Sometimes the food soars, and only the amateurish service keeps this restaurant from playing in the big leagues. ♦ Californian/Japanese ♦ Daily dinner. 4243 18th St (between Collingwood and Diamond Sts). 626.7864; fax 626.7886

23 Ryan's Charcuterie This is one of the city's top carryout places, and chef and co-owner Lenore Nolan-Ryan stocks two cases with freshly made products. Chicken may be Jamaican barbecued, crusted with mustard, simply grilled, or roasted whole with herbs and lemon. You can always find roasted garlic bulbs (great spread over bread), artichokes stuffed with aioli and croutons, a wonderful chicken potpie, and an excellent version of *pasta primavera*. The dessert crumble, made with fresh fruit in season, is a particular favorite. ♦ Daily. 4230 18th St (between Collingwood and Diamond Sts). 621.6131

23 Ryan's Restaurant ★★$$ Few establishments have such a charming, speakeasy atmosphere as this restaurant, located above the carryout shop and accessed by a narrow, curving staircase that spills into a warren of rooms. The solid antique tables and chairs and white walls hung with modern art give the place distinction.

While the decor is classic, the food is imaginative. A game hen may be stuffed with gruyère cheese and served with a warm potato-and-wild-mushroom salad. Pork loin is coated with garlic and comes with soft polenta and a fresh-tasting marinara sauce. Sometimes the creativity can go a little too far in the appetizers, such as soft pork taco with chipotle, aioli, and coriander salad. But such desserts as the baked chocolate pudding and the fruit crumble are winners. ♦ Californian ♦ W-F dinner; Sa brunch and dinner; Su brunch. 4230 18th St (between Collingwood and Diamond Sts). 621.6131

23 Siam Grill $ The Thai food is nothing special but is better than most in the area. Specialties are the hot, red-curry dishes, especially chicken with cashews and a seafood blend of scallops, prawns, and mussels. ♦ Thai ♦ Daily dinner. 4248 18th St (between Collingwood and Diamond Sts). 552.1174

24 The Sausage Factory $ For almost 30 years, this local Italian restaurant has been dishing up pizzas, pastas, and salads in ample portions at reasonable prices. The dark wood paneling and narrow design of the winding dining rooms make for a cozy dinner but a rather dimly lit lunch. ♦ Italian ♦ Daily lunch and dinner. No credit cards accepted. 517 Castro St (between 19th and 18th Sts). 626.1250 &

24 The Patio Cafe $$ People love to knock the food here, but this is probably the most popular place in the Castro, thanks to the tree-shaded patio in back that fosters a pleasant atmosphere in good weather. It's particularly busy during the day for brunch, when 15 omelettes and a half-dozen kinds of pancakes are featured. There's something for everyone on the laundry-list menu, which leans toward sandwiches, burgers, and such generic American food as meat loaf, spaghetti, grilled chicken breast, and fried calamari. ♦ American ♦ Daily breakfast, lunch, and dinner. 531 Castro St (between 19th and 18th Sts). 621.4640 &

24 Anchor Oyster Bar ★★$$ Fresh seafood served in tiled, vaguely nautical surroundings is the draw of this small oyster bar with seating divided about equally between the counter and the stainless steel tables. The oysters are good, but what keeps customers coming back are the well-prepared clam chowder and the classic crab or shrimp Louis salad, made with a dressing that is similar to Thousand Island. ♦ Seafood ♦ M-Sa lunch and dinner; Su dinner. 579 Castro St (between 19th and 18th Sts). 431.3990

Castro/Noe Valley

25 Suzanne's Muffins This bakery has earned a reputation for big, fist-size muffins—more than 80 kinds. The top seller is the cakelike blueberry, followed by the likes of buttermilk spice and bran. Savory selections include "chile cheese corn" and "broccoli cheddar quiche." Those with a sweet tooth will find such dessert varieties as chocolate Grand Marnier and rum raisin. And many fans go for the "Very Very Lowfat Muffins," such as pumpkin, apple, banana walnut, and cranberry orange. ♦ Daily from 7AM. 564 Castro St (between 19th and 18th Sts). 864.4266 &

25 Pachá ★$ The setting of this tapas bar—the only one in the area—is whimsical and modern with bright colors and unusual chairs with squiggly legs. Some of the best dishes are the chunks of roasted potatoes drizzled with garlicky aioli; Chinese-style chicken with a bronzed exterior cut into irregular chunks; eggplant doused in an oregano-flecked tomato sauce and covered with cheese and green olives; plump shrimp accented with a spicy tomato sauce; and fried calamari enhanced by a lemony dipping sauce. Service can be erratic, though, and the quality of the food varies. ♦ Spanish ♦ Daily lunch and dinner. No credit cards accepted. 544 Castro St (between 19th and 18th Sts). 431.7622 &

26 Buffalo Whole Food & Grain Company Smaller than the Nob Hill branch, this health-food store is packed with select organic produce, plentiful breads, packaged convenience foods, and lots of vitamins and supplements. ♦ Daily. 598 Castro St (at 19th St). 626.7038; fax 626.7511 &. Also at: 1058 Hyde St (between Pine and California Sts). 474.3053 &

27 Castro Village Wine Co. Specializing in small California wine producers, the shop employs a knowledgeable staff to help the committed wine lover find just the right bottle. In the corner is a tasting bar featuring a different selection of varietals each week, and customers get a 10 percent discount on the purchase of a featured bottle. Rare wines might include a 1980 Stony Hill Chardonnay or a 1989 Groth Cabernet Sauvignon. There's also a small selection of premium spirits. Prices are competitive, often lower than other full-service shops in the area. ♦ Daily. 4121 19th St (at Castro St). 864.4411; fax 864.4411 &

28 Firefly ★★★$$ You might miss this small chef-owned place, tucked into a row of houses, if it weren't for the bumblebee-yellow door and the glowing firefly above the entrance. A comfortable eclectic spirit pervades the restaurant, started on a shoestring by Brad Levy and Veva Edelson. Despite the improvised decor—such as the mismatched tables and chairs from a garage sale—the look comes together. Levy characterizes his food as home cooking from around the world. That translates to pot stickers (Chinese dumplings) plump with shrimp and scallops, potato latkes with apple sauce, and chopped chicken livers. Main courses may be grilled tuna with *soba* (buckwheat) noodles, sesame orange–glazed yams, and wasabi aioli; hearty beef brisket; spicy gumbo; barbecued chicken with mashed potatoes; or cabbage stuffed with turkey in a sweet-and-sour sauce. Desserts are based on such down-home favorites as a dense chocolate chip cake layered with peanut butter. ♦ Californian ♦ Daily dinner. 4288 24th St (at Douglass St). 821.7652; fax 821.5812

29 Auntie Pasta All kinds of fresh, frozen, and packaged pasta and sauces are offered at this take-out emporium, along with wines and just about everything else needed to entertain at home. The ever-changing carryout menu might include Thai chicken rolls, baby crab cakes with jalapeño remoulade, shepherd's pie, or honey-glazed chicken breast. ♦ M-F 11AM-9PM, Sa-Su 11AM-8PM. 741 Diamond St (between 24th and Elizabeth Sts). 282.0738; fax 282.4205. Also at: 2139A Polk St (between Broadway and Vallejo St). 776.9420; fax 776.8512 &; 1501 Waller St (at Clayton St) 681.4242; fax 681.0227 &; 3101 Fillmore St (at Filbert St). 921.7576; fax 921.1547 &

29 Bacco Ristorante Italiano ★★★$$ Persimmon and pumpkin hues lend a modern, stylish Italian feel to this fairly new establishment. It covers several storefront spaces, and the three-tiered dining room faces a wall of windows overlooking the quiet side street. Although the menu seems pedestrian at first glance, the preparations are anything but. Try the gnocchi, tender and light, or the simply sauced pastas, cooked exactly as they should be with just a little bite. The main courses are as good as the rest of the meal, especially the lamb chops and any veal dish. For dessert the warm chocolate cake, with a slightly runny center, is a real winner. To top it all off, the consummate

Castro/Noe Valley

Italian waiters are efficient yet friendly, with a good sense of humor. ♦ Italian ♦ Daily dinner. Reservations recommended. 737 Diamond St (between 24th and Elizabeth Sts). 282.4969; fax 282.1315 &

30 Barney's Gourmet Hamburgers ★$
Barney's developed such a following in the East Bay that the owners decided to try their luck in Noe Valley. The specialty here is the big fat beef patty (one-third of a pound) with all kinds of toppings that span the globe for flavor inspiration. You can also find tofu burgers, chicken, and salads, if you're not a beef eater. Located in a Victorian house, the restaurant has given over the front yard to tables shaded by green canvas umbrellas, making it a prime alfresco dining spot.
♦ American ♦ Daily lunch and dinner. 4138 24th St (between Castro and Diamond Sts). 282.7770; fax 282.1920 &. Also at: 3344 Steiner St (between Lombard and Chestnut Sts). 563.0307 &

31 Miss Millie's ★★★$ Great word of mouth on this retro-looking diner has drawn customers from all over the city. Breakfast is a big deal here, featuring fat, sticky cinnamon rolls, citrus-flavored scones, and French toast topped with bananas, whipped butter, and real maple syrup. And don't miss the lemon ricotta pancakes with blueberry syrup—yum! More healthy alternatives are also available, such as the side dish of roasted root vegetables and the entrée of scrambled curried tofu. Lunch is also popular; try the great grilled cheese sandwich made with two kinds of cheddar (New York sharp, made with cow's milk, and goat cheese). There's a long wait at times, especially for Sunday brunch, but this place is worth it. ♦ American ♦ Tu-F breakfast and lunch; Sa-Su brunch. 4123 24th St (at Castro St). 285.5598; fax 585.5030

32 Tom's Peasant Pies An offshoot of a pie shop in Paris, this tiny bakery sells both sweet and savory pies, baked twice a day to ensure freshness. They're a real bargain, taste great at room temperature, and are ideal for picnics. The savories are reminiscent of piroshki. Generally four or five vegetable offerings are waiting to be snapped up, the most popular made of potato and onion laced with rosemary. Close behind are the seafood pies—shrimp, calamari, or clam. The fruit pies, made with a brown-sugar crust, are plumped with whatever is in season. Although most people prefer takeout, there's a counter with 10 seats and a bench outside. ♦ Daily. No credit cards accepted. 4108 24th St (at Castro St). 642.1316 &

33 Little Italy Ristorante ★★$$ If the food-labeling act extended to restaurants, the sign in front of this tiny eatery would read: "Garlic-shy diners should go elsewhere." The pungent aroma of the stinking rose is everywhere, and it shows up on just about every dish: At least a quarter-cup is strewn over the marvelous veal chop, and it's the main ingredient in the spaghetti with prawns and anchovies. Garlic even shows up on the stuffed artichoke, the asparagus side dishes, and the half chicken broiled with garlic vinegar and olive oil. To clean your palate, finish with the zabaglione, one of the top preparations in the city. ♦ Southern Italian ♦ Daily dinner. 4109 24th St (at Castro St). 821.1515

33 Rory's Twisted Scoop The idea here is to choose an ice-cream flavor and combine it with such add-ins as chunks of Reese's Peanut Butter Cups, M&Ms, and nuts. The scoopmaster plops the ice cream on a marble slab and cuts in customers' selections with paddles. The shop makes its own waffle cones and also features such nonfat yogurts as banana peanut butter and Ghirardelli chocolate. The original store on Fillmore Street is where they actually make the ice cream.
♦ M-Th, Su until 11PM; F-Sa until midnight. No credit cards accepted. 4101 24th St (at Castro St). 648.2837 &. Also at: 2015 Fillmore St (between Pine and California Sts). 346.3692

34 Hamano Sushi ★★$ The light wood used in the hand-tooled sushi bar and raised dining area in back give this narrow restaurant an understated feel of serenity. Full meals are offered, but the specialty is *makimono* (sushi rice roll), which includes tuna with green onions, salmon with avocado, or eel with cucumber. The equally impressive vegetarian rolls are filled with pickled burdock, radish sprouts, or fermented soybeans. Be sure to try the *mirugai* (giant geoduck clams) for their nutty flavor.
♦ Japanese ♦ Daily dinner. 1332 Castro St (between Jersey and 24th Sts). 826.0825

Castro/Noe Valley

35 Out of Hand American contemporary crafts are featured here, and shoppers should drop in regularly to keep abreast of the ever-changing merchandise. You might come upon a special exhibition/sale, such as the *Ultimate Ice Cream Dish Show*, a collection of glass and ceramic dishes commissioned from top artists across the United States, including Lisa Scroggins's *Original Sin*, an ice-cream goblet encircled with a snake. ♦ M-Sa 10:30AM-6:30PM; Su noon-6PM. 1303 Castro St (at 24th St). 826.3885; fax 510.526.1743

36 Noe Valley Bakery & Bread Co. Michael Gassen and Mary Gaylord-Gassen, who met at **Il Fornaio**, one of the city's premier Italian bakeries, took over this place in February 1995, and it already is destined to be one of the city's best. Their gorgeous breads, displayed in baskets, come in many unusual flavors: One chewy loaf is studded with figs, another with dried apricots and a whisper of ginger, another with cherries and chocolate. Cinnamon twists have a crackling glaze and a seductively buttery, spicy essence. The brioche is finely textured and barely sweet, and the bread sticks are crisp and flavorful. Focaccia is offered plain, with scallions, or with fresh rosemary. The scones are some of the best around; try the intense lemon almond or blueberry pecan versions. Other irresistible treats include oatmeal-raisin or chocolate chip cookies, lemon pound cake, fruit tarts, pear frangipani, and carrot cake. ♦ Daily. 4073 24th St (between Noe and Castro Sts). 550.1405; fax 550.1485

36 Caruso Wine and Liquor Store Steve Kerr has assembled a fine collection from small-production wineries, with special emphasis on California, French Rhône, and central Italian wines. He also stocks 40 kinds of single-malt scotches, a half-dozen premium tequilas, up to a dozen small-batch American whiskeys, and dozens of Cognacs and Armagnacs. Prices are good, considering the hand-picked nature of his collection. If you don't see what you want, just ask; Kerr stashes some of the rarer wines in back. ♦ Daily. 4011 24th Street (at Noe St). 282.3841; fax 282.6109

37 Panos' $$ Popular with neighborhood residents, this restaurant leans toward chic with its white walls, granite-topped wine bar, and black marble floor, although the Greek food is pretty standard and can be salty. Good bets are the grilled lamb, the avgolemono soup with its bright lemon kick, and the *spanikopita* (spinach pie). ♦ Californian/Greek ♦ Daily lunch and dinner. 4000 24th St (at Noe St). 824.8000

38 Herb's Fine Foods ★$ Since 1943 this has been the place to go for a longshoreman-style breakfast of eggs and bacon or corned beef hash. The sea of vinyl chairs, red-plaid Formica tabletops, and the horseshoe counter foster a comfortable, "Happy Days"–like atmosphere. ♦ Diner ♦ M-F 6:30AM-3:30PM; Sa-Su 7AM-4PM. 3991 24th St (between Sanchez and Noe Sts). 826.8937

38 Bakers of Paris Croissants and baguettes, crispy outside and soft and slightly airy inside, are the specialties of one of the city's best-known bakeries. On any given day you'll find more than a dozen kinds of bread, such as Alsatian rye or multigrain walnut. There's limited seating for those who want to sip a coffee while indulging in one of the delectable offerings. ♦ Daily. No credit cards accepted. 3989 24th St (between Sanchez and Noe Sts). 863.8725

38 The Chef Specialty Foods Hardly big enough to turn around in, this shop packs a lot into its small space. In addition to made-to-order sandwiches and salads, you'll find dried shiitake and morel mushrooms, crystallized ginger and candied violets, and all kinds of pâtés. Other specialty products include such jarred condiments as hot mango chutneys and a choice selection of coffee beans. ♦ Daily. 3977 24th St (between Sanchez and Noe Sts). 550.7982

38 Chocolate Covered This shop has a great assortment of chocolates and chocolate-covered goodies from 15 manufacturers and five countries. Among the tempting treats are candied fruits, creams, nuts, and espresso nuggets. Everything comes professionally wrapped, and if you buy enough items, the staff will place them in a beautiful tin. ♦ Hours are erratic; call ahead. 3961½ 24th St (between Sanchez and Noe Sts). 641.8123

39 Spinelli Coffee Company This is the original location, opened a decade ago, of the popular chain that's known for its strong coffee with a slightly bitter edge. The house blend is a medium-body mixture of Central

Castro/Noe Valley

American beans. There are also 15 coffees for takeout. ♦ Daily 6:30AM-9PM. 3966 24th St (between Sanchez and Noe Sts). 550.7416; fax 550.0301 ♿

Courtyard Café

40 Courtyard Cafe ★$$ The front of this Mediterranean delicatessen and cafe is given over to takeout, while the back is a restaurant. Painted to resemble a garden, the indoor dining room overlooks a brick terrace arranged around two lacy Japanese maples. On warm days, the outdoor tables are popular. Try the eggs Barcelona with bell peppers, tomatoes, and mushrooms. ♦ Mediterranean ♦ M-Sa breakfast, lunch, and dinner; Su breakfast and lunch. 3913 24th St (between Sanchez and Noe Sts). 282.0344

40 Panetti's Gifts On sale here is a charming selection of decorative accessories and some food-related products, such as place mats and napkins; jewelry in the shape of chilies, fruits, and other food motifs; copper cookie cutters; picnic baskets; mushroom-shaped garlic crushers; and blue-and-white tin plates. ♦ Daily. 3927 24th St (between Sanchez and Noe Sts). 648.2414

40 The Real Food Company The produce here is top-of-the-line organic, as it is at the other branches, but this shop is smaller. There's no meat or fish and the cheese selection is not as extensive. Service here is marginally better than at the other branches, though still indifferent. ♦ Daily. 3939 24th St (between Sanchez and Noe Sts). 282.9500; fax 282.9190 ♿. Also at: 2140 Polk St (between Broadway and Vallejo St). 673.7420; fax 673.1787 ♿; 1023 Stanyan St (at Carl St). 564.2800; fax 564.4882 ♿

After playing at Finocchio's nightclub one night in 1932, a hungry bandleader named Fortune Nelson "Bunny" Burson slipped into the nearby New Joe's restaurant for a bite. Because of the late hour, all the cook had left was a little hamburger, some spinach, and a couple of eggs. Burson said to mix them together and cook it up, which is how the Joe's Special—a San Francisco comfort food—was invented. New Joe's is long gone, but Joe's Special still can be ordered at Little Joe's and Original Joe's restaurants.

"It was in Paris that a world traveler said: 'San Francisco! That wonderful city where you can get the best there is to eat, served in a manner that enhances its flavor and establishes it forever in your memory.'"

Clarence Edwards,
Bohemian in San Francisco, 1914

---

41 Twenty-Fourth Street Cheese One of the best cheese shops in the city for both variety and price, this 20-year-old establishment has a quaint European atmosphere. The front window is decorated with wheels of gruyère and a barrel-size round of parmesan reggiano. Customers can choose among 250 kinds of cheese and about 30 types of crackers and bread sticks (including the much-admired Cuneo), as well as **Acme** bread, **Molinari** sausage, a small selection of wines, and a dozen varieties of olives. The shop also rents raclette ovens and sells fondue sets. ♦ Daily. 3893 24th St (at Sanchez St). 821.6650; fax 648.3361

42 Holey Bagel About 15 varieties of New York-style bagels are served at this bakery, along with 10 schmears made from cream cheese and other ingredients such as herbs and garlic or dates and walnuts. There's also an espresso bar and a full-service deli featuring a dozen types of smoked fish, including four kinds of lox. At press time, the chain was considering changing its name to **Manhattan Bagel.** ♦ Daily. No credit cards accepted. 3872 24th St (between Vicksburg and Sanchez Sts). 647.3334; fax 647.0824 ♿. Also at: 3218 Fillmore St (at Greenwich St). 922.1955; fax 626.2453 ♿; 1206 Masonic St (at Haight St). 626.9111; fax 626.2730; 1789 Fourth St (at Harvest Ave), Berkeley. 510/525.9445; fax 510/525.8105 ♿

42 Martha and Brothers Coffee Co. $ The coffee aroma lures people in; the earthy house blend of Sumatra and Guatemalan keeps them coming back. Fifty kinds of coffee are available at this coffee shop and cafe, but the staff are less informed about their beans than they should be. ♦ Cafe ♦ Daily. No credit cards accepted. 3868 24th St (between Vicksburg and Sanchez Sts). 641.4433; fax 641.0193. Also at: 1551 Church St (at Duncan St). 648.1166

43 Chloe's Cafe ★$ Marked with a blue awning, this small storefront is a neighborhood gathering place, especially for breakfast on the weekend. You sign up outside and wait your turn. Different configurations of couples touch and chat comfortably while babies in strollers create a traffic jam in the middle of the sidewalk; it's just another Noe Valley Sunday. Pancakes are the specialty here and might be banana nut or Swedish-style with oatmeal. Scrambled eggs are enhanced with such additions as bacon and tomato and served with ho-hum wedges of sautéed potatoes. ♦ American ♦ Daily breakfast and lunch. No credit cards accepted. 1399 Church St (at 26th St). 648.4116

44 Lady Sybil's Closet This shop, specializing in tea accessories, is as tiny as the name implies. The windows are filled with antique teapots, cups and saucers, hand-crocheted potholders, and embroidered dish towels; the interior is draped with all types of lace,

Castro/Noe Valley

crocheted doilies, and tablecloths. Most items are vintage and handmade. ◆ Th-Su 1-6PM. No credit cards accepted. 1484 Church St (at 27th St). 282.2088; fax 285.7452

45 What's for Dessert? ★$ Owner Mervyn Mark has acquired a faithful clientele for breakfast and lunch and is also the creator of the unique "Gâteau San Francisco," featuring an intricate chocolate design of the San Francisco skyline. The cookies, whether flavored with ginger or chocolate, are first-rate. ◆ Cafe ◆ Tu-Su breakfast and lunch. No credit cards accepted. 1497 Church St (at 27th St). 550.7465 &

46 Eric's ★★$ On most nights, this place has the atmosphere of a nightclub rather than a Chinese restaurant; purple and green neon lights up the outside and illuminates the milling throng waiting for tables. The interior features plain white walls and plank floors, and only the tasteful, hand-carved wood screen hints at the ethnic origin of the food. Some dishes miss the mark because of too much oil and cloying sweetness, but the hits can be sensational: Try the spicy eggplant with shrimp and loads of chilies or the walnut prawns (sugar-glazed walnuts with fried shrimp and creamy mayonnaise sauce served in a fried-potato nest). Among the more unusual dishes are the spicy smoked pork with leeks and the Shanghai chicken nuggets laced with crunchy seaweed. ◆ Chinese ◆ M-Sa lunch and dinner; Su dinner. 1500 Church St (at 27th St). 282.0919 &

47 Speckmann's ★$$ The food is traditional at this out-of-the-way *bierstube* that looks as if it was created for a movie set: dark paneling, austere wood chairs, and tables draped in red-and-white–checkered cloths, which are placed so close together that you brush up against the waiter's lederhosen as he serves. Cheerful music completes the stereotype. The sauerbraten is more sweet than sour, and so is the cabbage, but the crunchy potato pancakes are a welcome accompaniment. Wiener schnitzel, another specialty, is fried to a crisp and served with roasted potatoes and peas and carrots. Wash it down with an excellent German beer. All dinners come with soup: meaty lentil, thick potato leek, or goulash dense enough to sauce pasta. Desserts are mostly rich pastries. The deli in the front of the restaurant is the place to buy German sausages, cold cuts, cheeses, and specialty items. ◆ German ◆ Daily lunch and dinner. 1550 Church St (at Duncan St). 282.6850

48 Lehr's German Specialties This shop, chockablock with teacups, mugs, and beer steins, is one of the few businesses catering to the German community in the Bay Area. It sells everything German from bath salts to decorative accessories to salad dressings, cookies, and candies. ◆ M-Sa 10AM-6PM; Su noon-6PM. 1581 Church St (between 28th and Duncan Sts). 282.6803; fax 282.0565 &

49 Drewes Market With a history dating back to 1889, this landmark meat market has been selling free-range chickens for 20 years. The shop retains an old-fashioned look with blue and white hexagonal tiles and service counters that stretch along two walls. Benches line the opposite walls, so weary customers can sit while waiting their turn. The shop also prepares a meat loaf "ready for the oven" and stuffed pork chops. ◆ Daily 10AM-5PM. No credit cards accepted. 1706 Church St (at 29th St). 821.0555 &

50 Star Bakery Irish soda bread is the main reason to come to this 1950s-style bakery that's been in business 104 years. Whether you prefer your soda bread plain, with raisins, or with raisins and caraway, it makes great breakfast toast. Other items sold here can be chancy. ◆ Tu-Sa 6:30AM-6PM; Su 7:30AM-2PM. No credit cards accepted. 1701 Church St (at 29th St). 648.0785 &

51 Mikey Tom's Market In this small, chic grocery housed in a Deco-style building with bright yellow walls, a checkout stand doubles as an espresso bar. The limited but carefully chosen produce offers several upscale varieties of potatoes and mushrooms. Choice specialty products line the shelves, and in the refrigerated display case are such fresh carryout items as mustardy chicken potpies. ◆ Daily. 1747 Church St (at Day St). 826.5757; fax 695.7932 &

52 Valentine's Cafe ★★★$ Vegetarian food, superbly prepared and thoughtfully priced, is created at this delightfully cozy, out-of-the-way spot decorated with many gold-rimmed mirrors, a yellow and white color scheme, and a large picture window looking onto the street. Owners Kunal Mukkherjee and Daniel Morrison have put together a veggie menu with true international flair. The *samosas* come filled with curried potato and accompanied by herbal-mint chutney; vegetarian spring rolls, totally free of grease, are stuffed with glass noodles, sun-dried tomatoes, and wild mushrooms; and crisp-fried tofu with roasted root vegetables is eminently satisfying. The desserts are good, but not remarkable. ◆ Vegetarian ◆ W-Su lunch and dinner. 1793 Church St (at 30th St). 285.2257 &

53 Church Produce This corner shop provides a little bit of everything edible and offers an interesting selection of natural foods, breads, and produce. ◆ Daily. No credit cards accepted. 1798 Church St (at 30th St). 282.1153 &

The Haight/Cole Valley/ West Portal/Glen Park

The Haight is virtually synonymous with the psychedelic 1960s, and the philosophy and the aesthetic of the flower children who arrived here in droves back then still lives on. The bright blue, yellow, red, and green storefronts that line the streets are filled with used bookstores, occult shops, and ice-cream parlors; vintage-clothing shops display tie-dyed shirts and patent-leather go-go boots; and wafts of marijuana sometimes perfume the air. The last of the longhaired hippies pass time on the street corners, along with the homeless, new-wave hipsters, and ex–punk rockers, who are pierced and earringed to the nines.

Food is cheap and basic in the Haight, a neighborhood mainly populated by young college students and recent graduates. To appeal to these environmentally conscious (and relatively poor) residents, many of the restaurants here offer a good selection of vegetarian dishes on their menus. One of the few restaurants remaining from the hippies' heyday, **Dish** (then called the **Drugstore**), now attracts more affluent residents for hearty breakfasts and lunch. **Cha Cha Cha** features Latin and Caribbean food in a colorful setting filled with folk art, and **Eos**, one of the latest arrivals, is breaking new culinary ground with its Asian-fusion cuisine and stylish wine bar. There is an outpost for almost every kind of food: **Taqueria El Balazo** for burritos, **Zare** for Middle Eastern fare, and **Massawa Restaurant** for African specialties. And just off **Haight Street**, on **Divisadero Street**, is **Cookin'**, a tiny cookware shop stacked to the ceiling with used (and some vintage) baking and cooking accessories, appliances, glasses, and dishes.

While the Haight may be a tourist destination, the neighborhoods to its south tend to focus on the activities of everyday residential life. Just below the Haight lies Cole Valley, an up-and-coming district filled with charming shops and former hippie haunts gone mainstream. The original **Tassajara Bread Bakery** was started here by Zen Buddhists, and Cole Valley also boasts one of the city's finest natural-foods stores, **The Real Food Company**, along with a great cheese shop, **Say Cheese**. Its true culinary beacon, however, is **Ashbury Market**, which proffers the gamut of gourmet products and has earned a citywide reputation for its selection of fine wines.

Twin Peaks, south of Cole Valley and in the geographic center of the city, is the site of San Francisco's second- and third-tallest hills, which offer spectacular panoramas of the Bay Area. (Enjoy the views by car by following **Twin Peaks Boulevard**, which winds around the whole district, or on foot by mounting one of the steep stairways that rise from the streets to the slopes' magnificent terraces.) The neighborhood also is home to a not-to-be-missed supermarket, **Tower Market**, which boasts an enviable selection of specialty foods and high-quality meat, fish, and produce.

Middle-class West Portal, located to the southwest of Twin Peaks, is the main shopping district for **Sir Francis Woods** and **Forest Hill**, two of the city's more affluent neighborhoods. Its name derives from its location at the western entrance of the streetcar tunnel that was cut through the hills of Twin Peaks early in the century. Nestled at the base of three hills—including **Mount Davidson**, which, at 938 feet, is the city's highest spot—West Portal has the feel of a European village, with curvy streets, streetcars, and a romantic, foggy shroud. It's a charming place to spend an afternoon. For a taste of Eastern Europe, stop in at **Old Krakow**, the city's only Polish restaurant. The most popular neighborhood hangout is **Cafe for All Seasons**, which serves straightforward American cuisine with an emphasis on the freshest ingredients.

Glen Park, on the southeastern slope of Twin Peaks, is mostly residential. It still has no restaurants that would attract people from outside the neighborhood, but it's beginning to develop a shopping district. Among the spots of interest here are the **Cheese Boutique**, a bakery branch of the Twin Peaks district's **Creighton's Cheese & Fine Foods** (go for the marvelous sticky buns), and **Sweet Sue's** (don't miss the lemon pound cake).

The Haight/Cole Valley/West Portal/Glen Park

1 Cookin' Specializing in used merchandise, this is the best-stocked cookware shop in the city; it's the place food stylists call when they're looking for one-of-a-kind props. Although the owners had to clear up some of the clutter to provide access to people with disabilities, the merchandise is still arranged in piles on the floor and in stacks on baker's racks. It's an awesome sight. There are vintage dishes, glasses, and appliances from the 1940s and 1950s, but most of the store's merchandise is modern. One area is devoted to cast-iron skillets, another to an enviable selection of French pastry equipment—including intricate molds, cutting utensils, and pans. And you won't find a better selection of copper pots or Le Creuset cookware anywhere. ♦ Tu-Su. 339 Divisadero St (between Page and Oak Sts). 861.1854; fax 861.1971 &

2 Dish ★$ Back in the Flower Power days, this corner cafe was known as the **Drugstore** and the window boxes were filled with marijuana plants. Now it's more mainstream, and dishes—hundreds of plates bedecking the walls—have replaced drugs as conversation pieces. Although the cafe is open from morning till night, breakfast is the meal that attracts the most attention. The macadamia nut waffles with fruit toppings are legendary. There's also corned-beef hash, pork chops with eggs, and blueberry waffles. The lunch and dinner menus are all-American; the early-bird special includes salad and such main courses as orange chicken or prawns with feta, for a pittance. ♦ American ♦ Daily breakfast, lunch, and dinner. 1398 Haight St (at Masonic Ave). 431.3534 &

3 People's Cafe ★★$ This new spot was quickly embraced by the neighborhood, with its simple, light fare that attracts lines of fans at peak hours. The generous sandwiches are made with French rolls, and the salads are served in huge glass bowls. The stylish room has a tile floor, traditional bentwood chairs, and clever tables with coffee beans pressed under the glass tops. And it's immaculate—something of a rarity in this part of town. ♦ Cafe ♦ Daily breakfast, lunch, and dinner. 1419 Haight St (at Masonic St). 553.8842 &

3 Holey Bagel The home of jalapeño bagels, this bakery also has pumpkin, blueberry, onion, honey-corn, and about a dozen other kinds of bagels, plus an equal number of cream cheeses, including sun-dried tomato, herb and garlic, and vegetable. It also serves Caffé Trieste coffee (from a well-known North Beach roaster) and a few select pastries. At press time, the chain was considering changing its name to **Manhattan Bagel**. ♦ Daily. No credit cards accepted. 1206 Masonic St (at Haight St). 626.9111; fax 626.2730. Also at: 3872 24th St (between Vicksburg and Sanchez Sts). 647.3334; fax 647.0824 &; 3218 Fillmore St (at Greenwich St). 922.1955; fax 626.2453 &; 1789 Fourth St (at Harvest Ave), Berkeley. 510/525.944; fax 510/525.8105 &

4 Ben & Jerry's Locals have made it clear that chain stores are unwelcome in the Haight, but this ice-cream franchise is a different story. More than merely making Cherry Garcia a household name, the corporation has made its presence felt in the political arena as well—serving the community's heart as well as its stomach. The ice cream comes in almost every flavor imaginable, and patrons can linger at the tables over sundaes and baked goods. ♦ Daily. No credit cards accepted. 1480 Haight St (at Ashbury St). 249.4685; fax 249.4682 &. Also at: 543 Columbus Ave (between Green and Union Sts). 249.4684; fax 249.2655 &; 79 Jefferson St (at Mason St). 249.2662 &

5 Martin Macks Bar and Restaurant ★$ A traditional Irish bar in the heart of the Haight? Well, it *is* a diverse neighborhood. Sports fans fill the front bar area with a haze of smoke, but through the saloon doors in back is a kitchen/dining counter and tables. The bric-a-brac along the walls and the copper pots hanging from the latticework behind the counter give the place a Victorian feel, despite the movie-size screen that keeps fans abreast of the game. Weekend brunch may offer eggs Benedict with salmon or sautéed trout with a tarragon-and-mushroom sauce, served with eggs and home fries. The kitchen is also known for its fish-and-chips, hamburgers, shepherd's pie, and other substantial pub grub. ♦ English/Irish ♦ M-F lunch and dinner; Sa-Su brunch and dinner. 1568 Haight St (between Ashbury and Clayton Sts). 864.0124 &

The "Big Four" moguls behind the Central Pacific Railroad—the Ralstons, Crockers, Stanfords, and Hopkins—entertained in lavish style. At one party held at the Palace Hotel in 1876, the banquet hall was decorated with oversize mirrors, flower and fruit arrangements—including a small grove of banana and orange trees—a profusion of candles, and 18 cages filled with songbirds. At each place setting, the menu was engraved upon a plate of solid silver from the Comstock lode.

Lucius Beebe, a columnist for the *San Francisco Chronicle* at the turn of the century, once said, "Everything in San Francisco smells deliciously of money or sauce Mornay." And what goes into a Mornay sauce? Just add some good cheese, usually swiss or parmesan, to a béchamel or simple white sauce. Serve with eggs, fish, vegetables, or chicken.

The Haight/Cole Valley/West Portal/Glen Park

5 Massawa Restaurant ★$ The setting is uninspired—a bright blue, barnlike space broken up with rattan screens—but the aromatic East African fare is enticing. Everything is served with *injera,* a spongelike bread used to scoop up the stews that are this cuisine's staple. Choices include a thick chicken stew with red peppers, lamb and vegetables simmered with spices, and a tuna stew with spinach. About half the offerings are vegetarian. For those who want to avoid culinary adventures, there's spaghetti with meat sauce. ♦ East African ♦ Tu-Su lunch and dinner. 1538 Haight St (between Ashbury and Clayton Sts). 621.4129 &

6 Pork Store Cafe ★$ One of the most popular spots in the Haight, this place is known for its hearty breakfasts. No one seems to mind crowding in at the counter or the cramped tables for huge plates of eggs with all the traditional trimmings. The name, incidentally, comes from the meat market that once occupied the space. ♦ American ♦ Daily breakfast and lunch. 1541 Haight St (between Ashbury and Clayton Sts). 864.6981

7 Taqueria El Balazo ★★$ A relatively new kid on the block (it opened in 1993), this *taqueria* looks as though it's been around forever. There's a marble floor, a copper-topped counter, and a garish red, yellow, and orange paint job; the menu is printed on old-fashioned calendars decorated with Mexican scenes and images of buxom women with off-the-shoulder blouses. The top seller is the vegetarian burrito, given a meaty flavor by grilled vegetables, black beans, and saffron rice; it's served with tortilla chips and lime-cabbage salad. Full plates include fish tacos, enchiladas, vegetarian tamales, chicken mole, and *tortas* (Mexican sandwiches)—all very reasonably priced. ♦ Mexican ♦ Daily lunch and dinner. No credit cards accepted. 1654 Haight St (between Belvedere and Cole Sts). 864.8608 &

7 Zare ★$$ One of the few places to serve creative food in the Haight, it also has a more refined ambience than most. Sun-dried tomatoes are the principal flavoring for a smoked-chicken linguine, and a rich lamb ragout is thick with beans, tomatoes, and other vegetables. The baked brie appetizer is a dish of the 1970s, but for the frozen-in-time Haight, even that's progress. ♦ Middle Eastern ♦ M-F lunch and dinner; Sa-Su brunch and dinner. 1640 Haight St (between Clayton and Cole Sts). 861.8868

7 Coffee, Tea & Spice In business for more than 25 years, this coffee store does its own roasting; its distinctive house blend has slightly burned nuances. The coffee comes from Costa Rica, Ethiopia, Sumatra, Tanzania, and other countries that produce high-quality beans. The shop also sells various herbs and spices in bulk. A room upstairs—with a charming fireplace and tables for drinking brewed cups of coffee—also displays unusual mugs, coffeepots, and teapots for sale. ♦ Daily. 1630 Haight St (between Clayton and Cole Sts). 861.3953; fax 861.0535 &

8 Double Rainbow Ice Cream Long popular in the Haight, this local ice-cream purveyor offers dozens of flavors, as well as coffee drinks and other desserts. It has recently added items such as pizza and sandwiches to the menu. ♦ Daily. No credit cards accepted. 1724 Haight St (between Cole and Shrader Sts). 668.6690 &. Also at: 1653 Polk St (between Sacramento and Clay Sts). 775.3220 &; 407 Castro St (at Market St). 621.2350 &

9 Zona Rosa ★$ Compared with most others up and down the street, this upscale corner *taqueria* is a civilized place for a quick bite. A loyal clientele munches on the good burritos, with meats grilled to order, at the counters in front of the windows and down the center of the room. Fajitas, fried tacos, and nachos round out the limited menu. ♦ Mexican ♦ Daily lunch and dinner. No credit cards accepted. 1797 Haight St (at Shrader St). 668.7717

The Haight/Cole Valley/West Portal/Glen Park

10 Cha Cha Cha ★★★$ Bright, bold, Latin-inspired flavors make this the area's best and most popular restaurant. The wild interior, ablaze with color, is filled with altars and other Hispanic folk art. Weekend brunch consists of such dishes as polenta with grilled red bell peppers and eggs, or a guacamole omelette. Lunch and dinner selections might be roast leg of pork marinated with Cuban spices and served with rice and black beans, or marinated chicken with pimientos, capers, and olives. Among the dozen tapas offered are mussels in a saffron broth and barbecued-pork quesadillas. Service tends to be a little lax, but the food is excellent, and the people watching is delicious. It's a perfect place to absorb the Haight's atmosphere while eschewing the nitty-gritty. For dessert, go to **Ben & Jerry's** (see page 168) or **Double Rainbow Ice Cream** (see page 169). ♦ Latin ♦ Daily lunch and dinner. No credit cards accepted. 1805 Haight St (at Shrader St). 386.5758 &

11 Auntie Pasta When there's no time to cook, this take-out shop offers all kinds of pastas, sauces, breads, and accompaniments. It even has wine. Regulars rely on the daily specials for variety. ♦ Daily. 1501 Waller St (at Clayton St). 681.4242; fax 681.0227 &. Also at: 741 Diamond St (between 24th and Elizabeth Sts). 282.0738; fax 282.4205; 2139A Polk St (between Broadway and Vallejo St). 776.9420; fax 776.8512 &; 3101 Fillmore St (at Filbert St). 921.7576; fax 921.1547 &

12 Ashbury Market No other mom-and-pop grocery in the city can compare with this market. The exterior is reminiscent of France, with the name printed in gold on a burgundy background, white canvas umbrellas at the entrance, fresh raspberries and other produce on one side, and flowers on the other. Though the window displays Jolly Time Popcorn and Kool-Aid—after all, it's an all-purpose neighborhood market—the shop also proffers wonderful specialty merchandise. There are more than two dozen kinds of olive oil, hazelnut oil, truffle oil, and grape-seed oil with chilies; teas from the chic Republic of Teas; dozens of mustards; and boutique-bakery breads. A passageway leads to a wine shop and deli. The wine department is legendary, with the best in French, Italian, and California wines—and at competitive prices, too. The deli is filled with house-baked scones, salads, and such smoked fish and meats as lemon-pepper cod, duck breast, and trout. ♦ Daily. 205 Frederick St (at Ashbury St). 566.3134; fax 566.0266 &

13 The Ganges ★★$ Sari-clad waitresses serve customers who lounge on cushions at low tables at this vegetarian Indian spot. Top starters include a cilantro-and-potato puree, dipped in batter and fried until golden, or *pappadams,* crisp lentil-flour wafers with a touch of hot spice. Among the main courses, the curries get star billing: Try the *mater paneer,* fried cheese and peas in a rich tomato gravy with garam masala, a spice mixture with chilies. Another often-ordered dish is *kofta,* meatless "meatballs" made with black-eyed peas. Every dish is prepared from scratch, so the food has a lively, fresh taste. ♦ Indian ♦ Tu-Sa dinner. 775 Frederick St (between Arguello Blvd and Willard St). 661.7290; fax 661.4059

14 The Real Food Company The ground floor of this excellent natural-foods store is chock-full of organic produce and bins holding beans, flours, granola, rice, and other bulk goods. Upstairs is a storehouse of packaged goods and vitamins, and a small anteroom has a collection of natural-food cookbooks, coffees, teas, pastas, and spices sold in bulk. ♦ Daily. 1023 Stanyan St (at Carl St). 564.2800; fax 564.4882 &. Also at: 3939 24th St (between Sanchez and Noe Sts). 282.9500; fax 282.9190 &; 2140 Polk St (between Broadway and Vallejo St). 673.7420; fax 673.1787 &

14 The Real Food Company Deli Next door to the **The Real Food Company** (see above) is a fine selection of baked goods and a changing array of main courses and salads, all prepared in-house. The temptations may include *samosas* (fried pastries filled with vegetables or meat), curried vegetables, and Szechuan cabbage. The small wine collection in back is nothing to speak of, though, especially given the impressive wine shops down the street. ♦ Daily. 1001 Stanyan St (at Carl St). 564.1117; fax 564.4882 &. Also at: 2164 Polk St (between Broadway and Vallejo St). 775.2805; fax 673.1787 &

15 Sun Country Foods Nowhere else in the city can you pick up a bunch of flowers at midnight. With a splashy fire-engine red exterior and 20 feet of sidewalk lined with bouquets stacked four deep on risers, this corner grocery attracts attention. The utilitarian interior houses such goods as beans, flours, and grains in bulk, along with sandwiches and a small but nicely selected array of produce. ♦ Daily 6AM-midnight. 1100 Stanyan St (at Parnassus Ave). 566.2511; fax 566.1336 &

16 Zazie ★★$$ It's just a bit bigger than a shoe box, but this charming French bistro has plenty of dash. The green-and-yellow–painted concrete floor, brick wall, and gold

The Haight/Cole Valley/West Portal/Glen Park

accents make a fine setting for the impressive food, which is served by a cheerful staff. At breakfast, the Belgian waffles with caramelized pecans and the omelette specials win raves; lunch selections include a large variety of sandwiches. The dinner menu offers such hearty dishes as a bone-warming daube (a marinated beef stew), free-range chicken roasted with garlic and herbs, and trout prepared in a different way each day. The homey desserts include fruit crumble, served warm with crème fraîche in a handmade ceramic bowl, and a charlotte with chocolate mousse, ladyfingers, and raspberry sauce.
♦ French ♦ M-Sa breakfast, lunch, and dinner; Su breakfast and lunch. No credit cards accepted. 941 Cole St (between Parnassus Ave and Carl St). 564.5332

16 EOS Restaurant & Wine Bar ★★★$$ Arnold and Richard Wong, sons of the founder of the well-regarded **Ashbury Market** (see page 170), have opened Cole Valley's first truly upscale restaurant, a real change of pace from the casual, ethnic eateries that characterize this area. Lively and fun, this place is bustling and very noisy much of the time. The room has a modern, sleek look, with high ceilings, light-colored wood accents, and black granite tables. Arnold Wong's menu features fresh, California-grown ingredients and Asian influences. Dishes include shiitake mushroom dumplings and sake-lemongrass-steamed clams as appetizers, and five-pepper calamari, pan-roasted salmon, and free-range chicken with green onions as main courses. Don't miss the wine bar (whose entrance is around the corner), with 400 vintages from countries around the world. This is a terrific addition to the neighborhood. ♦ Asian/Fusion ♦ M-Sa dinner. Restaurant: 901 Cole St (at Carl St). Wine bar: Entrance at 101 Carl St (at Cole St). 566.3063; fax 566.2663 &

17 Taqueria la Coqueta ★$ When **The Creperty Cafe** folded at this sunny location, it was replaced by yet another San Francisco *taqueria*. But it's a good one, with huge portions of well-prepared Mexican dishes such as burritos, tacos, nachos, and various types of sandwiches. The prices are very reasonable, too. The dining room is small, cozy, and bright, with yellow tables and pictures of Mexican scenes on the walls; there's also outdoor seating, so you can soak up the sun while enjoying your meal.
♦ Mexican ♦ Daily lunch and dinner. 86 Carl St (at Cole St). 566.1274 &

18 Val de Cole Wines and Spirits A sea of boxes gives this shop the look of a well-organized grocery store. Spirits are lined up behind the counter, and a hundred or more kinds of beer can be found in a nook at the rear and in a refrigerator case. The wines, arranged down the center of the room, feature many hard-to-find labels and vintages. The wine display in the window includes many inexpensive options, and a rack of handpicked bargain wines sits by the cashier. ♦ M-Th; F-Sa until midnight. 906 Cole St (at Carl St). 566.1808; fax 566.3564 &

18 Say Cheese One of the best cheese shops in the city, it carries up to 400 types; look for those by Laura Chenel, the top specialty producer of goat cheese. The store also stocks caviar, salsas, crackers, breads, pâtés, sandwich meats, nine kinds of olives, goat-milk yogurt, marmalades, and vinegars, all carefully selected. It's a one-stop shop for gifts and elegant munchies for entertaining.
♦ Daily. 856 Cole St (at Carl St). 665.5020; fax 566.9776

19 Tassajara Bread Bakery ★$ Renowned for its fabulous rustic breads, this Zen bakery-cafe was created by the group that made **Greens** one of the country's best-known vegetarian restaurants. Although it is now owned by the local **Just Desserts** chain, it still carries products found nowhere else, such as a ginger-plum tart and a berry-cheese tart. A dozen kinds of bread are always on hand, as well as such **Just Desserts** staples as triple lemon cake and big, chewy cookies. The cafe tables are usually packed with people relaxing over a cup of coffee and a breakfast pastry, a simple salad, or a vegetarian sandwich (no meat is served). ♦ Cafe ♦ Daily breakfast, lunch, and dinner. 1000 Cole St (at Parnassus Ave). 664.8947; fax 664.3747 &

20 Adel's Wine Cellar Up the steps inside **17th & Cole Market,** this shop is chock-a-block with bottles—more than a thousand labels from California, France, and Italy. Prices are a bit higher here than at other wine shops in the city, but the selection of older vintages is better. There may be multiple vintages of Ridge Howell Mountain Zinfandel, or Pine Ridge or Steltzner Cabernet Sauvignon. We even found some bottles from the now-defunct Lytton Springs winery.
♦ M-Sa until 10:30PM; Su until 10PM. 1400 Cole St (at 17th St). 731.6319 &

The Haight/Cole Valley/West Portal/Glen Park

21 Creighton's Cheese & Fine Foods ★$ This deli-cafe supplies the Twin Peaks area with more than 140 kinds of cheeses, a modest selection of wine, a variety of coffee drinks, and prepared fare to take out or eat at one of the tables. Salads range from sesame noodle and celery root with crème fraîche, mustard, and mayonnaise, to tarragon chicken with walnuts and sour-cream dressing; the standard array of sandwiches includes turkey and roast beef. The deli also sells pastries and other treats produced at **Creighton's American Bakery**, its sister shop on Chenery Street (see page 173); the most popular is the lemon curd tart, its buttery crust flecked with cornmeal. ♦ Cafe/Takeout ♦ Daily breakfast and lunch. 673 Portola Dr (near O'Shaughnessy Blvd). 753.0750; fax 753.0938. Also at: 598 Chenery St (at Castro St). 239.5525; fax 753.0538 &

21 Tower Market One of the city's best supermarkets, this independently owned full-service store was opened in 1942 by Mark Pommon. His 76-year-old son, Daniel, now runs it. To compete with the grocery chains, the market emphasizes upscale products. It carries a fine supply of organic produce, an array of breads from boutique bakeries, cheeses as varied as at any specialty shop, and at least a dozen olive oils. The deli is a godsend for anyone short on time (or desire) to cook. The wine is selected by well-known wine merchant Wilfred Wong (of **Ashbury Market**) and by George Beard. The meat market is leased to John Vigglizzio, who has built a reputation on his high-quality cuts. Many of the staffers have been here for years and they know loyal customers by name. ♦ Daily. 635 Portola Dr (near O'Shaughnnesy Blvd). 664.1600, meats 664.1609, deli 661.7333; fax 664.7406 &

22 Spiazzo ★★$$ Stippled walls and an open kitchen make this the neighborhood's trendiest-looking spot; adding friendly service to the formula makes it a favorite gathering place. The pizzas, which are assembled before your eyes and baked in a brightly tiled wood-burning oven, boast a thin, slightly smoky crust. Simple toppings include sausage and prosciutto; and mushrooms, fresh tomatoes, and seasonal vegetables. Such pastas as penne with onions, tomatoes, red chili peppers, and pecorino cheese or linguine with smoked salmon, garlic, parmesan, tomato, and béchamel sauce are worth a try. The few grilled dishes—chicken and pork loin among them—are not the kitchen's strength. ♦ Italian ♦ Tu-Su dinner. 33 W Portal Ave (between Vicente and Ulloa Sts). 664.9511

23 Cafe for All Seasons ★★★$$ Donna Katzl, who studied with James Beard, carries on her teacher's romance with solid American fare at the eatery she owns with her husband, Frank. The light wood interior and the long kitchen that stretches along one wall provide an informal appeal in keeping with the straightforward food. There are wonderful salads and one of the best hamburgers in the city. The delicious main courses include grilled rainbow trout with herb butter and french fries; sautéed chicken breast with mushrooms, lemon, and a light cream sauce, served with orzo pasta; and pork, which is distinguished by a creamy mustard sauce. The pasta dishes are simply great; all of them are made with *capellini*, a long, flat, thin noodle, which may be served simply with garlic, fresh tomato, olive oil, and grated asiago cheese, or dressed up with a light cream sauce and an array of fresh vegetables. For dessert, the apple cake with warm caramel sauce is the favorite; a close second is the sweet molded French cream with fresh berries and raspberry sauce. ♦ American ♦ M-F lunch and dinner; Sa-Su brunch and dinner. 150 W Portal Ave (between Vicente St and 14th Ave). 665.0900 &

23 Shaw's Confections At one time, branches of this chain of candy shops, founded in 1931 were scattered all over the Bay Area. Now only two remain—this one and another at the manufacturing plant in Millbrae, where the company makes private-label chocolates. The selection here includes cream-filled chocolates, nuts, all kinds of gooey jelly candies, hard candies, and jelly beans. There are mugs and other gift items, and a fountain in back that serves ultrarich Mendocino ice cream. ♦ Daily. No credit cards accepted. 122 W Portal Ave (between Vicente St and 14th Ave). 681.2702 &

The Haight/Cole Valley/West Portal/Glen Park

24 Fuji Japanese Restaurant ★★$$
Adorned with bamboo umbrellas, *tansu* wooden chests, kimonos, and plants everywhere, this spot defies the minimalist decor of most other Japanese eateries. From his perch at the sushi counter, chef Makoto Kobayashi greets just about everyone who enters. The sashimi, particularly the tuna, has an exceptional buttery quality, and the *maki* (rolls of tidbits wrapped in rice and seaweed) are unusual; the one called Gilroy (after the garlic capital of California) combines marinated salmon with avocado and a hefty dose of fresh garlic. All the standard dishes—tempura, teriyaki, and sukiyaki—are well prepared, too. The pork *katsu* is superb, with a crisp coating and a pleasant, slightly smoky dipping sauce. To sample almost all the specialties, try the Fuji special, a combination platter for two or more people. ♦ Japanese ♦ M, Sa-Su dinner; Tu-F lunch and dinner. 301 W Portal Ave (at 14th Ave). 564.6360; fax 564.2247 &

25 Old Krakow ★★$$ As far as we know, this newcomer is San Francisco's only Polish restaurant. The antique wood tables and chairs (no two are alike), the original artwork by Polish artists, and the red swags at the windows and over the kitchen area re-create some of the atmosphere of a Krakow cafe. The food is homey: rich beef stew in a thick, tomato-infused broth; huge cabbage rolls stuffed with seasoned ground beef and rice; crisp crepes filled with finely chopped mushrooms; and tender pieces of boneless duck rolled around apples and prunes, served with red cabbage and potatoes. For dessert, the crumbly cheesecake is a perfect rendition of the European original. A dense poppy-seed cake (made from a breadlike dough) is prepared every Friday. ♦ Polish ♦ M dinner; Tu-Su lunch and dinner. 385 W Portal Ave (at 15th Ave). 564.4848 &

26 Sweet Sue's Although this bakery sells primarily to wholesale clients and is off the beaten path (as are most spots in the Glen Park area), it's worth seeking out. Try the lemon pound cake, which has an intense flavor and moist texture; the *rugelach* and seasonal pies are also winners. ♦ M-F. No credit cards accepted. 732 Chenery St (at Brompton St). 587.7837 &

27 Cheese Boutique Glen Park's first gourmet specialty store has quickly become a neighborhood favorite. Cheese lovers can choose among 170 varieties, all at lower-than-supermarket prices, and are welcome to taste before they buy. The packaged goods cover all the bases and most cuisines; there are several brands of *arborio* rice and polenta, for example. With a nod to the health-conscious, the shop also stocks juices and assorted dried fruits and vegetables. One of the most popular items is a locally made vegetarian ravioli. ♦ M-Sa. No credit cards accepted. 666 Chenery St (at Diamond St). 333.3390; fax 333.5450 &. Also at: 1298 12th Ave (at Irving St). 566.3155; fax 333.5450

28 Creighton's American Bakery The tiny branch of **Creighton's Cheese & Fine Foods** (see page 172) is devoted to the production and sale of delicious baked goods. People flock here for sticky buns and scones, as well as for lemon bars, orange-pecan bars, and the not-to-be missed fresh-fruit tarts, which are very reasonably priced. ♦ Daily. 598 Chenery St (at Castro St). 239.5525; fax 753.0538 &. Also at: 673 Portola Dr (near O'Shaughnnesy Blvd). 753.0750; fax 753.0938

Bests

Barbara Rodgers
News Anchor/Reporter, KPIX Television

It's really hard to come up with a list of favorites in San Francisco, since there are so many to choose from and food is my drug of choice. Because of my odd hours, I'm always looking for a take-out meal that is like real food.

MacArthur Park: It's one of the few places a southern (fried) girl like me can get fried catfish to go.

Hunan Restaurant: My favorite dishes are the noodles with pork meat sauce and vegetables and Diana's meat pie special with some hot-and-sour soup on the side.

Powell's Place: This place has great soul food—the kind my mamma made back home in Tennessee—and the best fried chicken anywhere.

Tom Dalldorf
Publisher, *Celebrator Beer News*

Gordon Biersch (brewery/restaurant): Situated almost under the **San Francisco Bay Bridge,** the food and the wine list are as impressive as the spectacular view.

Cafe Pacifica/Sankt Gallen Brewery: This unique brew pub offers Chinese dim sum served Japanese-style, accompanied by house-made English aloo. It's as cosmopolitan as San Francisco itself.

Suppenküche: This German restaurant features outstanding entrées, accompanied by the city's largest selection of German beer on draught.

> The food in this city is fantastic. Better than London.
> —John Lennon and Yoko Ono

The Sunset

The Sunset is one of the city's least explored areas, metaphorically—and literally—shrouded in fog. This residential neighborhood—the last one to be developed in San Francisco—is bordered by **Golden Gate Park** to the north, **Twin Peaks** to the east, and the ocean to the west. More popular with tourists than locals, it's best known for being the home of the **San Francisco Zoo** and for its proximity to **Golden Gate Park**.

Yet for those who love food, the Sunset is a rewarding destination. Through the years, the neighborhood has attracted people from Thailand, Japan, Greece, Mexico, the Middle East, and other foreign lands (including, most recently, Russia and Northern Ireland), and the shops and restaurants reflect these diverse ethnic heritages. One of the city's best grocery stores—**Andronico's Market**—is here; its staggering array of goods includes at least 10 varieties of dates, 18 types of olives, and 25 kinds of apples under one sleek, modern roof.

The Sunset also boasts two unique ice-cream purveyors: **Marco Polo**, offering Italian gelato in Asian-influenced flavors such as guava; and **Polly Ann Ice Cream**, which dishes up ice cream flavored with durian, a tasty exotic fruit that has such a pungent odor that it is actually banned from airplanes and some hotel rooms in its native Thailand. The area is also home to **Shaharazad Bakery**, one of the few bakeries that still makes phyllo dough by hand.

The main shopping area is along **Irving**, **Judah**, **Noriega**, and **Taraval Streets**, which are lined with great produce markets, Chinese and Middle Eastern delis, and all kinds of shops for the home cook. (Notice that the streets here—known as the "alphabet streets"—are named in alphabetical order from north to south, beginning with **Lincoln** and proceeding to **Wawona**.) Thanks to their proximity to the **University of California San Francisco Medical Center**, a teaching hospital, many spots cater to a student's budget and taste. One such place is the **Owl & Monkey Cafe**, a popular hangout. The outer edge of Sunset is a favorite destination for San Francisco residents from other neighborhoods, who shop at a number of

Asian, Middle Eastern, and European-American markets, including the venerable **22nd & Irving Market,** one of the best places for fresh produce. The Sunset's restaurants tend to be small and neighborhood-oriented, but that doesn't mean the kitchens are unambitious. There is **Marnee Thai,** a top Thai spot; a good Greek place, **Stoyanof's;** and two excellent Middle Eastern eateries, the stylish **YaYa Cuisine** restaurant and **Just like Home** deli/cafe. And **Raw Living Foods,** the newest kid on the block, features a menu consisting solely of uncooked food—and its daring cuisine has quickly won an enthusiastic local following.

Because of its proximity to the ocean, the Sunset can be gray, cold, and foggy sometimes. But on a sunny day, hopping from ethnic market to ethnic market and stopping for lunch at one of the great cafes in the area can make a visit here a heart- and stomach-warming adventure.

1 Cafe de Young ★★$ Located in the **M. H. de Young Memorial Museum** in **Golden Gate Park,** this boasts one of the city's most charming garden settings: Handsome metal tables with umbrellas are arranged around a small pool, all surrounded by lush rhododendrons and other flowers. Before settling in, diners make their choices—all prepared to order—at a short counter. The menu, which changes daily, showcases seasonal produce in such dishes as Greek-style salad with spirals of pasta, chunks of juicy chicken, chickpeas, roasted peppers, and feta, or tuna salad on soft sourdough bread with crisp coleslaw in a celery-seed dressing. For a light meal, adults can order from a children's menu of half sandwiches with soups. On the first Wednesday of each month, when the museum is open late and admission is free, dinner is served until 8PM.
♦ American ♦ T-Su lunch 10AM- 4PM. North side of the Music Concourse (off JFK Dr), Ground level. 752.0116; fax 752.3313 ♿

1 Teahouse in Japanese Tea Garden ★$ For more than a century, the five-acre tea garden has been a highlight of **Golden Gate Park.** It's a serene spot for reflective strolling along groomed paths winding past flowers, shrines, and pools. Complete a visit by relaxing at the teahouse over a steaming pot of tea and a plate of simple cookies, served by the traditionally costumed staff.
♦ Teahouse ♦ Daily. Next to the Asian Art Museum, north side of the Music Concourse (off JFK Dr). 752.1171

2 Hana Restaurant ★★$ One of the oldest Japanese restaurants in the area, it maintains a loyal following and a cheerful spirit, thanks to the longtime staff and the lively setting. Oversize round lanterns hang from the plum-colored ceiling above dark wood beams; the walls are a rich blue, accented with blue print fabric and black tile floors. In a little room next door, chefs at the sushi bar fashion sushi with firm, chewy rice and the freshest-tasting fish. Try the eponymous Hana roll, containing yellowtail, avocado, and rice flecked with flying-fish roe. The sukiyaki is a model of all the dish should be, with paper-thin beef, tofu, cabbage, carrots, onions, and a richly sweet sauce. The kitchen also does a great job with tempura, which has an almost buttery flavor.
♦ Japanese ♦ M-F lunch and dinner; Sa dinner. 408 Irving St (between Fifth and Sixth Aves). 665.3952 ♿

3 Mae-Thip ★$ Walk through an intricate Thai shrine to a cozy dining room with gray walls, blue-and-white dishes, and tapers flickering on each table. One of the best choices here is the soup, a clear broth with shrimp, mushrooms, the seductive, sour citrus taste of lemongrass, and a touch of spice from chilies. The rest of the menu tends to be humdrum; daily specials sometimes show creative twists, such as a deep-fried, bite-sized dumpling filled with curried sweet potatoes and served with a salad of tiny cucumbers in a sweet-and-sour sauce.
♦ Thai ♦ M-Sa lunch and dinner; Su dinner. 524 Irving St (between Sixth and Seventh Aves). 759.9644 ♿

4 Tart to Tart ★★★$ Few places in the city make pastries better than the ones here. The setup is basic—shoulder-high display cases of baked goods separate the kitchen from the cafe, which is a hodgepodge of wooden tables—but the aromas of freshly brewed coffee and pastries are irresistible. Fruit tarts are a specialty, with an almost runny pastry cream and a buttery, flaky crust; don't miss the Key lime tart, which has an intense, puckery richness. Other delights include thick peanut

The Sunset

butter cookies with concentrated flavor and a great, sandy texture; big, crumbly, and nutty chocolate chip cookies; and three-layer chocolate-mocha cake, with a light buttercream filling and whipped-cream frosting. For special occasions, there are two-layer sheet cakes in such flavors as apricot-mango, lemon-blueberry, or raspberry-coconut. Customers eating in-house can also choose among such sandwiches as curry chicken and roast turkey, a selection of salads, and a few hot dishes, including three-bean chili and vegetable pasties. ♦ Cafe ♦ Daily 6AM–2AM. 641 Irving St (between Seventh and Eighth Aves). 753.0643; fax 753.3274

5 Crepevine ★★$

Just about every neighborhood in the city seems to be getting its own creperie nowadays, but the budding competition will have to work hard to beat the crepes at this cafe. We're not talking teatime fare; these crispy crepes, served with home fries, make a complete meal. The Florentine version has a good, savory mix of cheddar, onions, spinach, and cottage cheese; the lasagna crepe is made with mozzarella, cottage cheese, eggplant, tomatoes, onions, and marinara sauce. Dessert crepes may be filled with apples and cheese; bananas and brown sugar; or strawberries and chocolate. A trio of soufflé-light omelettes, sandwiches, salads, and bagels with a variety of toppings round out the menu. The simple cafe is accented with tile floors, pine, and large, industrial-looking, copper chandeliers. ♦ Cafe/Creperie ♦ Daily breakfast, lunch, and dinner. No credit cards accepted. 624 Irving St (between Seventh and Eighth Aves). 681.5858

6 YaYa Cuisine ★★★$$

Many restaurants serve Middle Eastern fare, but we can name only one that mixes the food of Mesopotamia with a hefty dose of Californian creativity. Yahya Salih, who grew up near the ruins of Nineveh in northern Iraq, has created a beautiful retreat. An impressive mural stretches along one wall, expansive arches separate the dining areas, and decorative halogen lighting casts a glow over the stippled walls. He's inventively updated the traditional foods of his mother's kitchen, which are aromatically flavored with cardamom, sumac, dried limes, pomegranate syrup, cinnamon, and mint. Baby chicken is stuffed with rice, raisins, and cashews and served with an apricot sauce. Lamb stew is studded with chunks of eggplant and lifted by a sweet-sour pomegranate sauce. Other lamb dishes are perked up with onions, dried limes, and cinnamon, all blended to exotic dimensions. It's an amazing culinary reach, and at times the attempt doesn't quite make it, but the food is never boring. ♦ Middle Eastern ♦ Tu-Su dinner. 1220 Ninth Ave (between Irving St and Lincoln Way). 566.6966

6 Raw Living Foods ★$

In a city like San Francisco, which boasts just about every kind of restaurant, it's tough to come up with a new concept. But the folks here have done it: This New Age–style eatery serves nothing but raw food. (This is in keeping with a health-food philosophy that cooked food interferes with the body's natural balance.) So the only heated item you'll find here is the water for the herbal teas; the rest of the menu consists of things like fruit smoothies, organic salads, sandwiches, and pizzas that are topped with cured vegetables or dried fruit and then "baked" in the sun for six hours. You can enjoy your meal sitting on Japanese-style cushions at low tables or in more conventional seating. New Age music plays in the background, creating a very peaceful atmosphere. ♦ Vegan ♦ M-Th lunch; F lunch and dinner; Sa-Su dinner. 1224 Ninth Ave (between Irving St and Lincoln Way). 665.6519

6 Stoyanof's Cafe and Restaurant ★★★$$

One of only a handful of Greek restaurants in San Francisco, this place has earned a devoted following with its excellent cuisine. At lunch it has the air of a neighborhood cafeteria, but at night the room takes on a romantic glow, and the wooden tables are set with fresh flowers. The traditional starters are all great: avgolemono soup with chicken, rice, and loads of lemon; dolmas; hummus; and tabbouleh. Also try *taramasalata*, red mullet caviar whipped with olive oil and served with fresh lemon and pita, or the smoked eggplant blended with bell peppers, tomatoes, and olive oil. The *spanakopita* (spinach pie) and *tiropetes* (cheese pie), both made with phyllo, are superb. Main courses include grilled chicken in a creamy hazelnut sauce; grilled salmon; Greek fisherman's stew; and beef, lamb, or swordfish kabobs. The kitchen consistently produces some of the best leg of lamb in the city. Although Angel Stoyanof largely has taken over day-to-day operations,

The Sunset

his father, Georgi Stoyanof, still makes the pastries and his own phyllo dough. His quince tart is utterly delicious. ♦ Greek ♦ Tu-Su lunch and dinner. No credit cards accepted at lunch. 1240 Ninth Ave (between Irving St and Lincoln Way). 664.3664; fax 665.9914 ♿

6 The Coffee Merchant Few shops offer a more complete selection of teas and coffees. More than a hundred kinds of teas, both bagged and loose, and about 90 kinds of coffee are stacked so high behind a counter here that customers need assistance reaching them. Hundreds of mugs also line the wall, along with coffeepots and specialty food items. ♦ Daily. 1248 Ninth Ave (between Irving St and Lincoln Way). 665.1915; fax 665.1915

7 Noah's Bagels This bakery's products are steamed, not boiled in the traditional fashion. The resulting chewy texture has attracted a large following (though detractors say the bagels here are nothing more than bread with a hole in it). The franchise, which has just been bought by the Boston Market chain, has enjoyed tremendous success—there are outlets all over the city, with more planned. The bagels, which come in more than a dozen flavors, are fatter than the competition's, and there are plenty of go-withs available, including flavored cream-cheese spreads and whole smoked fish. ♦ Daily. No credit cards accepted. 742 Irving St (at Ninth Ave). 566.2761; fax 566.9258 ♿. Also at: 2075 Chestnut St (at Steiner St). 775.2910; fax 775.1243 ♿

8 PJ's Oysterbed ★★ $$ Lovers of Louisiana-style seafood have loyally patronized this nonstop Mardi Gras for some 15 years. Reservations are accepted, but people don't seem to mind arriving unannounced, putting their names on the list, and waiting for an hour or more; they simply head across the street for a drink at **Yancy's**. Once guests are seated, though, the open kitchen turns out mounds of food just as quickly as the Zydeco music bounces. Start with heaps of crayfish, or try the shrimp bisque with a dollop of jalapeño puree. And there's no better jambalaya in the city than the version here, made with rice, tomatoes, chicken, and spicy andouille sausage. **PJ's** also houses a thriving fish market and, next to the sales area, a counter where people can enjoy bowls of steaming clam chowder. ♦ Seafood ♦ Daily lunch and dinner. 737 Irving St (between Eighth and Ninth Aves). 566.7775; fax 566.8088 ♿

9 Owl & Monkey Cafe ★ $ This earthy coffeehouse, with the rough-hewn look of pine tables and plank flooring, is usually packed with college students. They congregate here mainly to meet and greet, but the food is good, too. Salads include Greek (with spinach, olives, and feta), chef's, and fruit. Among the hot dishes are enchilada casserole, potato skins with melted cheese and sour cream, vegetarian lasagna, and quiche. Sandwiches are standard, from chicken salad and turkey to tuna melts and egg salad. Live music plays Thursday, Saturday, and Sunday nights. ♦ Cafe ♦ Daily breakfast, lunch, and dinner. 1336 Ninth Ave (between Judah and Irving Sts). 665.4840

9 Tamnan Thai ★★ $ The story to wheedle out of the owners is what brought Mick Jagger to this small Thai place after a concert in October 1994. (A photo of the rock star posing with them graces the front window.) The answer could be the food. The sweetness of the silken *tom kha gai* (chicken and coconut-milk soup) is perfectly tempered by sour flavoring from lime juice. The traditional ground chicken with basil is above average, too, thanks to the profusion of herbs that provide a licorice aftertaste. Specials always include at least one curry, including one of the best we've had in any Thai restaurant: shrimp with fresh asparagus, doused in a green curry that's fragrant with basil. With a canopied service area in one corner, candles on the tables, and friendly service, enjoying a meal here is like eating in the home of a relative. ♦ Thai ♦ Tu-Su lunch and dinner. 1360 Ninth Ave (at Judah St). 564.5771 ♿

10 Howard's ★★ $ Although the original owner died in 1991, this retro spot still turns out three great square meals a day. Perch at the horseshoe-shaped counter in back with a view into the kitchen, or squeeze in at one of the tables in the dark-paneled dining room; they're so close together that you can whiff your neighbor's food, but nobody seems to mind. The omelettes are excellent, and the potatoes are beyond compare—cut paper-thin, fried until crisp, and sprinkled with scallions. All the beef for the quarter-pound burgers is ground in-house. ♦ American ♦ Daily breakfast, lunch, and dinner. 1309 Ninth Ave (at Irving St). 564.4723

The Sunset

ORGANIC GROUNDS

10 Organic Grounds ★★$ A relative newcomer to San Francisco's coffeehouse scene, this one is unique in that it uses only beans organically grown in Guatemala. Whether it's the way the beans are grown or just that these folks know how to make a cup of coffee, the brew is complex, full, and rich, with a touch of bitterness. The narrow shop has a stylish look, with light wood tables, banquettes lining cheery yellow walls, and a pretty wood floor. Health drinks also are served, including shots of wheat grass, smoothies (the orange, banana, and cinnamon smoothie has a bright and lively flavor and tastes as rich as a milk shake), and all kinds of vegetable juices. Even the bagels and granola are organic. ♦ Coffeehouse ♦ Daily. No credit cards accepted. 1307 Ninth Ave (at Irving St). 661.1255 ♿

10 Chika ★★$ The sushi chef at work in the shoe-box–size kitchen at this Japanese spot offers a good show. The dining room is spare and attractive, with a high-gloss, blond wood sushi bar and rice-paper screens softening the windows. Diners munch on complimentary plates of steamed beans as they peruse the menu, which offers the standard array of sushi (barbecued eel, tuna, and shrimp) and limited hot options, including tempura and teriyaki. The blackboard lists such specials as bonito, as well as paper-thin slices of lemon and salmon hand-rolled in rice. ♦ Japanese ♦ M-Tu, Th-Su dinner. 841 Irving St (at 10th Ave). 681.5539 ♿

11 Just Desserts The draw at this sweet shop—which has served only desserts for 13 years—is the long counter and soda fountain. It's the place for milk shakes, all kinds of sundaes in traditional fluted glass dishes, or sinful baked goods. Chocoholics will love the rich fudge cake. The bakery also has a way with lemon. Try the lemon tart; the triple lemon cake with layers of lemon sponge, lemon custard filling, and a lemon buttercream filling; or the densely textured lemon-buttermilk pound cake. ♦ Daily. 836 Irving St (at 10th Ave). 681.1277; fax 681.0308. Also at: 248 Church St (between 15th and Market Sts). 626.5774; fax 626.7212 ♿

12 New Eritrea Restaurant ★★$ From the front window this East African place appears to be a bar. But just beyond the quaffing space is a small, dark dining room with a pass-through window to the kitchen. Combination dinners appear on enameled platters the size of a small tabletop, laid with *injera* (spongy Ethiopian bread) and ringed with shredded romaine. The vegetarian combo includes okra with tomatoes and aromatic spices, a spicy vegetable curry, and zucchini and spinach. The meat combo has beef simmered in a red pepper sauce, chicken in clarified butter with a spicy red pepper sauce, lamb curry, and spinach. The braised dishes are fork tender and the flavors are excellent, although the sauces do begin to taste alike. ♦ East African ♦ Tu-Su lunch and dinner. 907 Irving St (at 10th Ave). 681.1288 ♿

13 Cheese Boutique A sister shop to the one in Glen Park, this neighborhood favorite boasts more than a hundred kinds of cheese and imported foods. Although the selection at **Andronico's Market** (see below) is more visually impressive, regulars here are loyal to the friendly staff and caring service. ♦ M-Sa. 1298 12th Ave (at Irving St). 566.3155; fax 333.5450. Also at: 666 Chenery St (at Diamond St). 333.3390; fax 333.5450 ♿

14 Andronico's Market This pricey supermarket has one of the best selections of upscale products in the city, beginning with 25 varieties of apples and 10 types of dates. Consider seven kinds of mushrooms, every fresh herb imaginable, and four varieties of pearl onions. On any given day, the store is likely to surprise customers with something they've never seen before, such as cocktail avocados—creamy, delicious baby avocados without pits. Chic chrome shelves are filled with oils and other essentials, and the terrific selection of bulk items includes 15 kinds of granola. The fresh meat cases display venison, and the fish tanks are swimming with carp, trout, catfish, lobsters, and crabs. Browse the deli for seven pâtés, cold cuts, and myriad take-out treats, the "Hofbrau" department for ribs and pastrami, and the "Hot Wok" for lemon chicken, *egg foo yong,* and barbecued pork. The bread department stocks loaves from most of the boutique bakeries in the area, and the bins are filled with three kinds of bread sticks and four flavors of croutons. We could go on and on, but we're still dizzy with delight. ♦ Daily. 1200 Irving St (at Funston Ave). 661.3220; fax 661.5294 ♿

15 Johnny Nipon's $ Since this place opened in 1979, its menu hasn't changed a bit—and neither, it seems, has the loyal clientele. Most of them begin with the shrimp bisque. Another good choice is Johnny's version of that San Francisco classic, cioppino; it's rich with crab, clams, and scallops in a tomato sauce. Frogs' legs are dipped in an egg batter and fried; such fish as rainbow trout and sand dabs can be broiled, grilled, or poached. Landlubbers might choose from chicken piccata, grilled pork loin with apples, calves' liver and onions, or veal Oscar with asparagus and crab meat. ♦ Seafood/Italian ♦ M-Sa

The Sunset

lunch and dinner; Su brunch and dinner. 1420 Irving St (between 15th and 16th Aves). 681.5778 ♿

16 Sagami-Ya Restaurant ★★$ Ignore the decor at this mom-and-pop Japanese cafe—it's a find. So what if the place looks a bit worn, and the chairs are covered in orange vinyl? It's all immaculate. Ask about the not-to-be-missed sukiyaki, and the cook will wax eloquent about the balance of sake, onions, and broth that flavor the paper-thin slices of beef. The *yosenabe*, an aromatic pot of broth brimming with seafood, is another specialty. Also try the *gyoza*, tasty pot stickers filled with plump shrimp and a hint of dill. Sushi selections are more limited than most, but are as fresh as the very best. ♦ Japanese ♦ Tu-Sa lunch and dinner; Su dinner. 1525 Irving St (between 16th and 17th Aves). 661.2434

17 Just Like Home ★★$ The food at this Middle Eastern cafe/deli is just as homey as the name implies. Up front is the deli, a wall of packaged products, and bins of rice and grains. Beyond an arched doorway lies the dining room, which has booth seating and few other amenities. The vegetarian combination includes the classics: tangy tabbouleh, creamy hummus, delicately flavored dolmas, refreshing cucumbers in yogurt with mint and garlic, and boldly seasoned falafel. Rustic meat dishes include chicken Musakhan (baked with grilled onions and spooned over pita bread) and lamb *shawarma* (thinly sliced rotisseried lamb served over hummus or rice). Wash it all down with the great house-made lemonade. ♦ Middle Eastern/Deli ♦ Daily lunch and dinner. 1924 Irving St (between 20th and 21st Aves). 681.3337 ♿

18 Irving Seafood Market Since its expansion into a second storefront, this market now carries more than seafood, but the fish here is particularly fresh. As many as 15 types of whole fish are available, as well as mussels, conch, oysters, and tanks of crabs, lobster, catfish, and rock cod. Packaged products including a shelf of Thai wonton wrappers, cram the other half of the store. ♦ Daily. No credit cards accepted. 2130 Irving St (between 22nd and 23rd Aves). 681.5000 ♿

18 Irving Little Cafe & Sandwiches ★$ *Bahn mi,* traditional Vietnamese sandwiches, are served at this tiny spot (just big enough for four tables and a counter). For a pittance, feast on half a French roll slathered with mayonnaise and a chili-based sauce, spiked with five-spice powder, peppers, shredded carrots, and cilantro, and filled with pâté, fried chicken, barbecued pork, sardines, or meatballs. It's a taste treat. The cafe also serves inexpensive rice and noodle dishes. ♦ Vietnamese ♦ Daily breakfast, lunch, and dinner until 6:30PM. No credit cards accepted. 2146 Irving St (between 22nd and 23rd Aves). 681.2326

19 22nd & Irving Market For over 25 years, this neighborhood market has attracted customers from all over the city. Fresh olives are just waiting to be brined and cured; the quince is picture-perfect; Italian chestnuts are ready for roasting; and the herbs are some of the freshest around. There are also bags of basmati and jasmine rice, nuts, dried fruits, and beans. The dairy department carries feta and Mexican cheese, and many of the makings for Latin and Asian fare are on hand—though **May Wah** (see page 180) is a better bet for stocking up on the most esoteric Asian ingredients. A couple of tables are available for eating takeout food from the other shops and cafes in the area. ♦ Daily. No credit cards accepted. 2101 Irving St (at 22nd Ave). 681.5212; fax 681.3285 ♿

19 Sunrise Deli and Cafe ★$ The falafel made here is sold to many of the corner markets around the city. These tasty croquettes are made from highly spiced, ground chickpeas that are deep-fried and either tucked into pita bread or served with a yogurt or tahini sauce. The front window showcases a spit of layered lamb slices, all brown, succulent, and ready to be carved. The deli also proffers salads, including tabbouleh. ♦ Middle Eastern ♦ Daily lunch and dinner. No credit cards accepted. 2115 Irving St (at 22nd Ave). 664.8210

Yum Yum Fish

19 Yum Yum Fish Shoppers in the know seek out this store for the freshest fish fillets in town. At the rear is a sushi counter, where more than a dozen first-rate sushi and sashimi items are prepared to order. You can get a sushi snack to go, too. The party trays are hugely popular. ♦ Tu-Su. No credit cards accepted. 2181 Irving St (between 22nd and 23rd Aves). 566.6433 ♿

19 New Hai Ky ★$ Cheap, good food attracts crowds to this popular spot. The window is full of mahogany-hued Peking ducks and other roasted meats that taste as good as they look; flavorful noodle soups are also a draw. It's enough to make you overlook the Formica tables and bare floors that contrast oddly with the sea of bright, crystal chandeliers above

179

The Sunset

them. ♦ Chinese ♦ Daily breakfast, lunch, and dinner. No credit cards accepted. 2191 Irving St (at 23rd Ave). 731.9948

20 May Wah Trading Compay A full-service Asian market, this store is more compact than its branches in Chinatown and Richmond. The narrow aisles and merchandise are stacked high. Those who can overcome their claustrophobia will find a grand selection of packaged products, produce, well-trimmed meat, up to a dozen kinds of fish, and everything else needed to put an Asian meal on the table. The younger staffers are helpful, but the older ones can be brusque. ♦ Daily. 2201 Irving St (at 23rd Ave). 665.4756 &. Also at: 547 Clement St (at Eighth Ave). 668.2583; fax 666.3933 &; 1230 Stockton St (between Pacific Ave and Broadway). 433.3095; fax 433.7876 &

20 Marnee Thai ★★$ The peaked room lined in bamboo and the walls covered in woven palm-frond mats give this Thai restaurant a tropical feel. Although it's one of the most popular in the city, the food has lost a bit of its edge recently. The signature dish is a fresh, thin corn-and-ginger cake deep-fried to a honey brown. Other top choices are raw spinach leaves filled with shrimp and ginger, and spicy green papaya salad with wedges of tomatoes and whole green beans. Among the main courses, the spicy chicken with cashews is studded with chunks of white onions, scallions, and red peppers. The chicken with chili sauce and fresh basil is another popular standby. For dessert, few can resist the fried bananas with a scoop of rich ice cream laced with coconut. ♦ Thai ♦ M, W-Su lunch and dinner. 2225 Irving St (at 23rd Ave). 665.9500

21 Thanh Long ★★$$ People travel from all over the city to feast on roast crab at this 26-year-old Vietnamese restaurant owned by Helene and Danny An, and for good reason. It's served either with sweet-and-sour sauce or "drunken" (in a vibrant wine broth with scallions). Diners, outfitted for battle with plastic bibs and nutcrackers, are amply rewarded with delighted palates, full stomachs, and hot towels to clean their fingers. Those who don't crave crab can opt for Saigon beef, the meat rolled around cooked onions and topped with more sweet, gooey onions, or lemongrass chicken with its edge of garlic. A good way to start is the multivitamin roll, a crisp-skinned imperial roll stuffed with pork and vegetables; also don't miss the garlic noodles. The dining room is always crowded, and it's not hard to understand why. ♦ Vietnamese/Seafood ♦ Tu-Su dinner. 4101 Judah St (at 46th Ave). 665.1146

22 Sweet Endings Cookies This all-purpose bakery has a retail outlet in front and a production facility in back, which supplies biscotti and other baked goods to many cafes in the city. Its biscotti (the dry Italian biscuit) are denser and not as crisp as most, but the flavors are just as good, particularly the chocolate. The ovens also turn out a variety of Middle Eastern cookies. ♦ Tu-Sa. No credit cards accepted. 1935 Lawton St (between 25th and 26th Aves). 665.4748 &

23 Casa Aguila ★$$ With paper decorations and streamers hanging from the beamed ceiling, mirrored walls, and friendly (if a bit slow) service, this eatery has a festive atmosphere. The food, although served in huge portions, is of uneven quality. The best choices are the appetizer of mushrooms baked with garlic, the consistently terrific guacamole, pork steak marinated in home-made jalapeño-apple jelly, *carne asada* (beef strips flavored with rosemary, cumin, and chilies and served with vegetables, rice, and pinto beans), and the brochette of shrimp, chicken, beef, or halibut served with potatoes, roasted vegetables, and melted cheese. More than a half-dozen Mexican beers are offered, along with tamarind-flavored mineral water and guava and other juices. ♦ Mexican ♦ Daily lunch and dinner. 1240 Noriega St (between 19th and 20th Aves). 661.5593

24 Shaharazad Bakery Making phyllo pastry by hand is a dying art, but it's practiced in its highest form here by Mihran and Rose Sagatelyan. The dough is stretched, pulled, and turned into a translucent sheet, resulting in a phyllo that is flakier and moister than any other. The cheery aqua-and-white bakery makes the most of the artful phyllo in such not-to-be missed treats as the *spanakopita*, baklava, apple turnover, or pistachio birds' nests, freshly made and dripping with honey. ♦ M-Sa. No credit cards accepted. 1586 Noriega St (at 23rd Ave). 661.1155 &

25 House of Coffee One of the first shops to introduce the city to the full range of fresh roasted coffees, this has been a popular neighborhood stop for 30 years. In addition to the coffees, roasted in the rear, it proffers coffeepots, espresso machines, and such specialty products as jars of baby eggplants, sour cherries, and Australian dried apricots. ♦ M-Sa. 1618 Noriega St (between 23rd and 24th Aves). 681.9363; fax 566.0768 &

The Sunset

26 Cheung Hing ★★$ The space is cramped, the decor utilitarian, but the wonderful aromas emanating from this little Chinese eatery have fans lining up even on Sunday nights, when other places wind down. Three frenzied workers behind the counter serve up roast pig, soy-sauce chicken, and barbecued pork and duck. And it seems almost everyone orders the lo mein noodles (try the ones topped with barbecued pork). All delicious, and for ridiculously low prices. ♦ Chinese/Barbecue ♦ Daily breakfast, lunch, and dinner. 2339 Noriega St (between 30th and 31st Aves). 665.3271

27 Hong Kong Seafood Restaurant ★★$ One of the best of the growing number of Hong Kong–style restaurants serving dim sum in the Sunset, it boasts Sunday-morning queues. People even line up at the take-out area, which has its own entrance and is separated from the dining room by a folding screen. The dim sum is terrific, each preparation given a slight twist: The pork in the *siu mai* dumpling is chopped into fairly large pieces along with equally large pieces of shrimp. Each *ha gow* (a shrimp dumpling made with a thin tapioca-flour casing) holds three shrimp smeared with a ginger-and-garlic paste. And the steamed dumplings' pork-and-cilantro filling is finely chopped, creating a creamy contrast to the al dente wrapping. The red swagged drapes at the storefront windows have faded to pink, but the room is a cut above most in the area, with tapestrylike upholstery and crystal chandeliers. ♦ Chinese/Dim sum ♦ Daily lunch and dinner; dim sum Sa-Su 9:30AM-2:30PM. 2588 Noriega St (at 33rd Ave). 665.8338 ♿

28 Polly Ann Ice Cream Unique in its decor and its ice cream, this parlor dishes up 400 flavors (50 on any given day), including passion fruit, litchi, guava, jackfruit, and taro. For less exotic tastes, owner Charles Wu offers Bumpy Road (his answer to Rocky Road) and coffee rum fudge. If it's too hard to decide what to order, spin the flavor wheel and hope you like what it lands on. The walls of the tiny shop are papered with slogans like "If there's anything a depressed person hates, it's a cheerful person." But it's hard not to feel cheerful at a place that offers a free ice-cream cone to any pup accompanied by a human customer. ♦ Daily. No credit cards accepted. 3142 Noriega St (between 38th and 39th Aves). 664.2472 ♿

29 Win's ★$ Roast ducks and spareribs hang in the window of this Chinese spot, and just inside the door cooks pull noodles and wontons from steaming pots. At eight pages, the menu is too long for the kitchen to manage consistently, but the duck is always a must-have. Start with pot stickers and barbecued baby pork ribs, served on a bed of lightly sauced white beans. The *congees,* rich rice soups that constitute a meal, are also very good—especially the combination with shrimp, scallops, squid, chicken, and pork. For a really inexpensive, filling meal, choose one of the rice plates topped with all kinds of stir-fries or curries. ♦ Chinese ♦ Tu-Sa lunch and dinner. 3040 Taraval St (between 40th and 41st). 759.1818

30 Rick's Restaurant & Bar ★★★$$ Richard and Victoria Oku's stylish place has a somewhat remote setting near the ocean, where it was sorely needed. The dining room resembles that of an exclusive cruise ship, with Philippine mahogany paneling, an ornate bar, gleaming brass trim, starched white tablecloths, bentwood chairs, and a forest green carpet. In keeping with the theme, brass porthole-framed mirrors are hung on the paneling. Oku, the former chef at the **Washington Square Bar and Grill** and a native of Hawaii, includes a few island-inspired dishes—such as *poki* (a tuna seviche) and *goliah* (a fish stew). But most of the fare is what he calls "San Francisco comfort food." That translates to lamb shanks with polenta, pork tenderloin over herbed bread stuffing, and New York steak with green-peppercorn sauce. Among the seafood selections are mahimahi with avocado-papaya salsa and red snapper in lime vinaigrette. Vegetarian dishes include ravioli with sun-dried tomatoes and almonds, and a mixed vegetable platter. ♦ American ♦ Daily dinner. Reservations recommended. 1940 Taraval St (between 29th and 30th Aves). 731.8900 ♿

Back in the 1890s, San Francisco's Ingleside Race Track was the first eatery in this country to offer enchiladas—that versatile Mexican dish featuring soft corn tortillas filled with meat and napped with a piquant tomato sauce. Today the race track is closed, but enchiladas appear on menus all over the country.

In the later part of the 19th century, San Francisco was home to "professor" Jerry Thomas, who tended bar at the Occidental Hotel. Thomas is credited with inventing both the martini and the Tom and Jerry, a warm mixture of rum or brandy blended with eggs and spices. Could it be that the professor named the latter drink after himself?

The Sunset

Tea Time

The delightful British tradition of afternoon tea is becoming increasingly popular on this side of the Atlantic, but a bit of linguistic confusion prevails. Perhaps because the experience can be so uplifting, it often is called "high tea." But any Englishman knows that high tea is a light supper of cold meats, fish, salads, and tea, usually served Sunday night.

Afternoon tea, by contrast, is a snack served late in the day that consists of tea, finger sandwiches, scones, and pastries. The Duchess of Bedford is said to have originated the tradition (partly to show off her beautiful tea services) in 1830. Since dinner was served quite late in those days, she decreed that tea be served at 5PM, and the late-afternoon restorative became all the rage.

Here are just some of the many spots in San Francisco where you can indulge in afternoon tea. Although most of them don't serve a proper English tea, they afford a pleasant alternative to the city's coffeehouses. Even the duchess would approve.

Just off the lobby of the **Westin St. Francis** (335 Powell St, at Geary St, 397.7000), the **Compass Rose Room** is so beautifully and tastefully appointed, they could serve Lipton's and no one would notice. Here's the picture: dramatic lighting, rich Oriental rugs, comfortable wing chairs, soaring wooden columns, draped valences, sprays of live orchids in sturdy wooden floor planters, a pianist tinkling in the background, and servers dressed as Russian Cossacks. The tea service is just as lovely. It includes a warm scone with butter and preserves, three finger sandwiches, a bowl overflowing with ripe strawberries napped with Grand Marnier whipped cream, and two petits fours. Choose from eight teas, or indulge in a glass of Champagne. Afternoon tea is served daily between 3PM and 5PM.

The **King George** (334 Mason St, at Geary St, 781.5050) is steeped in all the charm of a small European hotel, with a sedate lobby and such touches as a bowl of red, ripe apples at the front desk. Afternoon tea is served on the mezzanine Monday through Saturday from 3 to 6:30PM. Here, softly upholstered wing chairs surround tables set with the finest English floral china. A portrait of Queen Elizabeth II dominates the room, fresh flowers add dashes of color, and classical music is piped in. The server, costumed as an English maid, lays out the tea (a house blend) and a carousel of assorted finger sandwiches, biscuits, a crumpet, and jam. Silky tipsy trifle rounds out the generous offering.

The **Ritz-Carlton San Francisco** (600 Stockton St, at California St, 296.7465) was once an engineering college. Today this Greek Revival structure is one of a handful of hotels favored by visiting dignitaries and rock stars. The **Lobby Lounge**'s comfortable bar is decorated in a grand manner, with beautiful antique silk tapestries and 18th- and 19th-century portraits of high-society women flanking tall French windows. Afternoon tea is served daily from 2:30 to 5PM, followed by a sushi service, reflecting the hotel's international flavor. The menu for the "Pacific tea" includes a choice of 11 teas; such sandwich combinations as prosciutto and asparagus, or Norwegian salmon with caviar and pickled onions; scones; tea cakes; fruit tartlets; and cookies. In addition, there's a "light tea" that includes everything but the sandwiches.

With its contemporary-looking glass ceiling and airy garden atmosphere, the lobby-level **Nob Hill Terrace** at the **Mark Hopkins Inter-Continental** (999 California St, at Mason St, 392.3434) makes a fine setting for afternoon tea, which is served daily from 2:30 to 5:30PM. The tea includes an assortment of sandwiches (perhaps Scottish smoked salmon, or a combination of English cheddar, cucumber, and York ham), scones and fancy pastries, and a choice of darjeeling, Earl Grey, English breakfast, jasmine, or orange pekoe tea.

Mad Magda's Russian Tea Room & Mystic Cafe (579 Hayes St, between Octavia and Laguna Sts, 864.7654) creates an intimate atmosphere in which to enjoy a variety of brews. The tea is served in china pots and old-fashioned flowered cups, and there's a selection of tasty baked goods to go with it. Those with heartier appetites can enjoy entrées from the largely Russian menu, including borscht and blintzes; the restaurant also serves sandwiches and soups. You can even get a psychic reading here from early afternoon into the evening. The most pleasant area is the outdoor patio in back, decorated in a hodgepodge of tables and chairs, large patches of green plants, and brightly colored flowers. It's open daily.

Pure T (2238 Polk St, between Vallejo and Green Sts, 441.7878) is a stylish, sunny spot to enjoy a soothing pot of unusual tea: black currant, chamomile, or red-colored Thai tea, for example, all served with crisp cookies. Even more exotic are the tea-flavored ice creams the owners have created. Instead of a cuppa, how about a cone of Earl Grey, passion fruit, or jasmine? There's also a shop here selling teapots and loose teas. It's open daily from 11:30AM to 9PM.

Modeled after a European-style tea salon, **Teaz** (900 N Point St, Ghirardelli Square, Plaza level, 346.3483) has a 16-seat "tea bar" selling 75 to 100 teas from all over the world. Also offered are such typical tea-time accompaniments as cookies, scones, and flavored sugars. The interior is decked out in ivory and gold, and graced by painted Louis XIV-style furniture. A private room is available for tea parties, and tea-leaf readings are offered several times a week. It's open daily from 10AM to 6PM, with extended hours in the summer.

VIVANDE Ristorante (670 Golden Gate Ave, between Franklin St and Van Ness Ave, 673.9245) has a medieval Italian ambience—despite its location in a skyscraper. At lunchtime the place is taken over by City Hall's movers and shakers; dinner draws people en route to the Performing Arts Center. But between 2:30 and 5PM daily it makes a delightful refuge, with an afternoon tea that includes a savory and a sweet tray with such tempting treats as chocolate cake with raspberry puree, gelato, and semolina pudding.

The Sunset

Marco Polo

31 Marco Polo This parlor, an East-West hybrid, is aptly named for the explorer who supposedly brought ice cream to Europe from the Orient. Two signs stretch across the building: one in English printed with the colors of the Italian flag, the other with Chinese characters. The ice cream is Italian-style gelato, which is dense in texture and rich in taste; it comes in both Asian flavors (red bean, litchi, and guava) and such Italian classics as double chocolate and *arcobaleno* (rainbow), with its stripes of vanilla, chocolate, and pistachio. ♦ Daily. No credit cards accepted. 1447 Taraval St (at 25th Ave). 731.2833 &

32 Mr. Liquor The top wine shop in the Sunset, and one of the best in the city, it will meet or beat any competitor's prices. It's the only San Francisco outlet for Kermit Lynch wines (a well-known importer in Berkeley) and carries about two-thirds of the entire line. It also stocks a good selection of current-release wines, particularly from California. Many older Bordeaux and Californian wines are stored off-premises in a 10,000-square-foot warehouse; a newsletter lists what's available. The store also carries up to 130 beers and 60 single-malt scotches. The tasting bar by the front window offers self-service wine tastings at a minimal charge, and wine-tasting seminars are held regularly. To double-check your choices, consult the binders full of wine ratings by the *Wine Advocate*, *Grapevine*, *Connoisseur's*, and the *Wine Journal*. ♦ Daily. 250 Taraval St (between 12th and Funston Aves). 731.6222; fax 731.0155 &

33 Just Won Ton ★★$ That's what to order at this little restaurant: just won tons. They may well be the best you ever ate. The skin is almost translucent, and the fillings are delicately and bursting with flavor. The best bet is a bowl of broth brimming with the stuffed noodles and another ingredient, maybe fish balls or barbecued chicken or pork. Other noodles include *chow mei fun* (thick rice noodles) and chow mein. The white-painted room is nothing fancy and has fewer than a dozen tables covered with bright oilcloth. ♦ Chinese ♦ Tu-Su lunch and dinner. No credit cards accepted. 1241 Vicente St (between 23rd and 24th Aves). 661.2999

34 Leon's Bar-B-Q ★$ After spending a day at the **San Francisco Zoo**, head across the street to this diner. Specialties are greasy ribs with a sweet barbecue sauce, jambalaya, and housemade sweet-potato pie. All the barbecue comes with corn bread, baked beans, potato salad, coleslaw, and fries or spaghetti. For something a little different, try the barbecued smoked turkey sandwich. There are also branches on Fillmore Street and at Fisherman's Wharf. ♦ Barbecue ♦ Daily lunch and dinner. 2800 Sloat Blvd (at 47th Ave, across from the zoo entrance). 681.3071. Also at: 1911 Fillmore St (between Bush and Pine Sts). 922.2436 &; 2800 Leavenworth St (Anchorage Center, between Jefferson and Beach Sts). No phone

Bests

en Stevens
hief Concierge, Four Seasons Clift Hotel

think a civilized evening on the town starts with nner at **Julie Ring's Heart and Soul**. Julie has a mited but very good menu, and there's jazz and ancing. I also like the New Orleans decor—It's arm and so are the people who work there. Next d go to **Harry Denton's Starlight Room** on the top f the **Sir Francis Drake Hotel** to have a nightcap, nd for the spectacular view and music. Some ghts I also like to meander the **Wharf** and go to he **Mandarin** for a crispy Peking duck and then on **Lou's Pier 47 Club** for dancing to some of the st blues bands in the country.

iana Nelson
hief Concierge, Grand Hyatt Hotel

think **Fleur de Lys** is the best and most romantic staurant in the city, with divine foie gras and the st dessert sampler. **Bix** is sophisticated and xy. My favorite is the chicken hash. **Scala's**
Bistro is a newish spot with terrific decor, I love the mural. **Rumpus** is fun and laid-back. The pan-roasted chicken and mashed potatoes and the chocolate brioche cake are terrific. **Anjou**, a tiny bistro on **Campton Place**, has the best bargain—lunch for $10.

Gerald Asher
Wine Editor, Gourmet Magazine

When I go out to eat, I like **Zax** in **North Beach** and **Woodward's Gardens**. I like **Yank Sing** for Sunday lunch with my family and the **R & G Lounge**, now possibly the best [Chinese food] in the city. I like **Rubicon**, but need a table downstairs. **Stars**. . . there's all that glamor (real or virtually real) as condiment. I recently discovered **Thep Phanom**, which I find superior to other Thai restaurants in the city.

I'm a regular at the **Ferry Plaza Farmers' Market** on Saturday mornings, and I rely on the cheese shop at **Leonard's**.

The Richmond/ Presidio Heights

A largely residential district, the Richmond is family-oriented to be sure. But those families are a diverse lot, with roots that cover the globe. The traditions of Asia, the Middle East, and Eastern and Western Europe mingle in this excitingly varied community, making for a bracing cultural and culinary stew.

Russians were the first group to settle the area, when some 10,000 immigrants arrived here after the 1917 Revolution. Many second- and third-generation Russians gradually moved away from the city beginning in the 1970s, but they were replaced by a large number of Russian-Jewish émigrés who came here in the 1980s to escape repression in the former Soviet Union. In subsequent years, non-Jewish Russians came here as well. More than 25,000 strong today, this community clusters around the impressive, onion-domed **Holy Virgin Cathedral**, a Russian Orthodox church on **Geary Boulevard at 26th Avenue**. At least a half-dozen bakeries and several stores and delis have opened in the last few years to cater to this growing group of residents.

Many people of Japanese descent moved to the central areas of the Richmond after World War II, and today more Japanese-Americans live in this district than in any other part of the city. The Chinese have likewise put down deep roots here—so much so that the Richmond is often called the New Chinatown. Twenty years ago, the main shopping district of **Clement Street**,

The Richmond/Presidio Heights

from **Fourth** to **Tenth Avenues**, had one small dim sum restaurant and no Asian groceries. Today there are numerous shops and restaurants catering to the burgeoning Asian community. But stores in the "original" Chinatown generally carry products that appeal primarily to the Chinese cook, while Richmond merchants branch out to cater to a more diverse market.

At **El Chico Produce Market**, for example, Asian and Hispanic products share shelf space with bread and pastries from **Cinderella Restaurant and Bakery**, one of the city's oldest Russian bakeries. And at **Cinderella**'s restaurant, diners may accent an order of traditional stuffed cabbage with the soy sauce that always sits on the tables.

The ethnic diversity in the Richmond has also given rise to the city's first Burmese restaurant, **Mandalay**, as well as several three-star Hong Kong–style dim sum parlors, including **Hong Kong Flower Lounge Restaurant** and **Ton Kiang** (the branch on Geary Boulevard at **22nd Avenue**). These relative newcomers happily coexist with such neighborhood institutions as **Haig's Delicacies**, where people have stocked up on Middle Eastern goods for almost half a century, and **Shenson's**, renowned for its Jewish delicatessen fare. Western Europe is well represented here, too. Such French classics as coq au vin or sweetbreads in Madeira cream sauce are served at the romantic **Le Cyrano**; modern Mediterranean fare stars at **Socca Restaurant**, and the area even boasts a four-star French restaurant, **Alain Rondelli**. Some of the best cracker-crisp–crusted pizza in the city is offered at **Mescolanza**, along with great pasta and veal dishes. And you can get your Irish up debating the fine points of a soccer match at **Pat O'Shea's Mad Hatter**—or just have a brew and a lunch of roast salmon or leg of lamb rivaling that at any downtown establishment. A fine spot to appreciate the community's family spirit is the **Toy Boat Dessert Cafe**, where youngsters climb up on a mechanical horse, ogle the tin toys for sale, and slurp ice-cream cones. Their older siblings may prefer a burger and malted at **Mel's Drive-In**, while Mom and Dad can revisit the 1950s at **Bill's Place** burger joint.

The Richmond spills into one of the city's most affluent areas: Presidio Heights, home to some of its most distinguished citizens, including US senator Dianne Feinstein. West of Geary Boulevard are the expensive homes of **Seacliff**, with many wealthy and famous residents (such as actor-comedian Robin Williams). And **Laurel Village** offers some of the best shopping in the city—at very steep prices. **Wine Impression** stocks every vintage of BV Private Reserve Cabernet Sauvignon; the **Cal-Mart** supermarket proffers an impressive selection of goods, including breads from more than a half-dozen bakeries; **Bryan's** market sells top-quality meat, fish, and poultry (including the hard-to-find Prime grade of beef); and **Forrest Jones** was the first store in the country to carry Calphalon pots and pans among its wide range of fine housewares. The antiques stores that line **Sacramento Street** also provide ample opportunities to fantasize and window shop. Here, too, the clubby **Garibaldis** serves up a fine hamburger and Caesar salad; a more elegant dining option is **The Heights**, a four-star French-California eatery. Presidio Heights, Seacliff, and Laurel Village are decidedly upscale enclaves, but they harmonize nicely with the staunchly middle-class Richmond district. Together they provide another example of the unified diversity that is San Francisco.

The Richmond/Presidio Heights

1 Baker Street Bistro ★★$$ Classic French food is the draw of this cozy storefron dining room with only 24 seats and tables brightened by pots of herbs. Throughout the evening, the chef emerges from the kitchen to make sure everything is going smoothly. Selections include snails sautéed in garlic and cream, and a rich ragout of lamb with carrots and other vegetables. Fish specials are offered nightly, and might include yellowtail tuna in a brown butter sauce, served with vegetables and a crusty wedge of baked polenta. The four-course prix-fixe dinner is a great deal. On Friday and Saturday nights, the seating area spills over into a small space the owners recently acquired next door. At other times, they operate the extra room as a casual cafe, serving breakfast and lunch. The menu includes pastries, baguette sandwiches, salads, and egg dishes, among them a great quiche. ♦ French ♦ Tu-Su breakfast, lunch, and dinner. 2953 Baker St (at Lombard St). 931.1475 &

2 Liverpool Lil's ★$$ When the Presidio was an army base, military personnel as well as civilians hung out at this cozy English pub. Still popular, it's one of the few places in the city where you can indulge in a steak-and-kidney pie. Other traditional English fare includes fish-and-chips, beef ribs with barbecue sauce, and Manchester Wellington—ground chuck swaddled in ham and puff pastry and finished with béarnaise sauce. With the kitchen open until 1AM most nights (until midnight on Sundays), this is a great place for a late snack of sausage-stuffed mushrooms, French onion soup, or baked brie. ♦ English ♦ M-F lunch and dinner; Sa-Su brunch and dinner. 2942 Lyon St (between Greenwich and Lombard Sts). 921.6664; fax 921.1019

3 Sue Fisher King This is the place for beautiful, expensive linens, wonderful plates, and glass- and tableware. One area is devoted to hotel silver, many in classic Deco designs; there's also a collection of unusual napkin rings. Watch for announcements of sales—the buys can be great. ♦ M-Sa. 3067 Sacramento St (between Broderick and Baker Sts). 922.7276; fax 922.9241 &

3 Virginia Breier Whimsical, unique artwork is this shop's claim to fame. Some of the found-object sculptures incorporate silverware; shoppers with more traditional tastes will find incredible one-of-a-kind plates, cups, and saucers. ♦ M-Sa. 3091 Sacramento St (at Baker St). 929.7173; fax 929.7173 &

American Pie

4 American Pie This general store displays candles in an unimaginable range of colors. A candy counter at the back features hard candy, coffee beans, and candy cordials. ♦ Daily May-Oct; M-Sa Nov-Apr. 3101 Sacramento St (at Baker St). 929.8025 &

5 The Heights ★★★$$$ Chef Charles Solomon made a name for himself in New York before moving west and opening a charming restaurant in a converted house. One dining room faces the street, the other two overlook a garden. The decor is simple and pleasant; the chairs are slipcovered either in an attractive green linen, or patterned with black-and-white artichokes. Solomon is truly a genius at creating vibrant, light combinations for his à la carte and fixed-price menus, which change weekly. One perennial is a braised organic-vegetable pot-au-feu. In another innovative twist, he teams rich foie gras with sweet scallops, braised artichokes, and balsamic vinegar. Chunks of lobster sit on a bed of hedgehog mushrooms, served with a Port wine and balsamic vinegar sauce. Dish after dish comes out a masterpiece, even dessert, which might be an apple napoleon with green apple sorbet. ♦ French/ Californian ♦ Tu-Su dinner. Reservations recommended. 3235 Sacramento St (between Lyon St and Presidio Ave). 474.8890; fax 474.1713

6 Ella's ★★★$ Line up here on weekends for one of the best brunches in San Francisco. It's a comfortable place with an open kitchen, a dining counter that's always bedecked with fresh flowers, and simply set, closely placed tables. The housemade sticky buns alone are worth a visit. Other noteworthy items include chicken hash, buttermilk pancakes, and the fresh punch of ginger and orange juice. All the baking is done in-house. The lunch menu ranges from grilled fish of the day and chicken potpie to a warm spinach salad with bacon, mushrooms, and a sherry vinaigrette. ♦ American ♦ M-F breakfast, lunch, and dinner; Sa-Su brunch. 500 Presidio Ave (at California St). 441.5669

7 Forrest Jones A pioneer in the housewares industry, this 20-year-old shop was the first retail outlet for Calphalon pots and pans. The aisles are crammed with Chinese pots, lamps,

187

The Richmond/Presidio Heights

kitchen towels, dishes, kitchen equipment, and a variety of other high-quality but reasonably priced goods. ◆ Daily. 3274 Sacramento St (at Presidio Ave). 567.2483; fax 567.7604

8 Garibaldis ★★$$$ This charming neighborhood restaurant has an understated beige-and-white decor and windows that open onto Presidio Avenue. Great appetizers include grilled radicchio; fat crab cakes; and green beans sautéed with pancetta, garlic, hot chili oil, and oyster sauce. Burgers, skirt steak, and a Mediterranean lamb tenderloin marinated in Zinfandel are always good choices, and grilled salmon makes frequent appearances in different guises. Pastas comprise a large part of the menu, but they can be oversauced and overcomplicated with too many ingredients. ◆ Californian ◆ M-F lunch and dinner; Sa dinner; Su brunch and dinner. 347 Presidio Ave (at Sacramento St). 563.8841; fax 563.1227 &

9 Ken Groom's Dogs and cats deserve gourmet treats, too, so don't overlook this chic pet shop, which carries Bowser Brittle, Haute Canine Gourmet dog cookies, and huge, bone-shaped biscuits with oatmeal and raisins. There's also a selection of lead-crystal Waterford-inspired dishes for the truly pampered pooch. ◆ M-Sa. 3429 Sacramento St (between Walnut and Laurel Sts). 673.7708 &

10 Tuba Garden ★$ Popular for brunch, this place conjures sunny days and gracious living amid foggy weather. The hand-painted mural of a garden, fresh flower arrangements, and windows overlooking the patio create an alfresco atmosphere that's the next best thing to sitting outside on the terrace here. The menu offers plenty of sandwiches, soups, and large salads. Try the substantial onion soup or a robust consommé with cheese-filled ravioli. Spinach salad, heaped with tender green leaves, is sprinkled with bacon and egg. Daily specials include a fish dish, perhaps grilled halibut with creamed spinach. A good selection of wines by the glass is offered, or opt for the excellent cinnamon-scented iced tea or the refreshing iced coffee. ◆ American ◆ M-F lunch; Sa-Su brunch. 3634 Sacramento St (between Locust and Spruce Sts). 921.8822; fax 381.1447

An immigrant Chinese cook in San Francisco invented the dish that is called a Denver sandwich west of the Mississippi and a Western sandwich in the eastern US. Recipe: In a little oil, sauté some chopped ham with finely chopped onion and green bell pepper. Add one beaten egg and cook until set, turning once. Serve between two pieces of toast with a little ketchup.

---

10 Tortola ★★$ Healthful and tasty Southwestern and Mexican fare is the specialty of this casual place, which has spun off four quick-service shops in Northern California. It offers burritos, tostadas, and tacos with various fillings, but is known for its "cup tamale," a fresh *masa* (pasta) shell filled with chicken, moistened with a smoky chili sauce, and topped with black beans and salsa. Sausages from the Yucatán are mildly spiced with chilies and garlic and served with grilled polenta and black beans. Also try the stewlike Santa Fe pork, which wins the most accolades. ◆ Southwestern/Mexican ◆ Tu-Sa lunch and dinner; Su dinner. 3640 Sacramento St (between Locust and Spruce Sts). 929.8181; fax 929.8181 &

Rosmarino
RESTAURANT

11 Rosmarino ★★$$ Tucked away behind two buildings, this restaurant boasts a pretty, ivy-trimmed patio. Inside, the focal point is a whimsical metal sculpture of the Golden Gate Bridge and the city that stretches along one wall. Unfortunately, frequent changes in the kitchen make the food unpredictable, although ricotta gnocchi are always on hand, accompanied by various seasonal toppings. Other Italian-inspired dishes include whole sea bass rubbed with thyme and olive oil and sprinkled with orange zest and *niçoise* olives. Dessert might be a fresh-fruit crumble or buckwheat crepes bulging with fruit and served with a scoop of housemade ice cream. ◆ Mediterranean ◆ Tu-Sa lunch and dinner; Su brunch. 3665 Sacramento St (between Locust and Spruce Sts). 931.7710; fax 931.5013

11 Magic Flute $$ The best features of the dining experience here are the cozy French ambience and the outdoor patio. The service adds a warm note, too; it's professional and efficient without being pretentious. On recent visits the food was mediocre, but one dish always worth ordering is the polenta lasagna, which changes nightly; sandwiched between layers of polenta may be fillings of duck, ricotta, greens, tomatoes, and a mix of herbs, all topped with cheese. The Caesar salad is a good way to begin, but the desserts consistently disappoint. ◆ Italian/American ◆ M-F lunch and dinner; Sa dinner. 3673 Sacramento St (between Locust and Spruce Sts). 922.1225; fax 922.1225

12 Eppler's/Fantasia Once a magical name in San Francisco pastry making, **Fantasia** was bought several years ago by **Eppler's,** a high-volume, American-style bakery. However, the store continues to produce some of **Fantasia**'s most popular cakes, including espresso torte, "Ecstasy" (a flourless chocolate cake made with ganache), Black Forest cake, Grand Marnier Sacher torte, and "Better-than-sex," containing a layer each of dense chocolate, truffle cream, and chocolate ganache, all topped with a layer of fudge. Most of the other baked goods, including the Danish pastries and cookies, are **Eppler's** recipes. ♦ Daily. 3465 California St (at Locust St). 752.0825; fax 752.1251 &

12 Wine Impression The majority of the stock at this high-end wine store isn't on display; it's in a 10,000-bottle warehouse. There John Brennan, the fine-wine specialist and one of the owners, stores every vintage of BV Private Reserve dating back to 1936; other California wines date to 1890. The French collection begins with the 1870 vintage. These rare wines can be in the customer's hand within 24 hours. The store prides itself on having extraordinary wines from around the world at exceptional values. Within the shop is a display of incredible wines by varietal at very reasonable prices, as well as up to 50 single-malt scotches and as many Cognacs—and the selection nearly triples during holidays. ♦ Daily. 3461 California St (at Locust St). 221.WINE; fax 221.5505 &

12 Bryan's Since 1963, when it opened in **Cal-Mart** (see page 190), this meat market has catered to the carriage trade. It has since relocated to a freestanding space in the same shopping center, but still draws well-heeled customers looking for something special. The butchers are knowledgeable about Midwestern beef, milk-fed veal, foie gras, and such game as pheasant, squab, guinea hen, and free-range geese. This is also the only place in the city that stocks Prime grade beef, and sushi-grade *ahi*, Dover sole from France, and Russian caviar can be found in the fish department. And homemade stocks and *demi-glace* (rich brown sauce) are popular with home cooks trying to prepare a gourmet meal in a hurry. ♦ M-Sa. 3473 California St (at Locust St). 752.3430; fax 752.0714 &

13 Judith Ets-Hokin's Home Chef This comprehensive one-stop shop for the budding or experienced cook has been in business since 1972. In addition to a vast range of cookware, it offers classes in its fully equipped kitchen; enrolled students receive a 10 percent discount on their purchases. And on the first Monday of each month, customers can trade in old knives, pots, pans, and bakeware for discounts up to 20 percent on new Home Chef knives, All-Clad, Calphalon, and Zani cookware, and Kaiser LaForme bakeware. ♦ Daily. 3525 California St (between Locust and Spruce Sts). 668.3191; fax 668.0902 & (classes not &)

The Richmond/Presidio Heights

Sourdough Starter

San Franciscans lay such possessive claim to sourdough bread that many visitors assume it originated here. But the truth is the ancient Egyptians actually whipped up the first batch more than 4,000 years ago. Columbus supposedly carried a sour starter on his voyage to America, and the Pilgrims routinely used sour starters in bread making.

When commercially available yeasts and baking powders began to be produced in the 19th century, sour starter fell out of favor. The starter, a combination of fermented flour, water, and sugar that makes the dough rise, had to be sustained from batch to batch. Once cooks could readily purchase yeast and baking powder, the use of sour starters was limited to folks who lived far from settlements. During the Alaskan Gold Rush in the 1890s, for instance, prospectors used sour starters so extensively they earned the nickname "sourdoughs." Since many set sail for Yukon goldfields from San Francisco, the bread became linked with the city.

Although it is possible to bake sourdough bread anywhere, San Franciscans maintain that the flavor of their loaves cannot be duplicated. Chef and cookbook author Bernard Clayton, determined to test this chauvinistic assertion, imported samples of San Francisco starter to his home in Bloomington, Indiana. Each time, however, no matter how carefully he tried to preserve the integrity of the starter, the batch metamorphosed into what he called "Bloomington sourdough bread," which had a distinctly different flavor. "I came to appreciate," he finally lamented, "that to bake San Francisco sourdough bread consistently I would probably have to live there."

This view may actually have a scientific basis. In his book *On Food and Cooking—The Science and Lore of the Kitchen,* author Harold McGee says that the "mother dough," or starter, eventually becomes dominated by the microflora characteristic of the area it comes from. According to McGee, Bay Area scientists have concluded after extensive lab analysis that the acid in San Francisco sourdough is produced by a bacteria found only here (they even dubbed it *Lactobacillus sanfrancisco*).

In 1849 Isadore Boudin first fired up his ovens on **Grant Avenue,** and the bread his namesake bakery produces is still a star; **Boudin** presently makes 12,000 loaves of sourdough a day. Several years ago, in a taste test by the *San Francisco Chronicle*, **Boudin** was the winner among all commercially produced sourdoughs, followed by **Colombo** and **Francican,** the two other brands available in just about every shop at **Fisherman's Wharf** and at area airports. Recently, a number of smaller bakeries have come on the scene. **Acme,** which has its roots in **Chez Panisse,** has set the standard for crusty, rough-textured loaves; other bakeries that have won loyal followers include **Bread Workshop, Grace Baking, Semifreddi's, Metropolis, Tassajara,** and the **Italian/French Bakery.** Most of these breads are widely available throughout the Bay Area.

189

The Richmond/Presidio Heights

13 Cal-Mart A cruise down the aisles reveals that this is no run-of-the-mill supermarket. It's where the elite meet (or at least their maids do). The store has a fine selection of staples, and the produce section carries such items as lemon cucumbers and fava beans. The meat market offers a good selection of veal, including shanks for osso buco. Fresh bread comes in regularly from the best bakeries in San Francisco. There are also about two dozen olive oils, as well as walnut, hazelnut, almond, and avocado oils, every kind of vinegar, and endless rows of specialty jams, jellies, and packaged products. ♦ Daily. 3585 California St (at Spruce St). 751.3516; fax 751.2744

14 Ton Kiang ★★$ The long menu specializes in the food of China's Hakka region, but is rounded out with Cantonese and northern Chinese selections; the waiters will helpfully lead you through it all. Best bets are the claypot dishes: braised pork in a rich sauce lightened with tofu and vegetables, or delicious squares of pork-stuffed tofu stewed with carrots, celery, and pieces of pork. Other excellent choices include salt-baked chicken, served in a vinegar sauce with chilies and garlic, and wonderful fish balls, lightly seasoned and finely textured. A low brick building houses the two large dining rooms, which are brightly lit and separated from the kitchen by fish tanks. Tablecloths soften the look at dinner. A more elaborate sister restaurant, with the same name, serves dim sum (see page 197). ♦ Chinese ♦ Daily lunch and dinner. 3148 Geary Blvd (at Spruce St). 752.4440. Also at: 5821 Geary Blvd (at 22nd Ave). 386.8530

15 Straits Café ★★$$ Hairstylist-turned-cook Chris Yao has crafted a unique menu of foods from Singapore. For example, he stuffs trout with lemongrass and other herbs, wraps it in a banana leaf, then grills the package. The herbs and smoke permeate the fish, making for a complex combination of flavors. Whole okra is cooked in a slightly spicy chili sauce with dried shrimp—an earthy, unusual taste. And don't miss the curry dishes, especially the chicken version. The dining room evokes a village courtyard; there's a mural of houses with shutters and ornate roof ornaments and, draped across it, a real clothesline with baby clothes. ♦ Singaporean/Chinese ♦ Daily lunch and dinner. 3303 Geary Blvd (at Parker St). 668.1783; fax 668.3901

16 Mel's Drive-In ★$ A branch of this chain of glitzy diners (another is in the Marina district), it appeals to kids and those who once used "neat" to mean "cool." The fare includes respectable hamburgers and fries, sandwiches, meat loaf, pork chops, chicken-fried steaks, salads, and all the breakfast standards. Small jukeboxes sit on almost every table and dot the bowling alley–length counter. ♦ American ♦ Daily breakfast, lunch, and dinner. No credit cards accepted. 3355 Geary Blvd (at Stanyan St). 387.2244; fax 387.1259. Also at: 2165 Lombard St (between Fillmore and Steiner Sts). 921.3039; fax 921.3521

17 Pat O'Shea's Mad Hatter ★★$$ Don't be intimidated by the sign out front that says, "We cheat tourists and drunks." This popular, convivial Irish pub serves some of the best lunches in the city in a room chock-full of television sets and sports paraphernalia. Renowned chef Nancy Oakes of the glitzy **Boulevard** got her start here. Tony Ngo, then her sous-chef, now works the kitchen, turning out roast salmon on a bed of mushrooms infused with a tarragon vinaigrette; leg of lamb with pearl onions, fennel, and potatoes au gratin; and homey chicken potpie and pot roast with mashed potatoes. Dinner entrées include pan-seared duck breast and Louisiana gumbo. And the crème brûlée in this drinkers paradise is much better than average. ♦ American ♦ M-F lunch and dinner; Sa-Su brunch and dinner. 3848 Geary Blvd (at Third Ave). 752.3148; fax 751.2285

18 Le Soleil ★★$ This Vietnamese spot extends a warm family welcome amid pleasant surroundings. Tables are dressed with gray cloths and napkins, the walls with muted pink-and-aqua–striped wallpaper. The terrific appetizers include the chicken salad—a mound of steamed meat with a tangle of cabbage, carrots, and browned garlic—and the flavorful marinated-beef salad. Another top starter is the do-it-yourself imperial rolls: You roll up rice noodles, cilantro, mint, and fish sauce in lettuce leaves then bite into their excitingly varied tastes and textures. For main courses, try the aromatic five-spice chicken; spicy lemongrass chicken accented with citrus; or crunchy fried egg noodles topped with shrimp, chicken, mushrooms, sugar snap peas, carrots, and other vegetables. With more than 60 dishes on the menu, however, the kitchen is bound to have a weakness: It's seafood. ♦ Vietnamese ♦ Daily lunch and dinner. 133 Clement St (between Second and Third Aves). 668.4848; fax 751.2616

190

The Richmond/Presidio Heights

ALAIN RONDELLI
SAN FRANCISCO

19 Alain Rondelli ★★★★ $$$ Chef Alain Rondelli arrived in San Francisco from France with impressive credentials. He had worked for six years in Marc Meneau's three-star restaurant, cooked at Palais de L'Elysée (the French White House), and been executive chef at Le Mas de Chastelas in Saint-Tropez. However, San Francisco so captivated him that he gave up his quest for Michelin stars and took a job at **Ernie's**. Three years later he opened this intimate 48-seat establishment. The simple decor, with warm, gold-glazed walls and upholstered banquettes, provides a serene stage for Rondelli's creations. His changing menu features a half-dozen appetizers and as many main courses. Pears and roquefort with Champagne vinegar and black pepper make a stunning starter, as does foie gras molded around a black Mission fig and served with warm brioche. Monkfish is wrapped in bacon and accompanied by a fava bean puree punched up with sage and lemon; a gutsy braised pork shank may be treated to a ragout of leeks and onions in a vinegar and juniper-berry broth. Desserts are often preceded by a pink, billowy cone of cotton candy. Fantastic finales include warm chocolate cake with pecan pralines and citrus granita accented with thyme and black pepper and served with lemon macaroons. Six-, nine-, and 20-course tasting menus are available by prior arrangement. This is serious eating. ◆ French ◆ T-Su dinner. Reservations recommended. 126 Clement St (at Second Ave). 387.0408

20 Murasaki ★★★ $ Chef/owner Toshi Sasaki works with quiet intensity at this comfortable restaurant favored by local sushi chefs. He produces some of the freshest sushi in the city, including mellow *hamachi* (yellowtail) with its silken texture, more strongly flavored *saba* (pickled mackerel), and cake-cured velvety salmon. What also makes the sushi so wonderful is the perfect rice that has enough stickiness to hold the grains together, yet is not starchy or mushy. Other menu items include tempura and deep-fried, soft-shell crabs in season. The simple decor features white, battened walls, a well-worn carpet, and chairs adorned with cartoon characters. There are even pictures of Sasaki's children on the walls behind where he produces his wonders, and on slower nights you'll find his family here enjoying the fruits of his labors. ◆ Japanese ◆ Daily dinner. 211 Clement St (between Third and Fourth Aves). 668.7317

21 Fountain Court ★★ $ The Shanghai-inspired fare here is a delight. A good way to start is with the Shanghai steamed buns, which are filled with ginger-laced pork and herbs and set on thin slices of cucumber in a bamboo steamer. Braised beef, served in half-moon slices, is redolent of five-spice powder, and lion's head is a well-executed classic: Five browned balls of ground pork are arranged over crunchy bok choy and a pool of intensely flavored meat sauce. Another standout is plump prawns combined with rice wine, garlic, ginger, and minced pork. The friendly host will guide overwhelmed diners through the long menu. The only drawback: the glaring lightbulbs; choose seats on the more subdued lower level, where large windows overlook the street. ◆ Chinese ◆ Daily lunch and dinner. Reservations recommended. 354 Clement St (at Fifth Ave). 668.1100; fax 668.1123

22 New Golden Turtle ★ $$ Once, this and its sister restaurant (the **Golden Turtle** on Van Ness Avenue, in Pacific Heights) were *the* outposts for the city's best Vietnamese food. But the owners sold this location about a year ago, and although the menu has remained the same, the food no longer rates as highly as that found on Van Ness Avenue. The best dishes are crisp imperial rolls and five-spice chicken. The interior is an exotic oasis of plants and bamboo appointments, including a bamboo ship on the wall. ◆ Vietnamese ◆ M dinner; Tu-Su lunch and dinner. 308 Fifth Ave (at Clement St). 221.5285

23 Happy Supermarket If the name doesn't make you smile, surely the ceiling-high selection of Asian products will. The aisles are packed with all kinds of ingredients—Chinese, Thai, and Filipino. The produce is pristine, including mustard greens with their yellow flowers intact, big water chestnuts, and delicate pea shoots. Fresh meat and fish are featured, and frozen foods include sausages, dim sum, and grated coconut. Also available are durian (whole or cleaned), green soy beans, an array of canned and powdered curries, and hundreds of sauces. ◆ Daily. No credit cards accepted. 400 Clement St (at Sixth Ave). 221.3195; fax 221.8137 &

In the late 19th century two exotic restaurants (now, unfortunately, defunct) opened in San Francisco. One was the Cobweb Palace, located down at Meig's Wharf at the foot of Powell Street. Owner Abe Warner served seafood in three dining rooms whose ceilings were festooned with cobwebs. Odder still was the Cabaret de la Mort, where guests were seated at empty coffins instead of tables and the dining room was illuminated by candles stuck in skulls.

191

The Richmond/Presidio Heights

24 Toy Boat Dessert Cafe ★★$ Children's delighted squeals fill this classic ice-cream and dessert parlor. Kids love climbing onto the mechanical prancing horse in the center of the room, and they can't resist the vast collection of playthings, ranging from nostalgic tin toys to newfangled rubber figures, including the Lion King. In addition to ice cream, there are coffee drinks and some killer desserts with adult appeal. Try the peanut-butter-and-chocolate-cookie sandwich; the good old-fashioned blackberry pie with a flaky crust; the Black Satin cake; or the mildly tart Key lime pie. ♦ Coffeehouse/Ice-cream parlor ♦ Daily. 401 Clement St (at Fifth Ave). 751.7505

24 Taiwan Restaurant ★★$ Don't miss the pork-filled boiled dumplings, roasted chicken, or lion's head (big pork balls in a clay pot with cabbage) among the Shanghai dishes available here. Another winner is wok-fried Shanghai noodles—fat, doughy noodles topped with strips of pork and other vegetables. (But the quality of the Taiwanese offerings has slipped a bit recently.) The small dining room, cast in shades of pink, is packed with tables and always busy, so the waiters move at a frantic pace. Expect a wait unless you go early or late. The Chinatown branch is generally less busy and the food is tastier. ♦ Chinese ♦ Daily lunch and dinner; F-Sa until midnight. 445 Clement St (at Sixth Ave). 387.1789 ♿. Also at: 289 Columbus Ave (at Broadway). 989.6789

25 Café Riggio ★$$ The main challenge here is getting in; no reservations are accepted for parties smaller than six, so patrons squeeze into a small bar area to wait. Once seated in the dining room—which is decorated with photos of Italy and light fixtures made of inverted terra-cotta flowerpots—they're served at a rapid clip. It's good, but maybe not worth the wait. Spinach salad topped with marinated squid is a nice starter. Follow with pasta or one of the half-dozen veal dishes, including scallopini topped with a mound of mushrooms infused with basil, garlic, and sun-dried tomatoes. ♦ Italian ♦ Daily dinner. 4112 Geary Blvd (at Fifth Ave). 221.2114; fax 387.9119 ♿.

25 Brothers Restaurant ★★$$ One of the best Korean places featuring tabletop barbecues, this dining spot offers a long list of grilling possibilities, including beef hearts. The kimchi, a spicy pickled cabbage that tests a Korean kitchen's mettle, is excellent here. If you're not up for do-it-yourself cooking, several hot and cold noodle dishes are available. ♦ Korean ♦ Daily lunch and dinner. 4128 Geary Blvd (between Fifth and Sixth Aves). 387.7991

25 Le Cyrano ★★$ A charming French restaurant with tieback curtains separating the dining areas, gleaming chandeliers, and an atmosphere that encourages conversation, it's a throwback to another era. But the food isn't tired, just a tad indulgent: Many sauces are lavished with butter and cream, bringing harmony to the dish and a smile to the face. With a nod to today's restraint, the menu also offers a number of low-fat choices. Most of the entrées are very reasonably priced, and for a slight additional charge, rich onion soup, house salad, and a choice of desserts are included. Best bets include rack of lamb marinated with juniper berries and served with hunter's sauce (wine, shallots, and herbs); red snapper poached in wine with mushroom cream sauce; frogs' legs with garlic and tomatoes; and sweetbreads with Madeira cream sauce. For dessert, go for the classic profiteroles or the ambrosial Grand Marnier soufflé—you won't be sorry. ♦ French ♦ Tu-Su dinner. 4134 Geary Blvd (between Fifth and Sixth Aves). 387.1090; fax 387.1090

26 Angkor Wat ★★$$ Established a decade ago, this is thought to be the first Cambodian restaurant in the US. And it still remains one of the best today. Start with the minted carrots with peanuts, pork, and shrimp in a lemon dressing; the vegetable soup, which gets added texture from toasted rice; or the Cambodian-style crepe, filled with chicken, shrimp, bean sprouts, and other vegetables. Main courses include a duck curry with undercurrents of tropical fruit, and a fiery lamb curry in a rich, red sauce. The grilled chicken, marinated overnight, also is outstanding. The dining room has an exotic, cavelike feel, enhanced by the handsome folk art collection and the Cambodian dancer who performs on a stage in the rear. ♦ Cambodian ♦ M-Sa lunch and dinner; Su dinner. 4217 Geary Blvd (at Sixth Ave). 221.7887; fax 221.4408 ♿.

27 Cinderella Restaurant and Bakery ★$ For more than 30 years, this has been touted as one of San Francisco's top Russian bakeries and restaurants. Top items include *pelmeny*, Russian ravioli stuffed with seasoned beef and served in a pleasant chicken broth; lamb with kasha; and stuffed peppers and cabbage. The soft-crusted

The Richmond/Presidio Heights

house-baked breads are excellent examples of the Russian baking style. There's often a wait, but never for too long. ♦ Russian ♦ Tu-Su lunch and dinner. 436 Balboa St (between Fifth and Sixth Aves). 751.9690 ♿

KATIA'S

28 Katia's ★★$$ Although it calls itself a Russian tearoom, it's actually a full-fledged restaurant, serving home-style food lightened with a Californian touch. Start with smoked salmon or piquant marinated mushrooms to wake up the palate. Then there's *pozharski* (a patty of herbed, minced chicken), sautéed and served with roasted potatoes; beef stroganoff rich with mushrooms; golden, flaky piroshki; and cabbage stuffed with beef and rice, baked in an intense tomato sauce. And don't miss the housemade dill pickles. Desserts—perhaps cheesecake or berry pudding—are uneven in quality. The service tends to be friendly but inefficient. Cheerful African violets are set on each white-clothed table, and mirrors expand the tiny room. The floor-to-ceiling windows in front are opened in warm weather. ♦ Russian ♦ Tu-Su lunch and dinner. 600 Fifth Ave (at Balboa St). 668.9292 ♿

29 Jakarta ★★$$ Charming and popular, this Indonesian restaurant is painted white, a dramatic backdrop for its folk-art collection of hand puppets, masks, and figurines. Tables set with batik place mats under glass, upholstered chairs, and a burgundy carpet make a pretty setting for the often fiery food. Crisp shrimp cakes studded with corn, bean sprouts, and chilies are an excellent way to begin. Main courses are divided into vegetarian dishes, grills, and fried and braised options, and the kitchen handles each technique with aplomb. Chicken is soaked in a spicy marinade to produce a tongue-tingling treat; rock cod, wrapped in banana leaves and grilled, boasts a moist, silken texture; and oxtails, infused with a chili-laced coconut-milk sauce, come out fork tender. ♦ Indonesian ♦ Tu-F lunch and dinner; Sa-Su dinner. 615 Balboa St (at Seventh Ave). 387.5225; fax 387.0233

30 Mandalay ★★$ Opened in 1984, San Francisco's first Burmese restaurant is still one of the best. The storefront surroundings don't add much to the dining experience, but the pleasant service and exotic food certainly do. In general, the Burmese specialties are much better than the Mandarin (Chinese) selections. Start with the tea salad—piles of green tea leaves, toasted lentils, ground shrimp, fried garlic, green pepper, and sesame seeds, all tossed tableside in a sprightly vinaigrette. A similar rendition substitutes shredded fresh ginger for the tea and is just as enticing. Other attractions: Burmese-style fish chowder, thick with coconut milk and noodles; Mandalay squid, served steamed on a bed of spinach; fried onions in a hot-and-sour sauce; and crisp, stir-fried green beans. ♦ Burmese/Mandarin ♦ Daily lunch and dinner. 4348 California St (at Sixth Ave). 386.3895; fax 386.3895 ♿

GREEN APPLE BOOKS

31 Green Apple Books Lavish displays of glossy books aren't this bookstore's forte, but it has one of the best selections of new and used cookbooks in the city. There's even a full shelf of classics, which might include *Thoughts for Buffets*, published in 1950, *The Home Dietitian's Cook Book*, published in 1938; or *Cooking For Two*, first published in 1909. ♦ Daily. 506 Clement St (at Sixth Ave). 387.2272; fax 387.2377 ♿

32 Richmond New May Wah Market A branch of the Chinatown **May Wah Market**, this supermarket likewise offers all the essential products for Chinese, Korean, and Thai cooking. Fish is arranged on tubs in front of the display case, making it hard for two people to squeeze by, and kimchi is dished up from open containers in the refrigerator case. The produce aisles hold roots and tubers (including lotus, sweet potatoes, and onions), plus huge bins of Thai purple basil, lemongrass, and other specialty herbs. ♦ Daily. 547 Clement St (near Sixth Ave). 668.2583; fax 666.3933 ♿. Also at: 1230 Stockton St (between Pacific Ave and Broadway). 433.3095; fax 433.7876 ♿; 2201 Irving St (at 23rd Ave). 665.4756 ♿

32 6th Avenue Cheese Shop Blue and white checkered curtains freshen this tiny shop, which has a small selection of cheese, all kinds of take-out salads and sandwiches, breads, and other gourmet products. A few small tables in the front are available for eating in-house. ♦ Daily. 311 Sixth Ave (at Clement St). 387.1436

Chicago may have deep-dish pizza but San Francisco has "It's It," an ice-cream sandwich made from oatmeal cookies dipped in chocolate. Created in 1928 at Playland-at-the-Beach (which was torn down in 1972 to make way for condominiums), It's It is now available commercially. There are four flavors in addition to the original vanilla (still the best): chocolate, mint, strawberry, and cappuccino.

The Richmond/Presidio Heights

HAIG'S
Middle Eastern Specialty Foods

33 Haig's Delicacies This 38-year-old shop is the place to go for Middle Eastern take-out treats—sheep's milk feta from three countries, piquant dolmas, hummus, excellent tahini, falafel and *kufta* (a spiced hamburger) sandwiches, coffees and teas, and a half-dozen phyllo desserts. Customers can also eat at one of the tables in the front. It also stocks such unusual products as pomegranate syrup (great for marinating ducks or pork, or for sprinkling on desserts) and packaged soups from Turkey. ♦ M-Sa. 642 Clement St (between Seventh and Eighth Aves). 752.6283 &

The Village Market

34 The Village Market A popular destination for the Pacific Heights/Presidio folks, this chic natural-foods market boasts a giant fountain at the entrance. It offers a variety of organic fresh and frozen fruits and vegetables, coffees, specialty mustards, canned truffles, and some organic wines. ♦ Daily. No credit cards accepted. 4555 California St (at Eighth Ave). 221.0445 &

35 San Francisco Chicken/New On Sang Market Here's a Chinese spin on fast food, and it's also a study in cultural amalgamation. The decor is Western, with ceramic tiles, neon logos, and illuminated menu boards. And a rotisserie turns out stupendous herb-crusted chicken, served with corn on the cob, Caesar salad, and baked beans. But other sections display bins of raw chicken parts, trays of Chinese stir-fried dishes, and ribs and ducks hanging on hooks. The focal point, however, is a whole suckling pig; the chef hacks off pieces to your specifications, and the pork has a marvelous crisp skin, robust taste, and succulent texture. Takeout is the mainstay here, although there are a half-dozen stools and a low counter for eating in-house. This place is under the same ownership as Chinatown's **New On Sang** market. ♦ M-F 11AM-9PM; Sa-Su 4-9PM. 617 Clement St (at Seventh Ave). 752.4100; fax 750.8242 &. Also at: 1114 Grant Ave (at Pacific Ave). 982.9228 &

35 Clement Restaurant $ The sign proclaims that this modest spot has the best pork buns in town. That's debatable, but they do make a great place to grab a snack while you explore the ethnic wonders of Clement Street. ♦ Chinese ♦ Daily breakfast, lunch, and dinner. 621 Clement St (between Seventh and Eighth Aves). 752.9520

36 Cafe Maisonette ★★★$$ Chef Ronald Tseng turns out impressive French fare in his shoe-box–size restaurant (there are just nine tables), decorated with skyblue walls, lace curtains, and a latticework ceiling. The soups are excellent, and the duck confit salad with tiny greens is a classic. Tseng prepares a perfect rack of lamb with a port-and-shallot *demi-glace*, drizzled with a creamy dressing of chopped mint and served with garlic-thyme potato pancakes, a specialty. Pork medaillons get a zing from green peppercorns and mustard, and chicken is rolled around a spinach stuffing before being roasted to bronze perfection. Generally, a choice of two desserts is offered, perhaps truffle cake with Grand Marnier or a fresh fruit torte. And Tseng often presents each departing diner with a small box containing a triangle of rich chocolate cake. ♦ French ♦ Tu-Su dinner. Reservations recommended. 315 Eighth Ave (between Geary Blvd and Clement St). 387.7992

37 Clement Street Bar and Grill ★$$ In traditional San Francisco fashion, this grill has a masculine ambience, with dark wood paneling and white tablecloths. In addition to the simple grilled meats, poultry, and seafood it's one of the few places in the neighborhood that serve such creative pastas as rigatoni with fresh tuna, roasted peppers, and tomatoes, and asparagus ravioli with spinach, garlic, and parmesan. ♦ American ♦ Tu-F lunch and dinner; Sa-Su brunch. 708 Clement St (at Eighth Ave). 386.2200

38 Seafood Center On any given day, the dozen enormous fish tanks here are packed with live fish, shellfish, turtles, and frogs. There also are periwinkles, Manila and cherrystone clams, and green-lipped mussels, all at much-lower-than-supermarket prices. Iced and refrigerated cases hold octopus, Hawaiian *hasa hasa,* and other whole and filleted fish. ♦ Daily. No credit cards accepted. 831 Clement St (between Ninth and 10th Aves). 752.3496; fax 752.3518 &

39 Singapore Malaysian ★$ Malaysian food is quite distinct from other Asian cuisines, but it's not well represented in the United States. That's why this tiny restaurant is such a treat. It's known for its salad of fruit and vegetables, which is tossed in a dressing spiced with fermented shrimp, chilies, and sesame seeds. Green beans are sautéed until crisp with a fiery mixture of chilies, herbs, and spices, an interesting variation on a standard Chinese dish. Rice noodles, another specialty, are sautéed with any number of ingredients. ♦ Malaysian ♦ M, W-Su lunch and dinner. 836 Clement St (between Ninth and 10th Aves). 750.9518

The Richmond/Presidio Heights

CORIYA

39 Coriya ★★$ One of the area's newest restaurants, this Korean cook-it-yourself place was packed from opening day. Mirrored walls, white tile floors, and black accents give it a bright and modern appeal. Each table is equipped with a burner, a hot pot of steaming water, a foil-covered tray for sautéing, and a strong vent to disperse the cooking smoke. Diners line up at the all-you-can-eat buffet to choose their ingredients from the heaps of raw seafood, meat, poultry, eggs, vegetables, and condiments. It's amazingly inexpensive, and it's fun creating your own dishes. If you don't like the results, you know who's to blame. ♦ Korean ♦ Daily dinner. 852 Clement St (at 10th Ave). 387.7888 &

40 Royal Thai ★$ Although many claim this to be the city's best Thai restaurant, it's not nearly as good as the original outpost in San Rafael. The kitchen washes many of the dishes in sweetness and tones down the spicing. But all the standards are here, including chicken and coconut-milk soup; chicken with basil; and Thai crepe, an airy pancake filled with shrimp, pork, peanuts, and tofu. Regulars also like the pad thai and the green papaya salad with green beans, carrots, and peanuts. The room is divided into a bar and dining areas; tables by the windows are best. ♦ Thai ♦ M-F lunch and dinner; Sa-Su dinner. 951 Clement St (at 11th Ave). 386.1795 &

41 Boudin Bakery One of the best-known bakery chains in the Bay Area, it started at this modest location with a retail shop in front and the plant in back. The sourdough bread is a classic; also not to be missed is the *pain au chocolat,* a buttery croissant that is loaded with chocolate. Just skip the weak, bitter coffee. ♦ M-Sa. No credit cards accepted. 399 10th Ave (at Geary Blvd). 221.1210; fax 221.3854 &. Also at: 157 Jefferson St (between Mason and Taylor Sts). 928.1849; fax 776.1778; 619 Market St (between New Montgomery and Third Sts). 281.8200 &

Heavenly Hot Restaurant
天珠子
麻辣涮烤自助火鍋城

42 Heavenly Hot ★$$ Specializing in *shabu shabu* (the cook-it-yourself hot pots), this tiny, popular Korean place was originally owned by the same people who run **Coriya**. Its booths are separated by light wood screens that look like a cross between Korean and Craftsman. The buffet line is stocked with raw fish, meat, and vegetables; diners make their selections, take them back to the table, and cook them all up in a copper pot. Some tables are also equipped with an aluminum-foil tray for sautéing. ♦ Korean ♦ Daily lunch and dinner. 4627 Geary Blvd (between 10th and 11th Aves). 750.1818 &

43 Chiang Mai Thai ★★$$ Silk plants and flowers splash color all over this Thai cafe, where each table is set with a bright bouquet of silk posies. Other adornments include a rose-colored ceiling, intricate wood detailing, and paned windows in back that reveal a fountain and lush greenery. The food is fresh-tasting, too. The kitchen produces standard Thai dishes and isn't afraid to use spices liberally: Green-curry chicken, smoothed with coconut milk, is fiery enough to clear the sinuses. The sautéed ground pork is served in a bowl, accompanied by cooling cucumber slices. Beef salad, another standard menu item, has a wonderful balance of flavors and leans toward the savory rather than the sweet. Plus, the service is unusually accommodating. ♦ Thai ♦ M-F lunch; daily dinner. 5020 Geary Blvd (between 14th and 15th Aves). 387.1299

43 House of Bagels Popular for more than 30 years, this resembles a bakery warehouse, piled high with bags of bagels. In addition to the dozen or so kinds of bagels, it sells good bread, including egg twists, whole wheat, and corn. ♦ Daily. No credit cards accepted. 5030 Geary Blvd (between 14th and 15th Aves). 752.6000; fax 752.6003 &

44 Kabuto Sushi ★★★$$ By most accounts, this is the top place for sushi in the entire city; it's certainly the most entertaining and friendly sushi bar around. Owner Sachio Kojima and his young assistant are in constant motion, and the best views are from the long, curved counter (there is also table seating). Kojima always offers diners a complimentary tidbit, perhaps a bowl of cooked tuna pieces. Barbecued eel is served piping hot, and conch, cooked in its shell in a sake broth, is brought flaming to the table. Everything is fresh as can be. Among the exceptional offerings are white tuna and the flying-fish roe served with a raw quail egg nestled in the middle. A full Japanese menu is also available, but sushi is the main attraction. Upon leaving, you'll get a bow and a warm goodbye from the staff. ♦ Sushi/Japanese ♦ Tu-Su dinner. 5116 Geary Blvd (at 15th Ave). 752.5652; fax 668.0149

44 Shenson's The oldest Jewish deli in San Francisco, it's been around since 1933. The corned-beef sandwiches and egg creams are winners, and the dill pickles and pickled green tomatoes are the best in town. The deli also offers housemade soups and entrées for takeout, as well as frozen kreplach (chewy dumplings) for you to use in your own

The Richmond/Presidio Heights

chicken soup. ♦ Daily. 5120 Geary Blvd (between 15th and 16th Aves). 751.4699; fax 751.4794 ♿

45 Mike's Chinese Cuisine ★$$ Once considered one of the city's best Cantonese restaurants, this softly lit, pleasantly sleek place now seems somewhat generic and Americanized. But the roasted chicken is still not to be missed, with a crispier skin and a saltier, more intense flavor than most. The egg rolls and Mongolian beef also are popular dishes. The longtime waiters can be a bit abrupt at first, but in the end they become quite endearing. ♦ Chinese ♦ M, W-Su dinner. 5145 Geary Blvd (between 15th and 16th Aves). 752.0120 ♿

46 Russian Renaissance Restaurant $$$ The walls and ceiling here are something of a landmark—and even worth a visit in themselves. They're covered with colorful murals depicting scenes from Russian folklore and history, a 14-year labor of love by artist Serge Smernoff. Unfortunately, the food is rather heavy. Among the specialties are chicken Kiev and veal scallopini with eggplant and mushrooms. All entrées include soup, salad, coffee, and dessert. ♦ Russian ♦ Daily dinner. 5241 Geary Blvd (at 17th Ave). 752.8558 ♿

47 Dragon House Restaurant ★$ The pink tablecloths don't do much to warm up this stark, linoleum place, but the Shanghai-style noodle soups here do the job just fine. The intensely flavored chicken broth contains long, slightly doughy noodles; the version that's also topped with shreds of pork and crunchy pickled vegetables is even better. Another winner is panfried noodles with mustard greens. There's also great-tasting bok choy sautéed with shiitake mushrooms and oyster sauce. ♦ Chinese ♦ Daily lunch and dinner. 5344 Geary Blvd (between 17th and 18th Aves). 751.6545

Hong Kong Flower Lounge Restaurant

47 Hong Kong Flower Lounge Restaurant ★★★$$ Among the best and prettiest of the Hong Kong–style restaurants, this branch of the decade-old place on the Peninsula is always bustling. Glazed green tiles and red swagged valences add a dash of style to the warren of rooms. Fish tanks in back display the daily seafood selection, but don't expect much help from the harried staff. Top menu choices are Peking duck; crab bathed in wine sauce; minced squab in lettuce cups; wok-charred calamari topped with fried peppers;

roast chicken; dry-braised green beans; and roast baby pig with pickled vegetables (a frequent special). ♦ Chinese ♦ Daily lunch and dinner. 5322 Geary Blvd (at 17th Ave). 668.8998; fax 668.0318 ♿

48 Joe's ★★$ A classic ice-cream parlor, this utilitarian place makes its own ice cream. The chocolate–peanut butter and the mocha–chocolate chip versions win raves, as do just about all of the 40 flavors. The root beer swirl, something like a frozen float, is worth the visit alone. Or bite into the "It's It," a big scoop of vanilla ice cream sandwiched between two oatmeal cookies, all coated with chocolate. There's also a grill here, so if you prefer savory to sweet, opt for a good hot dog, grilled cheese sandwich, or hamburger. ♦ Ice-cream parlor/American ♦ M-Th, Su until 10PM; F-Sa until 11PM. No credit cards accepted. 5351 Geary Blvd (at 18th Ave). 751.1950 ♿

49 Tip Toe Inn Many Russian families make an Easter tradition of a trip to this 35-year-old shop to purchase *kulich* (a tall, cylindrical Russian fruitcake). While they're here, they might also pick up bread and select from a case of frozen main courses and classic Russian favorites, many of which are produced on site. ♦ M-Sa. No credit cards accepted. 5423 Geary Blvd (at 18th Ave). 221.6422

49 Odessa One of the Russian delicatessens to spring up in the last few years, this bright, clean shop offers a broad array of individually wrapped Russian candies; the selection fills most of one wall. Other products include Russian mineral water, farmer cheese, very rich Russian-style yogurt, at least a dozen kinds of smoked fish, and *pelmeny*. Most of the staff speaks little or no English, so you may have to point to what you want. ♦ Daily. No credit cards accepted. 5427 Geary Blvd (between 18th and 19th Aves). 666.DELI; fax 666.3370 ♿

50 Moscow and Tbilisi Bakery On Sunday afternoons, when most bake shops are quiet, customers line up at this new Russian bakery. It turns out at least eight kinds of breads, cream puffs, and other confections, as well as sweet yeast rolls and piroshki. The display case at the entrance holds such savory deli items as pickled tomatoes and sour cabbage. ♦ Daily. No credit cards accepted. 5540 Geary Blvd (between 19th and 20th Aves). 668.6959 ♿

51 Laghi ★★★$$$ The spirit of a true Italian trattoria is captured at this corner storefront. (Just overlook the decor: The blue-heart ceiling borders would be more at home in a Midwestern country kitchen.) The short menu—only a few appetizers, four pastas, five main courses, and two desserts—changes nightly, and every item's a winner.

The Richmond/Presidio Heights

All pasta is made in-house. The polenta, topped with a variety of mushrooms, is smooth and creamy. Equally good entrées might be a combination of roast duck and venison topped with sliced portobello mushrooms, or wonderful oxtails braised in red wine. And the service couldn't be more convivial; chef/owner Gino Laghi makes the rounds to see if diners are enjoying their meal, and he basks in their praise. ♦ Northern Italian ♦ Tu-Su dinner. 1801 Clement St (at 19th Ave). 386.6266

52 Vegi Food ★$ No dairy, meat, onions, or garlic are served at this Chinese vegetarian eatery, but the food still has a rib-sticking quality. Dumplings are plumped with cabbage, braised eggplant acquires a meaty flavor from its rich sauce, and brown rice mixed with mushrooms is moistened with an explosively spicy curry sauce. One of the best dishes on the menu is fried walnuts coated with a delicate sweet-and-sour sauce studded with carrot coins, pineapple, and bits of tomato and bell pepper. The spicy fare cries out for beer, but soft drinks will have to do, there's no liquor license. The servers are friendly, but the spartan decor (brown paneling, Formica tables, bare floors) doesn't encourage lingering. ♦ Chinese/Vegetarian ♦ Tu-Su lunch and dinner. No credit cards accepted. 1820 Clement St (at 19th Ave). 387.8111

53 Israel Kosher Meats The only kosher meat market in San Francisco, it has a homey feel—just a bit frayed around the edges, with boxes stacked helter-skelter. Long a gathering place for the area's Russian-Jewish population, it also draws shoppers from all over the city. A complete line of fresh beef, chicken, and lamb is cut to order. A freezer case holds fish and all kinds of kosher convenience foods, including frozen dinners. The deli department features a number of sandwich meats, freshly prepared pierogi and kugel, as well as desserts like strudel. Also available are packaged products and kosher wines. ♦ M-F, Su. 5621 Geary Blvd (between 20th and 21st Aves). 752.3064 &

54 Vishal India Restaurant ★$ Chef Surinder Kuman worked at **Gaylord India Restaurant** before opening this place, where vegetarian dishes are among the best choices. Garlic nan, onion *kulcha* (onion-filled nan), *baigan bharta* (eggplant with potatoes and peas), and *saag paneer* (spinach with cheese) are all winners. From the tandoori oven come chicken wings and boneless chicken breast marinated in mint and cilantro; both are excellent. The restaurant stretches over three rooms; the blue walls are bedecked with sequined hangings depicting the Taj Mahal. ♦ Indian ♦ Daily lunch and dinner. 5625 Geary Blvd (between 21st and 22nd Aves). 751.2975; fax 751.2979

55 Ton Kiang ★★★$$ A dressier and more ambitious version of its sister restaurant of the same name (see page 190), this Hakka-inspired, Hong Kong–style eatery is adorned with light wood booths, rose-colored walls, Chinese lanterns, patterned carpets, and white tablecloths. The dim sum, particularly the Shanghai dumplings, are excellent, and the kitchen adeptly prepares vegetables, be they bok choy, spinach, or *ong choy* (Chinese watercress). An entire menu of specialties is offered at night, but the one-page "special menu" highlights the best bets, perhaps tender pea shoots (in spring), thin slices of geoduck sautéed with chives and bean sprouts, or fresh frogs' legs served with ginger and asparagus. The delicious salt-baked chicken is always available. ♦ Chinese ♦ Daily lunch and dinner. 5821 Geary Blvd (at 22nd Ave). 386.8530 &. Also at: 3148 Geary Blvd (at Spruce St). 752.4440

55 Thom's Natural Foods In business for over 30 years (at this location for about eight), this market carries a fine selection of produce, including such hard-to-find items as Spanish black radishes and burdock root, as well as cheese and fresh chickens. Sunflower meal, soya flour, and protein powder are bagged and stored in the refrigerator section. A staffer is generally on hand to provide nutritional information and help customers choose from the wide selection of vitamins and herb extracts. There is also an excellent collection of natural-foods books. ♦ Daily. 5843 Geary Blvd (between 22nd and 23rd Aves). 387.6367; fax 387.9215

SOCCA

56 Socca Restaurant ★★★$$ This charming restaurant is named after the chickpea cake sold on the streets in southern France. The green-and-yellow–striped walls, lapis-colored bar, and tile floor have a modern, warm feel, making the dining room a fine showcase for John Caputo, former chef at the tony Jordan Winery in Sonoma and sous-chef at **Campton Place.** Caputo's food is much more complex than one might expect at a neighborhood spot, and it's only gotten better with time. The changing menu might list rich goose confit, topped with a stack of beer-battered, fried green beans, all moistened with an earthy truffle vinaigrette. Grilled pork chops, accompanied by crispy potato pancakes and creamy leeks, are the best in town. Lamb shank, browned and glazed, is served in a shallow pool of white beans with carrot spears, parsnips, and celery. And the

The Richmond/Presidio Heights

trio of crème brûlées—lime, maple, and pumpkin—is a great way to end a meal. ♦ Mediterranean ♦ Tu-Su dinner. 5800 Geary Blvd (at 22nd Ave). 379.6720; fax 379.9666

57 Yet Wah ★$$ Several **Yet Wah**s are scattered around the Bay Area, but they are all under different ownership and offer very different dining experiences. This outpost offers larger quarters and a more civilized ambience than the popular Chinatown branch. Specialties on the menu here include glazed walnut prawns, scallops with ginger and garlic, chicken chow mein, and lemon chicken. ♦ Chinese ♦ Daily lunch and dinner. 2140 Clement St (between 22nd and 23rd Aves). 387.8040; fax 387.8333

58 La Belle Saison ★★$$ East meets West at chef Tadayuki Tani's welcoming corner restaurant. The onion soup is classic Paul Bocuse, topped with flaky puff pastry; the seafood salad falls in the Japanese camp, coming bathed in a dressing of plum paste, rice vinegar, miso, and olive oil (after all, a little Italian flair never hurt anyone). Duck breast is splayed on a plate drizzled with blackberry sauce; salmon is brightened with tarragon and truffles. For dessert, the poached pear is a work of fine art, a perfect pear half filled with ice cream, perched on a pool of berry sauce. The dining room's not fancy, but makes a comfortable setting for the innovative and surprisingly moderately priced fare. ♦ Eclectic ♦ Tu-Su dinner. 200 23rd Ave (at California St). 751.7066; fax 751.7074

59 El Chico Produce Market The produce spilling onto the sidewalk and the milling crowds give this shop a farmers' market ambience. At times, the quality of the produce can be a bit suspect, but prices are good, and there are always a few surprises, such as fresh horseradish and arrowroot. In addition to basic products and breads and pastries from **Cinderella Bakery** (see page 192), it sells ingredients for Russian, Mexican, and Chinese cooking. ♦ Daily. No credit cards accepted. 2214 Clement St (at 23rd Ave). 752.7372 ♿

60 Mescolanza ★★★$$ Squeezed into a block of Chinese restaurants, this homespun eatery is easy to miss, but it's worth seeking out for the delicious Italian food. The pizza's cracker-crisp crust doesn't need fancy toppings, and the gnocchi rivals any Italian grandmother's. Pastas are excellent, but the kitchen tends to ladle on too much sauce; if you prefer a bit more restraint, tell the waiters. Standouts among the meat courses are roast chicken and the veal with lemon and capers. The understated decor includes gray-blue walls adorned with plates and copper pots, blue-and-white checkered tablecloths, and a china cabinet near the entrance. ♦ Italian ♦ M-Sa dinner. 2221 Clement St (between 23rd and 24th Aves). 668.2221; fax 668.1905 ♿

NARAI RESTAURANT

60 Narai ★★$ Glass bricks separating the kitchen from the dining room and metallic wallpaper are attractive enough, but the food here is much more stylish than the decor. The kitchen turns out both Thai and Chiu Chow Chinese dishes. Among the Thai offerings are chicken and coconut-milk soup and *larb ped*, chicken infused with lime and chilies. One of the Chinese delights is pompano, lightly breaded with rice flour, deep-fried, and sprinkled with garlic. The crisp fish comes with a choice of sauces, of which the best is the zingy lemon; it's accented with diced chilies, bell peppers, and carrots. Another standout is duck simmered in a sweet soy-based sauce and served with a puckery vinegar sauce. To round out the meal, try the Chinese broccoli, cooked to a tender crunch and laced with a confetti of fried garlic and strands of smoked fish. Attention, adventurous dessert eaters: This is one of the few places to sample durian; a spiky fruit with a pungent smell, it's served with taro pudding. ♦ Chinese/Thai ♦ Tu-Su lunch and dinner. 2229 Clement St (between 23rd and 24th Aves). 751.6363 ♿

60 San Wang Restaurant Number 2 ★★$$ Hand-pulled noodles are the thing to order at this Chinese spot, one of the few places in the city serving these delicacies. The chef pulls, stretches, doubles, and slaps a mass of dough on a table until long noodle strands miraculously begin to form; the noodles are never cut with a knife. The menu also features excellent boiled dumplings, dry-braised shrimp, pork salad, and noodles and seafood tossed with pork. ♦ Chinese ♦ Daily lunch and dinner. 2239 Clement St (between 23rd and 24th Aves). 221.1870. Also at: 1682 Post St (at Laguna St). 921.1453

61 Khan Toke Thai House ★★★$$ Far and away the prettiest Thai restaurant in the city, it resembles a serene Thai temple. Diners leave their shoes at the entrance and are seated at low, intricately carved tables positioned over pits that accommodate their legs. The rich

198

The Richmond/Presidio Heights

wood paneling and ceiling work exhibit the best Thai craftsmanship, and the patio filled with blooming orchids lends a tropical feel to the place. Coconut-chicken soup is a velvety broth with succulent pieces of chicken and mushrooms; the prawn salad tastes intensely of lime and lemongrass, with just a touch of heat, creating a wonderfully balanced blend; and the duck salad has an earthy flavor and texture, thanks to the powdered rice that is sprinkled on top. An unusual main course is clear, chewy noodles tossed with Napa cabbage, celery, pork, shrimp, and squid in a faintly sweet sauce of pickled garlic. For dessert, have the fried bananas topped with a scoop of ice cream, which is decorated with cashews and currants. With its good wine list and food prices only slightly higher than at the city's more modest Thai places, this makes a fine setting for special occasions. ♦ Thai ♦ Daily dinner. 5937 Geary Blvd (between 23rd and 24th Aves). 668.6654; fax 386.1352

62 Bill's Place ★$ Incongruously, crystal chandeliers hover above this venerable greasy spoon known for its great hamburgers. They come in more than two dozen guises. The Carol Doda (named for a famous topless dancer) features two patties, side by side, each topped with an olive; the Red Skelton is daubed with condiments that make the burger look like a clown's face. Also available are a half-dozen chicken burgers, patty melts (cheeseburgers), hot dogs, and milk shakes. In good weather, eat on the patio in back. ♦ Hamburgers/American ♦ Daily lunch and dinner. 2315 Clement St (at 24th Ave). 221.5262

62 Jasmine House ★★★$ San Franciscans can get very passionate about good crab restaurants—and this Vietnamese place ranks high on nearly everybody's list. Among chef Nhan Nguyen's best creations is an authentic Vietnamese roast crab; the huge crustacean is quartered, then cooked in a butter and black pepper sauce. The result is heavenly. Another tasty item featured on the menu is barbecued catfish—its crackling skin caramelized from the heat of the grill—served with thin rice crepes and a dipping sauce of ginger, lemon grass, sugar, and fish. If you're unfamiliar with Vietnamese food, the staff is happy to assist you. ♦ Vietnamese ♦ Daily lunch and dinner. 2301 Clement St p(at 24th Ave). 668.3382

63 Hong Kong Villa ★★★$$ Those in the know here start with prawns, scooped from a three-tiered fish tank, quickly steamed to sweet succulence, and served with a scallion-flecked soy dipping sauce. They're so good that diners don't mind having to do the messy chore of removing the heads, peels, and tails. Black cod, also netted from the tanks, is served salt-baked or steamed in sweet rice wine. Seafood is the prime attraction here, but don't ignore the crispy fried chicken, the claypot dishes, and the vegetable stir-fries (especially when pea shoots are in season). To end the meal, try the sweet soup of the day, which might be taro with swirls of egg whites and flecks of fresh water chestnuts. The lighting from two crystal chandeliers is harsh, but the room is softened by white tablecloths and walls painted in mint green and blue with pink trim. ♦ Chinese ♦ Daily lunch and dinner. 2332 Clement St (at 25th Ave). 752.8833

63 25th & Clement Produce Market Top-quality produce is the hallmark at this market; the selection isn't vast, but it's well chosen and maintained. There are also breads from some of the best bakeries, plus other specialty and everyday products. ♦ Daily. 2354 Clement St (at 25th Ave). 387.8222; fax 387.2437

64 Courtyard Bar and Grill ★$$ Bamboo furniture, leafy palms, skylights, and steel beams crisscrossing the ceiling imbue this expansive restaurant with the feel of a woodland retreat. The new chef, Tim Whalen, has created a straightforward menu featuring lots of salads, pastas, and such dishes as chicken stuffed with ham, petrale sole stuffed with crab in a lobster cream sauce, and grilled filet mignon with béarnaise sauce. Sports fans happily gather around the bar's oversize video monitor to watch their favorite teams in action. ♦ Californian ♦ Daily lunch and dinner. 2436 Clement St (between 25th and 26th Aves). 387.7616; fax 387.6227

64 Greco-Romana ★★$$ Greek and Italian specialties are offered in a courtyardlike setting, with shuttered windows and flowerpot-filled balconies. Pizzas, tossed in the air and shaped before your eyes, are as good as the show. The thin crust is substantial enough to stand up to the dozen toppings, which include Canadian bacon with pineapple, and pesto with pine nuts and sun-dried tomatoes. Pasta with meat sauce and pasta shells with tuna are just as tasty. On the Greek side, just about any lamb dish is a winner; try the moussaka with ground lamb and eggplant, or the flaky *spanakopita* (spinach pie). ♦ Mediterranean ♦ Tu-Su lunch and dinner. 2448 Clement St (between 25th and 26th Aves). 387.0626; fax 751.1964

65 Blue Point ★★$$ This stylish restaurant (formerly *La Marmite*) is a welcome addition to the neighborhood. It has a sleek, sophis-

The Richmond/Presidio Heights

Now You're Cookin'

Not only is San Francisco one of the dining meccas of America, it's a leader in culinary education. One of the country's most renowned chef-training programs, **California Culinary Academy (CCA)**, is located here, as are plenty of places where the hobbyist cook can discover a few new tricks.

The **California Culinary Academy** offers several professional culinary programs. Founded in 1977 by Danielle Walker, the academy's emphasis is on classic and modern techniques with special attention to nutrition and culinary theory. The primary course is a 16-month, four-semester training program, and students partake in a one-month culinary "externship" (usually at a restaurant) during the senior term. The academy also features a Consumer Education Program with approximately 80 classes a year for novice and professional cooks, as well as a 30-week baking and pastry course. More than 20 professionally trained European, American, and Asian chefs are on staff here, plus a visiting faculty of local professionals.

To schedule a tour of the academy or receive a brochure, call or write: **The California Culinary Academy, School For Professional Chef Training,** 625 Polk St, San Francisco, CA 94102; 771.3536, 800/BAY.CHEF.

Draeger's Culinary Center, located on the top floor of a chic supermarket in Menlo Park (30 miles south of San Francisco), is exclusively for the enthusiastic amateur chef. All classes are demonstration only and usually last two to three hours. Most of the best Bay Area chefs and food professionals have taught here, including Hubert Keller from **Fleur de Lys,** Gary Danko from the **Ritz-Carlton's Dining Room,** Julian Serrano of **Masa's,** and authors Harold McGee (*On Food and Cooking*) and Joyce Jue (*Asian Appetizers* and *Wok and Stir-Fry Cooking*). Classes cover many ethnic cuisines and all categories of cooking—breads, pastries, appetizers, and so forth. For information, call or write: **Draeger's Culinary Center,** PO Box C, Menlo Park, CA 94026; 688.0688.

Judith Ets-Hokin's **HomeChef Cooking School** in **Presidio Heights** features a 13-week basic cooking course and a series of one- to four-week classes for the home cook: Quick and Easy Dinner Party, How to Choose a Wine You Like, Chinese Food that Heals, Light Cooking Basics, or Ravioli and Filled-Pasta Workshop, to name just a few. Emphasis here is on the science of cooking—why and how things work. Judith Ets-Hokin, who started the school in 1972, is the author of the *Dinner Party Cookbook* and *The Homechef, Fine Cooking Made Simple.* She holds certificates from cooking schools in England, France, and Italy. Contact: **HomeChef Cooking School, Laurel Center,** 3525 California St, San Francisco, CA 94118; 668.3191; fax 668.0902.

Sugar 'n' Spice Cake Decorating School, established in 1973, offers more than 50 courses a year in cake decoration and candy making. There are five-session programs in beginner, intermediate, and advanced cake decorating. Other courses—ranging from one to six classes—cover gum paste roses, Australian and Nirvana methods, writing and airbrush techniques, and confections for holidays and celebrations. In addition to Jeanne Lutz, a graduate of **Edith Gate's Cake Decorating School,** there are occasional guest instructors. It's also a great place to stock up on baking utensils. For information, call or write: **Sugar 'n' Spice Cake Decorating School,** 3200 Balboa St, San Francisco, CA 94121; 387.1722.

Tante Marie's Cooking School gives demonstration and participation courses for beginning to professional cooks in a charming storefront near Telegraph Hill. Mary Risley, who studied at Cordon Bleu and La Varenne, founded the school in 1979. Catherine Pantsios, who has graced the kitchens of several of the city's top restaurants, is the primary teacher, but Ms. Risley brings in guest faculty each season. Six-month career courses are offered twice a year, beginning in March and September. This program teaches the basic techniques of French cooking, pastries, desserts, and ethnic cuisines. There is also a six-month, part-time program designed to train pastry chefs. There are a number of options for the hobbyist chef: The Basics (six sessions); Mediterranean Light (a weekend workshop); and Chocolate, Chocolate, Chocolate (a three-day workshop), for example. Contact: **Tante Marie's Cooking School, Inc.,** 271 Francisco St, San Francisco, CA 94133; 788.6699.

The Richmond/Presidio Heights

ticated look, with walls the color of pale buttercups, rich mahogany chairs and tables, and a serene atmosphere. Chef Tony Batchon offers a refined menu of classic seafood dishes like plump oysters on the half shell; house-smoked salmon served with *lebanni* (a Middle Eastern yogurt cheese); pasta with sautéed clams, prosciutto, sweet peas, and cream sauce; grilled salmon with Chardonnay sauce; and crab cioppino. And there's a succulent rib eye steak splashed with olive oil for confirmed carnivores. ♦ Seafood ♦ Tu-Su dinner. 2415 Clement St (between 25th and 26th Aves). 379.9216

66 Mayflower Seafood Restaurant ★★★$$
The four-page menu is filled with many Chinese favorites, but the specialty here is seafood. For a good sampling, try the seafood dinner (for four people), which includes steamed crab in wine sauce, sautéed conch, and scallops with tender greens. Other recommended dishes are minced squab; shrimp accompanied by fried milk (cubes of milk curd that are crisp outside and barely set inside); sweet shrimp and deep-fried milk dumplings, with a silky interior; and roast chicken. Tapioca makes a warm, comforting finale. At lunch, there's excellent dim sum. Crystal chandeliers dominate the large room, making it brighter than day, whatever the hour. ♦ Chinese/ Seafood ♦ Daily lunch and dinner. 6225 Geary Blvd (at 27th Ave). 387.8338; fax 387.1769

67 Shanghai King ★$ Don't be put off by the gaudy gold exterior or by the baskets of artificial plants hanging from the ceiling inside: This place makes some of the best dumplings in the city. Shanghai steamed dumplings as well as the boiled version with hot-and-spicy sauce will satisfy the most persnickety palates. Twenty soups are also featured, as well as nine chow mein dishes and a dozen noodle preparations, all at ridiculously low prices. ♦ Chinese ♦ Daily lunch and dinner. 3038 Clement St (at 32nd Ave). 751.8866; fax 751.6368

68 Sugar 'n' Spice At this unique 21-year-old shop, Jeanne Lutz carries baking and cake decorating to a high art. She sells a hand-selected cache of baking books, more than a thousand cookie cutters, scores of plastic chocolate molds, tart pans, and piping bags and tips. There are dozens of food colors in the paste form used by professionals, as many different food extracts, and edible glitter in about a dozen colors. The shop is so crowded with merchandise that two people can barely fit in comfortably. An accomplished teacher, Lutz also offers classes on dessert decorating, which are held in an adjoining room; call for the schedule. ♦ M-Sa. 3200 Balboa St (at 33rd Ave). 387.1722; fax 387.7133 ♿

69 Salad Basket $$ Located in the two-story **Cliff House**, a tourist destination perched overlooking the ocean, this deli-style cafeteria has a standard array of sandwiches (turkey, roast beef), salads, and crab and prawn cocktails. Table service is also available. ♦ American ♦ Daily lunch and dinner. 1090 Point Lobos Ave (at Geary Blvd), Ground floor. 386.3330; fax 387.7837 ♿

Cliff House — Since 1850 — Where San Francisco Begins

69 Upstairs at the Cliff House ★$$
Omelettes are served here from early morning to mid-afternoon. Among the 20 different combinations are Joe's Special, with ground beef, spinach, and onions, and a seafood version with shrimp, scallops, and mushrooms. The lunch menu also includes hot Reuben sandwiches, burgers, and cold sandwiches filled with tuna-pecan salad and shrimp salad. ♦ American ♦ Daily breakfast, lunch, and dinner. 1090 Point Lobos Ave (at Geary Blvd), Second floor. 386.3330; fax 387.7837

69 Seafood and Beverage Co. ★$$$
The **Cliff House**'s flagship restaurant, it has 140 seats and a touch of just about every decorating style since Queen Victoria's reign. The eclectic look comes together pretty well, though, thanks to grand views of the Pacific. Appetizers are the best bet, especially the bay shrimp cocktail or fried calamari. Otherwise, stick to the simple grilled fish—fillet of sole, Pacific red snapper, or salmon. The kitchen tries hard, and the pleasant waiters don't rush diners, but the star attraction is the spectacular seascape. ♦ Seafood ♦ Daily lunch and dinner. 1090 Point Lobos Ave (at Geary Blvd), Ground floor. 386.3330; fax 387.7837

In the 1860s, Robert B. Woodward, a noted restaurateur, opened a resort called Woodward Gardens at 14th and Mission Streets. In addition to the extensive gardens and an art gallery, the resort featured a menagerie, a sea lion pond, and balloon ascensions. In 1994 a new Woodward Gardens Restaurant opened not far from the original resort, at 1700 Mission Street.

201

Beyond the Bridges

All the culinary wealth of the Bay Area isn't confined to San Francisco. In fact, **Chez Panisse**—the restaurant generally considered to be the birthplace of California cuisine—is in **Berkeley**, in the **East Bay**. Today the East Bay area, north of the city, is still on the gastronomic cutting edge, boasting exciting new restaurants, such as **Rivoli**—also in Berkeley—and dining spots with proven staying power, like **Bay Wolf** in **Oakland**. The East Bay is also more multicultural than San Francisco, hosting some of the best ethnic restaurants in the area, including **Ajanta Restaurant** in Berkeley and **Le Cheval Restaurant** and **Battambang** in Oakland. Just minutes from San Francisco across the **Bay Bridge**, Berkeley and Oakland are appropriate places to begin an exploration of restaurants beyond the city limits. Also nearby—just north of the **Golden Gate Bridge**—are the rolling hills and quaint towns of **Marin County**, a place synonymous with hot tubs and New Age thinking, perhaps because the terrain is so magical. Many of Marin's restaurants have wonderful outdoor decks, all the better to enjoy a climate that is more reliably sunny than the city.

Currently, the hottest area for new culinary ventures is the grapevine-covered

Napa Valley, less than 100 miles northeast of San Francisco. In the northern part of the valley, the **Culinary Institute of America** has recently opened a campus geared to food industry professionals at the former **Greystone** winery and established the **Wine Spectator Greystone Restaurant** here. Staffed by **CIA** graduates, this dining room is a pleasant place to enjoy a Mediterranean lunch or dinner. In addition, a number of famous chefs have moved to the county: Current local heroes include Joachim Splichal, whose new **Pinot Blanc** dining room has raised the level of culinary excellence in the Napa Valley; Jeremiah Tower, who opened **Stars Oakville Cafe**, an outpost of **Stars** and **Stars Cafe** in downtown San Francisco; Jan Birnbaum, who left **Campton Place** to try his hand at his native Cajun food at **Catahoula Restaurant and Saloon** in **Calistoga**; and Thomas Keller, who made his reputation at Checkers Restaurant in Los Angeles and Rakel in New York before taking over the ever-popular **French Laundry** in **Yountville**.

Sprawling **Sonoma County**, birthplace of the California wine industry, is home to much of the state's general farmland. Perhaps the two best known areas are **Sonoma Valley** (which runs roughly from the town of **Sonoma** to **Santa Rosa**), and **Russian River Valley**, whose hub is the little town of **Healdsburg**. Only about an hour from San Francisco, the region abounds with charming country restaurants, from the tiny **East Side Oyster Bar & Grill** in the town of **Sonoma**, to the standard-setting **John Ash & Company** in Santa Rosa, to **Willowside Cafe** in **Guerneville**, which showcases the incredible bounty of locally grown meat and produce.

These areas are generally relaxed and informal, and most of the restaurants here follow suit, so you don't need to dress up. Reservations, however, are suggested for the more popular places.

The East Bay

In addition to the legendary **Chez Panisse** in **Berkeley**, the East Bay is also home to many other excellent and popular restaurants. This area is accessible via **Bay Area Rapid Transit (BART)**, by ferry, and by car over the **Bay Bridge**. Our coverage begins in **Oakland**, moves to Berkeley, then north to **Marin**.

1 Battambang ★★★$ This modest little restaurant, located on the ground floor of a high-rise condominium complex in downtown Oakland, is not just the best *Cambodian* restaurant in the Bay Area; it's one of the Bay Area's best restaurants, period. Here, you can explore the wonders of Cambodian food, which is similar to Thai and Vietnamese cuisine (but less spicy). The best way to sample a cross-section of Cambodian dishes is to order the inexpensive "Special Combo," which consists of a generous portion of shredded chicken breast in a shredded cabbage salad served in a lime vinaigrette with fresh mint; red lemongrass soup with pineapple, chilies, and chicken chunks in a coconut milk broth; a plate with grilled chicken, pork, and beef, plus a skewer threaded with prawns and vegetables; and a mound of rice, dipping sauce for the meats, and house-fried soft rice noodles with vegetables on the side. All of the above items are also available as separate entrées. The staff is friendly and very helpful. ♦ Cambodian ♦ Daily lunch and dinner. 850 Broadway (at Ninth St), Oakland. 510.839.8815 &

2 Le Cheval Restaurant ★★★$ Twenty years ago, when US immigration laws were relaxed, large numbers of Vietnamese people settled in Oakland. Many of the newcomers established successful businesses here, revitalizing the area. Among them was the Tran family, whose two branches of **Le Cheval Restaurant** have popularized Vietnamese cuisine in Oakland. (They originally opened in a downtown location, but it was damaged by an earthquake, and they moved to this modern, comfortable eatery a few years ago.) The creative menu gives an Asian flavor to such familiar staples as poultry, beef, pork, seafood, and tofu. One top choice is *cha gio*, a crispy egg roll wrapper made from rice flour and filled with noodles, shredded vegetables, and pork. The proper way to eat this dish is to wrap pieces of the roll in lettuce and dip them in a rice vinegar sauce. Or try an entrée of lemongrass beef (lean steak panfried with lemongrass, onions, and a touch of curry), or either *pho* or beef noodle soup (which is large enough to make a tasty meal in itself). The prices are incredibly low, especially considering the large size of the portions.
♦ Vietnamese ♦ M-Sa lunch and dinner; Su dinner. 1007 Clay St (near 10th St), Oakland. 510/763.8495; fax 510/763.0555 &

Beyond the Bridges

3 Citron ★★★$$$ Chef/owner Craig Thomas created a stir when he opened this pretty and simply decorated cafe in 1991, because the food was so good. It still is: Although the menu offers only five appetizers and five entrées, they would all be excellent choices for a fine meal. Mussels get a lift from Pernod, fennel, leeks, and wild mushrooms; and puffy artichoke fritters are served with shaved fennel, olives, and a tangerine-flavored aioli. Follow with a Moroccan *tajine* (casserole) of prawns, scallops, tuna, and roasted tomatoes, served over couscous; beef daube with wild mushrooms and Swiss chard; or Atlantic cod wrapped in pancetta and served with peppers and winter greens. ♦ Mediterranean ♦ Daily dinner. 5484 College Ave (at Taft Ave), Oakland. 510/653.5484; fax 510/653.9915

3 Bay Wolf ★★★$$$ A few years after Alice Waters launched the culinary revolution in Berkeley with **Chez Panisse**, Michael Wild followed suit in Oakland. This charming restaurant, perfectly situated in a converted house, has dark wainscoting lightened by cream walls and bright artwork. The dining rooms on either side of the bar are a perfect setting for the food. Duck is one of Wild's specialties and has a permanent place on the menu, which changes weekly: It can be grilled with bacon, chanterelles, and peas; or served over pasta with okra, corn, bell peppers, and andouille sausage. Duck liver also plays a major role—it may appear warm, in a salad of dandelion greens and hazelnuts; or as an ethereal flan. Other excellent dishes include artichoke fritters with an herbed rice timbale, grilled salmon with sorrel sauce, and a pan-seared pork chop with sherry vinegar. Desserts of the day might be a lemon almond tart or chocolate pecan cake. The wine list boasts a few unusual labels (especially European). ♦ Californian ♦ M-F lunch and dinner; Sa-Su dinner. 3853 Piedmont Ave (between MacArthur Blvd and 40th St), Oakland. 510/655.6004; fax 510/652.0429 ♿

3 Oliveto ★★★$$ Paul Bertolli, who was the chef for a decade at **Chez Panisse**, is now a partner at this ever-popular restaurant. The Tuscan-inspired menu is alive with rustic, straightforward flavors; nothing can beat the tongue-of-fire beans (beans that look like they are painted with red flames), cooked to tenderness and flavored with a garlic-anchovy vinaigrette, and accented with thin shavings of parmesan cheese and a sprinkling of parsley. Another traditional Italian dish is chicken cooked under a brick, which somehow results in a perfect crisp skin and a succulent interior. Sliced leg of lamb may be served with a gratin of artichoke, potato, and leek, or with a watercress salad. The dessert offerings vary with the season: luscious strawberries and cream atop an old-fashioned biscuit, or caramelized mango upside-down cake, served with an extraordinary lime sorbet. There's a traditional dining room upstairs; downstairs is a more casual cafe with an open kitchen, rustic terra-cotta–colored walls, open-beamed ceiling, and windows that overlook one of the most jam-packed food shopping areas in the East Bay. (Be sure to stop by the **Market Hall** a few doors down where there are all kinds of wonderful fresh and prepared products for sale.) ♦ Californian ♦ M-F lunch and dinner; Sa-Su dinner. 5655 College Ave (at Shafter St) Oakland. 510/547.5356; fax 510/547.4624 ♿

4 Chez Panisse ★★★★$$$ This restaurant has been turning out a set rustic French/Italian–style menu for more than 20 years, and the packed house at each of the nightly four seatings is the best evidence of its lasting success. Owner Alice Waters's philosophy is to find the best and to present it as simply as possible, and the results are outstanding. On Monday a three-course meal is offered; four courses are served Tuesday through Thursday; and a five-course dinner is offered on Friday and Saturday nights. A typical midweek, four-course meal might begin with grilled leeks and fennel served with olive toasts, followed by a green-garlic custard with Dungeness crab, and grilled pork loin accompanied by preserved lemons and a mélange of sautéed cabbage, potatoes, and leeks. An apple tart with pink-apple sherbet is a perfect ending to the meal. The California Craftsman–style interior mirrors the food, which is sophisticated and rustic at the same time. The open kitchen flows right into the dining room where copper light fixtures and wall sconces add a warming glow. The table settings are as straightforward as the food—no candles or flowers, just good wine glasses to showcase the fine wines from the carefully selected list. Hearty eaters, however, may be disappointed by the small portions. ♦ Californian ♦ M-Sa dinner. Reservations required. 1517 Shattuck Ave (between Cedar and Vine Sts), Berkeley. 510/548.5525; fax 510/548.0140

Beyond the Bridges

Upstairs from Chez Panisse:
Cafe at Chez Panisse ★★★★$$ Meals are served à la carte at this casual offspring of **Chez Panisse.** The brick oven, positioned behind a long service counter, turns out some of the best *pizzas* in Northern California. The toppings aren't elaborate, but everything tastes like it just came from the garden. Pastas and salads enticingly showcase seasonal vegetables, and simple meat dishes, grilled or baked, are succulent. Don't pass up dessert; the cookies, fruit tarts, cobblers, and ice creams are all marvelous. ♦ Californian ♦ M-Sa lunch and dinner. 510/548.5049; fax 510/548.0140

4 **O Chamé** ★★★$$ Chef David Vardy creates Japanese-style food with a California twist at this attractive and peaceful restaurant on Fourth Street, Berkeley's culinary center. Using local produce in addition to traditional Japanese foodstuffs, Vardy's menu consists of appetizers and salads and a selection of meals in a bowl, featuring *udon* (buckwheat) or *soba* (white) noodles, augmented with about four daily specials. Winning appetizers include young greens blanched and served with a sesame dressing, and delicately vinegared cucumbers enlivened with *wakame* seaweed. One particularly memorable dish features two pristine salmon fillets, wet-roasted in a wood oven to create an almost poached texture, tucked under tender carrots that have been roasted and glazed with sweet sake, and accompanied by chunks of grilled portobello mushrooms—all surrounded by a tomato-lemon broth. The focal point of the dining room is an Oriental carpet, centered under a long table that holds a vase with an arrangement of grasses and blooms as well as platters of wonderful cookies and a few baked goods. The Japanese country ambience is further enhanced by the straight-back rough wooden chairs and a round window inset with bamboo. There's also a tea kiosk outdoors where cookies, tea, and bento boxes are available at lunchtime—either to take away or enjoy at the heavy wooden table under a leafy green tree. ♦ Japanese ♦ M-Sa lunch and dinner. 1830 Fourth St (at Hearst Ave), Berkeley. 510/841.8723

4 **Mannix Café** ★★$ The bistro tables out front are popular on warm days, and the dark wood trim and marble counters indoors give this small cafe a bit of style. The sandwich selection is good, as are the empanadas, frittatas, and egg salad with sun-dried tomatoes. Pastries and gelato in more than a dozen flavors are also featured. ♦ Cafe ♦ Daily lunch until 5PM. 1809 Fourth St (at Hearst Ave), Berkeley. 510/644.3040; fax 510/644.3209

4 **Bette's Oceanview Diner** ★★$ The black-and-white floor and curved white walls create the ambience of a 1930s Deco diner. Customers can sit at the long counter overlooking the open kitchen or at one of the burgundy booths that line the wall. Breakfast covers all the ethnic bases: *huevos rancheros,* lox scramble, or a Philadelphia breakfast (poached eggs with scrapple). And don't miss the best buttermilk pancakes west of the Mississippi (probably east of it too). The sandwich selection is equally broad, ranging from a panfried fish fillet, to a chicken sandwich, to kosher New York franks. The diner is famous for its desserts, so leave room for the pie of the day, bread pudding, or fresh fruit crisp. ♦ American ♦ Daily breakfast and lunch; F-Su until 4PM. 1807 Fourth St (between Hearst and Virginia Aves), Berkeley. 510/644.3230; fax 510/644.3209

4 **Bette's-to-Go** Just as the name says, here you can get all of Bette's goodies, from fresh baked goods—rich double-chocolate pecan or moist peanut butter cookies, almond cakes, apple pie—to Chinese chicken salad, sandwiches, and pizza by the slice. Home chefs can pick up the famous buttermilk pancake mix, lemon-currant scone mix, and other essentials. ♦ Daily. 1804 Fourth St (between Hearst and Virginia Aves), Berkeley. 510/548.9494 510/644.3209

4 **Holey Bagel** The golden walls, painted gray-and-yellow floor, and black appointments give this bagel emporium a decidedly upscale look. Choose from 18 flavors of bagels—including blueberry—from the bins in front. Chopped chicken liver, lox, hummus, and knishes are also for sale. Enjoy it all at one of the tables outside. At press time, the chain was considering changing its name to **Manhattan Bagel.** ♦ Daily. 1789 Fourth St (at Hearst Ave), Berkeley. 510/525.9445; fax 510/525.8105 Also at: 3218 Fillmore St (at Greenwich St), San Francisco. 922.1955; fax 626.2453 ; 3872 24th St (between Vicksburg and Sanchez Sts), San Francisco. 647.3334; fax 647.0824 ; 1206 Masonic St (at Haight St), San Francisco. 626.9111; fax 626.2730

205

Beyond the Bridges

4 Crate & Barrel Outlet Store Here's the place to find terrific bargains on everything for the home, including good kitchen towels for as little as 50 cents each. There are loads of serving pieces, glasses, plates, stainless steel flatware, chefs' knives, mugs, candlesticks, and just about everything else. Area bargain hunters stop in at least once a month to see what's new. ♦ Daily. 1785 Fourth St (near Hearst Ave), Berkeley. 510/528.5500; fax 510/528.3466 &

4 Lalime's ★★★$$ This neighborhood restaurant forges a close bond with the community through special theme dinners, charity benefits, and a monthly newsletter that keeps its regulars abreast of what's going on in the kitchen. The à la carte menu changes daily, and there's also a fixed-price menu that varies in price and offerings every day. It might be a Spanish-influenced evening that begins with an assortment of tapas, followed by paella, and a refreshing blood-orange granita for dessert; or a French meal, with a *tajine* of mussels perfumed with coriander, followed by grilled Cornish hens with stuffed mushrooms and roast garlic mashed potatoes, and warm pear strudel. Although it's always crowded in the two-level dining room, the light colors give the space a restful, celebratory feeling. ♦ Mediterranean ♦ Daily dinner. 1329 Gilman St (near Neilson St), Berkeley. 510/527.9838; fax 510/527.1350 &

5 Ajanta Restaurant ★★★$ With this comfortable, refined Indian restaurant in one of North Berkeley's busiest shopping districts, owner Lachu Moorjani has achieved something very special. His menu (which changes monthly) goes beyond standard tandoori dishes, nan bread, and rice to offer interesting entrées from all over India, including Tamil Indian curry, flavored with poppy seeds and fennel; *lobhia aur khumbi*, a dish featuring fresh black-eyed peas with mushrooms, onions, tomatoes, garlic, and other spices; and chicken in coconut-onion-tomato sauce. The dining room is decorated in bright yellow fabrics accented with burnt sienna woodwork and carpeting; there are a number of striking murals depicting the Ajanta caves, a popular archaeological area in central India. ♦ Indian ♦ Daily lunch and dinner. 1888 Solano Ave (near Henry St), Berkeley. 510/526.4373; fax 510/526.3885

Sonoma County Farm Trails, founded in 1972, produces a map of small farms, wineries, and other food-related businesses that sell to the public. Free maps are available by writing: PO Box 6032, Santa Rosa, CA, 95406, or they can be picked up at member businesses throughout the county. Napa, Sonoma, Alameda, and other counties produce their own farm trail maps.

Rivoli RESTAURANT

5 Rivoli ★★★$$ Opened in 1994, this restaurant took off quickly, thanks to the reputations of chef/owner Wendy Brucker (**Stars, Square One, Ernie's**) and her husband and host, Roscoe Skipper (**Square One, Masa's, Bizou**). Start with portobello mushroom fritters with lemon aioli, shaved parmesan, peppery leaves of arugula, and caper vinaigrette. One of the best salads combines endive, pear, frisée (curly endive), and arugula with spiced hazelnuts, pickled onions, and a hazelnut-balsamic vinaigrette. Main courses include braised lamb shank, accompanied by pomegranate-and–bulgur wheat pilaf, accented with a mint-garlic yogurt sauce and cumin oil. The day's vegetarian plate might be potato-cauliflower curry, basmati rice, and a garden basket of steamed or grilled seasonal vegetables. Desserts are equally delectable, from blood-orange granita to chocolate *pots de crème* (custard) with hazelnut cookies. This is also a great place to learn the wonders of the sweet Meyer lemon, which stars here in a flaky tart with pistachio, cranberry, and apricot sauces. ♦ Californian ♦ Daily dinner. 1539 Solano Ave (at Peralta Ave), Berkeley. 510/526.2542; fax 510/525.8412

Marin County

This charming county has some of the prettiest villages and most dramatic vistas in the Bay Area. In **Sausalito** and **Tiburon**, visitors can spend the day strolling through quaint seaside villages, poking in shops and art galleries, and enjoying the sun that across the bay may be obscured by fog. The well-known **Lark Creek Inn**, in airy, Victorian surroundings in **Larkspur**, draws crowds for Bradley Ogden's American food with a twist. And travelers bogged down in traffic near the **Golden Gate Bridge** will be glad to stop for a bite at the **Buckeye Roadhouse** or **Frantoio Ristorante**, a new eatery that boasts its own working olive oil press. Marin is reachable from San Francisco by bus, ferry, and the Golden Gate Bridge, and from the **East Bay** via the **Richmond–San Rafael Bridge**. We start our tour in Sausalito and work north to **San Rafael**.

6 North Sea Village ★★$ This large Chinese restaurant, overlooking the bay and with gently rocking sailboats docked just outside the door, is a good place to try dim sum. It's off the beaten path, so diners don't

Beyond the Bridges

have to deal with the crush of tourists so common in San Francisco's dim sum houses. The trade-off is a more limited selection on weekdays; but on weekends there is the typical grand offering. The dumplings are excellent, as is anything with shrimp. To round out the meal ask the server for stir-fried bok choy in oyster sauce. The staff is cordial and extremely good at helping novices.
♦ Chinese/Dim Sum ♦ Daily lunch and dinner. 300 Turney St (at Bridgeway), Sausalito. 415/331.3300

7 Guaymas ★★$$ On a sunny afternoon take a ferry from The Embarcadero to Tiburon, where the boat debarks at the door of this pretty Mexican restaurant. Take a seat on the deck and enjoy an enchanting view of the San Francisco skyline while indulging in nachos and margaritas. You can dine outside if it's warm, or head inside to try some of the creative dishes that pepper the menu. Start with grilled shrimp, marinated in lime juice and cilantro, or tiny tamales filled with chicken and coated with a pumpkin-seed sauce. If there's a nip in the air (remember, you're on the water), try the tortilla soup with chunks of chicken and avocado floating in a rich smoky broth. Such main course offerings as slow-roasted pork sirloin or mesquite-grilled lamb loin with salsa can't be beat. ♦ Mexican
♦ Daily lunch and dinner. 5 Main St (at Tiburon Blvd), Tiburon. 415/435.6300; fax 435.6802

7 Tutto Mare Ristorante & Taverna ★★★$$ In the last few years, the town of Tiburon has become a popular dining center, and this place is just one of the reasons. Under the same ownership as **Guaymas** (see above), it's a bi-level replica of an Italian boathouse, only this one offers spectacular views of the San Francisco skyline. Another striking feature of the decor is the three-dimensional ceramic murals. The menu has everything you'd expect in an Italian seafood restaurant: fried calamari with aioli; seafood salad with shrimp, octopus, and vegetables; freshly shucked oysters; steamed shellfish; and whole baked fish. For landlubbers, there are pizzas, charcoal-grilled meat and poultry, and homemade pastas. The deck is a perfect place to sit and enjoy a sunny afternoon or watch the sun set in the evening.
♦ Italian/Seafood ♦ M-Sa lunch and dinner; Su brunch and dinner. 9 Main St (at the wharf), Tiburon. 415/435.4747; fax 435.4766

Mt. St. Helens, the mountain that looms above the Napa Valley (not to be confused with the one in Washington State), was an active volcano millions of years ago. Its ash and lava flows formed much of the rich substrata that make the surrounding acreage so suited to wine growing.

BUCKEYE
ROADHOUSE

8 Buckeye Roadhouse ★★$$ Owned by Real Restaurants, the same people who brought **Bistro Roti, Bix, Fog City Diner, Ristorante Tra Vigne,** and **Mustards Grill** to fruition, this popular roadhouse just on the other side of the Golden Gate Bridge has a lodgelike ambience. The high-pitched ceiling adds drama, but the massive rock fireplace holds center stage. The food style is a mélange of classic American, French, and Italian cuisine, with a few Asian touches. An appetizer of pan-roasted artichoke with creamy tarragon dip is an ideal way to celebrate California's favorite vegetable. Onion rings with homemade ketchup, and warm spinach salad with smoked bacon are other excellent ways to launch a meal. Barbecued baby back ribs accompanied by cole slaw and garlic mashed potatoes are delicious; as are the smoked half chicken and grilled pork chops. Don't miss the butter-scotch crème brûlée or baked lemon pudding for dessert. ♦ American ♦ M-Sa lunch and dinner; Su brunch and dinner. 15 Shoreline Hwy (near Hwys 101 and 1), Mill Valley. 415/331.2600; fax 331.6067

8 Piazza D'Angelo ★★★$$ One of the most popular spots in Marin, the patio or light-filled interior of this active restaurant is an ideal place to end a walk around Mill Valley (check out **Smith and Hawkins** for chic gardening finds, **Mill Valley Market** for gourmet foods, and several cookstores and accessory shops). For a light meal, two excellent choices are a simple *pizza margherita* with mozzarella, basil, and tomato sauce, and a heartier *pizza rustica* with calamata olives, sun-dried tomatoes, feta cheese, and arugula. The menu changes daily, but there's always a pasta dish—maybe penne with fresh tomatoes, artichokes, and wild mushrooms—and such entrées as whole baked trout with eggplant and mushrooms, and thin paillards of grilled chicken dressed with a drizzle of olive oil, oregano, and fresh lemon. Anything from the rotisserie is recommended: rabbit, duck with balsamic vinegar, or chicken. The chef is from Sardinia, so dishes from that area are worth a try, especially the *bottarga* (dried tuna roe) with spaghetti and garlic and the carpaccio with celery and touches of olive oil. ♦ Italian ♦ Daily lunch and dinner. 22 Miller Ave (between Sunnyside and Throckmorton Aves), Mill Valley. 415/388.2000; fax 388.1234

Beyond the Bridges

9 Frantoio Ristorante ★$$ The unique centerpiece of the dining room—a massive, working olive oil press—is second only to the distinctive Italian dishes served here. While you enjoy leg of lamb, homemade pasta, or osso buco served atop saffron risotto, you can watch olives being crushed by two 3,600-pound granite wheels. The appetizer of mussels and mashed potatoes flavored with saffron is generous enough to make a meal in itself. The wine list offers mainly Italian vintages. ♦ Italian ♦ Daily lunch and dinner. 152 Shoreline Hwy (near Hwy 1), Mill Valley. 415/289.5777; fax 415/289.5775 ♿

10 Lark Creek Inn ★$$$ A large and airy Victorian house surrounded by redwoods showcases chef Bradley Ogden's New American cuisine. Ogden, who earned his stripes at the American Restaurant in Kansas City and at **Campton Place** in San Francisco, has become known for his twists on familiar comfort food. For example, he grills double-cut pork chops and tops them with spiced apple-pear butter, then rounds out the plate with rich cheddar potatoes and braised red cabbage. Oven-roasted chicken is accompanied by buttered spinach and mashed red potatoes (which are unfortunately gummy), and braised lamb shank is dressed up with horseradish mashed potatoes and roasted root vegetables. Unfortunately, the quality of the food has gone down a bit in recent years. Desserts, however, are still worth a splurge: warm country apple tart with apple sherbet, butterscotch pudding with shortbread cookies, or devil's food cake with chocolate fudge frosting and double-chocolate espresso ice cream. When the weather permits, people can sit on the deck overlooking the proverbial babbling brook. ♦ Californian ♦ M-F lunch and dinner; Sa dinner; Su brunch and dinner. 234 Magnolia Ave (at William Ave), Larkspur. 415/924.7766; fax 924.7117 ♿

10 Left Bank ★★★$$ A little bit of Paris has been captured in this brasserie, which is partly owned by Roland Passot of **La Folie** in San Francisco. For this venture in charming downtown Larkspur, Passot has scaled back his grand style and offers stick-to-your-ribs fare. Stop at the ornate bar and order one of the fruit- or vegetable-infused vodkas (fennel, kumquat, or pear, to name a few), which are impressively displayed in huge glass jars. The menu changes seasonally; in spring two can share the generous warm new-potato salad with mussels and roasted artichoke; on a late summer's night nothing can beat the cooling salad of mixed organic greens and yellow wax beans with roasted peppers and vine-ripened tomatoes. You'll swear you're in France when you order salad *lyonnaise,* composed of *frisée* tossed with lardoons of bacon and topped with a poached egg. Steamed salmon glistens in an herbed broth with a medley of vegetables; duck confit is enriched with braised lentils; and roast chicken is a perfect foil to roasted vegetables. For dessert try the fruit shakes, or classic chocolate mousse. ♦ French ♦ M-Sa lunch and dinner; Su brunch and dinner. 507 Magnolia Ave (at Ward St), Larkspur. 415/927.3331; fax 927.3034 ♿

10 Chai of Larkspur ★★$ Just a stone's throw from **Left Bank** is this gem of a tea salon. Decorated by Candra Scott (who also designed **Vivande** in Pacific Heights), the room features tomato-red walls, oversize green wicker chairs, and persimmon accents. Owner Betty Shelton prepares a wide selection of sandwiches, pastries, and cookies to go with the tea service. There's also a shop selling more than 70 imported teas, accessories, and tea-themed gifts. ♦ Tea Salon ♦ Daily afternoon tea (F until 7PM). 25 Ward St (at Magnolia Ave), Larkspur. 415/945.7161; fax 415/945.7164 ♿

10 Fabrizio ★★$$ This restaurant just keeps getting better. The setting is light—track lighting, cream-colored walls hung with photographs of Italian doors and windows, and white-draped tables give an airy feeling—and the food has followed the same path. Risotto is always outstanding; but if it's your lucky day, the version with the sharp bite of gorgonzola and radicchio will be on the menu. Angel-hair pasta tossed with garlic, olive oil, basil, and chunks of tomato is simple and satisfying. The veal piccata is excellent, and the crisp cubed potatoes that accompany it are out of this world. Desserts aren't anything special, but the tiramisù is fine for those who like a boozy ending to a meal. ♦ Italian ♦ M-S lunch and dinner; Su dinner. 455 Magnolia Ave (between Ward and King Sts), Larkspur. 415/924.3332 ♿

11 Bay Area Certified Farmers' Market Started in 1983 as a Thursday market, it is now held on Sunday as well, year-round at the **Marin Civic Center.** On both days it draws thousands of people who relish the cornucopia of locally grown, mostly organic fruits, vegetables, and herbs, free-range poultry and lamb, ranch eggs, local honey, homemade jams, freshly squeezed juices, fresh fish and shellfish, multigrain breads, pastries, and specialty pastas, sauces, and vinegars. ♦ Th, Su 8AM-1PM. Marin Civic

Beyond the Bridges

Center, 3501 Civic Center Dr (Thursday in the parking lot of the Veterans Auditorium, at the Avenue of the Flags; Sunday in the main parking lot, parallel to Hwy 101), San Rafael. 415/456.FARM; fax 415/453.7502 ♿

11 Rice Table ★★★$ Rijsttafel (which means rice table in Dutch) is a traditional Indonesian multicourse banquet featuring appetizer-size portions of many different dishes. The delicious parade makes for a festive, and usually very inexpensive, meal. Here it begins with shrimp chips paired with three dipping sauces; followed by split-pea soup with nuances of licorice; then *sumpia* (deep-fried egg roll) and a salad. There's also delectable pork or chicken satay; *bihun goreng* (a dish with fried rice and noodles); clove-infused beef stew; and a mild chicken curry. The quiet room, divided by rattan screens, is filled with attractive Indonesian art. ♦ Indonesian ♦ W-Su dinner. 1617 Fourth Street (at G St), San Rafael. 415/456.1808 ♿

Napa Valley

Once a series of quiet little farm towns, today the Napa Valley wine-growing region gets almost as many tourists in a year as Disneyland. It boasts hundreds of wineries, shops, art galleries, and some of the hottest new restaurants in Northern California, all within a 1.5-hour drive of San Francisco. Some of the best dining spots in the valley are located along the **St. Helena Highway** (also called **Highway 29**) spine, starting from the city of **Napa** and extending north to **Calistoga**. The following are our top ten favorites.

12 Scala's ★★$$ Surrounded by vineyards, this Italian restaurant is owned by Donna and Giovanni Scala, who also have an interest in **Scala's Bistro** in San Francisco. A recent renovation has given the place a rustic look, with country fabrics, antique copper pots, Italian ceramics, a Mediterranean garden, and an outdoor fireplace. The food takes on the warm gutsy notes of Italian cooking. Start with fritto misto, fried crispy rock shrimp, purple onions, and green beans, served with spicy aioli on the side. The *pappardelle* (wide ribbon noodles) are a perfect bed for the stew of rabbit with baby artichokes. *Capellini* (thin spaghetti-like noodles) tossed with tomato, basil, and garlic make a simple, soul-satisfying dish. The lunch menu features several focaccia sandwiches—the grilled vegetable version is outstanding. Roast chicken is another winner, as is braised lamb shank with Tuscan white-bean stew. The wine list is dominated by California selections and includes Italian wines, Armagnacs, and grappas. ♦ Italian ♦ Daily lunch and dinner. Reservations recommended. 4110 St. Helena Hwy (north of Salvador Ave), Napa. 707/224.3300; fax 707/224.3395 ♿

13 Domaine Chandon ★★★★$$$$ On the grounds of this eponymous winery is one of the most impressive restaurants in Northern California, thanks to the cuisine of Philippe Jeanty who has been in charge of the kitchen since it opened in 1977, and the magnificent setting overlooking a pond and vineyards. During the day it's a magical experience to enjoy Jeanty's French/Californian creations on the patio with the gentle breeze tickling your face. At night the arch-roofed dining room glows with candlelit romance. The menu changes often but the chef might pair seared tuna crusted in black pepper with buttery mashed potatoes and a mustard sauce; tender slices of lamb tongue accented with warm potatoes, *frisée*, and capers; or quail presented over a rich risotto with caramelized mushrooms. Dessert may be a seductive warm chocolate cake with a trufflelike center, or crème brûlée sandwiched between perfect layers of puff pastry. As you would expect, the restaurant has one of the best wine lists in the valley for both selection and price. ♦ French/Californian ♦ M-Tu lunch, W-Su lunch and dinner May-Oct; W-Su lunch and dinner Jan-Apr, Nov-Dec. Reservations recommended; jackets required at dinner. 1 California Dr (off St. Helena Hwy), Yountville. 707/944.2892; fax 707/944.1123 ♿

13 French Laundry ★★★★$$$$ Thomas Keller has taken over this old stone laundry and has turned it into a fine-dining destination in the tradition of France. The dining room has an almost austere simplicity, in contrast to the luxurious style of the table settings with oversized napkins and sparkling crystal. Keller

209

Beyond the Bridges

has also added a touch of whimsy: a starched chef's coat hangs to "dry" over the fireplace, wooden laundry pins hold the napkins in place, and laundry tags are used to itemize the check. There are four- or five-course prix-fixe menus, with as many as five choices for each course and one all-vegetarian option. A fish choice could be a snowy fillet of sea bass moistened by a bright, fresh carrot broth—which gets its intense flavor from dehydrating the vegetables before juicing them—presented on a bed of couscous. Meat courses are particularly good, especially when Keller takes humble cuts and transforms them into heavenly creations. He roasts the breast of veal for hours, cools it, doubles it over, and cuts it into perfect rounds. It is then brushed with mustard and bread crumbs and seared, forming a crackling crust that creates an alluring contrast to the velvety meat. The wine list is one of the best in the wine country; it concentrates on Napa Valley and boasts a mix of classics and selections from small wineries. Also, 25 half-bottles are offered, allowing parties of two to match the wine with the food. And for dessert, you've surely never had "coffee and doughnuts" like this—a freshly made doughnut and a cup of cappuccino mousse topped with a froth of whipped cream. ♦ Californian ♦ Tu-Su dinner; call ahead about lunch hours, as they vary with the season. Reservations required. 6640 Washington St (at Creek St), Yountville. 707/944.2380; fax 707/944.1974 ♿

13 Mustards Grill ★★★$$ A popular restaurant from the day it opened over a decade ago, this low-slung, ranch-style building is still one of the best destinations for casual dining. The menu features such all-American standards as hamburgers and great onion rings, but with a twist; for example, the ketchup is homemade, as is everything else. Smoked salmon is given distinction with corn cakes spiced with mild *pasilla* chilies and topped by fresh dill cream cheese; wild mushrooms are baked in a flaky tart; and crab cakes are served with a three-pepper salad. Liver with caramelized onions and bacon is always on the menu, as is a delicious slab of barbecued baby back ribs served with corn bread and slaw. Occasionally braised lamb shanks with polenta, grilled rabbit with wild mushrooms, or a grilled pork chop with mashed potatoes appear as specials. There is an enticing selection of the more unusual wines produced in the Napa Valley, with more than a dozen good wines available by the glass. Prices tend to be a little high. Try the caramel apple cake with cinnamon ice cream, or the Jack Daniel's chocolate cake with an intense chocolate sauce. ♦ Californian ♦ Daily lunch and dinner. Reservations recommended. 7399 St. Helena Hwy (near Washington St), Yountville. 707/944.2424; fax 707/944.0824 ♿

14 Stars Oakville Cafe ★★$$$ Jeremiah Tower has re-created a little bit of San Francisco's **Stars Cafe** in the Napa Valley. The menu changes daily, crafted to the season, and may include house-smoked salmon with pickled red onions, oysters on the half shell, or a baby romaine salad. Salmon is grilled and served with vegetable-studded orzo; and grilled lamb sirloin is accompanied by baked white beans with spinach. Many meat dishes, including delectable chicken and duck, are prepared in the wood-burning oven. The 75 wines—Californian, French, and Italian—are a good mix of classics and more unusual bottles, but prices can be high, with few bargains to be found. The interior doesn't have the flash of its big-city brother, but the single room is given dimension by a cathedral ceiling at the entrance and a small bar area tucked next to the kitchen, which is separated from the dining area by glass so you can watch the action. In summer, a seating area is created on a tented outdoor patio and, beyond that, a white lattice fence encloses a garden filled with olive trees and lavender, centered with an aviary filled with doves. ♦ Cafe ♦ M, Th-Su lunch and dinner. Reservations recommended. 7848 St. Helena Hwy (near Oakville Rd), Oakville. 707/944.8905; fax 707/944.0469 ♿

15 Wine Spectator Greystone Restaurant ★★$$ When the **Culinary Institute of America** (based in Hyde Park, New York) wanted to create a Northern California campus a few years ago, they chose to take over the beautiful building that once housed the **Christian Brothers Winery–Greystone Cellars**. The new campus now features a restaurant staffed by **CIA** graduates and students; its name acknowledges a generous donation from the *Wine Spectator* magazine. The restaurant got off to a shaky start—the food was uneven, the wine list incomplete—but things improved rapidly. One good starter is pureed Mediterranean dips: garlicky yogurt dill, a bland chick pea hummus, and *muhammara*, a combination of red pepper and walnuts. Pizza prepared with cooked sweet onions, niçoise olives, and bits of anchovies on a crispy flat bread is another outstanding choice. Although tasty, the duck cooked on the rotisserie and flavored with honey and lavender was a little too fatty. The rich, dense Valrhona chocolate cake sitting on a sauce of espresso Sambuca and vanilla bean cream makes a fine finish. The dining room's rough stone walls (from the former winery) are brightened by the generous use of tile, wrought iron, and blond wood furnishings. The tasting and antipasto bar is a good place to watch the cooks on display in the open kitchen and to sample up to 16 wines by the glass. And the newly expanded wine list offe

Beyond the Bridges

helpful hints for beginners. But the staff can be a bit absentminded. ♦ Californian ♦ M, W-Su lunch and dinner. 255 Main St (north of Pratt Ave), St. Helena. 707/967.1010; fax 707/963.1113 ♿

16 Ristorante Tra Vigne ★★$$ No restaurant in the valley captures the feel of the wine country better than this impressive stone building in St. Helena which has grape vines on the front lawn. The restaurant is always crowded; you can sit outside on the impressive patio underneath fig trees, or inside, which sports a magnificent casual trattoria feel with an open kitchen hung with hams, strings of garlic, and garlands of herbs. Most products, including the prosciutto, sausage, and even the olive oil is produced in-house by chef Michael Chiarello. Because of the volume of business the food can sometimes be uneven. The regularly changing menu includes a list of thin-crusted pizzas, great pasta with interesting sauces—such as a mushroom ragout or braised rabbit—and many grilled dishes, like excellent lamb. The wine list includes Italian and Californian vintages (try one of the new Californian wines using the Italian varietals), but prices are a bit high. ♦ Italian ♦ Daily lunch and dinner. Reservations recommended. 1050 Charter Oak Ave (at Main St), St. Helena. 707/963.4444; fax 707/963.1233 ♿

Next to Ristorante Tra Vigne:

Cantinetta Tra Vigne ★★★$ This upscale deli and wineshop offers such simple fare as panini (Italian sandwiches on focaccia bread) and interesting salads that can be eaten outside on the patio or taken away for a glorious picnic. Wines, house-produced conserves, vinegars and oils, mustards, and some fresh produce items are also offered. ♦ Italian/Takeout ♦ Daily lunch and early dinner (until 6PM). 1050 Charter Oak Ave (at Main St), St. Helena. 707/942.8888 ♿

Terra ★★★★$$$$ Chef/owner Hiro Sone and his wife, Lissa Doumani, met at Spago in Los Angeles: He was on the line with Wolfgang Puck and she worked in the pastry kitchen. Their partnership has produced a magnificent cross-cultural restaurant where Italian and Asian flavors play against each other in a setting reminiscent of a Tuscan village. Located one block off the main street in St. Helena, the stone building has exposed rock walls, a terra-cotta floor, and bright modern art

that work together to create a simultaneously rustic and refined setting. The menu changes often, but the combinations are always creative—try the ragout of sweetbreads with prosciutto and mushrooms in a broth perfumed with white truffle oil. Follow with rack of lamb flanked by ratatouille, hummus, and a refreshing *raita* (yogurt and chopped cucumber). There's an extensive collection of Napa Valley wines, which are clearly labeled by varietal. Less common varietals are characterized as "the other side of red" on the wine list; French selections are called "intruders." The desserts are also unusual: Consider sampling the gently warmed strawberries in a Cabernet sauce spiked with black pepper, and cooled by a slowly melting scoop of vanilla ice cream. ♦ Asian/Mediterranean ♦ M, W-Su dinner. Reservations recommended. 1345 Railroad Ave (between Hunt and Adams Sts), St. Helena. 707/963.8931; fax 707/963.8933 ♿

Brava Terrace ★★★$$ The redwood deck overlooking the creek is the place to be in the summer at this dining spot; in the winter, it's in front of the massive rock fireplace that holds center stage in the peaked roof dining room. Fred Halpert, who made a name at the **Portman Hotel** in San Francisco before relocating to the wine country, offers a hearty Mediterranean menu, and many of his herbs and lettuces are fresh picked from the restaurant's adjacent garden. Long-cooked dishes are a standout, particularly the cassoulet. The menu includes several excellent sandwiches for lunch, and the risotto of the day is always superb. Halpert hosts interesting food and wine tastings as special events; for example, California Zinfandel paired with barbecue is a match made in heaven. Because the restaurant is located just north of St. Helena, it's often a bit less crowded than the places in the lower valley. ♦ Mediterranean ♦ Daily lunch and dinner May-Oct; M-Tu, Th-Su lunch and dinner Nov-Apr. Reservations recommended. 3010 St. Helena Hwy N (at Lodi La), St. Helena. 707/963.9300; fax 707/963.9581 ♿

Except for older established cities such as Palo Alto and Redwood City, most of the communities on the San Francisco Peninsula were developed after World War II. Other peninsula cities, especially in Santa Clara County, where prune orchards (with plums that are specifically cultivated to become prunes) once bloomed, became the epicenter of the high-tech industry.

Napa's grapevines were pulled out during Prohibition, and the area became known as the nation's prune capital.

Beyond the Bridges

17 Pinot Blanc ★★★$$ The latest celebrity chef to grace the Napa Valley is Joachim Splichal, the mastermind behind several Los Angeles restaurants, including Patina, Pinot Bistro, and Pinot Hollywood. With such impressive credentials, this brand-new dining spot (scheduled to open at press time) in the heart of St. Helena is sure to be a winner. The boxy-looking building is enhanced with a lovely pergola and grounds landscaped with olive trees, flowers, and an herb garden. The menu features French country bistro classics prepared with a California twist, including rotisserie beef and chicken; herring salad served with a potato pancake and mustard greens; caramelized onion tart with marinated salmon and cream; calf's liver with roasted fingerling potatoes; spinach casserole and sweet and sour shallot *jus;* and crispy duck leg confit with a warm salad of *frisée,* apples, and walnuts. ♦ French/Californian ♦ Daily lunch and dinner. 641 Main St (between Grayson and Vidovich Aves), St Helena. 707/963.6191; fax 707/963.6192

18 Wappo Bar Bistro ★★$$ This restaurant takes its name from a Native American tribe that used to occupy the area. Its decor is California Craftsman and the fare consists of continually changing offerings that span the globe: Mexican spicy meatball soup, Indian fish fritters, Spanish seafood vermicelli, and Asian grilled chicken with sesame-ginger sauce. American-influenced dishes include a homey rabbit pie and roast chicken with chive-mashed potatoes. The 40-bottle wine list is an eccentric mix containing unusual varietals that have clearly been selected to go with the spicy food. Desserts are formidable. The warm steamed chocolate cake with a brownielike texture and a straw-Wberry-rhubarb pie could win a prize at any state fair. The brick patio in back, with a grape arbor overhead and a wall of climbing vines with pink and yellow roses, makes this one of the loveliest outdoor stops in the upper Napa Valley. ♦ International/Californian ♦ M, W-Su lunch and dinner. Reservations recommended. 1226B Washington St (near Lincoln Ave), Calistoga. 707/942.4712; fax 707/942.4741

18 Catahoula Restaurant and Saloon ★★★★$$$; For this venture within the **Mount View Hotel,** Jan Birnbaum returned to his native Louisiana roots (where he worked for Paul Prudhomme) to create a host of spicy foods. Menu offerings range from spicy rooster gumbo to pizza with andouille sausage to hominy cakes with vegetables and smoked-onion vinaigrette. Locally raised lamb is encrusted with sassafras and served with potato-salsify pie; whole roast fish is stuffed with fennel and onion; braised short ribs are paired with mashed potatoes and pungent mustard greens; and, in an unusual combination, wild boar sausage is served with pecorino ravioli. There's an excellent wine list, and Birnbaum also offers food and wine tastings where he matches a dish with three different wines. Dessert could be buttermilk pie, rich apple grunt, or almond upside-down cake with caramelized mangoes. The restaurant's interior has an urban, sophisticated look: salvaged wood tables edged with wrought iron, rusted animal sculptures, and portraits of dogs (the catahoula is the state dog of Louisiana). A granite bar separates the open kitchen from the brick oven and the rest of the dining room. There's additional seating in the bar and around the pool in back. ♦ Contemporary Creole ♦ M, W-Su lunch and dinner; closed in January. Reservations recommended. 1457 Lincoln Ave (near Washington St), Calistoga. 707/942.2275; fax 707/942.5338

Sonoma County

Unlike the **Napa Valley,** where wine grapes are about the only crop, Sonoma County is an agricultural region that happens to grow grapes. The terrain is varied, with orchards scattered among the grapevines, and cows and lambs grazing just about everywhere you look. The setting is so bucolic it's easy to forget that you are only an hour or two from San Francisco. In the last few years, Sonoma has become a hotbed of restaurant activity. Here's a rundown of the best, starting from the town of **Sonoma** and heading north to **Healdsburg.**

Beyond the Bridges

19 East Side Oyster Bar & Grill ★★★$$

Charles Saunders was the chef of the **Sonoma Mission Inn** before he struck out on his own at this charming restaurant just off the town square. The intimate dining room has a marble fireplace and an Old World oyster-bar feeling, and there's a counter at the bar where diners sans reservations can grab a bite. But in warm weather the brick patio, a lush oasis of grape arbors and gurgling fountains, is the place to be. Saunders's offerings change often to make the best of local produce, and range over many cultures—lunch choices, for example, may include a duck burrito or a rock-shrimp and vegetable tempura. The dinner menu's signature dish is a lamb parfait: layers of succulent lamb, mashed chickpeas, onion confit, roasted tomatoes, and a crispy tangle of fried leeks. Other typical entrées include mussels poached with green lentils, ginger, coriander, and lemongrass; and sturgeon crusted with coriander and lemon and served on a cooling bed of lemon cucumbers.
♦ Californian/Seafood ♦ Daily lunch and dinner. Reservations recommended. 133 E Napa St (at First St E), Sonoma. 707/939.1266; fax 707/939.9845

19 Piatti ★★$$

The perfect meal here begins with grilled vegetables, including whole roasted garlic cloves that can be spread like butter. From there it's on to spinach-and-ricotta ravioli topped with lemon-infused cream sauce, or grilled meat from the rotisserie, such as a pork chop served with creamy mashed potatoes and a heady mushroom sauce. Those who are in the mood for a lighter midday snack can opt for tasty thin-crusted pizza. An open kitchen, terra-cotta floor, light walls painted with big fruits and vegetables, and massive chairs give this trattoria an Italian country look. The feeling is further enhanced by a wisteria-draped outdoor patio complete with a massive fig tree. For dessert, hope that a fruit ice is on the menu; if not, the tiramisù is rich, creamy, and refreshing. ♦ Italian ♦ Daily lunch and dinner. Reservations recommended. 405 First St W (at Spain St), Sonoma. 707/996.2351; fax 707/996.3148

20 Kenwood Restaurant and Bar ★★$$$

One of the most popular restaurants in this part of the valley is frequented by local wine folks, including gentleman farmer Tommy Smothers, who owns a winery in the area. The gently peaked roof lined in natural pine and large windows overlooking lush greenery combine with comfortable bentwood and bamboo chairs and bright art to create an airy feel. The food can be uneven, although the Caesar salad is a consistent winner, as is poached salmon served with a lemon cream sauce kissed with mustard. Sweetbreads are always on the menu in different guises, sometimes sprinkled with capers and accompanied by marinated mushrooms and an arugula salad. Fat crab cakes get a lift from an intense red bell pepper sauce, and duck is prepared with orange sauce and accompanied by wild rice or locally grown berries. Tapioca pudding with brandied cherries finishes the meal in a comforting fashion. ♦ Californian ♦ Tu-Su lunch and dinner. 9900 Sonoma Hwy (at Warm Springs Rd), Kenwood. 707/833.6326; fax 707/833.2238

20 Cafe Citti ★★$

It looks like a modest roadside eatery, but once you see the open kitchen, the deli case filled with great salads, and the glistening bronzed chickens on the rotisserie, you'll know you've found a winner. The chicken, redolent of rosemary, tastes as good as it looks. The place is frequented mostly by locals who swear by such fresh, simply sauced pastas as rigatoni with garlic, black-pepper pancetta, and olive oil. This is a good place to pick up wine and fixings for a picnic. If you decide to eat in, order, take a seat, and the food will be delivered to your table. The outside deck is close to the highway, but plantings block the traffic so you see only rustling trees and hillsides. ♦ Italian ♦ Daily lunch and dinner. No reservations accepted. 9049 Sonoma Hwy (at Shaw Rd), Kenwood. 707/833.2690

Thirty-four wineries in the Sonoma Valley produce 25 types of wine—more than 5 million cases yearly.

Beyond the Bridges

The Sporting Life

Baseball great Joe DiMaggio came from a long line of Sicilian fishermen; his father, Giuseppe Paolo DiMaggio, fished in **San Francisco Bay,** and the "Yankee Clipper" even worked on the boat with him. So when DiMaggio returned to his hometown in 1937, it was a natural for him to open a seafood restaurant on **Fisherman's Wharf. DiMaggio's** operated at 245 Jefferson Street until it was sold in 1984; it eventually became **Bobby Rubino's Place for Ribs,** which still is in business today.

Probably San Francisco's most famous eatery owned by a sports figure is **Lefty O'Doul's** (333 Geary St, between Mason and Powell Sts, 982.8900), near **Union Square.** O'Doul gained prominence as a pitcher for the **Boston Red Sox** in the 1920s. His restaurant opened in 1958 and to this day offers hofbrau-style fare in a room filled with sports memorabilia.

Dante Benedetti became a local hero—not for his 87 amateur prizefights, but as the coach of the **University of San Francisco** baseball team, which he led to victory from 1968 to 1989. In 1918 his family established the **New Pisa Restaurant** (550 Green St, between Grant and Columbus Aves, 989.2289), which carries on under new owner Tom Ginella. Dante's awards fill the Trophy Room, and Dante himself hosts at lunch most days and is happy to talk about old times with sports buffs. And when basketball superstar Nate Thurman retired from playing with the **Golden State Warriors** in 1990, he opened **Big Nate's Bar-B-Que** (1665 Folsom St, between 12th and 13th Sts, 861.4242; fax 861.1633 &) in the trendy SoMa district. The tangy sauces and smoked meats have made the place very popular, especially with young club-hoppers.

Of course San Francisco has numerous sports bars that, while not owned by former athletes, are magnets for sports fans. Even a stylish restaurant like **Moose's,** in **North Beach,** has two jumbo screens. Here's a list of some of the top sports bars; most have at least one large screen and several television monitors:

Barley & Hops ♦ Parc 55 Hotel, 55 Cyril Magnin St (near Market and Fifth Sts), Second floor. 392.8000

The Bus Stop ♦ 1901 Union St (between Laguna and Buchanan Sts). 567.6905

Gino & Carlo ♦ 548 Green St (between Columbus and Grant Aves). 421.0896

Greens Sports Bar ♦ 2239 Polk St (between Green and Vallejo Sts). 775.4287

Pat O'Shea's Mad Hatter ♦ 3848 Geary Blvd (at Third Ave). 752.3148

21 Buckley Lodge ★★★$$ Formerly the **Golden Bear Lodge** until 1994 when Michael Buckley purchased it, this newly refurbished restaurant is a real find. Buckley had fallen in love with Sonoma County after many annual wine-buying trips for Butterfield's, his restaurant in Los Angeles. The bright interior has light wood wainscoting and modern artwork; a tree-shaded deck overlooking a creek is a good spot to enjoy lunch or dinner in warm weather. The chef, Tony Marano, turns out such excellent dishes as a simple risotto with shiitake mushrooms, ground black pepper, and parmesan cheese; duck cooked to a succulent pink, drizzled with Port and green peppercorns, and served with a mix of green lentils and pearl-shaped pasta; and a tender lamb shank accented with barley, roasted tomatoes, and pomegranate juice. Desserts are less exciting and run the gamut from Grand Marnier cheesecake to a coconut-melon sorbet. The extensive wine list is very well-priced and includes some of the best unusual varietals produced in the county.
♦ Californian ♦ M, W-Sa lunch and dinner, Su brunch and dinner early-Feb–Dec. 1717 Adobe Canyon Rd (off Hwy 12), Kenwood. 707/833.5562 &

Beyond the Bridges

21 John Ash & Company ★★$$$$ Since its opening in 1980, this has been one of Northern California's most innovative restaurants. It remains so, even though founder John Ash is now only a consultant and spends his time running the culinary program at the Fetzer Wine & Food Center in Mendocino County. The food is expensive and the combinations can be a little far out; some work better than others. Generally the simpler the preparation, the better the dish, as evidenced by a delicious thick charred steak accented with a sauce of Jack Daniels and wild mushrooms. For starters try the excellent duck rillettes, made without fat or liver, served on crisp toast points. The wine list is expensively priced, but offers some hard-to-get Sonoma vintages. The modern building has cathedral ceilings that seem to parody the idea of a mecca of gastronomy, and the Southwestern decor looks a little stuck in the previous decade.
♦ Californian ♦ M dinner; Tu-Sa lunch and dinner; Su brunch and dinner. Reservations recommended. 4330 Barnes Rd (at River Rd), Santa Rosa. 707/527.7687; fax 707/527.1202 &

21 Cafe Lolo ★★★$$ Located in downtown Santa Rosa, this restaurant has a simple clean look, a convivial backdrop for the food of Michael Quigley, who was a sous chef at Meadowood in Napa Valley before venturing out on his own. The menu changes seasonally and might include rock shrimp with shaved raw artichokes and asiago cheese, topped with lemon dressing; or roasted beets with caramelized shallots, toasted walnuts, and frisée, bathed in sherry vinaigrette. Main courses could be a pork chop in Merlot sauce paired with Swiss chard, or roast duck with mushrooms and a rhubarb chutney. The sophisticated food and moderate prices have quickly made this place a local favorite.
♦ Californian ♦ M-F lunch and dinner; Sa dinner. Reservations recommended. 620 Fifth St (near D St), Santa Rosa. 707/576.7822

22 Willowside Cafe ★★★$$ This modest, low-slung barn-red roadhouse attracts little attention from the highway, but within it owners Michael and Carole Hale and chef Richard Allen have created one of the best restaurants in California wine country. The light paneled ceiling, whirling fans, dark wood floors, and copper-top tables add a dash of style, as do cheerfully painted wainscoting and bright oil paintings created by employees. The weekly changing menu might start with mussels coated with a mustardy broth thickened with crème fraîche. Leg of lamb, roasted to a perfect pink, is served on a bed of artichokes and barely crunchy onions with cheese and tarragon. The wine list is as refreshing as the menu and concentrates on unusual and hard-to-find selections. Desserts—intense lemon tart, angel food cake layered with lemon mousse, or chocolate silk pie with a nut crust—are delicious.
♦ Californian ♦ W-Su dinner. Reservations recommended. 3535 Guerneville Rd (at Willowside Rd), Guerneville. 707/523.4814

23 Bistro Ralph ★★★$$ Ralph Tingle's cutting-edge cuisine makes use of fresh local ingredients and takes its inspiration from the Southwest, Italy, and Asia. Never pass up the Szechuan pepper calamari, which is fried crispy and served with a lemon-ginger dipping sauce. Sonoma lamb stars in *niçoise* stew at dinner and as a lamb burger with goat cheese and delightful shoestring potatoes at lunch. Grilled *ahi* tuna is served with an olive sauce and horseradish-flavored mashed potatoes. The staff is friendly and well-informed, and there's a reasonably priced wine list.
♦ Californian ♦ M-F lunch and dinner; Sa-Su dinner. Reservations recommended. 109 Plaza St (on Healdsburg Plaza), Healdsburg. 707/433.1380 &

Sonoma County is home to four cheese manufacturers: Vella Cheese Company (known for its dry monterey jack), the Sonoma Cheese Factory, Laurel Chenel Cheese (which put goat cheese on the map in this country), and Joe Matos Cheese Factory (which produces St. George, a semihard cheese otherwise made only in the Azores).

There are 13,000 acres planted to grapes in the Sonoma Valley.

Index

A

Academy Grill $ 119
Accessibility for the disabled 6
Acquerello ★★★$$$ 75
Act IV $$$ 117
Adel's Wine Cellar 171
Adriano, Cafe 98
Ajanta Restaurant ★★★$ 206
Akimbo, Cafe 20
Alain Rondelli ★★★★$$$ 191
Albona Restaurant ★★★$$ 61
Alcatraz Bar and Grill ★$ 65
Alemany Farmers' Market 153
Alfred's ★★★$$$ 81
Ali Baba's Cave ★$ 110
Alioto's ★★$$$ 68
All Aboard 7
Allegria ★★$$ 97
Allegro Ristorante Italiano ★★$$$ 81
All Seasons, Cafe for 172
Alta Plaza Bar and Restaurant ★★$$ 91
Amazing Grace Vegetarian Restaurant ★$ 156
American Pie 187
Amici's East Coast Pizza ★★$ 94
Amira ★$$ 146
Anchor Oyster Bar ★★$$ 160
Andalé Taqueria ★★$ 100
Andronico's Market 178
Angkor Borei ★★$ 152
Angkor Wat ★★$$ 192
Anjou ★★$$ 20
Anna's Danish Cookies 148
Anthony's ★$$ 60
Aperto ★★★$$ 138
Appam Indian Cuisine ★$ 135
Aqua ★★★★$$$$ 29
Arabi $ 126
Armani Cafe ★★$$ 21
Aroma $ 126
Aromi ★★$$ 74
Ar Roi ★★$ 13
Art Institute Cafe ★$ 79
A. Sabella's Restaurant ★★★$$$ 67
Asakichi 107
Asakichi II 109
Ashbury Market 170
Asher, Gerald 183 (bests)
Asimakopoulos Cafe ★★$$ 138
Auntie Pasta (Castro) 161
Auntie Pasta (Cow Hollow) 96
Auntie Pasta (Russian Hill) 77
Auntie Pasta (The Haight) 170
Autumn Harvest 133
Aux Délices ★★$ 79

B

Babaloo Restaurant $ 97
Bacco Ristorante Italiano ★★★$$ 161
Backstage ★★$$$ 117
Bad Man Jose's ★★$ 159
Bagelry, The 77
Bakers of Paris 163
Baker Street Bistro ★★$$ 187
Balboa Cafe ★$$ 96
Barney's Gourmet Hamburgers (Noe Valley) ★$ 162
Barney's Gourmet Hamburgers (The Marina) ★$ 99
Basil ★★$$ 135
Basque Hotel and Restaurant ★$$ 50
Basta Pasta $$ 52
Bastille, Cafe 24
Baton Rouge Cajun Roadhouse $ 93
Battambang ★★★$ 203
Bay Area Certified Farmers' Market 208
Bayview-Hunter's Point 122 (chapter and map)
Bay Wolf ★★★$$$ 204
Bean There ★$ 111
Bechelli's Coffee Shop ★★$ 102
Belle Saison, La 198
Bell Tower ★★$ 76
Ben & Jerry's (Fisherman's Wharf) 67
Ben & Jerry's (North Beach) 58
Ben & Jerry's (The Haight) 168
Benihana of Tokyo ★$$$ 108
Benkyodo Confectioners ★$ 106
Bepples Pies 92
Bernstein, Sally 121 (bests)
Betelnut ★★★$$ 93
Bette's Oceanview Diner ★★$ 205
Bette's-to-Go 205
Beyond the Bridges 202 (chapter and map)
Bien Dong ★$ 120
Big Four, The 82
Big Nate's Bar-B-Que ★$ 136
Big Sky Ranch ★★$$ 71
Bill's Place ★$ 199
Biordi 51
Biscuits and Blues ★$$ 17
Bistro Clovis ★★$$ 114
Bistro M ★★$$$ 134
Bistro Ralph ★★★$$ 215
Bistro Rôti ★★★$$ 125
Bix ★★★$$$ 27
Bizou ★★$$ 129
Blackstone, Cammy 71 (bests)
Blue Chip Cookies (Fisherman's Wharf) 65
Blue Chip Cookies (SoMa) 126
Blue Point ★★$$ 199
Bob's Donut and Pastry Shop 75
Bocce Caffè ★$$ 53
Bodega, La 53
Bombay Bazar 146
Bonta Ristorante ★★★$$ 95
Boudin Bakery (The Richmond) 195
Boudin Sourdough Bakery & Café (Fisherman's Wharf) ★$ 67
Boudin Sourdough Bakery & Café (SoMa) ★$ 131
Boulevard ★★★$$$ 125
Bow Hon ★$ 34
Brandy Ho's ★$ 48
Brasserie Chambord ★$$ 25
Brasserie Savoy ★★★$$ 13
Brava Terrace ★★★$$ 211
Brazen Head Restaurant, The 93
Brew City Personal Brewery 96
Brothers Restaurant ★★$ 192
Bruno's ★★$$ 149
Bryan's 189
Buca Giovanni ★★$$$ 61
Buchanan Grill ★★$$ 103
Buckeye Roadhouse ★★$$ 207
Buckley Lodge ★★★$$ 214
Buena Vista Cafe ★$ 69
Buffalo Whole Food & Grain Company (Castro) 161
Buffalo Whole Food & Grain Company (Nob Hill) 85
Bugatti's Espresso Cafe ★$ 96
Burger Gourmet ★$ 126
Burger Joint ★$ 148
Burma House Cuisine ★$ 12
Byblos ★★$$ 97

C

Cadillac Bar and Grill ★$ 133
Cafe Adriano ★★$$ 98
Cafe Akimbo ★★$$ 20
Cafe at Chez Panisse ★★★★$$ 205
Cafe Bastille ★★$$ 24
Café Chaise ★★$$ 81
Cafe Citti ★★$ 213
Café Claude ★$$$ 23
Cafe Corbas ★$ 115
Cafe de la Presse ★★$ 23
Cafe de Paris L'Entrecôte ★$$ 93
Cafe de Young ★★$ 175
Cafe Dolci 21
Cafe Espresso ★★$ 19
Cafe Express $ 133
Cafe Flore $ 157
Cafe for All Seasons ★★★$$ 172
Cafe Istanbul $ 146
Cafe Jacqueline ★★★$$ 54
Cafe Kati ★★★$$ 106
Cafe Lolo ★★★$$ 215

216

Cafe Lupann's ★$$ 159
Cafe Macondo $ 147
Cafe Maisonette ★★★$$ 194
Cafe Majestic ★★$$$ 107
Cafe Marimba ★$$ 102
Cafe Pacifica/Sankt Gallen Brewery $ 24
Cafe Pescatore ★$$ 66
Cafe Rigatoni $$ 69
Café Riggio ★$$ 192
Cafe SFA ★★$$ 19
Cafe Tiramisù ★★$$ 24
Cafe Tisane ★★$$ 144
Cafe Titanic ★$ 12
Caffe Centro (SoMa) ★★$ 128
Caffe Centro (The Marina) ★★$ 99
Caffè Delle Stelle ★★$$ 115
Caffè Freddy's Eatery ★$ 61
Caffè Macaroni ★★$ 49
Caffè Malvina ★★$ 54
Caffè Museo ★★$ 131
Caffè Puccini ★$ 51
Caffè Roma Coffee Roasting Company ★$ 58
Caffè Sport ★★$$$ 56
Caffè Trieste ★$ 52
Caffe Trinity ★★$ 117
California Creole Cafe $$ 131
California Culinary Academy 119
California Pizza Kitchen ★$ 15
California Wine Merchant, The 100
Cal-Mart 190
Calzone's $$ 52
Campo Santo ★$ 49
Campton Place Restaurant ★★★$$$$ 19
Canasta, La 95
Candelier 22
Candy Barrel, The 67
Candy Jar Outlet, The (SoMa) 140
Candy Jar, The (Downtown) 23
Cannery, The 69
Cannery Wine Cellar and Gourmet Market 69
Cantinetta Tra Vigne ★★★$ 211
Canto do Brazil ★$ 148
Canton Restaurant ★★$ 130
Capp's Corner ★★$ 60
Careme Room ★$$$ 119
Caribbean Zone ★$$ 130
Carl's Pastry 148
Carnelian Room ★★$$$ 26
Carta ★★$$ 113
Caruso Wine and Liquor Store 163
Casa Aguila ★$$ 180
Casa de Fruta 65
Casa Felix 149
Casa Lucas 144
Casa Sanchez 144
Cassis Bistro ★★★$$ 97
Cass, Maxine 85 (bests)

Castro 154 (chapter and map)
Castro Cheesery 159
Castro Village Wine Co. 161
Catahoula Restaurant and Saloon ★★★★$$$ 212
Cedanna 88
Centerfolds ★★$$$ 48
Central, Le 23
Centro, Caffe (SoMa) 128
Centro, Caffe (The Marina) 99
Cha Cha Cha ★★★$ 170
Chai of Larkspur ★★$ 208
Chaise, Café 81
Chalkers Billiard Club ★$ 126
Champagne Exchange $$ 133
Chantilly, Le 89
Charles Nob Hill ★★★★$$$ 81
Charm, Le 132
Chava's Mexican Restaurant ★★$ 145
Cheese Boutique (Glen Park) 173
Cheese Boutique (The Sunset) 178
Chef Specialty Foods, The 163
Chestnut Street Grill, The 100
Cheung Hing ★★$ 181
Cheval Restaurant, Le 203
Chevys (Downtown) ★★$ 30
Chevys (SoMa) ★★$$ 132
Chez Michel ★$$$ 70
Chez Panisse ★★★★$$$ 204
Chez Panisse, Cafe at 205
Chiang Mai Thai ★★$$ 195
Chico Produce Market, El 198
Chika ★★$ 178
Child's Play 80
China Moon Cafe ★★$$$ 13
Chinatown 32 (chapter and map)
Chloe's Cafe ★$ 164
Cho-Cho Restaurant ★$$ 49
Chocolate Covered 163
Chocolate Heaven 65
Chong Imports 34
Christofle 22
Christophe ★$$$ 16
Church Produce 165
Ciao ★★$$ 29
Cinderella Restaurant and Bakery ★$ 192
Citron ★★★$$$ 204
Citti, Cafe 213
City Centre Grill $$ 133
City Discount 79
City Eats $ 25
City of Paris ★★$$ 13
City Picnic ★$ 115
Cityscape Restaurant ★★$$$ 14
City Tavern $$ 96
Civic Center 112 (chapter and map)
Claude, Café 23
Clement Restaurant $ 194
Clement Street Bar and Grill ★$$ 194

Cliff's Variety 159
Coconut Grove ★★★$$$ 73
Coffee Merchant, The 177
Coffee, Tea & Spice 169
Coit Liquors 59
Cole Valley 166 (chapter and map)
Collections Gift Store 128
Columbus Cutlery 51
Compass Rose ★$$$ 18
Confetti California Fruits and Nuts 69
Confetti le Chocolatier 31
Confetti's 69
Cookin' 168
Coppola, Francis Ford 103 (bests)
Corbas, Cafe 115
Cordon Bleu ★$ 74
Coriya ★★$ 195
Costco 137
Cost Plus World Market 66
Courtyard Bar and Grill ★$$ 199
Courtyard Cafe ★$$ 164
Cow Hollow 86 (chapter and map)
Crab Cake Lounge ★★$ 71
Crate & Barrel (Downtown) 21
Crate & Barrel Outlet Store (The East Bay) 206
Creighton's American Bakery 173
Creighton's Cheese & Fine Foods ★$ 172
Crepevine ★★$ 176
Crustacean ★$$$ 74
Cucina Paradiso ★★★$$ 103
Cypress Club ★★★$$$ 27
Cyrano, Le 192

D

Daily Grind, The 84
Daily Scoop, The 139
Dalldorf, Tom 173 (bests)
Dame—a restaurant ★★$ 155
D&M Liquors 90
Danilo Italian Bakery 53
Danto's Fresh Italian Seafood ★$$$ 66
David's Delicatessen ★$ 15
Delancey Street Restaurant ★$$ 127
de la Presse, Cafe 23
Delle Stelle, Caffè 115
de Paris L'Entrecôte, Cafe 93
Des Alpes Restaurant ★★$ 45
deStijl Cafe ★★$ 64
Dewey's ★$ 18
de Young, Cafe 175
Dianda's Bakery ★★$ 56
Dianda's Italian and American Pastries 151
Dick Lee Pastry 43
Disabled travelers, accessibility 6

Index

Dish ★$ 168
Doc's International Candy Shoppe 67
Doidge's ★★$ 94
Dojima An ★★$$ 18
Dolci, Cafe 21
Domaine Chandon ★★★★$$$$ 209
Dominguez Mexican Bakery 144
Dottie's True Blue Cafe ★$ 14
Double Rainbow Ice Cream (Castro) 157
Double Rainbow Ice Cream (Russian Hill) 75
Double Rainbow Ice Cream (The Haight) 169
Downtown 10 (chapter and map)
DPD Restaurant ★★$$ 38
Dragon House Restaurant ★$ 196
Drewes Market 165
Drinking 6
Dutch Kitchen $$$ 18

E

Eagle Cafe ★$ 65
E'Angelo Restaurant ★★$ 101
East Bay, The 203
Eastern Bakery 34
East Side Oyster Bar & Grill ★★$$ 213
Eastwind Books & Arts 41
Ecco, Ristorante 128
Eclipse Cafe $$ 31
Economy Restaurant Fixtures 141
Eddie Rickenbacker's ★★$$ 130
Eichelberger's $$ 145
El Chico Produce Market 198
11 Ristorante + Bar ★★$$ 136
Elite Cafe ★★$$ 89
Eliza's (Hayes Valley) ★★★$$ 114
Eliza's (SoMa) ★★★$ 139
Ella's ★★★$ 187
El Nuevo Frutilandia ★$ 152
El Pollo Supremo ★★$ 152
El Toro Taqueria ★★$$ 146
Embarcadero, The 62 (chapter and map)
Emerald Garden ★★$$ 74
Empress of China ★$$ 34
Enrico's ★★★$$ 48
EOS Restaurant & Wine Bar ★★★$$ 171
Epicurean Shop, The 20
Eppler's Bakery ★$ 21
Eppler's/Fantasia 188
Equinox $$$ 31
Eric's ★★$ 165
Esperpento ★★$ 150
Espresso Bar $ 21
Espresso, Cafe 19
Etheredge, Jeanette 71 (bests)
European Delights 57

Everyday Cafe ★$ 68
Everything You Ever Wanted to Know about Pairing Wine and Food, But Were Afraid to Ask 57
Express, Cafe 133

F

Fabrizio ★★$$ 208
Fabulous Food Festivals and Street Fairs 7
Fairmont Lobby, The 82
Farley's ★$ 139
Farmers' Markets 134
FAZ ★★$$ 25
Feng Huang Pastry 43
Ferry Plaza Farmers' Market 125
Figoni Hardware Co. 53
Fillamento 90
Fina Estanpa ★★$ 149
Fior d'Italia, Ristorante 55
Firefly ★★★$$ 161
Firenze, Ristorante 56
Fisherman's Wharf 62 (chapter and map)
Fishermen's Grotto ★$$$ 68
Fleur de Lys ★★★★$$$$ 13
Floogie's Swamp Cafe ★★$$ 114
Floréal 15
Flore, Cafe 157
Florence Ravioli 56
Flying Kamikazes ★★$$ 99
Flying Saucer, The 151
Fly Trap, The 130
Fog City Diner ★★$$ 65
Foggy's ★$ 66
Folie, La 79
Food Inc. ★★$ 89
Food tours 7
Fornaio, Il 64
Fornaio Panetteria, Il 95
Forrest Jones 187
42 Degrees ★★★$$ 141
Fountain Court ★★$ 191
Fournou's Ovens ★★$$$ 83
Four Sea Supermarket 39
Frantoio Ristorante ★$$ 208
Frascati Ristorante ★★$$ 80
Freddy's Eatery, Caffè 61
Freed Teller & Freed's (Downtown) 29
Freed Teller & Freed's (Nob Hill) 73
French Laundry ★★★★$$$$ 209
French Room ★★$$$$ 14
Fresh Choice (Downtown) $ 21
Fresh Choice (SoMa) $ 132
Fresh Market Cafe ★$ 21
Fringale Restaurant ★★★$$ 129
Fudge House, The 65
Fuji Japanese Restaurant ★★$$ 173
Full Moon Foods and Mercantile 94

G

Ganges, The 170
Garden Court ★★$$$$ 131
Garibaldis ★★$$$ 188
Garibaldi's Cafe $$ 138
Gaylord India Restaurant ★$$$ 71
Gebhart, Fred 85 (bests)
Gelato Classico ★$ 55
George's Global Kitchen ★$ 137
German Cook ★★$ 121
Geva's ★★$$$ 116
Ghirardelli Chocolate Manufactory ★★$ 70
Ghirardelli Chocolates 21
Ghirardelli Square 70
Ginn Wall Company 39
Ginseng Mania 157
Gira Polli ★★$ 59
Glen Park 166 (chapter and map)
Gloria Jean's 25
Goat Hill Pizza ★$ 138
Golden Flower Restaurant ★$ 38
Golden Gate Bakery 39
Golden Gate Fortune Cookie Company 43
Golden Gate Meat Company 42
Golden Turtle ★★★$ 77
Gold Leaf 15
Gold Mountain Restaurant ★★$ 40
Gold Spike $ 58
Good Life Grocery, The (SoMa) 140
Good Life Grocery, The (The Mission) 153
Gordon Bennett 94
Gordon Biersch Brewery Restaurant ★$$ 127
Gourmet Carousel ★★$ 91
Gourmet Kitchen 44
Graffeo Coffee 60
Grand Cafe ★★$$$ 14
Grand Central Market 89
Gravy, Wavy 121 (bests)
Grazie ★★$$ 56
Great Eastern Restaurant ★★★$$ 38
Greco-Romana ★★$$ 199
Greek American Food Imports 145
Green Apple Books 193
Greens Restaurant ★★$$ 103
Green World Mercantile 79
Grove, The 101
Guaymas ★★$$ 207
Gump's 22

H

Hacienda, La 147
Haig's Delicacies 194
Haight & Fillmore Whole Foods 110
Haight, The 166 (chapter and map)
Hai Ky Mi Gia ★$ 120

218

Index

Half Shell Restaurant and Oyster Bar ★★$$ **135**
Halprin & Associates, Lawrence **70**
Hamano Sushi ★★$ **162**
Hamburger Mary's ★$ **136**
Hana Restaurant ★★$ **175**
Happy Supermarket **191**
Happy Valley Chinese Seafood Restaurant ★★$$ **64**
Harbor Village ★★$$ **31**
Hard Rock Cafe ★$ **75**
Harris' Restaurant ★★★$$$ **76**
Harry Denton's ★$$ **125**
Harry Denton's Starlight Room ★★$$ **19**
Harvest Ranch Market **157**
Hawthorne Lane ★★★$$$ **130**
Hayes and Vine ★★$ **115**
Hayes Street Grill ★★$$$ **115**
Hayes Valley **112** (chapter and map)
Hazel's Kitchen **139**
Heavenly Hot ★★$$ **195**
Heights, The **187**
Helmand Restaurant, The **48**
Herb's Fine Foods ★$ **163**
Heritage House **140**
Hing Lung **41**
Hing Lung Chinese Cuisine ★★$ **41**
Holding Company, The **30**
Holey Bagel (Berkeley) **205**
Holey Bagel (Noe Valley) **164**
Holey Bagel (The Haight) **168**
Holey Bagel (The Marina) **97**
Home Plate ★★$ **100**
Homestead Ravioli **137**
Hong Kong Deli **42**
Hong Kong Flower Lounge Restaurant ★★★$$ **196**
Hong Kong Seafood Restaurant ★★$ **181**
Hong Kong Villa ★★★$$ **199**
Hop Sang Company **42**
Hot 'N' Hunky ★$ **159**
Hot Shop, The **23**
Hours **6**
House of Bagels **195**
House of Coffee **180**
House of Nanking $ **38**
House of Prime Rib, The **76**
House, The **50**
Howard's ★★$ **177**
H-P Seafood Market **45**
Hunan Homes ★★$ **38**
Hunan Restaurant ★$$ **48**
Hunters Point **122** (chapter and map)
Hyde Street Bistro ★★$$ **81**
Hyde Street Seafood House and Raw Bar ★$$ **81**

I

Icon Byte Bar & Grill $ **136**
Ideal Deli ★$ **135**
Ideale, Ristorante **52**
i Fratelli ★★$$ **81**
Il Fornaio ★★$$ **64**
Il Fornaio Panetteria **95**
Il Pollaio ★$ **58**
Imperial Tea Court **45**
Inca ★★$ **153**
Incontro ★$ **114**
India Oven ★★$$ **111**
Iroha ★★$$ **107**
Irving Little Cafe & Sandwiches ★$ **179**
Irving Seafood Market **179**
Isobune Sushi $ **108**
Israel Kosher Meats **197**
Istanbul, Cafe **146**
Isuzu Restaurant ★★$ **108**
Italian/French Bakery **54**
It'o Topo Coffee Shop ★★$ **155**
Ivy's Restaurant and Bar ★★$$$ **115**
Izzy's Steak & Chops ★★★$$ **99**

J

Jack's ★★★$ **26**
Jack's Bar $ **69**
Jack's Elixir Bar **147**
Jackson Fillmore Trattoria ★★★$$ **91**
Jackson Pavilion ★$ **38**
Jacqueline, Cafe **54**
Jakarta ★★$$ **193**
James & James Ribs 'n' Thangs ★★★$$ **140**
J & J Restaurant ★★★$ **35**
Japanese Tea Garden, Teahouse in **175**
Japantown **104** (chapter and map)
Jasmine House ★★★$ **199**
Jelly's: A Dance Cafe ★$$ **141**
Jimmy Bean's ★★$ **127**
Jivano's Cutlery Service **148**
Joe's ★★$ **196**
John Ash & Company ★★$$$$ **215**
John Cunin's No-Name Restaurant ★★★$$ **156**
Johnny Love's ★$$ **77**
Johnny Nipon's $ **178**
Johnny Rockets (Fisherman's Wharf) ★★$ **67**
Johnny Rockets (Pacific Heights) ★$ **88**
John's Grill ★$$ **17**
John Walker and Co. Liquors **25**
Jordan, Michele Anna **85** (bests)
Joseph Esherick & Associates **69**
J R New Orange Land **43**

J.T.'s Bistro ★★$$$ **118**
Judith Ets-Hokin's Home Chef **189**
Judy's Cafe ★$ **101**
Jug Shop **76**
Juicy News **91**
Julie Ring's Heart and Soul ★★$$ **75**
Julie's Supper Club ★★$$ **135**
Julius' Castle ★$$$$ **61**
Just Desserts (Castro) **156**
Just Desserts (The Sunset) **178**
Just For You Cafe ★$ **139**
Just Like Home ★★$ **179**
Just Won Ton ★★$ **183**

K

Kabuto Sushi ★★★$$ **195**
Kame Sushi ★★$ **109**
Kam (H.K.) Po Kitchen ★$ **45**
Kam Lok ★$ **44**
Kam Wah ★★★$ **121**
Kantaro ★$ **17**
Kate's Kitchen ★★$ **110**
Katia's ★★$$ **193**
Kati, Cafe **106**
Katz Bagels ★$ **147**
Kelly's on Trinity ★★$ **24**
Ken Groom's **188**
Kenwood Restaurant and Bar ★★$$$ **213**
Khan Toke Thai House ★★★$$ **198**
Kiki's Paris 1920 ★★$$ **76**
Kim Do Company **40**
Kinoko ★$$$ **132**
Kinokuniya Bookstore **109**
Kiss ★★$$$ **137**
Klein's Deli ★$ **140**
Koji Osakaya ★★$$ **108**
Korea House ★★$$$ **107**
Kowloon Vegetarian Restaurant ★$ **35**
Kuleto, Pat **70**
Kuleto's Italian Restaurant ★$$ **18**
Kushi Tsuru ★★$$ **109**
Kwong Jow Sausage Manufacturing Company **40**
Kyo-ya ★★★$$ **131**

L

La Belle Saison ★★$$ **198**
La Bodega ★$ **53**
La Canasta ★$ **95**
Lady Svbil's Closet **164**
LaFelce ★★$$ **55**
La Folie ★★★$$$$ **79**
Laghi ★★★$$$ **196**
La Hacienda **147**
Lalime's ★★★$$ **206**
La Méditerranée (Castro) ★★$ **157**
La Méditerranée (Pacific Heights) ★★$ **90**

219

Index

L & H Seafood **45**
La Nouvelle Patisserie (Cow Hollow) **94**
La Nouvelle Patisserie (SoMa) $ **133**
La Palma **144**
La Paz Restaurant and Pupuseria ★★$ **140**
La Posada ★$$ **90**
Lark Creek Inn ★$$$ **208**
La Rondalla ★$$ **148**
La Scene Cafe and Bar ★$$$ **15**
La Taqueria ★★$ **151**
Latin Freeze **151**
La Traviata ★★$$ **152**
La Victoria Mexican Bakery **144**
Lawrence Halprin & Associates **70**
Le Central ★★$$ **23**
Le Chantilly **89**
Le Charm ★★$ **132**
Le Cheval Restaurant ★★★$ **203**
Le Cyrano ★★$ **192**
Left Bank ★★★$$ **208**
Lehr Brothers Bistro & Grill ★★$$ **13**
Lehr's German Specialties **165**
Leonard's **76**
Leon's Bar-B-Q (Pacific Heights) ★$$ **87**
Leon's Bar-B-Q (The Sunset) ★$ **183**
Le Soleil ★★$ **190**
Le Trou ★★$$ **150**
Levy's Bagels & Co. **31**
Lhasa Moon ★★$ **102**
Liberty Cafe, The **153**
Lights, Camera, Dinner! **153**
Liguria Bakery **55**
Line-Up, The **135**
Little City Antipasti Bar ★$$ **59**
Little City Market/Meats **56**
Little Italy Ristorante ★★$$ **162**
Little Joe's ★$$ **50**
Little Paris Coffee Shop ★★$ **45**
Little Rio Cafe and Pizzeria ★$ **69**
Little Thai Restaurant ★$ **79**
Liverpool Lil's ★$$ **187**
Lobby Lounge, The **83**
Lo Coco's Restaurant ★★$ **54**
L'Olivier ★★$$$ **30**
Lolo, Cafe **215**
London Wine Bar $ **28**
L'Osteria del Forno ★★★$ **58**
Lotus Garden ★$ **33**
Lou's Pier 47 Club **69**
Lower Haight **104** (chapter and map)
Lucca Delicatessen **100**
Lucca Ravioli Co., Inc. **150**
Lucky Creation ★★$ **44**
Lucky Pork Store **149**

Luddy, Tom **71** (bests)
LuLu ★★★$$ **132**
Lumbini **128**
Lupann's, Cafe **159**

M

Macaroni, Caffè **49**
MacArthur Park ★$$$ **29**
Macondo, Cafe **147**
Macy's Cellar **21**
Mad Dog in the Fog, The **110**
Mad Magda's Russian Tea Room & Mystic Cafe ★$ **116**
Mae-Thip ★$ **175**
Mager's Wine Shop **139**
Magic Flute $$ **188**
Mainline Gifts **88**
Main Squeeze ★$ **74**
Maisonette, Cafe **194**
Majestic, Cafe **107**
Malai Lao Restaurant ★$ **147**
Malvina, Caffè **54**
Mama's Girl ★★$ **55**
Mandalay ★★$ **193**
Mandarin, The **70**
M & M Tavern ★$ **134**
Mangiafuoco ★★$$ **151**
Mannix Café ★★$ **205**
Manora's Thai Cuisine (SoMa) ★★$$ **136**
Manora's Thai Cuisine (The Mission) ★★$ **152**
Map key **6**
Mara's Italian Pastry ★$ **55**
Marco Polo **183**
Marimba, Cafe **102**
Marina, The **86** (chapter and map)
Marin County **206**
Mario's Bohemian Cigar Store Cafe (Russian Hill) ★★$ **78**
Mario's Bohemian Cigar Store (North Beach) ★★$ **58**
Marnee Thai ★★$ **180**
Martha and Brothers Coffee Co. $ **164**
Martin Macks Bar and Restaurant ★$ **168**
Maruwa Foods **108**
Masa's ★★★★$$$$ **19**
Ma-Shi-Ko Folkcraft **109**
Masons Restaurant ★★$$$ **82**
Massawa Restaurant ★$ **169**
Mastering the Dim Sum Experience **36**
Ma Tante Sumi ★★$$ **160**
Matterhorn Swiss Restaurant ★★$$$ **78**
Maxfield's $$ **131**
Max's Diner and Bakery ★$ **129**
Max's Opera Cafe ★$ **118**
Maya Taqueria ★$ **147**

Mayerson Food Company **39**
Maye's Oyster House $$ **73**
Mayflower Seafood Restaurant ★★★$$ **201**
Maykedeh ★★$$ **53**
May's Coffee Shop $ **109**
May Wah Trading Company (Chinatown) **41**
May Wah Trading Company (The Sunset) **180**
McCormick & Kuleto's ★$$$ **70**
McNair, James **121** (bests)
Mecca ★★$$ **156**
Méditerranée, La (Castro) **157**
Méditerranée, La (Pacific Heights) **90**
Mee Heong Bakery **45**
Mee On Company **35**
Meetinghouse, The **91**
Mel's Drive-In (The Marina) ★$ **97**
Mel's Drive-In (The Richmond) ★$ **190**
Meriwa ★★$ **42**
Mescolanza ★★★$$ **198**
Metro Bar and Restaurant ★$ **157**
Metro Foods Company **41**
Metropol ★★★$ **25**
Mi Burrito $ **89**
Michaelangelo Cafe ★$$ **59**
Mifune ★★$ **109**
Mike's Chinese Cuisine ★$$ **196**
Mikey Tom's Market **165**
Milano, Ristorante **81**
Millennium ★★$$ **118**
Mi Rancho Market **149**
Mission Market Fish & Poultry **149**
Mission Meat Market **150**
Mission Rock Resort ★$ **141**
Mission, The **142** (chapter and map)
Miss Millie's ★★★$ **162**
Miss Pearl's Jam House ★★$$ **120**
Mr. Liquor **183**
Mitchell's Ice Cream **152**
Moishe's Pippic ★$ **116**
Molinari Delicatessen **51**
Momi Toby's Revolution Cafe $ **117**
Mona Lisa #3: The Island of Garlic ★$$ **51**
Mondo Caffe ★★$ **130**
Moose's ★★$$ **55**
Morrow's Nut House **21**
Morton's of Chicago ★$$$$ **18**
Moscow and Tbilisi Bakery **196**
Mo's Gourmet Hamburgers ★★$ **53**
Moshi Moshi ★★$ **140**
Muddy's Coffee House (The Mission) $ **151**
Muddy Waters Coffee (Castro) $ **156**

220

Index

Murasaki ★★★$ 191
Murata's Café Hana ★$ 109
Museo, Caffè 131
Mustards Grill ★★★$$ 210
My Sister's Garden 18

N

N. Alioto ★★$ 67
Nanbantei ★★$$ 17
Napa Valley 209 (map)
Napa Valley Winery Exchange 14
Napper's ★★$ 20
Narai ★★$ 198
Nature Stop, The 53
Neecha Thai ★★$ 105
Nelson, Diana 183 (bests)
Neptune's Palace ★$$$ 66
NeverEnding Quails 42
New Asia ★$ 41
New Chieu Fong Company 120
New Delhi Restaurant ★$$ 17
New Eritrea Restaurant ★★$ 178
New Golden Daisy Company 44
New Golden Turtle ★$$ 191
New Hai Ky ★$ 179
New Hong Kong Noodle Company 45
New Hop Yick Meat Market 40
New Joe's $ 18
New On Sang Market/San Francisco Chicken 194
New On Sang Poultry Company 39
New Ping Yuen 43
New Pisa Restaurant ★$ 53
New Sun Hong Kong ★★$ 40
New Woey Loy Goey Restaurant ★$ 39
Nippon Sushi ★★$ 156
Noah's Bagels (The Marina) 98
Noah's Bagels (The Sunset) 177
Nob Hill 72 (chapter and map)
Nob Hill Cafe ★★$$ 82
Nob Hill Noshery Cafe ★$ 81
Nob Hill Restaurant ★★$$$$ 85
Noe Valley 154 (chapter and map)
Noe Valley Bakery & Bread Co. 163
North Beach 46 (chapter and map)
North Beach Pizza ★$ 52
North Beach Restaurant ★$$ 55
North End Caffè 53
North India Restaurant ★★★$$ 97
North Sea Village ★★$ 206
Nosheria ★$ 22
Nouvelle Patisserie, La (Cow Hollow) 94
Nouvelle Patisserie, La (SoMa) 133
Now You're Cookin' 200
Nuevo Frutilandia, El 152
Nuts About You 114

O

Occidental Grill ★★$$ 23

O Chamé ★★★$$ 205
Odessa 196
Old Krakow ★★$$ 173
Old Place, The 48
Old Swiss House ★★$$$ 66
Olive's Gourmet Pizza ★★$$ 102
Oliveto ★★★$$ 204
Olivier, L' 30
One Market Restaurant ★★$$$ 125
Operetta 71
OPTS Cafe ★★$$ 132
Orbit Room, The 155
Oriental Pearl Restaurant ★★$ 34
Orientation 4
Original Joe's Italian Restaurant ★$ 14
Oritalia ★★★$$ 88
Osome ★★$$ 88
Osteria del Forno, L' 50
Out of Hand 163
Owl & Monkey Cafe ★$ 177

P

Pachá ★$ 161
Pacific ★★★$$$ 16
Pacifica, Cafe 24
Pacific Court Cafe ★$ 42
Pacific Heights 86 (chapter and map)
Pacific Restaurant ★$ 120
Paella la Movida ★★$$ 148
Pagolac ★★$ 120
Palermo Ristorante ★$ 38
Palindrome ★$ 125
Palio d'Asti ★★★$$ 26
Palma, La 144
Palmtag, Ron 85 (bests)
Palomino Euro Bistro ★$$ 127
Pancho Villa Taqueria ★$ 146
Pane e Vino ★★$$ 95
Panelli Brothers' Delicatessen 56
Panetti's Gifts 164
Paninoteca Palio d'Asti ★★$ 26
Panos' $ 163
Paragon ★★$$ 102
Paris L'Entrecôte, Cafe de 93
Park Grill ★★$$$ 28
Parma Ristorante ★★$$ 98
Pasand Madras Cuisine ★$ 92
Pasha ★$$$ 76
Pasqua (Downtown) 29
Pasqua (SoMa) ★$ 131
Pasta Pomodoro (North Beach) ★★$ 59
Pasta Pomodoro (The Marina) ★★$ 98
Pasta Primer 158
Patio Cafe, The 160

Patisserie Delanghe 105
Pat O'Shea's Mad Hatter ★★$$ 190
Pauline's Pizza ★★$ 146
Pauli's Cafe ★$$ 91
Paz Restaurant and Pupuseria, La 140
Pazzia ★$ 129
Peet's Coffee & Tea 99
Pendragon Bakery and Cafe ★$ 115
People's Cafe ★★$ 168
Perry's ★★$$ 92
Perry's Downtown ★★$$ 25
Pescatore, Cafe 66
Phnom Penh ★★$ 120
Piatti ★★$$ 213
Piazza D'Angelo ★★★$$ 207
Picaro ★★$ 147
Pinot Blanc ★★★$$ 212
Pizza Inferno ★$ 106
PJ's Oysterbed ★★$$ 177
Place Pigalle ★$ 116
Planet Hollywood $$$ 21
Plaza ★$$ 20
Plout ★★★$$ 24
PlumpJack Cafe ★★$$ 96
PlumpJack Wines 96
Polk St. Beans and Cafe $ 75
Pollaio, Il 58
Pollo Supremo, El 152
Polly Ann Ice Cream 181
Pompei's Grotto ★$$ 68
Pork Store Cafe ★$ 169
Posada, La 90
Postrio ★★★$$$ 15
Potrero Hill 122 (chapter and map)
Pottery Barn (Downtown) 29
Pottery Barn (The Marina) 100
Powell's Place ★$ 116
Pozole ★★$ 157
Prego Ristorante $$ 93
Presidio Heights 184 (chapter and map)
Presse, Cafe de la 23
Prudente Meat Market and Deli 54
Pub, The 133
Puccini & Pinetti ★$ 17
Puccini, Caffe 51
Pure T ★★★$ 78

R

Racha Cafe ★$ 120
Radicchio ★★$$ 92
Radio Valencia Cafe ★$ 150
Rainbow Grocery 145
Rainbow Mall, The 42
Ralph, Bistro 215
Ramp, The 141
Rasselas ★★$$ 89
Raw Living Foods ★$ 176
Raza's $ 134
R & G Lounge ★★$$ 33

221

Index

Real Food Company Deli, The (Cole Valley) **170**
Real Food Company Deli, The (Russian Hill) **77**
Real Food Company, The (Cole Valley) **170**
Real Food Company, The (Noe Valley) **164**
Real Food Company, The (Russian Hill) **77**
Red's Java House ★$ **127**
Redwood Room ★★$$$ **14**
Rendezvous du Monde ★★$$ **23**
Reservations **6**
Restaurants, rating **6**
Restaurant 2001 ★★$$ **138**
Rex Cafe ★$$ **78**
R.H. **90**
Rice Table ★★★$ **209**
Richmond New May Wah Market **193**
Richmond, The **184** (chapter and map)
Rick's Restaurant & Bar ★★★$$ **181**
Rigatoni, Cafe **69**
Riggio, Café **192**
Rincon Center **126**
Ristorante Ecco ★★$$ **128**
Ristorante Fior d'Italia ★$$$ **55**
Ristorante Firenze ★$$ **56**
Ristorante Ideale ★★★$$ **52**
Ristorante Milano ★★$$ **81**
Ristorante Tra Vigne ★★$$ **211**
Ristorante Volare ★$ **58**
Rivoli ★★★$$ **206**
RoCocoa's Faerie Queene Chocolates **159**
Rodgers, Barbara **173** (bests)
Roma Coffee Roasting Company, Caffè **58**
Rondalla, La **148**
Roosevelt's Tamale Parlor ★★$ **144**
Rooster, The **150**
Rory's Twisted Scoop (Castro) **162**
Rory's Twisted Scoop (Pacific Heights) **88**
Rose Garden ★$ **110**
Rose Pistola ★★$$ **58**
Rosie's Cantina ★$ **159**
Rosmarino ★★$$ **188**
Rossi's Delicatessen **159**
Rotunda, The **20**
Royal Exchange, The **29**
Royal Ground Coffee **78**
Royal Jade ★$ **39**
Royal Thai ★$ **195**
Rubicon ★★★$$$ **28**
Rubin's $ **126**
Ruby's Pizza ★★$ **129**

Rue Lepic ★★$$$ **85**
Rumpus ★★★$$ **22**
Russian Hill **72** (chapter and map)
Russian Renaissance Restaurant $$$ **196**
Rustico ★$$ **138**
Ruth's Chris Steak House ★$$$ **74**
Ryan's Charcuterie **160**
Ryan's Restaurant ★★$$ **160**

S

Sagami-Ya Restaurant ★★$ **179**
Saigon Saigon ★★$ **150**
Saigon Sandwich ★★$ **120**
St. Francis Fountain ★★$ **144**
Saji Japanese Cuisine ★★★$$ **101**
Salad Basket $$ **201**
Sally's ★★$ **137**
Salonika ★$$ **78**
Sam's Grill ★★$$ **24**
Samui Thai Cuisine ★★$ **102**
Sam Woh $ **34**
San Francisco **2** (map)
San Francisco Area **202** (map)
San Francisco Bar-B-Que ★$ **139**
San Francisco Brewing Company **49**
San Francisco Centre **133**
San Francisco Chicken/New On Sang Market **194**
San Francisco Herb Company **145**
San Francisco Patisserie Cafe ★★$ **135**
San Francisco Public Transportation **237** (map)
San Francisco Tea and Coffee Co. **66**
Sanko Cooking Supply **107**
Sankt Gallen Brewery **24**
Sanppo ★★$$ **106**
San Wang Restaurant Number 2 ★★$$ **198**
Sapporo-ya ★$ **109**
Sausage Factory, The **160**
Savoy Tivoli **54**
Say Cheese **171**
Scala's ★★$$ **209**
Scala's Bistro ★★★$$ **19**
Scan Trends **71**
Scene Cafe and Bar, La **15**
Schroeder's ★$$ **30**
Scoma's ★★$$ **69**
Scott's Seafood (Downtown) ★$$$ **31**
Scott's Seafood (The Marina) ★$$ **102**
Seafood and Beverage Co. ★$$$ **201**
Seafood Center **194**
Sears Fine Foods ★★$$ **18**
See's Candy **74**
Seoul Garden ★★$$ **108**

SFA, Cafe **19**
s. f. gourmet **100**
SF Scone Works **119**
Shaharazad Bakery **180**
Shanghai King ★$ **201**
Shaw's Confections **172**
Shenson's **195**
Shopping in Chinatown—A Flavorful Adventure **43**
Siam Grill $ **160**
Silks ★★$$$ **28**
Silver Restaurant ★$ **35**
Sinclair's Petite Cafe ★★$ **80**
Singapore Malaysian ★$ **194**
6th Avenue Cheese Shop **193**
Slanted Door, The **146**
Slider's Diner ★$ **159**
Slow Club, The **145**
Smoking **7**
Snookies Cookies **28**
Snyderman, Nancy L. **121** (bests)
Socca Restaurant ★★★$$ **197**
Soko Hardware **107**
Soko Interiors **107**
Soleil, Le **190**
Sol y Luna ★★$$ **28**
SoMa (South of Market) **122** (chapter and map)
Some Like It Hot! A Fiery Food Emporium **101**
Sonoma County **212** (map)
Sonoma Valley Bagel Co. ★★$ **23**
Sophie's Cookhouse ★★★$ **27**
Sorabol Noodles ★$ **126**
Soups ★$ **121**
Sourdough Starter **189**
South Beach **122** (chapter and map)
South of Market (SoMa) **122** (chapter and map)
South Park Cafe ★★★$$ **128**
Spaghetti Western ★$ **110**
Specialty's Cafe and Bakery **24**
Speckmann's ★$$ **165**
Speedsters ★$ **126**
Spiazzo ★★$$ **172**
Spinelli Coffee Company **163**
Splendido ★★$$$ **31**
Sport, Caffè **56**
Sporting Life, The **214**
Spuntino ★$$ **118**
Square One ★★★$$$ **30**
Squat & Gobble Cafe ★★$ **111**
SRO! ★$ **31**
Stamp Francisco **137**
Star Bakery **165**
Starbucks Coffee (Cow Hollow) **92**
Starbucks Coffee (Russian Hill) **78**
Star Lunch ★$ **35**
Stars ★★★$$$$ **118**
Stars Cafe ★$$ **117**
Stars Oakville Cafe ★★$$$ **210**

222

Index

Stella Pastry **52**
Stelle, Caffè Delle **115**
Stelline ★**$ 116**
Steps of Rome ★**$ 51**
Stevens, Ken **183** (bests)
Stinking Rose, The **51**
Stoyanof's Cafe and Restaurant ★★★**$$ 176**
Straits Café ★★**$$ 190**
Straw, The Jar and The Bean, The **88**
Studio Cafe ★**$ 111**
Sue Fisher King **187**
Sugar 'n' Spice **201**
Sun Country Foods **170**
Sun Duck Market **43**
Sunrise Deli and Cafe ★**$ 179**
Sunset, The **174** (chapter and map)
Superior Trading Company **44**
Super Koyama **107**
Suppenküche ★★**$$ 117**
Suriya Thai Restaurant ★★**$$ 151**
Sushi-A ★★★**$$ 106**
Sushi Bune ★★**$ 17**
Sushi Chardonnay ★**$$ 91**
Suzanne's Muffins **161**
Swan Oyster Depot ★★★**$$ 74**
Sweet Endings Cookies **180**
Sweet Factory, The **68**
Sweet Heat ★★**$ 99**
Sweet Sue's **173**
Swensen's Ice Cream **79**

T

Tadich Grill ★★**$$ 30**
Tad's Steaks ★**$ 17**
Tai Chi Restaurant **$ 76**
Taiwan Restaurant (Chinatown) ★★★**$ 40**
Taiwan Restaurant (The Richmond) ★★**$ 192**
Tamnan Thai ★★**$ 177**
Tampico **$ 126**
Taqueria El Balazo ★★**$ 169**
Taqueria Goyaz ★**$ 151**
Taqueria, La **151**
Taqueria la Coqueta ★**$ 171**
Taqueria La Cumbre ★**$ 146**
Taqueria San Jose ★★★**$ 152**
Taqueria Zapata ★**$ 159**
Tarantino's **$$$ 67**
Tart to Tart ★★★**¢ 175**
Tassajara Bread Bakery ★**$ 171**
Tây Việt ★★**$ 98**
Tea & Company **90**
Teahouse in Japanese Tea Garden ★**$ 175**
Tea Time **182**
Tenderloin, The **112** (chapter and map)
Ten Ichi ★★**$$ 90**
Ten Ren Tea Company of San Francisco, Ltd. **39**
Terra ★★★★**$$$$ 211**
Terrace, The **83**
Teuscher Chocolates of Switzerland **22**
Thai BBQ ★★**$ 119**
Thai House Bar and Café ★**$ 156**
Thai House Restaurant ★**$ 157**
Thai-to-go **$ 126**
Thang Xuong Market **120**
Thanh Long ★★**$$ 180**
Thanya and Salee ★★**$ 138**
Thatcher's **126**
The Bagelry **77**
The Big Four ★★**$$$$ 82**
The Brazen Head Restaurant ★★**$$ 93**
The California Wine Merchant **100**
The Candy Barrel **67**
The Candy Jar (Downtown) **23**
The Candy Jar Outlet (SoMa) **140**
Tho Cannery **69**
The Chef Specialty Foods **163**
The Chestnut Street Grill ★**$ 100**
The Coffee Merchant **177**
The Daily Grind **84**
The Daily Scoop ★**$ 139**
The Dining Room ★★★★**$$$$ 83**
The East Bay **203**
The Embarcadero **62** (chapter and map)
The Epicurean Shop **20**
The Fairmont Lobby ★★**$$ 82**
The Flying Saucer ★★★**$$$ 151**
The Fly Trap ★★★**$$ 130**
The Fudge House **65**
The Ganges ★★**$ 170**
The Good Life Grocery (SoMa) **140**
The Good Life Grocery (The Mission) **153**
The Grove ★★**$ 101**
The Haight **166** (chapter and map)
The Heights ★★★★**$$$ 187**
The Helmand Restaurant ★★★**$$ 48**
The Holding Company ★**$$ 30**
The Hot Shop **23**
The House ★★★**$$ 50**
The House of Prime Rib ★★**$$ 76**
The Liberty Cafe ★★★**$$ 153**
The Line-Up ★**$$ 135**
The Lobby Lounge **83**
The Mad Dog in the Fog ★**$ 110**
The Mandarin ★**$$$ 70**
The Marina **86** (chapter and map)
The Meetinghouse ★★**$$ 91**
The Mission **142** (chapter and map)
The Nature Stop **53**
The Old Place ★★**$$ 48**
The Orbit Room ★**$ 155**
The Patio Cafe **$$ 160**
Thepin Thai Cuisine ★**$ 114**
Thep Phanom ★★★**$ 111**
The Pub **$ 133**
The Rainbow Mall **42**
The Ramp ★**$$ 141**
The Real Food Company (Cole Valley) **170**
The Real Food Company Deli (Cole Valley) **170**
The Real Food Company Deli (Russian Hill) ★**$ 77**
The Real Food Company (Noe Valley) **164**
The Real Food Company (Russian Hill) **77**
The Richmond **184** (chapter and map)
The Rooster ★★**$$ 150**
The Rotunda ★★**$$ 20**
The Royal Exchange **$ 29**
The Sausage Factory **$ 160**
The Slanted Door ★★**$ 146**
The Slow Club ★★**$$ 145**
The Sporting Life **214**
The Stinking Rose ★**$$ 51**
The Straw, The Jar and The Bean **88**
The Sunset **174** (chapter and map)
The Sweet Factory **68**
The Tenderloin **112** (chapter and map)
The Terrace ★★★**$$$ 83**
The Up & Down Club **$$ 135**
The Village Market **194**
The Waterfront Restaurant ★★**$$ 64**
The Wine House **129**
The Wok Shop **34**
Thirteen Views **$$ 31**
Thomas E. Cara, Ltd. **27**
Thom's Natural Foods **197**
Ti Couz ★★★**$ 147**
Timo's Tapas Bar ★★**$ 148**
Tipping **7**
Tip Top Inn **196**
Tiramisù, Cafe **24**
Tisane, Cafe **144**
Titanic, Cafe **12**
Todos Santos ★**$ 110**
Tokyo Sukiyaki Restaurant and Sushi Bar ★★**$$ 68**
Tommaso's ★**$ 49**
Tommy Toy's ★★**$$$ 27**
Tom's Peasant Pies **162**
Tonga Restaurant and Hurricane Bar **$$$ 82**
Ton Kiang (Presidio Heights) ★★**$ 190**
Ton Kiang (The Richmond) ★★★**$$ 197**
Top of the Mark **83**

Index

Toro Taqueria, El **146**
Tortola ★★**$ 188**
Tosca Cafe ★**$ 50**
Tours, food **7**
Tower Market **172**
Town's End Restaurant and Bakery ★★**$$ 128**
Toy Boat Dessert Cafe ★★**$ 192**
Trader Joe's **137**
Trattoria Contadina ★★**$$ 60**
Traviata, La **152**
Tra Vigne, Ristorante **211**
Tre Fratelli ★**$ 105**
Trieste, Caffè **52**
Trinity, Caffe **117**
Trio Cafe ★**$ 105**
Trou, Le **150**
Tuba Garden ★**$ 188**
Tutto Mare Ristorante & Taverna ★★★**$$ 207**
25th & Clement Produce Market **199**
Twenty-Fourth Street Cheese **164**
22nd & Irving Market **179**
Twenty Tank Brewery **136**
23rd and Mission Produce **151**
2001, Restaurant **138**

U

Union Square **10** (chapter and map)
Union Street Coffee Roastery ★**$ 94**
Universal Cafe ★★★**$$ 145**
Uoki K. Sakai Company **107**
Up & Down Club, The **135**
Upstairs at the Cliff House ★**$$ 201**
U.S. Restaurant ★★**$ 51**

V

Val de Cole Wines and Spirits **171**
Valencia Whole Foods **149**
Valentine's Cafe ★★★**$ 165**
VAL 21 ★★**$$ 148**
Vanessi's ★**$$$ 85**
Vegi Food ★**$ 197**
Vertigo Restaurant & Bar ★★★**$$$ 26**
Vesuvio ★**$ 50**
Via Veneto ★★**$$ 90**
Vicolo Pizzeria ★★**$ 117**
Victoria Mexican Bakery, La **144**
Victoria Pastry Co. **56**
View Lounge **132**
Village Market, The **194**
Village Pizza ★**$ 126**
VIP Coffee and Cake Shop **41**
Virginia Breier **187**
Vishal India Restaurant ★**$ 197**
VIVANDE Porta Via ★★★**$$ 89**
VIVANDE Ristorante ★★★**$$$ 119**
Volare, Ristorante **58**

W

WA-HA-KA! (Oaxaca Mexican Grill; Cow Hollow) **$ 93**
WA-HA-KA! (Oaxaca Mexican Grill; Russian Hill) ★**$ 77**
WA-HA-KA! (Oaxaca Mexican Grill; SoMa) ★★**$ 136**
Wappo Bar Bistro ★★**$$ 212**
Washington Square Bar and Grill ★★**$$ 59**
Waterfront Restaurant, The **64**
Wazam **$ 126**
We Be Knives **65**
West Portal **166** (chapter and map)
What's for Dessert? ★**$ 165**
Wheelchair accessibility **6**
White Horse Tavern ★**$ 16**
Who Says There's No Free Lunch? **92**
Williams-Sonoma (Downtown) **22**
Williams-Sonoma (SoMa) **133**
Williams-Sonoma (The Marina) **98**
Willowside Cafe ★★★**$$ 215**
Wine Club **134**
Wine House, The **129**
Wine Impression **189**
Wine Spectator Greystone Restaurant ★★**$$ 210**
Wing Lee Restaurant ★★**$ 75**
Wing Sun Market Seafood **42**
Win's ★**$ 181**
Wishart **13**
Wok Shop, The **34**
Woodward's Garden ★★★**$$ 137**
World Ginseng Center **35**
World Wrapps ★**$ 101**
Wren & Culpeper's Vintages **78**
Writer's Bookstore **94**
Wu Kong Restaurant ★★★**$$ 127**
Wurster, Bernardi & Emmons Inc. **70**
Wycen Foods Inc. **44**

Y

Yakety Yak Coffee House ★**$ 16**
Yakitori West **$$ 106**
Yamada Seika Confectionery **106**
Yank Sing Restaurant ★★**$ 29**
YaYa Cuisine ★★★**$$ 176**
Yee Cheong General Contractors **50**
Yet Wah (Fisherman's Wharf) ★**$ 66**
Yet Wah (The Richmond) ★**$$ 198**
Yong Kee **39**
Yoshida-Ya ★★**$$ 94**
Young, Cafe de **175**
Your Space **12**
YOYO Tsumami Bistro ★★★**$$ 108**
Yuen's Garden ★★**$ 40**
Yuet Lee Seafood ★**$ 41**
Yum Yum Fish **179**

Z

ZA Pizza ★**$$ 80**
Zare ★**$$ 169**
Zarzuela ★★★**$ 79**
Zax ★★★**$$ 61**
Zazie ★★**$$ 170**
Z-Gallerie **94**
Zinc Details **87**
Zingari ★★**$$$ 16**
Zona Rosa ★**$ 169**
Zuni Cafe ★★★**$$$ 114**

Restaurants by Star Ratings

Only restaurants with star ratings are listed below. All restaurants are listed alphabetically in the main (preceding) index. Always call in advance to ensure a restaurant has not closed, changed its hours, or booked its tables for a private party. The restaurant price ratings are based on the average cost of an entrée for one person, excluding tax and tip.

★★★★ An Extraordinary Experience
★★★ Excellent
★★ Very Good
★ Good

$$$$ Big Bucks ($25 and up)
$$$ Expensive ($15-$25)
$$ Reasonable ($10-$15)
$ The Price Is Right (less than $10)

★★★★

Alain Rondelli $$$ **191**
Aqua $$$$ **29**
Cafe at Chez Panisse $$ **205**
Catahoula Restaurant and Saloon $$$ **212**
Charles Nob Hill $$$ **81**
Chez Panisse $$$ **204**
Domaine Chandon $$$$ **209**
Fleur de Lys $$$$ **13**
French Laundry $$$$ **209**
Fringale Restaurant $$ **129**
La Folie $$$$ **79**
Masa's $$$$ **19**
Postrio $$$ **15**
Terra $$$$ **211**
The Dining Room $$$$ **83**
The Heights $$$ **187**

★★★

Acquerello $$$ **75**
Ajanta Restaurant $ **206**
Albona Restaurant $$ **61**

224

Index

Alfred's $$$ **81**
Aperto $$ **138**
A. Sabella's Restaurant $$$ **67**
Bacco Ristorante Italiano $$ **161**
Battambang $ **203**
Bay Wolf $$$ **204**
Betelnut $$ **93**
Bistro Ralph $$ **215**
Bistro Rôti $$ **125**
Bix $$$ **27**
Bonta Ristorante $$ **95**
Boulevard $$$ **125**
Brasserie Savoy $$ **13**
Brava Terrace $$ **211**
Bruno's $$ **149**
Buckley Lodge $$ **214**
Cafe for All Seasons $$ **172**
Cafe Jacqueline $$ **54**
Cafe Kati $$ **106**
Cafe Lolo $$ **215**
Cafe Maisonette $$ **194**
Cafe Tiramisù $$ **24**
Campton Place Restaurant $$$$ **19**
Cantinetta Tra Vigne $ **211**
Cassis Bistro $$ **97**
Cha Cha Cha $ **170**
Citron $$$ **204**
Coconut Grove $$$ **73**
Cucina Paradiso $$ **103**
Cypress Club $$$ **27**
East Side Oyster Bar & Grill $$ **213**
Eliza's (Hayes Valley) $$ **114**
Eliza's (SoMa) $ **139**
Ella's $ **187**
Enrico's $$ **48**
EOS Restaurant & Wine Bar $$ **171**
Firefly $$ **161**
42 Degrees $$ **141**
Golden Turtle $ **77**
Great Eastern Restaurant $$ **38**
Harris' Restaurant $$$ **76**
Hawthorne Lane $$$ **130**
Hong Kong Flower Lounge Restaurant $$ **196**
Hong Kong Villa $$ **199**
Izzy's Steak & Chops $$ **99**
Jack's $ **26**
Jackson Fillmore Trattoria $$ **91**
James & James Ribs 'n' Thangs $$ **140**
J & J Restaurant $ **35**
Jasmine House $ **199**
John Cunin's No-Name Restaurant $$ **156**
J.T.'s Bistro $$$ **118**
Kabuto Sushi $$ **195**
Kam Wah $ **121**
Khan Toke Thai House $$ **198**
Kyo-ya $$ **131**
Laghi $$$ **196**
Lalime's $$ **206**

Le Cheval Restaurant $ **203**
Left Bank $$ **208**
L'Osteria del Forno $ **58**
LuLu $$ **132**
Mayflower Seafood Restaurant $$ **201**
Mescolanza $$ **198**
Metropol $ **25**
Miss Millie's $ **162**
Murasaki $ **191**
Mustards Grill $$ **210**
North India Restaurant $$ **97**
O Chamé $$ **205**
Oliveto $$ **204**
Oritalia $$ **88**
Pacific $$$ **16**
Palio d'Asti $$ **26**
Piazza D'Angelo $$ **207**
Pinot Blanc $$ **212**
Plouf $$ **24**
Pure T $ **78**
Rice Table $ **209**
Rick's Restaurant & Bar $$ **181**
Ristorante Ideale $$ **52**
Rivoli $$ **206**
Rubicon $$$ **28**
Rumpus $$ **22**
Saji Japanese Cuisine $$ **101**
Scala's Bistro $$ **19**
Socca Restaurant $$ **197**
Sophie's Cookhouse $ **27**
South Park Cafe $$ **128**
Square One $$$ **30**
Stars $$$$ **118**
Stoyanof's Cafe and Restaurant $$ **176**
Sushi-A $$ **106**
Swan Oyster Depot $$ **74**
Taiwan Restaurant (Chinatown) $ **40**
Taqueria San Jose $ **152**
Tart to Tart $ **175**
The Flying Saucer $$$ **151**
The Fly Trap $$ **130**
The Helmand Restaurant $$ **48**
The House $$ **50**
The Liberty Cafe $$ **153**
Thep Phanom $ **111**
The Terrace $$$ **83**
Ti Couz $ **147**
Ton Kiang (The Richmond) $$ **197**
Tutto Mare Ristorante & Taverna $$ **207**
Universal Cafe $$ **145**
Valentine's Cafe $ **165**
Vertigo Restaurant & Bar $$$ **26**
VIVANDE Porta Via $$ **89**
VIVANDE Ristorante $$$ **119**
Willowside Cafe $$ **215**
Woodward's Garden $$ **137**
Wu Kong Restaurant $$ **127**

YaYa Cuisine $$ **176**
YOYO Tsumami Bistro $$ **108**
Zarzuela $ **79**
Zax $$ **61**
Zuni Cafe $$$ **114**

★★

Alioto's $$$ **68**
Allegria $$ **97**
Allegro Ristorante Italiano $$$ **81**
Alta Plaza Bar and Restaurant $$ **91**
Amici's East Coast Pizza $ **94**
Anchor Oyster Bar $$ **160**
Andalé Taqueria $ **100**
Angkor Borei $ **152**
Angkor Wat $$ **192**
Anjou $$ **20**
Armani Cafe $$ **21**
Aromi $$ **74**
Ar Roi $ **13**
Asimakopoulos Cafe $$ **138**
Aux Délices $ **79**
Backstage $$$ **117**
Bad Man Jose's $ **159**
Baker Street Bistro $$ **187**
Basil $$ **135**
Bechelli's Coffee Shop $ **102**
Bell Tower $ **76**
Bette's Oceanview Diner $ **205**
Big Sky Ranch $$ **71**
Bistro Clovis $$ **114**
Bistro M $$$ **134**
Bizou $$ **129**
Blue Point $$ **199**
Brothers Restaurant $$ **192**
Buca Giovanni $$$ **61**
Buchanan Grill $$ **103**
Buckeye Roadhouse $$ **207**
Byblos $$ **97**
Cafe Adriano $$ **98**
Cafe Akimbo $$ **20**
Cafe Bastille $$ **24**
Café Chaise $$ **81**
Cafe Citti $ **213**
Cafe de la Presse $ **23**
Cafe de Young $ **175**
Cafe Espresso $ **19**
Cafe Majestic $$$ **107**
Cafe SFA $$ **19**
Cafe Tisane $$ **144**
Caffe Centro (SoMa) $ **128**
Caffe Centro (The Marina) $ **99**
Caffè Delle Stelle $$ **115**
Caffè Malvina $ **54**
Caffè Museo $ **131**
Caffè Sport $$ **56**
Caffe Trinity $ **117**
Canton Restaurant $ **130**
Capp's Corner $$ **60**
Carnelian Room $$$ **26**
Carta $$ **113**

Index

Centerfolds $$$ **48**
Chai of Larkspur $ **208**
Chava's Mexican Restaurant $ **145**
Cheung Hing $ **181**
Chevys (Downtown) $ **30**
Chevys (SoMa) $$ **132**
Chiang Mai Thai $$ **195**
Chika $ **178**
China Moon Cafe $$$ **13**
Ciao $$ **29**
City of Paris $$ **13**
Cityscape Restaurant $$$ **14**
Coriya $ **195**
Crab Cake Lounge $ **71**
Crepevine $ **176**
Dame—a restaurant $ **155**
Des Alpes Restaurant $ **45**
deStijl Cafe $ **64**
Dianda's Bakery $ **56**
Doidge's $ **94**
Dojima An $$ **18**
DPD Restaurant $$ **38**
E'Angelo Restaurant $ **101**
Eddie Rickenbacker's $$ **130**
11 Ristorante + Bar $$ **136**
Elite Cafe $$ **89**
El Pollo Supremo $ **152**
El Toro Taqueria $$ **146**
Emerald Garden $$ **74**
Eric's $ **165**
Esperpento $ **150**
Fabrizio $$ **208**
FAZ $$ **25**
Fina Estanpa $ **149**
Floogie's Swamp Cafe $$ **114**
Flying Kamikazes $$ **99**
Fog City Diner $$ **65**
Food Inc. $ **89**
Fountain Court $ **191**
Fournou's Ovens $$$ **83**
French Room $$$$ **14**
Fuji Japanese Restaurant $$ **173**
Garden Court $$$$ **131**
Garibaldis $$$ **188**
German Cook $ **121**
Geva's $$$ **116**
Ghirardelli Chocolate Manufactory $ **70**
Gira Polli $ **59**
Gold Mountain Restaurant $ **40**
Gourmet Carousel $ **91**
Grand Cafe $$$ **14**
Grazie $$ **56**
Greco-Romana $$ **199**
Greens Restaurant $$ **103**
Guaymas $$ **207**
Half Shell Restaurant and Oyster Bar $$ **135**
Hamano Sushi $ **162**
Hana Restaurant $ **175**
Happy Valley Chinese Seafood Restaurant $$ **64**
Harbor Village $$ **31**
Harry Denton's Starlight Room $$ **19**
Hayes and Vine $ **115**
Hayes Street Grill $$$ **115**
Hing Lung Chinese Cuisine $ **41**
Home Plate $ **100**
Hong Kong Seafood Restaurant $ **181**
Howard's $ **177**
Hunan Homes $ **38**
Hyde Street Bistro $$ **81**
i Fratelli $$ **81**
Il Fornaio $$ **64**
Inca $ **153**
India Oven $$ **111**
Iroha $$ **107**
Isuzu Restaurant $ **108**
It's Tops Coffee Shop $ **155**
Ivy's Restaurant and Bar $$$ **115**
Jakarta $$ **193**
Jimmy Bean's $ **127**
Joe's $ **196**
John Ash & Company $$$$ **215**
Johnny Rockets (Fisherman's Wharf) $ **67**
Julie Ring's Heart and Soul $$ **75**
Julie's Supper Club $$ **135**
Just Like Home $ **179**
Just Won Ton $ **183**
Kame Sushi $ **109**
Kate's Kitchen $ **110**
Katia's $$ **193**
Kelly's on Trinity $ **24**
Kenwood Restaurant and Bar $$$ **213**
Kiki's Paris 1920 $$ **76**
Kiss $$$ **137**
Koji Osakaya $$ **108**
Korea House $$$ **107**
Kushi Tsuru $$ **109**
La Belle Saison $$ **198**
LaFelce $$ **55**
La Méditerranée (Castro) $ **157**
La Méditerranée (Pacific Heights) $ **90**
La Paz Restaurant and Pupuseria $ **140**
La Taqueria $ **151**
La Traviata $$ **152**
Le Central $$ **23**
Le Charm $ **132**
Le Cyrano $ **192**
Lehr Brothers Bistro & Grill $$ **13**
Le Soleil $ **190**
Le Trou $$ **150**
Lhasa Moon $ **102**
Little Italy Ristorante $$ **162**
Little Paris Coffee Shop $ **45**
Lo Coco's Restaurant $$ **54**
L'Olivier $$$ **30**
Lucky Creation $ **44**
Mama's Girl $ **55**
Mandalay $ **193**
Mangiafuoco $$ **151**
Mannix Café $ **205**
Manora's Thai Cuisine (SoMa) $$ **136**
Manora's Thai Cuisine (The Mission) $ **152**
Mario's Bohemian Cigar Store Cafe (Russian Hill) $ **78**
Mario's Bohemian Cigar Store (North Beach) $ **58**
Marnee Thai $ **180**
Masons Restaurant $$$ **82**
Ma Tante Sumi $$ **160**
Matterhorn Swiss Restaurant $$$ **78**
Maykedeh $$ **53**
Mecca $$ **156**
Meriwa $ **42**
Mifune $ **109**
Millennium $$ **118**
Miss Pearl's Jam House $$ **120**
Mondo Caffe $ **130**
Moose's $$ **55**
Mo's Gourmet Hamburgers $ **53**
Moshi Moshi $ **140**
N. Alioto $ **67**
Nanbantei $$ **17**
Napper's $ **20**
Narai $ **198**
Neecha Thai $ **105**
New Eritrea Restaurant $ **178**
New Sun Hong Kong $ **40**
Nippon Sushi $ **156**
Nob Hill Cafe $$ **82**
Nob Hill Restaurant $$$$ **85**
North Sea Village $ **206**
Occidental Grill $$ **23**
Old Krakow $$ **173**
Old Swiss House $$$ **66**
Olive's Gourmet Pizza $$ **102**
One Market Restaurant $$$ **125**
OPTS Cafe $$ **132**
O'Reilly's Bar & Restaurant $$ **60**
Organic Grounds $ **178**
Oriental Pearl Restaurant $ **34**
Osome $$ **88**
Paella la Movida $$ **148**
Pagolac $ **120**
Pane e Vino $$ **95**
Paninoteca Palio d'Asti $ **26**
Paragon $$ **102**
Park Grill $$$ **28**
Parma Ristorante $$ **98**
Pasta Pomodoro (North Beach) $ **59**
Pasta Pomodoro (The Marina) $ **98**

Index

Pat O'Shea's Mad Hatter $$ **190**
Pauline's Pizza $ **146**
People's Cafe $ **168**
Perry's $$ **92**
Perry's Downtown $$ **25**
Phnom Penh $ **120**
Piatti $$ **213**
Picaro $ **147**
PJ's Oysterbed $$ **177**
PlumpJack Cafe $$ **96**
Pozole $ **157**
Radicchio $$ **92**
R & G Lounge $$ **33**
Rasselas $$ **89**
Redwood Room $$$ **14**
Rendezvous du Monde $$ **23**
Restaurant 2001 $$ **138**
Ristorante Ecco $$ **128**
Ristorante Milano $$ **81**
Ristorante Tra Vigne $$ **211**
Roosevelt's Tamale Parlor $ **144**
Rose Pistola $$ **58**
Rosmarino $$ **188**
Royal Jade $ **39**
Ruby's Pizza $ **129**
Rue Lepic $$$ **85**
Ryan's Restaurant $$ **160**
Sagami-Ya Restaurant $ **179**
Saigon Saigon $ **150**
Saigon Sandwich $ **120**
St. Francis Fountain $ **144**
Sally's $ **137**
Sam's Grill $$ **24**
Samui Thai Cuisine $ **102**
San Francisco Patisserie Cafe $ **135**
Sanppo $$ **106**
San Wang Restaurant Number 2 $$ **198**
Scala's $$ **209**
Scoma's $$ **69**
Sears Fine Foods $$ **18**
Seoul Garden $$ **108**
Silks $$$ **28**
Sinclair's Petite Cafe $ **80**
Sol y Luna $$ **28**
Sonoma Valley Bagel Co. $ **23**
Spiazzo $$ **172**
Splendido $$$ **31**
Squat & Gobble Cafe $ **111**
Stars Oakville Cafe $$$ **210**
Straits Café $$ **190**
Suppenküche $$ **117**
Suriya Thai Restaurant $$ **151**
Sushi Bune $ **17**
Sweet Heat $ **99**
Swedish Grill $$ **30**
Taiwan Restaurant (The Richmond) $ **192**
Tamnan Thai $ **177**
Taqueria El Balazo $ **169**
Tay Viêt $ **98**

Ten Ichi $$ **90**
Thai BBQ $ **119**
Thanh Long $$ **180**
Thanya and Salee $ **138**
The Big Four $$$$ **82**
The Brazen Head Restaurant $$ **93**
The Fairmont Lobby $$ **82**
The Ganges $ **170**
The Meetinghouse $$ **91**
The Old Place $$ **48**
The Rooster $$ **150**
The Rotunda $$ **20**
The Slanted Door $ **146**
The Slow Club $$ **145**
The Waterfront Restaurant $$ **64**
Timo's Tapas Bar $ **148**
Tokyo Sukiyaki Restaurant and Sushi Bar $$ **68**
Tommaso's $ **49**
Ton Kiang (Presidio Heights) $ **190**
Tortola $ **188**
Town's End Restaurant and Bakery $$ **128**
Toy Boat Dessert Cafe $ **192**
Trattoria Contadina $$ **60**
U.S. Restaurant $ **51**
VAL 21 $$ **148**
Via Veneto $$ **90**
Vicolo Pizzeria $ **117**
WA-HA-KA! (Oaxaca Mexican Grill; SoMa) $ **136**
Wappo Bar Bistro $$ **212**
Washington Square Bar and Grill $$ **59**
Wine Spectator Greystone Restaurant $$ **210**
Wing Lee Restaurant $ **75**
Yank Sing Restaurant $ **29**
Yoshida-Ya $$ **94**
Yuen's Garden $ **40**
Zazie $$ **170**
Zingari $$$ **16**

★

Alcatraz Bar and Grill $ **65**
Ali Baba's Cave $ **110**
Amazing Grace Vegetarian Restaurant $ **156**
Amira $$ **146**
Anthony's $$ **60**
Appam Indian Cuisine $ **135**
Art Institute Cafe $ **79**
Balboa Cafe $$ **96**
Barney's Gourmet Hamburgers (Noe Valley) $ **162**
Barney's Gourmet Hamburgers (The Marina) $ **99**
Basque Hotel and Restaurant $$ **50**
Bean There $ **111**
Benihana of Tokyo $$$ **108**

Benkyodo Confectioners $ **106**
Bien Dong $ **120**
Big Nate's Bar-B-Que $ **136**
Bill's Place $ **199**
Biscuits and Blues $$ **17**
Bocce Caffè $$ **53**
Boudin Sourdough Bakery & Café (Fisherman's Wharf) $ **67**
Boudin Sourdough Bakery & Café (SoMa) $ **131**
Bow Hon $ **34**
Brandy Ho's $ **48**
Brasserie Chambord $$ **25**
Buena Vista Cafe $ **69**
Bugatti's Espresso Cafe $ **96**
Burger Gourmet $ **126**
Burger Joint $ **148**
Burma House Cuisine $ **12**
Cadillac Bar and Grill $ **133**
Café Claude $$ **23**
Cafe Corbas $ **115**
Cafe de Paris L'Entrecôte $$ **93**
Cafe Lupann's $$ **159**
Cafe Marimba $$ **102**
Cafe Pescatore $$ **66**
Café Riggio $$ **192**
Cafe Titanic $ **12**
Caffè Freddy's Eatery $ **61**
Caffè Macaroni $$ **49**
Caffè Puccini $ **51**
Caffè Roma Coffee Roasting Company $ **58**
Caffè Trieste $ **52**
California Pizza Kitchen $ **15**
Campo Santo $ **49**
Canto do Brazil $$ **148**
Careme Room $$$ **119**
Caribbean Zone $$ **130**
Casa Aguila $$ **180**
Chalkers Billiard Club $ **126**
Chez Michel $$$ **70**
Chloe's Cafe $ **164**
Cho-Cho Restaurant $$ **49**
Christophe $$$ **16**
Cinderella Restaurant and Bakery $ **192**
City Picnic $ **115**
Clement Street Bar and Grill $$ **194**
Compass Rose $$$ **18**
Cordon Bleu $ **74**
Courtyard Bar and Grill $$ **199**
Courtyard Cafe $$ **164**
Creighton's Cheese & Fine Foods $ **172**
Crustacean $$$ **74**
Dante's Fresh Italian Seafood $$$ **66**
David's Delicatessen $ **15**
Delancey Street Restaurant $$ **127**
Dewey's $ **18**

227

Index

Dish $ **168**
Dottie's True Blue Cafe $ **14**
Dragon House Restaurant $ **196**
Eagle Cafe $ **65**
El Nuevo Frutilandia $ **152**
Empress of China $$ **34**
Eppler's Bakery $ **21**
Everyday Cafe $ **68**
Farley's $ **139**
Fishermen's Grotto $$$ **68**
Foggy's $ **66**
Frantoio Ristorante $$ **208**
Frascati Ristorante $$ **80**
Fresh Market Cafe $ **21**
Gaylord India Restaurant $$$ **71**
Gelato Classico $ **55**
George's Global Kitchen $ **137**
Goat Hill Pizza $ **138**
Golden Flower Restaurant $ **38**
Gordon Biersch Brewery Restaurant $$ **127**
Hai Ky Mi Gia $ **120**
Hamburger Mary's $ **136**
Hard Rock Cafe $ **75**
Harry Denton's $$ **125**
Heavenly Hot $$ **195**
Herb's Fine Foods $ **163**
Hot 'N' Hunky $ **159**
Hunan Restaurant $$ **48**
Hyde Street Seafood House and Raw Bar $$ **81**
Ideal Deli $ **135**
Il Pollaio $ **58**
Incontro $ **114**
Irving Little Cafe & Sandwiches $ **179**
Jackson Pavilion $ **38**
Jelly's: A Dance Cafe $$ **141**
Johnny Love's $$ **77**
Johnny Rockets (Pacific Heights) $ **88**
John's Grill $$ **17**
Judy's Cafe $ **101**
Julius' Castle $$$$ **61**
Just For You Cafe $ **139**
Kam (H.K.) Po Kitchen $ **45**
Kam Lok $ **44**
Kantaro $ **17**
Katz Bagels $ **147**
Kinoko $$$ **132**
Klein's Deli $ **140**
Kowloon Vegetarian Restaurant $ **35**
Kuleto's Italian Restaurant $$ **18**
La Bodega $ **53**
La Canasta $ **95**
La Posada $$ **90**
Lark Creek Inn $$$ **208**
La Rondalla $$ **148**
La Scene Cafe and Bar $$$ **15**
Leon's Bar-B-Q (Pacific Heights) $$ **87**

Leon's Bar-B-Q (The Sunset) $ **183**
Little City Antipasti Bar $$ **59**
Little Joe's $$ **50**
Little Rio Cafe and Pizzeria $ **69**
Little Thai Restaurant $ **79**
Liverpool Lil's $$ **187**
Lotus Garden $ **33**
MacArthur Park $$$ **29**
Mad Magda's Russian Tea Room & Mystic Cafe $ **116**
Mae-Thip $ **175**
Main Squeeze $ **74**
Malai Lao Restaurant $ **147**
M & M Tavern $ **134**
Mara's Italian Pastry $ **55**
Martin Macks Bar and Restaurant $ **168**
Massawa Restaurant $ **169**
Max's Diner and Bakery $ **129**
Max's Opera Cafe $ **118**
Maya Taqueria $ **147**
McCormick & Kuleto's $$$ **70**
Mel's Drive-In (The Marina) $ **97**
Mel's Drive-In (The Richmond) $ **190**
Metro Bar and Restaurant $ **157**
Michaelangelo Cafe $$ **59**
Mike's Chinese Cuisine $$ **196**
Mission Rock Resort $ **141**
Moishe's Pippic $ **116**
Mona Lisa #3: The Island of Garlic $$ **51**
Morton's of Chicago $$$$ **18**
Murata's Café Hana $ **109**
Neptune's Palace $$$ **66**
New Asia $ **41**
New Delhi Restaurant $$ **17**
New Golden Turtle $$ **191**
New Hai Ky $ **179**
New Pisa Restaurant $ **53**
New Woey Loy Goey Restaurant $ **39**
Nob Hill Noshery Cafe $ **81**
North Beach Pizza $ **52**
North Beach Restaurant $$ **55**
Nosheria $ **22**
Original Joe's Italian Restaurant $ **14**
Owl & Monkey Cafe $ **177**
Pachá $ **161**
Pacific Court Cafe $ **42**
Pacific Restaurant $ **120**
Palermo Ristorante $ **38**
Palindrome $ **125**
Palomino Euro Bistro $$ **127**
Pancho Villa Taqueria $ **146**
Pasand Madras Cuisine $ **92**
Pasha $$$ **76**
Pasqua (SoMa) $ **131**
Pauli's Cafe $$ **91**

Pazzia $ **129**
Pendragon Bakery and Cafe $ **115**
Pizza Inferno $ **106**
Place Pigalle $ **116**
Plaza $$ **20**
Pompei's Grotto $$ **68**
Pork Store Cafe $ **169**
Powell's Place $ **116**
Puccini & Pinetti $ **17**
Racha Cafe $ **120**
Radio Valencia Cafe $ **150**
Raw Living Foods $ **176**
Red's Java House $ **127**
Rex Cafe $$ **78**
Ristorante Fior d'Italia $$$ **55**
Ristorante Firenze $$ **56**
Ristorante Volare $ **58**
Rose Garden $ **110**
Rosie's Cantina $ **159**
Royal Thai $ **195**
Rustico $$ **138**
Ruth's Chris Steak House $$$ **74**
Salonika $$ **78**
San Francisco Bar-B-Que $ **139**
Sapporo-ya $ **109**
Schroeder's $$ **30**
Scott's Seafood (Downtown) $$$ **31**
Scott's Seafood (The Marina) $$ **102**
Seafood and Beverage Co. $$$ **201**
Shanghai King $ **201**
Silver Restaurant $ **35**
Singapore Malaysian $ **194**
Slider's Diner $ **159**
Sorabol Noodles $ **126**
Soups $ **121**
Spaghetti Western $ **110**
Speckmann's $$ **165**
Speedsters $ **126**
Spuntino $$ **118**
SRO! $ **31**
Star Lunch $ **35**
Stars Cafe $$ **117**
Stelline $ **116**
Steps of Rome $ **51**
Studio Cafe $ **111**
Sunrise Deli and Cafe $ **179**
Sushi Chardonnay $$ **91**
Tad's Steaks $ **17**
Taqueria Goyaz $ **151**
Taqueria la Coqueta $ **171**
Taquería La Cumbre $ **146**
Taqueria Zapata $ **159**
Tassajara Bread Bakery $ **171**
Teahouse in Japanese Tea Garden $ **175**
Thai House Bar and Café $ **156**
Thai House Restaurant $ **157**
The Chestnut Street Grill $ **100**
The Daily Scoop $ **139**

228

Index

The Grove $ **101**
The Holding Company $$ **30**
The House of Prime Rib $$ **76**
The Line-Up $$ **135**
The Mad Dog in the Fog $ **110**
The Mandarin $$$ **70**
The Orbit Room $ **155**
Thepin Thai Cuisine $ **114**
The Ramp $$ **141**
The Real Food Company Deli (Russian Hill) $ **77**
The Stinking Rose $$ **51**
Todos Santos $ **110**
Tommy Toy's $$$ **27**
Tosca Cafe $ **50**
Tre Fratelli $ **105**
Trio Cafe $ **105**
Tuba Garden $ **188**
Union Street Coffee Roastery $ **94**
Upstairs at the Cliff House $$ **201**
Vanessi's $$$ **85**
Vegi Food $ **197**
Vesuvio $ **50**
Village Pizza $ **126**
Vishal India Restaurant $ **197**
WA-HA-KA! (Oaxaca Mexican Grill; Russian Hill) $ **77**
What's for Dessert? $ **165**
White Horse Tavern $ **16**
Win's $ **181**
World Wrapps $ **101**
Yakety Yak Coffee House $ **16**
Yet Wah (The Richmond) $$ **198**
Yuet Lee Seafood $ **41**
Za Pizza $$ **80**
Zare $$ **169**
Zona Rosa $ **169**

Restaurants by Description

The following index lists restaurants by the type of food served. All restaurants are listed alphabetically in the main index (above) and restaurants with stars are listed in the ratings index (also above).

Afghan
The Helmand Restaurant **48**

African
Massawa Restaurant **169**

East African
New Eritrea Restaurant **178**

Ethiopian
Asselas **89**

Moroccan
Asha **76**

American
Academy Grill **119**
Alcatraz Bar and Grill **65**
Art Institute Cafe **79**
Backstage **117**
Balboa Cafe **96**
Barney's Gourmet Hamburgers (Noe Valley) **162**
Barney's Gourmet Hamburgers (The Marina) **99**
Baton Rouge Cajun Roadhouse **93**
Bechelli's Coffee Shop **102**
Bell Tower **76**
Bette's Oceanview Diner **205**
Big Nate's Bar-B-Que **136**
Big Sky Ranch **71**
Bill's Place **199**
Bix **27**
Buchanan Grill **103**
Buckeye Roadhouse **207**
Buena Vista Cafe **69**
Burger Gourmet **126**
Cafe de la Presse **23**
Cafe de Young **175**
Cafe Express **113**
Cafe for All Seasons **172**
Cafe Tisane **144**
Cafe Titanic **12**
Caffè Freddy's Eatery **61**
Campton Place Restaurant **19**
Centerfolds **48**
Chalkers Billiard Club **126**
Chloe's Cafe **164**
City Picnic **115**
City Tavern **96**
Clement Street Bar and Grill **194**
Coconut Grove **73**
Cypress Club **27**
Dame—a restaurant **155**
Delancey Street Restaurant **127**
Dish **168**
Doidge's **94**
Dottie's True Blue Cafe **14**
Dutch Kitchen **18**
Eagle Cafe **65**
Eclipse Cafe **31**
Eddie Rickenbacker's **130**
Eichelberger's **145**
Ella's **187**
Equinox **31**
Everyday Cafe **68**
Fog City Diner **66**
Fournou's Ovens **83**
Fresh Choice (Downtown) **21**
Hamburger Mary's **136**
Hard Rock Cafe **75**
Harry Denton's **125**
Harry Denton's Starlight Room **19**
Home Plate **100**
Hot 'N' Hunky **159**

Howard's **177**
Icon Byte Bar & Grill **136**
It's Tops Coffee Shop **155**
Jack's **26**
Jackson Pavilion **38**
Joe's **196**
John Cunin's No-Name Restaurant **156**
Johnny Love's **77**
Johnny Rockets (Fisherman's Wharf) **67**
Johnny Rockets (Pacific Heights) **88**
John's Grill **17**
J.T.'s Bistro **118**
Judy's Cafe **101**
Julie's Supper Club **135**
Kate's Kitchen **110**
Leon's Bar-B-Q (Pacific Heights) **87**
Leon's Bar-B-Q (The Sunset) **183**
MacArthur Park **29**
Magic Flute **188**
Mama's Girl **55**
M & M Tavern **134**
Masons Restaurant **82**
Maxfield's **131**
Max's Diner and Bakery **129**
Mel's Drive-In (The Marina) **97**
Mel's Drive-In (The Richmond) **190**
Mission Rock Resort **141**
Miss Millie's **162**
Mo's Gourmet Hamburgers **53**
Napper's **20**
Occidental Grill **23**
Pacific Court Cafe **42**
Paragon **102**
Pat O'Shea's Mad Hatter **190**
Perry's **92**
Perry's Downtown **25**
Planet Hollywood **21**
Plaza **20**
Pork Store Cafe **169**
Raza's **134**
Red's Java House **127**
Restaurant 2001 **138**
Rex Cafe **78**
Rick's Restaurant & Bar **181**
Rumpus **22**
St. Francis Fountain **144**
Salad Basket **201**
Sally's **137**
Sam's Grill **24**
Sears Fine Foods **18**
Sinclair's Petite Cafe **80**
Slider's Diner **159**
Sonoma Valley Bagel Co. **23**
Soups **121**
Speedsters **126**
Squat & Gobble Cafe **111**
Studio Cafe **111**
Tad's Steaks **17**

229

Index

The Burger Joint **148**
The Chestnut Street Grill **100**
The Holding Company **30**
The House of Prime Rib **76**
The Liberty Cafe **153**
The Meetinghouse **91**
The Patio Cafe **160**
The Pub **133**
The Ramp **141**
The Royal Exchange **29**
The Stinking Rose **51**
The Waterfront Restaurant **64**
Thirteen Views **31**
Town's End Restaurant and Bakery **128**
Tuba Garden **188**
Upstairs at the Cliff House **201**
U.S. Restaurant **51**
Woodward's Garden **137**
Zuni Cafe **114**

Asian

Betelnut **93**
EOS Restaurant & Wine Bar **171**
Oritalia **88**
Silks **28**
Terra **211**
The House **50**
The Rooster **150**
The Slanted Door **146**
Tonga Restaurant and Hurricane Bar **82**

Burmese

Burma House Cuisine **12**
Mandalay **193**

Cambodian

Angkor Borei **152**
Angkor Wat **192**
Battambang **203**
Phnom Penh **120**

Chinese

Bow Hon **34**
Brandy Ho's **48**
Cafe Pacifica/Sankt Gallen Brewery **24**
Canton Restaurant **130**
Cheung Hing **181**
China Moon Cafe **13**
Clement Restaurant **194**
DPD Restaurant **38**
Dragon House Restaurant **196**
Eliza's (Hayes Valley) **114**
Eliza's (SoMa) **139**
Empress of China **34**
Eric's **165**
Fountain Court **191**
Gold Mountain Restaurant **40**
Gourmet Carousel **91**
Great Eastern Restaurant **38**
Hai Ky Mi Gia **120**

Happy Valley Chinese Seafood Restaurant **64**
Harbor Village **31**
Hing Lung Chinese Cuisine **41**
Hong Kong Flower Lounge Restaurant **196**
Hong Kong Seafood Restaurant **181**
Hong Kong Villa **199**
House of Nanking **38**
Hunan Homes **38**
Hunan Restaurant **48**
J & J Restaurant **35**
Just Won Ton **183**
Kam (H.K.) Po Kitchen **45**
Kam Lok **44**
Kam Wah **121**
Kowloon Vegetarian Restaurant **35**
Lotus Garden **33**
Lucky Creation **44**
Mandalay **193**
Mayflower Seafood Restaurant **201**
Meriwa **42**
Metro Bar and Restaurant **157**
Mike's Chinese Cuisine **196**
Narai **198**
New Asia **41**
New Hai Ky **179**
New Sun Hong Kong **40**
New Woey Loy Goey Restaurant **39**
North Sea Village **206**
Oriental Pearl Restaurant **34**
R & G Lounge **33**
Royal Jade **39**
Sam Woh **34**
San Wang Restaurant Number 2 **198**
Shanghai King **201**
Silver Restaurant **35**
Star Lunch **35**
Straits Café **190**
Tai Chi Restaurant **76**
Taiwan Restaurant (Chinatown) **40**
Taiwan Restaurant (The Richmond) **192**
The Mandarin **70**
Tommy Toy's **27**
Ton Kiang (Presidio Heights) **190**
Ton Kiang (The Richmond) **197**
Vegi Food **197**
Wing Lee Restaurant **75**
Win's **181**
Wu Kong Restaurant **127**
Yank Sing Restaurant **29**
Yet Wah (Fisherman's Wharf) **66**
Yet Wah (The Richmond) **198**
Yuen's Garden **40**
Yuet Lee Seafood **41**

Indian

Ajanta Restaurant **206**
Appam Indian Cuisine **135**
Gaylord India Restaurant **71**
India Oven **111**
New Delhi Restaurant **17**
North India Restaurant **97**
Pasand Madras Cuisine **92**
The Ganges **170**
Vishal India Restaurant **197**
Wazam **126**

Indonesian

Jakarta **193**
Rice Table **209**

Japanese

Benihana of Tokyo **108**
Benkyodo Confectioners **106**
Chika **178**
Cho-Cho Restaurant **49**
Dojima An **18**
Dutch Kitchen **18**
Flying Kamikazes **99**
Fuji Japanese Restaurant **173**
Hamano Sushi **162**
Hana Restaurant **175**
Iroha **107**
Isobune Sushi **108**
Isuzu Restaurant **108**
Kabuto Sushi **195**
Kame Sushi **109**
Kantaro **17**
Kinoko **132**
Koji Osakaya **108**
Kushi Tsuru **109**
Kyo-ya **131**
Ma Tante Sumi **160**
Mifune **109**
Moshi Moshi **140**
Murasaki **191**
Nanbantei **17**
Nippon Sushi **156**
O Chamé **205**
Osome **88**
Sagami-Ya Restaurant **179**
Saji Japanese Cuisine **101**
Sanppo **106**
Sapporo-ya **109**
Sushi-A **106**
Sushi Bune **17**
Sushi Chardonnay **91**
Ten Ichi **90**
Tokyo Sukiyaki Restaurant and Sushi Bar **68**
Yakitori West **106**
Yoshida-Ya **94**
YOYO Tsumami Bistro **108**

Korean

Brothers Restaurant **192**
Coriya **195**
Heavenly Hot **195**

Index

Korea House **107**
Seoul Garden **108**
Sorabol Noodles **126**

Laotian
Malai Lao Restaurant **147**

Malaysian
Singapore Malaysian **194**

Singaporean
Straits Café **190**

Thai
Ar Roi **13**
Basil **135**
Chiang Mai Thai **195**
Khan Toke Thai House **198**
Little Thai Restaurant **79**
Mae-Thip **175**
Malai Lao Restaurant **147**
Manora's Thai Cuisine (SoMa) **136**
Manora's Thai Cuisine (The Mission) **152**
Marnee Thai **180**
Narai **198**
Neecha Thai **105**
Racha Cafe **120**
Royal Thai **195**
Samui Thai Cuisine **102**
San Francisco Bar-B-Que **139**
Siam Grill **160**
Suriya Thai Restaurant **151**
Tamnan Thai **177**
Thai BBQ **119**
Thai House Bar and Café **156**
Thai House Restaurant **157**
Thai-to-go **126**
Thanya and Salee **138**
Thepin Thai Cuisine **114**
Thep Phanom **111**

Tibetan
Lhasa Moon **102**

Vietnamese
Aux Délices **79**
Bien Dong **120**
Cordon Bleu **74**
Emorald Garden **74**
Golden Flower Restaurant **38**
Golden Turtle **77**
Giving Little Cafe & Sandwiches **179**
Jasmine House **199**
Nam Wah **121**
Le Cheval Restaurant **203**
Le Soleil **190**
Little Paris Coffee Shop **45**
New Golden Turtle **191**
Pacific Restaurant **120**
Pagolac **120**
Rose Garden **110**
Saigon Saigon **150**
Saigon Sandwich **120**
Tuy Việt **98**

Thanh Long **180**

Austrian
Hyde Street Bistro **81**

Barbecue
Big Nate's Bar-B-Que **136**
Cheung Hing **181**
El Pollo Supremo **152**
James & James Ribs 'n' Thangs **140**
Leon's Bar-B-Q (Pacific Heights) **87**
Leon's Bar-B-Q (The Sunset) **183**

Basque
Basque Hotel and Restaurant **50**
Des Alpes Restaurant **45**

Bistro
Anjou **20**
Bistro Clovis **114**
Cafe Bastille **24**
City of Paris **13**
Plouf **24**

Brewery/Pub/Wine Bar
Cafe Pacifica/Sankt Gallen Brewery **24**
Dewey's **18**
EOS Restaurant & Wine Bar **171**
Gordon Biersch Brewery Restaurant **127**
Hayes and Vine **115**
Liverpool Lil's **187**
London Wine Bar **28**
Martin Macks Bar and Restaurant **168**
O'Reilly's Bar & Restaurant **60**
The Mad Dog in the Fog **110**
The Orbit Room **155**
The Pub **133**
Vesuvio **50**

Cafe
Armani Cafe **21**
Boudin Sourdough Bakery & Café (Fisherman's Wharf) **67**
Boudin Sourdough Bakery & Café (SoMa) **131**
Cafe Corbas **115**
Cafe Espresso **19**
Caffe Centro (SoMa) **128**
Caffe Centro (The Marina) **99**
Caffè Malvina **54**
Caffè Trieste **52**
Caffe Trinity **117**
Creighton's Cheese & Fine Foods **172**
Crepevine **176**
Dianda's Bakery **56**

Eppler's Bakery **21**
Espresso Bar **21**
Food Inc. **89**
Fresh Market Cafe **21**
Garibaldi's Cafe **138**
Katz Bagels **147**
La Nouvelle Patisserie (Cow Hollow) **94**
La Nouvelle Patisserie (SoMa) **133**
Little Paris Coffee Shop **45**
Main Squeeze **74**
Mannix Cafe **205**
Mario's Bohemian Cigar Store Cafe (Russian Hill) **78**
Mario's Bohemian Cigar Store (North Beach) **58**
Martha and Brothers Coffee Co. **164**
May's Coffee Shop **109**
Mondo Caffe **130**
Muddy Waters Coffee **156**
ORTS Cafe **132**
Owl & Monkey Cafe **177**
Pasqua (SoMa) **131**
Pendragon Bakery and Cafe **115**
People's Cafe **168**
Place Pigalle **116**
Radio Valencia Cafe **150**
Sally's **137**
SRO! **31**
Stars Oakville Cafe **210**
Steps of Rome **51**
Tart to Tart **175**
Tassajara Bread Bakery **171**
Trio Cafe **105**
Universal Cafe **145**
What's for Dessert? **165**

Cafeteria
Fresh Choice (SoMa) **132**
Kelly's on Trinity **24**

Cajun/Creole
Baton Rouge Cajun Roadhouse **93**
California Creole Cafe **131**
Catahoula Restaurant and Saloon **212**
Elite Cafe **89**
Floogie's Swamp Cafe **114**
Just For You Cafe **139**

Californian
Act IV **117**
Alta Plaza Bar and Restaurant **91**
Bay Wolf **204**
Bell Tower **76**
Bistro M **134**
Bistro Ralph **215**
Bistro Rôti **125**
Boulevard **125**
Buckley Lodge **214**

Index

Cafe Akimbo **20**
Cafe at Chez Panisse **205**
Cafe de Paris L'Entrecôte **93**
Cafe Flore **157**
Cafe Kati **106**
Cafe Lolo **215**
Cafe Lupann's **159**
Cafe Majestic **107**
Cafe SFA **19**
California Creole Cafe **131**
Careme Room **119**
Champagne Exchange **133**
Chez Michel **70**
Chez Panisse **204**
China Moon Cafe **13**
Ciao **29**
City Centre Grill **133**
City of Paris **13**
Cityscape Restaurant **14**
Compass Rose **18**
Courtyard Bar and Grill **199**
deStijl Cafe **64**
Domaine Chandon **209**
East Side Oyster Bar & Grill **213**
Eliza's (Hayes Valley) **114**
FAZ **25**
Firefly **161**
Fleur de Lys **13**
42 Degrees **141**
French Laundry **209**
Garibaldis **188**
George's Global Kitchen **137**
Gordon Biersch Brewery Restaurant **127**
Grand Cafe **14**
Hawthorne Lane **130**
Hyde Street Bistro **81**
Ivy's Restaurant and Bar **115**
Jimmy Bean's **127**
John Ash & Company **215**
Julie Ring's Heart and Soul **75**
Kenwood Restaurant and Bar **213**
Kiss **137**
La Folie **79**
Lark Creek Inn **208**
Ma Tante Sumi **160**
Metropol **25**
Moose's **55**
Mustards Grill **210**
Nob Hill Restaurant **85**
Oliveto **204**
One Market Restaurant **125**
Pacific **16**
Panos' **163**
Park Grill **28**
Pauli's Cafe **91**
Pinot Blanc **212**
PlumpJack Cafe **96**
Postrio **15**
Puccini & Pinetti **17**
Redwood Room **14**

Rivoli **206**
Rubicon **28**
Ryan's Restaurant **160**
Silks **28**
Spaghetti Western **110**
Square One **30**
Stars **118**
Stars Cafe **117**
The Big Four **82**
The Dining Room **83**
The Flying Saucer **151**
The Fly Trap **130**
The Heights **187**
The House **50**
The Rotunda **20**
The Slow Club **145**
The Up & Down Club **135**
VAL 21 **148**
Vertigo Restaurant & Bar **26**
Wappo Bar Bistro **212**
Washington Square Bar and Grill **59**
Willowside Cafe **215**
Wine Spectator Greystone Restaurant **210**

Caribbean/Tropical
Caribbean Zone **130**
Cha Cha Cha **170**
Geva's **116**
Miss Pearl's Jam House **120**

Cuban
Babaloo Restaurant **97**
El Nuevo Frutilandia **152**

Puerto Rican
El Nuevo Frutilandia **152**

Coffeehouse
Aroma **126**
Bean There **111**
Bugatti's Espresso Cafe **96**
Cafe Macondo **147**
Caffè Puccini **51**
Caffè Roma Coffee Roasting Company **58**
Farley's **139**
Foggy's **66**
Mara's Italian Pastry **55**
Momi Toby's Revolution Cafe **117**
Muddy's Coffee House **151**
Murata's Café Hana **109**
Organic Grounds **178**
Palindrome **125**
Polk St. Beans and Cafe **75**
San Francisco Patisserie Cafe **135**
The Grove **101**
The Orbit Room **155**
Tosca Cafe **50**
Toy Boat Dessert Cafe **191**
Union Street Coffee Roastery **94**

Vesuvio **50**
Yakety Yak Coffee House **16**

Contemporary
Catahoula Restaurant and Saloon **212**
Charles Nob Hill **81**
Garden Court **131**
John Cunin's No-Name Restaurant **156**

Continental
Act IV **117**
Grand Cafe **14**
Icon Byte Bar & Grill **136**
Julius' Castle **61**
Old Swiss House **66**
The Brazen Head Restaurant **93**

Deli
David's Delicatessen **15**
Just Like Home **179**
Klein's Deli **140**
Mad Magda's Russian Tea Room & Mystic Cafe **116**
Max's Opera Cafe **118**
Moishe's Pippic **116**
Nob Hill Noshery Cafe **81**
Rubin's **126**
The Real Food Company Deli (Russian Hill) **77**

Diner
Bette's Oceanview Diner **205**
Fog City Diner **65**
Herb's Fine Foods **163**
Max's Diner and Bakery **129**
Slider's Diner **159**

Eastern European

Istrian
Albona Restaurant **61**

Polish
Old Krakow **173**

Russian
Cinderella Restaurant and Bakery **192**
Katia's **193**
Russian Renaissance Restaurant **196**

Eclectic
Cafe Kati **106**
Johnny Love's **77**

English
Liverpool Lil's **187**
Martin Macks Bar and Restaurant **168**
The Mad Dog in the Fog **110**

232

Index

The Pub **133**
White Horse Tavern **16**

French

Alain Rondelli **191**
Anjou **20**
Baker Street Bistro **187**
Bistro Clovis **114**
Bistro M **134**
Bistro Rôti **125**
Bizou **129**
Boulevard **125**
Brasserie Chambord **25**
Brasserie Savoy **13**
Café Chaise **81**
Café Claude **23**
Cafe de la Presse **23**
Cafe de Paris L'Entrecôte **93**
Cafe Jacqueline **54**
Cafe Maisonette **194**
Carome Room **119**
Carnelian Room **26**
Cassis Bistro **97**
Chez Michel **70**
Christophe **16**
Crepevine **176**
Domaine Chandon **209**
Emerald Garden **74**
Fleur de Lys **13**
Fringale Restaurant **129**
Kiki's Paris 1920 **76**
Kiss **137**
La Belle Saison **198**
La Folie **79**
La Scene Cafe and Bar **15**
Le Central **23**
Le Charm **132**
Le Cyrano **192**
Left Bank **208**
Le Trou **150**
L'Olivier **30**
LuLu **132**
Maca's **19**
Nob Hill Restaurant **85**
Pinot Blanc **212**
Redwood Room **14**
Rendezvous du Monde **23**
Rue Lepic **85**
South Park Cafe **128**
Squat & Gobble Cafe **111**
The Big Four **82**
The Dining Room **83**
The Heights **187**
Ti Couz **147**
Tommy Toy's **27**
YOYO Tsumami Bistro **108**
Zax **61**
Zazie **170**

Fusion

EOS Restaurant & Wine Bar **171**

German

German Cook **121**
Schroeder's **30**
Speckmann's **165**
Suppenküche **117**

Greek

Asimakopoulos Cafe **138**
Panos' **163**
Salonika **78**
Stoyanof's Cafe and Restaurant **176**

Health Food/ Vegetarian

Amazing Grace Vegetarian Restaurant **156**
Greens Restaurant **103**
Kowloon Vegetarian Restaurant **35**
Lotus Garden **33**
Lucky Creation **44**
Millennium **118**
Raw Living Foods **176**
Valentine's Cafe **165**
Vegi Food **197**

Ice-cream Parlor

Gelato Classico **55**
Ghirardelli Chocolate Manufactory **70**
Joe's **196**
Pure T **78**
St. Francis Fountain **144**
The Daily Scoop **139**
Toy Boat Dessert Cafe **191**

International

French Room **14**
Jelly's: A Dance Cafe **141**
Wappo Bar Bistro **212**
World Wrapps **101**

Irish

Martin Macks Bar and Restaurant **108**
O'Reilly's Bar & Restaurant **60**
The Mad Dog in the Fog **110**

Italian

Acquerello **75**
Allegro Ristorante Italiano **81**
Anthony's **60**
Aperto **138**
Aromi **74**
Bacco Ristorante Italiano **161**
Basta Pasta **52**
Bocce Caffè **53**
Bonta Ristorante **95**
Buca Giovanni **61**
Cafe Adriano **98**
Cafe Citti **213**
Cafe Pescatore **66**
Cafe Rigatoni **69**
Café Riggio **192**
Cafe Tiramisù **24**
Caffè Delle Stelle **115**
Caffè Freddy's Eatery **61**
Caffè Macaroni **49**
Caffè Sport **56**
Calzone's **52**
Cantinetta Tra Vigne **211**
Capp's Corner **60**
Ciao **29**
Cucina Paradiso **103**
E'Angelo Restaurant **101**
11 Ristorante + Bar **136**
Enrico's **48**
Fabrizio **208**
Frantoio Ristorante **208**
Frascati Ristorante **80**
Fratelli **81**
Gira Polli **59**
Gold Spike **58**
Grazie **56**
Il Fornaio **64**
Il Pollaio **58**
Incontro **114**
Jackson Fillmore Trattoria **91**
Johnny Nipon's **178**
Kuleto's Italian Restaurant **18**
LaFelce **55**
Laghi **196**
La Traviata **152**
Little City Antipasti Bar **59**
Little Italy Ristorante **162**
Little Joe's **50**
Lo Coco's Restaurant **54**
L'Osteria del Forno **58**
LuLu **132**
Magic Flute **188**
Mangiafuoco **151**
Mario's Bohemian Cigar Store Cafe (Russian Hill) **78**
Mario's Bohemian Cigar Store (North Beach) **58**
Mayo's Oyster House **73**
Mescolanza **198**
Michaelangelo Cafe **59**
Mona Lisa #3: The Island of Garlic **51**
Mondo Caffe **130**
Moose's **55**
New Joe's **18**
New Pisa Restaurant **53**
Nob Hill Cafe **82**
North Beach Restaurant **55**
Nosheria **22**
Olive's Gourmet Pizza **102**
Original Joe's Italian Restaurant **14**
Oritalia **88**
Palermo Ristorante **38**
Palio d'Asti **26**
Pane e Vino **95**

233

Index

Paninoteca Palio d'Asti **26**
Parma Ristorante **98**
Pasta Pomodoro (North Beach) **59**
Pasta Pomodoro (The Marina) **98**
Pazzia **129**
Piatti **213**
Piazza D'Angelo **207**
Pompei's Grotto **68**
Prego Ristorante **93**
Puccini & Pinetti **17**
Radicchio **92**
Rendezvous du Monde **23**
Ristorante Ecco **128**
Ristorante Fior d'Italia **55**
Ristorante Firenze **56**
Ristorante Ideale **52**
Ristorante Milano **81**
Ristorante Tra Vigne **211**
Ristorante Volare **58**
Rose Pistola **58**
Ruby's Pizza **129**
Scala's **209**
Scala's Bistro **19**
Spiazzo **172**
Spuntino **118**
Stelline **116**
The Sausage Factory **160**
The Stinking Rose **51**
The Terrace **83**
Tommaso's **49**
Trattoria Contadina **60**
Tre Fratelli **105**
Tutto Mare Ristorante & Taverna **207**
U.S. Restaurant **51**
Vanessi's **85**
Via Veneto **90**
VIVANDE Porta Via **89**
VIVANDE Ristorante **119**
Washington Square Bar and Grill **59**
Zingari **16**

Mediterranean

Brava Terrace **211**
Bruno's **149**
Caffè Museo **131**
Carta **113**
Citron **204**
Courtyard Cafe **164**
Enrico's **48**
Greco-Romana **199**
Lalime's **206**
La Méditerranée (Castro) **157**
La Méditerranée (Pacific Heights) **90**
La Scene Cafe and Bar **15**
Palomino Euro Bistro **127**
PlumpJack Cafe **96**
Rosmarino **188**
Socca Restaurant **197**
Splendido **31**

234

Square One **30**
Terra **211**
The Rooster **150**
Zax **61**

Mexican

Andalé Taqueria **100**
Bad Man Jose's **159**
Cadillac Bar and Grill **133**
Cafe Marimba **102**
Campo Santo **49**
Casa Aguila **180**
Chava's Mexican Restaurant **145**
Chevys (Downtown) **30**
Chevys (SoMa) **132**
El Pollo Supremo **152**
El Toro Taqueria **146**
Guaymas **207**
Ideal Deli **135**
La Canasta **95**
La Posada **90**
La Rondalla **148**
La Taqueria **151**
Maya Taqueria **147**
Mi Burrito **89**
Pancho Villa Taqueria **146**
Pozole **157**
Roosevelt's Tamale Parlor **144**
Rosie's Cantina **159**
Sweet Heat **99**
Tampico **126**
Taqueria El Balazo **169**
Taqueria Goyaz **151**
Taqueria la Coqueta **171**
Taquería La Cumbre **146**
Taqueria San Jose **152**
Taqueria Zapata **159**
The Line-Up **135**
Todos Santos **110**
Tortola **188**
WA-HA-KA! (Oaxaca Mexican Grill; Cow Hollow) **93**
WA-HA-KA! (Oaxaca Mexican Grill; Russian Hill) **77**
WA-HA-KA! (Oaxaca Mexican Grill; SoMa) **136**
Zona Rosa **169**

Middle Eastern

Ali Baba's Cave **110**
Amira **146**
Arabi **126**
Cafe Istanbul **146**
FAZ **25**
Just Like Home **179**
La Méditerranée (Castro) **157**
La Méditerranée (Pacific Heights) **90**
Pasha **76**
Sunrise Deli and Cafe **179**
YaYa Cuisine **176**

Zare **169**

Lebanese
Byblos **97**

Persian
Maykedeh **53**

Miscellaneous
City Eats **25**

Pizza

Amici's East Coast Pizza **94**
California Pizza Kitchen **15**
Goat Hill Pizza **138**
Little Rio Cafe and Pizzeria **69**
North Beach Pizza **52**
Pauline's Pizza **146**
Pizza Inferno **106**
Ruby's Pizza **129**
Rustico **138**
Vicolo Pizzeria **117**
Village Pizza **126**
ZA Pizza **80**

Seafood

Alioto's **68**
Anchor Oyster Bar **160**
Anthony's **60**
Aqua **29**
A. Sabella's Restaurant **67**
Blue Point **199**
Cafe Pescatore **66**
Crab Cake Lounge **71**
Crustacean **74**
Dante's Fresh Italian Seafood **66**
East Side Oyster Bar & Grill **213**
Fishermen's Grotto **68**
Floogie's Swamp Cafe **114**
Half Shell Restaurant and Oyster Bar **135**
Hayes Street Grill **115**
Hyde Street Seafood House and Raw Bar **81**
Izzy's Steak & Chops **99**
Jack's Bar **69**
Johnny Nipon's **178**
Mayflower Seafood Restaurant **201**
McCormick & Kuleto's **70**
N. Alioto **67**
Neptune's Palace **66**
PJ's Oysterbed **177**
Scoma's **69**
Scott's Seafood (Downtown) **31**
Scott's Seafood (The Marina) **102**
Seafood and Beverage Co. **201**
Swan Oyster Depot **74**
Tadich Grill **30**
Tarantino's **67**
Thanh Long **180**
The Waterfront Restaurant **64**

Index

Tutto Mare Ristorante & Taverna **207**
Yuet Lee Seafood **41**

South/Central American

Argentine
Il Pollaio **58**

Brazilian
Canto do Brazil **148**
Little Rio Cafe and Pizzeria **69**
Taqueria Goyaz **151**

Peruvian
Inca **153**

Salvadoran
La Paz Restaurant and Pupuseria **140**

Southern
Biscuits and Blues **17**

Soul Food
James & James Ribs 'n' Thangs **140**
Miss Pearl's Jam House **120**
Powell's Place **116**

Spanish
Allegria **97**
Esperpento **150**
Fina Estanpa **149**
La Bodega **53**
Pachá **161**
Paella la Movida **148**
Picaro **147**
Sol y Luna **28**
Timo's Tapas Bar **148**
Zarzuela **79**

Steak
Alfred's **81**
Benihana of Tokyo **108**
Harris' Restaurant **76**
Izzy's Steak & Chops **99**
Morton's of Chicago **18**
Ruth's Chris Steak House **74**

Swiss
Matterhorn Swiss Restaurant **78**
Old Swiss House **66**

Takeout
Big Nate's Bar-B-Que **136**
Cantinetta Tra Vigne **211**
Creighton's Cheese & Fine Foods **172**
Food Inc. **89**
Ideal Deli **135**
Kam (H.K.) Po Kitchen **45**
New Asia **41**
Palindrome **125**
Pasqua (Downtown) **29**
San Francisco Patisserie Cafe **135**
The Real Food Company Deli (Russian Hill) **77**
VIVANDE Porta Via **89**

Teahouse
Cafe Tisane **144**
Chai of Larkspur **208**
Mad Magda's Russian Tea Room & Mystic Cafe **116**
Pure T **78**
Teahouse in Japanese Tea Garden **175**
The Fairmont Lobby **82**

Features
All Aboard **9**
Child's Play **80**
Everything You Ever Wanted to Know about Pairing Wine and Food, But Were Afraid to Ask **57**
Fabulous Food Festivals and Street Fairs **7**
Farmers' Markets **134**
Lights, Camera, Dinner! **153**
Mastering the Dim Sum Experience **36**
Now You're Cookin' **200**
Pasta Primer **158**
Shopping in Chinatown—A Flavorful Adventure **43**
Sourdough Starter **189**
Tea Time **182**
The Daily Grind **84**
The Sporting Life **214**
Who Says There's No Free Lunch? **92**

Bests
Asher, Gerald (Wine Editor, *Gourmet Magazine*) **183**
Bernstein, Sally (Editor, "Sally's Place," an Internet Web Site Dedicated to Food, Wine, and Travel) **121**
Blackstone, Cammy (On-air Personality, KFRC Radio) **71**
Cass, Maxine (Travel Writer; Co-author, *On the Road Around California*) **85**
Coppola, Francis Ford (Film Director/Producer) **103**
Dalldorf, Tom (Publisher, *Celebrator Beer News*) **173**
Etheredge, Jeanette (Owner, Tosca Cafe) **71**
Gebhart, Fred (Travel Writer; Co-author, *On the Road Around California*) **85**
Gravy, Wavy (Activist/Clown) **121**
Jordan, Michele Anna (Author, *The Good Cook's Book;* Freelance Restaurant Critic) **85**
Luddy, Tom (Film Producer, American Zoetrope) **71**
McNair, James (Cookbook Author/Food Photographer) **121**
Nelson, Diana (Chief Concierge, Grand Hyatt Hotel) **183**
Palmtag, Ron (Chief Concierge, Park Hyatt Hotel) **85**
Rodgers, Barbara (News Anchor/Reporter, KPIX Television) **173**
Snyderman, Nancy L., M.D. (Surgeon; Medical Correspondent, ABC News) **121**
Stevens, Ken (Chief Concierge, Four Seasons Clift Hotel) **183**

Maps
Bayview **122**
Beyond the Bridges **202**
Castro **154**
Chinatown **32**
Civic Center **112**
Cole Valley **166**
Cow Hollow **86**
Downtown **10**
Fisherman's Wharf **62**
Glen Park **166**
Hayes Valley **112**
Hunters Point **122**
Japantown **104**
Lower Haight **104**
Map key **6**
Napa Valley **209**
Nob Hill **72**
Noe Valley **154**
North Beach **46**
Pacific Heights **86**
Potrero Hill **122**
Presidio Heights **184**
Russian Hill **72**
San Francisco **2**
San Francisco area **202**
San Francisco Public Transportation **237**
SoMa (South of Market) **122**
Sonoma County **212**
South Beach **122**
The Embarcadero **62**
The Haight **166**
The Marina **86**
The Mission **142**
The Richmond **184**
The Sunset **174**
The Tenderloin **112**
Union Square **10**
West Portal **166**

235

ACCESS®
The Neighborhood Guide

Other Destinations:

- Boston
- Cape Cod, Martha's Vineyard & Nantucket
- Caribbean
- Chicago
- Florence/Venice/Milan
- Hawaii
- Las Vegas
- London
- Los Angeles
- Mexico
- Miami/S. Florida
- Montreal & Quebec City
- New York Restaurant
- Orlando/Central Florida
- Paris
- Rome
- San Francisco
- San Francisco Restaurant
- Santa Fe/Taos/Albuquerque
- Seattle
- Ski Country Eastern US
- Ski Country Western US
- Wine Country France

Pack lightly and carry the best travel guides going: ACCESS®. Arranged by neighborhood and featuring color-coded entries, ACCESS® guides are designed to help you explore—not to leave you standing on the corner thumbing madly through an index. Whether you are visiting Philadelphia or Paris, you'll need a sturdy pair of walking shoes and plenty of ACCESS®.

HarperReference
A Division of HarperCollinsPublishers

SAN FRANCISCO PUBLIC TRANSPORTATION

Credit

Writer and Researcher
GraceAnn Walden

Writer and Researchers (Previous Edition)
Michael Bauer
Dan Bowe
Jay Rhoderick
Juan Carlos Weiss

ACCESS®PRESS

Editorial Director
Lois Spritzer

Managing Editor
Laura L. Brengelman

Senior Editors
Mary Callahan
Beth Schlau

Associate Editors
Patricia Canole
Gene Gold
Susan McClung

Map Coordinator
Marcy S. Pritchard

Editorial Assistant
Susan Cutter Snyder

Contributing Editor
Nancy Cohen

Senior Art Director
C. Linda Dingler

Design Supervisor
Joy O'Meara

Designers
Alexandra Lindquist
Elizabeth Paige Streit

Map Designer
Patricia Keelin

Associate Director of Production
Dianne Pinkowitz

Director, Electronic Publishing
John R. Day

Cover Photo©
Richard Pierce

Special Thanks
Ann Roberti
  Librarian,
  Alice S. Statler
  Culinary Library
San Francisco City
  College

The publisher and authors assume no legal responsibility for the completeness or accuracy of the contents of this book nor any legal responsibility for the appreciation or depreciation in the value of any premises, commercial or otherwise, by reason of inclusion in or exclusion from this book. All contents are based on information available at the time of publication. Some of the maps are diagrammatic and may be selective of street inclusion..

ACCESS®PRESS does not solicit individuals, organizations, or businesses for inclusion in our books, nor do we accept payment for inclusion. We welcome, however, information from our readers, including comments, criticisms, and suggestions for new listings. Send all correspondence to: **ACCESS**®PRESS, 10 East 53rd Street, 18th Floor, New York, NY 10022

Printed in the United States

ACCESS® Guides

Order by phone, toll-free: 1-800-331-3761

Travel: Promo # R00111

Name _____ Phone _____
Address _____
City _____ State _____ Zip _____

Please send me the following ACCESS® Guides:

- [ ] **ATLANTA** ACCESS® $18.50
  0-06-277156-6
- [ ] **BARCELONA** ACCESS® $17.00
  0-06-277000-4
- [ ] **BOSTON** ACCESS® $18.50
  0-06-277143-4
- [ ] **BUDGET EUROPE** ACCESS® $18.50
  0-06-277171-X
- [ ] **CAPE COD** ACCESS® $18.50
  0-06-277159-0
- [ ] **CARIBBEAN** ACCESS® $18.50
  0-06-277128-0
- [ ] **CHICAGO** ACCESS® $18.50
  0-06-277144-2
- [ ] **FLORENCE/VENICE/MILAN** ACCESS® $18.50
  0-06-277170-1
- [ ] **HAWAII** ACCESS® $18.50
  0-06-277142-6
- [ ] **LAS VEGAS** ACCESS® $18.50
  0-06-277177-9
- [ ] **LONDON** ACCESS® $18.50
  0-06-277161-2
- [ ] **LOS ANGELES** ACCESS® $18.50
  0-06-277131-0
- [ ] **MEXICO** ACCESS® $18.50
  0-06-277127-2
- [ ] **MIAMI & SOUTH FLORIDA** ACCESS® $18.50
  0-06-277178-7
- [ ] **MONTREAL & QUEBEC** ACCESS® $18.50
  0-06-277160-4
- [ ] **NEW ORLEANS** ACCESS® $18.50
  0-06-277176-0
- [ ] **NEW YORK CITY** ACCESS® $18.50
  0-06-277162-0
- [ ] **NEW YORK CITY RESTAURANT** ACCESS® $13.00
  0-06-277191-4
- [ ] **ORLANDO & CENTRAL FLORIDA** ACCESS® $18.50
  0-06-277175-2
- [ ] **PARIS** ACCESS® $18.50
  0-06-277163-9
- [ ] **PHILADELPHIA** ACCESS® $18.50
  0-06-277155-8
- [ ] **ROME** ACCESS® $18.50
  0-06-277150-7
- [ ] **SAN DIEGO** ACCESS® $18.50
  0-06-277185-X
- [ ] **SAN FRANCISCO** ACCESS® $18.50
  0-06-277121-3
- [ ] **SAN FRANCISCO RESTAURANT** ACCESS® $13.00
  0-06-277192-2
- [ ] **SANTA FE/TAOS/ALBUQUERQUE** ACCESS® $18.50
  0-06-277148-5
- [ ] **SEATTLE** ACCESS® $18.50
  0-06-277149-3
- [ ] **SKI COUNTRY** ACCESS® Eastern United States $18.50
  0-06-277125-6
- [ ] **SKI COUNTRY** ACCESS® Western United States $18.50
  0-06-277174-4
- [ ] **WASHINGTON DC** ACCESS® $18.50
  0-06-277158-2
- [ ] **WINE COUNTRY** ACCESS® France $18.50
  0-06-277151-5
- [ ] **WINE COUNTRY** ACCESS® Northern California $18.50
  0-06-277164-7

Prices subject to change without notice.

Total for **ACCESS®** Guides:	$
Please add applicable sales tax:	
Add $4.00 for first book S&H, $1.00 per additional book:	
Total payment:	$

- [ ] Check or Money Order enclosed. Offer valid in the United States only. Please make payable to HarperCollins*Publishers*.
- [ ] Charge my credit card [ ] American Express [ ] Visa [ ] MasterCard

Card no. _____ Exp. date _____
Signature _____

Send orders to: HarperCollins*Publishers*
P.O. Box 588
Dunmore, PA 18512-0588

Bring Home a Taste of Northern California.

ALICE WATERS

CHEZ PANISSE VEGETABLES

Acclaimed restaurateur and author Alice Waters pays tribute to the riches of the garden's bounty with more than 250 of the spirited recipes that have delighted eaters at Chez Panisse.

"Say 'vegetables' in America and you think of Alice Waters."
—Patricia Wells

HarperCollins*Publishers*
Also available from HarperCollinsCanadaLtd

At bookstores now.